To Bobby Green —

A gift from the
Lord of which we are
very grateful.

Jerry C White

Oct 2000

HE SHALL HAVE DOMINION

Other books by Kenneth L. Gentry, Jr.

The Christian Case Against Abortion, 1982, rev. 1989
The Christian and Alcoholic Beverages: A Biblical Perspective, 1986, rev. 1990
The Charismatic Gift of Prophecy, 1986, rev. 1989
The Beast of Revelation, 1989, 1994
Before Jerusalem Fell: Dating the Book of Revelation, 1989, 1997
House Divided: The Break-up of Dispensational Theology (with Greg L. Bahnsen), 1989
The Greatness of the Great Commission: The Christian Enterprise in a Fallen World, 1991, rev. 1994
Lord of the Saved: Getting to the Heart of Lordship Salvation (1992)
God's Law in the Modern World, (1992)
The Great Tribulation: Past or Future? (with Thomas D. Ice), 1997

Contributions to:

David L. Bender, ed., *The Welfare State: Opposing Viewpoints* (1982)
Gary North, ed., *Theonomy: An Informed Response* (1992)
Darrell L. Bock, ed., *Three Views of the End of History* (1997)
C. Marvin Pate, ed., *Four Views of the Book of Revelation* (1997)

HE SHALL HAVE DOMINION
A Postmillennial Eschatology
(Second Edition)

Kenneth L. Gentry, Jr.

Institute for Christian Economics
Tyler, Texas

Library of Congress Cataloging-in-Publication Data

Gentry, Kenneth L.
    He shall have dominion / Kenneth L. Gentry
      p. cm.
    Includes bibliographical references and indexes.
    ISBN 0-930464-62-1 (alk. paper) : $19.95
    1. Eschatology. 2. Millennialism. 3. Postmillennialism.
    4. Dominion theology. 5. Calvinism. 6. Reformed Church
    – Doctrines.
    I. Title
    BT821.2.G46 1992   92-15890
    236'.9–dc20   CIP

Institute for Christian Economics
P.O. Box 8000, Tyler, TX 75711

TABLE OF CONTENTS

First Edition Dedicated to the Memory of
two servants of Christ:

Dr. Cornelius Van Til

(who taught me to think as Christian)

and

Dr. Loraine Boettner

(who taught me to hope as a Christian)

Second Edition Dedicated to the Memory of
my mentor:

Dr. Greg L. Bahnsen (1948-1996)

(who instructed me in these two themes)

Christ shall have dominion Over land and sea;
Earth's remotest regions Shall His empire be;
They that wilds inhabit Shall their worship bring,
Kings shall render tribute, Nations serve our King.

When the needy seek Him He will mercy show;
Yea, the weak and helpless Shall His pity know;
He will surely save them From oppression's might
For their lives are precious in His holy sight.

Ever and forever Shall His name endure,
Long as suns continue It shall stand secure;
And in Him forever All men shall be blest,
And all nations hail Him King of Kings confessed.

Unto God Almighty Joyful Zion sings;
He alone is glorious, Doing wondrous things.
Evermore, ye people, Bless His glorious name;
His eternal glory Through the earth proclaim.

FOREWORD TO THE SECOND EDITION

Gary North

O how love I thy law! it is my meditation all the day. Thou through thy commandments hast made me wiser than mine enemies: for they are ever with me. I have more understanding than all my teachers: for thy testimonies are my meditation. I understand more than the ancients, because I keep thy precepts. (Psalm 119:97-100)

The words of two familiar Protestant hymns stand in judgment of all of modern Protestantism, whether evangelical, fundamentalist, Lutheran, or Reformed, every time a congregation sings either of them. The first has to do with God's law: "O how love I thy law; O how love I thy law; It is my meditation all the day." If "consternation" were substituted for "meditation," the hymn would be somewhat more representative of Protestant belief, except that the law of God is not in the minds of Christians all the day, either for meditation or consternation. They ignore it. The second chorus is this one: "Onward, Christian soldiers, marching as to war, with the cross of Jesus going on before." *He Shall Have Dominion* shows why these two great hymns are linked, not merely theologically but covenantally.

I decided to publish this book in 1992 because I recognized that it was the first systematically covenantal study of biblical eschatology. This is not merely a publisher's hyperbole; I mean every word. But how can this book be the first truly comprehensive study of the topic? Aren't there many hundreds of such volumes going back for almost two millennia? In a word, *no.*

Ken Gentry's various books on eschatology, which culminate in this comprehensive treatise, are not competing with a massive body of theological literature stretching back to the early Church. Because modern evangelicals live in a ghetto subculture that is suffused with prophetic speculation, they tend to forget how recent eschatology is as a separate theological sub-discipline. Neither Calvin nor Luther wrote commentaries on the Book of Revelation. The Roman Catholic Church and Eastern Orthodoxy have long avoided eschatology like the plague. Only in the nineteenth century did eschatology gain the prominence that it enjoys today, and really only in the second half of the century, and mainly in the United States.

Interest in the broader topic of biblical eschatology has been fueled almost entirely by interest in prophecy. The Protestant fundamentalist world has wanted to hear uplifting (literally) stories about the imminent return of Christ, a literary preference that has led both Charles Colson and Pat Robertson to write novels about the last days. Christian novelist Frank Perretti's huge success with *This Present Darkness* and its follow-up volumes paved the way. We theonomic postmillennialists used to tease dispensationalists for having written novels disguised as popular theological treatises, but now they are writing theological treatises disguised as novels. Having failed to defend their eschatology exegetically, they have adopted the strategy of defending it imaginatively. Tactically, this is wise; strategically, it will fail. Man does not live by novels alone.

One of the major psychological motivations for this continuing interest in prophecy is the evangelical Protestant world's weariness in marching as Christian soldiers with the cross of Jesus going on before. They are tired of carrying that cross. They seek acceptable ways of sitting down. One way is to take up residence in cultural ghettos where the comprehensive cultural requirements of the Great Commission[1] are redefined to

---

1. Kenneth L. Gentry, Jr., *The Greatness of the Great Commission: The Christian*

mean little more than attending weekly worship services and handing out an occasional gospel tract. These days, there are not very many gospel tracts still in print. To justify life in the ghetto, evangelicals have proclaimed their commitment to pre-Darwinian humanism's "natural law" social theories,[2] political pluralism,[3] and ghetto eschatologies.[4] They have self-consciously rejected the theonomists' suggestion that biblical law is still valid in New Covenant times. If theonomy is valid, then Christians have received a far larger assignment from God: to subdue the whole earth to His glory by means of His Bible-revealed law.[5] Christians have proclaimed, "Let it never be!"

The Great Commission

People sometimes ask me what I think is the most important book on Christian social ethics ever written. I do not hesitate to answer: Dr. Gentry's *The Greatness of the Great Commission*. This book sets forth briefly, clearly, and powerfully, the comprehensive covenantal claims of Jesus Christ in history. Christ lays claim to more than men's souls. He lays claim to entire civilizations. He lays claim to all the earth:

And Jesus came and spake unto them, saying, All power is given unto me in heaven and in earth. Go ye therefore, and

Enterprise in a Fallen World (Tyler, Texas: Institute for Christian Economics, 1990). Second edition, 1995.

2. This has been going on in the Church since the days of the early Church. Luther adopted Roman Catholicism's natural law theory as the basis of his views. After the intellectual and cultural triumph of Unitarian Isaac Newton in the late seventeenth century, Protestants substituted Newtonian natural law theory for medieval Scholasticism's traditional version.

3. Gary North, *Political Polytheism: The Myth of Pluralism* (Tyler, Texas: Institute for Christian Economics, 1989).

4. Gary North, "Ghetto Eschatologies," *Biblical Economics Today*, XIV (April/ May 1992), published by the Institute for Christian Economics.

5. Gary North, *The Dominion Covenant: Genesis* (2nd ed.; Tyler, Texas: Institute for Christian Economics, 1987); North, *Tools of Dominion: The Case Laws of Exodus* (Tyler, Texas: Institute for Christian Economics, 1990).

teach all nations, baptizing them in the name of the Father, and
of the Son, and of the Holy Ghost: Teaching them to observe all
things whatsoever I have commanded you: and, lo, I am with
you alway, even unto the end of the world. Amen. (Matt. 28:18-
20)

In *The Greatness of the Great Commission*, Dr. Gentry makes it
clear that the gospel's scope of authority is as broad as the fall
of man. The gospel has the power to heal every area of life that
man's sin has corrupted. This means that **God's kingdom in
history is as extensive as Satan's kingdom in history**. Furthermore, as surely as Satan's human representatives can rule in
history as his kingdom's agents, so are Christians called on by
God to exercise dominion in His name. As surely as Satan does
not need to sit upon an earthly throne in order to exercise his
kingdom's rule through his covenantal agents, so Jesus Christ
does not need to sit upon an earthly throne in order to exercise
His kingdom's rule through His covenantal agents. Simple, isn't
it? But this simple suggestion is emphatically rejected by modern evangelicals. Premillennialists implicitly (and sometimes
even explicitly) insist that the power of sin in history is so great
that without Jesus' bodily presence on an earthly throne, sin
will remain culturally dominant. Amillennialists say the same
thing, except that they deny that He will ever sit on an earthly
throne in history. Amillennialists are, in R. J. Rushdoony's
classic phrase, premillennialists without earthly hope.

Premillennial and amillennial theologians are suspiciously
silent regarding the social effects in history of Christ's historical
ascension to heaven. This is because they do not want to say in
public what they believe in private, namely, that the bodily ascension of Jesus Christ in history has left His people in a less
influential position in history than they were in national Israel
under Joshua and David. They believe that the Davidic throne
in Israel possessed more authority and power than Jesus'
throne in heaven. They do not deny that Jesus sent the Holy

Spirit to the Church to lead the Church into all truth after His ascension,[6] yet they believe that the Church possesses far less authority or ability to speak to the daily affairs of life than the Old Covenant's Mosaic priesthood did. But because they are so embarrassed – as well they should be – by this theologically necessary conclusion from their views regarding both biblical law and biblical eschatology, they refuse to say any of this in public. They believe it, but they refuse to admit it. Discretion is the better part of pessimillennial valor.

He Shall Have Dominion is a companion volume to *The Greatness of the Great Commission*. Its presentation is far more detailed. I published this book in 1992 because I wanted to force theonomy's critics to admit in print what they believe in private about the cultural irrelevance of Christ's bodily ascension in history. But I was willing to settle for second-best: merely to silence them. I predicted in my Foreword to the first edition that theonomy's critics would not comment publicly on this book. So far, I have been correct. They have refused. Why? First, they cannot answer it theologically. Second, they cannot answer it honestly without admitting publicly what they really believe about the inevitable impotence in history of both Jesus' heavenly throne and the Church under the Holy Spirit's guidance.

Their silence is the theonomists' opportunity. Once again, we can come before our supporters and point out the graveyard-like silence of our critics. As I predicted in the earlier edition's Foreword, this book will reduce them to murmuring in private. So far, it has. They cannot answer it. They have not even tried to answer it. Instead, they pretend that they have never heard of Gentry, just as they have never heard of Chilton's *Days of Vengeance*. Professional theologians never quite get around to hearing about books they cannot answer.

---

6. "I have yet many things to say unto you, but ye cannot bear them now. Howbeit when he, the Spirit of truth, is come, he will guide you into all truth: for he shall not speak of himself; but whatsoever he shall hear, that shall he speak: and he will shew you things to come" (John 16:12-13).

Eschatology

Eschatology is that part of systematic theology which deals with "final things." It is a much broader topic than prophecy, for it involves ethics. As I have already argued, only very recently have Protestant evangelical theologians begun to deal with the first things about the last things. We have not had a developed, comprehensive, exegetically defended presentation of exactly how the Church of Jesus Christ is required by God to conduct itself ethically as it moves from the here and now to those "last things." Nor have we had a detailed presentation of exactly what the Church should expect to happen along the way if it conducts itself according to God's ethical requirements, or what will happen when it refuses to do so.

But that was before *He Shall Have Dominion* was published. It remedies the problem, and does this comprehensively, exegetically, and in a style that is easy to follow for the reader who pays attention. It fills the gap as no other book ever has.

Take a look at the book's contents. There are a lot of Bible verses cited: thousands. There are a lot of footnotes to books and articles. It had to be this way. Dr. Gentry is arguing for an ancient and respected view of eschatology: postmillennialism. This places him at a disadvantage. There have not been many theologians in the twentieth century who have held this view of the comprehensive future success of the gospel. This was not the case a century ago, but it is the case today. Thus, he comes before an audience that is disinclined to believe him. He has to overcome their resistance. Like a conservative college student in a liberal classroom, who must outperform liberal students in the class in order to receive the same grade, so is Dr. Gentry.

He is also doing his best to overcome a lot of misinformation that has been taught in conservative seminary classrooms for many decades. He knows; he attended two of them: one dispensational, the other amillennial. Although Dr. Gentry has made the postmillennial position clear in previous books, and although the Institute for Christian Economics has sent out copies of these books free of charge to offending faculties, the same misinformation continues to be presented in the class-room to vulnerable, trusting students. (I much prefer the word *lies* to "misinformation," since this gets across to the reader what is really going on in seminary classrooms, but I am trying to be a Christian gentleman, since Dr. Gentry is.)[7]

Because he has meticulously documented everything he writes about the Bible and what other theologians have written on eschatology, Dr. Gentry has done his best to gain the rea-der's confidence in what he is saying. What appears to be over-kill with respect to the volume of citations is necessary in a pioneering book of this nature. Some of postmillennialism's less intellectually gifted critics (one in particular) used to complain that there has never been a successful exegetical defense of the position – not just theonomic postmillennialism but postmillen-nialism in general. I had them in mind when I published this book. Its volume of citations conforms to my long-term pub-lishing strategy: *to stuff the critics' mouths with footnotes*.

He has expended considerable effort to accomplish the fol-lowing goals: (1) to persuade the reader that his analysis is correct; (2) to provide supporting evidence for *every* statement; (3) to avoid exaggeration; (4) to present a positive case for what he believes; (5) to summarize accurately the arguments against

---

7. Here is an example of this systematic, deliberate misinformation. Three students at Dallas Theological Seminary came to Tyler to videotape me and Ray Sutton in 1985. The very first question that the interviewer asked was this: "Why do you say that Israel is identical to the Church?" We replied (approximately): "We don't. We believe that Israel will be brought to Christ prior to the millennium. This has been taught by Robert Haldane, Charles Hodge, and John Murray. It is the view of Scottish Presbyterianism. The Westminster Larger Catechism instructs us to pray for the Jews: Answer 191." The interviewer was so stunned that he had his partner shut off the video camera. (I kept my audio cassette recorder running.) He then told us that they had all been taught in class that Christian Reconstructionists believe that Israel is identical to the Church. I had argued against this view in my 1981 book, *Unconditional Surrender: God's Program for Victory* (Tyler, TX: Geneva, 1981), p. 199. They had never been told of the traditional Scottish postmillennial interpretation of Romans 11. This is unconscionable. It is also typical. It is this lack of both integrity and scholarship that is steadily undermining traditional Scofieldian dispensationalism.

his position; (6) to refute the major critics of postmillennialism; (7) to present the implications of his position; and (8) to state the implications of rival positions. This is why the book is long. I know of no book that presents the case for any view of eschatology that is equally painstaking and comprehensive.

Notice, too: his book has a positive aspect and a negative aspect. As with the gospel, this book has a two-fold goal: reconciliation and condemnation. There is no escape from these goals. When we share the gospel, we are bringing God's covenantal lawsuit, just as Jonah brought it before the people of Nineveh. This lawsuit offers blessings and cursings. Therefore, *He Shall Have Dominion* is designed to achieve the following results: (1) to give confidence and greater information to those who already believe its general position; (2) to persuade those who have not yet made up their minds; (3) to persuade those who are still open to new evidence; (4) to silence the critics.

An honest critic, if he goes into print against *He Shall Have Dominion*, should do the following: (1) show how Gentry has generally misinterpreted biblical eschatology, i.e., demonstrate a *pattern* of misinterpretation; (2) provide several examples of this pattern; (3) refer the reader to equally detailed and equally comprehensive studies in eschatology that offer biblical solutions to the problems that Gentry raises; (4) show how Gentry either ignored this missing book or completely misrepresented it. While a short book review cannot match Gentry's massive documentation, the reviewer had better be able to point the reader to a book or books of equal or greater exactness as *He Shall Have Dominion*. If he fails to do the third task – suggest an exegetically superior book – he is implicitly admitting that Gentry has offered the most exegetically impressive case that anyone has made so far. My belief is that no reviewer will publicly identify *the* definitive book on eschatology; this would involve too much commitment on his part. No reviewer today trusts any book on eschatology unless it is his own, but reviewers rarely have the *chutzpa* to say this in print. So, Gentry wins.

This leads me to a discussion of the state of eschatological writing in this, the final decade of the second millennium after the life, death, resurrection, and ascension of Jesus Christ, the Second Person of the Trinity, the perfect son of man. The year 2000 is fast approaching, yet the Church has not done its eschatological homework. To prove this statement, I need to go into a brief history of a long series of inconclusive debates over the earthly future of the Church. To explain why *He Shall Have Dominion* is so important, I need to show what has preceded it.

An Incomplete Case for Every Previous Position

It is true that there has not been a recent, definitive, comprehensive, detailed exegetical presentation of the case for postmillennialism – a book about which large numbers of postmillennialists have said with confidence: "Yes, here is our book. Sink this, and you will have seriously damaged our position." What needs to be pointed out is that the postmillennialists are in no worse shape in this regard than historic premillennialists, dispensational premillennialists, and amillennialists. The fact is, *none of the four major Protestant eschatological positions has been defended exegetically by a large body of scholarly, comprehensive books.* All eschatological positions in the twentieth century have rested on a comparative handful of books that at best sketch the broad exegetical case for their respective positions. None of these books has developed a comprehensive worldview based on its particular system. (I exempt here the Christian Reconstructionists, who have been self-conscious about the comprehensive nature of their system, which is why the Reconstructionists have made so many enemies in so many camps.)

I need to suggest something. What I am about to say should not be very controversial. It is this: *biblical eschatology provides God's people with a philosophy of history.* Any objections? Any cries of "this is an outrageous exaggeration"? No? Fine. Let me add a corollary: any eschatological system that does not offer a comprehensive philosophy of history that is theologically consistent with the its system of interpretation is in an incomplete state. This has long been the situation facing every traditional view of eschatology: no public philosophy of history. Until now.

Is Your Life's Work Prophetically Doomed in History?

Let me ask you three questions. *First,* do you hope that your work on earth will leave a positive legacy to future generations, no matter how small the legacy is, even if no one in the future remembers who you were or what you did? Of course you do. *Second,* does God's Word return to Him void? No. *Third,* as a covenant-keeper, can you legitimately expect that your good words and good deeds will have more impact in the future than your evil words and evil deeds? I am not speaking merely of building up treasures in heaven; I am speaking also of your legacy in history to earthly heirs. I am speaking of *inheritance* in the broadest sense. If you answer *yes,* I think you have the right attitude about yourself and your work in God's kingdom. If you answer *no,* I think you are in need of professional Christian counseling. You are headed for a mental crisis. First, you have a problem with your lack of self-esteem (and covenant-keepers have a right to self-esteem as legally adopted sons of God: Ephesians 1:5). Second, you have a problem with your lack of confidence regarding God's willingness to bless your work. You have neglected God's promise: "Wherefore the LORD God of Israel saith, I said indeed that thy house, and the house of thy father, should walk before me for ever: but now the LORD saith, Be it far from me; for them that honour me I will honour, and they that despise me shall be lightly esteemed" (1 Sam. 2:30).

The three questions I have asked here with respect to your legitimate expectations about the historical outcome of your *personal* efforts also need to be asked with respect to Christianity in general: *the kingdom (civilization) of God.* When we begin to seek Bible-based answers to these three questions regarding the kingdom of God in history, we have necessarily raised the issue of a biblical philosophy of history. Each of the major views of eschatology has a specific philosophy of history. This connection is not always discussed in public. In most cases, the implications of eschatology for a philosophy of history are implicit rather than explicit, since the defenders of the various positions tend not to discuss these implications. But there is no escape from those implications. There is no eschatological neutrality. This is one of the themes in *He Shall Have Dominion*.

Historic Premillennialism

Historic premillennialists are not dispensationalists. They do not believe in a coming secret "rapture" or the supposed seven-year absence of the Church from the earth after the return of Jesus to "rapture" the Church into heaven. They believe that Jesus will come back to the earth to rule for a thousand years before the final judgment. They believe that the Great Tribulation is still in the future: it will precede the return of Christ to set up His kingdom. They are therefore *post-tribulationists*.

There are not many historic premillennialists these days. Two centuries ago, there were far more people who held this position. In the late nineteenth century, the Baptist Calvinist Charles Haddon Spurgeon was a well-known historic premillennialist, although his language was often very optimistic with respect to the spread of the gospel, and he believed in the familiar postmillennial doctrine of the future conversion of the Jews. He did not have much use for millennial theories. "I am not now going into millennial theories, or into any speculation as to dates. I do not know anything about such things, and I am not sure that I am called to spend my time in such researches. I am rather called to minister the gospel than to open prophecy."[8] In our day, the most famous American historic premillennialist has been the Calvinist Presbyterian author, Francis Schaeffer, although he rarely wrote about his Calvinism,

---

8. Charles Haddon Spurgeon, "The Restoration and Conversion of the Jews" (June 16, 1864), Sermon No. 582, *Metropolitan Tabernacle Pulpit*, vol. 10 (1864) p. 429.

his Presbyterianism, or his premillennialism. (It does present a problem for historic premillennialists when their most famous representatives prefer not to write about eschatology.)

Historic premillennialists can appeal to recent books by George Eldon Ladd. But I am aware of no book that discusses the premillennial view of the era of the Church prior to Christ's return to earth to set up His kingdom, i.e., no book on the premillennial philosophy of history. The focus of all historic premillennial works is on the Second Coming: the great future discontinuity that supposedly will inaugurate the judicially visible phase of Christ's kingdom in history, when Jesus will reign in person on earth. Only then does the idea of Christian civilization become significant in historic premillennialism. Christendom is ignored until after the Second Coming.

Even with respect to this future millennial era, there is never any detailed discussion of ethical cause and effect in history, i.e., a biblical philosophy of history. There is no discussion of how Jesus Christ will rule on earth through His people. Will there still be politics? Will government be entirely bureaucratic? What laws will Jesus require governments to enforce? What penalties will be imposed? Will civil judges and juries still hand down sentences? How will appeals be conducted? Will the line of justice-seekers in front of Jesus' headquarters be a thousand times longer than the line in front of Moses' tent (Exo. 18:13)? We are not told – not by historic premillennialists or dispensational premillennialists.

Dispensationalism

The question facing historic premillennialism also faces dispensational premillennialism: *What is the premillennial philosophy of history?* What is the relationship between the faithful preaching of the gospel and the extension of Christ's kingdom in history? What are the cultural effects of this extension of Christ's kingdom in history, and why? This is another way of asking: What is the relationship between ethics and authority in history? Is there a *predictable* cause-and-effect relationship, long term, between *personal* righteousness and success, and personal unrighteousness and failure? What about *corporate* righteousness? What about corporate unrighteousness?

In the spring of 1956, Alva J. McClain, the president of Grace Theological Seminary, wrote an essay for *Bibliotheca Sacra*, the journal published by Dallas Theological Seminary. Both schools were (and are) dispensational. The essay was titled, "The Premillenial Philosophy of History." It was only five and a half pages long. Most of it was devoted to criticizing other views. When he had finished with them, he had only half a page remaining to present the premillennial view. He did not say what it is. All he said was this: "The Premillennial philosophy of history makes sense. It lays a Biblical and rational basis for a truly optimistic view of human history." But he never explained what he meant by "history." Since dispensationalism teaches that the Church will not succeed in converting large numbers of people to Christ in the "Church Age," and that it will suffer increasing persecution until the rapture, McClain must have been defining *history* as the post-rapture *millennial dispensation*. But this totally new era will begin only after the rapture and after the seven-year Great Tribulation, meaning *after every trace of the gospel's effects in history will be blotted out*. So, what legitimate optimism does dispensationalism offer to a Christian regarding the long-term historic effects of his life's work? McClain did not say, but the answer is obvious: none.

Dispensationalists can appeal to modern books on eschatology and the millennial kingdom written by McClain and John Walvoord, but the major presentation of their eschatological position is found in *Things to Come* (1958) by Dallas Seminary professor J. Dwight Pentecost. Unknown to most readers, he has significantly revised the book in a key area, and in doing so, he has abandoned the traditional dispensational case for the inevitable defeat of the Church in what the dispensationalists call the "Church Age." In the original edition, he argued for the eventual triumph of unbelief in this, the "Church Age." He wrote that Jesus' parable of the mustard seed (Matt. 13:31-32) points to the expansion of an *evil* tree in history, "a monstrosity. . . . The parable teaches that the enlarged sphere of profession has become inwardly corrupt. This is the characteristic of the age" (p. 147). In his exposition of the parable of the leaven, he argued: "This evidently refers to the work of a false religious system. . . . This figure is used in Scripture to portray that which is evil in character. . ." (p. 148). Summarizing, he wrote: "The mustard seed refers to the perversion of God's purpose in this age, while the leaven refers to a corruption of the divine agency, the Word, through which this purpose is realized" (p. 148). Pentecost's focus here was *ethics*: the progressive triumph of evil through time, during the "Church Age." This could at least serve as the foundation of a dispensational philosophy of history: *the defeat of the saints*. His book did not provide a developed philosophy of history; it provided only a starting point.

Three decades later, he abandoned this view, but very few of his followers are aware of the fact. The 1987 reprint is not a reprint but *a strategically revised edition*. It is nowhere identified as such. Dr. Pentecost had the typesetter carefully superimpose a crucial revised section. The switch is almost undetectable, yet it is a devastating admission for dispensationalism. Here is his revised exposition of Christ's kingdom during the "Church Age." *Mustard Seed*: "This part of the parable stresses the great growth of the kingdom when once it is introduced. The kingdom will grow from an insignificant beginning to great proportions" (p. 147). There is not a word about its ethical corruption. *Leaven*: "When leaven is used in Scripture it frequently connotes evil. . . . Its use in the sacrifices that represent the perfection of the person of Christ (Lev. 2:1-3) shows that it is not always so used. Here the emphasis is not on leaven as though to emphasize its character, but rather that the leaven has been hidden in the meal, thus stressing the way leaven works when once introduced into the meal" (p. 148). *There is no mention here of evil*: not one word about any evil effects of either the mustard seed or the leaven. Today, his focus is on the growth of the kingdom of Christ in history – a *post***millennial focus**: "The parable of the mustard and the leaven in meal, then, stress the growth of the new form of the kingdom" (p. 148).

If Christ's kingdom is not being corrupted in our dispensation, then it is either ethically neutral (the kingdom of Christ as ethically neutral?!?) or positive. Pentecost's theological problem is obvious: *there can be no ethical neutrality*. If the necessarily expanding kingdom of Christ is not being steadily undermined by theological and moral perversion, then it must be growing in righteousness. This interpretation is the postmillennial view of the kingdom of God: expansion over time. Matthew 13 is not discussing Satan's kingdom; it is discussing Christ's. Dr. Pentecost has very quietly overthrown the heart and soul of the traditional dispensational system's account of the inevitable progress of evil in this, the "Church Age."[9] I am aware of no dispensational theologian who has discussed in print the implications of this radical alteration by Pentecost, or explained exactly how it has not, if correct, overthrown the dispensational system. **Traditional dispensationalism has been quietly abandoned by younger theologians who now lead the movement.**[10]

Amillennialism

Amillennialism is the most widely held interpretation of prophecy, primarily because Roman Catholics generally hold it, although they rarely discuss eschatology. Lutherans also hold it. Episcopalians, like Roman Catholics, have rarely emphasized eschatology, so amillennialism has won by default. European

---

9. Gary DeMar spotted this shift in early 1992. He looked up Pentecost's section on leaven in the 1987 edition. He found that it was not what Gentry had quoted. He called Gentry, who looked it up in the 1958 edition. The two versions differed.

10. Gary North, *Rapture Fever: Why Dispensationalism Is Paralyzed* (Tyler, Texas: Institute for Christian Economics, 1993), ch. 8.

Calvinists have held it for the last two centuries. Dutch Calvinists have been amillennialism's major expositors.

The amillennialist believes that the next major eschatological
event will be the Second Advent of Jesus Christ at the final
judgment. The series of cosmic events which is called the rapture by dispensationalists is identified by the amillennialist as
immediately preceding the final judgment. Like the premillennialist and the postmillennialist, he believes in the coming of
Christ from the sky, to where the living and dead in Christ will
be raised. Like the postmillennialist, but unlike the premillennialist, he does not believe that this unified event will take place
a thousand years before the final judgment. It will take place
on the day of final judgment. That is to say, he denies that
there will be any eschatological discontinuity between today and
just before the Second Advent (final judgment). There will be
historical continuity for the gospel. Unlike the postmillennialist,
but like the premillennialist, he insists that this is *a continuity of
cultural decline and defeat for Christianity* until Jesus comes again.

Amillennialist authors have written short books that mix
personal eschatology (death, resurrection, and final judgment)
with cosmic eschatology (New Testament prophecy, the Church,
the Second Advent, final judgment, and the world beyond).
What is conspicuously absent in all of them is a detailed exposition of the New Testament era from the fall of Jerusalem in
A.D. 70 to the Second Advent. Anthony Hoekema's *The Bible
and the Future* (1979) attempts this, but not in any systematic or
comprehensive exegetical fashion, and it is virtually alone in
attempting even this much. This is not to say that amillennialists do not have a philosophy of history. They do, but it is
rarely discussed and never developed in detail or used to develop a distinctly amillennial social theory.

Let me offer an example of the amillennial approach to
questions of the outcome of the gospel in history. There is a

book by an amillennialist titled, *A New Heaven and a New Earth*.[11] The title is taken from a biblical eschatological phrase. This phrase appears twice in the New Testament (2 Pet. 3:13; Rev. 21:1) and twice in the Old Testament (Isa. 65:17; 66:22). The passage in Isaiah 65 prophesies of a coming era on earth and before the final judgment (since sinners will still be active) in which there will be great external blessings, including very long life spans. Here is the complete passage:

> For, behold, I create new heavens and a new earth: and the former shall not be remembered, nor come into mind. But be ye glad and rejoice for ever in that which I create: for, behold, I create Jerusalem a rejoicing, and her people a joy. And I will rejoice in Jerusalem, and joy in my people: and **the voice of weeping shall be no more heard in her, nor the voice of crying**. There shall be no more thence an infant of days, nor an old man that hath not filled his days: **for the child shall die an hundred years old; but the sinner being an hundred years old shall be accursed**. And they shall build houses, and inhabit them; and they shall plant vineyards, and eat the fruit of them. They shall not build, and another inhabit; they shall not plant, and another eat: for as the days of a tree are the days of my people, and mine elect shall long enjoy the work of their hands. **They shall not labour in vain, nor bring forth for trouble**; for they are the seed of the blessed of the LORD, and their offspring with them. (Isa. 65:17-23, emphasis added)

A postmillennialist can interpret this passage literally: a coming era of extensive millennial blessings *before* Jesus returns in final judgment. So can a premillennialist: the era after Jesus returns to earth but before final judgment. But the amillennialist cannot admit the possibility of such an era of literal, culture-wide blessings in history. His eschatology denies any literal,

---

11. Archibald Hughes, *A New Heaven and a New Earth* (Philadelphia: Presbyterian & Reformed, 1958).

culture-wide triumph of Christianity in history. Therefore, he has to "spiritualize" or allegorize this passage.

So, how did the author explain this passage? He didn't. He simply ignored it. "It isn't in *my* Bible," he seemed to be saying. In a 233-page book on the new heavens and the new earth, there is no discussion of Isaiah 65:17-23. The Scripture index refers the reader to pages 139 and 157. On page 139 there is a reference to Isaiah 65:17-25, but not one word of commentary. On page 157, there is neither a reference nor a comment. The book is filled with thousands of Bible references, but nowhere does the author comment on the one passage, *more than any other passage in the Bible*, that categorically refutes amillennialism. Yet this book is regarded by amillennial theologians as a scholarly presentation of their position. There are very few other books that present a detailed exegetical case for amillennialism.

Most amillennial discussions of ethical cause and effect in history are limited to the unpleasant conclusion that evil men will get ever-more powerful culturally, while the righteous will become progressively weaker culturally.[12] In other words, the progressive sanctification of God's people will lead to their progressive enslavement and isolation from culture. This means that the amillennial view of history rests on a view of ethical cause and effect in which *right makes weakness* and *unrighteousness makes might*. This conclusion is so unpleasant – and so despairing – that amillennialists prefer not to discuss it, which leaves them without a publicly articulated philosophy of history. About the only exception to this statement is Meredith G. Kline's 1978 essay, in which he argued that God's sanctions in history are ethically random from the human point of view.[13] But since we live in an era in which the Church is on the defensive, there

---

12. This was Cornelius Van Til's view, presented in his book, *Common Grace* (1947). It has been reprinted by Presbyterian & Reformed in a larger book, *Common Grace and the Gospel* (1972).

13. Meredith G. Kline, "Comments on an Old-New Error," *Westminster Theological Journal*, XLI (Fall 1978), p. 184.

can be no legitimate hope on Kline's basis of a comprehensive victory. He has been quite willing to admit this.

Historic Postmillennialism

There have been numerous presentations of various aspects of postmillennialism over the years. There was David Brown's *Christ's Second Coming: Will It Be Premillennial?*, published in 1842 and reprinted in 1990.[14] There was the traditional Scottish postmillennial interpretation of Romans 11: the conversion of the Jews, which will launch a great era of God's blessing on the Church. This interpretation has appeared repeatedly in Calvinist expositions, such as in the commentaries by Robert Haldane, Charles Hodge, and John Murray. There was the huge *Commentary on the Prophecies of Isaiah* by Princeton Seminary theologian J. A. Alexander, which is not well known because of its enormous bulk and detailed argumentation. There were the theological writings of Benjamin B. Warfield, another Princeton Seminary theologian, who carried on the Princeton eschatology until his death in 1921.

In many respects, these earlier defenses of postmillennialism also failed to present a case for ethical cause and effect in history. The future era of blessing was seen as the result of the outpouring of the Holy Spirit, which it surely will be, but not the product also of ethical transformation. God's law and God's covenantal sanctions – blessing and cursing – were rarely discussed. This was especially true of the type of postmillennialism preached by Jonathan Edwards in the mid-eighteenth century. Except in the writings of seventeenth-century Puritans prior to 1660, postmillennialism has long been stripped of any necessary connection between God's Bible-revealed law and God's corporate sanctions in history. This view of God's predictable sanctions in history is an extension of the "no New Covenant back-up"

---

14. Edmonton, Alberta; Canada: Still Water Revival Books (1882 edition).

argument regarding covenant lawsuits. This form of postmillennialism is inherently antinomian: denying the willingness of God to defend His covenant law through the imposition of historical sanctions. Consistent men ask: "If God will not apply sanctions, then how can Christians dare to apply them?" But if God's judicial sanctions are not applied, then Satan's judicial sanctions will be. There is no judicial neutrality in history.

By refusing to acknowledge either God's revealed law or God's predictable corporate sanctions in history, defenders of postmillennialism have generally abandoned a philosophy of history. They have proclaimed a pietistic postmillennialism rather than covenantal postmillennialism.[15] They have proclaimed Christianity's victory in history, but without specifying the legal foundations of the kingdom (civilization) of God.

The Key Issue: Ethics With Historical Sanctions

Ethics cannot successfully be divorced from eschatology, *but neither can the question of God's sanctions in history*. The **unified** question of ethics and corporate sanctions must not be evaded. The eschatological issue is this: Do Christians have legitimate hope for the positive historical effects of their efforts, both personal and corporate, in history? Do their sacrifices really make a difference in history? Of course they make a difference in eternity; this is not the question. Do Christians' individual and corporate efforts make a positive difference *in history?*

If all that Christians can accomplish in history is to present God's covenant lawsuits against individuals, allowing the Holy Spirit to pull a few people out of the eternal fire, then why should they go to college, except to serve as witnesses to college students? Why should they become lawyers, except to witness to

---

15. Ray R. Sutton, "Covenantal Postmillennialism," *Covenant Renewal*, III (Feb. 1989); Sutton, "A Letter from Loraine; or a Covenantal View of the Millennium" *Covenant Renewal*, III (May 1989). Copies are available on request from the Institute for Christian Economics, P. O. Box 8000, Tyler, TX 75711.

lawyers? Is everything we do or build doomed to destruction, either in some future Great Tribulation or in the final rebellion of Satan's forces at the end of time? Does everything we leave behind get swallowed up by Satan's historically successful kingdom (civilization)? Should every dollar that Christians spend today on education above the twelfth grade be sent instead to missionaries? Are our struggling little Christian colleges nothing more than very expensive dating and marriage broker services? (I would have said "universities," but evangelicals and fundamentalists do not have one: a state-accredited institution that grants the Ph.D. in the liberal arts and sciences.) Are Christians supposed to live in a cultural ghetto forever, either premillennial or amillennial, praying for the Second Coming as their only means of escape from predestined historic impotence?

Recent Defenses of Postmillennialism

Roderick Campbell, a Canadian layman and businessman, wrote *Israel and the New Covenant* in the early 1950's. It was published in 1954 by Presbyterian & Reformed Publishing Company. These were the years before *The Genesis Flood* (1961) and *Competent to Counsel* (1970) provided P&R with a much wider market and a lot more income. Campbell's book did not receive much attention. Reformed (Calvinist) theological books written by businessmen rarely do – a lesson that I have personally learned, painfully and expensively.

Campbell's book is a masterpiece: short chapters, tightly written, filled with Bible verses and clear exposition. It is a little over 350 pages long, so the average reader has no excuse for not finishing it. The book's Preface was written by O. T. Allis, one of the greatest Old Testament scholars of all time, author of *The Five Books of Moses* (1943) and *Prophecy and the Church* (1945), a devastating exegetical critique of dispensationalism that has yet to be answered in equal or greater detail, half a century after its publication.[16] Contrary to Charles Ryrie, Allis was a postmillennialist, not an amillennialist – a true heir of the theology of the old (pre-1929) Princeton Theological Seminary, including its eschatology. This is why he was so enthusiastic about *Israel and the New Covenant*. The book went out of print in the late 1960's. It was reprinted jointly by P&R and Geneva Divinity School Press in 1981. It is again out of print. But this is not to say that it never was in print, which is why the critics are wrong when they assert that there has never been an exegetical case for postmillennialism.

There is also Loraine Boettner's book, *The Millennium* (1958), which presents a defense of the traditional Princeton eschatology, as well as a critique of amillennialism (brief) and premillennialism. There is R. J. Rushdoony's *Thy Kingdom Come* (1970). There is J. Marcellus Kik's *An Eschatology of Victory* (1971). Last, but hardly least, there is David Chilton: *Paradise Restored* (1985), *The Days of Vengeance* (1987), and *The Great Tribulation* (1987). (Some scholars would include Geerhardus Vos in this list.)[17] There have also been lesser-known defenders throughout the twentieth century. Dr. Gentry mentions some of them in Chapter 2.

---

16. Charles C. Ryrie's short book, *Dispensationalism Today* (Chicago: Moody Press, 1965), attempted a generation ago to refute Allis' case for continuity in New Testament history – that is, no dispensational "secret" rapture in the midst of history, no premillennial Second Advent of Christ prior to the final judgment – by citing ultradispensationalism's arguments for discontinuity in history. Then he used Allis-type arguments for prophetic continuity in order to refute ultradispensationalism's arguments that the Church did not begin in Acts 2 or Acts 4, but later, after Paul was called to minister to the Gentiles. For a more detailed consideration of the issues raised by Ryrie, see my comments in Publisher's Foreword, Greg L. Bahnsen and Kenneth L. Gentry, Jr., *House Divided: The Break-Up of Dispensational Theology* (Tyler, TX: Institute for Christian Economics, 1989), pp. xxiv-xxv.

17. Vos wrote in some passages as though he held to postmillennialism, most notably in his comments on Romans 11: the conversion of the Jews. He specifies that the conversion of the Jews must take place before the Second Advent, and that this conversion will inaugurate "seasons of refreshing." Vos, "Eschatology of the New Testament," *International Standard Biblical Encyclopedia*, 5 vols. (Grand Rapids: Eerdmans, [1929] 1943), II, p. 983. He is usually regarded as amillennial.

One thing is sure: postmillennialism, contrary to Alva J. McClain's 1956 assertion, has not disappeared.[18] What has disappeared are systematic, detailed defenses of dispensationalism written by theologians teaching at dispensational seminaries.[19]

The Missing Link: A Biblical Philosophy of History

Prior to the theonomists, what had been absent in every eschatological camp except the Puritans was a self-conscious presentation of an explicitly biblical philosophy of history. There had been no such presentation based on a comprehensive exegesis of the Bible – specifically, a philosophy of history derived from the biblical doctrine of the last things. In the field of systematic theology, eschatology is obviously the section in which such a discussion of history should be presented, yet such a discussion has long been missing. This is, to put it mildly, a bit peculiar. This glaring hole is not something that seminary-based theologians have often discussed in public.

Furthermore, a biblical philosophy of history is a necessity for any eschatology that is designed for those still living in this world. The absence of a detailed presentation of a philosophy of history does not keep Christians from having one. They inevitably adopt one. They just do not adopt one that has been systematically developed from the Bible. For example, they have strong opinions about such matters as the legitimacy and wisdom of social action in the name of Christ. They have strong opinions on what the Church can expect in the future. The more pessimistic these expectations, the more ready those who hold them are to imagine that the Church has very little time

---

18. Alva J. McClain, "Premillennialism as a Philosophy of History," *Bibliotheca Sacra*, CXIII (1956), p. 113.

19. The last full-scale defense of the original dispensational system was Charles C. Ryrie's *Dispensationalism Today* (1965): 212 pages of text. In 1995, a "revised and expanded" edition appeared: *Dispensationalism*. Ryrie added one page of text. Some revision! He still incorrectly identifies Allis as an amillennialist (p. 215). In any case, Ryrie was dismissed by Dallas Seminary well over a decade ago.

remaining. Facing (they believe) the threat of persecution in the future, and facing also (they believe) the *inevitable (predestined) historical irrelevance* of their efforts to turn back the satanic tide, Christians who hold to either premillennialism or amillennialism place their hope in a future, discontinuous, supernatural escape from the cares of this world, meaning an *escape from personal and institutional responsibility in this world.* I do not mean that they place their hope in death; I mean they place hope in "getting out of life alive": the dispensational rapture or the amillennial Second Advent. "It's just around the corner!"

The eschatological concern of evangelical, Protestant Christianity in the twentieth century has not been on ethics and Christians' responsibility – ethical cause and effect in history – but rather on the transcending of Christians' responsibility through a future divine intervention into history, either to set up Jesus' One World State bureaucracy (premillennialism) or to remove sinners from history by ending history (amillennialism). The eschatological focus has been on our legitimate (because eschatologically inevitable) escape from corporate responsibility as Christians. The psychological motivation has been the quest for theological justification for the Christians' escape from any obligation to work to extend the kingdom (civilization) of God in history: **bystander Christianity**.

Eschatology has been used to justify retroactively the sad fact that Protestant churches have accomplished virtually nothing in presenting an explicitly biblical alternative to the two major humanist worldviews of the West: the right-wing Enlightenment humanism of the liberal English Whigs and the left-wing Enlightenment humanism of the French Revolution. Protestants have defended one or the other viewpoint in the name of a religiously neutral political pluralism that supposedly is conformable to the Bible. They have not turned to the Bible for social answers. There is a reason for this lack of an alternative: the missing link – a theory of covenantal cause and effect in history. *He Shall Have Dominion* supplies this missing link.

Ethical Cause and Effect: Historical Sanctions

The missing eschatological link has been a theory of New Covenant history that is forthrightly based on ethical cause and effect. The Old Covenant saints had such an ethics-based theory of history, which is outlined in Leviticus 26 and Deuteronomy 28: blessings in history for those who obey God's Bible-revealed law, and cursings in history for those who disobey God's Bible-revealed law.[20] Today, the premillennialists and the amillennialists agree: such a system of ethical cause and effect no longer operates in New Covenant history. Thus, biblically speaking, ethical cause and effect either leads nowhere in particular (God's random sanctions in history) or, more widely believed, it leads to the cultural defeat of Christianity in history until Jesus comes again in person to judge His enemies.

This is an odd view of history, theologically speaking. We know that God backed up His prophets in the Old Covenant era. When they brought a covenant lawsuit, God would prosecute it. But, we are assured, this is no longer the case in the New Covenant. The Church can no longer successfully invoke such divine power in history. Question: If Jesus' death, resurrection, and ascension to the right hand of God has left His Church even more powerless than the Church was in Mosaic Israel, *then what have been the **culturally significant effects** (if any) of Jesus' death, resurrection, and ascension to the right hand of God?* Both the amillennialists and the premillennialists avoid answering this question at all costs, for they keep coming up with this highly embarrassing answer: *almost no effects whatsoever.* This is just too embarrassing to admit in public. They must be pushed, and pushed hard, to get them to admit it. (I do the pushing.)

The postmillennialist insists that Jesus' ascension to the throne of God is the transcendent mark of His absolute sover-

---

20. Gary North, *Leviticus: An Economic Commentary* (Tyler, Texas: Institute for Christian Economics, 1994), chaps. 32-35; *Sanctions and Dominion: An Economic Commentary on Numbers* (Tyler, Texas: Institute for Christian Economics, 1996).

eignty over history. The postmillennialist argues that Jesus will not leave this throne to return to earth until all His enemies are subdued (1 Cor. 15:24-28).[21] But *supernatural* postmillennialism has not been taken seriously in the twentieth century. Today, theonomic postmillennialism raises two very divisive issues: (1) personal and corporate responsibility; (2) legitimate avoidance thereof. To take this eschatology seriously raises questions regarding the Church's responsibility for the transformation of culture. This raises even more questions regarding the level of personal responsibility in the lives of Christians. Christians today fear what the answers might be. So, they prefer to avoid considering the biblical case for theonomic postmillennialism.

The standard response to covenantal (theonomic) postmillennialism is to argue that the world cannot improve ethically until Jesus comes again to rule with a rod of iron. But why should this be the case? How strong is Satan's rod in New Covenant history? I know of no premillennialist who argues that Satan must sit on an earthly throne in order for his kingdom to be manifested in history. They all understand that Satan's kingdom is manifested *representatively* through his human disciples. Yet they all insist that for Christ's kingdom to be "truly" manifested in history, Jesus Christ must return bodily from heaven to sit on an earthly throne, probably in Jerusalem. Question: Why does the Son of God need to be bodily present in order to enable His human servants to rule effectively in history, when the human servants of the devil, who was *defeated definitively* at Calvary, have no problem whatsoever in ruling over Christ's representatives in history? To put it starkly, *why has the sending of the Holy Spirit left Christianity culturally impotent in history?*

The amillennialists and premillennialists refuse to respond to this question. One can hardly blame them. It is so much easier to sit quietly and pray silently that the postmillennialist who

---

21. Gary North, *Millennialism and Social Theory* (Tyler, Texas: Institute for Christian Economics, 1990), pp. 280-282.

keeps asking it will either go away soon or else Jesus will come again, thereby shutting the mouths of all postmillennialists. But neither event takes place: I keep asking the question, and Jesus remains on His heavenly throne.

The amillennialists and the premillennialists agree: Christians can leave nothing of significance behind that will survive the horrors of the satanic oppression that inevitably lies ahead. Only the institutional Church will survive, and a besieged and shrinking institution it will be until Jesus arrives in person.

Dr. Gentry says they are wrong. He also says that the Bible says they are wrong.[22] As I wrote in 1992, it is now incumbent on premillennial and amillennial theologians to refute him: point by point, verse by verse. Silence is no longer golden.

The Significance of This Book

Dr. Gentry has already defended exegetically the comprehensive implications and applications of Jesus' Great Commission. In doing so, he has offered the culturally retreatist and defeatist theology of pietism its most detailed exegetical challenge in the twentieth century. He has also documented in exhaustive detail the dating of the Book of Revelation: before A.D. 70.[23] This has removed the most significant criticism of the preterist (past tense, i.e., *historically completed*) interpretation of the Book of Revelation. The preterists argue that all the

---

22. Gentry is a pastor in the Presbyterian Church in America (PCA), which left the Presbyterian Church of the U.S. (Southern Presbyterians) in the early 1970's when the PCUS became far more liberal theologically. Gentry is an heir of the postmillennial tradition of Southern Presbyterian theologians James Thornwell and Robert Dabney. Both of these theologians prior to 1861 had been members of the Presbyterian Church in the U.S.A. (Northern Presbyterians), sometimes known as the Old School Presbyterians, whose chief theologians taught at Princeton Seminary: Charles Hodge, A. A. Hodge, J. A. Alexander, and B. B. Warfield. They were also postmillennial. On the postmillennialism of nineteenth-century Southern Presbyterianism, see James B. Jordan, "A Survey of Southern Presbyterian Millennial Views Before 1930," *Journal of Christian Reconstruction*, III (Winter 1976-77).

23. Kenneth L. Gentry, Jr., *Before Jerusalem Fell: Dating the Book of Revelation* (Tyler, TX: Institute for Christian Economics, 1989).

prophecies regarding the Great Tribulation were fulfilled with the fall of Jerusalem in A.D. 70.[24] The preterist interpretation was easily criticized by those who argued that the Book of Revelation was written in A.D. 96. This counter-argument can no longer be easily sustained. He demolished it in *Before Jerusalem Fell*. So far, there has been no detailed published refutation.

In 1992, Dr. Gentry came with the first explicitly theonomic case for postmillennialism. No longer would the question of ethical cause and effect stripped out of postmillennialism. God's Bible-revealed laws *and their appropriate sanctions in history* lie at the very heart of his discussion of postmillennialism. It is not just that Dr. Gentry argues here for the continuing authority of God's law – what might be called **barebones theonomy**. It is not just that he argues for postmillennialism – what might be called **barebones postmillennialism**. What is significant about *He Shall Have Dominion* is that it links together these two positions by means of a covenantal doctrine of God's predictable historical sanctions in history.[25] Dr. Gentry defends the continuation of God's sanctions in history as a *theologically necessary* component of postmillennialism's doctrine of the comprehensive triumph of the kingdom of God in history. Without this link, there can be no ethics-based Christian philosophy of history. Paraphrasing the philosopher Immanuel Kant, "Theonomy without postmillennialism is impotent; postmillennialism without theonomy is blind." Theonomic postmillennialism is a unified system.

This is why *He Shall Have Dominion* is so important. As I wrote in 1992, from this point forward, this book will represent the position known as theonomic postmillennialism. All future expositions in the name of this position will have to build self-consciously on *He Shall Have Dominion*. As the old advertisement used to put it, "Accept no substitutes!"

---

24. David Chilton, *The Days of Vengeance: An Exposition of the Book of Revelation* (Ft. Worth, TX: Dominion Press, 1987); Chilton, *The Great Tribulation* (Ft. Worth, TX: Dominion Press, 1987).

25. Chapters 6 and 10.

The Task of Theonomy's Critics (Still Being Avoided)

Consider the wealth of documentation in this book. It will not be sufficient for a critic to conclude in some two-page review that "Gentry's book just does not prove his case." If anyone tries this stunt, the careful reader should ask: "Then what theologian *has* produced an equally comprehensive book that defends a rival position?" At this stage of history – approaching the year 2000 – to refute this book will require a comprehensive positive case presenting a rival eschatology with equal or greater diligence. The critics should not expect to be able to refute something this comprehensive with anything less comprehensive and detailed. They need a positive alternative. So far, they do not have one, although they write confidently as if they did. I must remind the critics of an old political slogan: **"You can't beat something with nothing."**

First, let me remind the reader of the disastrous attempts so far by a few theologians to refute both theonomy and postmillennialism. Westminster Seminary's attack, *Theonomy: A Reformed Critique* (1990), called forth my book, *Westminster's Confession* (1991), Bahnsen's *No Other Standard* (1991), and the collection of essays I edited, *Theonomy: An Informed Response* (1991). In it, Dr. Gentry refuted amillennialist critic Richard Gaffin's essay, point by point.[26] He had already refuted in great detail the embarrassingly weak criticisms of postmillennialism that were set forth by Rev. Thomas D. Ice in Ice's section of the co-authored and ill-fated book, *Dominion Theology: Blessing or Curse?*[27]

---

26. For a forthcoming jointly authored book on the four views of eschatology, Dr. Gaffin has recruited a co-author for his chapter on amillennialism. I do not blame him a bit. The editor picked Dr. Gentry to write the postmillennial chapter and to respond to the other authors. Dr. Gaffin has already suffered one such response all by himself. He does not want to suffer another.

27. H. Wayne House and Thomas D. Ice, *Dominion Theology: Blessing or Curse?* (Portland, OR: Multnomah, 1988). House left Dallas Seminary the next year to join the faculty of an obscure Baptist college in Oregon. In 1992, he departed from that school because of a dispute. I think House should write another book, *Dispensational Professorships: Blessing or Curse?*

There was nothing left of substance in Ice's critique after Gentry finished his polite, scholarly dissection.[28]

Second, and more important, premillennial and amillennial critics will not be able to appeal successfully to some well-developed body of theological opinion in order to buttress their rejection of Dr. Gentry's thesis. There is no such body of published opinion. *The footnotes are not there.* Each respective school of eschatological opinion has been flying exegetically by the seat of its pants for over a century. (Dispensationalism appeared only around 1830.) There has been no integrated, exegetical presentation by any school of eschatological opinion that (1) offers a detailed, Bible-based defense of its position and (2) applies this eschatological viewpoint to the relationships among the Church, Christian culture, anti-Christian rivals, and the future effects of the gospel prior to the Second Coming of Christ. Such a book does not exist in any of the rival camps. In short, there is not a single eschatological treatise in any of the rival competing camps – let alone dozens of treatises – which answers Francis Schaeffer's ethical question: "How Shall We Then Live?" (He did not answer it, either.)

This is why *He Shall Have Dominion* is unique. It brings together three themes: biblical ethics, God's historical sanctions, and the future of Christianity. It provides what no previous book on eschatology has provided, namely, a theologically integrated system of eschatology: ethics, sanctions, and prophecy.

Conclusion

From this time forward, as surely as critics of postmillennialism will have to respond in detail to Chilton's *Days of Vengeance*, so will they also have to respond to Gentry's *He Shall Have Dominion*. In my Publisher's Preface to Chilton's book, I predicted that critics would not be able to handle Chilton theologically

---

28. Bahnsen and Gentry, *House Divided*, Part II.

or stylistically. Since that time, I have yet to see a published exception to my prediction. That book's one weakness – Chilton's failure to defend in detail the pre-A.D. 70 authorship of the Book of Revelation – was solved by Gentry's *Before Jerusalem Fell*. I predicted in 1992 that pessimillennial theologians would be unable to handle this book theologically. So far, my prediction has been on target. Their continuing silence is a public admission of defeat: **their inability to defend their systems**.

[I wrote in 1992:] Perhaps a few theologians may yet take up my challenge, although I doubt it. If they are to look their students in the eye and tell them that "Chilton's *Paradise Restored*, Chilton's *Days of Vengeance*, Gentry's *Before Jerusalem Fell*, and Gentry's *He Shall Have Dominion* are without theological merit," they must first prove their case in print, where Gentry can respond. Murmuring in private conversations is not an academic argument. Neither are authoritative proclamations by seminary professors to captive students behind closed doors. Neither is the tried and true refrain, "I shall not dignify such shoddy and amateurish scholarship with a reply." Theonomy is now too well established for that response to work. Theonomists have too many books on the table.

Critics, it is time to reply. Silence in the face of this book and the others is no longer a wise strategy. Word is getting out. The brighter seminary students are figuring out what is going on. Representatives of the various schools of eschatological opinion had better start producing their own comprehensive books on these topics. It is too late for critics to expect to bottle up theonomic postmillennialism by ignoring it or murmuring about it in private. If the critics cannot answer these books in print, then the theonomists will win the debate by default.

I have in mind primarily amillennialist critics, and more to the point, Calvinists. Historic premillennialism barely exists today, and its public defenders are few. Meanwhile, dispensational premillennialism is in a never-ending transition. Its public defenders are mostly writers of paperback books on Bible prophecy. Few of them are trained theologians. They are more often accountants, lawyers, or cable television evangelists. Those few defenders of dispensationalism who are academic theologians are either at the end of their careers (e.g., Walvoord, Pentecost, Ryrie) and are no longer willing or able to interact with academic critics, or else they are younger seminary professors who are involved in an on-campus, semi-private, seemingly never-ending revision of the original dispensational system. They never present anything like an integrated, completed version of their "new, improved" dispensationalism. They never demonstrate how the traditional dispensational system can be revised without collapsing. They keep tinkering with the unraveling system. They never present a finished product.

Younger dispensational seminary professors are well aware that traditional Scofield-Chafer-Ryrie dispensationalism has become defenseless. They just want to keep their jobs. Arminian dispensationalist professors do not need to respond to Calvinistic Christian Reconstructionists in order to keep their jobs, so they keep silent. Thus, my challenge is directed primarily to Calvinistic amillennialists. Calvinist seminary professors have a problem: their brighter students read. We theonomists keep picking off these bright students, since we write, and not only write: we speak to the burning social issues of our day. Nobody expects dispensational professors to speak with authority to the issues of the day; their system declares the futility of doing so. Calvinist theologians are expected to.[29] *But amillennialism offers no blueprints, no solutions, and no earthly hope.* Theonomy does.

One thing is certain: the next time some critic says to me, "There has never been an exegetical case made for postmillennialism," I shall not reply, "What about Roderick Campbell's?" I shall instead try to sell him a copy of *He Shall Have Dominion*.

---

29. Gary DeMar, "Calvinism and Theonomy," Part I of *Theonomy: An Informed Response*, edited by Gary North (Tyler, TX: Institute for Christian Economics, 1991).

PREFACE TO THE SECOND EDITION

I have been gratified with the response to and acceptance of the first edition of *He Shall Have Dominion*. It has been used as a textbook in some Christian colleges and seminaries and has been placed on eschatological resource reading lists in others. So it is with great joy that I present this second edition of *He Shall Have Dominion* to the world of biblical studies. I am thankful to Dr. Gary North for his encouragement in producing this second edition — and for his important ministry at the Institute for Christian Economics.

The changes in the second edition are relatively minor. No positions have changed and the presentational flow is virtually identical in format and argument with the original. The reader of the first edition will probably remember with some pain the several typographical and layout errors that appeared in the original. These errors have been corrected (hopefully!) in this new edition. Some heading and paragraph changes at some junctures should make for easier reading.

Of course, in any new edition it is important to include more recent works in the presentation. Consequently, there are a number of new bibliographic resources employed to fill out and update the argument. Most of these will appear in the footnotes, though a few have altered the text itself by providing important new information. The time lapse between the first edition (1992) and the second (1996), however, is not sufficiently long enough to require a wholesale re-orientation of the argument.

The reader will also notice a new appendix providing a general critique of the hyper-preterist movement. Though I appreciate much of the "consistent preterist" research and insight into eschatology, I am convinced that they have gone too far. And I hope they will, with further study and analysis, make the necessary corrections and return to a more orthodox view of the Second Advent and the Resurrection. But since that movement is making its presence felt and I receive correspondence asking for my thoughts, I deemed it necessary to provide at least a brief analysis of some of the problems I have with its positions. Especially since some dispensationalists confuse my orthodox preterism wither their heterodox form.

The postmillennial reader will be encouraged to know that Zondervan will be publishing a three views book on eschatology in 1997. That work, under the editorship of Darrell L. Bock of Dallas Theological Seminary, will present the progressive dispensational viewpoint (Craig Blaising, Dallas Theological Seminary), the amillennial viewpoint (Richard B. Gaffin, Westminster Theological Seminary), and the reconstructionist postmillennial viewpoint (me, Kenneth L. Gentry, Jr.). The postmillennial viewpoint, assumed by many to be dead, is coming back — as any postmillennialist would expect. Therefore we remember with joy and hope that we must not "despise the day of small things" (Zech. 4:10).

Kenneth L. Gentry, Jr., Th.D.

June 28, 1996

PREFACE TO FIRST EDITION

It was the best of times, it was the worst of times. So begins Charles Dickens' *A Tale of Two Cities*. And such is an appropriate introduction to the present work. For this study in eschatology is also a tale of two cities: the City of God and the City of Man. And we today may declare that in many respects it is the best of times, while in other respects it is the worst of times.

As I write this book, modern man is witnessing remarkable world events. It has not been too many months since the Berlin Wall dividing the two Germanys fell (1989), Eastern Europe freed itself from Soviet Communist domination (1990), and East and West Germany reunited (1991). The Beirut hostage crisis has finally come to an end, after many years of frustration (1991). Within the past few weeks of my writing these words, the Soviet Union has officially vanished, having broken into twelve independent democratic republics (1992). In addition, there are remarkable revivals of Christianity in various Third World countries, as well as in the former Soviet Union. Such would suggest the best of times.[1] Five years ago, who would have thought that these world-shaking events would occur? The bleak shadow that the Soviet Bear cast over the earth has vanished with the dawn of a new day. In many respects, these events signal the best of times for those long afflicted by Communism and the rest of us who were threatened with nuclear destruction by its existence.

But these are also the worst of times. The Chinese Communists are still brutally repressing free speech. Not long ago, Iraq's Saddam Hussein started (and lost) a cruel and potentially disastrous war, but he still remains in power (1992). There is fear

---

1. Not all would agree that these are good signs. Dispensationalist theologian Robert P. Lightner comments: "Even the present evident failure of atheistic, communistic governments brings great fear and uncertainty." Lightner, *The Last Days Handbook: A Comprehensive Guide to Understanding the Different Views of Prophecy* (Nashville: Thomas Nelson, 1990), p. 161. Amillennialist John Heys agrees: "At the moment what is happening in Russia, and for us because of the 'changes' in Russia (which some trust), seems to say that the antichrist is not far away, to realize the one-world kingdom in which he will, because of the inventions, and the satellites which he will have placed in the sky, be able to rule the whole world and know whether all the citizens of his kingdom have that mark of the beast on their right hand or forehead." Heys, "Our Hope for Our Savior's Return," *Standard Bearer* 66:7 (Jan. 1, 1990) 152.

that the turbulent Middle East will buy up the brains and weaponry of the former Soviet Union. Abortion still ranks as one of
America's leading surgical procedures and is widely practiced
throughout the world. The AIDS epidemic shows no signs of
abating, but rather of increasing; the same is true of the nearly
incurable strain of tuberculosis that now accompanies AIDS.
The federal government's debt is enormous and growing rapidly. Though there are bright historical and social rays of hope,
these are too often eclipsed by the clouds of political gloom and
the smoke of cultural upheaval.

One day the world events listed above will be understood in
terms of the all-controlling plan of God. "Our God is in heaven;
He does whatever He pleases" (Psa. 115:3). For right now we
can only surmise what God might be doing and what the end
result will be. But I have not written this work as a prophetic
commentary on the times; I am not interested in newspaper
exegesis. Christianity has been embarrassed by too many failed
prophets in this century.[2]

Yet I believe there is a system of biblical eschatology that has
in the past and will yet again demonstrate itself a valid force in
the development of world events. And that eschatology is postmillennialism.

For the last fifty years many Christians (wrongly) deemed
postmillennialism a theologically dead issue.[3] It held too optimistic a prospect for the future for those who lived in an era
that witnessed the rise of Communism and two World Wars.
But postmillennialism has begun to make headway once again
as a theologically credible alternative to the more popular eschatologies of despair. And it is important to realize that its
remarkable resurgence antedates the collapse of Soviet and

---

2. See: Dwight Wilson, *Armageddon Now! The Premillenarian Response to Russia and
Israel Since 1917* (Tyler, TX: Institute for Christian Economics, [1977] 1991); Gary
DeMar, *Last Days Madness: The Folly of Trying to Predict When Christ Will Return* (Brent-
wood, TN: Wolgemuth and Hyatt, 1991).

3. See discussion in Chapters 4 and 18.

Eastern Bloc communism. These events cannot be laid down as the psychological bases for the modern resurgence of postmillennial optimism.

The market for works on eschatology is ripe. Many of the best-selling Christian works in the last few years have dealt with prophecy. In this work I hope to set forth compelling reasons for a return to postmillennialism by evangelical Christians. These reasons will be shown to be pre-eminently exegetical and theological. For the Christian, exegesis and theology should provide the basis of expectation for the future, not current events.

I would like to thank several friends for assisting me in proofreading the chapters: Bill Boney, Edmond Sandlin, and Kim Conner. Their friendship, assistance, advice, and encouragement are much appreciated. They are Christians who are persuaded that *He Shall Have Dominion*. Thanks also to my son Stephen for spending several days helping me to double-check direct quotations for accuracy.

PART I

INTRODUCTION

1

THE SIGNIFICANCE OF ESCHATOLOGY

Remember the former things of old, for I am God, and there is no other; I am God, and there is none like Me, Declaring the end from the beginning, and from ancient times things that are not yet done, saying, "My counsel shall stand, and I will do all My pleasure." (Isaiah 46:9-10)

The English term "eschatology" is a fairly late theological term, apparently not used before the nineteenth century.[1] "Eschatology" is derived from the compounding of two Greek terms: *eschatos*, which means "last," and *logia*, which means "word, discourse." Etymologically, then, eschatology is "the study of the last things."[2] The term is derived from certain Scriptural passages that speak of "the last days" (2 Tim. 3:1; Heb. 1:2), "the last time" (1 Pet. 1:20; Jude 18), "the last hour" (1 John 2:18), and other comparable statements. We find simi-

---

1. Oscar Cullmann and W. Georg Kümmel, "Eschatology," *The Oxford Dictionary of the Christian Church*, F. L. Cross and E. A. Livingstone, eds. (2nd ed.; Oxford: Oxford University Press, 1974), p. 469. *The Compact Edition of the Oxford English Dictionary*, 2 vols. (Oxford: Oxford University Press, 1971), 1:893, cites George Bush's *Anastasis; or the Doctrine of the Resurrection of the Body*, written in 1845, as the earliest work employing the term "eschatology."

2. Some theologians and dictionaries define it as: "The department of theological science concerned with 'the four last things: death, judgement, heaven, and hell'." *OED*, 1:893. See also: Cullmann and Kümmel, *Oxford Dictionary of the Christian Church*, p. 469.

lar examples in the Septuagint, the second-century, B.C., Greek translation of the Old Testament.[3]

Eschatology is generally divided into two categories. There is that branch that we may call "cosmic eschatology," which deals with the consummational history of the world system and the human race.[4] Cosmic eschatology involves the study of the biblical data regarding the providentially governed flow of history as it develops toward its foreordained consummation. Cosmic eschatology especially focuses on the developmental unfolding of the kingdom of God in history, the Second Advent of Christ, the resurrection of the dead, the final judgment, and the eternal state.

Then there is what we may call "personal eschatology," which is concerned with the destiny of the individual at death.[5] This necessarily involves a study of physical death, the immortality of the soul, and the intermediate state. Of course, because it ushers the individual out of the temporal and into the eternal world, it also involves a consideration of heaven and hell.

The present treatise will focus on cosmic eschatology. Eschatology is vitally important to a proper understanding of the biblical revelation. As Geerhardus Vos notes regarding Paul's theology, "not only Christology but also the Soteriology of the Apostle's teaching is closely interwoven with the Eschatology, that, were the question put, which of the strands is more cen-

---

3. See the Septuagint *eschatai hemerai* (Gen. 49:1; Isa. 2:2; Jer. 37:24; Ezek. 38:16; Hos. 3:5; Mic. 4:1; Dan. 10:14) and *eschaton ton hemeron* (Num. 24:14; Deut. 4:30; 31:29; Jer. 23:20; 25:18).

4. Berkhof calls it "general eschatology"; Murray and Vos call it "collective eschatology"; Bruce calls it "world eschatology." L. Berkhof, *Systematic Theology* (Grand Rapids: Eerdmans, 1941), p. 666. John Murray, "The Last Things," in *Collected Writings of John Murray*, 4 vols. (Edinburgh: Banner of Truth, 1977), 2:403. Geehardus Vos, *The Pauline Eschatology* (Phillipsburg, NJ: Presbyterian & Reformed, [1930] 1991), p. 5. F. F. Bruce, "Eschatology," *Baker's Dictionary of Theology*, Everett F. Harrison, ed. (Grand Rapids: Baker, 1960), p. 188.

5. Berkhof, Murray, Vos, and Bruce prefer "individual eschatology." Berkhof, *Systematic Theology*, p. 667. Murray, "The Last Things," 2:401. Vos, *Pauline Eschatology*, p. 5. Bruce, "Eschatology," p. 187.

tral, which more peripheral, the eschatology would have as good a claim to the central place as the others. In reality, however, there is no alternative here; there is backward and forward movement in the order of thought in both directions."[6]

Although eschatological matters have always been before the Church,[7] they have only fairly recently come to prominence as an area of *systematic* inquiry. Berkhof notes in this regard: "When Klieforth wrote his *Eschatologie,* he complained about the fact that there had never yet appeared a comprehensive and adequate treatise on eschatology as a whole. . . . In general it may be said that eschatology is even now [1941] the least developed of all the loci of dogmatics."[8] This concern has come very late in Church history.

Though this deficiency has been somewhat alleviated of late,[9] unfortunately the field of eschatology is largely dominated by writers offering either rationalistic assessments (e.g., Rudolf Bultmann, Jürgen Moltmann, Wolfhart Pannenberg), dispensationalistic novelties (e.g., Charles C. Ryrie, John F. Walvoord, J. Dwight Pentecost), or sensationalistic prognostications (e.g., Hal Lindsey and Dave Hunt). Of course, there are exceptions (e.g., Anthony Hoekema and George Eldon Ladd). Nevertheless, a careful and systematic presentation of the *opti-*

---

6. Vos, *Pauline Eschatology,* p. 29.

7. Some of the earliest of post-apostolic Christian literature dealt with eschatological issues. See especially *The Shepherd of Hermas (ca.* A.D. 80s); Barnabas *(ca.* A.D. 100), *Epistle,* ch. 15; Papias *(ca.* A.D. 60-130), *Against Heresies* 5:33; Justin Martyr *(ca.* A.D. 100-165), *Dialogue with Trypho the Jew,* chaps. 32, 51, 110 and *Apology* 1:50-52; and Irenaeus *(ca.* A.D. 100-200), *Against Heresies* 5:23-26. Many early creeds and liturgies alluded to eschatological issues. See the Apostles' Creed, the Nicene Creed, Clementine liturgy, liturgy of James, and the liturgy of Mark in Philip Schaff, *History of the Christian Church* (5th ed.; Grand Rapids: Eerdmans, [1910] 1985), 2:598.

8. Berkhof, *Systematic Theology,* p. 664.

9. In the third edition of Charles L. Feinberg, *Millennialism: The Two Major Views* (3rd ed.; Chicago: Moody Press, 1980), p. 32, we read: "Eschatology remains a much neglected field of theological study and research. If one were to scan the standard work of theology, he would be surprised to find the little attention that is given to eschatology." This, apparently, is from the earliest edition (1936) and was not amended in the 1980 version.

mistic eschatology of Scripture remains a genuine need within the Church.[10] I hope this work will partially meet that need.

Some lament the introduction of new ideas or the re-systematization of older views in the eschatogical marketplace. One theologian writes that "we do not need another defense of a particular view of the future and certainly not a new view."[11] Another comments in a review of a new work on eschatology that he "sincerely questions . . . the necessity of adding a fifth position to an already overcrowded rapture debate."[12] Yet it is vitally important that continued inquiry, systematization, and correction be made in our understanding of this important field of theology. Let me present three justifications for a new work on eschatology.

The Priority of Scripture

Paul informs us in 2 Timothy 3:16 that "All scripture is given by inspiration of God, and is profitable for doctrine, for reproof, for correction, for instruction in righteousness." Consequently, the study of any of Scripture's doctrines will be beneficial to the Christian. And eschatology is certainly one of the major fields of biblical theology. Scripture, not experience, must be the foundation of our eschatology.

As I will demonstrate in more detail later, the material of biblical eschatology begins at the very genesis of universal history and extends to its ultimate consummation. Thus, its sweep encompasses the whole of time and the entirety of the biblical record. As Jürgen Moltmann puts it: "From first to last, and not

---

10. Even here there is no *total* lack, though there is no really full-blown systematic theological treatment. See: Roderick Campbell, *Israel and the New Covenant* (Tyler, TX: Geneva Divinity School Press, [1954] 1981); Loraine Boettner, *The Millennium* (Philadelphia: Presbyterian & Reformed, 1957); David Chilton, *Paradise Restored: A Biblical Theology of Dominion* (Ft. Worth, TX: Dominion Press, 1985).

11. Robert P. Lightner, *The Last Days Handbook* (Nashville: Nelson, 1990), p. 93.

12. Gerald B. Stanton, "A Review of *The Pre-Wrath Rapture of the Church*," *Bibliotheca Sacra* 148 (Jan./March 1991) 90.

merely in the epilogue, Christianity is eschatology, is hope, forward looking and forward moving, and therefore also revolutionizing and transforming the present."[13] J. J. Van Oosterzee agrees: "All true Theology is at the same time Teleology, which must of itself lead to Eschatology."[14] Or, to put the matter statistically in this econometric age, some research suggests that the prophetic element in Scripture accounts for more than one-fourth, or about 27% of the biblical record, because predictive prophecy is found in 8,352 of the Bible's 31,124 verses.[15]

Berkhof puts the significance of eschatology in proper perspective regarding its relation to the other branches of systematic (or dogmatic) theology:

> In theology it is the question, how God is finally perfectly glorified in the work of His hands, and how the counsel of God is fully realized; in anthropology, the question, how the disrupting influence of sin is completely overcome; in christology, the question, how the work of Christ is crowned with perfect victory; in soteriology, the question, how the work of the Holy Spirit at last issues in the complete redemption and glorification of the people of God; and in ecclesiology, the question of the final apotheosis of the Church. All these questions must find their answer in the last locus of dogmatics, making it the real capstone of dogmatic theology.[16]

---

13. Jürgen Moltmann, *Theology of Hope*, trans. by J. W. Leitch (New York: Harper & Row, 1967), p. 16. Berkhof also laments the epilogical placement of eschatology: "In such a scheme eschatology could only appear as the finale of history, and not at all as one of the constitutive elements of a system of truth." Berkhof, *Systematic Theology*, p. 664.

14. J. J. Van Oosterzee, *Christian Dogmatics*, 2 vols. (New York: Scribner's, n.d.), 2:581.

15. J. Barton Payne, *Encyclopedia of Biblical Prophecy* (New York: Harper & Row, 1973), pp. 675, 681. Of course, this is not to say that all of these prophecies are future to *our* time.

16. Berkhof, *Systematic Theology*, p. 665.

McDonald boldly asserts of Jesus' teaching: "It is much more than a mere paradox to say that the first things in the Gospels is their presentation of the last things. Their theology, like any sound theology which is true to its biblical perspective, involves an eschatology, a doctrine of end events."[17]

For the evangelical Christian, the Scripture holds a dominant sway over his worldview.[18] Given the heavy biblical emphasis on matters of eschatological significance, we must not overlook this field of study. In fact, this leads me to my next, related concern: the philosophy of history.

The Christian Philosophy of History

Does history have any meaning, purpose, or significance? Is there a unified movement in history? Is history going anywhere? These are important questions as we begin a study of biblical eschatology; the first two prepare for and the last one speaks of cosmic eschatology. After all, the issue of eschatology is "not just one of how to interpret Rev. 20, but one that bears on the entire philosophy of history."[19]

Carl Henry observes that "Judeo-Christian revelation has nurtured a universal conviction that no theology or philosophy can be comprehensive unless it deals with the direction of history and the goal of the universe, with the matter of man's ultimate destiny and the problem of death."[20] Vos notes:

It is no wonder that such energetic eschatological thinking tended towards consolidation in an orb of compact theological structure. For in it the world-process is viewed as a unit. The end is

---

17. H. D. McDonald, *Living Doctrines of the New Testament* (Grand Rapids: Zondervan, [1971] 1972), p. 116.

18. See Chapter 5, below.

19. G. C. Berkouwer, *The Return of Christ* (Grand Rapids: Eerdmans, 1972), p. 234n.

20. Carl F. H. Henry, *God Who Stands and Stays: Part Two*, in Henry, *God, Revelation, and Authority*, 6 vols. (Waco, TX: Word, 1983), 6:492.

placed in the light of the beginning, and all intermediate developments are construed with reference to the purpose *a quo* and the terminus *ad quem*. Eschatology, in other words, even that of the most primitive kind, yields *ipso facto* a philosophy of history, be it of the most rudimentary sort. And every philosophy of history bears in itself the seed of a theology. . . . [A]ll eschatological interpretation of history, when united to a strong religious mentality cannot but produce the finest practical theological fruitage. To take God as source and end of all that exists and happens, and to hold such a view suffused with the warmth of genuine devotion, stands not only related to theology as the fruit stands to the tree: it is by reason of its essence a veritable theological tree of life.[21]

Although I will not flesh out a full philosophy of history, we must be at least generally aware of its significance.[22] Basically, three approaches to history are significant to our inquiry, as presented by Reinhold Niebuhr and Arthur F. Holmes.[23] These views are the pagan cyclical view, the Christian linear view, and the secular evolutionary view.

A Brief Historical Sketch

The study of history is a complicated task. The difficulty of arranging all the evidence we have (which gives us but a fraction of all that occurred) is truly imposing. Tolstoy once commented that "History would be an excellent thing if only it were true."[24] In the late 1600's, systematic historical Pyrrhonism arose, which discounted the value of history due to the

---

21. Vos, *Pauline Eschatology*, p. 61.

22. For a helpful introduction to some of the elements of a Christian philosophy of history, see: Rousas John Rushdoony, *The Biblical Philosophy of History* (Nutley, NJ: Presbyterian & Reformed, 1969). For an historical study see: D. W. Bebbington, *Patterns in History: A Christian View* (Downer's Grove, IL: Inter-Varsity Press, 1979).

23. Reinhold Niebuhr, *Faith and History* (New York: Scribner's, 1949), p. 17. Arthur F. Holmes, *Contours of a Christian Worldview* (Grand Rapids: Eerdmans, 1983).

24. Cited by Bebbington, *Patterns in History*, p. 8.

philosophical skepticism regarding all human knowledge.[25]
Developing an explicitly biblical philosophy of history is a task
of great significance for the Christian.

Although "societies have existed, and continue to exist,
where there is little awareness of the ongoing historical process,"[26] there eventually arose in the ancient pre-Christian
world a cyclical view of history.[27] The cyclical interpretation of
history held (and in some cases still holds) a strong influence in
the East: China, India, and Persia. This cyclical view of history
influenced the West through Greece and Rome.[28] Based on
the seasonal rhythm of nature, it presented history as an endless, recurring series of cycles.

Given the pagan conception of recurring cycles and the
unconnectedness of reality under competing gods, there could
be no unified conception of reality. Such a view destroyed any
hope of historical progress, thereby trapping men in a dead-
end universe of relentless political cycles.[29] In Greece, there
was a "rigorously anti-historical metaphysics,"[30] as a result of
the influence of Aristotle's concern with the eternal.

Aristotle wrote: "For indeed time itself seems to be a sort of
circle" (*Physics* 4:14). The Roman historian Cornelius Tacitus

25. La Mothe le Vayer in 1668 was an early systematizer of historical Pyrrhonism. Pyrrhonism is based on the philosophy of the Greek skeptic Pyrrho (365-275
B.C.), who argued that all knowledge, including knowledge based on the senses, is
uncertain.

26. Bebbington, *Patterns in History*, p. 21.

27. For a fuller discussion of the cyclical view of history, see: Bebbington, *Patterns
in History*, ch. 2. John Marsh, *The Fullness of Time* (London: Nisbet, 1952) and Hendrikus Berkhof, *Christ the Meaning of History*, trans. by L. Buurman (4th ed.; Richmond: John Knox, 1966).

28. The three fundamental eastern forms were Chinese dynasticism, the recurrent world cycle, and the Persian pattern of decline from a golden age. See Bebbington, *Patterns in History*, p. 33.

29. For a brief discussion of the debate over whether the Greeks held to historical progress, see: Gary North, *Moses and Pharaoh: Dominion Religion Versus Power
Religion* (Tyler, TX: Institute for Christian Economics, 1985), ch. 17: "The Metaphor
of Growth: Ethics."

30. R. G. Collingwood, *The Idea of History* (Oxford: Clarendon, 1946), p. 20.

(A.D. 56-117) wrote that "not only the seasons but everything else, social history included, moves in cycles" (*Annals* 3:55). Marcus Aurelius Antoninus (A.D. 121-180), the Stoic philosopher and Roman emperor, clearly expressed the cyclical view: "Future generations will have nothing new to witness, even as our forefathers beheld nothing more than we of today, but that if a man comes to his fortieth year, and has any understanding at all, he has virtually seen – thanks to their similarity – all possible happenings, both past and to come" (*Meditations* 11:1).

The philosophically and ethically self-conscious Christian has a wholly different conception of reality. His realistic conception of history gives rise to a distinctive and meaningful philosophy of history. Aurelius Augustine, Bishop of Hippo (A.D. 354-430), may rightly be called the father of the philosophy of history.[31] He set forth a philosophy of history that had its meaning rooted in the redemptive work of Jesus Christ, which is an important aspect of the eternal plan of Almighty God, Creator of heaven and earth.

Eventually, the calendar of the West was dated *Anno Domini*, "in the year of our Lord." This was first done by Dionysius Exiguus in 525. It was not until the eighteenth century that the preceding era was designated "B.C.," Before Christ. Cullmann observes: "Our system of time does not number the years in a continuous forward moving series that begins at a fixed initial point. . . . Our history . . . does not proceed from an initial point, but from a *center*. . . . This event is the birth of Jesus Christ of Nazareth."[32]

Augustine argued that what gave meaning to history was the providential intervention of God. In addition, "since, according to Augustine, human history is but the unfolding of the divine

---

31. However, we should understand that Augustine was not the first Christian thinker to oppose the pagan cyclical worldview. See: Justin Martyr, *The Dialogue with Trypho the Jew* 1:5. Cited in Bebbington, *Patterns in History*, p. 52.

32. Oscar Cullmann, *Christ and Time: The Primitive Christian Conception of Time and History*, trans. by Floyd V. Filson (3rd ed.; Philadelphia: Westminster, 1964), p. 17.

drama, history has direction."[33] He saw that history is moving
to a glorious conclusion; hence, he viewed history as linear
rather than cyclical.[34] In fact, since Augustine "central . . . to
the early Christian theological tradition is what has been called
a 'linear' view of history: the conviction that history has an origin
and an end, both rooted in the plan and the power of God. So
both the Gnostic contempt of the temporal world and Origen's
apparent flirtation with the possibility of future cycles of salva-
tion-history were sharply rejected by most Orthodox writers as
making the gospel absurd. Sixth-century apologists contested,
with equal fervor, Platonic theories on the eternity of the world.
In order to be a history of salvation, time must have its limits
and must move unrepeatably in a single direction."[35] The four
basic elements of a Christian view of history are: (1) Creational
beginning, (2) linear movement, (3) divine intrusion, and (4)
teleological orientation.

The Christian, Augustinian view of universal history reigned
with great influence throughout the Medieval period. It was
largely displaced by a secular philosophy of history influenced
by the Renaissance concern with classical antiquity. For a brief
time in 1792, the leaders of the French Revolution attempted to
impose a new calendar on France to rid themselves of the
Christian-based calendar. In fact, the very designations "Middle
Ages," "Medieval Period," "Dark Ages," and so forth, evidence
a bias against the Christian influence on history. The period of
the dominant influence of Christianity in the Middle Ages is
considered to be a dark period separating the golden days of

33. W. T. Jones, *The Medieval Mind*, vol. 2 in *A History of Western Philosophy* (2nd ed.; New York: Harcourt, Brace, & World, 1969), p. 135.

34. Although secularist intellectuals are still debating the origin of the linear conception of history, most accept that it derives from the Bible. Victor Ferkiss, *Technological Man* (New York: Mentor, 1969), pp. 22, 43-44. See also: Cullmann, *Christ and Time*, chaps. 1-2.

35. Brian E. Daley, *The Hopes of the Early Church: A Handbook of Patristic Eschatology* (Cambridge: University Press, 1991), p. 219.

pagan Greece and Rome from their glorious modern heirs in secular humanism. Notice the dim view that the Marquis de Condorcet had of the Middle Ages: "Man's only achievements were theological day-dreaming and superstitious imposture, his only morality religious intolerance."[36] But ancient pagan and modern secular history are not glorious at all.[37]

Christian historian C. Gregg Singer relates an experience he had at an annual meeting of the American Historical Association in the early 1970s. He was at an informal small group meeting with several leading historians. The subject under discussion was the meaning and purpose of history. The six other historians present were convinced that history "lacks any decisive meaning and any discernible purpose."[38] Singer responded: "If this be the case, then why do we teach history?" His query was met with surprise and disgust, the group broke up, and all the historians went to their various discussion seminars on the subject they teach in colleges, but which by their own estimation has no inherent meaning.

According to the various competing modern, secular, evolutionary views, history can really have no meaning, purpose, value, or direction.[39] The floor of reality is Chance. In such a

---

36. Marquis de Condorcet, *Sketch for a Historical Picture of the Progress of the Human Mind*, trans. by June Barraclough (London, [1795] 1955), p. 77.

37. It is more than a little interesting that this century, which has been praised as the age of the triumph of humanism, is also noted for being the bloodiest century known to man. See: Gil Elliot, *The Twentieth Century Book of the Dead* (New York: Scribner's, 1972). See also: Kenneth L. Gentry, Jr., "The Greatness of the Great Commission," *Journal of Christian Reconstruction* 7:2 (Winter 1981) 19-24.

38. C. Gregg Singer, "History," *Foundations of Christian Scholarship: Essays in the Van Til Perspective*, Gary North, ed. (Vallecito, CA: Ross House, 1976), p. 53.

39. The modern Western intellectual rules out in principle "the possibility that the universe might be ordered teleologically." Huston Smith, *Chance and Necessity* (New York: Vintage, 1972), p. 21. In some circles the cyclical view of history was revived in mild forms since the Renaissance, such as in Niccolo Machiavelli's *The Discourses*. And "although no fully articulated cyclical theory is popular in the West today," it should be noted that "cyclical theory is not dead." Bebbington, *Patterns in History*, p. 40. In fact, some physicists who hold to the Big Bang fluctuation theory of the universe do hold to a cyclical view of reality. See Gary North, *Is the World Run-*

system, the ultimate foundation of the rational, therefore, becomes the irrational. Thus, not only is there no ultimate meaning and purpose, but no foundation for ethics, i.e., for moral values. The chaos of modern culture is the fruit of the widespread permeation of this modern philosophy of history.

Presuppositions of the Christian Philosophy of History

The presuppositions undergirding the Christian philosophy of linear history include the following several elements, which will be only briefly stated. It is important that we bear these in mind from the outset. Eschatological inquiry will be radically altered and thrown into hopeless confusion if these presuppositions to our study are not properly understood as givens. These will undergird my treatment of the biblical eschatological system. The fundamental presuppositions of the Christian philosophy of history, which appear in both testaments,[40] are: God, creation, providence, fall, redemption, revelation, and consummation.

God. God exists and is absolutely independent and wholly self-sufficient. In Exodus 3:14, He defines Himself via His special covenantal name "YHWH" ("Jehovah"). Here He identifies Himself as "I am that I am." This self-designation is peculiarly important to our understanding of God. This statement is found in the imperfect tense in Hebrew, thereby emphasizing a constantly manifested quality. From this name we may discern certain of God's intrinsic qualities: (1) His *aseity*: God exists of Himself. He is wholly uncreated and self-existent. There is no principle or fact back of God accounting for His existence (John 5:26). (2) His *eternity*: He is of unlimited, eternal duration. The

---

ning Down? Crisis in the Christian Worldview (Tyler, TX: Institute for Christian Economics, 1988), ch. 2.

40. There are those who (wrongly) argue that the Old Testament operates from a cyclical view of history. J. B. Curtis, "A Suggested Interpretation of the Biblical Philosophy of History," *Hebrew Union College Annual* 34 (1963).

combination of the verb tense (imperfect) and its repetition ("I am" / "I am") emphasize His uninterrupted, continuous existence (Psa. 90; 93:1-2; Isa. 40:28; 57:15). (3) His *sovereignty*: He is absolutely self-determinative. He determines from within His own being. As the Absolute One, He operates with unfettered liberty. He is not conditioned by outward circumstance. He is what He is because He is what He is. He is completely self-definitional and has no need of anything outside of Himself (Isa. 40:9-31).

Creation.[41] There is a personal, moral, sovereign origin of all of reality. The Christian's creational viewpoint puts man under God and over nature (Gen. 1:26-27; Psa. 8). It imparts transcendent meaning to temporal history and sets before man a high calling.[42] The entire universe from the smallest atomic particle to the largest and farthest flung galaxy was created *ex nihilo*. It exists solely because of the exercise of God's creative will, and was brought into being by His sovereign, successive divine fiats (Gen. 1:1; Exo. 20:11; Heb. 11:3). All facts and laws, all people and materials, trace their origin, meaning, and purpose back to God.[43]

Providence. God has an eternally decreed, minutely detailed, sovereignly determined, and unfailingly certain plan for the universe; this plan is personally and intimately administered by Him and for His own glory.[44] Providence imparts transcendent meaning into the control of history. God works all things after the counsel of His holy will (Eph. 1:11; cf. Psa. 33:11; Isa. 45:10-11). Providence is the alternative to the Chance and brute factuality (i.e., the unrelatedness of reality) of the non-Christian viewpoint.

---

41. See Chapter 9, below, for more detail.
42. Rushdoony, *Biblical Philosophy of History*, p. 3.
43. Psa. 24:1; John 1:4; Rom. 11:36ff; Col. 1:16-17; Rev. 4:11.
44. Psa. 115:3; Prov. 16:1-4, 9; Dan. 4:35; Matt. 10:29, 30.

Fall. Because of God's testing of Adam, which resulted in Adam's Fall (Gen. 3:1-8), history has become the battleground of Christ and Antichrist (Gen. 3:15). Sin affects every aspect of human endeavor, distorting all of reality. We cannot understand our historical situation apart from the intrusion of sin as an unnatural factor. Neither may we think of man's fundamental problem as ontological, related to his finite being. Adam's pre-Fall abilities were remarkable (Gen. 2:15, 19-20), as will be our post-temporal existence (1 Cor. 15:42-53). Man's fundamental problem is an ethical one, related to His rebellion against the Law of God (Rom. 5:10; 8:7-8). Because of this he labors under God's curse (Gen. 3:15; Rom. 5:12-19; Gal. 3:10). But history is not abandoned by God due to man's Fall. It does, however, witness the rise of a new factor: redemption.

Redemption. The major motif of history is the redemptive activity of God in reconciling creation back to Himself (Gen. 3:15; Col. 1:19-23). This will very strongly and directly affect our understanding of biblical eschatology. God has established the plan of redemption in order to bring wayward man back to himself. No proper understanding of historical progress and direction can be held with reference only to the Fall of man. We must take into account also the restorative acts of God in redemption.[45] The division of history into B.C. and A.D. is indicative of the realization that Christ is the focal point of the historical process.[46] Such an historical designation has theological implications. That some scholars opt for B.C.E. and C.E. dating is a sign of an anti-Christian bias.[47]

---

45. North, *Is The World Running Down?*

46. Cullmann, *Christ and Time*, pp. 18-19.

47. Before the Common Era and Common Era. For instance, see the practice and debate in *Biblical Archaeology Review* 15:2 (March/April 1989) 56; 15:4 (July/ Aug. 1989) 16-17, 46; 16:4 (July/Aug. 1990) 12.

Revelation.[48] God has revealed Himself and various aspects of His will infallibly and inerrantly in His Holy Word, the Bible (John 10:35; 2 Tim. 3:16,17; 2 Pet. 1:20,21). The providential governance of history employs the causative prophetic word of the Creator. God's eternal decree, from which His prophetic Word springs into history, is neither abstract nor random; it is concrete and rational. It is not raw force, but structured power. God's Word gives intelligible construction to all things (Psa. 33:11; 148:5; Heb. 1:3; 11:3). The objective revelation of God in Scripture is foundational to a truly Christian eschatology.

Consummation. Not only does history have a beginning, but it is being guided providentially to a particular end (Isa. 46:10; 55:11). Our labor in the Lord here on earth is not in vain (1 Cor. 15:58). We labor in the present with a view to the future and ultimately to the consummation and the eternal state. In fact, "it was the Christian view of history that gave western civilization its remarkably widespread conviction that the future offers hope."[49]

I can afford no more space to this important matter of the philosophy of history. But I urge the reader to keep these general statements in mind as he reads this study of biblical eschatology. We are dealing with a very important matter: *the Christian philosophy of universal history.* We must recognize that "Scripture affirms that all history has a purpose and goal, that history is unrepeatable, and that it moves toward the final triumph of the good."[50] To read much of popular eschatological literature, one could surmise that the Bible is an eschatological jigsaw puzzle, a grand trivial pursuit.[51] Such is not the case.

---

48. This factor of the Christian philosophy of history will be brought to bear more precisely regarding the eschatological question in Chapter 5, below.

49. Bebbington, *Patterns in History*, p. 42.

50. Henry, *God, Revelation, and Authority*, 6:493.

51. Samuel Bacchiocchi, *Hal Lindsey's Prophetic Jigsaw Puzzle: Five Predictions That Have Failed!* (Berrien Springs, MI: Biblical Perspectives, 1987). T. Boersma, *Is the Bible a Jigsaw Puzzle: An Evaluation of Hal Lindsey's Writings* (St. Catherines, Ontario:

Whether or not the entire course of world history is under the absolutely sovereign administration of the infinitely personal God of Scripture means everything to eschatological inquiry. It is of fundamental consequence whether or not we view the universe as the creature of God designed for His glory. If God were not absolutely sovereign, some competing God or some countervailing principle or some unforeseen fortuity could throw a dark blanket of obscurity over the ultimate eschatological outcome of universal history and human existence. This would undermine any hope for a moral conclusion to world and universal history.[52]

Regarding the facts of eschatological eventuation, it is extremely important that we understand this: God has an eternal plan that absolutely governs the origin, process, and outcome of history. A Christian philosophy of history must insist that His will is determinative rather than responsive. God is not merely responding to forces inherent within the processes of history, whether resultant from a competing spiritual being or beings, or in consequence of autonomous human activity, or due to "natural" phenomena. It matters immensely whether or not God has graciously and objectively revealed Himself and His will to man. If neither of these biblical "givens" is true, then, hoplessness prevails. Denying the former, God Himself cannot certainly know the future, because it would be definitionally random and unknowable. Denying the latter, we could have no hope ourselves of lifting the veil of the future; our inquiry would be pure guess-work.

The Cultural Implications of Eschatology

As will become increasingly evident in the following chapters, eschatology has a tremendous effect on the Christian's world-

---

Paideia, 1978).

52. See Greg L. Bahnsen, "The Problem ot Evil," *Biblical Worldview* 7:10 (Oct. 1991) and 7:12 (Dec. 1991).

view and, consequently, on his practical, daily living. In this
book, I will highlight one particular eschatological theme that
is especially dominant in the entire prophetic Scriptures and
that is most influential in promoting a full-orbed Christian
witness and Bible-based social activism: *the gospel victory theme*.

The omission of the gospel victory theme in much of modern eschatology should be lamented. Its replacement with a defeatist scheme for Christian enterprise has paralyzed the Christian cultural enterprise, emptied the Christian worldview of
practical significance, and given Christians a sinful "comfort in
lethargy," because it tends "to justify social irresponsibility."[53]
It has left the earth (which is the Lord's, Psa. 24:1[54]) to a conquered foe and the enemy of our Lord and Savior, Jesus
Christ. This paralysis is all the more lamentable because it has
caused the forfeiture of great gains made by the tireless and
costly labors of our Christian forefathers, particularly from the
Reformation era through the early 1900s.

Eschatological Pessimism

Three of the four major evangelical eschatological systems
may be categorized as "pessimistic," whereas the view set forth
in the present work may be seen as "optimistic." In categorizing
them as pessimistic, I am speaking of the following issues:

(1) As systems of gospel proclamation, each teaches the gospel
of Christ will not exercise any major influence in the world
before Christ's return;
(2) As systems of historical understanding, each holds that the
Bible teaches prophetically determined, irresistible trends downward toward chaos in the outworking and development of history; and therefore

53. Ted Peters, *Futures: Human and Divine* (Atlanta: John Knox, 1978), pp. 29,
28.
54. Exo. 9:29; 19:5; Lev. 25:23; Deut. 10:14; 1 Sam. 2:8; 1 Chron. 29:11, 14; 2
Chron. 29:11, 14; Job 41:11; Psa. 24:1; 50:12; 89:11; Psa. 115:16; 1 Cor. 10:26, 28.

(3) As systems for the promotion of Christian discipleship, each dissuades the Church from anticipating and laboring for wide-scale success in influencing the world for Christ during this age.

The pessimism/optimism question has very much to do with the *practical* endeavors of Christians in the world *today*.[55] Of course, all evangelical Christians are optimistic in the *ultimate* sense that God will miraculously win the war against sin and Satan. This will occur at the end of history by direct, supernatural intervention, either in an earthly millennial kingdom introduced by Jesus at the Second Coming[56] or at the final judgment, which introduces the New Heavens and New Earth.[57]

Dispensationalism. The Dispensationalist urges believers to accept the view that "the church age will end in apostasy, not revival" because it is destined by God.[58] Furthermore, believers today are taught by this view that "this current world is headed toward judgment. After that judgment, Christ will take control of the world and rule it. But until that happens, the message and activities for believers should be, 'Flee the wrath to

55. Gary North observes that Christians who are either premillennial or amillennial tend to become operational postmillennialists when they begin to get involved in social action projects, whether or not these are political activities. North, "Ghetto Eschatologies," *Biblical Economics Today* 14:3 (April/May 1992) 3-4, 6. He points out that dispensational activists in the United States after 1975 ceased discussing in public the details of their eschatology (p. 3).

56. For example: "The Bible expects the world to be conquered not by Christianity, but only by the second coming of Christ." John F. Walvoord, "Review of House Divided," *Bibliotheca Sacra* (July/Sept. 1990) 372. "The premillennialist sees Christ intervening catastrophically in a moment of history, resulting in an establishment of his mediatorial rule." H. Wayne House and Thomas D. Ice, *Dominion Theology: Blessing or Curse?* (Portland, OR: Multnomah, 1988), p. 140.

57. Hoekema has written: "*Old Testament prophecies interpreted by postmillennialists as referring to a future millennial golden age picture the final state of the redeemed community . . . [in] a new heaven and a new earth.*" Anthony Hoekema, *The Bible and the Future* (Grand Rapids: Eerdmans, 1979), p. 177. Cf. Vos, *Pauline Eschatology*, p. 33.

58. House and Ice, *Dominion Theology*, pp. 390, 378.

come by finding safety in Jesus Christ.' "[59] "We are witnessing in this twentieth century the collapse of civilization. It is obvious that we are advancing toward the end of the age. . . . I can see no bright prospects, through the efforts of man, for the earth and its inhabitants."[60] As this book was going to press, another sample of pessimism crossed my desk: "This present world is rapidly coming to an end. It is on an irreversible collision course with destiny."[61]

Because of this, dispensationalists dogmatically teach their followers: "Christians have no immediate solution to the problems of our day."[62] In fact, they aver that "to attempt to establish a long-term change of institutions before Christ returns will only result in the leaven of humanism permeating orthodox Christianity"[63] and "that our main business should be to rescue people out of the mess and not try to improve it or preserve its good characteristics."[64] Dispensationalists are prone to lament: "Without the hope of our Lord's return . . . what future do any of us have?"[65]

I am not taking these statements out of context. They are quite conventional. The language of social and political disengagement is basic to the dispensational outlook. Hal Lindsey[66]

---

59. *Ibid.*, p. 356.

60. Lehman Strauss, "Our Only Hope," *Bibliotheca Sacra* 120 (April/June 1963) 154.

61. Jack Van Impe, "There Is Hope!" (Troy, MI: Jack Van Impe Ministries International, December, 1991), p. 1.

62. John F. Walvoord, "Why Are the Nations in Turmoil?" *Prophecy and the Seventies*, Charles Lee Feinberg, ed. (Chicago: Moody Press, 1971), p. 212. Walvoord continues: "A solution to this unrest and turmoil is provided in the Bible, and there is no other. That solution is that Jesus Christ Himself is coming back to bring peace and rest to the world." *Ibid.*, p. 210.

63. House and Ice, *Dominion Theology*, p. 340.

64. George H. Dollar, *A History of Fundamentalism in America* (Greenville, SC: Bob Jones University Press, 1973), p. 278.

65. Salem Kirban, *Your Last Goodbye* (Wheaton, IL: Tyndale, 1969), p. 252.

66. Lindsey is best known for his 35-million best-seller, *The Late Great Planet Earth* (Grand Rapids: Zondervan, 1970), the largest-selling book of the 1970s. Consequently, his ideas exercise a great influence over untold numbers of Christians.

states the situation about as strongly as can be: "Christ died for us in order to rescue us from *this present evil age*. These verses show what our *focus*, *motivation*, and *hope* should be *in this present age*. We are to live with the constant expectation of the any-moment appearing of our LORD to this earth."[67] In fact, he writes, "the world will progressively harden its heart against the Gospel and plunge itself into destruction."[68] His call to Christians is: "We should be living like persons who don't expect to be around much longer."[69] As Reuben A. Torrey put it: "The darker the night gets; the lighter my heart gets."[70] Christianity has no future in this view, for "we are in the time of the end."[71]

Dispensationalists have no practical, long-range hope for the Christian in the here and now. "It would appear the great Judge is poised on the threshold of a new age just ready to usher in the next major movement in His plan for the world (James 5:9). . . . [E]very saint should be standing on tiptoe in anticipation."[72] Charles C. Ryrie[73] denies any optimistic gospel victory, when he teaches that "defection and apostasy, among other things, will characterize [the] entire period" of

---

67. Hal Lindsey, *The Road to Holocaust* (New York: Bantam, 1989), p. 279.

68. *Ibid.*, p. 36.

69. Lindsey, *Late, Great*, p. 145.

70. Cited from Dwight L. Wilson, *Armageddon Now! The Premillenarian Response to Russia and Israel Since 1917* (Tyler, TX: Institute for Christian Economics, [1977] 1991), p. 37. The implication of the theological necessity of cultural withdrawal cannot easily be evaded, and American dispensationalists until the mid-1970's did not seek to evade it. From the mid-1970s on, this language of cultural retreat created a problem for dispensational activists. In 1982, Gary North warned that this would create a major crisis in dispensationalism: North, "The Intellectual Schizophrenia of the New Christian Right," *Christianity and Civilization* 1 (Spring 1982) 1-40.

71. Feinberg, *Millennialism*, p. 31.

72. Herman Hoyt, *The End Times* (Chicago: Moody Press, 1969), p. 13.

73. Ryrie is perhaps the most influential dispensationalist theologian alive today. He is a former Dallas Theological Seminary professor, who has trained hundreds of evangelical pastors. His best-selling *Ryrie Study Bible* alone gives him an influence well beyond other dispensationalist theologians.

Church history.[74] Dave Hunt[75] argues that "only a small percentage of mankind is willing . . . to come to Christ in repentance and be born again by the Spirit of God" and that "the vast majority of people will continue to reject Christ in the future just as they have in the past."[76]

The dispensationalist is alarmed at the thought of Christian cultural transformation. In his view, to attempt such "is to err so grievously as to lead one into a program that is hopeless; it calls necessarily for the adopting of means that are unauthorized, and the setting of a goal that is unattainable as it is unscriptural. Herein lies the great mistake of the 'kingdom builders' (their tribe decreases) who have as their goal a vision of Christianizing the world."[77]

Historic premillennialism. Historic premillennialists would join in the denial of the gospel victory theme. J. Barton Payne believes that "evil is present in our world as predicted in the Holy Books" (of the Bible). This evil must occur because it is a forecast of Christ's imminent return.[78] Robert H. Mounce laments that "it is difficult to see from history alone any cause for optimism." He is certain a "persecuted church will witness the victorious return of Christ"[79] rather than a world-conquering Church. George Eldon Ladd concurs: "In spite of the fact that God had invaded history in Christ, and in spite of the fact that it was to be the mission of Jesus' disciples to evangelize the entire world (Matt. 24:14), the world would remain an evil

---

74. Charles C. Ryrie, *Basic Theology* (Wheaton, IL: Victor, 1986), p. 461.

75. Hunt is a best-selling author whose books are found in virtually every Christian bookstore in America.

76. Dave Hunt, *Whatever Happened to Heaven?* (Eugene, OR: Harvest House, 1988), pp. 178, 274.

77. Charles E. Stevens, "The Church of Christ and the Kingdom of Christ in Contrast," *Prophecy and the Seventies*, p. 101.

78. J. Barton Payne, *Biblical Prophecy for Today* (Grand Rapids: Baker, 1978), p. 10.

79. Robert H. Mounce, *The Book of Revelation* (*New International Commentary on the New Testament*) (Grand Rapids: Eerdmans, 1977), p. 47; cf. p. 44.

place. False christs would arise who would lead many astray. Wars, strife, and persecution would continue. Wickedness would abound so as to chill the love of many."[80]

Amillennialism. Among amillennialists we discover the same sort of despair. William Hendriksen comments that "the majority will ever be on the side of the evil one."[81] Cornelis Vanderwaal writes that "I do not believe in inevitable progress toward a much better world in this dispensation" and God's "church has no right to take an optimistic, triumphalistic attitude."[82] H. de Jongste and J. M. van Krimpen forthrightly declare: "there is no room for optimism: towards the end, in the camps of the satanic and the anti-Christ, culture will sicken, and the Church will yearn to be delivered from its distress."[83]

Van Riessen writes that "Babylon will be the city of the end."[84] Amillennialist Donald Guthrie, according to dispensationalist John F. Walvoord, "readily agrees that the biblical point of view is pessimistic, that is, the world as it is now constituted will not be revived and improved, but instead, will be destroyed and replaced."[85] Hendrikus Berkhof notes the effect of such thinking on the average Christian: "The average Christian does not expect to see any positive signs of Christ's reign in the world. He believes that the world only becomes worse and races in the direction of the antichrist."[86] Dale H. Kuiper

---

80. George Eldon Ladd, *The Last Things: An Eschatology for Laymen* (Grand Rapids: Eerdmans, 1978), p. 58.

81. William Hendriksen, *More Than Conquerors* (Grand Rapids: Baker, [1939] 1967), p. 228.

82. Cornelis Vanderwaal, *Hal Lindsey and Biblical Prophecy* (St. Catherine's, Ontario: Paideia, 1978), pp. 44, 45.

83. H. de Jongste and J. M. van Krimpen, *The Bible and the Life of the Christian* (Philadelphia: Presbyterian & Reformed, 1968), p. 27.

84. Hendrik van Riessen, *The Society of the Future* (Philadelphia: Presbyterian & Reformed, 1957), p. 233. See a similar sentiment in Raymond O. Zorn, *Church and Kingdom* (Philadelphia: Presbyterian & Reformed, 1962), pp. 182-184.

85. John F. Walvoord, "Review of Donald Guthrie, *The Relevance of John's Apocalypse*" *Bibliotheca Sacra* 147 (April/June 1990) 251.

86. Berkhof, *Christ the Meaning of History*, p. 174.

blasts postmillennialists because "they are fiercely opposed to speaking of a parallel development of good and evil, of God's kingdom and Satan's kingdom, of the world becoming progressively worse and falling away, of the church's tribulation increasing and the end of the world finding the church lonely and sorely beset."[87] Hanko insists that "we must indeed expect an age when the powers of darkness shall rule in the earth." Consequently, "there is nothing optimistic here or filled with hope for the future."[88]

An entire issue of *The Standard Bearer* of the amillennial Protestant Reformed Church is dogmatic in its despair. "The hope of the Reformed Christian is not in any kingdom in this sorry world. Why, after all, would he *want* to place it there? For, what is the Taj Mahal, even . . . compared to the mansion prepared for him in heaven. . . . Another decade has ended. We are a step closer [to the end]. We do well to meditate on that."[89] "In all his or her 'sorrows and persecutions,' the child of God living in January, A.D. 1990 longs for one thing, and one thing only: the coming of Christ to judge the living and the dead, by which he and all Christ's chosen ones shall be translated to Christ. . . . All other hopes are miserable delusions and pipe dreams."[90]

The woe continues: The "world [is] filled with sin and getting worse, a hopeless situation beyond repair and impossible to

---

87. Dale H. Kuiper, "What Constitutes Victory? An Analysis of the Postmillennialism Espoused by Chalcedon, Especially in Rushdoony's *God's Plan for Victory*" (unpublished conference paper: South Holland, IL: South Holland Protestant Reformed Church, 1978), pp. 51-52.

88. Herman Hanko, "An Exegetical Refutation of Postmillennialism" (unpublished conference paper: South Holland, IL: South Holland Protestant Reformed Church, 1978), pp. 22, 23.

89. Don Doezema, "In This Issue. . . ," *Standard Bearer* 66:7 (Jan. 1, 1990) 146.

90. David J. Engelsma, "The Reformed Faith – Theology of Hope," *ibid.* 149. This dramatic overstatement reduces all Christian hope to one event: the Second Advent. It effectively undermines the missionary and evangelistic hope of bringing others to Christ – as well as other such hopes – in that "*all* other hopes are delusions."

salvage" is before us. Thus, the postmillennial hope of the growth of the true Christian faith to dominance "holds before us an illusory hope. . . . It is a mirage, therefore, a false hope. . . . It is a mirage because the kingdom which the Postmillennialists described is, in fact, the kingdom of Antichrist. . . . The hope of the believer, and for this I am profoundly grateful, is not on any kingdom in this sorry world, but is fastened with eagerness, with longing and with great optimism, on the everlasting kingdom of righteousness which shall be realized only in the new heavens and in the new earth where sin shall be no more."[91] "Because of God's curse, man lies in the midst of death with no escape. Man goes in a circle, a vicious circle. He has made progress, but his progress consists only in that he runs his miserable circle at a faster pace. The best of man's earthly life is labor and sorrow (Psalm 90:10). Nothing is free from becoming dust."[92] "Apostasy grows worse and worse as time goes on. We live in the last days and we know that our Lord prophesied that in our days there would be few in the world that believe."[93]

Conclusion

Few things have been more destructive to the implementation of a well-rounded, biblically grounded Christian worldview than an incorrect perspective on the end times. A classic, though inadvertent, illustration of this is available in a 1977 interview with premillennial evangelist Billy Graham:

Q. If you had to live your life over again, what would you do differently?

---

91. Herman Hanko, "The Illusory Hope of Postmillennialism," *ibid.*, 159, 160.

92. Ronald VanOverloop, "The Hope of Every Believer Regarding His Future Earthly Life," *ibid.* 162.

93. Arie denHartog, "Hope and the Protestant Reformed Churches' Mission Calling," *ibid.* 165.

A. One of my great regrets is that I have not studied enough. I wish I had studied more and preached less. . . . Donald Barnhouse said that if he knew the Lord was coming in three years he would spend two of them studying and one preaching. I'm trying to make it up.[94]

A similar problem is admitted by Tim LaHaye. Many Christians are committed to the approaching end of the age, with all of its horror (according to their dispensational view):

Most knowledgeable Christians are looking for the Second Coming of Christ and the tribulation period that He predicted would come before the end of the age. Because present world conditions are so similar to those the Bible prophesies for the last days. . . , they conclude that a takeover of our culture by the forces of evil is inevitable; so they do nothing to resist it.[95]

Such pessimistic outlooks are not conducive to the promotion of a full-orbed Christian worldview. A *Christianity Today* book review further illustrates this mindset. There we read that "Myers calls us 'not to change the world, but to understand it.'" The review also notes that author Myers writes: "If we cannot expect our culture to be a holy enterprise, we can at least try to avoid participating in its profanities."[96]

It is not unusual for the defenders and extenders of pessimistic eschatologies to speak of suffering and sorrow as the lot of Christians *throughout* the Christian history, with no hope of a let up. Writes amillennialist professor Richard Gaffin of Westminster Theological Seminary: "Over the interadvental period *in its entirety*, from beginning to end, a *fundamental* aspect of the church's existence is (to be) 'suffering with Christ'; *nothing*, the

---

94. "Taking the World's Temperature" (interview), *Christianity Today* (Sept. 23, 1977) 19.

95. Tim LaHaye, *The Battle for the Mind* (Old Tappan, NJ: Revell, 1980), p. 217.

96. Steve Rabey, "Review of Kenneth A. Myers, *All God's Children and Blue Suede Shoes: Christians and Popular Culture*," *Christianity Today* 34:12 (Sept. 10, 1990) 43.

New Testament teaches, *is more basic* to its identity than that."[97] "The normal situation for the community of Jesus is not to be influential and prosperous but poor and oppressed."[98] "The church is called to suffer in this world."[99] "Such tolerance as [Christians] receive on the part of the world is due to this fact that we live in the earlier, rather than in the later, stage of history."[100]

The study of eschatology is a worthy Christian endeavor. Its significance to the Christian worldview is evident in the large role it plays in Scripture, which holds priority in the developing of a truly Christian worldview. It is also crucial to the development of a distinctively Christian philosophy of history, which is fundamental to the Christian understanding of the here and now. In addition, eschatology significantly impacts the Christian's cultural endeavors because it sets before the Christian the foreordained pattern of the future. If that pattern is one of pessimism, it will tend to discourage and thwart the Christian social enterprise.[101]

In this work, I will set forth a biblical eschatology that gives prominence to the gospel victory theme. The optimistic eschatological perspective from which I write is that of postmillennialism – a postmillennialism generated neither by a contemporary Reagan-era optimism nor by a Kierkegaardian leap of faith, but by a careful exegetical and theological study of the eschatological data of Scripture.

---

97. Richard B. Gaffin, "Theonomy and Eschatology: Reflections on Postmillennialism," *Theonomy: A Reformed Critique*, William S. Barker and W. Robert Godfrey, eds. (Grand Rapids: Zondervan, 1990), pp. 210-211 (emphasis mine).

98. Van Riessen, *Society of the Future*, p. 234.

99. John R. Muether, "The Era of Common Grace: Living Between the 'Already' and the 'Not Yet,' " *RTS Ministry* 9 (Summer 1990) 18. This magazine is published by Reformed Theological Seminary.

100. Cornelius Van Til, *Common Grace and the Gospel* (Nutley, NJ: Presbyterian & Reformed, 1972), p. 85.

101. See: North, *Is the World Running Down?* and James B. Jordan, ed., *Christianity and Civilization* 1 (Spring 1982): "The Failure of American Baptist Culture."

I believe, with Roderick Campbell, that "the church today needs this kind of vision – the vision of her reigning Lord with all the resources of heaven and earth under His command for the help and protection of His church and the ingathering of His elect."[102] In the *Foreword* to that book, O. T. Allis wrote:

[M]y own studies in this and related fields have convinced me that the most serious error in much of the current 'prophetic' teaching of today is the claim that the future of Christendom is to be read not in terms of Revival and Victory, but of growing impotence and apostasy, and that the only hope of the world is that the Lord will by His visible coming and reign complete the task which He has so plainly entrusted to the church. This claim . . . is pessimistic and defeatist. I hold it to be unscriptural. The language of the Great Commission is world-embracing; and it has back of it the authority and power of One who said: "All power is given unto Me in heaven and in earth. Go ye therefore and make disciples of all nations." The duty of the church is to address herself to the achieving of this task in anticipation of the Lord's coming, and not to expect Him to call her away to glory before her task is accomplished.[103]

---

102. Campbell, *Israel and the New Covenant*, p. 79.
103. Allis, "Foreword," in *ibid.*, p. ix.

2

THE PURPOSE OF THIS TREATISE

Sanctify the Lord God in your hearts, and always be ready to give a defense to everyone who asks you a reason for the hope that is in you, with meekness and fear. (1 Peter 3:15)

The writer of Ecclesiastes remarks that "of making many books there is no end" (Eccl. 12:12a). Today this seems especially true with eschatological books. As I noted in the preceding chapter, there are those who complain about the fielding of additional material relating to the "overcrowded field" of eschatology.

It is necessary to provide a chapter setting forth the purpose and rationale of the present work. In this book I intend to accomplish the following goals. First, to furnish helpful information on the eschatological debate, since the debate still rages within evangelicalism and is increasing as we draw closer to the year 2000. Second, to give careful exposition to major eschatological themes in the Bible, since they carry the eschatological weight in Scripture. Third, to set forth a detailed vindication of that eschatological position generally known as postmillennialism, since it has been so neglected in the latter half of this century. Finally, to provide a biblical invitation to the reader to adopt the postmillennial eschatology, since its optimism is so needed in our time. I have therefore divided this chapter into four sections that encompass these four goals: information, exposition, vindication, and exhortation.

Information

I begin with the question of the theological awareness of contemporary Christians.

Theological Awareness

Christians should be aware of contemporary theology, particularly evangelical formulations. Too few Christians today have an adequate grasp of the doctrines of Scripture. This is due to a widespread disinterest in doctrinal preaching and deep reading. John A. Sproule laments: "The tragedy today . . . is the apparent disinterest in the preaching of doctrine in the church. . . . Caught up in the craze for 'Christian' entertainment and psychology, the church is worse off for it."[1] This problem, though intensified in our day, is not new: "The growth of ignorance in the Church is the logical and inevitable result of the false notion that Christianity is a life and not also a doctrine; if Christianity is not a doctrine then of course teaching is not necessary to Christianity."[2]

Regarding the material in Christian bookstores, R. C. Sproul comments: "My guess is that in the current Christian bookstore the simplistic books outweigh the simple books by at least 10 to 1. I've often wondered where Jesus would apply His hastily made whip if He were to visit our culture. My guess is that it would not be money-changing tables in the temple that would feel His wrath, but the display racks in Christian bookstores."[3]

---

1. John A. Sproule, "A Tribute to S. Lewis Johnson, Jr.: Theologian and Preacher," *Continuity and Discontinuity: Perspectives on the Relationship Between the Old and New Testaments*, John S. Feinberg, ed. (Westchester, IL: Crossway Books, 1988), p. 318.

2. J. Gresham Machen, *Christianity and Liberalism* (New York: Macmillan, 1923), p. 177. Reprinted by William B. Eerdmans Co., Grand Rapids.

3. R. C. Sproul, *Lifeviews* (Old Tappan, NJ: Revell, 1986), p. 184.

Much of the doctrine evangelical Christians today have picked up has been through informal instruction that is largely inadequate and often downright heretical.[4]

The doctrine of eschatology, because of its theological complexity, historical breadth, and practical implications, requires intense study and careful reflection. The need of care in this area is evidenced by the proliferation of "last day" cults over the last 150 years, such as Seventh-Day Adventists, Church of Jesus Christ of Latter-Day Saints (i.e., Mormons), Jehovah's Witnesses, Herbert W. Armstrong's Worldwide Church of God, the Children of God, the Unification Church, and others.

A divine lament in Scripture is quite apropos today: "My people are destroyed for lack of knowledge" (Hos. 4:6). Christians are urged to "be diligent to show themselves approved, workmen of God that need not to be ashamed, handling accurately the word of truth" (2 Tim. 2:15). Light is an emphasized metaphor of the Christian faith;[5] consequently, obscurantism and ignorance are not virtues for the people of God.[6] We need to get things bright and clear, theologically and ethically.

Because of both our sin and our finitude, we cannot know anything *exhaustively* (though we can know truly what we do know).[7] Consequently, no one knows all there is to know re-

---

4. Michael Horton, ed., *The Agony of Deceit: What Some TV Preachers Are Really Teaching* (Chicago: Moody Press, 1990).

5. The word "light" occurs seventy-six times in the New Testament. It is used metaphorically most often.

6. The call to "know" is a frequent refrain in the New Testament, particularly in Paul's writings, where it occurs no less than sixty-one times. The rebuke "know ye not" occurs fifteen times; see: Rom. 6:3, 16; 7:1; 1 Cor. 3:16; 5:6; 6:2, 3, 9, 15, 16, 19; 9:13, 24; 2 Cor. 13:5; Jms. 4:4. "I would not have you ignorant [i.e., unknowing]" occurs seven times; see: Rom. 1:13; 11:25; 1 Cor. 10:1; 12:1; 2 Cor. 1:8; 2:11; 1 Thess. 4:13. "We/ye know" occurs thirty times; see: Rom. 3:19; 7:14, 18; 8:22, 26, 28; 1 Cor. 2:12, 14; 8:1, 2, 4; 12:2; 15:58; 16:15; 2 Cor. 5:1; 8:9; 13:6; Gal. 3:7; 4:13; 3:19; Eph. 5:5; Phil. 2:22; 4:15; 1 Thess. 3:3; 4:2; 5:2; 2 Thess. 2:6; 3:7; 1 Tim. 1:8; 3:5. "I would have you know/that ye may know" occurs nine times; see: 1 Cor. 11:3; 2 Cor. 2:4; Eph. 1:18; 6:21, 22; Col. 4:6; 1 Thess. 4:4; 1 Tim. 3:15; 2 Tim. 3:1.

7. Cornelius Van Til, *The Defense of the Faith* (3rd ed.; Philadelphia: Presbyterian & Reformed, 1967), ch. 3.

garding Scripture, so we always need to study it more in order to gain a better understanding of it.[8] The Scripture teaches that "a wise man will hear, and will increase learning" (Prov. 1:5). And the better we apprehend and apply Scripture, the closer will be our walk with God, for sanctification comes through the means of the Word of God: "Sanctify them through thy truth: thy word is truth."[9]

All Christians, therefore, should "desire the sincere milk of the word, that [they] may grow thereby" (1 Pet. 2:2). As we grow in the knowledge of the Word of Truth, we should strive to reach a level of understanding that would equip us to be competent teachers of the Word (Heb. 5:12-14; contra John 3:10). None of us "knows it all." Thus, the study of issues of contemporary concern is always practically beneficial to the Christian. And the labor of diligent and systematic study of Scriptural issues is essential to the Christian's pleasing God.

My concern in this work is with an evangelical audience. Consequently, I will give only occasional and passing reference to the various eschatological formulations by liberal theologians, such as might be discovered in process theology, liberation theology, and the like. This approach does not imply that a study of the errors involved in rationalistic eschatological formulations is unneeded.[10] For a full-orbed Christian witness, we should strive to understand and be able to respond to those who would subvert doctrine within the church. Nevertheless, due to space limitations, I will not engage such in the present work.

---

8. Psa. 1:2-3; 119:97; Matt. 13:23; Acts 17:11.

9. John 17:17; cf. John 8:32; 15:3; Eph. 5:26; 2 Thess. 2:13; Jms. 1:21.

10. For helpful introductions to liberal eschatological views, see: Millard J. Erickson, *Contemporary Options in Eschatology: A Study of the Millennium* (Grand Rapids: Baker, 1977), chaps. 1-2, and Erickson, *Christian Theology*, 3 vols. (Grand Rapids: Baker, 1985), 3:1155ff. Anthony Hoekema, *The Bible and the Future* (Grand Rapids: Eerdmans, 1979), pp. 288-315 (Appendix: "Recent Trends in Eschatology"). John N. Oswalt, "Recent Studies in Old Testament Eschatology and Apocalyptic," *Journal of the Evangelical Theological Society* 24:4 (Dec. 1981) 289-302.

Hasty Postmortems

Many evangelical treatments of eschatology obscure the facts of contemporary options, sometimes through ignorance, sometimes through overstatement. Whatever the reason, a great disservice is done to the unsuspecting reader who inadvertently adopts and then labors under a delusion.

For instance, it is often stated that postmillennialism is dead, supposedly having totally collapsed because of World War I. Although it is true that postmillennialism fell upon hard times after World Wars I and II, it is not true that it totally disappeared from the Church. Here are several statements from different decades regarding the alleged death of postmillennialism. These are at best misleading overstatements and at worst downright erroneous.[11]

In 1936, Lewis Sperry Chafer stated: "postmillennialism is dead. . . . [I]t is *dead* in the sense that it offers *no living voice* in its own defense when the millennial question is under discussion."[12] "It exists only in the limited literature which it created and with no living voice to defend it" (1948).[13] In 1956, Culbertson and Centz observed: "Devout Postmillennialism has virtually disappeared."[14] In 1958, J. Dwight Pentecost wrote that "Postmillennialism is *no longer an issue* in theology. . . . Postmillennialism finds *no defenders or advocates* in the present

---

11. For a brief analysis of the theological problems inherent in such statements, see: R. J. Rushdoony, "Introduction," in J. Marcellus Kik, *An Eschatology of Victory* (n.p.: Presbyterian & Reformed, 1971), pp. vii-ix. Although the three statements to follow all come from dispensationalists, the problem is not one limited to that school of thought. Premillennialists and amillennialists are also guilty of such hasty postmortems. See for example, amillennialist Jay E. Adams, *The Time Is at Hand* (Nutley, NJ: Presbyterian & Reformed, 1966), pp. 2, 4, 96.

12. Lewis Sperry Chafer, "Foreword to the First Edition [1936]," in Charles L. Feinberg, *Premillennialism or Amillennialism*. This work is entitled *Millennialism: The Two Major Views* (3rd ed.; Chicago: Moody Press, 1980), p. 9 (emphasis mine).

13. Lewis Sperry Chafer, *Systematic Theology*, 8 vols. (Dallas: Dallas Theological Seminary Press, 1948) 4:281. This set went out of print in 1988.

14. W. Culbertson and H. B. Centz, ed., *Understanding the Times* (Grand Rapids: Zondervan, 1956), p. 22.

chiliastic discussions within the theological world."[15] In 1959, Walvoord suggested that "Postmillennialism is not a current issue in millennarianism" and that "in eschatology the trend away from postmillennialism became almost a rout with the advent of World War II."[16] In 1961, Merrill F. Unger claimed of postmillennialism: "This theory, largely disproved by the progress of history, is practically a dead issue."[17] In 1970, Hal Lindsey commented: "There *used to be* a group called 'postmillennialists'. . . . *No* self-respecting scholar who looks at the world conditions and the accelerating decline of Christian influence today is a 'postmillennialist.' "[18] As late as 1990, John Walvoord wrote: "Postmillennialism largely died out in the first quarter of the 20th century. World War I dashed the hopes of those who said the world was getting better and Christianity was triumphing."[19]

The impression left by such statements is simply false. In fact, the statements were incorrect when originally made. Chafer's 1936 statement demonstrates little awareness of the strong postmillennialism current in Southern Presbyterian circles in the 1920's leading up to the era of his statement.[20] Important articles on postmillennialism were published after World War I in *Union Seminary Review* by Eugene C. Caldwell in 1922[21] and

---

15. J. Dwight Pentecost, *Things to Come: A Study in Biblical Eschatology* (Grand Rapids: Zondervan, 1958), pp. 386, 387 (emphasis mine).

16. John F. Walvoord, *The Millennial Kingdom* (Findlay, OH: Dunham, 1959), p. 9.

17. Merrill F. Unger, "Millennium," *Unger's Bible Dictionary* (2nd ed.; Chicago: Moody Press, 1961), p. 739.

18. Hal Lindsey, *The Late Great Planet Earth* (Grand Rapids: Zondervan, 1970), p. 176 (emphasis mine).

19. John F. Walvoord, "Review of *House Divided*," *Bibliotheca Sacra* 147 (July/Sept. 1990) 371.

20. The following material and bibliographic data regarding Southern Presbyterian postmillennialism is derived from James B. Jordan, "A Survey of Southern Presbyterian Millennial Views Before 1930," *Journal of Christian Reconstruction* 3:2 (Winter 1976-77) 106-121.

21. Eugene C. Caldwell, "A Kingdom That Shall Stand Forever," *Union Seminary*

T. Cary Johnson in 1923.[22] A postmillennial book by Russell
Cecil was published in 1923.[23] And sometime after 1921 David
S. Clark published a postmillennial commentary on Revelation.[24] J. Gresham Machen, who died in 1937, was a widely
known writer, who fought valiantly against encroaching liberalism in the Church and in society. He also was a postmillennialist.[25] Chafer was simply in error when he stated that postmillennialism was "dead" and had "no living voice" in his time.

J. Dwight Pentecost had even less reason in 1958 to assert
postmillennialism's total demise. In the 1940s, premillennialist
D. H. Kromminga and amillennialist Floyd E. Hamilton were
contending with postmillennialists. Kromminga wrote in 1945:
"That all three major eschatological views are still persisting
among Protestants and in our country, Floyd E. Hamilton

Review 33 (Jan. 1922) 112. Caldwell was professor of Greek New Testament at Union
Theological Seminary.

22. T. Cary Johnson, "The Signs of the Times," *ibid.* 35 (Oct. 1923) 47ff. Johnson
was professor of systematics at Union. This was written after World War I and in
spite of it to show that Christ "is going to disciple all the nations of the earth. . . .
[F]urther triumph is ahead for the church."

23. Russell Cecil, *Handbook of Theology* (Richmond: The Presbyterian Committee
of Publication, 1923), p. 101.

24. David S. Clark, *The Message from Patmos: A Postmillennial Commentary on the
Book of Revelation* (Grand Rapids: Baker, rep. 1989). The book is undated, but on
page 9 he refers to the "very recent" publication of A. S. Peake's commentary on
Revelation, which was published in 1919, and on page 39 he refers to a 1921 article
in *Century Magazine*.

25. See: Ned B. Stonehouse, *J. Gresham Machen: A Biographical Memoir* (3rd ed.;
Philadelphia: Westminster Theological Seminary, [1954] 1978). Machen urges Christians to go forth joyfully, enthusiastically to make the world subject to God" (p. 187).
"And despite all ridicule of peace movements I cherish the hope that the gospel is
going to win" (p. 245). "I do believe that there is going to be a spiritual rebellion of
the common people throughout the world which if taken at the flood may sweep
away the folly of war" (p. 261). See also: Machen, *Christianity and Liberalism*, pp. 49,
152, 178, 180. Gary North writes: "I once asked [Paul] Woolley what eschatological
views were held by J. Gresham Machen. . . . Woolley replied that he had been a
postmillennialist, to the extent that he ever announced his views, which I gathered
was infrequently." North, "Editor's Introduction," *Journal of Christian Reconstruction*
3:2 (Winter 1976-77), 3-4. Professor Norman Shepherd subsequently told North that
Woolley had said much the same thing to him about Machen's views.

makes clear."[26] O. T. Allis, an important defender of the faith and a writer well-known to Pentecost[27], was defending post-millennialism in 1947 and 1954, just prior to Pentecost's *Things to Come*.[28] Not long before Pentecost's statements, J. M. Kik (1948, 1954), Allan R. Ford (1951), Roderick Campbell (1954), and Loraine Boettner (1958) made important contributions to the eschatological debate.[29] In 1952, premillennialist George E. Ladd (in a book referenced in Pentecost's *Things to Come*) admitted that "the postmillennial interpretation . . . is not altogether dead."[30] In 1953, there was enough interest in postmillennialism to justify reprinting David Brown's postmillennial work, *Christ's Second Coming*. Pentecost's statements simply were not justified by the evidence.

In the case of the statement by popular prophecy writer, Hal Lindsey, there is no excuse for the error. In 1989, fellow dispensationalist Thomas Ice admits that "the last *twenty years* has seen an upsurge of postmillennialism."[31] Just two years after

---

26. D. H. Kromminga, *Prophecy and the Church: Studies in the History of Christian Chiliasm* (Grand Rapids: Eerdmans, 1945), p. 257. See: Floyd E. Hamilton, *The Basis of the Millennial Faith* (Grand Rapids: Eerdmans, 1942).

27. The first two quotations and six of the thirty-four quotations in the first chapter of Pentecost's *Things to Come* were from Allis' *Prophecy and the Church*.

28. We can point to at least two postmillennial contributions to the debate by Allis, one in 1947, the other in 1954. O. T. Allis, "The Parable of the Leaven," *Evangelical Quarterly* 19:4 (Oct. 1947) 254-273 and Allis, "Foreword," in Roderick Campbell, *Israel and the New Covenant* (Tyler, TX: Geneva Divinity School Press, [1954] 1981), pp. vii-x.

29. J. Marcellus Kik produced two book-length contributions to the discussion. See: *Eschatology of Victory*. This book is a collection of two smaller books by J. M. Kik dated 1948 and 1954 (as well as a short series of lectures given at Westminster Seminary in 1961). For the two earlier dates see: Loraine Boettner, *The Millennium* (Philadelphia: Presbyterian & Reformed, 1958), pp. 12, 385. See also: Allan R. Ford, "The Second Advent in Relation to the Reign of Christ," *Evangelical Quarterly* 23 (1951) 30-39; Campbell, *Israel and the New Covenant*; Boettner, *The Millennium*.

30. George E. Ladd, *Crucial Questions About the Kingdom of God* (Grand Rapids: Eerdmans, 1952), pp. 47-48. In 1978, he spoke of it as "a minority view today." Ladd, *The Last Things: An Eschatology for Laymen* (Grand Rapids: Eerdmans, 1978), pp. 108-110.

31. H. Wayne House and Thomas D. Ice, *Dominion Theology: Blessing or Curse?*

Pentecost's work and a decade before Lindsey's, E. F. Kevan wrote: "There are many evangelical believers who hold these post-millennial views. . . ."[32] The classic dispensational commentary on Revelation by one of Lindsey's seminary professors, John Walvoord, clearly pointed out in 1966 that Boettner's postmillennial work "has revived" postmillennialism.[33]

By Lindsey's time, postmillennialism had begun to make its reinvigorated presence strongly felt. John Murray's postmillennial commentary on Romans was published in 1965.[34] Erroll Hulse's postmillennial work, *The Restoration of Israel*, preceded Lindsey's book by two years.[35] Boettner's book had gone through six printings by the time Lindsey published his statement. The Banner of Truth Trust was established in the 1950s and had been republishing many Puritan postmillennial books for more than a decade before Lindsey. It was also republishing postmillennial articles in its popular magazine.[36] In fact, postmillennial contributions in *The Banner of Truth Magazine* in the year Lindsey published his book (1970) included articles by Donald Macleod, Donald Dunkerley, Iain Murray, Alexander

(Portland, OR: Multnomah, 1988), p. 210. Emphasis mine.

32. Ernest Frederick Kevan, "Millennium," *Baker's Dictionary of Theology*, Everett F. Harrison, ed. (Grand Rapids: Baker, 1960), p. 353.

33. John F. Walvoord, *The Revelation of Jesus Christ* (Chicago: Moody Press, 1966), p. 289.

34. John Murray, *The Epistle to the Romans* (*New International Commentary on the New Testament*), vol. 2 (Grand Rapids: Eerdmans, 1965). Richard B. Gaffin, Jr., seems to be mistaken as to Murray's amillennialism, based on reviewing Murray's earlier work (1954) rather than his later work (1965). Gaffin, "Theonomy and Eschatology: Reflections on Postmillennialism," *Theonomy: A Reformed Critique*, William S. Barker and W. Robert Godfrey, eds. (Grand Rapids: Zondervan, 1990), p. 199.

35. Erroll Hulse, *The Restoration of Israel* (Worthing, Sussex: Henry E. Walter, 1968).

36. In the very year of the publication of Lindsey's book (1970), issues 76 through 88 of the monthly *Banner of Truth* were published. In the first article these neo-Puritans mentioned their numbers had "grown steadily over the last decade," despite widespread liberalism and defection around them. Anonymous, "The End of the Sixties," *Banner of Truth*, No. 76 (Jan. 1970) 3.

Somerville, S. M. Houghton, and W. Stanford Reid.[37] Also, 1970 witnessed the publication of R. J. Rushdoony's postmillennial book *Thy Kingdom Come* and Peter Toon's *Puritans, the Millennium and the Future of Israel*.[38] In the next year was published a major postmillennial work that had already been advertised and promoted in 1970: Iain Murray's *The Puritan Hope: Revival and the Interpretation of Prophecy*.[39]

To quote Mark Twain, the postmillennial system could well complain, "The rumours of my death are greatly exaggerated." Dispensationalists have only recently even begun to admit the presence of postmillennialism.[40]

The Waxing and Waning of Eschatological Systems

Despite the extreme exaggerations of some regarding the demise of postmillennialism, it is true that by the mid-1900s its fortunes had been greatly reduced from its earlier times of near dominance (the 1600s-1800s).[41] Through most of the 1800s,

---

37. Donald Macleod, "The Second Coming of Christ," *Banner of Truth*, Nos. 82/83 (July/August 1970) 16-22. Donald Dunkerley, "Review of *The Time Is at Hand*," *ibid.*, Nos. 83/83 (July/Aug. 1970) 46-47. Iain Murray, "The Hope and Missionary Activity," *ibid.*, No. 84 (Sept. 1970) 7-11. This is a reprint of Alexander Somerville's nineteenth century article, "The Evangelisation of the World," *ibid.*, No. 84 (Sept. 1970) 31-35. S. M. Houghton, "Maintaining the Prayer for the World-wide Outreach of the Gospel," *ibid.*, No. 84 (Sept. 1970) 36-37. W. Stanford Reid, "Christian Realism and Optimism," *ibid.*, No. 85 (Oct. 1970), 3-6.

38. R. J. Rushdoony, *Thy Kingdom Come: Studies in Daniel and Revelation* (n.p.: Presbyterian & Reformed, 1970). Peter Toon, *Puritans, the Millennium, and the Future of Israel* (London: James Clark, 1970).

39. Iain Murray, *The Puritan Hope: Revival and the Interpretation of Prophecy* (Edinburgh: Banner of Truth, 1971). See the advance notice through publication of a chapter entitled "The Hope and Missionary Activity," *Banner of Truth*, No. 84 (Sept. 1970) 7-11.

40. See: House and Ice, *Dominion Theology*; John F. Walvoord, *The Prophecy Knowledge Handbook* (Wheaton, IL: Victor, 1990), p. 17; Robert P. Lightner, *The Last Days Handbook: A Comprehensive Guide to Understanding the Different Views of Prophecy* (Nashville: Thomas Nelson, 1990), p. 85.

41. For a brief history of postmillennialism, see Chapter 4, below. "Postmillennialism became the eschatological position of the theologians who dominated theological thinking for the past several centuries." J. Dwight Pentecost, *Things to Come*, p.

postmillennialism could be called "the commonly received doctrine," as it was in 1859.[42] Historians can state that the various premillennial views "were scattered throughout the major denominations, but none of those successfully challenged the hegemony of postmillennialism before the last decades of the century."[43] Such has certainly not been the case in the 1900s.

Although any historical analysis of the decline of postmillennialism is complex, there does appear to be merit in the view that "in a word, the erosion of postmillennialism was part of the waning of supernaturalism" in the early 1900s.[44] Evangelical postmillennialism held to a high supernaturalism that could shake heaven and earth. With the decline of a widespread commitment to supernaturalism in conjunction with the arising of various radical critical theories, interest in postmillennialism waned.

Nevertheless, "postmillennialism, since 1965, has experienced a renaissance."[45] As indicated above, an ever increasing stream of postmillennial literature has begun. In the 1980s, that stream became a flood. Today, at least partly because of the renewal of postmillennial advocacy, there is evidence of a de-

---

386. An illustration of this change of fortunes for postmillennialism may come from comparing W.E.B.'s [William E. Blackstone] 1878 *Jesus is Coming* (Old Tappan, NJ: Revell, [1898, 1908, 1932]) with Charles L. Feinberg's 1936 (first edition) *Premillennialism or Amillennialism*, republished as *Millennialism: The Two Major Views*. Blackstone's 1878 work defended premillennialism against postmillennialism only; Feinberg's 1936 book defended premillennialism against amillennialism, with virtually no mention of postmillennialism.

42. James H. Moorhead, "Millennialism in American Religious Thought," *Journal of American History* 71:3 (Dec. 1984) 525.

43. *Ibid*. See also: "History of Opinions Respecting the Millennium," *American Theological Review* 1 (Nov. 1859) 655. George M. Marsden, *The Evangelical Mind and the New School Presbyterian Experience: A Case Study of Thought and Theology in Nineteenth-Century America* (New Haven: Yale University Press, 1970), pp. 185ff.

44. James H. Moorhead, "The Erosion of Postmillennialism in American Religious Thought, 1865-1925," *Church History* 53 (1984) 76.

45. Gary North, "Towards the Recovery of Hope," *Banner of Truth*, No. 88 (Jan. 1971) 12.

cline in adherence to premillennialism, the dominant evangelical view of the 1900s.

Some recent dispensational works have begun mentioning the slipping of the numbers of premillennialists. One dispensationalist writes that "today, a growing number of Christians are [sic] exchanging the hope for the rapture for a new hope." Of dispensational adherents, he laments: "the numbers are dwindling."[46] Two other recent dispensational writers comment: "In fact, the premillennial position is probably more on the decline at the present time than the other two views."[47] Still another observes that "in the last quarter of the 20th century a movement has begun to return to the Reformation as a basis of theology, and with it an abandonment of dispensationalism and premillennialism."[48] Another bemoans that "premillennialism, though still entrenched within many local churches, is *no longer* being taught from the pulpit and is rapidly falling from favor."[49]

As with the decline of postmillennialism, the ascertaining of the exact reasons for premillennialism's decline are certainly numerous and complex. Yet a case can be made that premillennialism – particularly its young offspring, dispensationalism – is being *embarrassed to death*. The temptation to date-setting is just too ingrained in the premillennial mindset to resist, particularly as the year 2000 approaches.[50] One premillennialist admits:

---

46. Dave Hunt, *Whatever Happened to Heaven?* (Eugene, OR: Harvest House, 1988), back cover copy; p. 9. See also: pp. 31, 68, 70, 72.

47. House and Ice, *Dominion Theology*, p. 210.

48. Walvoord, "Review of *House Divided*," 372.

49. Douglas Shearer, *Political Power: Battle for the Soul of the Church* (Sacramento, CA: New Hope Christian Fellowship, 1988), p. 16.

50. "As the year 2000 approaches there will undoubtedly be increased interest in premillenarian ideas and even more hazardous speculation that this third millennium will be the Thousand Year Kingdom of Christ." Dwight Wilson, *Armageddon Now! The Premillenarian Response to Russia and Israel Since 1917* (Tyler, TX: Institute for Christian Economics, [1977] 1991), p. 13. Examples of a tendency to a mild form of date-setting among noted dispensationalist scholars may be found in Charles C. Ryrie, *The Living End* (Old Tappan, NJ: Revell, 1976), pp. 128-129; Herman A. Hoyt, "Dispen-

"The premillenarians' credibility is at a low ebb because they succumbed to the temptation to exploit every conceivably possible prophetic fulfillment. . . . It is not likely that the situation will change greatly."[51] In the late 1980s, there was an agreement signed by a number of dispensationalists, urging against such a lamentable situation:

1988 Manifesto on Date Setting

Whereas the Scripture clearly says that no man can know the day or hour of the Lord's coming, thus indicating that date-setting serves no good purpose,

And whereas date-setting has historically always proven to be false prophecy which is damaging to the cause of Christ,

And whereas we are living in the *last days and nothing must be* allowed to detract from the nobility and power *or the message of* endtime Bible prophecy,

Therefore we, the undersigned hereby demand that all date-setting and date-suggesting cease immediately. Let abstinence from this type of speculation prevail until the Lord comes.

But the addiction continues.[52]

Even those dispensationalists less prone to date-setting admit the problem. Lightner comments: "Sometimes individuals who

---

sational Premillennialism," *The Meaning of the Millennium: Four Views*, Robert Clouse, ed. (Downer's Grove, IL: Inter-Varsity Press, 1977), p. 63; and John F. Walvoord, *The Nations, Israel, and the Church in Prophecy* (Grand Rapids: Zondervan, 1988), p. xiv.

51. Dwight Wilson, *Armageddon Now!*, p. 218. As I write these words, just a couple of weeks after the conclusion of the Allied victory in the Gulf War of 1991, I am aware of a large number of books pointing to Saddam Hussein and Babylon as harbingers of the end. *Christianity Today, Newsweek,* and other magazines have run articles on the flood of evangelical doom sayers. Joe Maxwell, "Prophecy Books Become Big Sellers," *Christianity Today* 34:3 (March 11, 1991) 60. Some of the titles mentioned in *Christianity Today* are: John Walvoord, *Armageddon, Oil and the Middle East*, an update of his 1974 book; Charles H. Dyer, *The Rise of Babylon: Sign of the End Times*; Edgar C. James, *Arabs, Oil and Armageddon*; Charles C. Ryrie, *Crisis in the Middle East*.

52. See: David Allen Lewis, "Prophecy Intelligence Digest" (Springfield, MO: Dave A Lewis Ministries, 1988), vol. 6, no. 3.

embrace a particular view of end-time events embarrass others who hold the same view and they even put the view in poor light by their radical and extreme viewpoints. . . . I refer particularly to date setting for Christ's return."[53] He specifically mentions Edgar C. Whisenant's *Why the Rapture Could Be in 1988* and Hal Lindsey's *1980's: Countdown to Armageddon.* Thomas D. Ice laments: "[J]ust this week (the week before Christmas) I received in the mail from an anonymous sender, a book entitled *Blessed Hope, 1996* . . . by someone from the Houston area named Salty Doc. You guessed it, the Rapture is slated for 1996. . . . Unfortunately, both advocates and antagonists of dispensationalism are woefully ignorant that the very Biblical assumptions underlying dispensationalism are themselves hostile to the date-setting of the Rapture. Much harm has been done by the supposed friends, not to mention the critics of dispensationalism by these distortions."[54]

For instance, dispensational theologian John F. Walvoord is dogmatic that the rapture of the Church must be always imminent, when he writes: "There is no teaching of any intervening event. The prospect of being taken to heaven at the coming of Christ is not qualified by description of any signs or prerequisite events."[55] Yet he could not resist the excitement generated by the Gulf War (the "100-day war"). In an interview in *U.S.A. Today*, we read his words: "Bible prophecy is being fulfilled every day. . . . Q. So the prophetic clock is ticking? A: Yes."[56] In one of his recent books, Walvoord includes a table recording "Predicted Events Relating to the Nations." Among those "predicted events" he lists: "1. United Nations organized as first

53. Lightner, *The Last Days Handbook*, p. 171. A 1991 offender is John Walvoord.

54. Thomas D. Ice, "Dispensationalism, Date-Setting and Distortion," *Biblical Perspectives* 1:5 (Sept./Oct. 1988) 1.

55. John F. Walvoord, *The Rapture Question* (2nd ed.; Grand Rapids: Zondervan, 1979), p. 73. See Chapter 14, below, for a critique of the imminence doctrine.

56. Barbara Reynolds, "Prophecy clock is ticking in Mideast," *U. S. A. Today* (Jan. 19, 1991), Inquiry section.

step toward world government in 1946. . . . 6. Red China becomes a military power. . . . 8. The Arab oil embargo in 1973,"
and other such "predicted events."[57]

It is likely that a continuing flood of failed expectations will
eventually sink premillennial views. It would seem that the
current decline (halted only temporarily by the Gulf War) of
premillennialism might be attributable to failed expectations.

Exposition

I have in mind several major reasons for the publication of
the present book. My first desire is to set forth in the contemporary debate a careful, exegetically rigorous foundation for
postmillennialism. Care will be taken to treat the major eschatological passages of Scripture in establishing the case for postmillennialism. There are some Christians, including Christian
scholars, who seem remarkably unaware of the existence of an
exegetical case for postmillennialism.[58] Others doubt that postmillennialism can be demonstrated from the New Testament,
although they recognize a certain plausibility based on Old
Testament exegesis. (The case can be made from the New
Testament, but even if it could not, does this mean that we
should therefore ignore the Old Testament?)

Complaints Against Postmillennialism

Two Dutch Reformed pastors complained: "Postmillenarians
can not produce a single passage of Scripture in defense of

---

57. Walvoord, *Prophecy Knowledge Handbook*, p. 400.

58. Some of this problem is being rectified since the first edition of this book.
See: Darrell L. Bock, ed., *Three Views of the End of History* (Grand Rapids: Zondervan,
1997). I am the contributor for the postmillennial position. See also: Ronald Nash,
Great Divides: Understanding the Controversies That Come Between Christians (Colorado
Springs, Colo.: NavPress, 1993). Stanley J. Grenz, *Millennial Maze: Sorting Our
Evangelical Options* (Downers Grove, IL: InterVarsity, 1992).

their spiritualizing system – NOT ONE. This is a great difficulty."[59] Dale H. Kuiper lodges as his first complaint against postmillennialism: "In the first place, we do not find a careful exegesis of Scripture which takes into account the nature of prophecy and vision. . . . We do not find exegesis of passages which would seem to oppose postmillennialism."[60]

L. S. Chafer writes off postmillennialism as wholly devoid of biblical foundations: "Doubtless the stress upon Bible study of the present century has served to uncover the unscriptural character of this system. Its advocates have not been able to meet the challenge made to them to produce one Scripture which teaches a millennium before the advent of Christ, or that teaches an advent of Christ after the Millennium."[61]

John Walvoord protests in a similar vein: "[T]he contenders for postmillennialism never set up their own view in a solid way. After all, the issue is whether postmillennialism is taught in the Bible."[62] Thomas D. Ice complains: "After fourteen years of study it is my belief that there is not one passage anywhere in Scripture that would lead to the postmillennial system. The best postmillennialism can come up with is a position built upon an inference."[63] Richard A. Young writes: "The primary weakness of postmillennialism . . . is that it lacks exegetical support."[64]

After citing an optimistic, postmillennial conception of history, amillennialist George Murray complains of the doctrine's

---

59. John T. Demarest and William R. Gordon, *Christocracy: Essays on the Coming and Kingdom of Christ* (3rd ed.; New York: R. Brinkerhoff, 1878), p. 378.

60. Dale H. Kuiper, "What Constitutes Victory? An Analysis of the Postmillennialism Espoused by Chalcedon, Especially in Rushdoony's *God's Plan for Victory*" (unpublished conference paper: South Holland, IL: South Holland Protestant Reformed Church, 1978), p. 54.

61. Chafer, *Systematic Theology*, 4:281.

62. Walvoord, "Review of *House Divided*," 370.

63. House and Ice, *Dominion Theology*, pp. 9-10.

64. Richard A. Young, "Review of *Dominion Theology: Blessing or Curse?*" *Grace Theological Journal* 2:1 (Spring 1990) 115.

absence in the New Testament. "One cannot but regret, however, that with the Bible in his hand, the writer did not produce chapter and verse to prove his contention. The obvious reason is that no such plain promise could be quoted from the New Testament, for neither Jesus Christ nor His apostles gave the slightest indication of any real rest for the church until she enters upon the rest prepared for the people of God on the other side of death."[65] Erickson largely agrees: "Perhaps more damaging to postmillennialism is its apparent neglect of Scriptural passages (e.g., Matt. 24:9-14) that portray spiritual and moral conditions as worsening in the end times. It appears that postmillennialism has based its doctrine on very carefully selected Scriptural passages."[66]

Amillennialist Richard B. Gaffin also doubts the New Testamental validity of postmillennialism, when he criticizes postmillennial advocacy. "Briefly, the basic issue is this: Is the New Testament to be allowed to interpret the Old – as the best, most reliable interpretive tradition in the history of the church (and certainly the Reformed tradition) has always insisted? . . . Will the vast stretches of Old Testament prophecy, including its recurrent, frequently multivalent apocalyptic imagery, thus be left without effective New Testament control and so become a virtual blank check to be filled out in capital, whatever may be its source, that is something other than the result of sound exegesis?"[67]

In addition, some passages of less significance for the establishment of postmillennialism per se are of great interest to the student of biblical prophecy. Some of these are familiar passages that are being abused today by seeking to apply them with-

---

65. George Murray, *Millennial Studies: A Search for Truth* (Grand Rapids: Baker, 1948), p. 86.

66. Erickson, *Contemporary Options in Eschatology*, p. 72.

67. Gaffin, "Theonomy and Eschatology: Reflections on Postmillennialism," *Theonomy: A Reformed Critique*, pp. 216-217.

out biblical warrant to contemporary fulfillments. Many of these intriguing passages will be covered, as well.

An Apologetic for Postmillennialism

As my second goal, I hope to provide a book that is a worthy apologetic of postmillennialism through a careful, systematic, theological, and historical development of the postmillennial system. There are many contemporary systematic eschatological works on the various non-postmillennial systems. Unfortunately, systematic formulations of postmillennialism tend to be either somewhat dated[68] or, if contemporary, more introductory than thorough.[69] Thomas Finger is not too far wrong when he comments: "Postmillennialism has not been expounded in as minute detail as has dispensationalism."[70] I hope that this work will serve as a foundational text for postmillennialism in the contemporary debate.

Interaction With Rival Views

Third, a major design of the present work is to provide a comparison and interaction with the other major evangelical millennial views. Too often today, writers of popular millennial literature make unwarranted assumptions implying the universal recognition of a particular view, without informing the

---

68. See: Loraine Boettner's rather thorough, though politically flawed, *The Millennium* (1957) and Roderick Campbell's thematic *Israel and the New Covenant* (1954).

69. Helpful recent postmillennial works include: John J. Davis' excellent (though small) introductory work, *Christ's Victorious Kingdom: Postmillennialism Reconsidered* (Grand Rapids: Baker, 1986). David Chilton's extremely helpful, symbolism-based approach to eschatological optimism themes, entitled *Paradise Restored: A Biblical Theology of Dominion* (Ft. Worth, TX: Dominion Press, 1985). Also see: Greg L. Bahnsen and Kenneth L. Gentry, Jr., *House Divided: The Break-up of Dispensational Theology* (Tyler, TX: Institute for Christian Economics, 1989), Part 2. But none of these is a full-blown systematic theology textbook on postmillennialism.

70. Thomas N. Finger, *Christian Theology: An Eschatological Approach* (Nashville: Thomas Nelson, 1985), p. 114.

reader of competing systems. This is particularly true in dispensational circles — and especially among the popular proponents, more so than among the theologians. Thus, I will interact with the non-postmillennial systems, attempting to summarize their salient features and expose their flaws, as understood from a biblically based postmillennial viewpoint.

Interestingly (or perhaps, tragically), the resurgence of postmillennialism has been rather harshly attacked recently by some dispensationalist writers.[71] The underlying assumption in these works is always dispensationalism's implicit monopolistic claim to orthodoxy.[72] There is a distressing ignorance in too many Christians today regarding the existence of non-premillennial eschatologies among Bible-believing, evangelical Christians.[73] A kind of blackout exists within dispensational circles.

Hunt, with historical naïveté, castigates the resurgent postmillennialism of the 1980s: "When confronted with an alleged key doctrine that men and women of God have failed to uncover from Scripture in 1900 years of church history, we have good reason to be more than a little cautious. After all, this is the stuff of which cults are made. It takes a certain arrogance to claim to have discovered a vital teaching that the entire church has overlooked for 1900 years."[74] This, you understand, comes from a man who defends an eschatological position, pre-tribula-

---

71. A helpful corrective and rebuke to such may be found in Bob and Gretchen Passantino, *Witch Hunt* (Nashville: Thomas Nelson, 1990), see especially Chapter 8. It needs to be pointed out that the authors were premillennialists when this work was written. See also: Nash, *Great Divides*, ch.8.

72. Hunt, *Whatever Happened to Heaven?*; Hal Lindsey, *The Road to Holocaust* (New York: Bantam, 1989).

73. In a taped program in February of 1989, I was interviewed with dispensationalist Thomas D. Ice on a Christian radio program in Austin, Texas. The dialogue regarded dispensationalism and postmillennialism. On several occasions the interviewer, who tried (at first) to be "objective" in his interview, kept referring to dispensational distinctives in common dispensationalism parlance: he called these "dispensational truths." Who can argue with truth?

74. Hunt, *Whatever Happened to Heaven?*, p. 224.

tional dispensationalism, whose origin which can be traced back no earlier than the 1820s, and probably no earlier than 1830.

Vindication

One of the frustrating barriers that postmillennialists face in the modern debate is the tendency by some to distort postmillennialism. Many of the average Christians-in-the-pew have such a flawed view of postmillennialism that it is sometimes difficult to gain a hearing with them. Postmillennialism is deemed to be utterly "this-worldly" in an unbiblical sense. It is often considered an aspect of the "social gospel" of liberalism. Or it is thought to throw out valid hermeneutical procedures to bend and twist Scripture into a liberal system. Still others wrongly assume postmillennialism involves a union of Church and State. Again, popularizers of other viewpoints are generally the source of the problem.[75]

Even worse, there are some fundamental misunderstandings of postmillennialism, even by noteworthy theologians. And some of these published errors have been in print for decades without any attempt at correction. This deserves exposure because it is the tendency of many simply to pick up on confident statements found in published works and promote them as truth. Such errors will be dealt with in detail in later chapters.

Exhortation

Finally, I have a strong concern to exhort evangelical Christians to adopt the Christ-promoting, optimistic, culture transforming postmillennial eschatology. I do not desire to produce an academic work which merely presents the case for postmillennialism, but one that will in fact promote its adoption. If there is a strong biblical case for postmillennialism (and I be-

---

75. See Part Five, "Objections," below.

lieve there is), and if that case can be convincingly presented
(which I pray I will do), then the Christian reader must let the
biblical case have its ultimate influence in his thinking. He must
not merely maintain his former position because of ecclesiastical, social, or familial pressures.

It is difficult to cast off one's eschatology in order to adopt a
new one. I know; I have done it.[76] It is difficult intellectually,
as well as ecclesiastically and socially. Intellectually, an eschatological system affects every realm of one's theological understanding and philosophical worldview. A correction in eschatology necessarily produces far-reaching effects throughout one's
system of thought and conduct. Ecclesiastically, a systemic correction in one's eschatological position can have disruptive
effects in some church circles (particularly those requiring
dispensational adherence among its officers). Socially, such a
change can cost one his fellowship with some Christians (again,
this is particularly true among dispensationalists who convert
from the system). Yet the Scripture urges: "Let God be true,
but every man a liar" (Rom. 3:4a). If the case for postmillennialism can be effectively presented, the challenge is issued.

Practically, with the presentation of the postmillennial system, there is set forth a challenge to Christian social activism.[77]
With the adoption of a full-orbed, biblical worldview based on
postmillennialism, the Christian is urged to confront secular
society with the radical claims of Christ by means of personal
evangelism, church revitalization, and cultural transforma-

---

76. See my testimony in the Preface (entitled "Why I Could Not Remain a
Dispensationalist") to Bahnsen and Gentry, *House Divided*, pp. xlvii-lii.

77. See Gary North, *Millennialism and Social Theory* (Tyler, TX: Institute for
Christian Economics, 1990), pp. 254ff. This 400-page work presents a challenge to
pessimistic eschatologies regarding the call to practical Christian activism in the
world.

tion.[78] Some critics of reconstructionist postmillennialism[79] recognize the strongly practical element in postmillennialism.

Postmillennialist Iain Murray writes: "In the light of history we can hardly say that matters prophetic are too secondary to warrant our attention. The fact is that what we believe or do not believe upon this subject will have continual influence upon the way in which we live. The greatest spiritual endeavors and achievements in the past have been those energized by faith and hope."[80] R. J. Rushdoony has provided an excellent brief study of the impact of a positive, optimistic eschatology on Christian endeavor. In that study, he notes: "A study of hospital patients in relationship to their life expectancy reportedly came to the conclusion that there was a strong correlation between life expectancy and future oriented thinking. A man whose mind looked ahead to activities a year hence was more likely to live than one whose thinking was only in terms of the daily hospital routine. Those without a future in mind had no future, as a rule."[81] His historical analysis following this statement demonstrates the same truth on the cultural level regarding society's future orientation. For such a reason, Milne has admitted: "There is one aspect of postmillennialism however which *is* worth retaining. That is its optimism concerning the work of the gospel."[82] His problem is the problem of all amillennialists and all premillennialists: How to retain this optimism, which is contrary to the implications of their eschatological systems.

---

78. Rousas John Rushdoony, *God's Plan for Victory: The Meaning of Postmillennialism* (Fairfax, VA: Thoburn Press, 1977).

79. See discussion of reconstructionist and pietistic postmillennialism in Chapter 4 below.

80. Murray, *Puritan Hope*, p. xxii.

81. Rushdoony, *God's Plan for Victory*, p. 17.

82. Bruce Milne, *What the Bible Teaches About the End of the World* (Wheaton, IL: Tyndale, 1979), p. 81.

Conclusion

Christianity, and only Christianity, is the world's legitimate hope. Postmillennialism sets forth a vibrant, biblically based, life-changing, culture-transforming Christianity. My concern with the advancement of the postmillennial eschatology is not merely academic; it is intensely practical. When there is ignorance and confusion regarding the optimistic hope of Scripture, there is a consequent ebbing of the power and vitality from the Christian faith itself. I am convinced that there is a relationship between the rise and acceptance of dispensationalism in the nineteenth century and the decline of Christian influence in American society in the twentieth. It is my heartfelt desire to encourage the adoption of the biblical eschatology: postmillennialism.

3

THE PESSIMISTIC MILLENNIAL VIEWS

Therefore, when they had come together, they asked Him, saying, "Lord, will You at this time restore the kingdom to Israel?" (Acts 1:6)

The discussion of cosmic eschatology necessarily involves the entire sweep of history, including the spiritual forces that impel the forward movement of history toward its God-predestined consummation. It also includes the complex series of events associated with the end of history. There is one aspect of the popular debate, however, that has risen to dominance. This is the idea of the *millennium*, which has been called "one of the most controversial and intriguing questions of eschatology."[1]

The Millennial Idea

The word "millennium" is derived from the Latin, being a combination of *mille* (thousand) and *annus* (year). This theological *term*, employed as early as 1638 by Cambridge scholar Joseph Mede,[2] is ultimately based on the reference to the "thousand years" of Christ's reign in Revelation 20:2-7. The Greek-based derivation is *chiliad*, from the Greek "thousand" (*chilias*). "Millennialism" and "chiliasm" etymologically have the same

---

1. Alan F. Johnson, *Revelation* (Grand Rapids: Zondervan, 1983), p. 180.

2. "Millennium," *The Compact Edition of the Oxford English Dictionary* (Oxford: Oxford University Press, 1971), 1:1797.

connotation and are used interchangeably in eschatological discussion, although the term "millennialism" is far more common today.

Though common in modern discussion and debate, the reference to a thousand-year millennium as associated with the divine kingdom in history is rare in Scripture. In fact, it is found only in the first few verses of one chapter in all of Scripture. Oftentimes it seems the eschatological debate is somewhat hampered due to the inordinate influence of Revelation 20.[3] Princeton Seminary's postmillennial theologian Benjamin B. Warfield commented on this as long ago as 1915: "The term 'Millennium' has entered Christian speech under the influence of the twentieth chapter of the book of Revelation. From that passage, imperfectly understood, there has also been derived the idea which is connected with this term. . . . 'Pre-millennial,' 'post-millennial' are therefore unfortunate terms, embodying, and so perpetuating, a misapprehension of the bearing of an important passage of Scripture."[4] Hoekema notes that "the Book of Revelation speaks of certain individuals who are said to live and reign with Christ a thousand years (chap. 20:4). Divergent interpretations of this passage have led to the formation of

---

3. "Certainly one of the most controversial and intriguing questions of eschatology is that of the legitimacy of the expectation of a thousand-year reign – the millennium – before the return of Christ. . . . Obviously one's view of the thousand years of Revelation 20 is intimately connected with the rest of his eschatology. How he thinks of this passage gives a specific color and structure to his expectation." G. C. Berkouwer, *The Return of Christ* (Grand Rapids: Eerdmans, 1972), p. 291. For a brief interpretation of the Revelation 20's millennium, see Chapter 14, below. Of Revelation 20, when compared to the broad sweep of Pauline eschatology, Vos writes: "The minor deliverances ought in the harmonizing process be made to give way to the far-sweeping, age-dominating program of the theology of Paul." Geerhardus Vos, *The Pauline Eschatology* (Phillipsburg, NJ: Presbyterian & Reformed, [1930] 1991), p. 226.

4. Warfield, "The Gospel and the Second Coming" (1915), *The Selected Shorter Writings of Benjamin B. Warfield - I*, John E. Meeter, ed. (Nutley, NJ: Presbyterian & Reformed, 1970), p. 348.

at least four major views about the nature of the *millennium* or the *millennial reign* here described."[5]

It is often the case that premillennial theologians and dispensational theologians are more enamored with Revelation 20 than are others.[6] Writing of some of the great non-premillennial Christian theologians of this century, dispensationalist L. S. Chafer derides such exegetes because of their view of Revelation 20: "Their abandonment of reason and sound interpretation has but one objective in mind, namely, to place *chiloi* ('thousand') years – six times repeated in Revelation, chapter 20 – back into the past and therefore something no longer to be anticipated in the future. The violence which this interpretation imposes upon the whole prophetic revelation is such that none would propose it except those who, for lack of attention, seem not to realize what they do. . . . In sheer fantastical imagination this method surpasses Russellism, Eddyism, and Seventh Day Adventism. . . ." He speaks of "antimillennialism" as a "strange theory, the origin of which is traced to the Romish notion that the church is the kingdom."[7]

In a calmer tone, historic premillennialist Ladd admits: "We must recognize frankly that in all the verses cited thus far it would seem that the eschatological Kingdom will be inaugurated by a single complex event, consisting of the Day of the Lord, the coming of the Son of Man, the resurrection of the dead, and the final judgment. However, in the one book which is entirely devoted to this subject, the Revelation of John, this time scheme is modified. . . . The theology that is built on this passage is millennialism or chiliasm. . . . This is the most natu-

5. Hoekema, *The Bible and the Future* (Grand Rapids: Eerdmans, 1979), p. 173.

6. "There are some who connect with the advent of Christ the idea of a millennium, either immediately before or immediately following the second coming. While this idea is not an integral part of Reformed theology, it nevertheless deserves consideration here, since it has become rather popular in many circles." Louis Berkhof, *Systematic Theology* (Grand Rapids: Eerdmans, 1941), p. 708.

7. Lewis Sperry Chafer, *Systematic Theology*, 8 vols. (Dallas: Dallas Theological Seminary Press, 1948), 4:281-282.

ral interpretation of the [Rev. 20] passage, and it is the view of
the present author. One thing must be granted: this is the only
place in Scripture which teaches a thousand-year reign of
Christ."[8]

The Standard Millennial Positions

In developing a systematic eschatology, the standard evangelical viewpoints have tended to be sorted out along millennial
lines. The term "millennium" is used in association with pre-
fixes that tend to modify the Second Coming of Christ as to its
relation to the millennium: *a*millennial, *pre*millennial, and *post*-
millennial. The privative *a* in "amillennialism" emphasizes that
there will be no earthly millennial kingdom as such.[9] The
prefix *pre* indicates that system of eschatology that expects there
to be a literal earthly millennial kingdom that will be *introduced*
by the Return of Christ before (pre) it. The prefix *post* points to
the view of the millennium that holds there will be a lengthy
(though not a literal thousand years) earthly era of righteous
influence for the kingdom that will be *concluded* by the Return
of Christ. Puritan era postmillennialism tended to expect a
literal thousand-year millennium introduced by the conversion

---

8. George Eldon Ladd, *The Last Things: An Eschatology for Laymen* (Grand Rapids: Eerdmans, 1978), pp. 108-110.

9. Many amillennialists are disturbed by the negative prefix: "The term amillennialism is not a very happy one. It suggests that amillennialists either do not believe
in any millennium or that they simply ignore the first six verses of Revelation 20,
which speak of a millennial reign. Neither of these two statements is correct." Hoekema, *Bible and the Future*, p. 173. Hamilton, Adams, and Hughes agree. Philip E.
Hughes, *Interpreting Prophecy: An Essay in Biblical Perspectives* (Grand Rapids: Eerdmans, 1976), pp. 99-100 and Floyd E. Hamilton, *The Basis of the Millennial Faith*
(Grand Rapids: Eerdmans, 1942), p. 35. See the discussion of the problem with a
proposed solution to it in: Jay E. Adams, *The Time Is at Hand* (Nutley, NJ: Presbyterian & Reformed, 1966), pp. 7-11. There are amillennialists, however, who do not
mind the term, *when literally interpreted*: The word 'amillennial' is "a term which
indicates a denial of any future millennium of one thousand years' duration." George
L. Murray, *Millennial Studies: A Search for Truth* (Grand Rapids: Baker, 1948), p. 87.
See also Berkhof, *Systematic Theology*, p. 708.

of the Jews (rather than the Return of Christ) as the last stage of Christ's earthly kingdom. Modern postmillennialism tends to see the thousand years as a symbolic figure covering the entirety of the Christian era.[10]

There is an important sub-class in the premillennial view that has arisen since the 1830s. It is known as "dispensationalism." It is worth noting that historic premillennialists strongly disavow any systemic commonality with dispensationalism. Premillennialist George E. Ladd vigorously protests the equation of dispensationalism and historic premillennialism. He even calls any equating of the two a "mistake."[11] This explains why the popular book edited by Robert G. Clouse is entitled *The Meaning of the Millennium: Four Views*.[12]

Dispensationalists are aware of their own distinctive differences, as well.[13] Ryrie even comments: "Perhaps the issue of premillennialism is determinative [for dispensationalism]. Again the answer is negative, for there are those who are premillennial who definitely are not dispensational. The covenant premillennialist holds to the concept of the covenant of grace and the central soteriological purpose of God. He retains the idea of the millennial kingdom, though he finds little support for it in the Old Testament prophecies since he generally assigns them to

---

10. Some postmillennialists have accepted the possibility that there may be a future millennial era of unique blessings within the general millennial era of the New Covenant. See Gary North, *The Sinai Strategy: Economics and the Ten Commandments* (Tyler, TX: Institute for Christian Economics, 1986), pp. 86-92: "The Sabbath Millennium."

11. George E. Ladd, *The Blessed Hope* (Grand Rapids: Eerdmans, 1956), pp. 31ff; Ladd, *Crucial Questions About the Kingdom of God* (Grand Rapids: Eerdmans, 1952), p. 49.

12. Robert G. Clouse, ed., *The Meaning of the Millennium: Four Views* (Downer's Grove, IL: Inter-Varsity Press, 1977). See my discussion in Greg L. Bahnsen and Kenneth L. Gentry, Jr., *House Divided: The Break-up of Dispensational Theology* (Tyler, TX: Institute for Christian Economics, 1989), pp. 234-238.

13. See also: Rolland Dale McCune, "An Investigation and Criticism of 'Historic' Premillennialism from the Viewpoint of Dispensationalism" (unpublished Th.D. dissertation, Grace Theological Seminary, 1982). Gleason L. Archer, *et al.*, *The Rapture: Pre-, Mid-, or Post-Tribulational* (Grand Rapids: Zondervan, 1984).

the Church. The kingdom in his view is *markedly different* from that which is taught by dispensationalists since it loses much of its Jewish character due to the slighting of the Old Testament promises concerning the kingdom."[14]

There is a helpful theological sorting device, created by O. T. Allis and modified by Jay Adams, that works generally well in classifying the three basic millennial positions.[15] Two questions tend to sort the positions into one of the three most basic schools. These questions are: (1) What is the *chronology* of the kingdom? (2) What is the *nature* of the kingdom? The question of chronology has to do with the timing of Christ's Second Advent in relation to the establishment of the kingdom. If His coming is *before* the kingdom, then the position is premillennial; if it is *after* the kingdom, then it may be either amillennial or postmillennial. The question as to the nature of Christ's kingdom has to do with the historical character of the kingdom. If the kingdom is to have a radical, objective, transforming influence in human culture, it is either premillennial or postmillennial; if it is not to have such, it is amillennial.

I will now turn to a summary of the millennial positions and a brief listing of some their leading advocates. The positions will be considered in alphabetical order. Three millennial positions will be defined in this chapter; postmillennialism will be dealt with in the following chapter and in somewhat more detail. Two qualifications need to be borne in mind as the list of adherents is surveyed. First, the ancient examples of the various millennial views hold to certain distinctive features of the millennial views, and would not necessarily adhere to a full-blown systematic presentation. Second, it should be understood that any particular adherent to one of the following views may disagree with some aspect as presented in my summation. There

---

14. Charles C. Ryrie, *Dispensationalism Today* (Chicago: Moody Press, 1965), p. 44 (emphasis mine).

15. O. T. Allis, *Prophecy and the Church* (Philadelphia: Presbyterian & Reformed, 1945), p. 4. Adams, *Time Is at Hand*, pp. 8-11.

are always differences of nuance among adherents to any particular system. Nevertheless, the presentation attempts to portray accurately the salient features of the systems.

Amillennialism

Definition. Hoekema describes amillennialism in the following words:

> . . . Amillennialists interpret the millennium mentioned in Revelation 20:4-6 as describing the present reign of the souls of deceased believers with Christ in heaven. They understand the binding of Satan mentioned in the first three verses of this chapter as being in effect during the entire period between the first and second comings of Christ, though ending shortly before Christ's return. They teach that Christ will return after this heavenly millennial reign.
>
> Amillennialists further hold that the kingdom of God is now present in the world as the victorious Christ is ruling his people by his Word and Spirit, though they also look forward to a future, glorious, and perfect kingdom on the new earth in the life to come. Despite the fact that Christ has won a decisive victory over sin and evil, the kingdom of evil will continue to exist alongside of the kingdom of God until the end of the world. Although we are already enjoying many eschatological blessings at the present time (inaugurated eschatology), we look forward to a climactic series of future events associated with the Second Coming of Christ which will usher in the final state (future eschatology). The so-called 'signs of the times' have been present in the world from the time of Christ's first coming, but they will come to a more intensified, final manifestation just before his Second Coming. The amillennialist therefore expects the bringing of the gospel to all nations and the conversion of the fullness of Israel to be completed before Christ's return. He also looks for an intensified form of tribulation and apostasy as well as for the appearance of a personal antichrist before the Second Coming.

The amillennialist understands the Second Coming of Christ to be a single event, not one that involves two phases. At the time of Christ's return there will be a general resurrection, both of believers and unbelievers. After the resurrection, believers who are then still alive shall be transformed and glorified. These two groups, raised believers and transformed believers, are then caught up in the clouds to meet the Lord in the air. After this 'rapture' of all believers, Christ will complete his descent to earth, and conduct the final judgment. After the judgment unbelievers will be consigned to eternal punishment, whereas believers will enjoy forever the blessings of the new heaven and the new earth.[16]

Engelsma adds:

> As the theology of hope, the Reformed faith [amillennialism] directs the saints' expectation to the great good in the future that is the genuine object of hope. This is not some event within time and history, but the event that is the end of time and history: the coming of Jesus Christ. . . . Faithful to its calling as the theology of hope, the Reformed truth [amillennialism] vigorously uproots all false hopes that spring up among Christians: earthly success; establishing the kingdom of Christ on the earth in a carnal form, before the Day of Christ (utopia). . . .[17]

Descriptive Features. 1. The Church Age is the kingdom era prophesied by the Old Testament prophets.[18] The people of God are expanded from Israel of the Old Testament to the universal Church of the New Testament, becoming the Israel of God.

---

16. Hoekema, *Bible and the Future*, p. 174.

17. David J. Engelsma, "The Reformed Faith – Theology of Hope," *Standard Bearer* 66:7 (Jan. 1, 1990) 149.

18. Unlike earlier amillennialists, Hoekema sees the fulfillment of the kingdom prophecies in the New Heavens and New Earth, rather than in the Church: *Bible and the Future*, ch. 20.

2. Satan is bound during Christ's earthly ministry at His First Coming. His binding prevents him from totally hindering the proclamation of the gospel. This allows for the conversion of great numbers of sinners to Christ and insures some restraint upon evil.

3. Christ now rules spiritually in the hearts of believers. There will be but occasional, short-lived influences of Christianity on culture, where Christians live out the implications of their faith.

4. History will gradually worsen as the growth of evil accelerates toward the end. This will culminate in the Great Tribulation, with the arising of a personal Antichrist.

5. Christ will return to end history, resurrect and judge all men, and establish the eternal order. The eternal destiny of the redeemed may be either in heaven or in a totally renovated new earth.

Representative Adherents. In the ancient church, the following are non-millennialists, who seem best to fit in with the amillennial viewpoint: Hermas (first century), Polycarp (A.D. 69-105), Clement of Rome (A.D. 30-100), and Ignatius (*ca.* A.D. 107).[19] In the modern church, we may note the following: Jay E. Adams, Louis Berkhof, G. C. Berkouwer, William E. Cox, Richard B. Gaffin, W. J. Grier, Floyd E. Hamilton, Herman Hanko, William Hendriksen, Jesse William Hodges, Anthony A. Hoekema, Philip E. Hughes, Abraham Kuyper, R. C. H. Lenski, George L. Murray, Albertus Pieters, Vern S. Poythress, Herman Ridderbos, Ray Summers, E. J. Young, and Bruce K. Waltke.[20]

---

19. This is according to the research of dispensationalist Alan Patrick Boyd, "A Dispensational Premillennial Analysis of the Eschatology of the Post-Apostolic Fathers (Until the Death of Justin Martyr)" (Dallas: Dallas Theological Seminary Master's Thesis, 1977), p. 50 (n. 1), 91-92. Premillennialist D. H. Kromminga provides evidence in this direction, as well, in his book, *The Millennium in the Church: Studies in the History of Christian Chiliasm* (Grand Rapids: Eerdmans, 1945), pp. 267ff. See also: Louis Berkhof, *The History of Christian Doctrine* (Edinburgh: Banner of Truth, [1937] 1969).

20. Adams, *The Time Is at Hand* (1966). Louis Berkhof, *The Second Coming of Christ*

Dispensationalism

Definition. Ryrie, the leading "classic dispensational"[21] theologian of our time, defines dispensationalism in the following manner:

> *Premillennialists* [sc., dispensationalists] believe that theirs is the historic faith of the Church. Holding to a literal interpretation of the Scripture, they believe that the promises made to Abraham and David are unconditional and have had or will have a literal fulfillment. In no sense have these promises made to Israel been abrogated or fulfilled by the Church, which is a distinct body in this age having promises and a destiny different from Israel's. At the close of this age, premillennialists believe that Christ will return for His Church, meeting her in the air (this is not the

---

(1953). G. C. Berkouwer, *The Return of Christ* (1972). William E. Cox, *Amillennialism Today* (1966). Richard B. Gaffin, "Theonomy and Eschatology: Reflections on Postmillennialism" in William S. Barker and W. Robert Godfrey, eds., *Theonomy: A Reformed Critique* (1991). W. J. Grier, *The Momentous Event* (1945). Floyd E. Hamilton, *The Basis of the Millennial Faith* (1942). Herman C. Hanko, "The Illusory Hope of Postmillennialism," *Standard Bearer*, 66:7 (Jan. 1, 1990). William Hendriksen, *Israel in Prophecy* (1974). J. W. Hodges, *Christ's Kingdom and Coming* (1957). Anthony A. Hoekema, *The Bible and the Future* (1979). P. E. Hughes, *Interpreting Prophecy* (1976). Abraham Kuyper, *Chiliasm, or the Doctrine of Premillennialism* (1934). R. C. H. Lenski, *the Interpretation of St. John's Revelation* (1943). George Murray, *Millennial Studies* (1945). Albertus Pieters, *The Seed of Abraham* (1937). Vern S. Poythress, *Understanding Dispensationalists* (1987). Herman Ridderbos, *The Coming of the Kingdom* (1962). Ray Summers, *Worthy Is the Lamb* (1950). Bruce K. Waltke, "Kingdom Promises as Spiritual," in John S. Feinberg, ed., *Continuity and Discontinuity* (1988). E. J. Young, *The Prophecy of Daniel* (1945).

21. A new form of dispensationalism is presently beginning to make its presence felt in eschatological discussion. It is called "progressive dispensationalism." See: Craig L. Blaising and Darrell L. Bock, *Dispensationalism, Israel and the Church* (Grand Rapids: Zondervan, 1992). Craig L. Blaising and Darrell L. Bock, *The Search for Definition* (Grand Rapids: Zondervan, 1992); *Progressive Dispensationalism: Up-to-Date Handbook of Contemporary Dispensational Thought* (Wheaton, IL: Bridgepoint, 1993). Robert Saucy, *Case for Progressive Dispensationalism: Interface Between Dispensational & Non-Dispensational Theology* (Grand Rapids: Zondervan, 1993). This newer position has yet to captivate the large installed dispensational audience and is, in fact, resisted by "classic dispensationalists": Wesley R. Willis and John R. Master, eds., *Issues in Dispensationalism* (Chicago: Moody, 1994).

Second Coming of Christ), which event, called the rapture or translation, will usher in a seven-year period of tribulation on the earth. After this, the Lord will return to the earth (this is the Second Coming of Christ) to establish His kingdom on the earth for a thousand years, during which time the promises to Israel will be fulfilled.[22]

Elsewhere he defines the idea of a "dispensation" within the dispensational schema of history:

A dispensation is a distinguishable economy in the outworking of God's purpose. If one were describing a dispensation he would include other things, such as the ideas of distinctive revelation, testing, failure, and judgment.[23]

Descriptive Features. 1. The Davidic Kingdom, an earthly, political kingdom, was offered by Christ in the first century. It was rejected by the Jews and thereby postponed until the future.[24]

2. The Church Age is a wholly unforseen and distinct era in the plan of God. It was altogether unknown to and unexpected by the Old Testament prophets. It is called a "parenthesis."

3. God has a separate and distinct program and plan for racial Israel, as distinguished from the Church. The Church of Jesus Christ is a parenthetical aside in the original plan of God.

4. The Church may experience occasional small scale successes in history, but ultimately she will lose influence, fail in

---

22. Charles C. Ryrie, *The Basis of the Premillennial Faith* (Neptune, NJ: Loizeaux Bros., 1953), p. 12.

23. Ryrie, *Dispensationalism Today*, p. 29.

24. There is a growing fragmentation in dispensationalism today over the notion of the kingdom. Some have recently begun to teach a "now and not yet" approach to the kingdom, which allows for a spiritual presence of the kingdom in the present. See: Robert L. Saucy, "The Presence of the Kingdom and the Life of the Church," *Bibliotheca Sacra* 145 (Jan./March 1988) 33ff; John S. Feinberg, "Systems of Discontinuity," and Walter C. Kaiser, Jr., "Kingdom Promises As Spiritual and National," *Continuity and Discontinuity*, chaps. 3 and 13.

her mission, and become corrupted as worldwide evil intensifies toward the end of the Church Age.

5. Christ will return secretly in the sky to rapture living saints and resurrect the bodies of deceased saints (the first resurrection). These will be removed out of the world before the Great Tribulation. The judgment of the saints will be accomplished in heaven during the seven-year Great Tribulation period before Christ's bodily return to the earth.

6. At the conclusion of the seven-year Great Tribulation, Christ will return to the earth in order to establish and personally administer a Jewish political kingdom headquartered at Jerusalem for 1,000 years. During this time, Satan will be bound, and the temple and sacrificial system will be re-established in Jerusalem as memorials.

7. Toward the end of the Millennial Kingdom, Satan will be loosed and Christ surrounded and attacked at Jerusalem.

8. Christ will call down fire from heaven to destroy His enemies. The resurrection (the second resurrection) and judgment of the wicked will occur, initiating the eternal order.

Representative Adherents. In the ancient church: none (created *ca.* 1830).[25] In the modern church: Robert Anderson, Gleason L. Archer, Jr., Charles F. Baker, Emery H. Bancroft, Donald G. Barnhouse, W. E. Blackstone, James M. Brookes, Richard H. Bube, L. S. Chafer, John Nelson Darby, M. R. DeHaan, William Evans, Charles Lee Feinberg, John S. Feinberg, Paul Feinberg, A. C. Gaebelein, Norman Geisler, James M. Gray, Harry A. Ironside, Walter C. Kaiser, Jr., William Kelly, Hal Lindsey,

---

25. "Indeed, this thesis would conclude that the eschatological beliefs of the period studied [to A.D. 150] would be generally inimical to those of the modern system (perhaps, seminal amillennialism, and not nascent dispensational premillennialism ought to be seen in the eschatology of the period)." "This writer believes that the Church *rapidly* fell from New Testament truth, and this is very evident in the realm of eschatology. Only in modern times has New Testament eschatological truth been recovered. Dispensational premillennialism is the product of the post-Reformation progress of dogma." Boyd, "Dispensational Premillennial Analysis," pp. 90-91. See also: Harry A. Ironside, *The Mysteries of God* (New York: Loizeaux, 1908), p. 50.

Robert P. Lightner, Alva J. McClain, G. Campbell Morgan, J. Dwight Pentecost, Charles C. Ryrie, C. I. Scofield, Henry C. Thiessen, John F. Walvoord, and Warren Wiersbe.[26]

Premillennialism

Definition. George Eldon Ladd, a leading advocate of historical premillennialism in recent times, defines the system for us:

> . . . Premillennialism is the doctrine stating that after the Second Coming of Christ, he will reign for a thousand years over the earth before the final consummation of God's redemptive purpose in the new heavens and the new earth of the Age to Come. This is the natural reading of Revelation 20:1-6.
>
> Revelation 19:11-16 pictures the Second Coming of Christ as a conqueror coming to destroy his enemies: the Antichrist, Satan and Death. Revelation 19:17-21 pictures first the destruction of Antichrist and the hosts which have supported him in opposition to the kingdom of

26. Gleason L. Archer, Jr., in *The Rapture: Pre-, Mid-, or Post-Tribulational?* (1984). Charles Baker, *A Dispensational Theology* (1971). Donald Gray Barnhouse, *His Own Received Him Not, But...* (1933). William E. Blackstone, *Jesus Is Coming* (1878). Lewis S. Chafer, *Dispensationalism* (1951). J. N. Darby, *Synopsis of the Books of the Bible* (1857-1867). M. R. DeHaan, *The Jew and Palestine in Prophecy* (1950). William Evans, *Great Doctrines of the Bible* (1949). Charles Lee Feinberg, *Millennialism: Two Major Viewpoints* (1980). John S. Feinberg, *Continuity and Discontinuity* (1989). Paul D. Feinberg, in *The Rapture: Pre-, Mid-, or Post-Tribulational?* (1984). William Kelly, *Lectures on the Gospel of Matthew* (1868). Arno C. Gaebelein, *The Harmony of the Prophetic Word* (1907). Norman Geisler, "A Premillennial View of Law and Government," *Moody Monthly* (Oct. 1985) James M. Gray, *Prophecy and the Lord's Return* (1917). Harry A. Ironside, *The Great Parenthesis* (1943). Walter C. Kaiser, Jr. in *Continuity and Discontinuity* (1989). Robert P. Lightner, *The Last Days Handbook: A Comprehensive Guide to Understanding the Different Views of Prophecy* (1990). Hal Lindsey, *The Road to Holocaust* (1989). Alva J. McClain, *The Greatness of the Kingdom* (1959). J. Dwight Pentecost, *Thy Kingdom Come* (1990). Charles C. Ryrie, *Basic Theology* (1986). C. I. Scofield, *Rightly Dividing the Word of Truth* (1920). Henry Thiessen, *Will the Church Pass Through the Tribulation?* (1941). John F. Walvoord, *Prophecy Knowledge Handbook* (1990). Warren W. Wiersbe, *The Bible Exposition Commentary* (1989).

God. Revelation 20 then relates the destruction of the evil power behind the Antichrist. . . . [T]his occurs in two stages.

First, Satan is bound and incarcerated in 'the bottomless pit' (Rev. 20:1) for a thousand years. . . . At this time occurs the 'first resurrection' (Rev. 20:5) of saints who share Christ's rule over the earth for the thousand years. After this Satan is loosed from his bonds, and in spite of the fact that Christ has reigned over the earth for a thousand years, he finds the hearts of unregenerated men still ready to rebel against God. The final eschatological war follows when the devil is thrown into the lake of fire and brimstone. Then occurs a second resurrection of those who had not been raised before the millennium. . . .[27]

Elsewhere he adds:

> The gospel is not to conquer the world and subdue all nations to itself. Hatred, conflict, and war will continue to characterize the age until the coming of the Son of Man. . . . [E]vil will mark the course of the age.[28]

Descriptive Features.

1. The New Testament era Church is the *initial* phase of Christ's kingdom, as prophesied by the Old Testament prophets.

2. The New Testament Church may win occasional victories in history, but ultimately she will fail in her mission, lose influence, and become corrupted as worldwide evil increases toward the end of the Church Age.

---

27. George E. Ladd, "Historic Premillennialism," *Meaning of the Millennium*, p. 17.

28. George Eldon Ladd, *Theology of the New Testament* (Grand Rapids: Eerdmans, 1974), pp. 202, 203.

3. The Church will pass through a future, worldwide, unprecedented time of travail. This era is known as the Great Tribulation, which will punctuate the end of contemporary history. Historic premillennialists are post-tribulational.

4. Christ will return at the end of the Tribulation to rapture the Church, resurrect deceased saints, and conduct the judgment of the righteous in the "twinkling of an eye."

5. Christ then will descend to the earth with His glorified saints, fight the battle of Armageddon, bind Satan, and establish a worldwide, political kingdom, which will be personally administered by Him for 1,000 years from Jerusalem.

6. At the end of the millennial reign, Satan will be loosed and a massive rebellion against the kingdom and a fierce assault against Christ and His saints will occur.

7. God will intervene with fiery judgment to rescue Christ and the saints. The resurrection and the judgment of the wicked will occur and the eternal order will begin.

Representative Adherents. In the ancient church: Papias (60-130), Justin Martyr (100-165), Irenaeus (130-202), and Tertullian (160-220). In the modern church: Henry Alford, E. B. Elliott, W. J. Erdman, A. R. Faussett, Henry W. Frost, F. Godet, H. G. Guinness, S. H. Kellog, D. H. Kromminga, George Eldon Ladd, Philip Mauro, J. Barton Payne, George N. H. Peters, Alexander Reese, R. A. Torrey, S. P. Tregelles, Nathaniel West, and Theodor Zahn.[29]

---

29. Henry Alford, *The Greek Testament* (1872), 4:732ff. William J. Erdman, *The Parousia of Christ a Period of Time; or, When Will the Church be Translated?* (1880). A. R. Faussett, *Commentary, Critical and Explanatory* (ca. 1885). Henry W. Frost, *The Second Coming and Christ* (1934). F. Godet, *Studies on the New Testament* (1873), pp. 294ff. H. Grattan Guinness, *The Approaching End of the Age* (1880). George Eldon Ladd, *The Blessed Hope* (1956). S. H. Kellogg in *Premillennial Essays* (1957). Philip Mauro, *The Gospel of the Kingdom* (1929). George N. H. Peters, *The Theocratic Kingdom* (1884). J. Barton Payne, *Bible Prophecy for Today* (1978). Alexander Reese, *The Approaching Advent of Christ* (1932). S. P. Tregelles, *The Hope of Christ's Second Coming* (1886). R. A. Torrey in Archer, *The Rapture* (ca., 1910). Nathaniel West, "Introduction," *Premillennial Essays of the Prophetic Conference Held in the Church of the Holy Trinity, New York City, Oct. 30–Nov. 1, 1878* (1879). Theodor Zahn, *Introduction to the New Testament* (1909).

Conclusion

Certainly each of the millennial views presented above has characteristic features that are different enough to distinguish them. These differences are of no small consequence. Yet one thing unifies these millennial views: overall pessimism regarding the hope for Christian civilization in present history. Such pessimism is a fundamentally important matter when men attempt to develop and promote a Christian worldview. It is this *intrinsic pessimism* that is a characteristic distinctive of these views when classed together in opposition to postmillennialism.

In the next chapter I will consider postmillennialism in a somewhat fuller manner. As I do it will be important to appreciate the optimism inherent in postmillennialism – an optimism that is of the very essence of a genuinely Christian worldview and which is so essential to the building of a Christian civilization. The kingdom of God in history is a civilization as surely as the kingdom of Satan in history is a civilization. Both kingdoms are spiritual; both are civilizations. One wins in history.

4

INTRODUCTION TO POSTMILLENNIALISM

The LORD said to my Lord, "Sit at My right hand, Till I make Your enemies Your footstool." (Psalm 110:1)

We do not hold with the philosophy of linguistic analysis that problems of definition lie at the heart of all ambiguity.[1] Yet often enough, carefully defining a theological position will help correct many unnecessary misconceptions. Probably more than any of the three other evangelical views, postmillennialism has suffered distortion through improper definition by its opponents. In this chapter, I will set forth a succinct theological explanation of postmillennialism, as well as briefly engage the question of postmillennialism's historical origins.

Confusion Regarding Postmillennialism

It is remarkable that there are some noted theologians who do not appear to have an adequate working definition of post-millennialism. This leads them to misclassify certain postmillen-

---

1. Ludwig Wittgenstein wrote in his preface to his *Tractatus Logico-Philosophicus* that "what can be said at all can be said clearly." Wittgenstein, *Tractatus Logico-Philosophicus*, trans. by D. F. Pears and B. F. McGuinness (New York: Humanities Press, 1961), p. 3.

nial scholars. For instance, dispensational theologians are notorious for classifying leading postmillennial scholars Benjamin B. Warfield and O. T. Allis as amillennialists. One has even misidentified W. G. T. Shedd as an amillennialist.[2] In Warfield's case, this misconception is based largely on his view of Revelation 20, despite his many clear statements elsewhere regarding postmillennialism. (This illustrates anew the inordinate role of Revelation 20 in the eschatological debate.) In Allis' case, his silence regarding his eschatological persuasion in his classic *Prophecy and the Church* seems to be partly responsible for the confusion. He is assumed by many to be amillennial, since postmillennialism, which some critics do not understand, is presumed dead.

Walvoord writes in this regard: "A new type of amillennialism has arisen, however, of which Warfield can be taken as an example which is actually a totally new type of amillennialism."[3] Chafer (1948), Ryrie (1953), Pentecost (1958), Culver (1977), Feinberg (1980), Johnson (1983), and Lightner (1990) promote the same Warfield-as-amillennialist error.[4] Ryrie con-

---

2. Charles F. Baker, *A Dispensational Theology* (Grand Rapids: Grace Bible College, 1981), p. 617.

3. Walvoord, "The Millennial Issue in Modern Theology," *Bibliotheca Sacra* 106 (Jan. 1948) 44. Strangely, Walvoord apparently comes to realize the true position of Warfield, but does not inform any of his colleagues at Dallas Theological Seminary: "Warfield is more optimistic, hence is usually classified as a postmillenarian." John F. Walvoord, *The Revelation of Jesus Christ: A Commentary* (Chicago: Moody Press, 1966), p. 286. If he is "usually" so classified, why do we not hear such from dispensationalists?

4. Lewis Sperry Chafer, *Systematic Theology*, 8 vols. (Dallas, TX: Dallas Theological Seminary, 1948), 4:281; 7:238. Chafer seems to be the source of this error. See also: Charles C. Ryrie, *The Basis of the Premillennial Faith* (Neptune, NJ: Loizeaux Bros., 1953), p. 30; J. Dwight Pentecost, *Things to Come: A Study in Biblical Eschatology* (Grand Rapids: Zondervan, 1958), p. 387; Robert D. Culver, *Daniel and the Latter Days* (2nd ed.; Chicago: Moody Press, 1977), p. 24; Charles Lee Feinberg, *Millennialism: The Two Major Views* (3rd ed.; Chicago: Moody Press, 1980), p. 314; Alan F. Johnson, *Revelation* (Grand Rapids: Zondervan, 1983), pp. 181-182; Robert P. Lightner, *The Last Days Handbook: A Comprehensive Guide to Understanding the Different Views of Prophecy* (Nashville: Thomas Nelson, 1990), p. 77.

tinues his earlier error, when he comments (1986): "Though Augustinian amillennialism is generally followed in this modern time . . . another form of amillennialism arose. B. B. Warfield . . . taught that the Millennium is the present state of the saints in heaven."[5]

Of Allis, Pentecost writes: "Amillennialism today is divided into two camps. (1) The first, of which Allis and Berkhof are adherents. . . ."[6] Walvoord follows suit: "However, in view of the evidence that many amillenarians consider it, as Allis does. . . ."[7] Culver (1977), C. Feinberg (1980), Ryrie (1986), J. Feinberg (1988), and Lightner (1990) concur.[8]

It is clear from Warfield himself,[9] as well as other eschatological writers[10], that he was a postmillennialist. While expressly discussing the "premillennial" and "postmillennial" positions, Warfield writes of his own view: "[T]he Scriptures do promise to the church a 'golden age,' when the conflict with the forces

---

5. Charles Caldwell Ryrie, *Basic Theology* (Wheaton, IL: Victor, 1986), p. 449.

6. Pentecost, *Things to Come*, p. 387.

7. John F. Walvoord, *The Nations, Israel, and the Church in Prophecy*, 3 vols. in 1 (Grand Rapids: Zondervan, 1988), 2:56. See also: Walvoord, *The Revelation of Jesus Christ*, p. 286. Walvoord, "Revelation," *The Bible Knowledge Commentary: New Testament Edition*, Walvoord and Roy B. Zuck, eds. (Wheaton, IL: Victor, 1983), p. 978.

8. Culver, *Daniel and the Latter Days*, p. 24. Feinberg, *Millennialism*, p. 49. Ryrie, *Basic Theology*, p. 449. John S. Feinberg, "Systems of Discontinuity," *Continuity and Discontinuity: Perspectives on the Relationship Between the Old and New Testaments*, Feinberg, ed. (Westchester, IL: Crossway, 1988), p. 67. Lightner, *Last Days Handbook*, 91.

9. See: Warfield, "Jesus Christ the Propitiation for the Sins of the Whole World" (1921), in *Selected Shorter Writings – I*, John E. Meeter, ed. (Nutley, NJ: Presbyterian & Reformed, 1970), pp. 167-177. "Antichrist" (1921), *ibid.*, pp. 356-364. "The Importunate Widow and the Alleged Failure of Faith" (1913), in *SSW-II* (Nutley, NJ: Presbyterian & Reformed, 1973), pp. 698-711. Warfield, *Biblical and Theological Studies*, Samuel E. Craig, ed. (Philadelphia: Presbyterian & Reformed, 1952): "Are There Few That Be Saved?" (1915), pp. 334-350; "The Prophecies of St. Paul" (1886), pp. 463-502; "God's Immeasurable Love" (n.d.), pp. 505-522. Warfield, *Biblical Doctrines* (New York: Oxford University Press, 1929), pp. 663ff. Warfield, "The Millennium and the Apocalypse," *Princeton Theological Review* (Oct. 1904).

10. For example see: historic premillennialist Ladd, *Crucial Questions*, pp. 46-47. Amillennialist Anthony A. Hoekema, *The Bible and the Future* (Grand Rapids: Eerdmans, 1979), pp. 176ff.

of evil in which it is engaged has passed into victory. . . . [T]he 'golden age' of the church is the adorning of the bride for her husband, and is the preparation for his coming. . . . [P]recisely what the risen Lord, who has been made head over all things for his church, is doing through these years that stretch between his first and second comings, is conquering the world to himself; and the world is to be nothing less than a converted world." "The ministry which Paul exercised, and which everyone who follows him in proclaiming the gospel exercises with him, is distinctively the ministry of reconciliation, not of testimony merely, but of reconciliation. It has as its object, and is itself the proper means of, the actual reconciliation of the whole world."[11]

Interestingly, Allis, in his book that is widely cited by dispensationalists, even calls Warfield a "postmillenarian who looked for a future golden age of the Church on earth."[12] More interesting is the resistance of one dispensationalist to admit what he suspects may be the case in this regard. Speaking of "modern amillennialism – B. B. Warfield School," Culver writes: "I have called Warfield an amillennialist because he denies any connection of the 'thousand years' with a reign of Christ or His saints on earth, either after Christ's second coming or before it. It may be true, as former students of his classes have told me, that he regarded himself as a postmillennialist."[13]

That Allis was postmillennial is evident, as well. In his *Foreword* to Roderick Campbell's postmillennial work, *Israel and the New Covenant*, Allis wrote: "[M]y own studies in this and related

---

11. Warfield, "The Gospel and the Second Coming," *Selected Shorter Writings – I*, pp. 349-350. This essay was originally published in *The Bible Magazine* 3 (1915) 303-309. It is a strong polemic against the premillennial position. In this article, he specifically called himself a postmillennialist. This should remove all confusion about his eschatological position.

12. O. T. Allis, *Prophecy and the Church* (Philadelphia: Presbyterian & Reformed, 1945), p. 287.

13. Robert D. Culver, *Daniel and the Latter Days* (2nd ed.; Chicago: Moody Press, 1977), p. 213.

fields have convinced me that the most serious error in much of the current 'prophetic' teaching of today is the claim that the future of Christendom is to be read not in terms of Revival and Victory, but of growing impotence and apostasy. . . . The language of the Great Commission is world-embracing; and it has back of it the authority and power of One who said: 'All power is given unto me in heaven and in earth. Go ye therefore and make disciples of all nations.' The duty of the church is to address herself to the achieving of this task in anticipation of her Lord's coming, and not to expect Him to call her away to glory before her task is accomplished."[14] Although his postmillennialism is not clearly spelled out in his classic study *Prophecy and the Church*, it is in this *Foreword* and elsewhere.[15]

A careful definition of an eschatological system will help keep one from making such mistaken identifications. Hence, the significance of this chapter.

A Definition of Postmillennialism

The dispensational error in defining non-premillennial eschatological systems is traceable to its focusing on Revelation 20, in its assumption that this passage controls those systems (as is evident in the Culver quotation above).[16] The postmillennialist, however, is reluctant to begin systemic definition with one of the last and most symbolic books of the Bible. Consequently, the much debated Revelation 20 passage is, frankly, not determinative for postmillennialism.[17]

---

14. O. T. Allis, "Foreword," Roderick Campbell, *Israel and the New Covenant* (Tyler, TX: Geneva Divinity School Press, [1954] 1981), p. ix.

15. See also: Allis, "The Parable of Leaven," *Evangelical Quarterly* 19:4 (Oct. 1947) 254-273.

16. See Footnote 6 regarding Berkhof in the preceding chapter. Cf. Richard B. Gaffin, "Theonomy and Eschatology: Reflections on Postmillennialism," *Theonomy: A Reformed Critique*, William S. Barker and W. Robert Godfrey, eds. (Grand Rapids: Zondervan, 1990), p. 199. Walvoord speaks of Revelation 20 as "one of the great chapters of the Bible." Walvoord, *Revelation*, p. 282.

17. This is *not* to say that the passage is unimportant. It is just to say that this

An appropriate, systematic definition of postmillennialism would include a number of key elements. It should be understood, of course, that ancient church fathers who held optimistic expectations for the progress of Christianity, and who may be called "postmillennial," would not hold to a full-blown systematic postmillenialism as outlined below. This is as true for postmillennialism as for premillennialism. "It must be conceded that the advanced and detailed theology of pretribulationism is not found in the Fathers, but neither is any other detailed and 'established' exposition of premillennialism. The development of most important doctrines took centuries."[18] Bearing this in mind, let us consider the nature of postmillennialism.

First, postmillennialism is that system of eschatology which holds the Messianic kingdom was founded upon the earth during the earthly ministry and through the redemptive labors of the Lord Jesus Christ. This establishment of the "kingdom of heaven" was in fulfillment of Old Testament prophetic expectation. The kingdom which Christ preached and presented was not something other than that expected by the Old Testament saints. In postmillennialism, the Church becomes the fulfilled/-transformed Israel, being called "the Israel of God" (Gal. 6:16).[19]

Second, the fundamental nature of that kingdom is essentially redemptive and spiritual rather than political and corporeal. Although it has implications for the political realm, postmillennialism is not essentially political, offering a kingdom in competition with geo-political nations for governmental rule. Christ

---

one passage has been allowed unduly to dominate the eschatological discussion.

18. John F. Walvoord, *The Rapture Question* (Grand Rapids: Zondervan, 1957), p. 52.

19. See: David E. Holwerda, *Jesus and Israel: One Covenant or Two?* (Grand Rapids: Eerdmans, 1995). The church as the elect of God existed in the Old Testament, despite dispensational claims. Jerry W. Crick, "The Church and the Kingdom" (ordination thesis) (Greenville, SC: Calvary Presbytery, 1990), pp. 1-6. See below, pages 171-178.

rules His kingdom spiritually in and through His people in the world (representation), as well as by His universal providence.

Third, because of the intrinsic power and design of Christ's redemption, His kingdom will exercise a transformational socio-cultural influence in history. This will occur as more and more people are converted to Christ, not by a minority revolt and seizure of political power. "[T]he *essential distinctive* of postmillennialism is its scripturally derived, sure expectation of gospel prosperity for the church during the *present* age."[20]

Fourth, postmillennialism, thus, expects the gradual, developmental expansion of the kingdom of Christ in time and on earth. This expansion will proceed by means of the full-orbed ministry of the Word, fervent and believing prayer, and the consecrated labors of His Spirit-filled people. Christ's personal presence on earth is not needed for the expansion of His kingdom. All of this kingdom expansion will be directed and blessed by the ever-present Christ, Who is now enthroned as King at the right hand of God, ruling and reigning over the earth.

Fifth, postmillennialism confidently anticipates a time in earth history (continuous with the present) in which the very gospel already operative in the world will win the victory throughout the earth in fulfillment of the Great Commission. "The thing that distinguishes the biblical postmillennialist, then, from amillennialists and premillennialists is his belief that the Scripture teaches *the success of the great commission in this age of the church*."[21] During that time the overwhelming majority of men and nations will be Christianized, righteousness will abound, wars will cease, and prosperity and safety will flourish. Of the postmillennial kingdom at its fullest expression David Brown writes: "It will be marked by the *universal reception of the true religion, and unlimited subjection to the sceptre of Christ*." "It shall be

---

20. Greg L. Bahnsen, "The *Prima Facie* Acceptability of Postmillennialism," *Journal of Christian Reconstruction* 3:2 (Winter 1976-77) 66.

21. *Ibid.*

a time of *universal peace.*" "It will be characterised by great *temporal prosperity.*"[22]

It should be noted at this juncture that there are some important differences between two types of postmillennialism today: pietistic and theonomic postmillennialism. "Among current postmils, to be sure, there are some who are not reconstructionists. . . . Nonreconstructionist postmils would naturally deny any such connection" between theonomic ethics and postmillennialism.[23] Pietistic postmillennialism (as found in Banner of Truth circles)[24] denies that the postmillennial advance of the kingdom involves the total transformation of culture through the application of biblical law. Theonomic postmillennialism affirms this.

Seventh, possibly "we can look forward to a great 'golden age' of spiritual prosperity continuing for centuries, or even for millenniums, during which time Christianity shall be triumphant over all the earth."[25] After this extended period of gospel prosperity, earth history will draw to a close by the personal, visible, bodily return of Jesus Christ (accompanied by a literal resurrection and a general judgment) to introduce His blood-bought people into the consummative and eternal form of the kingdom. And so shall we ever be with the Lord.

---

22. David Brown, *Christ's Second Coming: Will it be Premillennial?* (Edmonton, AB: Still Waters Revival, [1882] 1990), pp. 399, 401.

23. Gaffin, "Theonomy and Eschatology," *Theonomy: A Reformed Critique*, p. 197. For more detail see: Rousas John Rushdoony, *God's Plan for Victory: The Meaning of Postmillennialism* (Fairfax, VA: Thoburn, 1977). Greg L. Bahnsen and Kenneth L. Gentry, Jr., *House Divided: The Break-up of Dispensational Theology* (Tyler, TX: Institute for Christian Economics, 1989). Gary North, *Millennialism and Social Theory* (Tyler, TX: Institute for Christian Economics, 1990), especially Chapter 10.

24. The Calvinists who are associated with this group are self-consciously identified with the revivalistic postmillennialism of Jonathan Edwards rather than with the theonomic postmillennialism of the colonial American Puritans. See: Iain Murray, *The Puritan Hope: A Study in Revival and the Interpretation of Prophecy* (Edinburgh: Banner of Truth, 1971). The reprints of Puritan works issued by the Banner of Truth are pietistic rather than Cromwellian, introspective rather than cultural.

25. Loraine Boettner, *The Millennium* (Philadelphia: Presbyterian & Reformed, 1958), p. 29.

Confusion Regarding Millennial Development

Unfortunately, serious errors have brought distortion into the understanding of the historical rise of millennial views. A recent work comments: "The early church was solidly chiliastic until the time of Augustine."[26] Another boldly asserts that "the church from the beginning was premillennial in belief."[27] Still another states that "a premillennial belief was the *universal* belief in the church for two hundred and fifty years after the death of Christ."[28] This is commonly heard today.

Frequently the false historical data is traceable to the seriously flawed, long-discredited claims of George N. H. Peters.[29] Peters commented on premillennialism in history: "Now let the student reflect: here are *two* centuries . . . in which positively no direct opposition whatever arises against our doctrine."[30] His claims, though still persisting and highly regarded by some, have been shown to be quite erroneous.[31] Because my primary concern is to provide data for tracing the rise of postmillennialism, I will only briefly comment on the general historical confusion regarding postmillennialism. But it does deserve at least passing comment.

---

26. H. Wayne House and Thomas D. Ice, *Dominion Theology: Blessing or Curse?* (Portland, OR: Multnomah, 1988), p. 200.

27. Paul Enns, *The Moody Handbook of Theology* (Chicago: Moody Press, 1989), p. 389.

28. Pentecost, *Things to Come*, p. 374 (italics his). But then he quotes Schaff as saying it was not creedally endorsed by the church, but was "widely current" among distinguished teachers. How he leaps from "widely current" to "universal" we probably will never know.

29. George N. H. Peters, *The Theocratic Kingdom*, 3 vols. (New York: Funk and Wagnalls, 1884).

30. Pentecost, *Things to Come*, p. 375, citing Peters, *Theocratic Kingdom*, 1:494-496.

31. Walvoord calls it "a classic work." John F. Walvoord, *The Millennial Kingdom* (Findley, OH: Dunham, 1959), p. 119. Other dispensationalists employ his findings. See: Chafer, *Systematic Theology*, 4:270-274; J. Dwight Pentecost, *Things to Come*, pp. 373-384; and Leon J. Wood, *The Bible and Future Events* (Grand Rapids: Zondervan, 1973), pp. 35ff.

The errors of Peters' analysis and others like it have been exposed by a number of scholars. The three leading, most detailed, and helpful are: Alan Patrick Boyd (a dispensational-ist), D. H. Kromminga (a premillennialist), and Ned Stonehouse (an amillennialist).[32] Also noteworthy are studies by Louis Berkhof, Philip Schaff, Albertus Pieters, and W. J. Grier.[33] Kromminga carefully examines the sub-apostolic writings, in-cluding: Clement of Rome's *1 Clement*, the pseudo-Clementine *2 Clement*, *The Didache*, the Ignatian epistles, Polycarp's *Epistle*, *The Letter of the Church at Smyrna on the Martyrdom of Polycarp*, Barnabas, Hermas, Diognetus, Fragments of Papias, and *Reli-ques of the Elders*. He convincingly shows that *only Papias among the sub-apostolic fathers is premillennial*. He concludes that "an inquiry into the extent of ancient chiliasm will serve to show the untenableness of the claim that this doctrine was held with practical unanimity by the Church of the first few centuries."[34]

Put in the best light, the most that Peters could say is: "[I]t would seem that very early in the post-apostolic era millenar-ianism was regarded as a mark neither of orthodoxy nor of heresy, but as one permissible opinion among others within the range of permissible opinions."[35] Dispensationalist Lightner has admitted that "None of the major creeds of the church include premillennialism in their statements."[36] Not even the

---

32. Alan Patrick Boyd, "A Dispensational Premillennial Analysis of the Eschatolo-gy of the Post-Apostolic Fathers (Until the Death of Justin Martyr)" (Dallas: Dallas Theological Seminary master's thesis, 1977); D. H. Kromminga, *The Millennium in the Church* (Grand Rapids: Eerdmans, 1945), pp. 29-112; Ned Stonehouse, *The Apocalypse in the Ancient Church* (Goes, Holland: Oosterbaan and LeCointre, 1929), pp. 13ff.

33. Louis Berkhof, *The History of Christian Doctrines* (Grand Rapids: Baker, [1937] 1975), p. 262; Philip Schaff, *History of the Christian Church*, 8 vols. (5th ed.; Grand Rapids: Eerdmans, [1910] n.d.), 2:615; Albertus Pieters, two articles: "Chiliasm in the Writings of the Apostolic Fathers" (1938), cited by Kromminga, *Millennium*, p. 41; W. J. Grier, *The Momentous Event* (London: Banner of Truth, [1945] 1970), pp. 19ff.

34. Kromminga, *Millennium*, pp. 30, 41, 42.

35. Jaroslav Pelikan, *The Christian Traditions*, vol. 1 (Chicago: University of Chicago Press, 1971), p. 125.

36. Lightner, *Last Days Handbook*, p. 158.

second-century Apostles' Creed.[37] In fact, "early millennialism was held mostly among Jewish converts. A few Apostolic Fathers held it as individuals, but those who do not mention the millennium had greater weight of authority and influence: Clement, Ignatius, Polycarp."[38] This is borne out by premillennialism's failure to receive creedal status. Even Tertullian and Irenaeus (who were premillennial) record brief creeds with no allusions to a millennium.[39] What has happened to the evidence for "pervasive" premillennialism?

Peters' mistakes were powerfully analyzed and conclusively rebutted in a 1977 Dallas Theological Seminary master's thesis by (then) dispensationalist Alan Patrick Boyd. According to Boyd, he "originally undertook the thesis to bolster the [dispensational] system by patristic research, but the evidence of the original sources simply disallowed this." He ends up lamenting that "this writer believes that the Church *rapidly* fell from New Testament truth, and this is very evident in the realm of eschatology. Only in modern times has New Testament eschatological truth been recovered."[40] As a consequence of his research, Boyd urges his fellow dispensationalists to "avoid reliance on men like Geo. N. H. Peters . . . whose historical conclusions regarding premillennialism . . . in the early church have been proven to be largely in error."[41]

Boyd goes on to admit that "it would seem wise for the modern [i.e., dispensational] system to abandon the claim that

---

37. A. Harnack, "Apostle's Creed," *The New Schaff-Herzog Encyclopedia of Religious Knowledge*, 3 vols. (Grand Rapids: Baker, [1907] 1949), 1:242.

38. W. G. T. Shedd, *A History of Christian Doctrine*, 2 vols. (Minneapolis, MN: Klock & Klock, [1889] 1978), 2:390-391. Papias' famous passage on the millennium was taken from the Jewish Apocalypse of Baruch 29:1-8. See Geerhardus Vos, *The Pauline Eschatology* (Phillipsburg, NJ: Presbyterian & Reformed, [1930] 1991), p. 233.

39. Irenaeus, *Against Heresies* 1:10; 3:4; Tertullian, *Virgin* 1; *Against Praexus* 2; *The Prescription Against Heretics* 13.

40. Boyd, "Dispensational Premillennial Analysis," p. 91n.

41. *Ibid.*, p. 92.

it is the historical faith of the Church."[42] Of Ryrie's bold statement that "Premillennialism is the historic faith of the Church,"
he states: "It is the conclusion of this thesis that Dr. Ryrie's
statement is historically invalid within the chronological framework of this thesis."[43] Boyd even states: "This validates the
claim of L. Berkhof. . . . '[I]t is not correct to say, as Premillenarians do, that it (millennialism) was *generally* accepted in the
first three centuries. The truth of the matter is that the adherents of this doctrine were a rather limited number.' "[44]

It is clear upon reading certain of the ancient advocates of
premillennialism that they faced opposition from orthodox non-
millennialists. For instance, consider Justin Martyr's response to
Trypho regarding the hope of "a thousand years in Jerusalem,
which will then be built." Justin replied: "I admitted to you
formerly, that I and many others are of this opinion, and [be-
lieve] that such will take place, as you assuredly are aware; but,
on the other hand, I signified to you that *many* who belong to
the pure and pious faith, and are true Christians, think otherwise."[45] Note the reference to "many" who "think otherwise."
There was no unanimity regarding the millennium.

Another premillennialist, Irenaeus (*ca.* A.D. 180), observes
that "some who are reckoned *among the orthodox*" do not hold to
his premillennial views.[46] Eusebius (*ca.* A.D. 325) points to
premillennialist Papias (A.D. 60-130) in explaining the spread
of premillennialism: "But it was due to him that so many [not
"all"!] of the Church Fathers after him adopted a like opinion,

---

42. *Ibid.*
43. *Ibid.*, p. 89.
44. *Ibid.*, p. 92, n 1.
45. Justin Martyr, *Dialogue with Trypho the Jew* 80 (emphasis mine).
46. Irenaeus, *Against Heresies* 5:31:1 (emphasis mine). W. G. T. Shedd comments on this statement: "Irenaeus . . . speaks of opposers of Millenarianism who held the catholic faith, and who agreed with the Gnostics only in being Anti-Millenarians; although he is himself desirous to make it appear that Anti-Millenarianism is of the nature of heresy." Shedd, *History of Christian Doctrine*, 2:394.

urging in their own support the antiquity of the man."[47] The fact that premillennialism was in no way approaching "universal" in extent is evident also in that Dionysius (A.D. 190-264) successfully dealt with "this doctrine" in a certain area where it prevailed and split "entire churches." He won the day in that Egyptian district and turns the majority away from premillennialism.[48] Later, Epiphanius (A.D. 315-403) wrote: "There is indeed a millennium mentioned by St. John; but the most, and those pious men, look upon those words as true indeed, but to be taken in a spiritual sense."[49]

The Origins of Postmillennialism

Concomitant with a confusion in properly identifying certain modern postmillennialists and an unbalanced perception of the early influence of premillennialism is a widespread confusion regarding the origins of postmillennialism. One dispensationalist has stated of postmillennialism: "Its advocates admit that it was first taught in the seventeenth century."[50] There are also those who wrongly assume that postmillennialism may be traced back only as far as Daniel Whitby in 1703. Often Whitby is alleged to be "the originator of what is known as postmillennialism."[51] This is the argument of Wayne House (at the time a Dallas Seminary professor) and Thomas Ice:

Daniel Whitby first put forth his view in a popular work entitled *Paraphrase and Commentary on the New Testament* (1703). It was at the end of this work that he first set forth what he calls in his

---

47. Eusebius, *Ecclesiastical History* 3:39. Pelikan observes: Eusebius "was certainly speaking for a large body of theological opinion in the East when he called Papias's millenarianism 'bizarre' and 'rather mythological.' " Pelikan, *Christian Traditions*, vol. 1, p. 125.
48. Eusebius, *Ecclesiastical History* 7:24; cf. Dionysius 5:6.
49. Epiphanius, *Heresies* 77:26.
50. Baker, *Dispensational Theology*, p. 623.
51. Chafer, *Systematic Theology*, 4:280-281.

own words 'A New Hypothesis' on the millennial reign of Christ. Thus, the system called postmillennialism was born in the early 1700s as a hypothesis. Whitby and his modern followers present their arguments and explanations based upon unproved assumptions – assumptions resulting in a hypothesis rather than something which is the fruit of the study of Scripture or even the voice of the church.[52]

It should be noted that Whitby was not the founder of postmillennialism – even of its more systematic, modern expression. Rodney Peterson writes that "this perspective had undergone changes, particularly since Thomas Brightman (1562-1607)."[53] Brightman, who died in 1607, was one of the fathers of Presbyterianism in England. His postmillennial views were set forth in detail in his book, *A Revelation of the Revelation*. In fact, this work is considered the "most important and influential English revision of the Reformed, Augustinian concept of the millennium."[54] This was a century before Whitby's 1703 article.

Whitby was helpful in "popularizing"[55] postmillennialism because he presented postmillennialism's "most influential formulation."[56] Ball categorically denies Whitby's foundational role.[57] Whitby was simply *not* the "founder" of postmillennialism; he was a modern systematizer. At this very late date, it is time for dispensational authors to retract their previous statements regarding Whitby as the founder of postmillennialism.

---

52. House and Ice, *Dominion Theology*, p. 209.

53. Rodney Peterson, "The Debate Throughout Church History," *Continuity and Discontinuity*, p. 31.

54. Peter Toon, ed., *Puritans, the Millennium and the Future of Israel* (Cambridge: James Clarke, 1970), p. 26. See also: Bryan W. Ball, *A Great Expectation: Eschatological Thought in English Protestantism to 1660* (Leiden, Holland: E. J. Brill, 1975).

55. John J. Davis, *Christ's Victorious Kingdom: Postmillennialism Reconsidered* (Grand Rapids: Baker, 1986), pp. 16-17.

56. R. G. Clouse, "Millennium, Views of the," *Evangelical Dictionary of Theology* (Grand Rapids: Baker, 1984), p. 717.

57. W. Ball, *A Great Expectation*, p. 170n.

Early Origins of Postmillennialism

Clearly postmillennialism has undergone much systematization in the post-Reformation era. In its simplest form, however, adumbrations of it appear in antiquity. Simply put, postmillennialism teaches that Christ will return to the earth *after* the Spirit-blessed Gospel has had *overwhelming success* in bringing the world to the adoption of Christianity. Obviously, systematization is developmental, issuing from the diligent labors of many minds over a period of time as they build on the research of those who have gone on before. There should be no problem with the slow, developmental systematization, for dispensationalists can even write: "The futurist interpretation is the approach used by the earliest church fathers. We do not argue that they had a sophisticated system, but the clear futurist elements were there."[58] I argue similarly for postmillennialism. After all, did not Ryrie argue regarding dispensationalism's "recency": "Informed dispensationalists . . . recognize that as a system dispensationalism was largely formulated by Darby, but that outlines of the dispensationalist approach to the Scriptures are found much earlier"?[59]

There are indicators in antiquity of a genuine hope for the progress of the gospel in history. Premillennialist Kromminga notes that although most Montanists were premillennialists, "others were at least containing also the germs for later fullfledged Postmillennialism."[60] This nascent postmillennialism arose from the hope (rooted in Scripture) of the Holy Spirit's dominance in the affairs of history.[61] This perspective on the future of the Church had considerable influence in the thinking of other Church fathers.

---

58. House and Ice, *Dominion Theology*, p. 275.
59. Charles Ryrie, *Dispensationalism Today* (Chicago: Moody Press, 1965), p. 66.
60. Kromminga, *Millennium*, p. 76.
61. *Ibid.*, p. 84.

Origen (A.D. 185-254)

Although much in Origen is unacceptable, he is a noteworthy church father of considerable influence. As Philip Schaff notes, Origen had a place for a great evidencing of the power of the gospel: "Such a mighty revolution as the conversion of the heathen emperor was not dreamed of even as a remote possibility, except perhaps by the far-sighted Origen." "Origen seems to have been the only one in that age of violent persecution who expected that Christianity, by continual growth, would gain the dominion over the world."[62]

Origen comments: "[I]t is evident that even the barbarians, when they yield obedience to the word of God, will become most obedient to the law, and most humane; and every form of worship will be destroyed except the religion of Christ, which will alone prevail. And indeed it will one day triumph, as its principles take possession of the minds of men more and more every day."[63] This represents the essence of postmillennial optimism.

Eusebius (A.D. 260-340)

Eusebius provides an even fuller expression of hope. In Book 10 of his *Ecclesiastical History*, he is convinced he is witnessing the dawning of the fulfillment of Old Testament kingdom prophecies. Of Psalms 108:1,2 and 46:8,9, which he specifically cites, he writes that he is "Rejoicing in these things which have been clearly fulfilled in our day."[64] Later in chapters 4 through 7 of Book 10 he cites dozens of other such passages as coming to fulfillment. He writes: "For it was necessary and

---

62. Schaff, *History of the Christian Church*, 2:591, 122. He cites Neander, *General History of the Christian Religion and Church* (12th ed.), 1:129.

63. Origen, *Against Celsus* 8:68.

64. Eusebius, *Ecclesiastical History* 10:1:6. See: Donald G. Bloesch, *Essentials of Evangelical Theology: Life, Ministry, and Hope*, 2 vols. (San Francisco: Harper and Row, 1979). 2:192.

fitting that as her [the Church's] shepherd and Lord had once tasted death for her, and after his suffering had changed that vile body which he assumed in her behalf into a splendid and glorious body, leading the very flesh which had been delivered from corruption to incorruption, she too should enjoy the dispensations of the Saviour."[65]

After quoting several passages from Isaiah, Eusebius writes: "These are the things which Isaiah foretold; and which were anciently recorded concerning us in sacred books; and it was necessary that we should sometime learn their truthfulness by their fulfillment."[66]

Of Christ he writes:

> What god or hero yet, as he has done, has set aside all gods and heroes among civilized or barbarous nations; has ordained that divine honors should be withheld from all, and claimed obedience to that command: and then, though singly conflicting with the power of all, has utterly destroyed the opposing hosts; victorious over the gods and heroes of every age, and causing himself alone, in every region of the habitable world, to be acknowledged by all people as the only Son of God?. . . What god or hero, exposed, as our Saviour was, to so sore a conflict, has raised the trophy of victory over every foe?[67]

After discussing Psalm 110:1 and how "even to this day [Christ] is honored as a King by his followers throughout the world,"[68] he writes:

---

65. *Ibid.* 10:4:46:

66. *Ibid.* 10:4:53; cf. sections 46-52. Citing Isaiah 51:10-11; 54:4; 54:6-8; 51:17,18,22-23; 52:1,2; 49:18-21.

67. Eusebius, *The Oration of the Emperor Constantine* 17:13-14. Though obviously prematurely, he sees in the spread of Christianity the anticipated conquest of the world, *Church History* 1:3:12; 2:3:1; 8:1:1-2, 6.

68. Eusebius, *Church History* 1:3:19.

It is admitted that when in recent times the appearance of our Saviour Jesus Christ had become known to all men there immediately made its appearance a new nation; a nation confessedly not small, and not dwelling in some corner of the earth, but the most numerous and pious of all nations, indestructible and unconquerable, because it always receives assistance from God. This nation, thus suddenly appearing at the time appointed by the inscrutable counsel of God, is the one which has been honored by all with the name of Christ.[69]

Following this, he cites Genesis 12:3, regarding the Abrahamic promise of Christ's blessing all nations.[70] Eusebius later states:

Long since had his passion, as well as his advent in the flesh, been predicted by the prophets. The time, too, of his incarnation had been foretold, and the manner in which the fruits of iniquity and profligacy, so ruinous to the works and ways of righteousness, should be destroyed, and the whole world partake of the virtues of wisdom and sound discretion, through the almost universal prevalence of those principles of conduct which the Saviour would promulgate, over the minds of men; whereby the worship of God should be confirmed, and the rites of superstition abolished.[71]

Athanasius (A.D. 296-372)

Athanasius has been called "the patron saint of postmillennialism."[72] He was certain of the victory of Christ for now "the Saviour works so great things among men, and day by day is invisibly persuading so great a multitude from every side, both from them that dwell in

---

69. *Ibid.* 1:4:2-3.

70. *Ibid.* 1:4:13.

71. Eusebius, *Constantine*, 16.

72. David Chilton, *The Days of Vengeance: An Exposition of the Book of Revelation* (Ft. Worth, TX: Dominion Press, 1987), p. 5.

Greece and in foreign lands, to come over to His faith, and all to obey His teaching. . . ."[73] "For where Christ is named, and His faith, there all idolatry is deposed and all imposture of evil spirits is exposed, and any spirit is unable to endure even the name, nay even on barely hearing it flies and disappears. But this work is not that of one dead, but of one that lives – and especially of God."[74] In fact, regarding idols, Christ "chases them away, and by His power prevents their even appearing, yea, and is being confessed by them all to be the Son of God."[75] Athanasius goes on to exult in Christ's continuing victory:

> The Saviour does daily so many works, drawing men to religion, persuading to virtue, teaching of immortality, leading on to a desire for heavenly things, revealing the knowledge of the Father, inspiring strength to meet death, shewing Himself to each one, and displacing the godlessness of idolatry, and the gods and spirits of the unbelievers can do none of these things, but rather shew themselves dead at the presence of Christ, their pomp being reduced to impotence and vanity; whereas by the sign of the Cross all magic is stopped, and all witchcraft brought to nought, all the idols are being deserted and left, and every unruly pleasure is checked, and every one is looking up from earth to heaven. . . . For the Son of God is 'living and active,' and works day by day, and brings about the salvation of all. But death is daily proved to have lost all his power, and idols and spirits are proved to be dead rather than Christ.[76]

Athanasius applies prophecies of the triumph of Christ to the Church age and even rhetorically asks: "But what king that ever was, before he had strength to call father or mother, reigned and gained triumphs over his enemies?"[77] He then

---

73. Athanasius, *Incarnation* 30:4.

74. *Ibid.* 30:6.

75. *Ibid.* 30:7.

76. *Ibid.* 31:2-3. This is particularly significant in that idolatry was a world-wide phenomenon (2 Kgs. 17:29; 1 Chron. 16:26; Psa. 96:5) in which Satan exercised control of men through demonic power (Lev. 17:7; Deut. 32:17; Psa. 106:37; 1 Cor. 10:19-20). Satan's binding (Rev. 20:2-3; Matt. 12:28-29) is increasing "day by day."

77. *Ibid.* 36:1. He cites sections from Num. 24:5-17; Isa. 8:4; Isa. 19:1 (Sec. 33

writes: "All heathen at any rate from every region, abjuring their hereditary tradition and the impiety of idols, are now placing their hope in Christ, and enrolling themselves under Him."[78] He continues:

> But if the Gentiles are honouring the same God that gave the law to Moses and made the promise to Abraham, and Whose word the Jews dishonoured, – why are [the Jews] ignorant, or rather why do they choose to ignore, that the Lord foretold by the Scriptures has shone forth upon the world, and appeared to it in bodily form, as the Scripture said. . . . What then has not come to pass, that the Christ must do? What is left unfulfilled, that the Jews should not disbelieve with impunity? For if, I say, – which is just what we actually see, – there is no longer king nor prophet nor Jerusalem nor sacrifice nor vision among them, but even the whole earth is filled with the knowledge of God, and the gentiles, leaving their godlessness, are now taking refuge with the God of Abraham, through the Word, even our Lord Jesus Christ, then it must be plain, even to those who are exceedingly obstinate, that the Christ is come, and that He has illumined absolutely all with His light. . . . So one can fairly refute the Jews by these and by other arguments from the Divine Scriptures.[79]

> . . . [I]t is right for you to realize, and to take as the sum of what we have already stated, and to marvel at exceedingly; namely, that since the Saviour has come among us, idolatry not only has no longer increased, but what there was is diminishing and gradually coming to an end: and not only does the wisdom of the Greeks no longer advance, but what there is is now fading away. . . . And to sum the matter up: behold how the Saviour's doctrine is everywhere increasing, while all idolatry and everything opposed to the faith of Christ is daily dwindling, and losing power,

[context = Secs. 30-31]); Dan. 9:24ff; Gen. 49:10 (Sec. 40); Isa. 2:4 (Sec. 52:1); 11:9 (Sec. 45:2; *Discourse Against the Arians* 1:59); Psa. 110:1 (*Discourse Against the Arians* 2:15:14, 16); etc.

78. *Ibid.* 37:5.

79. *Ibid.* 40:5, 7.

and falling. . . . For as, when the sun is come, darkness no longer prevails, but if any be still left anywhere it is driven away; so, now that the divine Appearing of the Word of God is come, the darkness of the idols prevails no more, and all parts of the world in every direction are illumined by His teaching.[80]

The great progress of the gospel is expected, according to Athanasius' view of Scripture (Isa. 11:9; Matt. 28:19; John 6:45:): "And then, from Dan to Beersheba was the Law proclaimed, and in Judea only was God known; but now, unto all the earth has gone forth their voice, and all the earth has been filled with the knowledge of God, and the disciples have made disciples of all the nations, and now is fulfilled what is written, 'They shall be all taught of God.' "[81]

The adumbrations of the ultimate pacific influence of the gospel are being felt in his day:

Who then is He that has done this, or who is He that has united in peace men that hated one another, save the beloved Son of the Father, the common Saviour of all, even Jesus Christ, Who by His own love underwent all things for our salvation. For even from of old it was prophesied of the peace He was to usher in, where the Scripture says: 'They shall beat their swords into ploughshares, and their pikes into sickles, and nation shall not take the sword against nation, neither shall they learn war any more.' And this is at least not incredible, inasmuch as even now those barbarians who have an innate savagery of manners, while they still sacrifice to the idols of their country, are mad against one another, and cannot endure to be a single hour without weapons: but when they hear the teaching of Christ, straightway instead of fighting they turn to husbandry, and instead of arming their hands with weapons they raise them in prayer, and in a word, in place of fighting among themselves, henceforth they

---

80. *Ibid.* 55:1-3.
81. Athanasius, *Four Discourses Against the Arians* 59:8.

arm against the devil and against evil spirits, subduing these by self-restraint and virtue of soul.[82]

Many other such references could be cited from Athanasius.[83] There is insufficient space at this point to do so.

We have yet to hear from the most influential theologian among the ancient church fathers: Augustine.

Augustine (A.D. 354-430)

Augustine looms as the greatest Christian thinker in the early church. Although many assume his views correspond more closely with amillennialism, there is evidence of postmillennial-type thinking in his writings, as scholars have noted.[84] Augustine taught that history "would be marked by the ever-increasing influence of the church in overturning evil in the world before the Lord's return."[85] Historic premillennialist Erickson admits Augustine is postmillennial and that "all three millennial positions have been held virtually throughout church history."[86] He cites Augustine's *Sermon* 259:2 as evidence of post-millennialism.

---

82. Athanasius, *Incarnation* 52.

83. For example, *Ibid.* 46-48; 50; 53-55.

84. John O'Meara, "Introduction," in Augustine, *City of God*, trans. By Henry Bettensen (New York: Penguin, 1984), viii. William Sanford LaSor, *The Truth About Armageddon: What the Bible Says About the End Times* (San Francisco: Harper & Row, 1982), p. 160. D. W. Bebbington, *Patterns in History: A Christian View* (Downers Grove, IL: Inter-Varsity, 1979), p. 54. Adolf von Harnack, "Millennium," *Encyclopedia Britannica* (9th ed.; New York: Scribner's, 1883), 16:314ff. Thomas N. Finger, *Christian Theology: An Eschatological Approach* (Nashville: Thomas Nelson, 1985), pp. 113-115. Gary North, *Millennialism and Social Theory* (Tyler, TX: Institute for Christian Economics, 1990), pp. 19, 22, 161, 239. Boettner, *Millennium*, p. 10. Paul Erb, *Bible Prophecy: Questions and Answers* (Scottdale, PA: Herald, 1978), pp. 101-102. Even Walvoord is aware of these tendencies in Augustine: *Millennial Kingdom*, p. 8.

85. Wendy Murray Zoba, "Future Tense," *Christianity Today*, October 2, 1995, 20.

86. M. J. Erickson, *Christian Theology*, 3 vols. (Grand Rapids: Baker, 1985), 3:1206-07.

A number of statements in Book 18 of *The City of God* certainly give the appearance of a postmillennial optimism. Of Nahum 1:14 and 2:1, Augustine states: "Moreover, we already see the graven and molten things, that is, the idols of the false gods, exterminated through the gospel, and given up to oblivion as of the grave, and we know that this prophecy is fulfilled in this very thing" (*City of God* 18:31). " 'The tents of Ethiopia shall be greatly afraid, and the tents of the land of Midian;' that is, even those nations which are not under the Roman authority, being suddenly terrified by the news of Thy wonderful works, shall become a Christian people. 'Wert Thou angry at the rivers, O Lord? or was Thy fury against the rivers? or was Thy rage against the sea?' This is said because He does not now come to condemn the world, but that the world through Him might be saved" (18:32).

He comments on Haggai 2:6: " 'Thus saith the Lord of hosts, Yet one little while, and I will shake the heaven, and the earth, and the sea, and the dry land; and I will move all nations, and the desired of all nations shall come.' The fulfillment of this prophecy is in part already seen, and in part hoped for in the end. . . . so we see all nations moved to the faith; and the fulfillment of what follows, 'And the desired of all nations shall come,' is looked for at His last coming. For ere men can desire and wait for Him, they must believe and love Him" (*City of God*, 18:35). His comments on Psalm 2 could also be cited.

Indeed, Augustine taught that history "would be marked by the ever-increasing influence of the church in overturning evil in the world before the Lord's return."[87] This would eventually issue forth in a "future rest of the saints on earth" (*Sermon* 259:2) "when the Church will be purged of all the wicked ele-

---

87. Wendy Murray Zoba, "Future Tense," *Christianity Today*, October 2, 1995, 20. Cp. John O'Meara, "Introduction," in Augustine, *City of God*, trans. By Henry Bettensen (New York: Penguin, 1984), viii.

ments now mixed among its memebers and Christ will rule peacefully in its midst."[88]

Medieval Postmillennialists

Somewhat later in history, but still pre-Whitby, is the case of the medieval Roman Catholic Joachim of Florus (1145-1202). Several non-postmillennial scholars cite him as a postmillennialist,[89] due to his view of a coming outpouring of the Spirit, initiating the Age of the Spirit.[90] As Kromminga puts it: "In fact, modern Postmillenarianism of the orthodox type with its expectation of a glorious final Church Age, brought about through the ordinary operation of the Word and the Spirit, embodies nothing but this Pure Church ideal, dissociated from Joachim's expectation of a future coming of the Holy Spirit."[91] Strangely, Walvoord points to Joachim as a postmillennialist, then speaks of postmillennialism "originating in the writings of Daniel Whitby," despite Whitby's writing five centuries later![92]

Other postmillennialists well before Whitby include the following: the Franciscans Peter John Olivi (d. ca. 1297) and Abertino de Casale (fl. 1305); the Dominicans Ghehardinus de Burgo (fl. 1254), Mechthild of Magdeburg (d. 1280), Fra Dolcino (fl. 1330); another Roman Catholic scholar Arnaldus of Villanova (fl. 1298); and the forerunner of John Huss, Jan Miliciz of Kremsier (fl. 1367).[93]

---

88. Brian E. Daley, *The Hope of the Early Chuch: A Handbook of Patristic Eschatology* (Cambridge: University Press, 1991), 133.

89. See: Kromminga, *Millennium*, pp. 20; 129ff; he cites Benz, *Zeitschrift für Kirchengeschichte*, 1931. See also: W. Möller, in Philip Schaff, *A Religious Encyclopedia* (rev. ed.; New York: Funk & Wagnalls, 1883), 2:1183. Ryrie, *Basic Theology*, p. 443.

90. Joachim of Florus, *Concordia Veteris et Novi Testamenti*, *Expositio super Apocalypsin*, and *Psalterium Decem Chordarum*.

91. Kromminga, *Millennium*, p. 132.

92. Walvoord, *Millennial Kingdom*, pp. 7, 19.

93. Kromminga, *Millennium*, pp. 135-136, 159ff, who cites the following sources: Johann Heinrich Kurtz, Henry Hart Milman, J. A. W. Neander, and Johann Jacob Herzog. See also: Möller in Schaff, *Religious Encyclopedia*, 2:1183; Williston Walker, *A

A century and a half before Whitby, John Calvin (1509-1564) held optimistic prophetic views that are commonly associated with postmillennialism. Such postmillennial expectations may be found at various places in his commentaries, such as at Isaiah 2:2-4; 65:17; Matthew 24:26; 28:18-20; Romans 11:24. "John Calvin's commentaries give some scholars cause for concluding that he anticipated the spread of the gospel and true religion to the ends of the earth."[94] Indeed, in his Prefatory Address to King Francis I of France, Calvin writes: "Our doctrine must tower unvanquished above all the glory and above all the might of the world, for it is not of us, but of the living God and his Christ whom the Father has appointed King to 'rule from sea to sea, and from the rivers even to the ends of the earth. . . . And he is so to rule as to smite the whole earth with its iron and brazen strength, with its gold and silver brilliance, shattering it with the rod of his mouth as an earthen vessel, just as the prophets have prophesied concerning the magnificence of his reign."[95] This is not the language of eschatological pessimism; and it was adopted by Calvin's Puritan and postmillennial successors. They had good reasons to see in Calvin a postmillennial optimism.

I have already mentioned the most important systematizer of English postmillennialism, Thomas Brightman (1562-1607). In addition to him, there was a growing and influential number of

---

History of the Christian Church (3rd ed.; New York: Scribner's, 1970), p. 237; Kenneth Scott Latourette, *A History of Christianity*, 2 vols. (rev. ed.; New York: Harper & Row, 1975), 1:435.

94. J. A. DeJong, *As the Waters Cover the Sea: Millennial Expectations in the Rise of Anglo-American Missions 1640-1810* (Kampen: J. H. Kok, 1970), p. 8. See also: J. T. McNeill, ed., Calvin's *Institutes of the Christian Religion*, trans. by Ford Lewis Battles (Philadelphia: Westminster Press, 1960), 2:904; Murray, *Puritan Hope*, pp. 89ff; Bloesch, *Evangelical Theology*, 2:199-200; Greg L. Bahnsen, "The *Prima Facie* Acceptability of Postmillennialism," pp. 69-76; James R. Payton, Jr., "The Emergence of Postmillennialism in English Puritanism," *Journal of Christian Reconstruction* 6:1 (Summer 1979) 87-106; Aletha Joy Gilsdorf, *The Puritan Apocalyptic: New England Eschatology in the 17th Century* (New York: Garland, 1989).

95. John Calvin, *Institutes of the Christian Religion*, 1:12.

English Puritans who held postmillennial views well before
Whitby, as a number of important historical works have amply
demonstrated.[96] We think of William Perkins (1558-1602),
William Gouge (1575-1653), Richard Sibbes (1577-1635), John
Cotton (1585-1652), Thomas Goodwin (1600-1679), George
Gillespie (1613-1649), John Owen (1616-1683), Elnathan Parr
(d. 1632), Thomas Brooks (d. 1662), John Howe (d. 1678),
James Renwick (d. 1688), Matthew Henry (1662-1714), and
others. John Cotton's *The Churches Resurrection, or the Opening of
the Fift and Sixt Verses of the 20th. Chap. of the Revelation* [*sic.*],
written in 1642, was quite influential and shows obvious influence by Brightman.[97]

The Westminster Standards (1640s) set forth a postmillennial
hope. The kingship of Christ is demonstrated to God's people
by Christ's "overcoming all their enemies, and powerfully ordering all things for his own glory" (Larger Catechism, 45).
Indeed, "Christ executeth the office of a king, in subduing us to
himself, in ruling and defending us, and in restraining and
conquering all his and our enemies" (Shorter Catechism, 26).
The evidence of His exaltation is made visible to His Church
when He does "gather and defend his church, and subdue
their enemies" (Larger Catechism, 54).

According to the Westminster Standards, the second petition
of the Lord's Prayer beseeches God "that the kingdom of sin
and Satan may be destroyed, the gospel propagated throughout
the world, the Jews called. . . [and] the fullness of the Gentiles
brought in."[98] This follows the first petition in which prayer is
righteously made "that he would prevent and remove atheism,

---

96. Toon, *Puritans, the Millennium and the Future of Israel*; Richard H. Popkin, ed.,
Millennialism and Messianism in English Literature and Thought 1650-1800 (Leiden,
Holland: Brill, 1988); Ball, *Great Expectation*. See also: the previous references to
historical works by Iain Murray, J. A. DeJong, James R. Payton, Greg L. Bahnsen, A.
J. Gilsdorf.

97. Ball, *A Great Expectation*, pp. 160-161.

98. LC 191.

ignorance, idolatry, profaneness, and whatsoever is dishonorable to him; and, by his over-ruling providence, direct and dispose of all things to his own glory."[99]

Congregationalism's Savoy Declaration of 1658 is a strong and unambiguous postmillennial document. It promises that "in the latter days, antichrist being destroyed, the Jews called, and the adversaries of the kingdom of His dear Son broken, the churches of Christ being enlarged and edified through a free and plentiful communication of light and grace, [they] shall enjoy in this world a more quiet, peaceable, and glorious condition than they have enjoyed."[100]

After a lengthy and informative discussion of a host of names, premillennialist Kromminga concludes: "In actual fact there is quite a strain of Postmillennialism in Reformed theology from Coccecius [1603-1669] onward. . . . Reformed theology can therefore in view of these phenomena not well be said to have been uniformly amillenarian, as is rather frequently assumed."[101] And as was shown in the preceding chapter, some of the great reformed scholars of the last 100 years have been postmillennial.

Simply put: Daniel Whitby was not the "founder" of postmillennialism. Postmillennialism's distinctive theme of gospel victory in history is hoary with age.

Representative Adherents to Postmillennialism

As in the earlier chapter, here I will summarily list some noteworthy adherents to postmillennialism. In the ancient church: Eusebius (A.D. 260-340), Athanasius (A.D. 296-372),

---

99. LC 190.

100. Philip Schaff, *The Creeds of Christendom, With a History and Critical Notes*, 3 vols. (6th ed.; New York: Harper & Bros., 1919), 3:723. Reprinted by Baker Book House, Grand Rapids, 1990.

101. Kromminga, *Millennium*, p. 303.

94 HE SHALL HAVE DOMINION

and Augustine (A.D. 354-430). In the modern, post-Puritan church: Jonathan Edwards (1703-1758), William Carey (1761-1834), Robert Haldane (1764-1842), Archibald Alexander (1772-1851), Charles Hodge (1797-1878), Albert Barnes (1798-1870), David Brown (1803-1897), Patrick Fairbairn (1805-1874), Richard C. Trench (1807-1886), J. A. Alexander (1809-1860), J. H. Thornwell (1812-1862), Robert L. Dabney (1820-1898), William G. T. Shedd (1820-1894), A. A. Hodge (1823-1886), Augustus H. Strong (1836-1921), H. C. G. Moule (1841-1920), B. B. Warfield (1851-1921), O. T. Allis (1880-1973), J. Gresham Machen (1881-1937), John Murray (1898-1975), Loraine Boettner (1903-1989), J. Marcellus Kik (1903-1965), and Greg L. Bahnsen (1948-1995). In addition, many contemporary writers defend the viewpoint, such as: Reuben Alvarado, Carl Bogue, David Chilton, Curtis Crenshaw, Jerry W. Crick, John Jefferson Davis, Gary DeMar, J. Ligon Duncan III, John R. deWitt, Kenneth L. Gentry, Jr., George Grant, Grover E. Gunn, Stephen J. Hayhow, Erroll Hulse, Douglas Kelly, Francis Nigel Lee, Peter J. Leithart, Donald Macleod, Joseph C. Morecraft III, Henry Morris III, Iain Murray, Gary North, Stephen C. Perks, Willard Ramsey, Rousas J. Rushdoony, Andrew Sandlin, Steve Schlissel, Roger Schultz, Norman Shepherd, Ray R. Sutton, Kenneth G. Talbot, Jack Van Deventer, James West, Douglas Wilson, and Colin Wright.[102]

---

102. See: Bloesch, *Essentials,* 2:189-204. J. A. Alexander, *Commentary on Isaiah* (1847). O. T. Allis, "Foreword," Roderick Campbell, *Israel and the New Covenant* (1954). Greg Bahnsen, "The *Prima Facie* Acceptability of Postmillennialism," *op. cit.* (1977). Albert Barnes, *Isaiah* (1860). Loraine Boettner, *The Millennium* (1957). David Brown, *Christ's Second Coming: Will It Be Premillennial?* (1849). Robert L. Dabney, *Lectures in Systematic Theology* (1878). John Jefferson Davis, *Christ's Victorious Kingdom* (1986). Jonathan Edwards, *The Works of Jonathan Edwards* (1834). Matthew Henry, *Matthew Henry's Commentary* (1714). A. A. Hodge, *Outlines of Theology* (1860). Charles Hodge, *Systematic Theology* (1871). Erroll Hulse, *The Restoration of Israel* (1968). Francis Nigel Lee, *Will Christ or Satan Rule the World?* (1977). Marcellus Kik, *An Eschatology of Victory* (1971). J. Gresham Machen, in Ned Stonehouse, *J. Gresham Machen: A Biographical Memoir* (1954), pp. 187, 245, 261. George C. Miladin, *Is This Really the End?* (1972). Iain Murray, *The Puritan Hope* (1971). John Murray, *Romans* (1965). Gary

Conclusion

Systematization of the various theological loci naturally developed over time, engaging the gifts and minds of spiritually sensitive Christian thinkers. Most biblical theologians would agree that eschatology is one of the loci that has undergone the most development in history. As I indicated earlier, eschatology is extremely deep and involved, intertwining itself with the very essence of Christianity itself. Because of this, the antiquity of an eschatological *system*, as such, is not absolutely essential to its orthodoxy. Nevertheless, the eschatological factors in Scripture cannot have been without some apparent impact upon the nascent development of early Christendom's perception of the flow of history. An eschatology lacking *any* historical rooting in antiquity is rightly suspect.

Much popular literature leaves the impression that postmillennial thought is a recent novelty. I have shown that postmillennialism has ample historical precedent in the early centuries of the Christian Church. Indeed, it has been the framework of some of the Church's noted thinkers. The crucial elements of postmillennialism – the presence of a biblically informed, historically relevant, and ultimately optimistic temporal hope – is clearly present in antiquity.

Furthermore, the postmillennial position has been held in more recent centuries by noted and devout defenders of the faith. Postmillennialism is not a fringe eschatology. It has been

---

North, *Millennialism and Social Theory* (1990). John Owen, *The Works of John Owen*, vol. 8 (1850-1853). R. J. Rushdoony, *God's Plan for Victory* (1977). Steve Schlissel, *Hal Lindsey and the Restoration of the Jews* (1990). W. G. T. Shedd, *Dogmatic Theology* (1888). Norman Shepherd, in *Zondervan Pictorial Bible Dictionary*, 4:822-823 (1975). Augustus H. Strong, *Systematic Theology* (1907). J. H. Thornwell, *Collected Writings*, vol. 4 (1871). Richard C. Trench, *Notes on the Miracles and Parables of Our Lord* (1875). B. B. Warfield, *Selected Shorter Writings* (1970). Willard A. Ramsey, *Zion's Glad Morning* (Simpsonville, S.C.: Millennium III, 1990). Note: On the Puritans, see: Peter Toon, *Puritans, the Millennium and the Future of Israel* (1970). See: Bloesch, *Evangelical Essentials*, 2:197.

particularly influential in reformed circles, as the list on page 94 demonstrates.

When postmillennialism is properly defined, it expresses the glorious hope of all of Scripture. When its advocates are carefully read, its antiquity and influence may be better understood. The widespread confusion regarding postmillennialism's nature, origins, and advocates is lamentable. The modern Church, sapped of the power of hope, largely through poor exegesis and a lack of an understanding of Church history, is the weaker for it.

PART II

INTERPRETATION

5

THE REVELATION OF TRUTH

So shall My word be that goes forth from My mouth; it shall not return to Me void, but it shall accomplish what I please, and it shall prosper in the thing for which I sent it. (Isaiah 55:11)

An important element in the Christian philosophy of history, as I noted in Chapter 1, is revelation. God has revealed Himself and His will for man in the Scriptures of the Old and New Testaments. I will not provide an apologetic for the orthodox view of Scripture here – that would take us well beyond our focus.[1] Nevertheless, it is important that the orthodox view of Scripture from which I operate as a postmillennialist be stated and applied to the subject at hand.

God's Word is Inerrant

The sixty-six books of Scripture are personally and directly revealed by God to the human writers through the inspiration of the Holy Spirit of God (2 Tim. 3:16; 2 Pet. 1:20-21). As Calvin says, the Scriptures have come to us "by the ministry of men from God's very mouth."[2] God so carefully revealed His

---

1. But see: Benjamin B. Warfield, *The Inspiration and Authority of the Bible* (Philadelphia: Presbyterian & Reformed, 1948). Edward J. Young, *Thy Word Is Truth: Some Thoughts on the Biblical Doctrine of Inspiration* (Grand Rapids: Eerdmans, 1957). J. I. Packer, *God Has Spoken* (Downer's Grove, IL: Inter-Varsity Press, 1979).

2. John Calvin, *The Institutes of the Christian Religion* (1559) 1:7:5.

Word to His prophets that it might be stated of the prophet: "I will put my words in his mouth; and he shall speak unto them all that I shall command him" (Deut. 18:18b[3]). Consequently, a constant refrain of Scripture is, "Thus saith the Lord."

Being the personally revealed Word of the Living and True God, the Scriptures are inerrant in their original autographa in anything they assert. This is as true in historical matters as in spiritual.[4] Christ affirms: "Thy word is truth" (John 17:17). God's wisdom is infinite and unsearchable.[5] There is no limitation or imperfection in His knowledge (Job 37:16). He knows all things fully and exhaustively.[6] His Word is inerrant and will always be demonstrated as such in history. Thus, the eschatological prophecies of Scripture, when properly interpreted, must absolutely come to pass.

If the Bible teaches that anything is true and to be expected, then no matter how difficult for us to imagine, no matter how strongly arrayed against it are the historical forces of Satan, we must bow to the authority of Scripture. "With God all things are possible" (Matt. 19:26). No historical or philosophical argument counterpoised against Scriptural revelation regarding eschatological eventuation should prevail in the thought of the Christian. The fundamental framework of the Christian eschatology must be rooted firmly in the Bible if it is to be realistic and true.

---

3. Cf. Jer. 1:9, 17; John 14:26; Rom. 3:2; 1 Cor. 2:13; 1 Thess. 2:13. Although it is true that the ultimate reference of Deut. 18:18 is to the Great Prophet, Jesus Christ, it is also true that this reference involves all the divinely commissioned prophets of Scripture, establishing and authorizing the prophetic line. See: Gentry, *The Charismatic Gift of Prophecy: A Reformed Response to Wayne Grudem* (2nd ed.; Memphis: Footstool, 1990), ch. 1.

4. Greg L. Bahnsen, "Inductivism, Inerrancy, and Presuppositionalism," *Evangelicals and Inerrancy*, Ronald F. Youngblood, ed. (Nashville: Thomas Nelson, 1984), pp. 199-216.

5. Job 11:7-8; 37:5, 14, 23; Isa. 40:28; 55:10ff; Rom. 11:33-36.

6. Psa. 147:5; Prov. 15:3; Acts 15:18; 1 John 3:20.

The Scriptures stand as absolute authority over man, providing a sure record of supernaturally revealed, propositional truth. For instance, the apostles of the New Testament insisted on the acceptance of their authority.[7] The commands of Scripture compel obedience for the believer, despite and against the wisdom of man and the power of Satan. "The weapons of our warfare are not carnal, but mighty through God to the pulling down of strong holds," therefore we are obliged to "cast down imaginations, and every high thing that exalteth itself against the knowledge of God, and bring into captivity every thought to the obedience of Christ" (2 Cor 10:4-5). Indeed, Paul commands: "Be not conformed to this world: but be ye transformed by the renewing of your mind, that ye may prove what is that good, and acceptable, and perfect, will of God" (Rom 12:2).

The Word of God is not only the *theoretical* foundation of the Christian worldview, but is a *practical* revelation of Truth, serving as a motivation to action in terms of that Truth. It spiritually and intellectually equips the believer for every task in every realm of human endeavor. "All scripture is given by inspiration of God, and is profitable for doctrine, for reproof, for correction, for instruction in righteousness: That the man of God may be perfect, thoroughly furnished unto all good works" (2 Tim. 3:16-17).[8] Because of this the godly labor of the believer is "not in vain in the Lord" (1 Cor. 15:58).[9] When the prophetic data of Scripture compel us to a particular historical hope and certain course of action, we are in error when we refuse them. We also stand in sinful unbelief when we fearfully doubt them.

---

7. 1 Cor. 14:37; 2 Cor. 11:3ff; 13:2-10; Gal. 1:6-9; 1 Thess. 1:5; 2:13; 2 Thess. 2:13-15; 3:6-15; 2 Tim. 2:1ff; 3:13ff; Titus 1:9; 2 Pet. 1:12-2:3; 1 John 2:21-24.

8. See also Heb. 13:21; 2 Tim. 2:21.

9. Cf. 1 Cor. 10:13; 2 Cor. 9:8; Phil. 4:13.

God's Word is Powerful

The very Word of God which maps out the plan of history is also the causative power insuring the success of that plan. This may be seen from several angles.

The Creative Word

The Bible opens with a strong and determinative statement regarding the absolute power of God's spoken Word. The universe exists solely because of the exercise of God's creative will, and was brought into being by His sovereign, successive divine fiats. By His Word the universe was created: "and God said" is a significant recurring element in the creation record.[10] The creation record sets forth a creation *ex nihilo* in six literal days.[11] Such is the causative power of God's Word. The universe is not a self-evolving, non-personal, naturalistic phenomenon lacking meaning or purpose.

The relationship between the creative Word of God and the revelatory Word is important to grasp. The Scriptures clearly tie the two together. The clearest evidence of this is found in Psalm 33:4-6: "For the [revelatory] word of the LORD is right;

---

10. Gen. 1:3, 6, 9, 11, 14, 20, 24, 26, 28, 29. See also later confirmation of this in Neh. 9:6; Psa. 33:6; Acts 17:24; Heb. 11:3.

11. Each of the six days of creation was a literal twenty-four-hour day: (1) "Day" is qualified by "evening and morning" (Gen. 1:5, 8, 13, 19, 23, 31), which specifically limits the time-frame. (2) The very same word "day" is used on the fourth day to define a time period that is governed by the sun, which must be a regular day (Gen. 1:14). (3) In the 119 instances of the Hebrew word "day" (*yom*) standing in conjunction with a numerical adjective (first, second, etc.) in the writings of Moses, it never means anything other than a literal day. Consistency would require that this structure must so function in Genesis 1 (Gen. 1:5, 8, 13, 19, 23, 31). (4) Exodus 20:9-11 patterns man's work week after God's original work week, which suggests the literality of the creation week. (5) In Exodus 20:11 the plural for the "days" of creation is used. In the 702 instances of the plural "days" in the Old Testament, it never means anything other than literal days. (6) Had Moses meant that God created the earth in six ages, he could have employed the more suitable Hebrew term *olam*. See the mass of scientific literature produced by the Creation Research Society, El Cajon, California. See also: Kenneth L. Gentry, Jr., "Reformed Theology and Six Day Creationism," *Christianity & Society*, 5:4 (October, 1995): 25-30.

and all his works are done in truth. He loveth righteousness
and judgment: the earth is full of the goodness of the LORD .
By the [creative] word of the LORD were the heavens made;
and all the host of them by the breath of his mouth."

The Providential Word

The universe is providentially upheld by God's Word
through the continued application of its inherent power. The
God of Scripture is no deistic Creator; He is intimately and
personally involved in every aspect of His creation to maintain
and preserve it by His active Word. The divine Christ is said to
be "upholding all things (*ta panta*) by the word of his power"
(Heb. 1:3; cf. 2 Pet. 3:7). His Word will never pass away (Matt.
24:35).

The sovereignty of God has a great bearing upon this matter. The Scripture teaches that the Triune God is in total and
absolute control of every eventuation in every corner of the
universe. God's total, absolute, unchangeable control of all
things is rooted in His predetermined plan from eternity past.
God is not a finite creature, limited to the confines of time, the
succession of moments, and the competition of other forces. He
is the Eternal Now, existing always in the present (Exo. 3:14).
"God, from all eternity, did, by the most wise and holy counsel
of his own free will, freely, and unchangeably ordain whatsoever comes to pass: yet so, as thereby neither is God the author of
sin, nor is violence offered to the will of the creatures; nor is
the liberty or contingency of second causes taken away, but
rather established" (Westminster Confession of Faith 3:1).

God controls the universe as a system and rules the "natural" phenomena on earth.[12] "And He is before all things, and
in Him all things consist" (Col. 1:17; cf. Isa. 45:7a; Heb. 1:3).
For the Christian "natural law" is but a convenient phrase to

---

12. Nah. 1:3-6; Isa. 45:7b; Psa. 29; 104:21; Job 36:32; 37:3; 28:23-27; 38:12-
39:30; Amos 4:7; Matt. 5:45; 6:28-30; Acts 14:17.

explain the phenomena of the universe in terms of their order-liness. Since the universe is permeated by the very presence of God (1 Kgs. 7:17; Jer. 23:23-24), the Christian worldview neces-sitates that we live in an ultimately personal universe (Prov. 15:3; Acts 17:28; Heb. 4:13). On the Christian view the universe does not operate under its own internal power (naturally), but under the constant direction of the ever-present God (supernat-urally). What scientists call "natural law" is actually "divine providence."

God governs the ebb and flow of history[13] and determines the purpose and the end of all things.[14] He "works all things according to the counsel of His will" (Eph. 1:11b). The universe and earth history exist for the glory of God and are controlled to that end. The universe exists neither of itself nor for itself. God's omnipotence and omniscience guarantee that the ulti-mate outcome of the sum total of all the events of history will conform to His plan or counsel, despite the railings of man and resistance of Satan. God's will cannot be thwarted.

God controls even the minute details of life.[15] His plan is not merely a general sketch of the course of historical develop-ment, but a detailed plan that evidences in its every phase His own absolute sovereignty. All the parts of the plan are mar-shalled forth in subservience to the whole. Considered in terms of ultimate reality, there is neither accident nor luck. All things occur according to the plan of God, despite their random or fortuitous appearance from the perspective of man.

This sovereign control by God includes even the free acts of men.[16] Man has "free moral agency." But he cannot do just

---

13. Ezra 6:22; 7:6; Psa. 115:2; 135:6; Pro. 21:1; Isa. 44:28; 54:16; 55:11; Jer. 27:5; Dan. 2:21; 4:17, 35; Eccl. 3:1-8, 11; Rom. 8:28; 13:1,4.

14. Psa. 24:1; 33:11; Prov. 16:4; Isa. 43:7; 46:10; Rom. 11:36; Rev. 4:11.

15. 1 Kgs. 22:28, 34; Job 1:21; 2:10; 14:5; Psa. 37:23; 139:16; Prov. 16:33; Eccl. 7:14; Isa. 46:10-11; Jer. 10:23; Lam. 3:37-38; Matt. 6:26; 10:29, 30; Acts 17:24-26; Rom. 8:28; Eph. 1:11.

16. Gen. 45:5-8; Deut. 2:30; Ezra 7:6; Prov. 16:1; 19:21; John 19:11.

anything by an act of his will; he is limited and can only act in terms of his nature. Man is not floating about in a vacuum with nothing to "push" against; he operates within the all-encompassing plan of God. It is up against the plan of God that he gets his "footing." God's control of man, however, is not "across the board," as our control of another would have to be. Rather it is a control that cuts across planes: God above and man below. Such a control guarantees man true significance (he is no automaton), while guaranteeing God's true sovereignty (all things issue forth under the direction of His wise counsel). This is not contradiction but mystery – mystery rooted in God's transcendence.

God's control governs both the evil acts of free moral agents,[17] as well as their righteous acts.[18] The classic evidence of this is Peter's statement: "For truly against Your holy Servant Jesus, whom You anointed, both Herod and Pontius Pilate, with the Gentiles and the people of Israel, were gathered together to do whatever Your hand and Your purpose determined before to be done" (Acts 4:27-28).

Though our holy and righteous God is not implicated in sin, nevertheless, He ordains it and controls it toward a good end.[19] God not only ordains all the events of history, he has also ordained the free moral agency of man and the secondary causes associated with all events. The evil act is always that of the individual agent performing it; nevertheless it is also always under the all-controlling power of God. Those who act in an evil manner thereby admit their own responsibility, despite God's ultimate control. Of course, the classic illustration of this

---

17. Gen. 50:20; Exo. 4:21; 9:12,16; Josh. 11:20; Jdgs. 9:23; 1 Sam. 2:25; 16:14; 2 Sam. 17:14; 24:1, 10; 1 Kgs. 12:11, 15; 22:20-23; Matt. 21:42; Luke 22:22; John 12:39-40; 17:12; Acts 3:18; 4:27-28; 13:27-29; Rom. 9:22; 11:8; 1 Pet. 2:8; 2 Pet. 2:12; Jude 4; Rev. 17:17.

18. John 15:5, 16; 1 Cor. 12:6; 15:10; Eph. 1:12; 2:10; Phil. 1:6; 2:12, 13; Heb. 13:21.

19. Greg L. Bahnsen, "The Problem of Evil" (Parts I and II), *Biblical Worldview* 3:9 (Oct. 1991) and 3:11 (Dec. 1991).

is in the crucifixion of Christ, which is definitely the most evil act of history. Yet, it was prophesied and foreordained of God (Acts 2:23; 4:26-28).

The Prophetic Word

It is just this powerful, determinative Word of God that issues forth in prophecy. And that prophecy is not a mere prescience, but is a constantly active, irresistibly causative power in history. "So shall my word be that goeth forth out of my mouth: it shall not return unto me void, but it shall accomplish that which I please, and it shall prosper in the thing whereto I sent it" (Isa. 55:11; cf. Isa. 46:10-11). That powerful word even slays His enemies.[20]

The Restorative Word

As regards the material of prophetic expectation, I will demonstrate in the course of this work that God's Word is also *restorative*. We should note that immediately upon the Fall of Adam in Eden (whence sin entered the human race), the Lord immediately spoke a restorative word of redemption. "And the LORD God said unto the serpent, Because thou hast done this, thou art cursed above all cattle, and above every beast of the field; upon thy belly shalt thou go, and dust shalt thou eat all the days of thy life: I will put enmity between thee and the woman, and between thy seed and her seed; it shall bruise thy head, and thou shalt bruise his heel" (Gen. 3:14-15).[21] Hence the presence of Edenic terminology in many eschatological passages, as we shall see.[22]

---

20. 2 Thess. 2:8; Rev. 19:15; cf. Psa. 2:9 (Rev. 19:15); Isa. 45:23; Jer. 5:14; 23:29; Ezek. 20:47.

21. See fuller discussion of the *protoevangelium* in Chapter 9 below.

22. See: David Chilton, *Paradise Restored: A Biblical Theology of Dominion* (Ft. Worth, TX: Dominion Press, 1985), Part Two: "Paradise: The Pattern for Prophecy."

Conclusion

Thus, God's Word is creative, providential, prophetic, and restorative. There is a real and important sense in which history is "his story." God created the world and man for His own glory (Rom. 11:36; Rev. 4:11). The Scriptures teach that God is in control of history by the exercise of His almighty wisdom and power. In fact, the whole idea of *predictive prophecy* is dependent upon this view of history, in that for any prophesied events to occur requires that all preceding and concurrent related events throughout the world and history must fall into place according to plan, as well. Almost always (Christ and John Baptist being notable exceptions) the person involved in the fulfillment of prophecy is *unaware* that his free action is fulfilling the predetermined prophecy of God.

The Word of the sovereign God is creatively constructive. That is, it brought reality into existence (Gen. 1; Heb. 11:3) and it directs the outworking of all historical processes (Isa. 46:10; 55:11). This two-fold reality – the creative Word and the providential Word – ties in the authority of God's Word to human life. The psalmist notes that the Word of the Lord both sovereignly made and providentially governs the heavens and the earth (Psa. 33:6-11). He also notes that it is His creative and sovereign Word that is the revelation to man of righteousness and justice: "For the word of the Lord is upright; and all His work is done in faithfulness. He loves righteousness and justice" (Psa. 33:4-5a). The word/command of God is the standard of right and wrong obligations, as it was in the garden of Eden.

Even Adam, while untainted by sin, was not an ultimate moral standard, but a derivative one. As Van Til says, Adam was receptively reconstructive of God's Word, rather than creatively constructive. He was to think God's thoughts after Him, on the creaturely level. Even in his unfallen state, he knew that he was created to live by supernatural, positive revelation, not autonomously. The method by which Adam was to know good and evil was to be due to God's interpretive word/command.

6

THE COVENANTS OF REDEMPTION

At that time you were without Christ, being aliens from the commonwealth of Israel and strangers from the covenants of promise, having no hope and without God in the world. (Ephesians 2:12)

Structuring the relationship of God to man and exercising a great influence on the redemptive flow of history is the biblical idea of "covenant." Biblical theologian Geerhardus Vos writes that "redemption and eschatology are co-eval throughout biblical history,"[1] so the covenant concept has a tremendous bearing on eschatology.

Covenantal Scripture

Covenant Defined

A covenant may be defined as *a legal bond, which establishes a favorable relation between parties based on certain specified terms, and which promises blessings for faithful adherence to those terms, while threatening curses for unfaithful departure from them.*[2]

---

1. Geehardus Vos, *The Pauline Eschatology* (Phillipsburg, NJ: Presbyterian & Reformed, [1930] 1991), p. 325.

2. Helpful studies of the covenant in Scripture are found in Ray Sutton's, *That You May Prosper: Dominion By Covenant* (2nd ed.; Tyler, TX: Institute for Christian Economics, 1992) and O. Palmer Robertson, *The Christ of the Covenants* (Phillipsburg, NJ: Presbyterian & Reformed, 1980). Sutton's work demonstrates the formal structure of the

In a covenant, the parties are solemnly sworn to maintain the specified obligations. Scripture notes of God's covenant with Abraham: "Since He could swear by no one greater, He swore by Himself" (Heb. 6:13). As *legal obligations*, favorable covenantal relations can be maintained only by the faithful keeping of the stipulated terms. Of the covenant set before Israel under Moses, we read: "I have set before you today life and prosperity, and death and adversity. . . . I have set before you life and death, the blessing and the curse" (Deut. 34:15,19). Obedience to covenantal demands brings blessings; disobedience brings cursings. Thus, a covenant establishes a *legal* bond that establishes and protects specified rights.[3]

Covenant and Scripture

The Bible is very much a covenant document, as even a cursory reading of Scripture demonstrates. The biblical words for "covenant" appear often in Scripture. The Hebrew *berith* occurs 285 times in the Old Testament, while the Greek word *diatheke* appears thirty times in the New Testament.[4] Thus, it might well be said that "the Biblical category which does the greatest justice to the persistence of God's activity among his

---

covenant from various portions of Scripture. Robertson's work outlines the particular divine covenants as a unifying principle for the structuring of redemptive history. See also: C. Van Der Waal, *The Covenantal Gospel* (Neerlandia, Alberta: Inheritance, 1990).

3. In fact, the Hebrew word for "covenant" (*berith*) is probably from the Akkadian root *beritu*, which means "clasp or fetter," indicating a bond. Moshe Weinfeld points out the difficulty of ascertaining its etymology, but opts for this derivation as the better one. Weinfeld, "*berith*," in G. Johannes Botterwick and Helmer Ringgren, eds., *Theological Dictionary of the Old Testament*, trans. by John T. Willis (Grand Rapids: Eerdmans, 1975), 2:255. A common biblical representation of covenantal inauguration is "to cut" a covenant, indicating the self-maledictory oath and consequent binding obligation resultant therefrom (1 Sam. 11:1, 2; 20:16; 22:8; 1 Kgs. 8:9; 2 Chr. 7:18; Psa. 105:9; Hag. 2:5).

4. Sometimes the Hebrew *berith* is translated either "confederacy" (Oba. 7) or "league" (Josh. 9:6ff; 2 Sam. 3:12ff) In the King James Version New Testament the Greek word for "covenant" (*diatheke*) is sometimes rendered "covenant" and other times (poorly) "testament."

people is *the covenant relation.*[5] That the covenant idea is a dominant biblical theme is held by a host of Bible scholars.[6]

Mutually established covenants were common among the ancients, examples of which are plentiful both in Scripture and in ancient non-biblical texts.[7] By way of example, we might notice the covenants between Abraham and Abimelech (Gen. 21:22-32), Isaac and Abimelech (Gen. 26:26-31), Jacob and Laban (Gen. 31:43-55), Joshua and the Gibeonites (Josh. 9:3-15), and Solomon and Hiram (1 Kgs. 5:12). Such mutually established covenants are similar to modern contracts and treaties, although with some important differences.[8] These human covenants were between roughly equal parties: man to man.

Also revealed in Scripture are the much more important sovereignly established divine covenants. The parties in these are decidedly unequal: the infinite God and finite man. The history-structuring divine covenants of epochal significance in

5. C. H. Dodd, cited by Alan Richards and W. Schweitzer, eds., *Biblical Authority for Today* (London: SCM Press, 1951), p. 201. This is not to say that "covenant" is the unifying principle of Scripture, or of Reformed theology. The Scripture is much too rich and complex to be organized around one principle.

6. For example: Walter Eichrodt, *Theology of the Old Testament*, trans. by J. A. Baker, vol. 1 (Philadelphia: Westminster Press, 1961); Ludwig Köhler, *Old Testament Theology*, trans. by A. S. Todd (Philadelphia: Westminster, 1957), pp. 60ff; Gerhard Von Rad, *Old Testament Theology*, trans. by D. M. G. Stalker, vol. 1 (New York: Harper & Row, 1962); Richardson and Schweitzer, *Biblical Authority for Today*; Robertson, *The Christ of the Covenants*; Willem Van Gemeren, "Systems of Continuity," *Continuity and Discontinuity*, John S. Feinberg, ed. (Westchester, IL: Crossway, 1988), ch. 2. (For a helpful bibliography of historical treatments of covenant theology, see his footnote 1.) T. C. Vriezen, *An Outline of Old Testament Theology*, trans. by S. Neuijen (3rd ed.; Oxford: Blackwell, 1970), pp. 139ff.

7. See M. G. Kline, *Treaty of the Great King* (Grand Rapids: Eerdmans, 1963). G. E. Mendenhall, *Law and Covenant in Israel and the Ancient Near East* (Pittsburgh: Biblical Colloquium, 1955). Delbert R. Hillers, *Covenant: The History of a Biblical Idea* (Baltimore: Johns Hopkins University Press, 1969).

8. Covenant and contract cannot be equated. Contracts are not established by a self-maledictory oath under God. See Gary North, *The Sinai Strategy: Economics and the Ten Commandments* (Tyler, TX: Institute for Christian Economics, 1986), pp. 65-70. See also: Robertson, *Christ of the Covenants*, pp. 127. John Murray, *The Covenant of Grace* (Phillipsburg, NJ: Presbyterian & Reformed, [1953] 1988), pp. 5ff.

Scripture are those established with Adam (Hos. 6:7), Noah (Gen. 6:18),[9] Abraham (Gen. 15:18),[10] Israel (Exo. 24:8), and David (Psa. 89:3).[11] Off in the future from the Old Testament perspective lay the glorious, final, consummative "New Covenant" (Jer. 31:31-34). These divine covenants are unique to the biblical record, for "outside the Old Testament we have no clear evidence of a treaty between a god and his people."[12]

The significance of these covenants for Scripture will be dealt with below in the section demonstrating the relationship of "Covenant and Redemption."

Covenant and Creation

Even the very creation of the world must be understood in terms of covenant. The creation account portrays a covenantal action,[13] even though it does not employ the word "covenant" (*berith*).[14] I argue this on three bases.

First, the *elements* of a covenant are there, even though the word is lacking. When God created Adam, he entered into a blessed relationship (Gen. 1:26-27) with him that established a legal bond on the basis of specified terms (Gen. 2:15-17). In that bond, God promised life for obedience and death for disobedience (Gen. 2:16-17; cf. 3:15-21). This forms the essence of a covenantal relation.

---

9. The nature of that covenant is expanded in Gen. 6:17-22; 8:20-22; 9:1-17.

10. See also: Gen. 12:1-4; 17:1ff.

11. 2 Sam. 7; 23:5; 2 Chr. 6:14-17; 21:7; Psa. 89:3-4; 132:11-18.

12. Ronald E. Clements, *Abraham and David: Genesis 15 and Its Meaning for Israelite Tradition* (Naperville, IL: Allenson, 1967), p. 83.

13. See: Robertson, *The Christ of the Covenants*, pp. 19-21. Willem Van Gemeren, *The Progress of Redemption* (Grand Rapids: Zondervan, 1988), p. 60.

14. The word "covenant" is first used in Genesis 6:18. This should not be assumed an insuperable problem for covenant theology, even by anti-covenantal dispensationalists. One of the universally recognized covenants of Scripture, the Davidic Covenant, lacks the word "covenant" in the accounts of its establishment. See: 2 Sam. 7; 1 Chr. 17.

Second, *later references* actually employing covenantal terminology speak of the creation as a covenantal action.[15] In Jeremiah, we read: "Thus saith the LORD, If ye can break my covenant of the day, and my covenant of the night, and that there should not be day and night in their season" (Jer. 33:20). "Thus saith the LORD, If my covenant be not with day and night, and if I have not appointed the ordinances of heaven and earth" (Jer. 33:25).

As Robertson carefully points out,[16] in Jeremiah 33:25 the Hebrew structure of the verse parallels "ordinances (*huqot*) of heaven and earth" with the "covenant (*berith*) with day and night,"[17] pointing back to the orderly creation ordained of God. This seems clearly to harken back to Genesis 1:14a: "And God said, Let there be lights in the firmament of the heaven to divide the day from the night."

Some might see this as an indicator of the Noahic Covenant mentioned in Genesis 8:22: "While the earth remaineth, seedtime and harvest, and cold and heat, and summer and winter, and day and night shall not cease."[18] But in a passage pressing the same point elsewhere, Jeremiah employs the term "ordinance" (*huqoth*) to speak of the sun, moon, and stars *as bearers of light* (Jer. 31:35), as does Genesis 1, but not Genesis 8. Even the reference to "stars" is lacking in Genesis 8, though appearing in Jeremiah 31:35.

Third, Hosea 6:7a is another passage employing "covenant" in reference to the creation. Speaking of Israel God declares:

---

15. As in the case of the Davidic covenant, it is called a "covenant," even though it is not so designated at its establishment. 2 Sam. 23:5; Psa. 89:3; Isa. 55:3; Jer. 33:21.

16. Robertson, *Christ of the Covenants*, pp. 18-21.

17. *Berith* and *huqoth* are paralleled elsewhere in Scripture: Lev. 26:15; Josh. 24:25; 1 Kgs. 11:11; 2 Kgs. 17:15; Psa. 50:16; 105:10.

18. Interestingly, in Genesis 6:18 the term employed of the "establishment" (Heb., *qum*) of the Noahic covenant may literally mean "*re*-establish." If this is the case, the Noahic covenant would clearly harken back to a formal covenant in the creation in Genesis 1-2. See: W. J. Dumbrell, *Covenant and Creation* (Nashville: Thomas Nelson, 1984), pp. 16-20.

"they like Adam have transgressed the covenant." Although the Hebrew term *adam* may be translated either "Adam" (in particular) or "man" (in general), either would point back to the original covenant with Adam in Eden.[19] Yet the particular man "Adam" seems to be in view here for several reasons.

In the first place, the significance of Adam's sin would bring out the force of the comparison with Israel's rebellion more specifically. Adam's role as the great sinner is familiar to the Jews (Gen. 3). Job 31:33 serves as a parallel: "If I covered my transgressions as Adam, by hiding mine iniquity in my bosom." Furthermore, if "man" were adopted in Hosea 6:7, the verse would be "altogether expressionless."[20] How else could they have sinned than like men? In addition, the reference (*"they* have transgressed") is to Ephraim and Judah (Hos. 6:4), not to the priests. Thus, the contrast is not one between priests and ordinary men, but between "Ephraim and Judah" and the historical Adam.

Certainly the Scriptures are pre-eminently a covenant document. Even the pattern for creation is developed covenantally in the revelation of God.

Covenant and Redemption

The unity of Scripture may be traced in the unity of the covenants, which set forth the overarching Covenant of Grace. The heart of God's "covenants of the promise" (*diathekon tes epaggelias*, Eph. 2:12) is: "I will be your God and you will be My

---

19. For an historical study of the various interpretations of the passage, see: Benjamin B. Warfield, "Hosea vi.7: Adam or Man?" (1903), *The Selected Shorter Writings of Benjamin B. Warfield – I*, John E. Meeter, ed. (Nutley, NJ: Presbyterian & Reformed, 1970), pp. 116-129. Though not unanimously so, according to A. Cohen, Jewish commentators have generally taken the position that Adam's sin in Eden is the historical reference here. See Cohen, *The Twelve Prophets, Hebrew Text, English Translation and Commentary* (London: Soncino Press, 1948), pp. 23ff.

20. Keil and Delitzsch, *The Book of Job* (Grand Rapids: Eerdmans, [1966] 1975), 2:193.

people." This idea occurs a great number of times in Scripture.[21] The redemptive covenants are established in order to
secure a favorable relationship between God and His people.[22]
By means of the covenant, the covenant people become intimately related to the Lord of heaven and earth.[23]

Covenantal development is onion-like, layer upon layer:
"[E]ach successive covenant supplements its predecessors."[24]
We may easily see this in comparing the structural and thematic
continuity between the covenants.[25] For instance, in preparing
for the establishment of the Mosaic covenant, we learn that
"God remembered his covenant with Abraham" (Exo. 2:24).[26]
Under the Davidic Covenant, we find reference to and deliver-

---

21. Gen. 17:7; Exo. 5:2; 6:7; 29:45; Lev. 11:45; 26:12,45; Deut. 4:20; 7:9; 29:13-15;
2 Sam. 7:24; Psa. 105:9; Isa. 43:6; Jer. 24:7; 31:33; 32:38; Ezek. 11:20; 34:24; 36:28;
37:23; Hos. 1:10; Zech. 8:8; 13:9; 2 Cor. 6:18; Rev. 21:3, 7. God's people are his
"special treasure," His "own possession," "his people," and the like, Exo. 19:4,5; Deut.
4:20; 9:26, 29; 32:9; 1 Kgs. 8:51, 53; 2 Kgs. 11:17; 2 Chr. 23:16; Psa. 28:9; 33:12;
78:71; 94:14; Isa. 19:25.

22. This, of course, would not include the pre-Fall Creation Covenant.

23. The covenantal structure of redemption is reflected in the forensic terminology
associated with redemption, such as "judgment/condemnation" (krinein), "justification"
(dikaio), "imputation" (logizomai), "judgment seat" (bema), God as "judge" (dikaois),
judgment based on "law" (nomos), etc. In Acts 16:4 the dogmata kekrimena ("decrees
having been decided upon") is "court-terminology." Vos, Pauline Eschatology, p. 268.

24. Robertson, Christ of the Covenants, p. 28. An earlier dispensationalist position
was that "the dispensation of promise was ended when Israel rashly accepted the law."
The Scofield Reference Bible (New York: Oxford University Press, [1909] 1917), p. 20n.
Rashly accepted? Though recanted by later dispensationalists, this bold statement ("Israel
rashly accepted the law") well illustrates what is still a continuing tendency in dispensationalism to a strong discontinuity between the covenants.

25. In passing, I will note only briefly that the three initial covenants could be
included in the survey to follow, as well. They are all foundational to the outworking of
God's redemptive purpose: The Creation Covenant establishes man as the image of God,
whom God will redeem (Gen. 1:26-28). The Adamic Covenant accounts for the sinfulness of man and the actual initiation of the redemption that will overcome that sin (Gen.
3:15). The Noahic Covenant is a preservative for the world, so that God's redemptive
purpose might be realized (Gen. 8:22).

26. A number of Scriptures speak of the conquest of the Promised Land under the
Mosaic covenant as a development of the Abrahamic: Exo. 3:16, 7; 6:4-8; Psa. 105:8-12,
42-45; 106:45.

ance under the Mosaic Covenant frequently mentioned,[27] as well as to the Abrahamic.[28] And, of course, the relationship of the New Covenant with earlier covenants is contained in the very formula of the New Covenant: "Behold, the days come, saith the LORD, that I will make a new covenant with the house of Israel, and with the house of Judah" (Jer. 31:31[29]).

Interestingly, Ezekiel combines the Abrahamic, Mosaic, and Davidic Covenants in the chapters in which he deals with the New Covenant:

> And David my servant shall be king over them [Davidic]; and they all shall have one shepherd: they shall also walk in my judgments, and observe my statutes, and do them [Mosaic]. And they shall dwell in the land that I have given unto Jacob my servant, wherein your fathers have dwelt [Abrahamic]; and they shall dwell therein, even they, and their children, and their children's children for ever: and my servant David shall be their prince for ever [Davidic]. Moreover I will make a covenant of peace with them; it shall be an everlasting covenant with them [New]: and I will place them, and multiply them, and will set my sanctuary in the midst of them for evermore. (Ezek. 37:24-26)

In the New Covenant era itself, we discover *continuity* with the preceding covenants. Romans 16:20 harkens back to the Adamic Covenant. Second Peter 3:5-7 draws a parallel with the Noahic Covenant. Romans 4:16 founds the New Covenant on the Abrahamic. Romans 3:31 demonstrates the validity of the Mosaic. Romans 15:12 harkens back to the Davidic Covenant. As mentioned above, Paul summed up the various Old Testament covenants as being "the covenants [plural] of the promise [singular]" (Eph. 2:12). There is both a basic unity undergird-

---

27. 2 Sam. 7:6, 23; 1 Kgs. 2:3ff.; Psa. 77:20; 103:7; 105:26; Dan. 9:11, 13; Mic. 6:4.

28. 1 Kgs. 18:36; 2 Kgs. 13:23; 1 Chr. 16:15-18; 29:18; 2 Chr. 20:7; 30:6; Neh. 9:7; Psa. 105:6,9,42; Isa. 41:8; 51:2; Jer. 33:26.

29. See also Ezek. 34:20ff, where the New Covenant is related to the Davidic.

ing the divine covenants, as well as a progressive development in them. Thus, with the coming of the New Covenant in the ministry of Christ, "the fullness of time" has been reached (Gal. 4:4).[30] And these concern redemption – a redemption, as we shall see, that shall overwhelm the world.[31]

The major competitor to covenantal theology among evangelicals today is dispensationalism.[32] Dispensationalism allows the historic, biblical covenants to play a large role in its theology.[33] Yet dispensational theology and covenantal theology are, in the final analysis, "irreconcilable."[34] Indeed, "reformed covenant doctrine cannot be harmonized with premillenarianism"[35] because the dispensationalist's "dispensations are not stages in the revelation of the covenant of grace, but are distinguishingly different administrations of God in directing the affairs of the world."[36] Thus, the major difference between covenantal theology and dispensational theology is that coven-

---

30. "That the Covenant is a basic assumption throughout the New Testament is evident from such passages as: Luke 1:72; 22:20; Matt. 26:28; Mark 14:24; Luke 24:25-27; John 6:45; Acts 2:39; 3:25; Rom. 11:27; 1 Cor. 11:25; 2 Cor. 3:6ff; Gal. 3:14-17; Eph. 2:12; Heb. 7:22; 8:6-13; 9:1, 15-20; 10:16; 12:24; 13:20. The basic idea, nature, and purpose of the covenants made with Abraham, Israel, and David are carried over into the New Covenant and require no explicit repetition in the New Testament." Roderick Campbell, *Israel and the New Covenant* (Tyler, TX: Geneva Divinity School Press, [1954] 1981), p. 53n.

31. See Chapter 10 for the postmillennial significance of these covenants.

32. See Chapter 3 for a definition of dispensationalism.

33. The role of covenants in dispensationalism produces a strange anomaly in the system: it results in a pandemonium of history-structuring devices. History is divided by dispensations, while at the same time it is structured by covenants – *covenants that do not always coincide with the dispensations!* For instance, the Abrahamic Covenant is considered unconditional and everlasting, but the dispensation of promise (the Abrahamic era) is closed by the giving of the Law. See: Robertson, *Christ of the Covenants*, pp. 202ff, 211.

34. Charles Lee Feinberg, *Millennialism: The Two Major Views* (3rd ed.; Chicago: Moody Press, 1980), p. 87.

35. *Ibid.*, p. 69.

36. Charles C. Ryrie, *Dispensationalism Today* (Chicago: Moody Press, 1965), p. 16.

antal theology traces a relentless forward moving, unified, and developmental progress of redemption, generally understood in Reformed theology as the Covenant of Grace. Dispensational theology, however, moves forward rather fitfully, backing up in the final dispensation to a Jewish era involving a temple and (memorial) sacrificial cultus, the millennium.[37]

For better or for worse, the very system name "dispensationalism" tends to throw the focus on the system's discontinuous, compartmental view of history, despite the protests of dispensationalists.[38] This is because "a dispensation is a distinguishable economy in the outworking of God's purpose. If one were describing a dispensation he would include other things, such as the ideas of distinctive revelation, testing, failure, and judgment."[39] So, as noted in the preceding paragraph, dispensations "are not stages in the revelation of the covenant of grace, but are distinguishingly different administrations of God in directing the affairs of the world."[40]

---

37. And this is only after leaping over the parenthetical Church Age, during which the "prophetic time clock" is stopped. Feinberg, *Millennialism*, p. 150.

38. Of covenant theologians, Pentecost writes: "These theologians claimed that they alone had a system that unified the Scriptures into a consistent whole; any other, they insisted, destroyed the unity of the Bible." J. Dwight Pentecost, *Thy Kingdom Come: Tracing God's Kingdom Program and Covenant Promises Throughout History* (Wheaton: Victor, 1990), p. 9.

39. Ryrie, *Dispensationalism Today*, p. 29. This definition is really not true to the system and contradicts Ryrie's assertions elsewhere. For dispensationalism posits *two* purposes in history: "The dispensationalist believes that throughout the ages God is pursuing two distinct purposes: one related to the earth with earthly people and earthly objectives involved, which is Judaism; while the other is related to heaven with heavenly people and heavenly objectives involved, which is Christianity." Ryrie (p. 45) citing Chafer. It is remarkable that this statement allows the *religion of Judaism* (not just Israel the people) to have an equal role in history with the Christian religion – even in the future, post-Christian millennium! And even more remarkable is Ryrie's expressed satisfaction following this statement: "This is probably the most basic theological test of whether or not a man is a dispensationalist, and it is undoubtedly the most practical and conclusive" (p. 45)!

40. *Ibid.*, p. 16.

This necessarily has a fragmenting effect on biblical history. In fact, as one dispensationalist notes, "the more one moves in the continuity direction, the more covenantal he becomes; and the more he moves in the discontinuity direction, the more dispensational he becomes."[41] Certainly, then, *discontinuity in redemptive history* is a major effect of dispensationalism. I will show later that this has a major bearing on the development of the redemptive purpose of God in history and thus on the eschatology of Scripture, when I compare the catastrophically introduced millennial kingdom of dispensationalism and the gradually developed kingdom of postmillennialism.[42]

Although there are many covenants specified and implied in Scripture, the overarching redemptive purpose of God throws a special emphasis on a select few of these. These covenants include the Abrahamic, Mosaic, Davidic, and Christ's New Covenant. It is unfortunate that dispensationalism suggests a secular understanding of some of these covenants, rather than a redemptive one (e.g., the Creation, Adamic, and Noahic Covenants). I will prove this in a later chapter when I focus on the postmillennial outworking of redemption.[43]

Covenantal Obligation

Due to the covenantal influence in Scripture, we learn that man's obligations are not fundamentally individualistic, but rather corporate. As we shall see in later chapters, this fits well with a postmillennial eschatology and its strong view of social responsibility.[44] Here I will outline the case for the societal obligations of covenantalism.

---

41. John S. Feinberg, "Preface," *Continuity and Discontinuity*, p. xii; see also p. 64. Feinberg is a dispensationalist.

42. See Part Three, below.

43. See Chapter 10.

44. See Gary North, *Millennialism and Social Theory* (Tyler, TX: Institute for Christian Economics, 1990). R. J. Rushdoony, *God's Plan for Victory: The Meaning of Postmillennialism* (Fairfax, VA: Thoburn, 1977).

Man was purposefully created as an organic, unified race.[45] Whereas all mankind traces its origin back to Adam, including Eve herself (Gen. 2:21-22; Acts 17:26), animals were created *en masse* (Gen. 1:20-25). Even angels were created *en masse* as nonprocreative individuals (Matt. 22:30).

The organic unity of the human race is vitally important to the redemptive plan of God, as seen in Romans and 1 Corinthians. Adam was the *federal head* of all mankind: a *legal representative*. In him, we are legally and judicially dead (Rom. 5:12-19; 1 Cor. 5:22). Christ is the federal head of all those "chosen out of" (*eklektos*) mankind. In Him, we are legally and judicially declared alive (Rom. 5:15-19; 1 Cor. 15:22). Christ became flesh in order that He might attach himself to the unified race and become its Redeemer (Phil. 2:5ff; Heb. 2:14).[46]

That God's covenant has societal implications may be seen in its being established with Abraham *and his seed* (Gen. 12:1-4). The significance of Israel's organic connection is illustrated in her portrayal as a vine (Psa. 80:8-16; Isa. 5:1-7). In addition, when God made covenant with Israel in the wilderness, it included future generations (Deut. 5:3).

Because of this, God specifically promises covenant blessings and warns of covenant curses running in communities of people. Deuteronomy 28 and Leviticus 26 detail specifics of community curses and blessings, transported from generation to generation and expansively covering the broad community. This covenantal factor is also demonstrated in Israel's history. For example, the whole nation of Israel suffered defeat in war due to the grievous sin of Achan (Josh. 7:1). They were learning corporate responsibility through this "lesson" from God.

---

45. The development of the seed-line in history is a significant aspect of the biblical revelation, as the genealogies of Scripture attest. See especially Matthew 1 and Luke 3.

46. There is no corporate guilt for angels, but neither is there salvation for fallen angels.

Outside of Israel, pagan communities were destroyed for their corporate evil.[47]

Neither may Christianity be properly understood in terms of radical individualism. By God's grace, we are in covenant with Him as a community. This may be seen from a number of angles. (1) We are grafted into the *community* of God's people as a branch into a tree (Rom. 11:17-18). (2) We are adopted into the *commonwealth* of Israel and partake of the covenants of "the promise" (singular, Eph. 2:12-16). Thus, we are included in the "household" of God (Eph. 2:19-22) as stones in a building (1 Pet. 2:5). (3) We are constituted one, inter-related body (1 Cor. 12:12-27). (4) We are part of one, connected vine (John 15:1-8). (5) Our blessings as members of the Christian community flow from our Head, Jesus Christ, through the body to us (Eph. 1:20ff).

The common societal unit among men is the family. Family solidarity involves covenantal succession, as is evident from the following: (1) Marriage, the world's first institution (Gen. 1:26-28; 2:18-24; Matt. 19:4), was established as a permanent obligation among men (Matt. 19:5,6; Gen. 2:24). (2) Adam's fulfillment of his mandate to subdue the earth required family procreation and solidarity (Gen. 1:28). (3) The principle of family solidarity is clearly illustrated in God's sparing the *families* of righteous men during judgments. See the cases of Noah, Abraham, and Lot.[48] (4) Due to this covenant, responsibilities centered around the family. Diligent child training was commanded (Deut. 6:4ff; Psa. 78:1ff; Proverbs, *passim*). Family protection was mandated (Prov. 13:22; 19:14; 1 Tim. 5:8). Three of the Ten Commandments specifically guard the family while the

---

47. Josh. 2:10; 6:21; Exo. 20:16-18; Josh 8:1,2,24-29; 10:29-43; 1 Sam. 15:3. Cf. Lev. 18:24-27. See: Kenneth L. Gentry, Jr., *God's Law in the Modern World: The Continuing Relevance of Old Testament Law* (Phillipsburg, NJ: Presbyterian & Reformed, 1992), ch. 6. Greg L. Bahnsen, *Theonomy in Christian Ethics* (rev. ed.; Presbyterian & Reformed, 1984), Part 7.

48. Gen. 6:8,9,18; 7:1,7; 12:1-3; 17:1,2,7; 19:12-16.

others relate to the family (Exo. 20:12,14,17). (5) Families are declared to be an heritage from the Lord.[49] Fruitfulness is a blessing, whereas barrenness is lamented.[50] (6) God's blessings run in family generations, as may be seen in the cases of Noah, Japheth, Abraham, Rahab, and covenant people in general.[51] By the same token, God's curses also run in family generations.[52]

Because of God's covenantal love, He graciously sanctifies the offspring of the covenant faithful (1 Cor. 7:14; Rom. 14:17). In the New Testament, even, His blessings are framed in terms inclusive of family generations, rather than terms excluding family generations (Acts 2:38,39; 16:31; 11:14).

In all of this, we learn something of the wider obligations of the Christian faith. "We should always bear in mind that there is a collective responsibility, and that there are always sufficient reasons why God should visit cities, districts or nations with dire calamities."[53] In the soil of covenantal corporate responsibility, postmillennial eschatology takes root and grows in the light of God's Word.

Objective Blessedness

The covenantal foundation of the eschatological hope encourages anticipation of God's historical blessings in history.[54] The biblical worldview is concerned with the material world, the here and now. Christianity's interest in the material here and now is evident in that God created the earth and man's

---

49. Psa. 127; 128; Gen. 33:5; 48:9; Isa. 8:18.

50. Gen. 25:41; Exo. 23:26; Deut. 7:14; Psa. 113:9.

51. Gen. 9:9; 9:27; 17:2-7; Josh. 2:12-14; Psa. 103:17,18; 105:8; 115:13,14; 37:25, 26; Prov. 3:33.

52. Exo. 20:5; 34:6,7; Deut. 5:9. Note: Gen. 9:24-25; Hos. 9:11-17; Psa. 109:1,2,9,10; Prov. 3:33.

53. Louis Berkhof, *Systematic Theology* (Grand Rapids: Eerdmans, 1941), p. 260.

54. See Chapter 6, below. See also: North, *Millennialism and Social Theory.*

body as material entities, and all "very good,"[55] Christ came in the flesh to redeem man,[56] His Word directs us in how to live in the present, material world,[57] and God intends for us to remain on the earth for our fleshly sojourn and does not remove us upon our being saved by His grace.[58] As is obvious from these four observations, Christians have a genuine concern with their objective environment.

At death, all men enter the spiritual world, the eternal realm (either heaven or hell).[59] But prior to our arrival in the eternal state, all men live before God in the material world,[60] which He has created for His own glory, as the place of man's habitation.[61] His covenant sanctions (blessings for the righteous; curses for the unrighteous) may, therefore, be expected in history. That is to say, these sanctions are predictable.

The *objectivity* of covenantal blessing, which undergirds the postmillennial eschatology, is clearly set forth in Deuteronomy 28 and Leviticus 26. When God's covenant people are faithful to His Law-word, He will bless them in all areas of life.[62] When they fail Him, His curses will pursue them to overtake them (Deut. 28:15-68; Lev. 26:21-39).

Such blessings are alluded to in a number of places and under a variety of images. Among these blessings are the reduction of disease,[63] abundant food production,[64] temporal lon-

---

55. Gen. 1:1-31; 2:7.

56. Rom. 1:3; 9:5; 1 John 4:1-3.

57. Rom. 12:1-2; Eph. 5:15-17; 2 Tim. 3:16-17.

58. John 17:15; Job 14:5; 2 Cor. 5:9-10.

59. 2 Cor. 5:8; Phil. 1:23; Luke 16:22-23. See Chapter 13 below.

60. 2 Chr. 16:9; Psa. 33:13-15; Prov. 15:3; Acts 17:28; Heb. 4:13. No U. S. Supreme Court "right-to-privacy" decision can alter this truth.

61. Psa. 24:1; 115:16; Prov. 15:3; Dan. 5:23; Acts 25:24-31; Rev. 4:11.

62. Deut. 28:1-14; Lev. 26:3-20, 40-46. Cf. Psa. 37:25; 112:1-3; Prov. 13:22.

63. Exo. 15:26; 23:25; Deut. 7:15; Psa. 103:3.

64. See Exo. 23:24-25; Deut. 8:7-9; Psa. 67:6; Isa. 30:23-24; 65:21-23; Jer. 31:12; Ezek. 34:26-27; 36:29-38; Amos 9:13; Zech. 8:12ff.

gevity,[65] blessings upon offspring,[66] economic prosperity,[67] national stability and peace.[68] In fact, such passages provide the biblical basis of progress in history, not just linear movement, but upward linear progression.[69]

The material things of life must be kept in perspective, but Christ promises they will be given to His people: "But seek first the kingdom of God and His righteousness, and all these things shall be added to you" (Matt. 6:33). He even promises His people that if they leave all for Him, they will receive many times more in this life: "Then Peter said, 'See, we have left all and followed You.' So He said to them, 'Assuredly, I say to you, there is no one who has left house or parents or brothers or wife or children, for the sake of the kingdom of God, who shall not receive many times more in this present time, and in the age to come everlasting life'" (Luke 18:28-30).

Conclusion

The various covenants in Scripture are equally "the covenants of the promise" (Eph. 2:12). The covenant concept runs throughout Scripture. It frames God's creational process, structures His dealings with man, and, most important for this book's thesis, *insures the success of His divine program in history.* This program is not about the defeat of Christ's redemptive work in history. The gospel of salvation, the building of His

---

65. Deut. 4:40; 5:33; 32:46,47; Isa. 65:20; Zech. 8:4.

66. Deut. 5:29; 7:13.

67. Deut. 7:12-16; 8:18; 28:1-15; Psa. 112:3; Prov. 13:22. See Gary North, "An Outline of Biblical Economic Thought," in North, *An Introduction to Christian Economics* (Nutley, NJ: Craig, 1973), ch. 18.

68. Josh. 1:5; Isa. 2:4; Mic. 4:3; Isa. 11:6-9.

69. See the path-breaking economic commentaries on the Bible by Gary North, *The Dominion Covenant* (1982), *Moses and Pharaoh: Dominion Religion Versus Power Religion* (1985), *The Sinai Strategy: Economics* (1986), *Tools of Dominion: The Case Laws of Exodus* (1990). All are published by Institute for Christian Economics.

Church, and the establishment of His comprehensive, world-wide kingdom lead to Christendom.[70]

The decline of covenant theology since the late nineteenth century has led to the decline of Christian influence in society. *Postmillennialism is fundamentally covenantal, presenting a full-orbed Christianity in its pristine authority and power.* The specific covenants of the Old and New Testaments support the postmillennial position, as I will show in greater detail in Chapter 10.

---

70. Kenneth L. Gentry, Jr., *The Greatness of the Great Commission: The Christian Enterprise in a Fallen World* (Tyler, Texas: Institute for Christian Economics, 1990)

7

THE RIGHTEOUSNESS OF GOD

Ye are the salt of the earth: but if the salt have lost his savour, wherewith shall it be salted? it is thenceforth good for nothing, but to be cast out, and to be trodden under foot of men. Ye are the light of the world. A city that is set on an hill cannot be hid. (Matthew 5:13-14)

In the familiar words of our Lord cited above, we learn that Christianity is to act as "salt" and "light" in the world. Covenantal obligations involve both the individual and the community, as I noted in the last chapter. Consequently, the Christian faith ought to have a distinctive, redemption-based, covenant-framed, revelation-controlled system of ethics for both personal and social morality. Because we are commanded to be perfect and holy on the basis of the divine Exemplar (Matt. 5:48; 1 Pet. 1:15), our personal walk and our social theory must reflect the very righteousness of God. But because of dependence on the fallen mind and heart (Eph. 4:17ff; Rom. 1:18ff), a nonbiblical ethic cannot be expected to produce either a righteous personal ethic or righteous social theory. Christianity alone can do this.

Unfortunately, the Christian ethic of our era is confused and disoriented. For instance, a prominent liberal denominational leader has commented: "Biblical ethics and Christian ethics for the church today are not the same thing." Consequently, his church committee was proposing "new moral standards for

sexual behavior" for his denomination.[1] There also are evangelicals who reveal confusion about ethics when they suggest
that the Christian "is not under the law as a rule of life," but
under "wisdom." They state that "law can govern any area of
life, such as civil, family, personal, and religious institutions. On
the other hand, wisdom is advice with no legal penalties."[2]
This leads to an ambiguous and optional ethic: "This is not to
say that you cannot obey the laws given to Moses, but you are
not obligated to them in order to be faithful to God."[3]

This problem in Christian ethics is due to a variety of factors.
One factor, which is perhaps a summation of these, is rooted in
the whole idea of the biblical worldview and its implications for
the Christian approach to culture. Broadly speaking, there have
been three approaches to culture in Christian history. These
approaches may be identified as the *Identificationist Model*, the
Separationist Model, and the *Transformationist Model*.[4]

Three Models for the Christian Worldview

The Identificationist Model essentially represents the position of the left wing of Christianity. It sees the Church's role as
flowing alongside of and sanctifying the evolutionary changes in

---

1. John Carey, Chairman, Special Committee on Human Sexuality, Presbyterian
Church USA. Quoted by Randy Frame in "Sexuality Report Draws Fire: Presbyterian
Church (USA)," *Christianity Today* 35:5 (April, 29, 1991) 37. Charles prefers "Biblical
ethics" in defense of capital punishment: "In the present essay I wish to propose a
test case for the application of Biblical ethics. (It should be noted that the preference
for my choice of terms – a 'Biblical' rather than merely 'Christian' framework – is not
incidental. It suggests a unified ethic that encompasses the full range of Biblical
data.)" J. Daryle Charles, "Crime, the Christian, and Capital Justice," *Journal of the
Evangelical Theological Society*, 38:3 (Sept., 1995): 431.

2. H. Wayne House and Thomas D. Ice, *Dominion Theology: Blessing or Curse?*
(Portland, OR: Multnomah, 1988), pp. 184, 186.

3. *Ibid.*, p. 86.

4. After I had completed this chapter, I came across J. Gresham Machen's article,
"Christianity and Culture," *Princeton Theological Review* 11 (1913) 1-15; reprinted in
What Is Christianity? He also identified these three views: subordination to the prevail-
ing anti-supernatural culture, destruction of culture, and consecration of culture.

culture, and adapting to them. It is wholly this-world in orientation. It adopts the contemporary worldview. Consequently, an unchanging ethic based on Scripture is deemed anathema. The ethic of the Old Testament and the ethic of the New Testament are seen to be but stages in evolving culture, phases in the religious self-awareness of man. Liberation theology and main line denominations are contemporary representatives of this view.

The Separationist Model is representative of the right wing of Christianity. It sees the Church's calling as keeping itself wholly separated from contemporary culture. The focus of this view is on heavenly citizenship, seeing the Church as but a pilgrim community passing through this world to a greater world above. It is essentially retreatist, recognizing the power of sin at work in the world and seeking to avoid staining itself with such tendencies. It concentrates on what it calls a New Testament ethic. Fundamentalism is a notable contemporary representative of this view.

When contrasted to the two views above, the Transformationist Model may be seen to be represented in the truly centrist position of historic, orthodox Christianity. It sees the Church's calling as that of leading human culture to the unfolding of God's creation according to the directives of the Word of God. Such is done with a view to the ethical and spiritual transformation of every area of life. The Transformationist Model sees the significance of this world in light of the world above and seeks to promote God's will being done on earth as it is in heaven. It promotes godly culture in the stead of an ungodly culture. It concentrates on a whole Bible ethic, including God's Law, as opposed to a truncated, separationist, "New Testament only" ethic. Confessional Presbyterianism has been representative of this view. Machen was typical (note 4, above).

Realizing these varying approaches, let us turn to a biblico-theological consideration of the question of the continuing validity of the Law of God in the New Covenant era. Has God changed His covenantal demands in the New Covenant era so as to abolish the Law as the normative standard of Christian ethics? Approaching the question of ethical righteousness from a covenantal perspective, we can discern a transformationist ethic known as Theonomic Ethics.[5] Such an ethic works hand-in-glove with a Bible-based postmillennial eschatology.

The Ultimate Source of Ethics

As I emphasized in the last chapter, the Lord God is a covenant God, and the covenant idea necessarily involves *social* structure. The Law-word of God, therefore, mandates what a moral *person* and a moral *society* should be like. Man has both a personal and a corporate responsibility before God, according to the covenantal structure of God's Law-word. This ultimately is traceable to the very being of God, for He is a tri-unity (hence the Trinity). As the One-in-Three, God is equally interested in individuals (the many: diversity) and in social life (the one: unity).[6]

Our primary concern in this chapter is to concentrate on the matter of formal obligation in ethics: to consider the normative perspective of ethics in our inquiry into the substance of godly morality. What is the ultimate source of moral authority? From whence may we derive a just and defensible moral authority which is at the same time relevant and practical? Is the Christian ethic (what ought to be) practical in light of the Christian eschatology (what will be)?

---

5. For fuller information, see: Greg L. Bahnsen, *By This Standard: The Authority of God's Law Today* (Tyler, TX: Institute for Christian Economics, 1985). See also: R. J. Rushdoony, *The Institutes of Biblical Law* (Nutley, NJ: Craig, 1973) and *Law and Society* (Vallecito, CA: Ross House, 1982). For more succinct introductions, see: Gentry, *God's Law in the Modern World: The Continuing Relevance of Old Testament Law* (Phillipsburg, NJ: Presbyterian & Reformed, 1992). William O. Einwechter, *Ethics & God's Law: An Introduction to Theonomy* (Mill Hall, PA: Preston/Speed, 1995).

6. R. J. Rushdoony, *The One and the Many: Studies in the Philosophy of Order and Ultimacy* (Fairfax, VA: Thoburn Press, [1971] 1978).

The Ultimate Standard of Righteousness

The Christian ethic is a theistic ethic that traces the ultimate source of ethical authority to the transcendent yet also immanent, self-contained ontological Trinity.[7] He alone supplies man with valid law. Consequently, only Christianity can provide universal statements of moral obligation, on the basis of the being of this God. This truth is fundamental to a transformationist ethic and a Reconstructionist postmillennial eschatology.

If there is any moral attribute of God that might be considered a controlling attribute, it is *holiness*. Considering the extreme ends of the spectrum, God's love and His wrath are both controlled by His holiness. Indeed, some systematic theologians deem holiness not to be a moral attribute at all, but rather the consummate perfection of all His moral attributes. The Scripture teaches that our God is a *thrice-holy God* (Isa. 6:3) who cannot look favorably upon iniquity (Hab. 1:13). Because God is such a holy God, ethics is fundamentally important for us as Christians. Not only must we ourselves "prove what the will of the Lord is" (Rom. 12:2) in order to please Him, but also we must be a testimony to the nations, a light for all the world (Matt. 5:14). Ecclesiastes 12:13-14 summarizes man's ethical obligation well when it states: "The conclusion, when all is heard, is: fear God and keep His commandments, because this applies to every person. Because God will bring every act to judgment, everything which is hidden, whether it is good or evil." Furthermore, "the earth is the Lord's, and all it contains, the world, and those who dwell in it. For He has founded it" (Psa. 24:1, 2a). Consequently men owe it to God to seek His good pleasure. Next to justification by the grace of God, that which is most needful to man is *sanctification* by the Holy Spirit

---

7. Cornelius Van Til, *Christian Theistic Ethics* (n.p.: den Dulk Foundation, 1974). R. J. Rushdoony, *By What Standard?* (Tyler, TX: Thoburn Press, [1959] 1983). Greg L. Bahnsen, *Theonomy in Christian Ethics* (2nd ed.; Phillipsburg, NJ: Presbyterian & Reformed, 1984), Part III.

of God, "for without holiness, no man shall see the Lord" (Heb. 12:14). And sanctification necessarily involves the question of ethics.

In addition, Reformed Christians are not interested in "ethics in general." We believe in a supernatural God to Whom we must answer on Judgment Day. Autonomous, neutral ethics is a myth; it must be renounced, as we will see momentarily. But neither are we concerned ultimately with a merely theistic ethic. We believe in the one true God Who has created all things and has graciously revealed Himself in Scripture and in Christ. The God we believe in is the Triune God of Scripture. Theistic forms of non-Christian ethics are as useless and dangerous as atheistic ethics. Our ethical concern, therefore, is with *Christian* theistic ethics.

As Christians, we necessarily have a distinctive metaphysics. We understand all of reality on the basis of the Creator God of Scripture "Who works all things after the counsel of His own will" (Eph. 1:11). Given our distinctive metaphysics, it must follow that we also have a distinctive meta-ethics. Our ethic is rooted in our theology. *It is impossible to have a "neutral" meta-ethic*, contrary to what most secularists have claimed. Ethics is either autonomous (based on self-law) or theonomous (based on divine law). Meta-ethics deals with the principles or philosophy behind ethics. It gives the *ultimate justifications* for ethical theory. Van Til has stated that "the key motif in humanistic ethics is away from the True God." As Van Til argues, all unbelieving systems posit false dichotomies: unsolvable contradictions.

The absolute, infinite, eternal, personal God of Scripture has a character of infinite moral goodness, perfection, and purity. Summarily stated, God is infinitely holy,[8] good,[9] and righteous.[10] He is such *in and of Himself*. His own intrinsic being is

---

8. 1 Sam. 2:2; Isa. 57:15; Psa. 99:9; John 17:11; Rev. 15:4.

9. Psa. 145:9-16; Matt. 5:45; Mark 10:18.

10. Ezra 9:15; Psa. 145:17; Jer. 12:1.

the standard of "holiness," "goodness," and "righteousness." If He were not the standard, there would be a principle independent of and more ultimate than God; God would cease to be God. Thus, God sovereignly determines right and wrong from within His own moral being and character. Good is good because God says so, based on His character.

The Proximate Standard of Righteousness

A fundamental theological assertion of orthodoxy is: the unity of God. Consequently, no reason flows from this unified God that either compels us or predisposes us to expect that His one creation has two plans operative in its historical progress. We should reject all ethical systems that propose two systems of law or two decrees of God. I have in mind here the dualistic theory of a universally logical natural law for non-Christians (Gentiles) and Bible-revealed law for Christians.

Man's sanctification (moral restoration) is *definitive, progressive, and final*. One God, one covenant law: through time and across borders. The successive covenants of Scripture really record for us a gradual historical unfolding of *one overarching covenant*, rather than the successive, compartmental establishing of distinctively different capsule covenants. This is clearly expected in the initial covenant directive of God for history that flows out of the Genesis 3:15 curse, which mentions only one basic struggle between two seeds, the Satanic and the Messianic.

This also is clearly asserted in Paul's argument in Ephesians, chapter 2. In this passage, Paul speaks not of the establishing of a new and distinct community separate from Israel, but of God's annexing of additional people – the Gentiles – into His one people. He speaks in verse 12 of "the covenants of the promise" (Greek), which defined His singular purpose. In verses 14-16, he speaks of the removal of the dividing wall between Jew and Gentile, so that the Gentiles might be included in God's one redemptive purpose. In verses 19-22, he speaks of *the merging of these two peoples into one, indivisible temple*.

Thus, the very unity of God's covenantal dealings with man flows out of the unitary being of God, as well as the explicitly revealed plan of God. These truths should predispose us to assume *continuity*, as opposed to discontinuity, in the ethical dictates of God.

We may summarily state that God's Law is binding (in that we are obliged to obey it for our sanctification), relevant (in that all our Lord does is governed by all-wisdom and all-knowledge, thus making His Word practical for all times and applicable for all situations), when properly interpreted (taking into account the full significance, purpose, and situation of the original intent of the various laws individually considered) and properly applied (the unfolding of redemptive history must be taken into account and the New Testament precepts and principles must be given their full significance). Thus, the details of the Law are essential to law-keeping (they form an essential part of the Law, as parts to the whole), and are meant to be equitably observed by man on the personal, social, and civil levels of human existence.

The focal standard of Christian theistic ethics, then, is the Law of God. God's Law is the transcript of His holiness, as is evident from its own nature:

(1) The Law represents the presence of God. God's Law is the revelational expression of His holy character and the moral representation of His presence to man. The summary statement of His Law, the Ten Commandments, was written by the very finger of God, as no other portion of Scripture was.[11] Consequently, bearing His own divine imprint, it necessarily shares His moral perfections. This truth is underscored by the fact that the Ark of the Covenant, which was housed in the Holy of Holies in the center of Israel, contained within it the summary of the Law of God, the Ten Commandments written on

---

11. Exo. 31:18; 32:16; Deut. 4:13; 9:10; 10:4.

stone.[12] At the most holy place of Israel, where the Shekinah glory of God was resident, God's Law was housed as an expression of God's holy presence among and will for His people.

(2) The Law reflects the character of God. The Law which He gives to His people is a transcript of His holy character, possessing the very moral attributes of God Himself. God is good,[13] holy,[14] perfect,[15] righteous,[16] just,[17] and spiritual.[18] Likewise, His Law is good,[19] holy,[20] perfect,[21] righteous,[22] just,[23] and spiritual[24]

(3) The Law expresses the legal relation between God and His people. The Law of God is described in Scripture as the Book of the Covenant (Heb. 9:19). Because of this, the Law of God lies at the heart of the New Covenant, which has been in effect since the crucifixion of Christ.[25] "I will put *my law*[26] in their inward parts, and write it in their hearts (Jer. 31:33). The biblical ethic, therefore, is constituted as a *covenantal theonomy*. The normative center of Christian ethics and morality can be noth-

---

12. Deut. 10:5; 31:25ff.

13. Psa. 143:10; Mark.10:18.

14. Isa. 6:3; Rom. 7:12; Rev. 15:4.

15. 2 Sam. 22:31; Psa. 18:30; Matt. 5:48.

16. Deut. 32:4; Ezra 9:15; Psa. 116:5.

17. Deut. 32:4; Psa. 25:8, 10; Isa. 45:21.

18. John 4:24; Jer. 31:3.

19. Deut. 12:28; Psa. 119:68; Rom. 7:12, 16.

20. Num. 15:40; Rom. 7:12.

21. Psa. 19:7; Jms. 1:25 (cf. 2:8-12).

22. Deut. 4:8; Psa. 19:7; Rom. 2:26; 8:4.

23. Prov. 28:4, 5; Zech. 7: 9-12; Rom. 7:12.

24. Rom. 7:14; 1 John 3:24; Rom. 8:4.

25. Matt. 26:28; Mark 14:24; Luke 22:20; 1 Cor. 11:25; 2 Cor. 3:7ff; Heb. 8:6ff.

26. The Law of Moses is identified time and time again as the Law of Jehovah: e.g., Deut. 30:10; Josh. 24:26; 2 Kgs. 10:31; 17:13; 21:8; 1 Chr. 22:12; 2 Chr. 6:16; 31:21; Ezra 7:6, 12, 14, 21; Neh. 8:8, 18; 9:3; 10:28, 29; Psa. 78:1; 81:4; 89:30; 119:34, 77, 92, 97, 109, 174; Isa. 1:10; Jer. 6:19; 9:13; 16:11; 26:4; 31:33; 44:10; 22:26; Dan. 6:5; Hos. 4:6; 8:1.

ing less than the whole law of God as revealed in Scripture, including the Mosaic Law.

The Continuing Validity of God's Law

It is important to recognize that the Law continues as the moral standard of righteousness into the New Testament and throughout the New Covenant era. In broad evangelicalism today, as in the past, there is a tendency to reduce or deny the role of the Mosaic law in discussions of social righteousness. In fact, there is widespread antipathy to the Mosaic law. Yet a strong and compelling case can be made for its use today.

In Matthew 5:13-16, Christ calls His Church to exercise cultural significance.[27] He sovereignly declares that His followers are to be "the salt of the earth." *Salt* is both a preservative and a flavor-enhancer. The imagery here portrays the Church's calling to preserve the good of human culture and to enhance all of life. We are not called to be wholly separate from the world in the sense of avoiding involvement in it. Rather, we are to be a vital and distinctive aspect of it, just as salt is distinctively present in the flavoring of food. Indeed, He says that if we do not do so we are "good for nothing" (v. 13). In short, Christ has denied the moral legitimacy of the Separationist Model.

In verses 14-16, He calls us to be "the light of the world." *Light*, the first aspect of the original Creation, is a positive and penetrating energy that dispels darkness and brings things into clear focus. The Christian's light exhibits the glory of God (v. 16). Light is essential for life itself and for direction. Paul re-

---

27. For a detailed exposition of the passage, see: Bahnsen, *Theonomy in Christian Ethics*, ch. 2, and Bahnsen, *No Other Standard: Theonomy and Its Critics* (Tyler, TX: Institute for Christian Economics, 1991), Appendix A: "The Exegesis of Matthew 5." J. Daryl Charles, "The Function of Matthew 5:17-20 in the Mathean Gospel," *The Journal of the Evangelical Theological Society*, 12:2 (1989): 213-266. Greg L. Bahnsen, "Theonomy," in Willem VanGemeren, ed., *The Law, the Gospel, and the Modern Christian: Five Views* (Grand Rapids: Zondervan, 1993). For a catalog of Greg L. Bahnsen tapes and educational materials on the topic, write to: Covenant Media Foundation, 4425 Jefferson Ave., Suite 108, Texarkana, AR 71854.

flects this idea in Ephesians, chapters 4-5. In Ephesians 5:11, he calls us to "expose the works of darkness."

But these are general exhortations to holy living before God and to His glory. A pair of specific normative questions remain: (1) How may we properly be the salt of the earth? (2) How may we properly be the light of the world? Jesus gave answers. Immediately following upon these general directives, the Lord provides the specifics needed, when He directly affirms the Law's validity in Matthew 5:17-19.

> Think not that I am come to destroy the law, or the prophets: I am not come to destroy, but to fulfil. For verily I say unto you, till heaven and earth pass, one jot or one tittle shall in no wise pass from the law, till all be fulfilled. Whosoever therefore shall break one of these least commandments, and shall teach men so, he shall be called the least in the kingdom of heaven: but whosoever shall do and teach them, the same shall be called great in the kingdom of heaven.

In the context of this statement, Jesus speaks of ethical conduct and urges righteousness in order to glorify God (cf. Matt. 5:16, 21ff). In this regard, He specifically says He has not come to "destroy" the "law or the prophets." The word "destroy" (*kataluo*, v. 17) means to "do away with, abolish, annul, make invalid."[28] Instead, He has come to do the very opposite, for He employs the strong adversative "but" (*alla*, v. 17) to set up a contrast. He has not come to destroy but "to fulfill" (v. 17). Jesus here contrasts "fulfill" with "destroy."

"Fulfill" cannot in this context mean "to live out" or "complete" the Law, so as to do away with it, for it is contrasted with "destroy." It provides strong contrast, as in Matthew 10:34, which exactly parallels the Matthew 5:17 structure. There Jesus

---

28. W. F. Arndt and F. W. Gingrich, *A Greek-English Lexicon of the New Testament and Other Early Christian Literature* (Chicago: University of Chicago Press, 1957), p. 415.

says: "Think not that I am come to send peace on earth: I came not to send peace, but a sword." Just as sending a sword is the opposite of sending peace, so "to fulfill" is the opposite of "to destroy."

The fulfillment in view here, then, must mean either one of two things: (1) It may mean Christ came to "confirm" or "establish" the Law.[29] If this is the meaning (and it certainly fits the context), it parallels Romans 3:31: "Do we then make void the law through faith? God forbid: yea, we establish the law" (Rom. 3:31). And surely Christ would not be contradicted by Paul. Or: (2) it may mean "fill up to full measure."[30] This would indicate restoring it to its true meaning, in opposition to Pharisaic distortions (Matt. 5:20[31]). Both of these interpretations are compatible, as well as contextually justifiable.

"For" (*gar*, v. 18) introduces an explanation of the statement in verse 17. Christ here emphatically declares *the continuing validity of the Law*, for it will last until "heaven and earth pass away" (v. 18). This indicates the greater stability of the Law in comparison to that of the world (cf. Eccl. 1:4; Psa. 104:5; 119:-90).

His reference to the "jot" and "tittle" (v. 18) is important. This statement emphatically declares that the smallest aspects of the Law will not be annulled. "Till all be fulfilled" (v. 18) parallels "heaven and earth pass away" and may literally be translated: "Until all things be accomplished." His prohibition against any tampering with the "least commandment" (v. 19) repeats the emphasis of the small aspects of the Law in order to show its binding significance.

---

29. Dalman gives the meaning "confirm," according to Arndt and Gingrich, *Lexicon*, p. 677.

30. Under the "fulfill" nuances in the *pleroo* entry, Arndt and Gingrich note of Matthew 5:17: "[D]epending on how one prefers to interpret the context, *pleroo* is understood here either as *fulfill* = do, carry out, or as *bring to full expression* = show it forth in its true mng., or as *fill up* = complete." Arndt and Gingrich, *Greek-English Lexicon*, p. 677.

31. Cf. Matt. 15:3-9; 23:23.

Following this strong statement of the Law's validity, Christ rebuts scribal distortions of the Law: their adherence to oral tradition (Matt. 5:21ff). He is not criticizing adherence to the Law. Note: (1) The contrast drawn in Matthew 5:21-47 is between that which is "said of old" or "said by the ancients" (*ekousate hoti errethe tois archaiois*) and that which Christ says (*ego de lego*). The contrast is not between what "is written" (*gegraptai*, which is the normal manner of speaking of God's Word[32]) and what Christ says. The contrast is between *Christ's words* and *rabbinic tradition* (cf. Matt. 15:1-8). (2) He had just made a strong statement as to the Law's continuing validity. Exegetical consistency requires that Matthew 5:21ff not be viewed as undermining His teaching on the permanence of the Law of God.

Christ emphatically taught the Law's continuing relevance. Even the little tithes are important (Matt. 23:23). The Law is the Golden Rule of service to God and man (Matt. 7:12; 22:36-40). He even upholds the Law's civil function (Matt. 15:3-6).

The New Testament Confirmation of the Law

The broader New Testament confirmation of the Law may be illustrated from a number of angles.

The New Testament expressly confirms the Law. Christ based His teaching on the Law.[33] Even the details of the Mosaic case laws are cited by the Apostles as binding directives.[34] Paul, the Apostle of Faith, declares that faith confirms the Law (Rom. 3:31). He even speaks of the perfection of the Law for the New Testament people (Rom. 7:12, 14).

Christian conduct is based on Law obedience. Law obedience defines the Golden Rule of social conduct (Matt. 7:12) and

---

32. Matt. 2:5; 4:4, 6, 7, 10; 11:10; 21:13; 26:24, 31.

33. Matt. 7:12; 12:5; 19:4; Luke 10:26; 16:17; John 8:17.

34. 1 Tim. 5:17 (Deut. 25:4), 2 Cor. 6:14 (Deut. 22:10), Rom. 10:6-8 (Deut. 30:11-13), Acts 23:1-5 (Exo. 22:28; Lev. 19:15; Deut. 25:2); 1 Cor. 14:34.

characterizes the conduct of love.[35] Keeping God's commandments is important to holy living,[36] in that it promotes spirituality,[37] and evidences holiness, justice, and goodness.[38]

Gospel preaching depends on the relevance of the Law. The Law of
God has a multiple usefulness for the Christian today. It defines
sin[39] and then convicts men of sin,[40] condemns transgression,[41] drives men to Christ,[42] restrains evil,[43] guides sanctification,[44] and serves as the standard for Judgment Day.[45]
Consequently, he who is not subject to the Law of God in the
New Covenant era is at enmity with God (Rom. 8:7).

The Universality of the Law of God

A frequently heard objection to applying God's Law today is
that it was expressly designed and intended for use only in Old
Covenant Israel. Its relevance therefore was only for the special
redemptive nation in pre-Christian times, and for no other.
This view is inherently dispensational – even when argued by
Reformed theologians.

Dispensationalists argue: "The stipulations of Sinai were not
for the nations in general but to a people under grace. . . .
Since the nations around Israel were not called to adopt the
Mosaic Covenant, it seems evident that the pagan nations would

---

35. Matt. 22:36-40; Rom. 13:10; Gal. 5:14; Jms. 2:8.

36. 1 Cor. 7:19; 1 John 2:3,4; 5:3.

37. Rom. 7:12, 16; 8:3-4.

38. Rom. 2:13; Heb. 2:2; 1 Tim. 1:8-10; Heb. 8:10.

39. 1 John 3:4; Rom. 5:13; 7:7. Cf. Matt. 7:23; Titus 2:14; Rom. 3:20 ("iniquity"
is literally "lawlessness").

40. Matt. 19:16-24; John 7:19; Acts 7:53; Rom. 7:7, 9-11; Jms. 2:9; 1 John 3:4.

41. Deut. 11:26, 28; Rom. 4:15; 7:10; Gal. 3:10; Jms. 2:10.

42. Rom. 7:10; Gal. 3:24.

43. Psa. 119:11; 1 Tim. 1:8-10.

44. Lev. 20:8; Psa. 119:105; Prov. 6:23; Rom. 8:4; 1 Cor. 6:21.

45. Matt. 7:23; 13:41; Rom. 2:12-15; Jms. 2:10-12. For the Final Judgment, see:
Chapter 13 below.

not be judged by the law of Moses."[46] Even some reformed theologians suggest that: "Israel *as a nation* was chosen by God 'out of all the peoples on the face of the earth to be his people, his treasured possession' (Dt 7:6). No other nation of the ancient or modern world is like Israel in its place in redemptive history. . . . Before applying a case law from the Old Testament today, therefore, we must consider not only cultural adaptations but also discontinuities that result because of the difference in redemptive status between Israel and any modern society."[47]

The dispensationalist objection (above) confuses *moral commandments* and *covenantal form*. Theonomists have always insisted that the moral commands are distinguishable from the covenantal system in which they are found. For example, in both the New Testament and the Old Testament, we are commanded to love father and mother (cf. Deut. 5:16 and Eph. 6:2). This does not mean that the Old Covenant and the New Covenant are the same! The Old Covenant *form*, which included the sacrificial system and such-like, which was established *only* with Israel, encoded numerous divinely ordained moral requirements, which are the *perpetually obligatory commandments of God*. Moral requirements must be distinguished from the historical and redemptive trappings in which they are found. Moral commandments (justice-defining) are distinguishable from distinctive ceremonial laws (redemption-expounding).[48]

We may urge a *prima facie* reason when insisting upon a *continuity* between God's expectations for Israel's rulers and for pagan rulers outside of Israel: (1) God created the whole world

---

46. House and Ice, *Dominion Theology*, pp. 128, 129.

47. Tremper Longman III, "God's Law and Mosaic Punishments Today," *Theonomy: A Reformed Critique*, William S. Barker and W. Robert Godfrey, eds. (Grand Rapids: Zondervan, 1990), pp. 47, 48.

48. Hos. 6:6; 1 Sam. 15:22; Psa. 51:14-17; Prov. 21:3; Isa. 1:10-17. See: Bahnsen, in Bahnsen and Kenneth L. Gentry, Jr., *House Divided: The Break-up of Dispensational Theology* (Tyler, TX: Institute for Christian Economics, 1989), ch. 3. See also: F. F. Bruce, *Epistle to the Hebrews* (Grand Rapids: Eerdmans, 1964), pp. 28ff.

and has a right to its governance (Gen. 1; 18:25; Psa. 24:1). Thus, Scripture represents Him as the King of all nations.[49] (2) He is one God, with but one holy will (Deut. 6:4ff; Isa. 46:10ff). (3) He is no respecter of persons in terms of His justice.[50] (4) The Scripture is silent on any other ethical standard being applied to the nations beyond Israel. But the matter is not one left solely to *prima facie* considerations.

God's Law was, in fact, designed to be *a model for the nations:* "Therefore be careful to observe them; for this is your wisdom and your understanding in the sight of the peoples who will hear all these statutes, and say, 'Surely this great nation is a wise and understanding people.' For what great nation is there that has God so near to it, as the LORD our God is to us, for whatever reason we may call upon Him?"[51] The Law was a model for the nations beyond Israel (Deut. 4:5ff). It must be spoken before kings (Psa. 119:46; cf. 2:9ff). It is a "light" to the whole world (Isa. 51:4), despite the fact the entire earth has transgressed it (Isa. 24:5).[52] Were not the Canaanites judged for its breach (Lev. 18:24-27; Deut. 12:29-31[53])? By it are not all the wicked condemned (Psa. 119:118-119; Rom. 3:19)? Should not the nations follow it so as to receive God's blessings (Jer. 12:14-17)?

God is said to judge the world in *righteousness*, the fundamental ethical quality of God's Law (Psa. 9:7-8; 98:9; Amos 1:3-2:3) Interestingly, the rulers of Babylon were condemned on the same basis as those of Israel by the prophets (e.g., cf. Hab. 2:12 with Mic. 3:10). This indicates *a parity of standard* employed

---

49. Psa. 47:2, 7ff; 22:28; 83:18; 99:2; 113:4; Mal. 1:14.

50. Psa. 119:118; Rom. 2:11,12. See also: 2 Chr. 19:7; Job 34:19; 37:24; Eph. 6:9; 1 Pet. 1:17.

51. Deut. 4:6-7. See also: 1 Kgs. 10:1, 8-9; Isa. 24:5; 51:4; Psa. 2:9ff; 47:1-2; 97:1-2; Psa. 94:10-12; 119:46, 118-119; Prov. 16:12; Eccl. 12:13.

52. E. J. Young, *The Book of Isaiah* (Grand Rapids: Eerdmans, 1969), 2:156-157.

53. P. C. Craigie, *The Book of Deuteronomy* (NICOT) (Grand Rapids: Eerdmans, 1976), pp. 219-220.

in the judgment of both nations. As a matter of fact, God's judgment upon the pagan nations of the Old Testament was rooted in the universality and equity of His Law. Often the prophetic condemnations were applied to whole pagan cultures due to their disobedience to God (Isa. 14:4-20; 19:1, 13, 14, 22; 30:33). Sodom was a city that was destroyed for its "unlawfulness" (2 Pet. 2:6-8). Thus, Sodom serves as a paradigm in Scripture for God's just judgment upon unlawfulness (Deut. 19:23; Isa. 1:9-10; Jer. 23:14; Lam. 4:6; Ezek. 16:46-56; Amos 4:11; Zeph. 2:9; Matt. 10:15; Jude 7; Rev. 11:8). Nineveh was threatened with God's judgment for its wickedness in God's sight (Jon. 3; Luke 11:30, 32). His righteous standards applied to it.

In their better moments – under the influence of God's Spirit – pagan rulers acknowledged the just rule of God's Law. Cyrus of Persia commanded all the nations to serve God (Dan. 6:25ff). Nebuchadnezzar told the nations that God rules over all and demands righteousness from kings (Dan. 4:1, 25ff). Artaxerxes commanded Ezra to appoint magistrates "beyond the River" which would enforce God's Law (Ezra 7:25ff). Ezra then praised him for this (Ezra 7:27).

Most importantly, the moral justification for Israel's expulsion of the Canaanites from the land rests upon the Canaanites' breach of God's Law (Lev. 18:24-27). In this passage, Israel is threatened with the same punishment as the Canaanites if they commit the lawless acts of the Canaanites. Again, we clearly see a parity of standard employed in the judgment of pagan nations, as in the judgment of Israel.[54] This comports well with the universal call to submission to God's will in Psalm 2.

Thus, we see that the spiritual, temporal, and geographical separation of Israel from pagan states does not effect a separation of moral obligation. Because of this, the nations around Israel are often judged for breaching God's moral standards, but never for breaching the Mosaic covenantal form. They are

---

54. See also: Deut. 7:5-6, 16, 25; 8:11-20; 9:4-5; 12:1-4, 29ff.

judged for such things as slave trade, loan abuse, witchcraft, and other non-ritual sins.⁵⁵ The same truth may be seen earlier in Abraham's day in the judgment of Sodom and Gomorrah, Genesis 19:15 (2 Pet. 2:9). Are the Ten Commandments binding upon pagans, despite the Decalogue's beginning with a distinct reference to Israel's redemption from pagan bondage (Exo. 20:1-3; Deut. 5:6-7)?

People from all nations are under obligation to God's Law today: Romans 1:32 (this speaks of the complex of sins preceding, not any one particular sin); 2:12-15; 3:19; 12:19-13:10; 1 Timothy 1:8-11. This is expected in light of the coming of the Messiah (Isa. 2:3-4). God's Law in our era is considered to be "just" (Rom. 7:12; Heb. 2:2) and "good" (Rom. 7:12; 1 Tim. 1:8).⁵⁶

The Civil Magistrate and God's Law

Church and State were separate under the Mosaic Law. There was a distinction between the civil ruler, Moses, and the priestly head, Aaron; between the offices of priest and king; between the temple and palace: 1 Samuel 13:11; 2 Chronicles 19:5-11; 26:16-21. Yet the Law was the standard of civil justice. The same is true in the New Testament era, as an analysis of Romans 12 and 13 shows.

In Romans Paul speaks to the problem of evil in society: "Repay no one evil [*kakon*] for evil [*kakou*]" (Rom. 12:17). He urges them: "Beloved, do not avenge [*ekdikountes*] yourselves, but rather give place to wrath [*orge*]" (Rom. 12:19a). Why? "For it is written, 'Vengeance [*ekdikesis*] is Mine, I will repay,' says the Lord" (Rom. 12:19). Thus, he urges the Christian not to take

55. Lev. 18:24-27; Deut. 7:5-6, 16, 25; 12:1-4; 19:29-32; Amos 1:6 (Exo. 21:16; Deut. 24:7); Nah. 3:4 (Exo. 22:18; Lev. 19:21); Hab. 2:6 (Exo. 22:25-27; Deut. 24:6, 10-13); Hab. 2:12 (cf. Mic. 3:10).

56. See: David E. Holwerda, *Jesus & Israel: One Covenant or Two?* (Grand Rapids: Zondervan, 1995), pp. 138-139.

the law into his own hands: "Be not overcome of evil [*kakon*]" (Rom. 12:21). He then engages a discussion of the God-ordained role of the civil magistrate as God's avenger.[57]

In Romans 13 the matter of the civil magistrate is approached prescriptively, rather than descriptively.[58] As such, he has been "ordained of God" (Rom. 13:2) so that "he does not bear the sword in vain. He is, in fact, *God's minister*, an avenger [*ekdikos*] to execute wrath [*orgen*] on him who practices evil [*kakon*]" (Rom. 13:4). Clearly, then, the magistrate is to *avenge* the *wrath of God* against those who practice *evil* (Rom. 13:4, 6).

As he continues Paul makes express reference to the Law of God, citing four of the Ten Commandments (Rom. 13:9a) and a summary case law from Leviticus 19:18 (Rom. 13:9b). Finally, he concludes the thought regarding personal vengeance, which he began in Romans 12:17-19: "Love does no harm [*kakon*, "evil"] to a neighbor; therefore love is the fulfillment of the law" (Rom. 13:10). This involves appropriate social conduct that is incumbent upon all men, especially Christians – conduct that avoids "carousing and drunkenness" and "sexual promiscuity and sensuality" (Rom. 13:13).

His reference to God's Law[59] in this context is most important. Ultimately, God's eternal vengeance is according to His holy Law (cf. Rom. 2:3, 5-6, 12-15), a substantial portion of which is encoded in the Mosaic Law. Proximately and mediatorially, however, God's temporal "minister," the civil magistrate, must mete out the "just reward" (Heb. 2:2; cf. Rom. 7:12; 1 Tim. 1:8) for those for whom the penalties of the Law were designed: evil-doers. Paul specifies this even more particularly

---

57. The very contextual flow (Rom. 12:17ff leads directly to Rom. 13:1ff) is validated by lexical similarity between the two chapters.

58. Gentry, "Civil Sanctions in the New Testament," *Theonomy: An Informed Response*, Gary North, ed. (Tyler, TX: Institute for Christian Economics, 1991), ch. 6.

59. Earlier he deems this Law: the standard for Judgment Day (Rom. 2:12-16), "established" (Rom. 3:31) calls it "holy, just, and good" (Rom. 7:12), and the pattern of spiritual sanctification (Rom. 8:3-4).

elsewhere: "The Law is not made for a righteous person, but for the lawless and insubordinate, for the ungodly and for sinners, for the unholy and profane, for murderers of fathers and murderers of mothers, for manslayers, for fornicators, for sodomites, for kidnappers, for liars, for perjurers, and if there is any other thing that is contrary to sound doctrine."[60] And all of this was "according to the glorious gospel of the blessed God which was committed to my trust" (1 Tim. 1:9-11), not according to a passé example.

The theonomic position is that God's Law is the standard for justice in all areas of life, *including criminal penology* (if supported by careful exegesis of the text of each penal sanction and subject to New Testament controls). We may legitimately deduce this from the Romans 12-13 passage. In fact, a self-conscious refusal to comment on this passage is a common failure on the part of those who criticize theonomy's view of civil government.

Conclusion

Given the fact that God is Creator and Judge, and that man is His creature, the very fact that God has uttered the Law obligates man to keep it. God's Law is ethically self-attesting and cannot be questioned, appealed, ignored, or replaced. The *sanctity* of the Law is underscored by the covenantal warning (*sanctions*) attached, which prohibits its alteration by addition or subtraction (Deut. 4:2; 12:32). It is the covenantal Word of God, not of man; it must be kept inviolable.

In short, the Christian is obligated on the basis of the fact of God and His covenant to keep the whole law of God because it is a pattern for both personal sanctification and social right-

---

60. A case may be made for Paul's generally following the order of the Ten Commandments. H. D. M. Spence, "I and II Timothy," *Ellicott's Commentary on the Whole Bible*, Charles John Ellicott, ed., 8 vols. (Grand Rapids: Zondervan, rep. n.d.), 7:180. At the very least, it may be said that "the apostle now gives a summary of the law of the Ten Commandments." William Hendriksen, *I and II Timothy and Titus: New Testament Commentary* (Grand Rapids: Baker, 1957), p. 67.

eousness. The call to follow the biblical pattern of ethics is to follow it in all of its far-reaching details. Obedience must not be arbitrarily cut short by personal desire, preconceptions, or complacency, or by ecclesiastical, traditional, cultural situation, or emotional appeal. There is one covenant and one law.

God loves us in a specific and extensive fashion; He is concerned for the details of our lives (Matt. 10:24-33). He expects us to respond with an all-encompassing devotion to Him by loving Him with all our heart, soul, mind, and strength (Mark 12:33). We believe in the ubiquity of ethics: every word or deed is a moral action, whether we eat or drink or whatever we do (1 Cor. 10:31). This is because these are done in God's world either for or against Him.[61] All words and deeds are subject to judgment (Matt. 12:36; 2 Cor. 5:10).

Consequently, God does not deliver to us some broad, general, vague moral principles. Rather, He reveals to us in His Law very extensive, specific, and all-encompassing commands. The Law is explicit in regard to moral directives and correctives. Man is given concrete standards possessing ultimate authority over man's ethical guidance in personal and social ethics. Non-Christian ethics has long divided between facts and values. But such cannot be the case in Christian ethics. The Creator God of all facts is also the Righteous God of all values. There is no divorce between metaphysics and ethics in Christianity.

It is the well-known Law of God that the prophets saw as established in the future Messianic Kingdom (a consequence of the work of Christ and the spread of the gospel). In Isaiah 2:2-4, we read of the glory of the Messianic future:

> Now it shall come to pass in the latter days that the mountain of the Lord's house shall be established on the top of the mountains, and shall be exalted above the hills; and all nations shall

---

61. Matt. 12:30; Luke 9:50; 11:23.

flow to it. Many people shall come and say, "Come, and let us go up to the mountain of the LORD, to the house of the God of Jacob; he will teach us His ways, and we shall walk in His paths." For out of Zion shall go forth *the law*, and the word of the LORD from Jerusalem. He shall judge between the nations, and shall rebuke many people; they shall beat their swords into plowshares, and their spears into pruning hooks; Nation shall not lift up sword against nation, neither shall they learn war anymore.

In Jeremiah 31:33-34, we discover the spiritual application of that righteous Law to the very heart of man, as a vital aspect of the saving work of God:

"But this is the covenant that I will make with the house of Israel: After those days," says the LORD, "I will put My law in their minds, and write it on their hearts; and I will be their God, and they shall be My people. No more shall every man teach his neighbor, and every man his brother, saying, 'Know the LORD,' for they all shall know Me, from the least of them to the greatest of them," says the LORD. For I will forgive their iniquity, and their sin I will remember no more."

The postmillennial kingdom in history grows on the basis of the God-blessed – positive sanctions – proclamation of the gospel of God's saving grace. God's Word does not return to Him culturally void. As God's kingdom expands in history, it produces an explicitly Christian and biblical culture – Christendom – by means of the comprehensive application of biblical law. In this sense, the kingdom of God is a true civilization, one which rivals all other civilizations in history. It is a kingdom that has three aspects: heavenly, spiritual, and institutional.

The defenders of the various humanist kingdoms deny both the heavenly and the supernaturally spiritual aspects of civilization, while pietism denies the institutional aspect (outside of family and church). As Rushdoony says, humanism denies God but affirms history, while pietism affirms God but denies history. Theonomy affirms both God and history. It is in this sense a creationist worldview. It proclaims Calvin's view of history: the Creator God of the Bible decrees all that comes to pass in history. The connection between God and history is judicial: God's law-based, sanctions-governed covenant. This *covenantal view of history* can be summarized as follows:

> The absolutely sovereign Creator God governs every historical fact in terms of His authoritative revealed Word in history, the Bible, which declares His comprehensive, specially revealed law, with its judicially mandatory sanctions (both positive and negative), in order to implement progressively His universal kingdom (civilization) in history: Christendom.[62]

---

62. Gentry, "Whose Victory in History?" *Theonomy: An Informed Response*, ch. 8.

8

THE HERMENEUTIC OF SCRIPTURE

*Knowing this first, that no prophecy of Scripture is of any private
interpretation.* (2 Peter 1:20)

An issue that has received much attention in the eschatological debate among evangelicals is *hermeneutics*: the principle of
biblical interpretation. How are we to approach the prophecies
of Scripture? For instance, what are the historical expectations
of eschatological significance set forth by the Old Testament
prophets? Although I will not go deeply into hermeneutic
discussion,[1] it is necessary that certain aspects of the debate be
highlighted. There are full-length books that more than adequately set forth the principles of biblical interpretation.[2]
Three particularly relevant issues that I will consider are literalism, preterism, and Israel.

---

1. For the most part my hermeneutic will be *illustrated* below in the actual
exposition of key passages in Part III: Exposition.

2. An excellent study in prophetic hermeneutics is Hans K. LaRondelle's *The
Israel of God in Prophecy: Principles of Prophetic Interpretation* (Berrien Springs, MI:
Andrews University, 1983), even though he is premillennial (non-dispensational).See
also: Vern Poythress, *Understanding Dispensationalists* (Grand Rapids: Zondervan,
1987). Milton Terry's classic on the history of interpretation is also helpful: *Biblical
Hermeneutics: A Treatise on the Interpretation of the Old and New Testaments* (Grand
Rapids: Zondervan, [n.d] 1983). Moisés Silva, *Has the Church Misread the Bible? The
History of Interpretation in the Light of Current Issues* (Grand Rapids: Zondervan, 1987).
Walter C. Kaiser and Moisés Silva, *An Introduction to Biblical Hermeneutics: The Search
for Meaning* (Grand Rapids: Zondervan, 1994).

Literalism and Prophecy

Especially since the rise to prominence of dispensationalism in the late nineteenth century interpretive principles have become a major focus of eschatological discussion.[3] One of the classic dispensationalist's leading arguments is the claim to consistent interpretive literalism. Ryrie sets forth interpretive literalism as a *sine qua non* of this leading branch of dispensationalism: "Dispensationalists claim that their principle of hermeneutics is that of literal interpretation. . . . The dispensationalist claims to use the normal principle of interpretation *consistently* in *all* his study of the Bible."[4]

Since Ryrie is a prominent dispensationalist, a few examples of literalism from his writings serve as illustrations of the classic dispensational approach to hermeneutics. He chides Mickelsen for suggesting that the ancient weapons and chariots of Ezekiel 39 (which both Ryrie and Mickelsen deem to be in the future) are symbolic equivalents of modern weaponry: "If specific details are not interpreted literally when given as specific details, then there can be no end to the variety of the meanings of a text."[5] Here the principle of consistent literalism is so vigorously held that we are left with what non-dispensational evangelicals would consider an absurdity, despite formal explanations.[6]

---

3. For the evolution of literalism in fundamentalism, see: George M. Marsden, *Fundamentalism and American Culture: The Shaping of Twentieth-Century Evangelicalism, 1870-1925* (New York: Oxford University Press, 1980).

4. Charles C. Ryrie, *Dispensationalism Today* (Chicago: Moody Press, 1965), pp. 86, 89.

5. *Ibid.*, pp. 89-90. Elsewhere he suggests that horses will play a role in Armageddon because of Ezekiel 38:4, 15. Ryrie, *The Living End* (Old Tappan, NJ: Revell, 1976), p. 54.

6. "With the worldwide catastrophes evident during the first three and one-half years of Daniel's 70th Week (Matt. 24:6-8; Rev. 6), a reversion to more primitive methods of warfare might become possible." Charles H. Dyer, "Ezekiel," *The Bible Knowledge Commentary*, John F. Walvoord and Roy B. Zuck, eds., 2 vols. (Wheaton, IL: Victor, 1983), 1:1301.

Elsewhere, Ryrie writes: "Jerusalem will be exalted (Zech. 14:10), and there is no reason to doubt but that this will be literal and that the city by means of certain physical changes shall be exalted above the surrounding hills"![7] Of the "future" battle of Gog and Magog, Ryrie suggests: "A cavalry in this day of jets and atom bombs? It does seem unbelievable. But Ezekiel saw the mighty army from the north coming against the land of Israel on horses (Ezekiel 38:4, 15)."[8] Can anyone accept such views as reasonable, especially since it is so easy to understand these elements as figurative?

Ryrie gives three arguments for the literalistic hermeneutic.[9] (1) "Philosophically, the purpose of language itself seems to require literal interpretation. . . . If God be the originator of language and if the chief purpose of originating it was to convey His message to man, then it must follow that He, being all-wise and all-loving, originated sufficient language to convey all that was in His heart to tell man. Furthermore, it must also follow that He would use language and expect man to use it in its literal, normal, and plain sense." (2) "[P]rophecies in the Old Testament concerning the first coming of Christ – His birth, His rearing, His ministry, His death, His resurrection – were all fulfilled literally. There is no non-literal fulfillment of these prophecies in the New Testament."[10] (3) "If one does not use the plain, normal, or literal method of interpretation, all objectivity is lost."

7. Charles C. Ryrie, *The Basis of the Premillennial Faith* (Neptune, NJ: Loizeaux Bros., 1953), p. 148.

8. Ryrie, *The Living End*, p. 54.

9. Ryrie, *Dispensationalism Today*, pp. 87-88.

10. See also: Charles L. Feinberg, *Millennialism: The Two Major Views* (3rd ed.; Chicago: Moody Press, [1936] 1980), p. 41; J. Dwight Pentecost, *Things to Come: A Study in Biblical Eschatology* (Grand Rapids: Zondervan, 1958), p. 10; Robert P. Lightner, *Last Days Handbook* (Nashville: Thomas Nelson, 1990), pp. 126-127.

Despite the vigorous assertions of dispensationalists, "consistent literalism" is an impossible ideal. Consider the following problems for the Ryrie-style consistent literalist.

The Philosophy of Language Argument

The immediately striking point about Ryrie's first proof is that it is a preconceived hermeneutic. This is quite evident in Ryrie's statement that "principles of interpretation are basic and ought to be established before attempting to interpret the Word. . . ."[11] Does not his approach to language function disallow the possibility of a spiritual interpretation at the very outset? Why must we begin with the assumption of literalism? May not so rich a work as the Bible, dedicated to such a lofty and spiritual theme (the infinite God's redemption of sinful man), written by many authors over 1,500 years employ a variety of literary genres?

Even dispensationalists admit that biblical revelation often employs figures of speech. But this brings up the very controversy before us: *when* is prophecy to be interpreted literally, and when figuratively? Poythress rightly suspects that dispensationalists "may have conveniently arranged their decision about what is figurative *after* their basic system is in place telling them what can and what cannot be fitted into the system. The decisions as to what is figurative and what is not figurative may be a product of the system as a whole rather than the inductive basis of it."[12] This fact is evidenced in Ryrie's statement that "The understanding of God's differing economies is *essential* to a proper interpretation of His revelation within those various economies."[13] In other words, you must have a dispensational

---

11. Ryrie, *Dispensationalism Today*, p. 86.

12. Poythress, *Understanding Dispensationalists*, p. 53. For a discussion between Poythress and two leading dispensationalists over Poythress' arguments, see: *Grace Theological Journal* 10:2 (Fall 1989) 123-160.

13. Ryrie, *Dispensationalism Today*, p. 31.

framework ("understanding God's differing economies") in order to do "proper interpretation"![14] Feinberg agrees: "Every prophecy is a part of a wonderful scheme of revelation; for the true significance of any prophecy, the whole prophetic scheme must be kept in mind and the interrelationship between the parts in the plan as well."[15]

The dispensationalist presumption of a *consistent* literalism is unreasonable. "To assert, without express authority, that prophecy must always and exclusively be one or the other, is as foolish as it would be to assert the same thing of the whole conversation of an individual throughout his lifetime, or of human speech in general."[16]

In addition, Ryrie's first argument begs the question. Ryrie argues that because God created language, "the purpose of language itself seems to require literal interpretation" on the basis that "it must . . . follow that He would use language and expect man to use it in its literal, normal, and plain sense."[17] This is not very convincing.[18]

Finally, the dispensational practice of hermeneutics tends to be immune to criticism by its exclusion of countervailing evidence. As Poythress demonstrates, dispensationalists apply

---

14. This is despite Ryrie's complaint: "Thus the nondispensationalist is not a consistent literalist by his own admission, but has to introduce another hermeneutical principle (the 'theological' method) in order to have a hermeneutical basis for the system he holds." Ryrie, *Dispensationalism Today*, p. 94.

15. Feinberg, *Millennialism*, p. 40.

16. J. A. Alexander, *Commentary on the Prophecies of Isaiah*, 2 vols. in one (Grand Rapids: Zondervan, [1875] 1977), 1:30.

17. A problem of which dispensationalists seem to be unaware is the question as to *whom* a prophecy is "plain." The dispensational practice is to try to make it plain to the 20th-century reader. What about the ancient audience to whom it was written?

18. Pentecost follows suit: "Inasmuch as God gave the Word of God as a revelation to men, it would be expected that His revelation would be given in such exact and specific terms that His thoughts would be accurately conveyed and understood when interpreted according to the laws of grammar and speech. Such presumptive evidence favors the literal interpretation, for an allegorical method of interpretation would cloud the meaning of the message delivered by God to men." Pentecost, *Things to Come*, p. 10.

prophecies in a non-literal way by calling them "applications"[19] or "partial fulfillments,"[20] or by classifying them as spiritual level fulfillments,[21] or arguing that sometimes original prophecies contained figures themselves. Poythress queries, how can we know this in advance?[22] His point is well-taken.

The First-Coming Fulfillment Argument

This literalism argument is one of the most frequently employed. But it also suffers from question-begging. Pentecost holds that this is "one of the strongest evidences for the literal method." He vigorously asserts: "When the Old Testament is used in the New it is used only in a literal sense." "No prophecy which has been completely fulfilled has been fulfilled any way but literally."[23] Walvoord argues that "the literal fulfillment of promises pertaining to the first coming is a foreshadowing of the literal fulfillment of promises pertaining to the second coming."[24] They need to prove this, not just assume it.

The New Testament does not support this bold claim. To say that all prophecies fulfilled in the New Testament are fulfilled literally requires that one's system *already be in place*. In other words, there is no such thing as hermeneutical neutrality. The interpretation of a passage is grounded in the expositor's original presupposition. Literalism *definitionally* writes off all non-literal fulfillments. It ignores Old Testament prophecies of the kingdom that find fulfillment in the *ministry of Christ*, though

---

19. J. Dwight Pentecost, *Thy Kingdom Come* (Wheaton, IL: Victor, 1990), p. 80.

20. For example, Psa. 69:25 in Acts 1:20. Feinberg, *Millennialism*, p. 51.

21. For example, the Church's participation in the New Covenant. John F. Walvoord, *Prophecy Knowledge Handbook* (Wheaton, IL: Victor, 1990), pp. 502-503.

22. Poythress, *Understanding Dispensationalists*, pp. 53-55.

23. Pentecost, *Things to Come*, pp. 10-11. See also: H. Wayne House and Thomas D. Ice, *Dominion Theology: Blessing or Curse?* (Portland, OR: Multnomah, 1988), pp. 321-323.

24. John F. Walvoord, *The Nations, Israel, and the Church in Prophecy*, 3 vols. in 1 (Grand Rapids: Zondervan, 1988), 3:61.

not as a literalistic, political conception (Matt. 12:28; Luke 17:20-21).[25] These prophecies *must* find fulfillment beginning in the first century, for the prophecies of the outpouring of the Holy Spirit, which is associated with them, did come to pass (Acts 2).[26] Part III of this book will demonstrate this.

Even apart from the debate regarding Christ's kingdom, the dispensationalist argument is unfounded. For instance, although Matthew often interprets Old Testament prophecies literally, he does not always do so. Crenshaw and Gunn carefully demonstrate that "out of 97 OT prophecies only 34 were directly or literally fulfilled, which is only 35.05 percent."[27] They show there are other types of fulfillments than literal in the New Testament. Typical fulfillments are used by Matthew: God's calling Israel up out of Egypt (Hos. 11:1) was fulfilled when the young Jesus returned from His flight to Egypt (Matt. 2:15). Analogical fulfillments are also used, as when the weeping of Rachel for her children (Jer. 31:15) is fulfilled in Bethlehem's weeping for its children (Matt. 2:18).

Types are fulfilled in their *antitypes*. There are a number of types that come to fulfillment and are spiritually transformed in the New Testament. For instance, *historical Jerusalem* is typical of its antitype, *the heavenly city*. Paul sets the New Covenant over against the Old Covenant, and the heavenly Jerusalem over against the earthly Jerusalem in teaching that *Christianity represents the heavenly Jerusalem:* "For this Hagar is Mount Sinai in Arabia, and corresponds to Jerusalem which now is, and is in bondage with her children; but the Jerusalem above is free, which is the mother of us all" (Gal. 4:25-26; cf. 22-31). The writer of Hebrews does the same, when he says that New Cove-

---

25. This whole matter will receive careful exposition in Chapter 11 below.

26. See Isa. 32:14-17; Ezek. 36:25-27; Joel 2:28ff. Cf. John 7:39; 16:12ff.

27. Curtis Crenshaw and Grover Gunn, *Dispensationalism Today, Yesterday, and Tomorrow* (Memphis: Footstool, 1985), p. 22. See their helpful chart on pages 14-22. For an excellent analysis of the matter, see: David E. Holwerda, *Jesus & Israel: One Covenant or Two?* (Grand Rapids: Zondervan, 1995).

nant Christian converts (Heb. 12:24) from Old Covenant Judaism are now come "to Mount Zion and to the city of the living God, the heavenly Jerusalem, to an innumerable company of angels, to the general assembly and church of the firstborn who are registered in heaven, to God the Judge of all, to the spirits of just men made perfect" (Heb. 12:22-23). John sees the New Jerusalem coming down out of heaven to earth in the establishment of Christianity (Rev. 21:1, 2).[28] This was the heavenly city that Abraham ultimately sought beyond the temporal (and typical) Promised Land (Heb. 11:10, 16).

Premillennialist LaRondelle insightfully observes: "In dispensationalism we face the fact that the hermeneutic of literalism accepts Christian typology for some selected historical parts of the Old Testament. But it suddenly rejects each typological application of God's covenant with Israel to Christ's new covenant with His Church. This seems to be an arbitrary, speculative use of typology with the Old Testament."[29] This is a telling observation.

A classic and eschatologically relevant spiritual fulfillment of the Old Testament in the apostolic era is found in Acts 2.[30] Peter interprets the Davidic kingdom prophecies in general (Acts 2:30) and Psalms 16:8-11 (Acts 2:25-28) and 110:1 (Acts 2:34-35) specifically as coming to fulfillment in the ascension and session of Christ: "Therefore, being a prophet, and knowing that God had sworn with an oath to him that of the fruit of his body, according to the flesh, He would raise up the Christ to sit on his throne, he, foreseeing this, spoke concerning the resurrection of the Christ, that His soul was not left in Hades,

---

28. For a brief statement regarding the New Jerusalem/Church connection, see Chapter 17. It seems clear from the time statements in Revelation following the New Jerusalem imagery that this must come to pass not long after John wrote (Rev. 22:6, 7, 10). See my chapter in C. Marvin Pate, *Four Views of Revelation* (Grand Rapids: Zondervan, 1997).

29. LaRondelle, *The Israel of God in Prophecy*, p. 48.

30. Later in this chapter, I will treat another important passage: Acts 15:15-17.

nor did His flesh see corruption. This Jesus God has raised up, of which we are all witnesses. Therefore being exalted to the right hand of God, and having received from the Father the promise of the Holy Spirit, He poured out this which you now see and hear" (Acts 2:30-33).

Later, Paul preaches that the Davidic promise to Israel has been fulfilled in the resurrection of Christ: "And we declare to you glad tidings; that promise which was made to the fathers. God has fulfilled this for us their children, in that He has raised up Jesus. As it is also written in the second Psalm: 'You are My Son, today I have begotten You.' And that He raised Him from the dead, no more to return to corruption, He has spoken thus: 'I will give you the sure mercies of David' " (Acts 13:32-34).

The Objectivity Argument

Because of the alleged "objectivity" factor, it is common for dispensationalists to deem liberal any employment of a non-literal interpretation of any particular passage of Scripture:

> Although it could not be said that all amillennialists deny the verbal, plenary inspiration of the Scriptures, yet, as it will be shown later, it seems to be the first step in that direction. The system of spiritualizing Scripture is a tacit denial of the doctrine of the verbal, plenary inspiration of the Scriptures. . . . Thus the allegorical method of amillennialism is a step toward modernism.[31]

Elsewhere, we read that postmillennialism "is a system of theology based upon a subjective spiritualizing of Scripture" that "lends itself to liberalism with only minor adjustments."[32] Consequently, "it is a fact that there are few, if any, theologically

31. Ryrie, *Basis of the Premillennial Faith*, pp. 34, 35, 46.

32. John F. Walvoord, *The Millennial Kingdom* (Grand Rapids: Zondervan, 1959), pp. 34, 35.

liberal premillenarians because premillennialists follow the literal method of interpreting all the Bible."[33]

Of course, literalism is not necessarily protective of orthodoxy. It is easy to point out that many *cults* approach Scripture literalistically – and erroneously. Consider the Mormon doctrine that God has a literal, tangible body. After citing Genesis 1:26-27 regarding Adam's creation "in the image and likeness of God," LeGrand Richards, a former Apostle of the Church of Jesus Christ, Latter-day Saints, writes: "Attempts have been made to explain that this creation was only in the spiritual image and likeness of God. . . . Joseph Smith found that he was as literally in the image and likeness of God and Jesus Christ, as Seth was in the likeness and image of his father Adam."[34]

Besides being naive, the dispensational claim to *"consistent literalism"* is frustrating due to its *in*consistent employment. For instance, several Old Testament prophecies regarding David's reign in the millennium are not always literally understood. Dispensationalist H. A. Ironside writes: "I do not understand this to mean that David himself will be raised and caused to dwell on the earth as king. . . . [T]he implication is that He who was David's Son, the Lord Christ Himself is to be the King."[35] On what basis can a consistent literalist allow this view?

Neither is it necessary that Elijah's coming as prophesied in Malachi 4:5-6 be literally understood. Pentecost writes: "The prophecy is interpreted by the Lord as being fulfilled, *not in literal Elijah,* but in one who comes in Elijah's spirit and power."[36] Here he breaches two hermeneutic principles of his dis-

33. Lightner, *Last Days Handbook*, p. 106.

34. LeGrand Richards, *A Marvelous Work and Wonder* (Salt Lake City: Deseret, 1958), p. 16. There are even non-Mormons who point to the biblical references to God's "hand" as indicative of a body: F. J. Dake, *Annotated Reference Bible* (Atlanta: Dake Bible Sales, 1965), New Testament, p. 280.

35. Harry A. Ironside, *Expository Notes on Ezekiel the Prophet* (New York: Loizeaux Bros., 1949), p. 262, cited in J. D. Pentecost, *Things to Come*, pp. 498-499. Cf. Ryrie, *Basis of the Premillennial Faith*, p. 88. Walvoord, *Prophecy Knowledge Handbook*, p. 60.

36. Pentecost, *Things to Come*, pp. 311-313; cf. E. Schuyler English, "The Two

pensationalism: He allows the New Testament (Luke 1:17) to interpret the Old Testament (Mal. 4:5-6), and he drops his consistent literalism. This is convenient but illegitimate.

The "millennial" sacrifices in the prophecy of Ezekiel 45 are expressly said to "make reconciliation" (Ezek. 45:15, 17, 20), using the piel of the Hebrew *kaphar* (as in Lev. 6:30; 8:15; 16:6ff[37]). But Pentecost notes that "the sacrifices *will be memorial* in character."[38] Yet this question needs to be faced by self-professed literalists: what literalist, reading the phrase "make reconciliation," would surmise that this was only "memorial"? Where is the consistent literalism here?[39] Some dispensationalists allow that this passage "is not to be taken literally," but is merely "using the terms with which the Jews were familiar in Ezekiel's day."[40] This is convenient but illegitimate.

Isaiah 52:15 says of Messiah: "So shall he sprinkle many nations." The *New Scofield Reference Bible* comments: "Compare the literal fulfillment of this prediction in 1 Pet. 1:1-2, where people of many nations are described as having been sprinkled

---

Witnesses," *Our Hope* 47 (April 1941) 666.

37. Often sacrifices in Scripture speak figuratively of prayer (Psa. 141:2), praise (Psa. 44:6; Jer. 17:26; 33:11), thanksgiving (Psa. 107:22; 116:17), joy (Psa. 27:6), righteousness (Psa. 4:5; 51:19), confession (Psa. 66:13), contrition (Psa. 51:17), and so forth.

38. Pentecost, *Things to Come*, p. 525. See also Charles C. Ryrie, *The Ryrie Study Bible* (Chicago: Moody Press, 1980), p. 1299.

39. The whole idea of a re-instituted sacrificial system is repulsive to the biblical scheme of things (see Hebrews). The dispensational system presents an unnecessary confusion here. Consider: By Christ's appointment, the Lord's Supper is the sign of the New Covenant (Matt. 26:28; Mark 14:24; Luke 22:20; 1 Cor. 11:25). It is to be kept until He comes (1 Cor. 11:25-26). But in the dispensational system, when Christ comes to establish the New Covenant with Israel for a millennium, the Lord's Supper (which is the sign of the New Covenant) will be done away with while the sacrificial system (which is an Old Covenant foreshadowing of Christ's redemptive labor, Heb. 10:1-3) will be reinstituted as a "memorial." And this memorial will be done in His very presence!

40. *The New Scofield Reference Bible* (New York: Oxford University Press, 1967), p. 888, note 1 (at Ezek. 43:19).

with the blood of Christ."[41] Literal? When was Jesus' blood *literally* sprinkled on the nations? This sounds more like "spiritualizing" than "consistent literalism."

Of Isaiah 13:17-22, we learn that these verses "predict the destruction of the literal Babylon then existing. The verses also look forward to the destruction of both political Babylon and ecclesiastical Babylon in the time of the Beast."[42] At Revelation 18:2 we read: "The term 'Babylon' in prophecy is sometimes used in a larger sense than mere reference to either the ancient city or nation. . . ."[43] I agree. This is exactly the case. This same approach is true in many other such cases, as with Israel (Gal. 6:16; Heb. 8:6-13), David's throne (Luke 1:32; Acts 2:29-31), circumcision (Phil. 3:3; Col. 2:11), sacrifices (Rom. 12:1; 1 Pet. 2:5), the temple (1 Cor. 3:17; Eph. 2:19-22), the tabernacle (Acts 15:16; Heb. 9:11), and so forth. But when it suits them, dispensationalists vigorously argue for literalism. For instance, of Isaiah 9:7 we read: " 'The throne of David' is an expression as definite, historically, as 'the throne of the Caesars,' and does not admit of spiritualizing."[44]

The catastrophic judgment prophecy in Jeremiah 4:23-28, where the heavens become black and the mountains shake and all the birds flee, is not to be understood literally, according to dispensationalist Charles H. Dyer. "Jeremiah pictured God's coming judgment as a cosmic catastrophe – an undoing of creation. Using imagery from the Creation account (Gen. 1) Jeremiah indicated that no aspect of life would remain untouched." The universal catastrophe imagery had to do with

---

41. *Ibid.*, p. 758, note 3.

42. *Ibid.*, p. 724, n 3.

43. *Ibid.*, p. 1369.

44. *Ibid.*, p. 721. Poythress (p. 24n) cites many examples of non-literalism in the notes of the original *Scofield Reference Bible* (New York: Oxford University Press, [1909] 1917): Gen. 1:16; 24:1; 37:2; 41:45; 43:45; Exo. 2:2; 15:25; 25:1, 30; 26:15; Ruth Intro; Ezek. 2:1; Zech. 10:1; John 12:24. Poythress, *Understanding Dispensationalists*, p. 24n.

"the approaching army of Babylon."[45] John A. Martin, writing in the same dispensational commentary, explains the language of Isaiah 13:10-13, where the sun, moon, and stars are darkened and the earth is moved out of its place: "The statements in 13:10 about the heavenly bodies (*stars . . . sun . . . moon*) no longer functioning may figuratively describe the total turnaround of the political structure of the Near East. The same would be true of *the heavens* trembling *and the earth* shaking (v. 13), figures of speech suggesting all-encompassing destruction."[46]

Rather than such "objective" interpretations, the Christian exegete must allow the New Testament to interpret the Old Testament. "The Christian interpreter comes to the Old Testament with a different theological perspective than the Jewish expositor."[47] As Van Gemeren well states: "Christian students of the Old Testament *must pass by the cross of Jesus Christ on their return to the Old Testament*, and as such they can never lose their identity as a Christian."[48] Simply put: "We cannot forget what we have learned from Christ."[49] This approach to biblical interpretation allows the conclusive revelation of God in the New Testament authoritatively to interpret the incomplete revelation in the Old.

The dispensationalist resists this: "As a result of the covenant of grace idea, covenant theology has been forced to place as its most basic principle of interpretation the principle of interpreting the Old Testament by the New."[50] But the Scripture suggests that even the prophets could not always fathom their own

45. Charles H. Dyer, "Jeremiah," *Bible Knowledge Commentary*, 1:1136, 1135.

46. John A. Martin, "Isaiah," *ibid.*, 1:1059.

47. LaRondelle, *Israel of God in Prophecy*, p. 7.

48. Willem Van Gemeren, *The Progress of Redemption: The Story of Salvation from Creation to the New Jerusalem* (Grand Rapids: Zondervan, 1988), p. 21.

49. Poythress, *Understanding Dispensationalists*, p. 104.

50. Ryrie, *Dispensationalism Today*, p. 187.

predictions,[51] because of the nature of predictive prophecy (Num. 12:8). Nor could the pre-resurrection, pre-pentecostal disciples.[52] Nor could the last prophet of the Old Covenant era, John Baptist (Matt. 11:2-6). Why not? Because "with respect to eschatology, people in the Old Testament were not in the same position as they were for short-range prophecy. . . . The exact manner of fulfillment frequently could not be pinned down until the fulfillment came."[53] The conclusive New Testament revelation was needed (Heb. 1:1-2).

The Emmaus disciples, holding to current literalistic Jewish conceptions, need to have Christ open the Scriptures to them (Luke 24:32, 45). Christ rejects the *political Messianism* of the literalistic Jews.[54] The Jews had a dullness of understanding[55] that seems to be accounted for (at least partially) in that "the prevailing method of interpretation among the Jews at the time of Christ was certainly the literal method of interpretation."[56] After all, when Christ confronted Nicodemus, He pointed to this very problem: "Jesus answered and said to him, 'Are you the teacher of Israel, and do not know these things? . . . If I have told you earthly things and you do not believe, how will

51. 1 Pet. 1:10,11. See: Dan. 8:27; 12:8; Zech. 4:13; Rev. 7:13-14; 17:8-9. Young defends the view that Daniel did not understand his prophecies in Dan. 8:27 and 12:5. E. J. Young, *The Prophecy of Daniel* (Grand Rapids: Eerdmans, 1949), p. 182.

52. Matt. 16:21-22; Luke 18:31-34; John 2:22; 20:9,

53. Poythress, *Understanding Dispensationalists*, p. 107.

54. Matt. 23:37-38; Luke 19:41-42; 24:21-27; John 6:15; 18:36.

55. 2 Cor. 3:14; cf. Matt. 13:15; John 8:12; 12:46; Acts 28:26-27; Rom. 11:7-8. The dullness led eventually to their ascribing Satanic influence to Christ (Matt. 12:22-28).

56. Pentecost, *Things to Come*, p. 17. See also: Richard Longenecker, *Biblical Exegesis in the Apostolic Period* (Grand Rapids: Eerdmans, 1977), ch. 1. Bernard Ramm, *Protestant Biblical Interpretation* (Boston: W. A. Wilde, 1950), pp. 48f. In fact, the fundamental idea of a premillennial kingdom seems to be traceable back to the literalistic Jewish conception, and thus it may be said that "premillennialism is a descendent of ancient Judaism." William Masselink, *Why Thousand Years?* (Grand Rapids: Eerdmans, 1930), p. 20. See also: Leon Morris, *The Revelation of St. John* (Grand Rapids: Eerdmans, 1969), p. 234; Henry B. Swete, *Commentary on Revelation* (Grand Rapids: Kregal, [1906] 1977), p. cxxxiii; Feinberg, *Millennialism*, pp. 34-35.

you believe if I tell you heavenly things?' " (John 3:10, 12). Literalism plagued the Jews throughout Jesus' ministry.[57] Few would dispute the fact that the Jews of Christ's day looked for a political Messiah (John 6:14-15; 18:33-36). The Emmaus disciples were rebuked for just such a conception (Luke 24:17-21, 25-26). Christ suffered, then entered immediately into His glory.[58] The cause of Israel's rejection of Christ is due (at least partially) to their not knowing He fulfilled prophecy (Luke 19:42-44; Matt. 23:37, 38).[59]

Consequently, "it is irresponsible to jump unprepared into the area of end-time prophecies of Scripture. By considering such apocalyptic portions of Holy Scripture by themselves, in isolation from the total prophetic-messianic framework, one will necessarily fall into the pitfall of a geographic and ethnic literalism."[60] The whole concept of *progressive revelation* points to this truth. Thus, the historical-grammatical analysis "cannot be separated from interpretation 'in faith.' The Bible requires continual submission of our understanding to what the spirit of God has inspired (1 Cor. 2:12-15)."[61]

In recent years literalism – the previously popular, linchpin hermeneutical argument promoted earlier by leading Dallas Seminary dispensationalists – has been losing adherents. For instance, John S. Feinberg, a noted contemporary dispensational-

---

57. See: John 2:19-21; 3:5-7; 4:10-15, 31-38; 6:31-35, 51-58; 8:21-22, 32-36; 8:51-53; 9:39-40; 11:11-14; 13:33-37; 18:33-37.

58. Luke 24:26; 1 Pet. 1:11. Cf. John 12:23-24; Phil. 2:8-9.

59. Ultimately, their spiritual condition is the source of their rejection, with the misapprehension of prophecy a result of that.

60. LaRondelle, *Israel of God in Prophecy*, p. 7. As Young notes: "In speaking of the future or Messianic age, Isaiah, as a prophet of the Old Testament, uses the thought forms and the figures which were current in that age. It is obvious that the language of the prophet cannot be interpreted in a consistently literal sense. Rather, Isaiah takes the figures which were the property of the Old Testament economy and makes them the vehicles of expression for the truths of salvation and blessing which were the characteristics of the age of grace." E. J. Young, *Isaiah* (Grand Rapids: Eerdmans, 1965), 1:99.

61. Van Gemeren, *Progress of Redemption*, p. 27.

ist, has admitted that on hermeneutics, "Ryrie is too simplistic."[62] Craig A. Blaising of Dallas Theological Seminary warns that: "consistently literal exegesis is inadequate to describe the essential distinctive of dispensationalism."[63] Blaising and Bock note: "hermeneutical methodology has been rethought and is no longer perceived as an exclusively dispensational hermeneutic."[64] This is due to the "conceptual naivete" of Ryrie's hermeneutic which involves a "methodological deficiency in the very hermeneutic that it proposed," which is gravely serious in that "this hermeneutical deficiency was structured into the very meaning of dispensational thought and practice in its advocacy of clear, plain, normal, or literal interpretation."[65] Nevertheless, we find that less well-informed dispensational authors still insist on identifying a broader hermeneutic as *the* danger of a non-dispensational eschatology.[66]

Preterism and Prophecy

Another important hermeneutic issue (but one that does not have a necessary relation to the broader question of postmillennialism, in that not all postmillennialists adopt it) is *preterism*. The term "preterism" is based on the Latin *preter*, which means "past." Preterism refers to that understanding of certain eschatological passages which holds that *they have already come to fulfill-*

---

62. John S. Feinberg, "Systems of Discontinuity," *Continuity and Discontinuity: Perspectives on the Relationship Between the Old and New Testaments*, Feinberg, ed. (Westchester, IL: Crossway, 1988), p. 73. One major theologian who converted from dispensationalism is former Dallas Seminary professor S. Lewis Johnson, who warns of the anti-apostolic nature of literalism, which he says interprets "woodenly." S. L. Johnson, *The Old Testament in the New* (Grand Rapids: Zondervan, 1980), p. 83.

63. Craig A. Blaising, "Development of Dispensationalism," *Bibliotheca Sacra*, 579, p. 272.

64. Craig A. Blaising and Darrell L. Bock, eds., *Dispensationalism, Israel and the Church: The Search for Definition* (Grand Rapids: Zondervan, 1992), p. 378.

65. Ibid., p. 29.

66. House and Ice, *Dominion Theology*, ch. 14; Dave Hunt, *Whatever Happened to Heaven?* (Eugene, OR: Harvest House, 1988), ch. 12; Hal Lindsey, *The Road to Holocaust* (New York: Bantam, 1989), ch. 3.

ment. Actually, all Christians – even dispensationalists – are preteristic to some extent. This is necessarily so because Christianity holds that a great many of the Messianic passages have already been fulfilled in Christ's first coming.[67]

On these points, Christians differ from the "futurism" of Orthodox Judaism. Orthodox Jews today and also in antiquity have insisted that Christians are misapplying the Old Testament's Messianic prophecies to past events.[68] Of the incarnation as revealed in prophecy, early church father Athanasius wrote: "So the Jews are trifling, and the time in question, which they refer to the future, is actually come."[69]

The preterist approach teaches, for instance, that many of the prophecies of Revelation and the first portion of the Olivet Discourse have already been fulfilled. Matthew 24:1-34 (and parallels) in the Olivet Discourse was fulfilled in the events surrounding the fall of Jerusalem in A.D. 70.[70] In Revelation, most of the prophecies before Revelation 20 find fulfillment in the fall of Jerusalem (A.D. 70). The preterist has strong exegeti-

---

67. See the list of thirty-one such passages in House and Ice, *Dominion Theology*, pp. 321-322.

68. See for instance: Justin Martyr, *Dialogue with Trypho the Jew* in Alexander Roberts and James Donaldson, eds., *The Ante-Nicene Fathers*, 10 vols. (Grand Rapids: Eerdmans, rep. 1985), vol. 1. For example, of Isaiah 7:14 Trypho challenges Justin (chs 77ff): "Proceed then to make this plain to us, that we may see how you prove that that [passage] refers to this Christ of yours. For we assert that the prophecy relates to Hezekiah" (p. 237). For some helpful insights, see: D. S. Russell, *From Early Judaism to Early Church* (Philadelphia: Fortress, 1986) and Geza Vermes, *Jesus and the World of Judaism* (Philadelphia: Fortress, 1983).

69. Athanasius, *Incarnation* 40:1. Cf. P. Lapide and U. Luz, *Jesus in Two Perspectives: A Jewish-Christian Dialog* (Minneapolis: Augsburg, 1985).

70. In this I differ from some preterists who go much farther and claim *all* of the Olivet Discourse has been fulfilled, and even the Second Advent, resurrection, and judgment at the destruction of Jerusalem. See: Milton Terry, *Biblical Hermeneutics* (Grand Rapids: Zondervan, n.d.); J. Stuart Russell, *The Parousia: A Study of the New Testament Doctrine of Our Lord's Second Coming* (Grand Rapids: Baker, [1887] 1983). Max R. King, *The Cross and the Parousia of Christ: The Two Dimensions of One Age-Changing Eschaton* (Warren, OH: Writing and Research Ministry, 1987). See Appendix C: Brief Critique of Hyper-Preterism.

cal indicators undergirding his system, which I will briefly illustrate. But first I need to refer to my hermeneutic.

The Exegetical Basis of Preterism

It should always be the Christian's hermeneutic practice that: (1) the clearer (didactic discourse) statements interpret the less clear (figurative imagery) and (2) Scripture interprets Scripture. I will briefly illustrate the preteristic argument from the Olivet Discourse and Revelation, based on these two principles. I contend that rival views frequently dishonor both principles.[71]

The Olivet Discourse. The fulfillment of Matthew 24:4-33 in the destruction of Jerusalem is a most reasonable and even necessary conclusion. Even futurists are pressed to admit to some preteristic elements in the discourse. Dispensationalists generally hold that: "The Olivet discourse did predict the coming destruction of Jerusalem, which is today a past event, but at the same time the bulk of the passage deals with the yet future events of Christ's coming and the end of the age."[72] Amillennialists Hendriksen, Lenski, and Berkhof, as well as postmillennialists Alexander and Henry, hold that this passage merges both the A.D. 70 event with the Second Advent.[73]

---

71. For additional insights into the preteristic approach to the Olivet Discourse, see Chapter 15; for Revelation, see Chapter 17. See also: Gentry, *Perilous Times: A Study in Eschatological Evil* (forthcoming); Gentry in C. Marvin Pate, ed., *Four Views of Revelation* (Grand Rapids: Zondervan, 1997); David Chilton, *The Great Tribulation* (Ft. Worth, TX: Dominion Press, 1987); J. Marcellus Kik, *An Eschatology of Victory* (n.p.: Presbyterian & Reformed, 1971). An interesting dispensational flirtation with preterism is C. Marvin Pate and Calvin B. Haines, Jr., *Doomsday Delusions: What's Wrong with Predictions About the End of the World* (Downer's Grove, Ill.: Inter-varsity, 1995).

72. House and Ice, *Dominion Theology*, p. 271. See also: Pentecost, *Thy Kingdom Come*, p. 249. Warren W. Wiersbe, *Bible Exposition Commentary* (Wheaton, IL: Victor, 1989), 2:86. John F. Walvoord, *Prophecy Knowledge Handbook*, p. 381. Louis A. Barbieri, Jr., "Matthew," *Bible Knowledge Commentary*, 2:76. James F. Rand, "A Survey of the Eschatology of the Olivet Discourse," *Bibliotheca Sacra* 113 (1956) 166.

73. William Hendriksen, *The Gospel of Matthew* (*New Testament Commentary*) (Grand Rapids: Baker, 1973), pp. 867-869. R. C. H. Lenski, *Interpretation of Matthew's Gospel*

That Matthew 24:4-33 *en toto* has been fulfilled seems quite obvious on the two following bases.[74] First, its introductory *context* strongly suggests it. In Matthew 23, Jesus sorely rebukes the "scribes and Pharisees" *of His own day* (Matt. 23:2ff), urging *them* finally to "fill up then the measure of your fathers" who killed the prophets (23:31-32).[75] Christ says that they are a "generation" of vipers (23:33) that will persecute and slay His disciples (23:34). He notes that upon *them* will come all the righteous blood shed on the earth (23:35). He then dogmatically asserts: "[V]erily I say unto you, all these things shall come upon *this generation*" (23:36).[76]

Then, in Matthew 23:37-24:2, Jesus weeps over Jerusalem, and declares that its temple will be destroyed, stone-by-stone,

---

(Columbus: Wartburg, 1932), pp. 929-930. Louis Berkhof, *Systematic Theology* (Grand Rapids: Eerdmans, 1941), p. 704. Matthew Henry, *Matthew Henry's Commentary* (Old Tappan, NJ: Revell, [1721] n.d.), 5:356-360. Joseph A. Alexander, *The Gospel According to Mark* (Grand Rapids: Baker, [1858] 1980), p. 363.

74. The preterist view is held by amillennial theologians also: George L. Murray, *Millennial Studies: A Search for Truth* (Grand Rapids: Baker, 1948), p. 110; Alfred Plummer, *The Gospel According to St. Luke* (*International Critical Commentary*) (New York: Scribner's, 1910), p. 338. A. B. Bruce, *Synoptic Gospels* (*The Expositor's Greek Testament*) (Grand Rapids: Eerdmans, n.d.), p. 296. William L. Lane, *The Gospel of Mark* (*New International Commentary on the New Testament*) (Grand Rapids: Eerdmans, 1974), pp. 479-480. A dispensationalist has even been moved close to this view, and has stated: "The manner in which dispensationalism has traditionally handled this section is thus weak on several fronts. . . . Contemporary dispensationalists should rethink this area of NT exegesis." "It must be concluded that the futurist view, held by traditional dispensationalists, is unconvincing. It does not satisfactorily handle the contextual emphasis on the fall of Jerusalem. . . ." David L. Turner, "The Structure and Sequence of Matthew 24:1-41: Interaction with Evangelical Treatments," *Grace Theological Journal* 10:1 (Spring 1989) 7, 10.

75. As did John Baptist before Him (Matt. 3:1-12).

76. The phrase is found in Matthew 1:17; 11:16; 12:39-45; 16:4; 17:17; and 23:36. It is only with great difficulty that any of these references may be given a meaning other than the contemporary generation in Jesus' day. In the five other instances in Matthew where the word *genea* is coupled with the near demonstrative to read "this generation," it clearly refers to the generation *then living*. These passages are Matthew 11:16; 12:41, 42, 45; and 23:36. In Scripture the idea of a "generation" of people involves roughly twenty-five to forty years. A. T. Robertson, *Word Pictures in the New Testament*, 6 vols. (Nashville: Broadman, 1930), 1:194. See: Num. 32:13; Psa. 95:10.

despite His disciples' surprise. It is of these things that the disciples ask, "When shall these things be?" As a matter of historical record we know the temple was destroyed, stone by stone, in August, A.D. 70.

Second, its express temporal indicators demand it. We must not miss the clear references to the *contemporary expectation*. Enclosing the relevant portion of the discourse, we have Christ's own time-element designation. In 23:36, he dogmatically asserts "*all* these things shall come upon *this* generation." He closes the relevant portion of the prophecy by repetition of the time frame: Matthew 24:34 says, "Verily I say unto you, *this* generation shall not pass, till all these things be fulfilled." And just forty years later Jerusalem was destroyed. Contextually the "this generation" of Matthew 24:34 *must* speak of the same idea as that of Matthew 23:36.

In verse 34 the matter is solemnly affirmed by Christ. He is quite dogmatic when He begins a statement with: "verily." Thus, Christ emphatically draws the disciples' attention to what He is about to say, just as He did in 24:2, where He made the statement that led to the whole discourse.

In addition the dogmatism of His statement is further underscored. He does not just tell them; He emphatically introduces what He is about to say: "I tell you." He has not left the temporal expectation to them to figure out. Furthermore, the literal rendering of the Greek reads: "Truly I tell you that *by no means* passes away generation this until all these things happen."[77] The "by no means" is a strong, double negative (*ou me*). Jesus places it early in His statement for added emphasis. He is staking His credibility,[78] as it were, on the absolute certainty of this prophetic pronouncement.

---

77. Alfred Marshall, *The Interlinear Greek-English New Testament* (Grand Rapids: Zondervan, 1959), p. 108

78. He contrasts the durability and integrity of His prophetic word here with that of the material universe (24:35).

But what does He so dogmatically and carefully tell them? Whatever the difficult apocalyptic imagery in some of the preceding verses (e.g., vv. 29-31) may indicate, Jesus clearly says that "all these things" will occur *before* "this generation" passes away. He employs the near demonstrative for the fulfillment of verses 2-34: these events will come upon "*this* generation." He uses the far demonstrative in 24:36 to point to the Second Advent: "*that* day." The coming "tribulation" (24:21; cf. Rev. 1:9) was to come upon "this generation" (23:36; 24:34; cf. 1 Thess. 2:16) and was to be foreshadowed by certain signs (24:4-8). But the Second Advent was to be at "that" far day and hour, and was not to be preceded by particular signs of its nearness, for no man can know it (24:36).   Preterism is well-established in Matthew 24:3-34, as many early church fathers recognized.[79]

The Book of Revelation.[80] The past fulfillment of most of the prophecies in Revelation 4-19 is compellingly suggested by the various time indicators contained in its less symbolic, more didactic introduction and conclusion.

Revelation 1:1 opens the prophecies of Revelation and prepares the reader to understand them: "The Revelation of Jesus Christ, which God gave unto him, to shew unto his servants things which must *shortly* [*en tachei*] come to pass." He repeats this assertion using different, though synonymous, terminology in Revelation 1:3c, when he says "the time is at hand" (*kairos eggus*). He again repeats these ideas as he closes. Revelation

---

79. See especially Eusebius, *Ecclesiastical History* 3:7:1-2; *The Clementine Homilies* 3:15; and Cyprian, *Treatises* 12:1:6, 15. For more detail, see Greg L. Bahnsen and Kenneth L. Gentry, Jr., *House Divided: The Break-up of Dispensational Theology* (Tyler, TX: Institute for Christian Economics, 1989), pp. 276-282.

80. See Chapter 17 below for a brief outline survey of Revelation. For more detail regarding preterism in Revelation, see my *Before Jerusalem Fell: Dating the Book of Revelation* (2d. ed.: Bethsesda, MD.: Christian Universities Press, 1996) or my *The Beast of Revelation* (2d. ed.: Tyler, Tex.: Institute for Christian Economics, 1994). See also: Pate, ed., *Four Views of Revelation*.

22:6: "These sayings are faithful and true: and the Lord God of the holy prophets sent his angel to shew unto his servants the things which *must shortly be done*" (*genesthai en tachei*). Revelation 22:10: "And he saith unto me, Seal not the sayings of the prophecy of this book: for the *time is at hand*" (*ho kairos gar eggus estin*). The point is clear: John expected imminent fulfillment.

The text-bracketing temporal indicators, pointed to by preterists, cannot lightly be dismissed. John is writing to seven historical churches (Rev. 1:4, 11; 22:16), which are expecting troublesome times (Rev. 2-3). He testifies to being with them in "tribulation" (Rev. 1:9). He expects those very churches to hear and understand (Rev.1:3; 22:10) the revelation (Rev. 1:1) and to heed the things in it (Rev. 1:3; 22:7), because of the nearness of the events (Rev. 1:1, 3; 22:6, 10). One of the agonizing cries from his fellow sufferers receives emphasis. In Revelation 6, the martyred souls in heaven plead for God's righteous vindication: "They cried with a loud voice, saying, 'How long, O Lord, holy and true, until You judge and avenge our blood on those who dwell on the earth?' And a white robe was given to each of them; and it was said to them that they should rest *a little while longer*" (Rev. 6:10-11).

Original relevance, then, is the lock and the time-texts the key to opening the door of Revelation. What terms *could* John have used to speak of contemporary expectation other than those that are, in fact, found in Revelation 1:1, 3; 22:6, 10 and other places?[81]

Preterism has a sound basis in historical and textual exegesis, as illustrated from the Olivet Discourse and Revelation.

Israel and Prophecy

The role of Israel as a distinct people radically distinguished from the Church is the leading feature of dispensationalism —

---

81. For ancient preterist exposition, see: Andreas of Capadocia and Arethas. For more references see: Gentry, *Before Jerusalem Fell*, pp. 133-145.

both in its classic and progressive forms. In fact, as Poythress suggests, this theological presupposition is probably the *raison d'etre* of the literalistic hermeneutic: "The dualism of Israel and the church is, in fact, the deeper dualism determining when and where the hermeneutical dualism of 'literal' and 'spiritual' is applied."[82] Non-dispensational evangelical exegetes are in agreement against the radical Israel/Church dichotomy of dispensationalism.

It is important that non-dispensationalists grasp the significance of dispensationalism's understanding of Israel, for herein lies a fundamental error of the entire system. This crucial error distorts the entire idea of the progress of redemption, the unity of God's people, the fulfillment of prophecy, and the interpretation of Scripture.

Ryrie points to the distinctiveness of Israel as the first of the three *sine qua non* of dispensationalism: "A dispensationalist keeps Israel and the Church distinct."[83] Elsewhere, he is even more detailed:

(1) The Church is not fulfilling in any sense the promises to Israel. (2) The use of the word *Church* in the New Testament never includes unsaved Israelites. (3) The church age is not seen in God's program for Israel. It is an intercalation. (4) The Church is a mystery in the sense that it was completely unrevealed in the Old Testament and now revealed in the New Testament. (5) The Church did not begin until the day of Pentecost and will be removed from this world at the rapture which precedes the Second Coming of Christ.[84]

---

82. Poythress, *Understanding Dispensationalists*, p. 24.

83. Ryrie, *Dispensationalism Today*, p. 44. See also: Pentecost, *Thy Kingdom Come*, p. 9. Walvoord, *The Nations, Israel, and the Church in Prophecy*, "Nations" section, pp. 56ff. Feinberg, "Systems of Discontinuity," *Continuity and Discontinuity*, pp. 81ff. House and Ice, *Dominion Theology*, pp. 29ff.

84. Ryrie, *Basis of the Premillennial Faith*, p. 136.

The Scripture does not support such theological assertions, as I will demonstrate.

Israel in Scripture

The Israel of the Old Testament is the forerunner of and continuous with the New Covenant phase of the Church, which is the fruition of Israel.[85] Thus, New Testament Christians may even call Abraham our father (Rom. 4:16) and the Old Covenant people our "fathers" (1 Cor. 10:1). This clearly evinces a *spiritual* genealogical relation. Employing another figure, we are said to be grafted into Israel (Rom. 11:16-19) so that we become one with her, partaking of her promises (Eph. 2:11-20). In fact, the Lord appointed twelve apostles in order to serve as the spiritual seed of a New Israel, taking over for the twelve sons of Old Covenant Israel. Both the names of the twelve tribes (as the Old Covenant representatives) and the twelve apostles (as the New Covenant representatives) are incorporated into the one city of God, the New Jerusalem (Rev. 21:12, 14).

Dispensationalists strongly assert that "the Scriptures never use the term Israel to refer to any but the natural descendants of Jacob."[86] Nevertheless, we are designated by terms associated with the Old Covenant people: we are called the "seed of Abraham,"[87] "the circumcision,"[88] "a royal priesthood,"[89] "twelve tribes" (Jms. 1:1), "*diaspora*" (1 Pet. 1:1), the "temple of God."[90] Do not these terms clearly speak to the essence of Is-

---

85. See especially: David E. Holwerda, *Jesus and Israel: One Covenant or Two?* (Grand Rapids:
Eerdmans, 1995), chs. 1-4.

86. Feinberg, *Millennialism*, p. 230. See also: *The New Scofield Reference Bible*, p. 1223. "The term *Israel* is nowhere used in the Scriptures for any but the physical descendants of Abraham." Pentecost, *Things to Come*, p. 127.

87. Rom. 4:13-17; Gal. 3:6-9, 29.

88. Rom. 2:28-29; Phil. 3:3; Col. 2:11,

89. Rom. 15:16; 1 Pet. 2:9; Rev. 1:6; 5:10. See: Exo. 19:6.

90. 1 Cor. 3:16-17; 1 Cor. 6:19; 2 Cor. 1:16; Eph. 2:21.

rael's covenantal identity? The Jews trusted in and boasted of descendency from Abraham,[91] and circumcision was a distinguishing covenantal mark of the Jews[92] – yet these concepts are applied to Christians. Peter follows after Paul's thinking, when he designates Christians as "stones" being built into a "spiritual house" (1 Pet. 2:5-9). But he does more; he draws upon several Old Testament designations of Israel and applies them to the Church: ". . . a chosen generation, a royal priesthood, an holy nation."[93] He, with Paul, also calls Christians "a peculiar people" (1 Pet. 2:10; Titus 2:14), which is a familiar Old Testament designation for Israel.[94]

If Abraham can have Gentiles as his "spiritual seed,"[95] why cannot there be a *spiritual Israel*? In fact, Christians are called by the name "Israel": "And as many as walk according to this rule, peace and mercy be upon them, and upon the Israel of God" (Gal. 6:16). Although dispensationalists attempt to understand Galatians 6:16 as speaking of Jewish converts to Christianity "who would not oppose the apostle's glorious message of salvation,"[96] such is surely not the case, as we shall see.

The entire context of Galatians is set against claims to a special Jewish status or distinction, as urged by dispensationalists. "For you are all sons of God through faith in Christ Jesus. For as many of you as were baptized into Christ have put on Christ. There is neither Jew nor Greek, there is neither

91. We read often of "the God of Abraham" (Gen. 28:13; 31:42, 53; Exo. 3:6, 15-16; 4:5; 1 Kgs. 18:36; 1 Chr. 29:18; 2 Chr. 30:6; Psa. 47:9; Matt. 22:32; Mark 12:36; Luke 20:37; Acts 3:13; 7:32). The Jews expected blessings in terms of their Abrahamic descent (Matt. 3:9; 8:11; Luke 3:8; Luke 13:16, 28; Luke 16:23-30; 19:9; John 8:39, 53; Rom. 11:1; 2 Cor. 11:22).

92. Circumcision is *the* special sign of God's covenant with Abraham and Israel (Gen. 17:10, 13). Circumcision is mentioned 86 times in the Scriptures; the uncircumcised are mentioned 61 times.

93. 1 Pet. 2:9-10; Exo. 19:5-6; Deut. 7:6.

94. Exo. 19:5; Deut. 14:2; 26:18; Psa. 135:4.

95. *New Scofield Reference Bible*, p. 1223 (at Rom. 9:6).

96. *Ibid*. See also: Ryrie, *Dispensationalism Today*, p. 139; Pentecost, *Things to Come*, p. 89; Donald K. Campbell, "Galatians," *Bible Knowledge Commentary*, 1:611.

slave nor free, there is neither male nor female; for you are all one in Christ Jesus" (Gal. 3:26-28). In Christ, all racial distinction has been done away with. Why would Paul hold out a special word for Jewish Christians ("the Israel of God"), when he had just stated that there is no boasting at all, save in the cross of Christ (Gal. 6:14)? After all, "in Christ Jesus neither circumcision nor uncircumcision avails anything, but a new creation" (Gal. 6:15). That new creation is spoken of in detail in Ephesians 2:10-22, where Jew and Gentile are united in one body. This is the Church.

It is important to note, as does Poythress, that the Church is not a "straight-line" continuation of Israel. It fulfills Israel through Christ.[97] *All* God's promises are "yea" and "amen" in Christ (2 Cor. 1:20). Since we are all the sons of Abraham (Gal. 3:29) through Christ, we receive the fullness of blessing through Him (Rom. 8:17; Eph. 1:23; Col. 2:10).

The well-known and vitally important "New Covenant" is originally framed in Jewish terminology: "Behold, the days come, saith the LORD, that I will make a new covenant with the house of Israel, and with the house of Judah" (Jer. 31:31[98]). But despite the contortions dispensationalists go through to avoid the obvious – some even declaring there are two New Covenants[99] – this New Covenant specifically comes

---

97. Poythress, *Understanding Dispensationalists*, p. 126.

98. See also: Ezek. 11:16-21; Joel 2:32; Zeph. 3:12-13.

99. See Ryrie, *Basis of the Premillennial Faith*, ch. 6, and Pentecost, *Things to Come*, ch. 8, for more detail. There has been a serious division even within dispensational circles over the function of the New Covenant as illustrated in Ryrie's work. Those views are: (1) The Jews Only View. This is "the view that the new covenant directly concerns Israel and has no relationship to the Church" (p. 107). (2) The One Covenant/Two Aspects View: The one "new covenant has two aspects, one which applies to Israel, and one which applies to the church" (p. 107). (3) The Two New Covenants View. This is Ryrie's view; it actually "distinguishes the new covenant with Israel from the new covenant with the Church. This view finds two new covenants in which the promises to Israel and the promises to the Church are more sharply distinguished even though both new covenants are based on the one sacrifice of Christ" (p. 107).

to existence in the days of Christ. We should note that the New Covenant is specifically applied to the Church: (a) Pentecost is quite correct, when he writes of the establishment of the Lord's Supper: "In its historical setting, the disciples who heard the Lord refer to the new covenant . . . would certainly have understood Him to be referring to the new covenant of Jeremiah 31."[100] What could be more obvious? (b) In fact, the sudden appearance of the "New Covenant" designation in the New Testament record, without qualification or explanation, demands it refer to the well-known New Covenant of Jeremiah (Matt. 26:28; Mark 14:24; Luke 22:20; 1 Cor. 11:25). The apostle to the Gentiles even promotes the New Covenant as an important aspect of his ministry (2 Cor. 3:6). He does not say he is a minister of a "second new covenant" or "another new covenant."

Hebrews 8, on everyone's view, cites Jeremiah's New Covenant in a context in which he is speaking to New Testament Christians. Yet Ryrie argues that "the writer of the Epistle has referred to both new covenants"![101]

Though Ryrie dogmatically affirms "Israel means Israel" via his literalistic hermeneutic, he does so on the basis of an inconsistently applied principle. Elsewhere, Ryrie fails to demand that "David" means "David." He cites Jeremiah 30:8-9 as proof of Messiah's millennial reign: "They shall serve the Lord their God, and David their king, whom I will raise up unto them." Then he says: "[T]he prophet meant what he said – and what else can we believe. . . ?" He cites also Hosea 3:4-5, where "David their king" will be sought in the millennium, then comments: "Thus the Old Testament proclaims a kingdom to be established on the earth *by the Messiah*, the Son of David, as the heir of the Davidic covenant."[102]

100. Pentecost, *Things to Come*, p. 126.
101. Ryrie, *Basis of the Premillennial Faith*, p. 121.
102. *Ibid.*, pp. 86-87, 88 (emphasis mine).

Other passages illustrating how the Church fulfills prophecies regarding Israel are found in the New Testament. Citing Amos 9:11-12, James says God is rebuilding the tabernacle of David through the calling of the Gentiles (Acts 15:15ff).[103] In Romans 15:8-12, Paul notes that the conversion of the Gentiles is a "confirming of the promises to the fathers." And at least one of the verses brought forth as proof speaks of Christ's Messianic kingdom rule (Rom. 15:12). In Acts, the preaching of the gospel touches on the very hope of the Jews, which was made to the fathers (Acts 26:6-7). *The promises did not set forth a literal, political kingdom, but a spiritual, gospel kingdom.* Psalm 2 begins its fulfillment in the resurrection of Christ – not at the Second Advent (Acts 13:32-33). The prophecy was fulfilled.

Ryrie's argument that "Church" never includes the unsaved Israelites is not a good argument. Not only do we not discover unsaved Israelites in the Church, neither do we find unsaved Gentiles there – if by "Church" Ryrie means the invisible Church. But if he is speaking of the visible Church, there surely were unsaved Israelites in it, just as there were unsaved Gentiles caught up in it during the first century. The idea of the Church is not racial; it represents a *purified Israel* (Rom. 2:28-29), not a wholesale adoption of the Jewish race. Ryrie's argument is irrelevant. The Church fulfills Old Testament prophecy.

Regarding the "parenthesis" or intercalation view of the Church, I have already noted that there are Old Testament prophetic passages that apply to the calling of the Gentiles in the New Testament. They speak of the Church. Another illustration in addition to those given above is Paul's use of Hosea 1:9-10 and 2:23. In Romans 9:24-26 Paul interprets these very strong Jewish-contexted verses as referring to Gentile salvation in the New Covenant phase of the Church.

---

103. O. Palmer Robertson, "Hermeneutics of Continuity," *Continuity and Discontinuity*, ch. 4.

Neither should we deem the New Covenant era, international-al Church as a mystery that was "completely unrevealed in the Old Testament," as Ryrie does. The clarity of the revelation increases in the New Testament, and the audience that hears it expands, but the revelation itself *was* given in the Old Testament. The question is: *for whom* was the revelation a mystery?

Ephesians 3:3-6 reads: "By revelation he made known unto me the mystery . . . which in other ages was not made known unto the *sons of men*, as it is now revealed unto his holy apostles and prophets by the Spirit; that the Gentiles should be fellow-heirs, and of the same body, and partakers of His promise in Christ." In Romans 16:25-26, Paul points out that the "mystery" of Gentile salvation was hidden only from the *Gentiles* (which in Ephesians 3 Paul calls "the sons of men"), not from the Old Testament prophets, for he defends his doctrine of the mystery from "the scriptures of the prophets." He speaks of "the revelation of the mystery, which was kept secret since the world began, but now is made manifest, and *by the scriptures of the prophets*, according to the commandment of the everlasting God, *made known to all nations* for the obedience of faith." Paul says that the "mystery" that was kept secret is "now made manifest" to "*all* nations," not just to Israel. The Church is no "parenthesis."

In Luke 24:44-47 the Lord taught that it was necessary for Him to die in order to fulfill Scripture in bringing salvation to the Gentiles: "All things must be fulfilled, which were written in the law of Moses, and in the prophets, and in the psalms, concerning me. Then opened he their understanding, that they might understand the scriptures, and said unto them, Thus it is written, and thus it behoved Christ to suffer, and to rise from the dead the third day: and that repentance and remission of sins should be preached in His name among *all nations*."

The distinction between Jew and Gentile has *forever* been done away with. Paul points out this fact in Ephesians 2:11-16: "Wherefore remember, that ye being in time past Gentiles in the flesh . . . at that time ye were without Christ, being aliens from the commonwealth of Israel, and strangers from the covenants of promise, having no hope, and without God in the world: but now in Christ Jesus ye who sometimes were far off are made nigh by the blood of Christ. For he is our peace, who *hath made both one*, and *hath broken down the middle wall of partition between us*; Having *abolished* in His flesh the enmity, even the law of commandments contained in ordinances; for *to make in himself of twain one new man*, so making peace; And that he might reconcile both unto God in one body by the cross, *having slain the enmity thereby*."

Thus, "there is neither Jew nor Greek . . . for ye are all one in Christ" (Gal. 3:28) and "there is neither Greek nor Jew, circumcision nor uncircumcision" (Col. 3:11). Yet dispensationalists see the Church as a temporary parenthesis in God's plan. After the Great Tribulation, they teach, the Church will be superseded by a rebuilt Jewish temple and its animal sacrifices.

Many of the early church fathers – even those claimed as premillennialists by modern dispensationalists – understood the Church to be the recipient of Israel's promises. It is appropriate at this point to cite the Th.M. thesis of Dallas Seminary-trained historian Alan Patrick Boyd: "The majority of the writers/writings in this period [A.D. 70-165] completely identify Israel with the Church."[104] He specifically cites Papias, 1 Clement, 2 Clement, Barnabas, Hermas, the Didache, and Justin Martyr.[105] Boyd notes that "In the case of Barnabas, . . . he has totally disassociated Israel from the precepts of the Old Testament. In fact he specifically designates the Church to be the

---

104. Alan Patrick Boyd, "A Dispensational Premillennial Analysis of the Eschatology of the Post-Apostolic Fathers (Until the Death of Justin Martyr)" (Dallas: Dallas Theological Seminary Master's Thesis, 1977), p. 47.

105. Papias, *Fragment* 6; 1 Clement 3:1; 29:1-30:1; 2 Clement 2:1-3; 3:5; Barnabas, *Epistles* 2:4-6,9; 3:6; 4:6-7; 5:2,7; Hermas, *Similitudes* 9:16:7; 9:15:4; 9:12:1-13:2; the Didache (14:2,3), and Justin Martyr (*Dialogue* 119-120, 123, 125). See Boyd, "Dispensational Premillennial Analysis," pp. 46, 60, 70, 86.

heir of the covenantal promises made to Israel (4:6-7; 13:1-6; 14:4-5)."[106] Elsewhere, Boyd writes: "Papias applied much of the Old Testament to the Church."[107] Of Hermas he notes "the employment of the phraseology of late Judaism to make the Church the true Israel."[108] Justin Martyr, says Boyd, "claims that the Church is the true Israelitic race, thereby blurring the distinction between Israel and the Church."[109]

Conclusion

The Bible is the revelation of the holy and gracious God to sinful, rebellious man. It is a vast and deep work touching on time and eternity that was written over a period of fifteen centuries by "holy men of God [who] spoke as they were moved by the Holy Spirit" (2 Peter 1:21). Because of the richness of its expression and the glory of its content, it must be approached with a holy reverence for God and a fearful appreciation of its own majesty and grandeur. The Scripture is not a cold mathematical formula that may be scientifically worked out. It is the living Word of God to man concerning the plan of redemption.

There are, of course, general rules of interpretation that are essential to recognize if one is to understand its message. Postmillennialists follow the general evangelical approach to Scripture known as the grammatico-historical hermeneutic. This view is shared with evangelical premillennialists and amillennialists. Postmillennialists stand with these over against the peculiar literalism common to dispensationalism.

It is not always the case that the "plain and simple" approach to a passage is the correct one. This is why Jesus can be heard saying, "He that has ears to hear, let him hear." This is why He often was misunderstood in His preaching – as noted

---

106. Boyd, *ibid.*, p. 46.
107. *Ibid.*, pp. 60-61
108. *Ibid.*, p. 70.
109. *Ibid.*, p. 86.

in John. Biblical interpretation requires careful thought and reflection, rather than mechanical manipulation.

In the material presented above, I focused on three critical issues in order to illustrate the reasonableness of the postmillennial use of hermeneutics. Those issues were literalism in kingdom prophecy, preterism regarding certain judgment passages, and the function of Israel in Scripture. Objections are frequently urged against these views by some expositors, particularly dispensationalists. So, instead of rehearsing the common principles of biblical interpretation – principles that are found in many hermeneutics manuals – I concentrated on these points of contention. The remainder of the book will illustrate the postmillennial hermeneutic in action.

PART III

EXPOSITION

9

CREATION

For by Him all things were created that are in heaven and that are on earth, visible and invisible, whether thrones or dominions or principalities or powers. All things were created through Him and for Him. And He is before all things, and in Him all things consist. (Colossians 1:16-17)

We move now to the actual exposition of the postmillennial eschatology. A predominant and distinguishing theme of biblical eschatology is that of a *sure expectancy of gospel victory in time and on earth*. This may be seen in various ways in the Old Testament revelation.

We begin with the Creation record. The Christian faith has a genuine interest in the material world, as noted in Chapter 6. God created the earth and man's body as material entities, and all "very good" (Gen. 1:1-31; 2:7). Consequently, the record of Creation is important for developing a Christian worldview, and, therefore, for understanding biblical eschatology.

In order to understand a thing aright, it is always helpful to understand its purpose according to its designer and builder. Eschatology is a theological discipline that is concerned with *teleology*, with discovering the divinely revealed, long-range *purpose* of the world and of history. What will the consummation be? What are its precursors? How will it be brought about? When will it occur? By necessity, then, *eschatology must be con-*

cerned with creation, for it is the divinely decreed fruition of creation. In short, the end is tied to the beginning.[1]

Genesis is of primary significance to the Christian faith. The very title "Genesis" is derived from the Greek of the Septuagint translation of Genesis 2:4a: "This is the book of the generation [*geneseos*] of heaven and earth."[2] The word *geneseos* means "origin, source." The opening chapters of Genesis (chapters 1-3) provide the foundational elements of biblical eschatology. The end is found in the beginning. *Creation had a glorious purpose.*

The Edenic Expectation of Victory

God has created the world for a purpose. Despite the confusion brought into the question by certain leading dispensationalists,[3] Reformed theology sees as the ultimate goal of universal history, the glory of God.[4] His creational intent in bringing the world into being was for the manifestation of His own glory: "You are worthy, O Lord, to receive glory and honor and power; for You created all things, and by Your will they exist and were created" (Rev. 4:11).[5] All men live before God in the

---

1. Isa. 46:10. See the Edenic imagery in Rev. 2:7; 20:2; 21:6; 22:2, 13-14.

2. The term *geneseos* occurs frequently in Genesis as a heading to various sections. See: Gen. 5:1; 6:9; 10:1; 11:10; 11:27; 25:12; 25:19; 36:1; 36:9; 37:2.

3. "A third aspect of the *sine qua non* of dispensationalism is a rather technical matter which will be discussed more fully later (chapter 5). The covenant theologian in practice makes this purpose salvation, and the dispensationalist says the purpose is broader than that, namely, the glory of God." Charles C. Ryrie, *Dispensationalism Today* (Chicago: Moody, 1965), pp. 46-7.

4. Reformed theology's emphasis on God's glory is expressed in its most basic, covenantal creed: the Westminster Standards. See the Confession of Faith (3:3, 7; 4:1; 5:1; 6:1; 16:2, 7; 18:1; 33:12), the Larger Catechism (Q. 1, 12, 13, 190), and the Shorter Catechism (Q. 1, 2, 7, 47, 66, 101, 102, 107). See also: R. B. Caper, *God Centered Evangelism: The Presentation of the Scriptural Theology of Evangelism* (Grand Rapids: Baker, 1961), p. 93; Charles Hodge, *Systematic Theology*, 3 vols. (Grand Rapids: Eerdmans, rep. 1973), 1:535ff.

5. Psa. 8:1; 19:1-16; 89:11b; 82:8b; Rom. 11:36; Rev. 4:11.

material world,[6] which He has created for His own glory, as the place of man's habitation.[7]

At the very outset of history, God created man in His own "image and likeness" (Gen. 1:26). In its setting, the Creation Mandate occurs as the "swelling of jubilant song" at the accomplishment of God's creative activity.[8] At that time, the creation had just been completed and was about to be pronounced "very good" (Gen. 1:31-2:2). One vital aspect of that image is that of man's acting as ruler over the earth and under God. This is evident in the close connection between the interpretive revelation regarding man's creation in God's image and the divine command to exercise rule over the creation order: "Then God said, 'Let Us make man in Our image, according to Our likeness; let them have dominion over the fish of the sea, over the birds of the air, and over the cattle, over all the earth and over every creeping thing that creeps on the earth" (Gen. 1:26-27). Because man is the image of God, he has the capacity and responsibility for dominion.

The image of God in man is constitutive to man; it is prior to and definitive of man's duty, dominion.[9] Man, however, is not, nor was he ever, an absolute sovereign; he is God's vice-regent. God created him and granted him temporal sovereignty, putting him *under command* to act obediently in terms of

---

6. 2 Chr. 16:9; Psa. 33:13-15; Prov. 15:3; Acts 17:28; Heb. 4:13.

7. Psa. 24:1; 115:16; Prov. 15:3; Dan. 5:23; Acts 25:24-31; Rev. 4:11.

8. C. F. Keil and Franz Delitzsch, *The Pentateuch*, in *Commentary on the Old Testament* (Grand Rapids: Eerdmans, [n.d.] 1975), 1:64.

9. Amillennialist Herman Hanko insists that through the Fall, "the image of God was changed in him to the image of Satan" and "that the fall brought about a complete loss of the image." Herman Hanko, "An Exegetical Refutation of Postmillennialism" (unpublished conference paper: South Holland, IL: South Holland Protestant Reformed Church, 1978), pp. 23, 22. The Scripture, however, grants that even fallen man is still in the image of God, although it is a fragmented and corrupted image (Gen. 9:6; 1 Cor. 11:7; Jms. 3:9). This image testifies to him of his sin. It is renewed and strengthened in holiness and righteousness in a redeemed man (Col. 3:10; Eph. 4:24).

God's ultimate sovereignty.[10] All of this is done in generic worship to God, for "the setting of six days of labor in the context of one day of worship and rest indicates the true perspective from which man's dominion over the earth is to be viewed."[11] Thus, the temporal "sovereignty" of man must be understood as derivative and interpreted in terms of the absolute sovereignty of God: God created (Gen. 1:26), God blessed (Gen. 1:27), God gave (Gen. 1:28), and God commanded (Gen. 2:16); man is to worship God (Gen. 2:3; Exo. 20:11). Man lives up to His creational purpose as he multiplies (Gen. 1:28a) and acts as a social creature (Gen. 2:8) exercising righteous dominion (Gen. 1:28b) in the earth. God implanted within man the drive to dominion.[12]

The Creational (or Dominion) Mandate was given at the very creation of man, distinguishing him from and elevating him above the animal, vegetable, and mineral kingdoms and defining his task in God's world in accordance with God's plan. Adam's naming of the animals in Genesis 2 must be understood according to the Semitic sense: "In Israel as among other peoples there was awareness of the significance attached to a name, and of the power which resided in it. . . . By giving someone a name, one establishes a relation of dominion and possession towards him. Thus acc. to Gn. 2:19f. Adam names all the animals. This means that he exercises dominion over creation and relates it to his own sphere. To name a conquered city (2 S.

---

10. Gary North, *The Dominion Covenant: Genesis* (2nd ed.; Tyler, TX: Institute for Christian Economics, 1987), ch. 3.

11. O. Palmer Robertson, *Christ of the Covenants* (Phillipsburg, NJ: Presbyterian & Reformed, 1980), p. 80.

12. See: Francis Nigel Lee, *Culture: Its Origin, Development, and Goal* (Cape May, NJ: Shelton College Press, 1967); Abraham Kuyper, *Lectures on Calvinism* (Grand Rapids: Eerdmans, [1898] 1961); Henry R. Van Til, *The Calvinistic Concept of Culture* (Philadelphia: Presbyterian & Reformed, 1959); Francis Schaeffer, *How Should We Then Live?: The Rise and Decline of Western Thought and Culture* (Old Tappan, NJ: Fleming H. Revell, 1976).

12:28) or lands (Ps. 49:11) is to establish a right of possession and to subject them to one's power."[13]

We should not assume that Adam's sovereign dominion was to be limited to Eden. Eden was only his starting point. Adam was, in essence, to extend the cultured condition of Eden (Gen. 2:17) throughout the world (Gen. 1:26).

Not only was the Cultural Mandate given at creation *before* the Fall, but it remains in effect even *after* the entry of sin. This is evident in many ways. Consider just two of them. First, the revelational record of man's beginnings show him acting as a dominical creature and without disapprobation, subduing the earth and developing culture. Indeed, from the very beginning and continuing into the post-Fall world, Adam and his descendants exercised dominion. This dominion impulse operated at a remarkably rapid rate, contrary to the primitivist view of man held by evolutionary anthropologists.[14] Man quickly developed various aspects of social culture: raising livestock, creating music and musical instruments, crafting tools from metal, and so forth (Gen. 4:20-22). Because man is a social creature (Gen. 2:8), his culture-building includes the realm of political government, as well. This is evident in God's ordaining of governmental authority for his "good" (Rom. 13:1-4). At his very creation, not only was man commanded to develop all of God's creation, but he actually began to do so. Culture is not an accidental aside in the historical order. Any primitiveness that may be found in man's cultures is a record of the developmental consequence of sin and of estrangement from God, not of original creational status.

Second, the Creation Mandate is specifically repeated in Scripture. This assertion bothers Hanko, who argues: "Adam

---

13. Hans Bietenhard, "*onoma*," *Theological Dictionary of the New Testament*, Gerhard Kittel and Gerhard Friedrich, eds., 10 vols., trans. by Geoffrey W. Bromiley (Grand Rapids: Eerdmans, 1967), 5:253.

14. That apes, lemurs, and monkeys are called "primates" (from the Latin *primus*, "first") is indicative of the evolutionary view of man.

did not *abandon* the cultural mandate; sin and the curse made it impossible for Adam to continue it. This is not a mere quibbling over words; this strikes at the very heart of the [millennial] question. Forgotten is the fact that sin and the curse made it forever impossible for the cultural mandate to be fulfilled in this present world."[15]

The Cultural Mandate is repeated as still in force in both testaments (Gen. 9:1ff; Heb. 2:5-8).[16] Psalm 8 clearly evidences the Cultural Mandate: "What is man that You are mindful of him, And the son of man that You visit him? For You have made him a little lower than the angels, And You have crowned him with glory and honor. You have made him to have dominion over the works of Your hands; You have put all things under his feet" (Psa. 8:4-6).

The optimistic expectations of postmillennialism comport well with God's creational purpose as evidenced in the Cultural Mandate. They highlight the divine expectation of the true, created nature of man *qua* man. Postmillennialism expects the world as a system (*kosmos*)[17] to be brought under submission to God's rule by the active, sanctified agency of redeemed man, who has been renewed in the image of God (Col. 3:10; Eph. 4:24). In other words, postmillennial eschatology expects *in* history what God originally intended *for* history. It sees His plan as maintained and moving toward its original goal, but now on the new basis of God's sovereign and gracious redemption. Hanko's objection to postmillennialism's employment of the Cultural Mandate is rooted in a very deep sense of the genuine fearsome power of sin. The postmillennialist, however, sees God's continuance of the Cultural Mandate, but upon a

---

15. Hanko, "An Exegetical Refutation of Postmillennialism," p. 10.

16. See allusions elsewhere: Gen. 3:15-20; Eccl. 3:1-17; 5:18-19; 9:9, 10; 1 Cor. 10:31; 15:22-28; Heb. 4:9-16; 6:7-11; Rev. 20:12; 21:24-22:5.

17. *Kosmos* ("world") is the Greek word (used in the New Testament) that is expressive of the orderly system of the world; it is contrary to *chaos*. For a discussion of this concept, see Chapter 12.

new principle: the very real and even greater power of redemption in Christ.

The Post-Fall Expectation of Victory

The first genuinely eschatological statement in Scripture occurs very early: in Genesis 3:15. In keeping with the progressively unfolding nature of revelation, this eschatological datum lacks the specificity of later revelation. "Revelation is the interpretation of redemption; it must, therefore, unfold itself in installments as redemption does. . . . The organic progress [of redemptive revelation] is from seed-form to the attainment of full growth; yet we do not say that in the qualitative sense the seed is less perfect than the tree. . . . The truth is inherently rich and complex, because God is so Himself."[18] At that nascent stage of revelation, the identity of the coming Redeemer was not sharply exhibited; it would take later revelation to focus the picture, a picture not perfectly clear until Christ came. Yet the broad outlines drawn by this original eschatological statement are clear enough: "O.T. Revelation approaches the concept of a personal Messiah very gradually. It sufficed for fallen man to know that through His divine power and grace God would bring out of the human race victory over the serpent."[19]

Orthodox Christian Bible students recognize the reference in Genesis 3:15 as referring to the coming redemptive labor of Jesus Christ as the Promised Redeemer.[20] He is promised as One coming to crush His great enemy – undoubtedly Satan, the

---

18. Geerhardus Vos, *Biblical Theology: Old and New Testaments* (Grand Rapids: Eerdmans, 1948), pp. 14, 15, 16.

19. *Ibid.*, p. 55.

20. Some liberal scholars argue that this prophecy must be understood etiologically rather than messianically. Gerhard Von Rad, *Genesis*, trans. by John Marks (Philadelphia: Westminster Press, 1961), pp. 89-90.

head of a nefarious kingdom of evil.[21] This verse portrays in one sentence a mighty struggle between the woman's seed (Christ and His kingdom)[22] and the serpent's seed (Satan and his kingdom).[23] "[U]nless we want to separate the second part of the verse completely from the first part and apply the deeper meaning only to the second part while taking the first part strictly literally, we cannot escape the conclusion that the first part of the verse announces the ongoing spiritual conflict between the seed of the woman and the seed of the serpent. In other words, what we have portrayed here is the constant conflict between the children of the devil and the children of the kingdom."[24] "This first gospel promise, therefore, despite the terse and figurative language in which it is expressed, provides a true perspective of the whole sweep of human history."[25] This explains the struggle in history: God's creational purpose is being resisted. (It also helps to explain the Bible's concern with genealogies leading up to and culminating in Christ, Luke 3:23-38.)

This, then, is the establishment of the covenant of grace, for this is the first promise of a redeemer.[26]

---

21. Rev. 12:9, 14-15; 20:2; cf. John 8:44; Rom. 16:20; 2 Cor. 11:3, 14; 1 John 3:8.

22. Although there must be a specific reference to Christ as *the* Seed (the Hebrew suffix on "heel" is masculine singular), clearly here we have reference to a collective seed, as well. Eve is called the "mother of all living" (Gen. 3:20). Cf. Matt. 25:40, 45; Luke 10:18; John 8:44; 15:1-7; Acts 13:10; Rom. 16:20; 1 Cor. 12:12-27; 1 John 3:10; Rev. 12:7-9.

23. See the conflict between Adam and Satan, Abel and Cain, the Sethites and Cainites, Noah and Nimrod, Abraham and the Chaldeans, Israelites and Canaanites, Christians and pagans.

24. Gerhard Charles Aalders, *Genesis* (*Bible Student's Commentary*) trans. by William Heynen (Grand Rapids: Zondervan, 1981), 1:107. See also: Robertson, *Christ of the Covenants*, pp. 97ff.

25. Philip Edgcumbe Hughes, *Interpreting Prophecy: An Essay in Biblical Perspectives* (Grand Rapids: Eerdmans, 1976), p. 11.

26. Anthony Hoekema, *The Bible and the Future* (Grand Rapids: Eerdmans, 1979), p. 180.

Despite this great struggle in history, the fundamental point of this poetic datum is that of the *victorious issue* by the woman's seed, Christ. Later revelation in the New Testament shows that this prophecy begins to find fulfillment at the death and resurrection of Christ;[27] it is not awaiting some distant beginning of its fulfillment.

Yet, citing Genesis 3:15, Hoekema asserts that "the expectation of a future golden age before Christ's return does not do justice to the continuing tension in the history of the world between the kingdom of God and the forces of evil."[28] He draws too much out of this terse statement. Why may we not refer it to Christ's first coming in the establishment of His kingdom and Church (cf. Col. 2:15; Rom. 16:20)?[29] Later revelation developed the nature of the struggle and its outcome in history, as Hoekema himself admits: "We may say that in this passage God reveals, as in a nutshell, all of his saving purpose with His people. The further history of redemption will be an unfolding of the contents of the mother promise."[30] In addition, the verse seems clearly to relate Satan's death blow with Christ's heel-wound, i.e., with Christ's crucifixion, which occurs at His first coming.

Thus, here we have at the very inception of prophecy the certainty of victory. Just as the Fall of Adam had a world-wide negative effect, so does the salvation of God, on the basis of the resurrection of Christ, the Last Adam, have a world-wide positive effect (Rom 5:15ff; 1 Cor. 15:22, 45).[31] The crushing of Satan is not awaiting a consummative victory of Christ over Satan at the end of history. The idea (as we will see more fully later) is that Satan the Destroyer, his nefarious kingdom, and its

---

27. 1 John 3:8; Heb. 2:14; Col. 2:14,15.

28. Hoekema, *Bible and the Future*, p. 180.

29. On the binding of Satan, see below (chs. 12 and 17):

30. Hoekema, *Bible and the Future*, p. 5.

31. Gary North, *Is the World Running Down? Crisis in the Christian Worldview* (Tyler, TX: Institute for Christian Economics, 1988).

evil effects are overwhelmed progressively by the superior strength and glory of Almighty God the Creator through Jesus Christ.

Conclusion

The stage for the optimistic prospects of redemption is set in the opening chapters of Genesis. God creates man for the purpose of ruling the world under God and to His glory. God commands man to develop culture, to promote civilization, to exercise righteous dominion in the earth. Postmillennialism expects the fulfillment of this mandate.

Man falls from favor with God by the intrusion of the tempter, Satan. Rather than scrapping His original purpose for the world, the Lord *immediately* begins to work out His redemptive plan in history. The outcome of that plan is prophetically clear: the seed of the woman will crush the seed of the serpent. God's covenantal dominion will be extended in history through His covenant-keeping representatives in history. The spiritual heirs of the Second Adam will progressively fulfill the comprehensive task that was originally assigned to the First Adam. Redemption progressively triumphs in history over reprobation. The resurrection of Christ was and remains more powerful than the Fall of Adam: not just judicially but also culturally.

This understanding of the power of Christ's resurrection and His ascension to the right hand of God is denied by amillennialism.[32] The amillennialist sees the fall of Adam as by far the more powerful force in mankind's cultural development. He sees Christ's redemption as "souls-only, Church-only, Christian families-only." He draws the line at culture, which is to say, he draws a *judicial boundary* around the transforming power of the

---

32. It is also denied by premillennialism in its view of Church history prior to the bodily return of Jesus to set up his thousand-year earthly kingdom.

Gospel. This is because he has already drawn an *eschatological boundary* around the transforming power of the Gospel.[33]

The historical outworking of God's redemptive plan is covenantal, as I note in Chapter 6. The development of covenantal redemption is traceable from these opening chapters of Genesis throughout the Scriptures. Let us next trace the progress of redemption through the Old Testament revelation. Again, theonomic postmillennialism fits well with this prophetic expectation, co-ordinating the redemptive and creative actions of God.

---

33. Perhaps it is the other way around. Van Til argued that ethics is primary; intellectual error is secondary. Thus, Gary North suggests that it is Christians' desire to escape personal and corporate responsibility for fulfilling the terms of the Dominion Mandate that has led them to invent false, pessimistic eschatologies.

10

ANTICIPATION

And I will make of thee a great nation, and I will bless thee, and make thy name great; and thou shalt be a blessing: And I will bless them that bless thee, and curse him that curseth thee: and in thee shall all families of the earth be blessed. (Genesis 12:2-3)

As noted in the previous chapter, the divinely ordained calling of man to exercise dominion over the earth is given at Creation, while Adam's redemptive restoration to that calling begins immediately after his Fall. Following this, the revelation of God in Scripture begins tracing the line of the Redeemer, developing the hope-filled eschatological expectation of the comprehensive redemption that He will surely bring.

Anticipation in the Pre-Mosaic and Early Mosaic Eras

The Noahic Covenant

The various features of the Noahic Covenant are found in Genesis 6:17-22 and 8:20-9:17. In this covenant, we have a clear reaffirmation of the Cultural Mandate, which is funda-mental to the outworking of God's eschatological purpose through man.[1] We also have a continuance of God's gracious

---

1. Cf. the references to the birds, cattle, etc. (Gen. 6:20; 8:17 with Gen. 1:24, 25), the command to "be fruitful and multiply" (Gen. 9:1, 7 with Gen. 1:28), and the dominion concept (cf. Gen. 9:2 with Gen. 1:28).

redemptive relation as the ongoing basis of the Cultural Mandate, which is likewise necessary to eschatology.[2]

This covenant is established with God's people: the family of Noah, who alone escape the deluge by the grace of God. Thus, this is *not* solely a common-grace covenant, for it is directly made with God's people (Noah's family), is established on the basis of grace and redemptive sacrifice (Gen. 6:8; 8:20-22), and is united with God's other redemptive covenants (cf. Hos. 2:18 with Gen. 6:20; 8:17; 9:9ff).[3] The Cultural Mandate, then, has an especial relevance to the function of God's people in the world: the Noahic reaffirmation of the Mandate is expressly made with God's people, the "you" of Genesis 9:1-12. On the basis of divine covenant, God's people are called to the forefront of cultural leadership, with the religious aspects of culture being primary.

In the Noahic covenantal episode, we also witness the objectivity of God's relationship with man: the world is judged in history for its sin. The rainbow, which signifies God's covenant mercy, is established with Noah and all that are with him, and their seed (Gen. 9:12).[4] This indicates that the world will be protected from God's curse through the instrumentality of the Church (the people of God). This covenant is only made indirectly with unbelievers, who benefit from God's protection only as they are not opposed to God's people. Because of God's love for His people, He preserves the orderly universe (Gen. 8:20-22). His enemies serve His people (Gen. 9:10b).

Thus we see the *objective corporate sanction* of God against sin in the Flood, which also serves as a type of Final Judgment (2

---

2. O. Palmer Robertson, *The Christ of the Covenants* (Phillipsburg, NJ: Presbyterian & Reformed, 1980), p. 111. He refers to L. Dequeker, "Noah and Israel. The Everlasting Divine Covenant with Mankind," *Questions disputees d'Ancien Testament, Methode et Theologie* (Gembloux, 1974), p. 119.

3. James B. Jordan, "True Dominion," *Biblical Horizons*, Special Edition (Dec. 1990), p. 1. Cf. Robertson, *Christ of the Covenants*, p. 111.

4. It seems that the rainbow did not exist prior to this time. Apparently, the Flood is the first instance of rain (and the rainbow): Genesis 2:5-6.

Pet. 3:4-6). We also see God's judicial sanctions in history in His ordaining of capital punishment (Gen. 9:6). God's objective judgment therefore finds *civil expression* in the affairs of man. His grant of legitimate authority to the civil government to enforce capital punishment is based on a religious principle, namely, the image of God in man (Gen. 9:6), and is given to the world through the Church (i.e., Noah's family).[5] God ordains civil sanctions as a means for preserving the human race for His redemptive purposes (cf. Rom. 13:1-4; 1 Pet. 2:13-14; cp. 1 Tim. 2:1-4; Acts 25:11).

The Abrahamic Covenant

As the scarlet thread of redemption is progressively woven more distinctively into the fabric of Scriptural revelation and history, the eschatological pattern of redemptive victory becomes more evident and more specific. The patriarchal and Mosaic eras demonstrate this fact. Here I will survey a few of the more significant references in these eras.

In Genesis the Abrahamic Covenant continues the redemptive theme begun in Genesis 3:15 and traced through Genesis 6-9. The active redemptive restoration of the fundamental relationship between God and man is greatly intensified through God's establishing His gracious covenant with Abraham and his seed: "Now the LORD had said to Abram: 'Get out of your country, from your family and from your father's house, to a land that I will show you. I will make you a great nation; I will bless you and make your name great; and you shall be a blessing. I will bless those who bless you, and I will curse him who curses you' " (Gen. 12:1-3a).

---

5. This does not mean that the institutional Church has the authority to execute criminals.

The promise has three aspects: (1) a seed,[6] (2) a land,[7] and (3) the nations.[8] The land and seed promises are given prominence in Genesis 15:5 and 18: "Then He brought [Abram] outside and said, 'Look now toward heaven, and count the stars if you are able to number them.' And He said to him, 'So shall your descendants be.' On the same day the LORD made a covenant with Abram, saying: 'To your descendants I have given this land, from the river of Egypt to the great river, the River Euphrates' " (Gen. 15:18).

The divine promise clearly involved temporal blessings for Abraham, including a seed and a land. According to the emphatic declaration of the Scriptures, history witnesses the fulfillment of the national aspects of the temporal blessings of the seed[9] and the land[10] promises. "Judah and Israel were as numerous as the sand by the sea in multitude. . . . So Solomon reigned over all kingdoms from the River to the land of the Philistines, as far as the border of Egypt" (1 Kgs. 4:20-21). "So the LORD gave to Israel all the land of which He had sworn to give to their fathers, and they took possession of it and dwelt in it. . . . Not a word failed of any good thing which the LORD had spoken to the house of Israel" (Josh. 21:43, 45). "You also multiplied their children as the stars of heaven, and brought them into the land which You had told their fathers to go in and possess" (Neh. 9:23).

The dispensationalist argues for a future fulfillment based on the promise that God will give Abraham the land "forever" (Gen. 13:15), as an "everlasting" possession (Gen. 17:8). This

---

6. Gen. 12:2; 13:16; 15:5; 16:10; 17:2-6; 18:18; 22:17; cf. Gen. 20:4; 28:4, 14; 32:12.

7. Gen. 12:2, 7; 13:15, 17; 15:7, 18; 24:7; cf. Gen. 28:4.

8. Gen. 12:3; 18:18; 22:18; cf. Gen. 26:4; 28:14. See also the prophetic and New Testament era development of this universal theme.

9. Exo. 12:37; Num. 22:11; Deut. 1:10; 10:22; 1 Kgs. 4:20; 1 Chr. 27:23; 2 Chr. 1:9; Heb. 11:12. Notice that Christ is the special seed, John 8:56.

10. 1 Kgs. 4:21; 8:65-66; 2 Chr. 9:26.

argument is not persuasive, however. In the first place, there is a common use of *olam* ("forever/everlasting") where it is employed of long-term temporal situations.[11] Secondly, it is evident that God's covenants and promises are conditioned upon ethical obedience, even when this is not specifically stated. "It is the conditional nature of all prophecy that makes the outcome contingent on the ethical decisions of men."[12] For instance, God clearly tells Jonah that Nineveh would be overthrown in forty days (Jon. 3:4), yet God "repented" of His determination (v. 10). God informs Paul that no life will be lost on the ship (Acts 27:22), but later adds a condition (v. 31).[13]

The Abrahamic Covenant is conditioned on the ethical obligation to "keep the way of the Lord" (Gen. 18:17-19).[14] Israel's forfeiture of the Land promised in the Abrahamic Covenant was clearly possible, as God's Word makes abundantly clear.[15]

Consequently, we must understand the biblical view of the land. The land of Israel is *"His* holy Land" (Lev. 25:23; Psa. 78:54). It depends on His favor upon Israel (Hos. 9:3; Jer. 2:7) and His dwelling therein (Num. 35:34; Lev. 26), which continues as long as Israel is obedient to Him (Deut. 4:40; Isa. 1:19;

---

11. Exo. 12:14; 40:15; Num. 25:13; 2 Chr. 7:16. "Figuratively also the term is applied to objects of impressive stability and long duration, as mountains, hills (e.g. Gen 49:26; Hab 3:6)." James Orr, "Everlasting," *The International Standard Bible Encyclopedia*. James Orr, ed., 5 vols. (Grand Rapids: Eerdmans, [1929] 1956), 2:1041.

12. Gary North, *Millennialism and Social Theory* (Tyler, TX: Institute for Christian Economics, 1990), p. 120. B. B. Warfield, "The Prophecies of St. Paul" (1886), *Biblical and Theological Studies* (Philadelphia: Presbyterian & Reformed, 1952), pp. 470ff. Sidney Greidanus, *The Modern Preacher and the Ancient Text: Interpreting and Preaching Biblical Literature* (Grand Rapids: Eerdmans, 1988), pp. 232ff.

13. Cf. also 1 Sam. 2:30; Isa. 38:1-6; Jer. 26:13-19; Joel 2:13-14. See: Kenneth Jones, "An Amill Reply to Peters," *Journal of the Evangelical Theological Society* 24:4 (Dec. 1981) 333-341.

14. Cf. Gen. 17:9-14; 22:18; 26:5; Heb. 11:8.

15. Exo. 19:5; Deut. 28:15ff; 30:5-19; Lev. 26:14ff; Josh. 8:34; 24:20 1 Kgs. 2:3,4; 9:2-9; 11:11; 2 Kgs. 21:8; 1 Chr. 28:76; 2 Chr. 7:19-22; Jer. 18.

Jer. 15:13-14; 17:1-4). When Israel is rejected by God, the promise of the Land is rejected by God.

Furthermore, the Promised Land serves as a *type* of the whole earth (which is the Lord's, Psa. 24:1). It is, as it were, a *tithe* to the Lord of the entire earth.[16] As such, it pictures the rest brought by Christ's kingdom, which shall cover the earth (see Hebrews 3-4). "Hebrews 11:8-16 shows that although Abraham received the physical land of Canaan, he was looking forward to the eternal city and Kingdom of God. Canaan is a type of the new heavens and earth that began with the first advent of Christ, in seed form (Gal. 4:26; Heb. 12:22-29)."[17] In Psalm 37:11, the psalmist speaks of God's promise to His people: "But the meek shall inherit the land." But Jesus takes this promise and extends it over the entire earth in Matthew 5:5! Abraham apparently understood the land promise as a down payment representing the inheriting of the world (Rom. 4:13). Paul expands the Land promises to extend across all the earth, when he draws them into the New Testament (Eph. 6:3). In several divine covenants, we can trace the expansion of these Land promises: Adam was given a garden (Gen. 2:8); Abraham's seed was given a nation (Josh. 1); the New Covenant Church was given the world (Matt. 28:18-20).[18]

But the fundamental blessedness of the Abrahamic Covenant, like that of the Adamic Covenant before it, is essentially *redemptive* rather than political. The seed line is primarily designed to produce the Savior; the Land promise is typological of the Savior's universal dominion. The Abrahamic Covenant involves a right relationship with God, as indicated in Genesis 17:7: "And I will establish My covenant between Me and you

---

16. David E. Holwerda, *Jesus and Israel: One Covenant or Two?* (Grand Rapids: Eerdmans, 1995), ch. 4.

17. W. Gary Crampton, "Canaan and the Kingdom of God – Conclusion," *Journey* 6 (Jan./March 1991) 19.

18. See my *The Greatness of the Great Commission: The Christian Enterprise in a Fallen World* (Tyler, TX: Institute for Christian Economics, 1990), Part II.

and your descendants after you in their generations, for an everlasting covenant, to be God to you and your descendants after you." That which is most important in the plan of God is the spiritual relation, rather than the blood relation (John 8:44, cf. Matt. 12:47, 50). As Paul says, so it was even in the Old Testament era: "[H]e is not a Jew who is one outwardly, nor is that circumcision which is outward in the flesh; but he is a Jew who is one inwardly, and circumcision is that of the heart, in the Spirit, and not in the letter" (Rom. 2:28-29).[19]

Now let us consider the postmillennial victory expectations inherent in the Abrahamic Covenant. The redemptive line is here narrowed from "the seed of the woman" (i.e., the human race) to the family of Abraham. It will continue to narrow until it issues forth in the singular seed, Christ (Gal. 3:16; John 8:56; cf. Luke 3:23-38). Nevertheless, the redemptive promise ultimately would include "all the families of the earth."[20] The Hebrew word for "families" here is *mispachah*, which includes nations.[21] Thus, the Abrahamic Covenant will include the *nations* beyond Israel. The *ultimate purpose* of the Abrahamic Covenant, in keeping with the Adamic Covenant earlier, is nothing less than *world conversion* (as we shall point out more particularly in our next section), rather than Jewish exaltation, as per dispensationalism.[22] This should be expected since the Lord is

---

19. The internal and ethical are always back of the external and national, and hold priority. For instance, see the emphasis on the spiritual significance of the sacrifices: Psa. 40:6; 51:17; Isa. 1:10-18; 66:2-3; Jer. 6:19-20; Amos 5:21-24; Mic. 6:6-8; Mal. 1:10.

20. Gen. 12:2-3; 13:14-16; 15:5; 16:10; 18:18; 22:17-18; 26:4; 28:14.

21. Psa. 22:27-28; Jer. 1:15; Ezek. 20:32; Amos 3:2; Zech. 14:18.

22. According to dispensationalists, when the Abrahamic Covenant comes to fruition in the millennium: "The redeemed living nation of Israel, regenerated and regathered to the land will be head over all the nations of the earth. . . . So he exalts them above the Gentile nations. . . . On the lowest level there are the saved, living, Gentile nations." Herman Hoyt, "Dispensational Premillennialism," *The Meaning of the Millennium: Four Views*, Robert G. Clouse, ed. (Downer's Grove, IL: InterVarsity Press, 1977), p. 81. On this Zionistic tendency in dispensationalism, see ch. 11 below.

King of the whole earth[23] and desires the world to know Him.[24]

The New Testament clearly informs us of the spiritual implications of the seed, in terms of the blessings for the nations. Abraham has become "the father of circumcision to them who are not of the circumcision only, but who also walk in the steps of that faith of our father Abraham. . . . Therefore it is of faith, that it might be by grace; to the end the promise might be sure to all the seed; not to that only which is of the law, but to that also which is of the faith of Abraham; who is the father of us all" (Rom. 4:12, 16). "Know ye therefore that they which are of faith, the same are the children of Abraham. And the scripture, foreseeing that God would justify the heathen through faith, preached before the gospel unto Abraham, saying, In thee shall all nations be blessed. . . . If ye be Christ's, then are ye Abraham's seed, and heirs according to the promise" (Gal. 3:7-8, 29). Thus, as we shall see in our next section, the Old Testament kingdom prophecies anticipate the sharing of the covenantal glory with others universally.[25]

Due to redemption, the curse of Genesis 3 upon all men is countered by the Abrahamic covenant, in which begins the "nullifying of the curse."[26] The expectation of victory is so strong that we may find casual references based on confident expectation. The seed is promised victory in accordance with the original *protoevangelium*. Abraham's seed is to "possess the gates of the enemy" (cf. Gen. 22:17 with Matt. 16:18).[27] Gene-

---

23. Psa. 22:28; 27:5; 47:2, 7, 8, 29; 66:7; 96:10a; 97:1; 99:1; 103:19; Dan. 4:17, 25, 32.

24. 1 Kgs. 8:43, 60; 2 Chr. 6:33; Psa. 2:9-12; 83:18; Oba. 21.

25. Isa. 25:6; 45:22; 51:4-6; Mic. 4:1ff.

26. G. Charles Aalders, *Genesis*, trans. William Heynen, 2 vols., in *The Bible Student's Commentary* (rand Rapids: Zondervan, [n.d.] 1981), 1:270. See also: Hans K. LaRondelle, *The Israel of God in Prophecy* (Berrien Springs, MI: Andrews University, 1983), p. 91.

27. "Enmity" in Genesis 3:15 (*'ybah*) is related to the verb (*'yb*). In participial form it "occurs repeatedly, alluding frequently to the very struggle between God's and

sis 49:8-10 promises that Judah shall maintain the scepter of rule until Shiloh [Christ] shall come and then to Him "shall be the obedience of the peoples." We should notice the plural "peoples"; Shiloh's winning of obedience is not among the Jews only (the people, singular). Here is the first express mention of a personal redeemer, and that redeemer is promised rule over all the peoples. Ezekiel and Paul both allude to this reference with confidence – Ezekiel in anticipation (Ezek. 21:27), Paul in realization (Gal. 3:19).

Numbers 14:21 confirms the victorious expectation with a *formulaic oath:* "Truly, as I live, all the earth shall be filled with the glory of the LORD." Balaam harkens back to Jacob's prophecy in Genesis 49:10. He foresees an all-powerful, world-wide dominion for the Messiah:

> A star shall come forth from Jacob, and a scepter shall rise from Israel, and shall crush through the forehead of Moab, and tear down all the sons of Sheth. And Edom shall be a possession, Seir, its enemies, also shall be a possession, while Israel performs valiantly. One from Jacob shall have dominion, and shall destroy the remnant from the city (Num 24:17-19).

First Samuel 2:10 promises that "The adversaries of the LORD shall be broken in pieces; from heaven He will thunder against them. The LORD will judge the ends of the earth. He will give strength to His king, and exalt the horn of His anointed." Thus may it be said from the New Testament perspective: "For the promise that he would be the *heir of the world* was not to Abraham or to his seed through the law, but through the righteousness of faith" (Rom. 4:13).

Satan's people." Abraham possesses the gates of his enemies (Gen. 22:17). Judah overcomes his enemies (Gen. 49:8). God shatters His enemies (Exo. 15:6) and will be an enemy to Israel's enemies (Exo. 23:22). The Canaanites are Israel's enemies (Deut. 6:19). Robertson, *Christ of the Covenants*, p. 96n.

Anticipation in the Messianic Psalms

In the prophetic era we discover a rich development of the revelation of God's redemptive plan, and with it the sure promise of a glorious victory for the redeemed. I offer here only a brief consideration of a few of the leading psalmic references.

Psalm 2

Particularly significant in this regard are the Messianic Psalms. In Psalm 2, Jehovah God laughs at the opposition of man to Him and to His Messiah.[28] Psalm 2:2 and Daniel 9:26 show that the term "messiah" (i.e., anointed one) was commonly understood to designate the great Deliverer and King.[29] Kings were "anointed" in the Old Testament.[30] "King" and "Messiah" are used interchangeably in certain places in Scripture (John 1:41, 49; Mark 15:32; Luke 23:2).[31]

According to Peter the opposition of the "nations" to "the Lord and His Messiah" includes the Jews (Acts 4:25-28[32]) and occurs in the ministry of Christ, at His crucifixion. Hebrews 1:5 and 5:5 inform us that Christ fulfills Psalm 2:7. Rather than at the Second Advent,[33] this Psalm's fulfillment is spoken of in

---

28. For the theonomic implications of Psalm 2, see: Greg L. Bahnsen, "The Theonomic Position," *God and Politics: Four Views on the Reformation of Civil Government*, Gary Scott Smith, ed. (Phillipsburg, NJ: Presbyterian & Reformed, 1989), pp. 28-30.

29. J. A. Alexander, *The Psalms Translated and Explained* (Grand Rapids: Baker, [1873] 1977), p. 13.

30. 1 Sam. 10:1; 16:13,14; 2 Sam. 2:4, 7; 3:39; 5:3, 17; 12:7; 19:10; 1 Kgs. 1:39, 45; 5:1; 2 Kgs. 9:3, 6, 12; 11:12; 23:30; 1 Chr. 11:3; 14:8; 29:22; 2 Chr. 23:11; Psa. 18:50.

31. See also the close association of kingdom and Christ in Acts 8:12; Eph. 5:5; 2 Tim. 4:1; Rev. 11:15.

32. "According to Acts 4:25-28, vv. 1 and 2 have been fulfilled in the confederate hostility of Israel and the Gentiles against Jesus the holy servant of God and against His confessors." Franz Delitzsch, *The Psalms*, 3 vols. (Grand Rapids: Eerdmans, [1867] 1973), 1:90. Israel's priority in resisting Christ is indisputable. See: Matt. 22:33-46; 23:29-38; Luke 19:14; John 11:47; 19:14-15; Acts 5:17, 33; 1 Thess. 2:16.

33. Anthony Hoekema, *The Bible and the Future* (Grand Rapids: Eerdmans, 1979),

Acts 13:33-34 as set in motion with the resurrection of Christ: "God has fulfilled this for us their children, in that He has raised up Jesus. As it is also written in the second Psalm: 'You are My Son, today I have begotten You.' And that He raised Him from the dead, no more to return to corruption, He has spoken thus: 'I will give you the sure mercies of David.' " The exaltation of Christ (including His resurrection, ascension, and session) establishes Him as king (Rom. 1:4; Matt. 28:18). It is at *Jerusalem*, the location of Zion (Psa. 2:6), where Jesus is both crucified (suffering the resistance and rage of the nations, Psa. 2:1-3) and resurrected (Psa. 2:7; Acts 13:33). It is there also that the gospel is first preached in the New Covenant era (Luke 24:49-52; Acts 1-2).

The Messiah is promised dominion over the "nations" (not just one nation, Israel) and "the ends of the earth" (not just one region, Palestine) as His permanent "possession" (Psa. 2:8). Though they would resist Him (Psa. 2:1-3), He would break them in His dominion (Psa. 2:9). On the basis of this promise, the kings and judges of the earth are exhorted to worship and serve the Son (Psa. 2:10-12). It anticipates progressive fulfillment — in time and on earth.

Psalm 22

Psalm 22 prophesies that "all the ends of the earth [extensive] will remember[34] and turn to the Lord, and all the families [intensive] of the nations will worship before Thee" (v. 27).[35] Interestingly, like Psalm 2, this psalm opens with a reference to Christ's suffering. In fact, Psalm 22:1-21 is universally

---

p. 178. Allen P. Ross, "Psalms," *The Bible Knowledge Commentary: Old Testament*, John F. Walvoord and Roy B. Zuck, eds. (Wheaton, IL: Victor, 1985), p. 792.

34. They "remember" because of their being created in God's image (Gen. 1:26) and having an innate awareness of the Creator (Rom. 1:19-20).

35. Cf. Psa. 66:4; 68:31-32; 82:8; 86:9. In the Old Testament, worshiping before God meant worshiping in Jerusalem. But in Messiah's day it means worshiping anywhere: Matt. 18:20; John 4:21; Isa. 66:23; Mal. 1:11.

recognized among evangelicals as prophesying the crucifixion. Verse 1 is uttered by Christ in His agony on the cross (Matt. 27:46); verse 18 is also fulfilled at the cross (John 19:2). But it immediately makes its way to His glorious dominion (vv. 22-31), as per the pattern applied to His crucifixion and resurrection in the New Testament: sufferings, then glory (Luke 24:26; 1 Pet. 1:11). After the suffering His praise will be declared in the Church (Psa. 22:22; Heb. 2:12). That praise includes the Church ("great assembly," Heb. 12:23) proclaiming His victory (Psa. 22:27ff). The reason He will save the earth is that the earth is His by right (Psa. 22:28); He created the material earth for His glory.

Alexander and Hengstenberg both note the interesting collusion of Christ's concluding words on the cross ("It is finished") with the closing words of Psalm 22, which speaks of the cross and the glory to follow: "He has performed it."[36] The performance of His work is redemptive, including the cross and the crown. This obviously anticipates the fruition of the covenant of God given to Abraham and expanded in Moses and David. This cannot be understood amillennially as in heaven or in the New Earth, for it speaks of the earth as turning and remembering, i.e., *conversions*. It also speaks of death (v. 29) and later generations following their fathers (vv. 30-31).

Psalm 72

Here the Messianic victory theme is tied to pre-consummative history, before the establishment of the eternal New Heavens and Earth. "Let them fear Thee *while the sun endures*, and *as long as the moon*, throughout all *generations*. May he come down like rain upon the mown grass, Like showers that water the earth. In his days may the righteous flourish, and abundance of

---

36. Alexander, *Psalms*, p. 107; E. W. Hengstenberg, *Christology of the Old Testament*, 2 vols. (McLean, VA: MacDonald, [1854] n.d.), 1:396.

peace till the moon is no more, may he also rule from sea to
sea, and from the River to the ends of the earth" (vv. 5-8).

Psalm 72 is a "glowing description of the reign of the Messiah, as righteous (vv. 1-7), universal (vv. 8-11), beneficent (vv.
12-14), perpetual (vv. 15-17)."[37] It speaks of the social (vv. 2-4,
12-14) and economic benefits of His reign (v. 16), as well as the
spiritual benefits (vv. 5-7, 17). The imagery of pouring rain
here reflects the spiritual presence of Christ in the Person of
the Holy Spirit (Rom. 8:9; John 14:16-18) being poured out
upon the world from on high (Isa. 32:15; 44:3; Ezek. 39:29;
Joel 2:28-29; Zech. 12:10; Acts 2:17-18).

According to the Psalmist, kings of the various nations will
rule in submission to Him (vv. 10-11). Because of His beneficent reign, there will be a population increase (v. 16b; Zech.
2:4). The flourishing of the righteous (v. 7) in the city (v. 16)
indicates a rapid increase in population under His beneficence,
as wars and pestilence cease. Population increase is associated
with Messiah's reign in prophecy (Psa. 110:3; Isa. 9:2; 49:20;
Zech. 2:4). This is in harmony with the Cultural Mandate (Gen.
1:26ff) and covenantal blessing (Deut. 28:4; Lev. 26:9).[38]

Psalm 110

Psalm 110:1 is the Old Testament passage most frequently
quoted and alluded to in the New Testament.[39] It has a great
bearing on New Testament theology. Psalm 110:1-2 reads: "The
LORD said to my Lord, 'Sit at My right hand, Till I make Your
enemies Your footstool.' The LORD shall send the rod of Your
strength out of Zion. Rule in the midst of Your enemies!"

---

37. Alexander, *Psalms*, p. 301.

38. See also: Gen. 9:1, 7; 17:6; 28:3; 35:11; 48:4; Psa. 128:3; Jer. 23:3.

39. Quotations include: Matt. 22:44; 26:64; Mark 12:36; 14:62; Luke 20:42-43;
22:69; Acts 2:34-35; Heb. 1:13. Allusions may be found in: 1 Cor. 15:24; Eph. 1:20-
22; Phil. 2:9-11; Heb. 1:3; 8:1; 10:12, 13; 1 Pet. 3:22; Rev. 3:21. For a detailed study
of this psalm's impact in both Jewish and Christian literature, see David M. Hay,
Glory at the Right Hand: Psalm 110 in Early Christianity (Nashville: Abingdon, 1973).

The Psalm is purely prophetic, having no reference to David himself. This becomes obvious in Jesus' teaching in Matthew 22:42-45 and in that David was not a priest (v. 4). And it clearly anticipates Christ's enemies being subjugated by Him. But He does this while sitting at the right hand of God ("sit until"[40]), not in arising, leaving heaven, and returning to the earth at the Second Advent. That this Psalm is now in force, expecting the ultimate victory of Christ, is evident in both its numerous New Testament allusions and in that He is already the Melchizedekan priest, mentioned in verse 4 (cf. Heb. 7). This peculiar priest was one who was both king and priest, according to Genesis 14:18, as is Christ.

His strong rod will rule from Zion, which portrays the New Covenant-phase Church as headquartered at Jerusalem where the gospel was first preached. He rules through His rod, which is His Word (Isa. 2:3; 11:4). He leads His people onward into battle against the foe (v. 3). The allusion to kings in verse 5, following as it does the reference to Melchizedek in verse 4, probably reflects back on Abraham's meeting with Melchizedek after his conquest of the four kings in Genesis 14. Because "kings" is in the emphatic position in Hebrew, it indicates Christ will not only rule the lowly, but also kings and nations through His redemptive power, as in Psalms 2 and 72. His rule shall be over governments, as well as individuals; it will be societal, as well as personal.

Anticipation in the Prophets

The prophets greatly expand the theme of victory under the Messiah. I will highlight several of the prophetic pronouncements regarding victory. Due to space limitations only three of these from Isaiah will be given a fuller treatment.[41]

---

40. The Hebrew adverbial particle *'d* indicates duration. See: J. J. Stewart Perowne, *The Book of Psalms*, 2 vols. (Andover, MA: Warren F. Draper, 1894), 2:292-293.

41. For fuller helpful exposition see: Hengstenberg, *Christology of the Old Testa-*

Isaiah 2:1-4

In Isaiah 2, we learn that in the "last days," there will be a universally attractive influence of the worship of God, an international dispersion and influence of Christianity, issuing forth in righteous living on the personal level and peace on the international level: "He shall judge between the nations, And shall rebuke many people; They shall beat their swords into plowshares, and their spears into pruninghooks" (v. 4a). Isaiah indicates the "last days" will be the era that witnesses these things – not some era *after* these last days. The "last days" begin with the coming of Christ.[42] Isaiah's younger contemporary, Micah, repeats this prophecy almost verbatim (Micah 4:1-3).

Here the reference to "Judah and Jerusalem" stand for the people of God, as "Israel and Judah" do in Jeremiah 31:31, which is specifically applied to the Church in the New Testament.[43] The reference to the "mountain," the "house of the God of Jacob," and "Zion" refer to the Church, which, according to the express revelation of the New Testament, is the temple and house of God[44] and the earthly representation of the city of God (Heb. 12:22; 1 Pet. 2:6[45]) is set on a hill (Matt. 5:14; Heb. 12:22).[46] Again, we must remember that it was *in Jerusalem* where the historical redemption by Christ was

---

ment; J. A. Alexander, *Commentary on the Prophecies of Isaiah.*

42. That is, in the times initiated by Christ at His First Advent, Acts 2:16, 17, 24; 1 Cor. 10:11; Gal. 4:4; Heb. 1:1,2; 9:26; Jms. 5:3; 1 Pet. 1:20; 1 John 2:18; Jude 18. For a discussion of "the last days," see ch. 14 below.

43. See my previous discussion: ch. 8.

44. The Church is the "temple of God," 1 Cor. 3:16; 6:19; 2 Cor. 6:16; Eph. 2:19-22; 1 Pet. 2:5. She is specifically designated "the house of God," 1 Tim. 3:15; Heb. 2:6; 1 Pet. 4:17. See my discussion in ch. 15 below.

45. The heavenly city of God comes to earth in the establishment of Christ's kingdom and Church, Rev. 3:12; 21:2, 10, 14ff. See my brief discussion of Revelation 21-22 in ch. 17 below.

46. See discussion of "The Holy Mountain": David Chilton, *Paradise Restored: A Biblical Theology of Dominion* (Ft. Worth, TX: Dominion Press, 1985), ch. 4.

wrought (Acts 10:39; Rom. 9:33; 1 Pet. 2:6)[47] and where Christianity began (Acts 1-2).

Isaiah's statement that it will be "established" (Heb.: *kun*) in "the top of the mountains" indicates Christ's Church will be "permanently fixed, rendered permanently visible."[48] After the introductory phrase "last days," Isaiah places the word "established" first for emphasis. In the eschatological portrayals of Ezekiel and Zechariah, this house is gigantic (Ezek. 40:2); Jerusalem is seen towering over a plain (Zech. 14:10).

Christianity, the last stage of God's redemptive plan in history, will be so established as to be firmly fixed: "And I also say to you that you are Peter, and on this rock I will build My church, and the gates of Hades shall not prevail against it" (Matt. 16:18). "Therefore, since we are receiving a kingdom which cannot be shaken, let us have grace, by which we may serve God acceptably with reverence and godly fear" (Heb. 12:28).[49]

In Isaiah 2:2 and Micah 4:1, there is a niphal participle that "must be understood of *an enduring condition*, and the same is implied in the representation in vss. 3, 4 of Jehovah's teaching function, of his judging between many nations and of the state of peace and security prevailing, every man sitting under his vine and fig-tree and to make none of them afraid (the last in Micah only)."[50]

---

47. A well-known phenomenon in Luke's gospel is his emphasis on Jerusalem, particularly Christ's determination to go there for His crucifixion. It was eschatologically necessary for Him to die in Jerusalem, so that His redemption would flow from the "city of peace" to effect "peace with God" (Rom. 5:1; 15:33; 16:20; 2 Cor. 13:11; Phil. 4:9; 2 John 3): "Nevertheless I must journey today, tomorrow, and the day following; for it cannot be that a prophet should perish outside of Jerusalem" (Luke 13:33). See also: Conzelmann's discussion of Jerusalem in Luke's eschatology. H. Conzelmann, *The Theology of St. Luke* (New York: Harper & Row, 1957), pp. 132ff.

48. J. A. Alexander, *The Prophecies of Isaiah* (Grand Rapids: Zondervan, [1875] 1977), 1:97.

49. Matt. 7:24-27; 1 Cor. 3:11; Eph. 2:20; 2 Tim. 2:19; Rev. 21:9ff.

50. Geerhardus Vos, *The Pauline Eschatology* (Phillipsburg, NJ: Presbyterian & Reformed, [1930] 1991), p. 7.

To this eschatological phenomenon "all nations shall flow" (Isa. 2:2-3); it will witness "the gathering of the people" (Gen. 49:10) and shall enjoy the flowing in of "many people and strong nations" (Zech. 8:20-23).

The nations shall flow there like a river to worship the Lord as a result of the desire wrought in conversion; they shall be discipled in His ways and learn the strictures of holiness from His Law (Isa. 2:3). The coming of the eschatological fulfillment of redemption (Mark 1:15; Matt. 13:17; Acts 2:16ff; Gal. 4:4; Heb. 1:1, 2) leads to the permanent establishment of Christianity as an agency of gracious influence in the world unto salvation and sanctification. Evangelism is indicated in the flowing river of people urging others to "come, go ye" to the house of God (Isa. 2:3). With the overwhelming numbers being converted to a saving knowledge of Christ and being discipled in God's Law,[51] great social transformation naturally follows (Isa. 2:4). "It is a picture of universal peace that Isaiah gives, but it is a religiously founded peace."[52] The peace with God (vv. 2-3) gives rise to peace among men (v. 4).

Amillennialist Hanko disposes of this postmillennial text as treated by Boettner with an incredible sweep of the hand: "Now it is true that Mount Zion has a symbolic and typical meaning in Scripture. It is also true that the reference is often to the Church of Jesus Christ – as Boettner remarks in connection with Hebrews 12:22. But one wonders at the tremendous jump which is made from the idea of Mount Zion as symbolic of the Church to the idea that 'the Church, having attained a position so that it stands out like a mountain on a plain, will be prominent and regulative in all world affairs.' There is not so much as a hint of this idea in the text. The conclusion is wholly unwarranted."[53] Having granted that Mount Zion is "symbolic

51. See Gentry, *Greatness of the Great Commission*; North, *Millennialism and Social Theory*.

52. E. J. Young, *The Book of Isaiah* (Grand Rapids: Eerdmans, 1965), 1:107.

53. Herman Hanko, "An Exegetical Refutation of Postmillennialism" (South Hol-

of the Church," how can Hanko legitimately call the postmillennial argument a "tremendous jump" with "not so much as a hint" and "wholly unwarranted"? Hanko's argument is merely a loud denial rooted in his pre-disposition to amillennialism. What we need here is careful exegesis, not loud assertions as a substitute for exegesis.

Isaiah 9:6-7

To understand Isaiah 9:1-7 we need to notice the close connection between the birth of "the son" (His redemptive humiliation, v. 6) and the devolving of universal government upon Him (at His exaltation at the resurrection/ ascension). The promise is that *this kingdom will grow, issuing forth in peace* (v. 7). When Messiah is born into the world, He will be granted His kingdom. The preceding context points also to the first coming of Christ for the beginning of the fulfillment of this prophecy. The reference in verse 2 to the people in darkness who see a great light finds fulfillment in Christ. In fact, the great light is Christ (John 8:12; 12:46). According to Matthew 4:16 this begins to be fulfilled in the ministry of Christ.

In verse 3 the Lord promises to multiply Israel. This is according to the Abrahamic Covenant promise of a great seed and influence among the nations. It is accomplished by the calling of the Gentiles as the seed of Abraham (Gal. 3:29), which involves the ingrafting of them into the stock of Israel (Rom. 11:16-19), the merging of Jew and Gentile into one body (Eph. 2:11-17). The increase of Israel's joy (verse 3) indicates the joy in the coming of the Savior (Luke 2:10; John 3:29[54]). As in Isaiah 2:3-4 the coming of Christ will result in the cessation of oppression and war (verses 4-5), which is here portrayed in the burning of the garments of soldiers, symbolizing they will

---

land, IL: South Holland Protestant Reformed Church, 1978), p. 6.

54. Christ brings joy to His people, John 15:11; 16:20ff. Where Christianity goes, joy follows, Acts 8:8; 13:52; 15:3; Rom. 14:17; 15:13; 1 Pet. 1:8; 1 John 1:4.

no longer be needed,[55] just as the swords were cast off earlier (Isa. 2:4).

The reign of Christ over His kingdom, which was entered at His first coming,[56] will be "progressive and perpetual."[57] In prophecy Christ is referred to as the son or branch of David (Jer. 23:5; 33:13), or as David himself (Jer. 30:9; Ezek. 34:23, 23; 37:24; Hos. 3:5). At His resurrection, He is raised up to the throne of David (Acts 2:30-31), which represents the throne of the Lord (1 Chr. 28:5; 29:23). Again, *His reign brings peace*, for He is the "Prince of Peace" (Isa. 9:6). This peace grows incrementally through history: Christ "extends its boundaries far and wide, and then preserves and carries it forward in uninterrupted progression to eternity."[58] His righteous rule begins at His first coming (Mark 1:14-15; Luke 1:32-33).

Isaiah 11:9

Isaiah 11:1-10 speaks gloriously of the eschatological hope begun with Adam, flowing through Noah, and expanded with Abraham. The rod/branch from the stem/roots spoken of here continues the thought of the preceding context. The collapse of David's house and of the Jewish government is set in contrast to the fall of Assyria (Isa. 10). The remaining, nearly extinct house of David, reduced to a stump, still has life and will bud with a branch. That branch is Christ: He restores the house of David in the New Testament,[59] hence the emphasis in the New Testament on his genealogy from David (Matt. 1:1-17; Luke 3:23-38[60]).

---

55. Young, *Isaiah*, 1:328.

56. For argumentation, see Chapter 11, below.

57. Alexander, *Prophecies of Isaiah*, 1:205.

58. Calvin, *Commentary on the Book of the Prophet Isaiah*, trans. William Pringle (Grand Rapids: Eerdmans, [n.d.] 1948), 1:96. See later discussion of the principle of gradualism in Chapter 12, below.

59. Matt. 1:17,18; Mark 11:10; Acts 2:34-36; 13:34; 15:16.

60. See also: Luke 1:27, 32, 69; 2:4; 9:27; 12:23; 15:22; 20:30-31; 21:9, 15; Rom.

This coming of Christ (His First Advent as a stem or branch), is with the fullness of the Holy Spirit (Isa. 11:2)[61] and leads to judgment upon His adversaries (v. 4, particularly first-century Israel, Matt. 3:1-12; 24:2-34; Rev. 1-19). As in the other prophecies surveyed, righteousness and peace flow after Him. Isaiah describes the peace between men as a removal of the enmity between wolf and lamb, bear and cow, lion and calf, leopard and kid, serpent and child.[62] Their warring nature is changed by the grace of God (cf. Eph. 2:1-4).

The future of the earth is seen as glorious: "They shall not hurt nor destroy in all My holy mountain, for the earth shall be full of the knowledge of the LORD as the waters cover the sea" (Isa. 11:9).[63] This comes about *gradually*, beginning "in that day" when the "root of Jesse" shall stand as a banner (signal, place of rendezvous[64]) to the Gentiles (v. 10) followed by the conversion of the Jews (v. 11). The calling of the Gentiles to Christ beginning in the first century is clear evidence the fulfillment of verse 10 is underway, continuing even to this very day (Rom. 15:4-12, see especially v. 12). The future conversion of

---

1:3; Rev. 3:7; 5:5; 22:16.

61. Matt. 3:16-4:1; 12:17-21; Luke 4:14-21; John 3:34; Acts 10:38.

62. It may be that this imagery speaks of an actual domestication of wild animals (Calvin, Hengstenberg, and North). See North, *The Dominion Covenant: Genesis* (2nd ed.; Tyler, TX: Institute for Christian Economics, 1987), p. 113. In light of the paucity of the evidence for such elsewhere (this imagery occurs in Isaiah 11 and 65:25), the preceding Isaianic prophecies of international peace among men, and the limitation of the subject to "in my holy mountain" (where men worship) would seem counter to such a view, however. Several of these dangerous creatures are compared to Satan and sinners elsewhere: wolves (Ezek. 22:27; Zeph. 3:3; Matt. 7:15; 10:16), bears (Prov. 28:15; Lam. 3:10; Dan. 7:5; Rev. 13:2), serpents (Psa. 140:3; 2 Cor. 11:3; Rev. 12:9ff), leopards (Jer. 13:23; Dan. 7:6; Rev. 13:2), and lions (Jer. 12:8; Ezek. 22:25; Dan. 7:4; 1 Pet. 5:8; Rev. 13:2). Three of them converge in the Daniel 7 and Revelation 13 image of wicked rulers, perhaps suggesting that Isaiah speaks of the pacification of rulers through conversion.

63. The employment of the future tense in the first clause ("they shall not hurt or destroy") and a preterit in the second clause ("the earth shall be full of the knowledge of the Lord" suggests the initial fulfillment of the spread of righteousness through faith, followed by peace.

64. Cf. John 11:52; 12:32.

the Jews will conclude the fulfillment (Rom. 11:12-25).[65] We learn later that even the arch-enemies of God and His people, Egypt and Assyria, will be healed and will on an equal footing worship with Israel (Isa. 19:22-24). The God of the Bible is the Healer of the nations.

Additional Prophecies

Jeremiah foresees the day when the ark of the covenant will no longer be remembered, but in which "all the nations will be gathered before" the "throne of the Lord" (Jer. 3:16-17). The New Covenant (initiated by Christ, Luke 22:20; 1 Cor. 11:25) will issue forth in worldwide salvation (Jer. 31:31-34). Natural enemies of God's Old Testament people will be brought to blessing in the era of the last days: Moab (Jer. 48:47), Ammon (Jer. 49:6); Elam (Jer. 49:39).[66]

With Isaiah, Daniel sees the expansion of the kingdom to the point of worldwide dominion: "And in the days of these kings the God of heaven will set up a kingdom which shall never be destroyed; and the kingdom shall not be left to other people; it shall break in pieces and consume all these kingdoms, and it shall stand forever" (Dan. 2:44; cf. Isa. 9:6-7). Christ's kingdom shall crush the world kingdom, expressed in the Lord's day in the Roman Empire.[67] The Messiah's ascension and session will guarantee world dominion: "I was watching in the night vi-

---

65. See later discussion in Chapter 15. See also: Alexander, *Isaiah*, 1:257ff.

66. See also: Egypt and Assyria (Isa. 19:23-25); the Gentiles (Isa. 49:23); Edom (Amos 9:12); many nations (Zech. 2:11); the Philistines (Zech. 9:7).

67. Although the imagery in Daniel 2 suggests a rapid destruction of the image, it is not uncommon for the occurrence to come about gradualistically in prophecy (see ch. 12 below on the principle of gradualism in prophecy). "Thus the threatening against Babylon, contained in the thirteenth and fourteenth chapters of Isaiah, if explained as a specific and exclusive prophecy of the Medo-Persian conquest, seems to represent the downfall of the city as more sudden and complete than it appears in history." However, that prophecy should be "regarded as a panorama of the fall of Babylon, not in its first inception merely, but through all its stages till its consummation." Alexander, *Isaiah*, 1:30.

sions, and behold, One like the Son of Man, coming with the clouds of heaven! He came to the Ancient of Days, and they brought Him near before Him. Then to Him was given dominion and glory and a kingdom, that all peoples, nations, and languages should serve Him. His dominion is an everlasting dominion, which shall not pass away, and His kingdom the one which shall not be destroyed" (Dan. 7:13-14). We must notice that Daniel 7:13-14 speaks of the Christ's ascension *to the Ancient of Days*, not His return to the earth. It is from this ascension to the right hand of God[68] that there will flow forth universal dominion: days of prosperity, peace, and righteousness lie in the future.[69] Particularly in Isaiah and Ezekiel "the catholicity of the Church's worship is expressed by all nations flowing to Jerusalem, and going up to the mountain of the Lord, to the house of the God of Jacob; whereas in Malachi, *instead of them going to the temple, the temple is represented as coming to them. . . .* [W]e must understand both representations as designed to announce just the *catholicity* and *spirituality* of the Gospel worship."[70]

These and many other such references refer to the *interadvental age*, not to the Eternal State (as per the amillennial view), for the following reasons.

First, numerous prophetic references speak of *factors inappropriate to the eternal state*, such as the overcoming of active opposition to the kingdom (e.g., Psa. 72:4, 9; Isa. 11: 4, 13-15; Mic. 4:3), birth and aging (e.g., Psa. 22:30-31; Isa. 65:20; Zech. 8:3-5) the conversion of people (Psa. 72:27), death (e.g., Psa. 22:29; 72:14; Isa. 65:20), sin (e.g., Isa. 65:20; Zech. 14:17-19),

68. See later discussion of His present Kingship in Chapter 11 below.

69. Psa. 22:27; 46:8-10; 47:3; 66:4; 67:4; 86:9; 67:2; 72:11, 17; 82:8; 86:9; 102:15; Isa. 2:2-3; 25:6-7; 40:5; 49:6, 22-23; 52:15; 55:5; 60:1-7, 10-14; 61:11; 66:19-20; Jer. 3:17; 4:2; Dan. 7:14; Amos 9:11-15; Mic. 4:1-3; 5:2-4, 16-17; 7:16-17; Hab. 2:14-20; Hag. 2:7ff; Zeph. 3:10; Zech. 2:11; 8:22-23; 9:9-10; 14:16; Mal. 1:11; 3:1-12.

70. David Brown, *Christ's Second Coming: Will It Be Premillennial?* (Edmonton, Alberta: Still Waters Revival Books, [1882] 1990), p. 347.

suffering (e.g., Psa. 22:29; 72:2, 13, 17), and national distinctions and interaction (e.g., Psa. 72:10-11, 17; Isa. 2:2-4; Zech. 14:16-17).

Second, though reduced to minority proportions, the curse will continue, despite the dominance of victory (Isa. 65:25). Isaiah 19:18 may suggest a world ratio of five Christians to one non-Christian.[71]

Third, some prophetic language is indisputably applied to *the First Advent of Christ.* Isaiah 9:6 ties Christ's Messianic rule in with His birth: "For unto us a child is born, unto us a son is given: and the government shall be upon his shoulder: and his name shall be called Wonderful, Counsellor, The mighty God, The Everlasting Father, The Prince of Peace" (Isa. 9:6). In Daniel 2, He appears as the destroyer of the world empires in the days of the fourth kingdom, Rome (Dan. 2:35ff).

Fourth, some prophetic passages expect the *present, pre-consummative order of things* to continue into that glorious era, such as the continuance of the sun and the moon (Psa. 72:5, 7, 17). Yet 2 Peter 3 indicates the conflagration of the universe prior to its renewal for eternity.

Fifth, hermeneutically it would seem that *prophetic figures should not be figures of figures.* For instance, if the nations' breaking their bows and spears is a figure of peace, would the prophetic breaking of bows and spears be a figure of peace (the absence of carnal warfare), which would, in turn, be a figure of salvation (the absence of spiritual warfare with God)?

Conclusion

The Old Testament anticipates the coming, development, and victory in history of the Messianic kingdom. This hope is

---

71. This view is held by such commentators as: J. A. Alexander, *Commentary on the Prophecies of Isaiah* (Grand Rapids: Zondervan, [1875] 1977), 1:355-357. John Calvin, *Commentary on the Book of the Prophet Isaiah*, trans. by William Pringle (Grand Rapids: Eerdmans, rep. 1948), 68-71. Matthew Henry, *Matthew Henry's Commentary* (Old Tappan, NJ: Revell, [1712] n.d.), 4:108.

traceable from the earliest days of God's covenantal dealings with man. The divine covenants of the Old Testament frame in the covenantal hope of dominion, while the prophets fill out that Messianic expectation. The Old Testament expects universal acquiescence to the rule of Messiah. This rule is founded in the spiritual realm, but is not limited to it. His rule will have objective effects in *all* areas of life – not just the soul, the family, and the local church. Christ's redemption is as comprehensive as sin is, and more powerful. Christ's bodily resurrection was more powerful than death. So are the objective effects of His resurrection in history.

11

REALIZATION

After John was put in prison, Jesus came to Galilee, preaching the gospel of the kingdom of God, and saying, "The time is fulfilled, and the kingdom of God is at hand. Repent, and believe in the gospel." (Mark 1:14-15)

The Scriptures, being an infallible and unified revelation of God, continue the prophetic victory theme into the New Testament. This is despite the charges by some amillennialists that the postmillennial hope cannot be sustained in the New Testament: "Whatever support postmillennialism may draw from its own interpretation of the Old Testament, we question seriously whether the New Testament gives any valid encouragement to this theory."[1] As I shall show, such charges are wholly without merit. There is ample witness to the postmillennial hope in the New Testament revelation. While dispensationalism's Zionistic approach to the kingdom promises of the Old Testament runs into serious problems in the New Testament, such is not the case with postmillennialism.

On the one hand, it seems that premillennialism finds its greatest strength in the Old Testament, when divorced from

---

1. George L. Murray, *Millennial Studies: A Search for Truth* (Grand Rapids: Eerdmans, 1948), p. 86. See also: Richard B. Gaffin, "Theonomy and Eschatology: Reflections on Postmillennialism," *Theonomy: A Reformed Critique*, William S. Barker and W. Robert Godfrey, eds. (Grand Rapids: Zondervan, 1990), p. 217.

the New. This is undeniably the situation with dispensational premillennialism. On the other hand, amillennialism garners its strongest arguments from the New Testament, when interpreted apart from its Old Testament foundations. Postmillennialism alone relates *both* the Old and New Testament revelation into one unified eschatological framework. To test my assertion, let us then turn our attention to the New Testament record.

Inauguration

The Birth of the King

In paradigmatic, biblico-theological fashion, Luke, in the first chapter of his gospel, draws upon and arranges the Old Covenant expectations that were uttered in response to the announcement of Christ's birth. As he brings the Old Testament expectations over into the New Testament, he rephrases the prophecies in terms of their New Covenant fruition. Interestingly, most of these are in poetic-song format, indicating the joyousness of the expectations (Luke 1:46-55, 67-79; 2:14, 29-32)..

In the angelic annunciation to Mary of the nativity of her Son, Christ is promised the Davidic throne of rule, which will know no end: " 'He will be great, and will be called the Son of the Highest; and the Lord God will give Him the throne of His father David. And He will reign over the house of Jacob forever, and of His kingdom there will be no end' " (Luke 1:32-33). This is surely an "echo of the sublime prediction" in Isaiah 9:6-7.[2] We should remember from our earlier study that Isaiah 9:6-7 ties in *kingdom dominion* with the *birth of the king* as historically successive realities. As I will show later, Daniel 7:13 equates Christ's coronation with His historical ascension leading to His supra-historical session. Daniel 2 also speaks of His king-

---

2. David Brown, "Matthew," *A Commentary, Critical and Explanatory on the Old and New Testaments*, Robert Jamieson, A. R. Faussett, and David Brown, eds., 2 vols. (Hartford: S. S. Scranton, n.d.), 2:97.

dom coming in the days of the fourth kingdom, Rome (Dan. 2:40-45). The pattern of the New Testament is: humiliation followed *immediately* by exaltation (John 7:39; Luke 24:26; 1 Pet. 1:11). Later I will show that He presently rules as Messianic king and that His rule will extend into eternity. Christ has received "David's" throne ordained in prophetic imagery (Acts 2:29-36; 3:13-15; 5:29-31; Rev. 3:7).

The reference in Luke 1:33 to Christ's ruling over "the house of Jacob" is significant. Jacob was the father of the "twelve tribes of Israel." Thus, this reference should be understood as alluding to the totality of the "Israel of God," which includes all of the redeemed, Jew and Gentile alike. Luke's companion, Paul, makes this especially clear (Gal. 3:29; 6:16; Eph. 2:12-22).[3]

Mary's Magnificat (Luke 1:46-55) reverberates with the victory theme. In verses 47 and 48, she exalts the Lord as Savior, recognizing God's glorious blessing upon her: "From this time on all generations will count me blessed." Why this universal homage? Because "the Mighty One" (v. 49) has begun to move in history in a powerful way, using Mary for His glory. The prognostication is guided by the prophetic victory theme, not by despair, lamentation, and expectation of perpetual suffering. She recognizes that in the soon-coming birth of Christ, God will do "mighty deeds with His arm," He will "scatter the proud" (v. 51). He will "bring down rulers" and "exalt those who are humble" (v. 52). He will fill "the hungry with good things" (v. 53). He will do it through His people (v. 54) in keeping with the Abrahamic Covenant (v. 55). There is absolutely no intimation of defeat here.

Zacharias' prophecy continues the glad tidings. He sees Christ's birth as bringing tidings of victory for God's people

---

3. See my earlier discussion in ch. 8. Even the premillennialist admits that in their Millennium Christ rules over *all people*, not just the "house of Jacob" literally conceived.

over their enemies (Luke 1:68-71). This, again, is *in fulfillment of the Abrahamic Covenant* (v. 73; cf. Rom. 15:8-12). Christ is the sunrise that will "shine upon those who sit in darkness and the shadow of death" (vv. 78-79). Elsewhere this refers to the Gentiles (Isa. 9:1,2; Matt. 4:16). This light is later seen as a positive force, dispelling darkness in the present age (Rom. 13:11-13; 1 John 2:8). Because Christ has come, He will bring "peace *on earth*" (Luke 2:14a). It is His birth at His first coming that insures the peace *on earth*, not His second coming (although in the consummative New Earth this peace will come to perfect, eternal realization[4]).

The Approach of the Kingdom

In sure expectation of the fulfillment of the Old Covenant expectations and nativity prophecies, Christ's ministerial appearance on the scene of history is introduced with a pronouncement of the nearness of the kingdom.

John Baptist, Christ's divinely commissioned forerunner, preached: "Repent, for the kingdom of heaven is at hand" (Matt. 3:2). In Mark 1:14-15, Jesus took up the same theme: "And after John had been taken into custody, Jesus came into Galilee, preaching the gospel of God, and saying, 'The time is fulfilled, and the kingdom of God is at hand; repent and believe the gospel.' " This is a very important statement. Let us note three crucial aspects of this declaration.

First, Christ asserts "the time" is fulfilled. What is "the time" to which He refers here? The Greek term employed is *kairos*, which indicates "the 'fateful and decisive point,' with strong, though not always explicit, emphasis . . . on the fact that it is ordained by God."[5] This "time" surely refers to the propheti-

---

4. See ch. 13 below.

5. Gerhard Delling, "*kairos*," *Theological Dictionary of the New Testament*, Gerhard Kittel, ed., trans. Geoffrey Bromiley, 10 vols. (Grand Rapids: Eerdmans, 1965), 3:459.

cally anticipated time, the time of the coming of David's greater Son to establish His kingdom, for He immediately adds, "the *kingdom of God* is at hand." Christ was sent by the Father in "the fullness of time" (Gal. 4:4; Eph. 1:10),[6] to initiate the "favorable year of the Lord" (Luke 4:16-21).[7] This time is "the accepted time"/"the day of salvation" (2 Cor. 6:2). It is the very day righteous men and angels desired to see.[8]

Second, Christ clearly asserts that the time "is fulfilled." Actually, a better translation of the verb tense and voice here (the perfect passive) would be: "[T]he time has been fulfilled." Luke 4:21 is similar to Mark 1:14-15 in regard to the time fulfillment: "And He began to say to them, 'Today this Scripture is fulfilled in your hearing.' " The perfect tense (*peplerotai*, "has come to fulfillment") and emphatic position of "today" strongly emphasize that fulfillment has begun.[9] That which has begun to be fulfilled is Isaiah 61:1ff, from which Christ quotes. The "acceptable year of the Lord" had come.

Apparently John Baptist is significant for Christ as a sort of line of demarcation separating the fading *kingdom-expectation* era from the *kingdom-fulfillment* era, which begins dawning with John's demise. Earlier, John noted of Jesus: "He must increase, but I must decrease" (John 3:30). Jesus observes of John: "Assuredly, I say to you, among those born of women there has not risen one greater than John the Baptist; but he who is least in the kingdom of heaven is greater than he. And from the days of John the Baptist until now the kingdom of heaven

---

6. Of the Eph. 1:10 reference Hodge comments: "This phrase does not indicate a protracted period – *the times which remain* – but the termination of times; the end of the preceding and commencement of the new dispensation." Charles Hodge, *Commentary on the Epistle to the Ephesians* (Grand Rapids: Eerdmans, [1865] n.d.), p. 48. This was reprinted by the Banner of Truth in 1958 and later printings.

7. For a related discussion of "the last days," see ch. 14 below.

8. Matt. 13:17; Luke 2:28-30; 10:24; John 8:56; Heb. 11:13, 39-40; 2 Pet. 1:10-11.

9. See discussion in Herman Ridderbos, *The Coming of the Kingdom* (Philadelphia: Presbyterian & Reformed, 1962), p. 49.

suffers violence, and the violent take it by force. For all the prophets and the law prophesied until John. And if you are willing to receive it, he is Elijah who is to come" (Matt. 11:11-14; cf. Mark 2:18-19; Luke 16:16).

Third, at this historical juncture – the beginning of His ministry – Christ clearly and pointedly says the kingdom is "at hand." The root term (*eggus*) literally means "at hand." The word is derived from the compounding of *en* (in, at) and *guion* (limb, hand).[10]

The time Christ introduces as "at hand" is later called "the now time" (2 Cor. 6:2; cf. Rom. 3:21-26; Eph. 3:10; 2 Tim. 1:9-10). John and Jesus announce it, but Jerusalem does not recognize the coming of "the time" (Luke 19:44; cf. Matt. 23:37). This is a great tragedy for their pronouncement "summarized all that had been the object of Old Testament prophecy and of Israel's expectation of the future from the oldest times. . . . 'The time,' i.e., the great turning-point of history, promised by God himself for the full revelation of his kingly glory; the time for the liberation of his people and the punishment of his enemies."[11]

The early New Covenant biblical revelation of the kingdom, then, is of its *nearness* in time, not of its distance. Jesus promises that some of His disciples would live to see it acting in *great power* in history: "There are some of those who are standing here who shall not taste of death until they see the kingdom of God after it has come with power" (Mark 9:1). Here "come" is "not, as the English words may seem to mean, in the act of coming (till they see it come), but actually or already come, the only sense that can be put upon the perfect participle here

---

10. Joseph H. Thayer, *A Greek-English Lexicon of the New Testament* (2nd ed.; New York: American Book Co., 1889), p. 164. For a fuller discussion of imminence terminology, see: Gentry, *The Beast of Revelation* (Tyler, TX: Institute for Christian Economics, 1989), pp. 21-28.

11. Ridderbos, *Coming of the Kingdom*, p. 13.

employed."[12] Thus, His disciples are to expect its exhibition *in power*. This would not be immediately, for many of His disciples would die before it acted in power. Yet it is to be within the lifetimes of others, for "some" standing there would witness it. This seems clearly to refer to the A. D. 70 destruction of the temple and removal of the Old Testament means of worship (cf. Heb. 12:25-28; Rev. 1:1, 3, 9). This occurs as a direct result of Jesus' prophecies (John 4:21-23; Matt. 21:33ff; 23:31-34:34).

Such data as these set the stage for a clear elucidation of the victory theme. The long-awaited kingdom prophesied in the Old Testament era is about to break forth in history. Would its effect be wholly internal, limited to small pockets of the faithful? Or would it exhibit itself in powerful victory, transforming the mass of men in salvation, whole cultures by righteousness, and national governments for justice? I take the latter view.

The Establishment of the Kingdom

Because "the time" is "fulfilled" and the "kingdom of God" is "at hand," we should expect its appearance in the gospel record. God determines the "times" (Dan. 2:21; Acts 1:7); the time had come. Clear and compelling evidence exists that *the kingdom does in fact come in Christ's ministry*. Perhaps one of the "clearest proofs" in the gospel for the presence of the kingdom of heaven[13] is Matthew 12:28: "But if I cast out devils by the Spirit of God, then the kingdom of God is come unto you." The truth is, Jesus *did* cast out demons by the Spirit of God. The protasis of this "if/then" statement being true, then the apodosis follows: "the kingdom of God is come." The very fact that Satan's kingdom is being invaded and his possessions (de-

---

12. J. A. Alexander, *The Gospel According to Mark* (Grand Rapids: Baker, [1858] 1980), p. 230.

13. Ridderbos, *Coming of the Kingdom*, p. 107.

moniacs) are being carried off by Christ (Matt. 12:25-29) is proof that the kingdom had come.[14]

In Luke 17:20-21 we read: "Now when He was asked by the Pharisees when the kingdom of God would come, He answered them and said, 'The kingdom of God does not come with observation; nor will they say, "See here! or "See there!" For indeed, the kingdom of God is within you.' " Notice that Christ answers the Pharisees' question "when" the kingdom should come in the present tense: the kingdom *is* present. It is not awaiting a future, Armageddon-introduced manifestation; it exists now and among them, says Christ. Hence, even in Christ's ministry men are pressing into it (Luke 16:16).

The Triumphal Entry of Christ is interesting in this regard: "The next day a great multitude that had come to the feast, when they heard that Jesus was coming to Jerusalem, took branches of palm trees and went out to meet Him, and cried out: 'Hosanna! Blessed is He who comes in the name of the LORD!' The King of Israel!' Then Jesus, when He had found a young donkey, sat on it; as it is written: 'Fear not, daughter of Zion; behold, your King is coming, sitting on a donkey's colt'" (John 12:12-15). Here Christ is not only declared to be "king," but He accepts the public lauding of Himself as king, despite Pharisaic rebukes (Matt. 21:15-16), for it is in fulfillment of prophecy (Zech. 9:9).

During His trial and at the inquiry of Pilate, Christ specifically admits His kingship and the presence of His kingdom: "Jesus answered, 'My kingdom is not of this world. If My kingdom were of this world, My servants would fight, so that I should not be delivered to the Jews; but now My kingdom is not from here.' Pilate therefore said to Him, 'Are You a king then?' Jesus answered, 'You say rightly that I am a king. For this cause I was born, and for this cause I have come into the

---

14. See Chapter 12 below for the application to Christians.

world, that I should bear witness to the truth' " (John 18:36-37a; cf. Matt. 27:11; Mark 15:2; Luke 23:3).

Although He defines His kingdom as something other-worldly, rather than essentially political (as was Caesar's kingdom),[15] He nevertheless indicates His kingdom is present: He speaks of "my kingdom" (v. 36a). He claims to have His own "servants" (even though they do not fight with sword to defend Him, v. 36b). He clearly states "I am king" (v. 37a). And, as we might expect, given our previous study of Mark 1:14-15, He states that it was for that very purpose He was born into the world (v. 37b).

Application

The Coronation of the King

A frequent refrain in the New Testament is of the glorious and powerful enthronement of Christ, which the nativity prophecies anticipate. A number of passages speak of His ascending into heaven and being royally seated at the right hand of the throne of Almighty God, Creator of the heavens and the earth.

The anticipation of this enthronement is clearly evident in His post-resurrection, pre-ascension Great Commission.[16] In Matthew 28:18-20, we read a statement much in contrast to His earlier reservation and humility. No longer do we hear the familiar, "I can do nothing of Myself" (John 5:19, 30; 8:28; 12:49; 14:10). Rather, we hear a resoundingly powerful: "All authority has been given Me in heaven and on earth." A mighty transformation has taken place in the ministry of Christ as a direct result of His resurrection. Satan has been conquered;[17]

---

15. On "The Nature of the Kingdom," see below.

16. Kenneth L. Gentry, Jr., *The Greatness of the Great Commission: The Christian Enterprise in a Fallen World* (Tyler, TX: Institute for Christian Economics, 1990).

17. Matt. 12:26-29; Luke 10:18; John 12:31; Col. 2:15; Heb. 2:14; 1 John 3:8; 4:3,4.

Christ has overcome the world[18] to be "declared the Son of God with power" (Rom. 1:3, 4). The Great Commission is truly a postmillennial commission.

The "all" in "all authority" is here used in the distributive sense: *every form* of authority is at His command. He does not just have the authority of moral persuasion among individuals and in the inter-personal realm. He also has authority in the ecclesiastical and familial, as well as in the societal, political, economical, and all other realms. As Revelation 1:5 says of Him, in the days when John wrote: He is "the ruler of the kings of the earth." As Philippians 2:10 and Romans 14:11 teach, He has a Name "above every name," unto which they all will bow.

Following upon this claim of universal authority, He delivers to His few followers the obligation and plan for *universal conquest:* "Go therefore and make disciples of all the nations, baptizing them in the name of the Father and the Son and the Holy Spirit, teaching them to observe all that I commanded you" (vv. 19-20). The command of the resurrected Christ who possesses "all authority" is for His followers to bring all nations *as nations* to conversion and baptism. The word *ethne* is employed rather than *basileia* ("kingdom") to show that His concern is not for earthly political power. The word *anthropos* ("man") is passed by, demonstrating His concern is for the transformation of all of culture, rather than just individuals.

Not only does He command them on the basis of universal authority, but He closes with the promise that He will be with them to the completion of their task (Matt. 28:20b): "'and lo, I am with you always, even to the end of the age.' Amen." Here we find no inkling of failure for the Church or the obscurity of the faith. If we let the Old Testament passages speak for themselves, this Great Commission harmonizes perfectly with them.

---

18. John 16:33; Eph. 1:21-22; Rev. 1:5,6.

The victory motif is enhanced and emphasized by this command of the exalted Christ.

The very first of the enthronement passages in the post-resurrection age is Acts 2:30ff. This passage associates Christ's enthronement with His exaltation, which begins with His resurrection and proceeds to His session at the right hand of God. Concerning David's prophecy anticipating his seed who will sit upon the Davidic throne, Peter proclaims:

> Therefore being a prophet, and knowing that God had sworn with an oath to him, that of the fruit of his loins, according to the flesh, he would raise up Christ to sit on his throne; he seeing this before spake of the resurrection of Christ, that his soul was not left in hell, neither his flesh did see corruption. . . . Therefore being by the right hand of God exalted, and having received of the Father the promise of the Holy Ghost, he hath shed forth this, which ye now see and hear. For David is not ascended into the heavens: but he saith himself, The Lord said unto my Lord, Sit thou on my right hand, Until I make thy foes thy footstool. Therefore let all the house of Israel know assuredly, that God hath made that same Jesus, whom ye have crucified, both Lord and Christ. (Acts 2:30, 31, 33-36)

David's prophecy regarding One Who will sit on his throne is in regard to the "resurrection." Thus, Christ suffered ultimate humiliation on the cross and in the tomb. But then His resurrection initiates His exaltation in preparation for His ascension to the right hand of the throne of God, the place of universal rule and authority. There He was "crowned with glory" (Heb. 2:9) to begin His rule[19] by wielding "all authority and power" (Matt. 28:18).[20]

---

19. Rom. 8:34; Eph. 1:20; Col. 3:1; Heb. 12:2; 1 Pet. 3:22; Rev. 3:21.

20. Athanasius writes of Acts 2:36: "Therefore the Word Himself became flesh, and the Father called His Name Jesus, and so 'made' Him Lord and Christ, as much as to say, 'He made Him to rule and to reign.' " Athanasius, *Discourses Against the Arians* 2:15:16. Of Peter's Great Confession he writes: "He knew Him to be God's

A mighty transformation takes place in the ministry of Christ as a direct result of His resurrection. The pouring out of the Spirit (Acts 2:34-36) is a powerful exercise of regal authority. This is a celebration of His coronation in distributing gifts to His subjects, in the manner of a warrior-king returning triumphantly to his capital city upon his victory over the enemy (Acts 2:33; Eph. 4:7-12).[21] It promises His divinely royal assistance to His people (Rom. 8:34).

Christ's enthronement is an accomplished fact ever since His ascension. The confident refrain relative to His coronation and enthronement is replete in the New Testament record. We are not awaiting a future kingship of Christ: He is *now* already on His throne. Indeed, in the New Testament, the most quoted or alluded to Old Testament passages is Psalm 110. That passage records God the Father's word to Christ the Son: "Sit at my right hand until I make your enemies a footstool for your feet." In various forms it appears sixteen times in the New Testament.[22] The sitting at the "right hand" of God is a semantic equivalent to sitting on God's throne, as is evident in Revelation 3:21: "I also overcame and sat down with My Father on His throne." Contrary to Walvoord,[23] Revelation 3:21 does not require a millennial throne for Christ, which is both entirely future and wholly separate from God the Father's throne. It no more refers to two distinct themes than Jesus' statement to Mary in John 20:17 requires two distinct persons, when He speaks of "my Father and your Father." The throne of God and of Christ is *one* throne (Rev. 22:1, 3).

Son, confessing, 'Thou art the Christ, the Son of the Living God;' but he meant His Kingdom and Lordship which was formed and came to be according to grace, and was relatively to us." *Ibid.* 2:15:18.

21. Cf. Gen. 14; 1 Sam. 30:26-31; Jdgs. 5:30. See: Isa. 53:12.

22. Matt. 22:44; 26:64; Mark 12:36; 14:62; 16:19; Luke 20:42-43; 22:69; Acts 2:34-35; Rom. 8:34; 1 Cor. 15:25; Eph. 1:20; Col. 3:1; Heb. 1:3, 13; 8:1; 10:12.

23. John F. Walvoord, *The Revelation of Jesus Christ* (Chicago: Moody Press, 1966), pp. 98-100.

The Proclamation of the Kingdom

This is why there is so much "kingdom of God" proclamation in the New Testament.[24] In Acts 3:15 Peter preaches Christ as the "prince of life." In Acts 5:31a he asserts his obligation to disobey civil authority when it demands that he cease preaching Christ. His rationale is important: "Him God has exalted to His right hand to be Prince and Savior." The word "prince" here may literally be translated "leader, ruler, prince."[25] He is exalted as Prince or Ruler.

In Acts 17:7 we learn of the civil turmoil the early Christians cause. The charge against them is most interesting and must be based in reality, even if largely misunderstood by the unbelieving populace. Just as the Jews accuse Jesus of claiming to be a king,[26] so we read of the charge against His followers: "These all do contrary to the decrees of Caesar, saying that there is another king, one Jesus." Just as Jesus does in fact teach that He is a king (though in a non-political sense, John 18:36-37), his followers do the same.

According to Paul God "*put* all things under his feet" (Eph. 1:22). God *gave* Him a title/name higher than any that is named (Phil. 2:9). In both of these places, Paul employs aorist tense verbs, which speak of an action at a point in *past* time, i.e., at His resurrection-ascension-enthronement. Hence, the scores of references to Him as "Lord" throughout the New Testament. In fact, "Christ is Lord" evidently becomes a creedal statement of sorts in the apostolic era.[27]

Paul speaks to the Colossians in a way quite agreeable to this view of the coming of the kingdom. "Giving thanks unto the

---

24. See: Acts 8:12; 14:22; 19:8; 20:25; 28:23, 31; Rom. 14:17; 1 Cor. 4:20; 6:9-10; 15:50; Gal. 5:21; Eph. 5:5; Col. 1:13; 4:11; 1 Thess. 2:12; 2 Thess. 1:5; 2 Tim. 4:1; 4:18; Heb. 1:8; 12:28; Jms. 2:5; 2 Pet. 1:11.

25. W. F. Arndt and F. W. Gingrich, *A Greek-English Lexicon of the New Testament* (Chicago: University of Chicago Press, 1957), p. 112.

26. See: Matt. 27:29, 37; Mark 15:12, 26; Luke 23:3; John 18:33; 19:12, 15, 21.

27. Rom. 10:9; 1 Cor. 12:3; Phil. 2:11.

Father, which hath made us meet to be partakers of the inheritance of the saints in light: Who hath delivered us from the power of darkness, and hath translated us into the kingdom of his dear Son" (Col. 1:12, 13). Inarguably, He is speaking of Christ's kingdom, for He calls it "the kingdom of his dear Son." Just as clearly the "translation" of those saints nearly 2,000 years ago is considered a past fact, not a future prospect. Paul uses aorist tense verbs when he speaks of their being "delivered" and "translated"; he does the same in 1 Thessalonians 2:12. He even speaks of those who were his helpers in the ministry "for the kingdom of God" (Col. 4:10).

John follows suit in Revelation 1:6 and 9: "And [Christ] hath made us kings and priests unto God and his Father. . . . I, John, who also am your brother, and companion in tribulation, and in the kingdom and patience of Jesus Christ." In these verses John speaks of the Christians of the Seven Churches of Asia (Rev. 1:4, 11; 2-3) as already "made" (aorist tense) to be "a kingdom" (literally). In fact, John is already a fellow with them in the "kingdom" (Rev. 1:9).

The Building of the Kingdom

In light of the above, Christians now rule and reign with Him in the world. Ephesians 1:3 declares we are blessed "in heavenly places." Ephesians 2:6 specifically teaches: "And He hath raised us up together, and made us sit [aorist tense] together in heavenly places in Christ Jesus." We are, in the eyes of God, seated with Christ in heavenly places (which, in essence, is the idea of Rev. 20:4-6), i.e., *in regal position.*

Interestingly, the epistle to the Ephesians is virtually an anti-dispensational polemic by the Apostle Paul. Notice the teaching in Ephesians regarding matters antithetical to dispensationalism: Christ is presently in His position as a kingly Lord (1:19-22) and we are presently seated with Him (1:3; 2:6). Paul applies the application of "the covenants of *the* promise" (literally) to Gentiles in the Church (2:10-12). He emphasizes the removal of the distinction of the Jew and the Gentile (2:12-19). He refers to the building up of the Church as being the building of the temple (2:20-22[28]). Paul notes that the New Testament phase of the Church is taught in the Old Testament, although not with the same fullness and clarity (3:1-6). Christ's kingly enthronement is celebrated by the pouring out of gifts upon His Church/kingdom (4:8-11) with the expectation of the historical maturation of the Church (4:12-14). Paul mentions the kingdom in a way that indicates its spiritual, rather than political, nature (5:5).[29]

In 1 Corinthians 3:21-22, Christians are shown their noble status: "For all things are yours; whether Paul, or Apollos, or Cephas, or the world, or life, or death, or things present, or things to come; all are yours." Elsewhere we see the present kingly status of Christians (e.g., Rom. 5:17; Col. 3:3; 1 Tim. 2:11,12).

Interestingly, the initial excitement at Christ's first proclamation of the kingdom sees men and women crowding their way into it. "From the days of John the Baptist until now the kingdom of Heaven has been taken by storm and eager men are forcing their way into it" (Matt. 11:12, J. B. Phillips' translation). Calvin understood this as saying "so many sought it with burning zeal."[30]

The Kingdom's Spiritual Nature

Despite dispensationalism's confusion, the Scripture is quite clear regarding the spiritual nature of the kingdom. Dispensationalism asserts Christ offers to Israel a literal, political, earthly

---

28. Cf. 1 Pet. 2:4-5; 1 Cor. 3:16-17; 6:19; 2 Cor. 6:16; Rev. 3:12. See discussion below in ch. 15.

29. On this point, critics of the theonomist viewpoint have repeatedly misrepresented it. That theonomists speak of God's kingdom as a civilization does not mean that they do not see this civilization as grounded in spiritual regeneration.

30. John Calvin, *Matthew, Mark, and Luke* (1553), 3 vols. (Grand Rapids: Eerdmans, 1972), 2:7. See also: Ridderbos, *Coming of the Kingdom*, p. 54.

kingdom, but that the Jews reject it, thus causing its postponement.[31] This view of the kingdom is totally erroneous. As a matter of fact, it is just this sort of kingdom that the first-century Jews want and which Christ refuses: "When Jesus therefore perceived that they would come and take him by force, to make him a king, he departed again into a mountain himself alone" (John 6:15).

The disciples themselves miss His point, for the most part, while He is on earth. In the Emmaus Road encounter after the crucifixion, certain disciples lament: "But we trusted that it had been he which should have redeemed Israel: and beside all this, today is the third day since these things were done" (Luke 24:21). Jesus rebukes them for such foolishness: "Then he said unto them, O fools, and slow of heart to believe all that the prophets have spoken: Ought not Christ to have suffered these things, and to enter into his glory? And beginning at Moses and all the prophets, he expounded unto them in all the scriptures the things concerning himself" (Luke 24:25-27). They expected political deliverance and glory to come to Israel through this Messiah.[32] But Jesus speaks to them of the true meaning of the prophecies of the Old Testament, showing them that He *must* suffer and then enter His resurrected, heavenly glory.[33]

In response to the Pharisees, Christ specifically declares that the kingdom does not come visibly with temporal fanfare. "And when he was demanded of the Pharisees, when the kingdom of God should come, he answered them and said, The kingdom of God cometh not with observation: Neither shall they say, Lo here! or, lo there! for, behold, the kingdom of God is within

---

31. Charles L. Feinberg, *Millennialism: The Two Major Views* (3rd ed.; Chicago: Moody Press, 1980), ch. 8.

32. Cf. their hope that He would "redeem Israel" with the Old Testament declaration that God "redeemed" Israel by delivering them from Egypt to become an independent nation, Deut. 7:8; 9:26; 13:5; 15:15; 24:18; 1 Chr. 17:21; Mic. 6:4.

33. Surely it cannot be denied that at the resurrection and ascension Christ "entered His glory," which was evidenced by Pentecost: John 7:39; 12:16; 12:23; Acts 3:13. He is now the "Lord of glory," cf. Jms. 2:1; 1 Pet. 1:11; 2 Pet. 3:18; Heb. 2:9.

you" (Luke 17:20-21). Obviously this demands a spiritual conception of the kingdom, in contradiction to an Armageddon-introduced, geo-political kingdom.

This is why Christ goes about preaching the "*gospel* of the kingdom" (Matt. 4:23; 9:35; 24:14; Mark 1:14-15). He proclaims a redemptive, spiritual kingdom. Hence, being exalted to His throne leads to a spiritual effusion of grace, not the political establishment of an earthly government.[34]

The Jews make a major accusation against Jesus by saying that He promotes a political kingdom in competition with Caesar's empire. This explains why Jesus is concerned to discover the source of the accusation – He knows of the misconception of the Jews in this regard. His answer indicates the spiritual nature of the kingdom:

> Then Pilate entered the Praetorium again, called Jesus, and said to Him, "Are You the King of the Jews?" Jesus answered him, "Are you speaking for yourself on this, or did others tell you this about Me?" Pilate answered, "Am I a Jew? Your own nation and the chief priests have delivered You to me. What have You done?" Jesus answered, "My kingdom is not of this world. If My kingdom were of this world, My servants would fight, so that I should not be delivered to the Jews; but now My kingdom is not from here." Pilate therefore said to Him, "Are You a king then?" Jesus answered, "You say rightly that I am a king. For this cause I was born, and for this cause I have come into the world, that I should bear witness to the truth. Everyone who is of the truth hears My voice." (John 18:33-37)

He presents His kingship in terms of *meekness and lowliness* and not as a conquering, *political* entity. "All this was done, that it might be fulfilled which was spoken by the prophet, saying, Tell ye the daughter of Sion, Behold, thy King cometh unto thee, meek, and sitting upon an ass, and a colt the foal of an

---

34. Luke 24:44-49; Acts 2:30-35; 3:22-26; 8:12; Eph. 4:8-11.

ass" (Matt. 21:4, 5). In illustration of the Emmaus Road confusion, John adds regarding this triumphal entry in fulfillment of prophecy that "these things understood not his disciples at the first: but when Jesus was glorified, then remembered they that these things were written of him, and that they had done these things unto him" (John 12:15-16).

Paul picks up on and promotes the spiritual nature of the kingdom, when he writes that "the kingdom of God is not meat and drink; but righteousness, and peace, and joy in the Holy Ghost" (Rom. 14:17). He disavows any carnal conception of the kingdom. Likewise, he speaks of attaining an inheritance in the spiritual kingdom (the heavenly aspect of the kingdom) for those who are righteous (1 Cor. 6:9-10; 15:50; Gal. 5:21). He even says very plainly of the heavenly aspect of the kingdom: "Now this I say, brethren, that flesh and blood cannot inherit the kingdom of God; neither doth corruption inherit incorruption" (1 Cor. 15:50).

How could it be that an earthly, political kingdom would hold forth no inheritance for flesh-and-blood people? It is in salvation that we are "delivered from the power of darkness, and translated into the kingdom of his dear Son: In whom we have redemption through his blood, even the forgiveness of sins" (Col. 1:12, 13).

The Kingdom's Cosmic Advance

A distinctive feature of dispensationalism is that the millennial kingdom is fundamentally Jewish in character, even to the point of the rebuilding of the temple, setting up David's tabernacle, re-instituting the Jewish sacrificial system, and exalting the Jews over elect Gentiles. "This is the point: once Israel is restored to the place of blessing and the tabernacle of David is rebuilt, then will follow the third phase in the plan of God. That period will be the time of the millennium, when the nations will indeed by converted and ruled over by Christ."[35] We should not regard this as a deviant opinion of a pair of unrepresentative dispensational authors. On the contrary, it is a representative statement of the dispensational system. Dispensationalism surprisingly teaches such things as those found in the following citations:

"God has two distinct purposes – one for Israel and one for the Church."[36]

"Israel, regathered and turned to the Lord in salvation, will be exalted, blessed, and favored through this period."[37]

"The Gentiles will be Israel's servants during that age. . . . The nations which usurped authority over Israel in past ages find that downtrodden people exalted and themselves in subjection in their kingdom." And these are not unsaved Gentiles: "The Gentiles that are in the millennium will have experienced conversion prior to admission."[38]

"The redeemed living nation of Israel, regenerated and regathered to the land will be head over all the nations of the earth. . . . So he exalts them above the Gentile nations. . . . On the lowest level there are the saved, living, Gentile nations."[39]

"God will keep his original promises to the fathers and will one day convert and place Israel as the head of the nations."[40]

"Israel will be a glorious nation, protected from her enemies, exalted above the Gentiles. . . ." "In contrast to the present church age in which Jew and Gentile are on an equal plane of privilege, the millennium is clearly a period of time in which

---

35. H. Wayne House and Thomas D. Ice, *Dominion Theology: Blessing or Curse?* (Portland, OR: Multnomah, 1988), p. 169.

36. Charles Ryrie, *Dispensationalism Today* (Chicago: Moody Press, 1965), p. 95.

37. Charles C. Ryrie, *The Basis of the Premillennial Faith* (Neptune, NJ: Loizeaux Bros., 1953), p. 149.

38. J. Dwight Pentecost, *Things to Come: A Case Study in Biblical Eschatology* (Grand Rapids: Zondervan, 1958), p. 508.

39. Herman Hoyt, "Dispensational Premillennialism," *The Meaning of the Millennium: Four Views*, Robert G. Clouse, ed. (Downer's Grove, IL: Inter-Varsity Press, 1977), p. 81.

40. House and Ice, *Dominion Theology*, p. 175.

Israel is in prominence and blessing. . . . Israel as a nation will be exalted."[41]

Yet in Scripture Christ's kingdom is *pan-ethnic*, rather than Jewish. While on earth Christ clearly and forthrightly teaches that God would soon set aside national Israel as a distinctive, favored people in the kingdom. In Matthew 8:11-12, in the context of the Gentile centurion's faith, He expressly says that the "sons of the kingdom shall be cast out" while "many from the east and west" shall enjoy the Abrahamic blessings. In Matthew 21:43 He parabolically teaches the rejection of national Israel when He says: "Therefore I say to you, the kingdom of God will be taken away from you, and be given to a nation producing the fruit of it." In Matthew 23-24, He prophesies the removal of the spiritual heart of Israel, the temple. He says it will be left "desolate" (Matt. 23:38) during the Great Tribulation (Matt. 24:21) when men should flee Judea (Matt. 24:16). He emphatically notes that "all these things shall come upon this generation" (Matt. 23:36; 24:34).

It is true that racial Jews in great mass will be saved later in the development of the kingdom in history (Rom. 11:11-25), per postmillennialism.[42] The hermeneutical rub comes with Jews' being exalted over and distinguished from saved Gentiles, and the turning back of the redemptive progress to "the weak and beggarly elements" of the sacrificial system. As mentioned above, Isaiah 19:19-25 expressly alludes to pagan nations being brought into the kingdom on a basis of equality with righteous Jews: "In that day Israel will be the third party with Egypt and Assyria, a blessing in the midst of the earth" (v. 23). Here the former enemies receive an equal share of God's favor. In Zechariah 9:7 God speaks of His future favor upon other enemies of Israel. He refers to Ekron, one of the five chief cities of Philis-

---

41. John F. Walvoord, *The Millennial Kingdom* (Grand Rapids: Zondervan, 1959), pp. 136, 302-303.

42. See Chapter 12 below.

tia: "I will remove their blood from their mouth, and their detestable things from between their teeth. Then they also will be a remnant for our God, and be like a clan in Judah, and Ekron like a Jebusite." This Philistine enemy is to become like "a clan in Judah."

Israel's demise from dominance is directly related to her ethical conduct. *Israel crucified the Messiah.* Jesus makes this the point of His Parable of the Householder mentioned above (Matt. 21:33ff). The constant apostolic indictment against the Jews pertained to *this gross, conclusive act of covenantal rebellion.* Although it is true that the Romans are responsible for physically nailing Christ to the cross (John 18:30-31), nevertheless, when covenantally considered, the onus of the divine curse fell squarely upon those who instigate and demand it: the Jews of the first century. The biblical record is quite clear and emphatic: the *Jews* are the ones who seek His death (Matt. 26; 27; John 11:53; 18; 19). *This most heinous sin of all time, committed by the Jewish nation*, is a constant refrain in the New Testament (Acts 2:22-23, 36; 3:13-15a; 5:30; 7:52; 1 Thess. 2:14-15).

The New Testament-era Church is not a distinct body of people for a time. Rather, it is a newly organized fulfillment of the old body for *all* time. This Church is one with the Jewish forefathers, being grafted into the Abrahamic root and partaking of its sap (Rom. 11:17-18). Because of the redemptive work of Christ "there is neither Jew nor Greek . . . for ye are all one in Christ Jesus" (Gal. 3:28).

In Ephesians Paul is quite emphatic on this matter. Though in the past the Gentiles (Eph. 2:11) were "strangers to the covenants of promise" (2:12), Christ has brought them "near" (2:13) by breaking down the wall of separation between Jew and Gentile "through" redemption (2:14-15). This makes one people of two (2:16-17), who worship one God (2:18), making the Gentiles "fellowcitizens with the saints, and of the household of God" (2:19), being built upon one foundation (2:20-22).[43]

Conclusion

The New Testament portrays Christ as a King who comes sovereignly to establish His kingdom. At His birth there is an outburst of hymnic joy at the coming of the long prophesied King. In the winding down of John Baptist's ministry, we are presented the Christ who has come into Messianic fulfillment. Early in Christ's ministry He declares His kingdom's approach, and then sets out to establish it through preaching and teaching.

Upon His coronation Christ begins ruling judicially over the nations of the earth *through spiritual means* rather than by the sword. He rules representatively through His covenant people, just as Satan rules representatively through his people. Those who are redeemed are members of His kingdom. As they labor for Him, they rule by spiritual and ethical power. Their goal? To see all nations baptized in Christ. The essence of Christ's kingdom is spiritual and ethical, not political and racial. (This does not deny that the kingdom has objective ethical and judicial implications; it does, in the same way that the conversion of a person's soul has objective ethical and judicial implications.)

43. David E. Holwerda, *Jesus and Israel: One Covenant or Two?* (Grand Rapids: Eerdmans, 1995).

12

EXPANSION

Another parable He put forth to them, saying: "The kingdom of heaven is like a mustard seed, which a man took and sowed in his field, which indeed is the least of all the seeds; but when it is grown it is greater than the herbs and becomes a tree, so that the birds of the air come and nest in its branches." Another parable He spoke to them: "The kingdom of heaven is like leaven, which a woman took and hid in three measures of meal till it was all leavened." (Matthew 13:31-33)

I have shown that the Messianic kingdom prophesied in the Old Testament is introduced during the earthly ministry of the Lord Jesus Christ. The Old Testament vision is of a massive universal influence for the kingdom.

Though the New Testament era does witness a remarkable expansion of the faith, it does not experience a universal dominance. Yet it is clear that the New Testament also anticipates the worldwide victory of the gospel in the same era in which it is inaugurated. The New Testament clearly expects an era of Christian dominion to occur prior to the Second Advent of the Lord Jesus Christ in power at the final judgment. This era of dominion will produce the worldwide transformation of society through the preaching of the gospel and individuals' widespread positive response to the message of redemption.

Some recoil today at the mention of the word "dominion,"[1]

---

1. Hal Lindsey, *The Road to Holocaust* (New York: Bantam, 1989), ch. 2; H.

when applied to the progress of the gospel. Yet the concept of dominion is a revealed expectation. The word "dominion" is used in significant ways in Scripture.[2] God's providential rule over the universe is His "dominion" over His kingdom (Psa. 145:13; Dan. 4:3). The Old Testament anticipates Christ's "dominion" in history (Psa. 72:8; Dan. 7:14; Zech. 9:10). Of course, those who lament the employment of "dominion" are not concerned about its reference to God's rule, but to the rule of His people in contemporary history. Yet, as we saw in Chapter 9, "dominion" is a general calling given to man as God's image (Gen. 1:26-28; Psa. 8:6). The expectation of "dominion" specifically for God's redeemed is also legitimate in that we currently have a kingship based on Christ's "dominion" (Rev. 1:6). Ours is a derivative, subordinate dominion under God and over His creation, and as such is representative.

Unfortunately, due to imprecise thinking by some, dominion is wrongly thought to imply a carnal militarism (such as in Islamic fundamentalism) or an ecclesiocracy (such as in medieval Romanism). Nevertheless, dominion is both commanded and assured in the New Testament record.

Dominion Commanded

The postmillennial view is the *only* one of the four major evangelical eschatologies that builds its case on the very charter for Christianity, the Great Commission (Matt. 28:18-20). David Brown wrote over a century ago:

Wayne House and Thomas D. Ice, *Dominion Theology: Blessing or Curse?* (Portland, OR: Multnomah, 1988), chaps. 1, 15; Dave Hunt, *Whatever Happened to Heaven?* (Eugene, OR: Harvest House, 1988), chaps. 10-11. Tim LaHaye, *No Fear of the Storm: Why Christians Will Escape All the Tribulation* (Sisters, OR.: Multnomah, 1992), p. 9. Roy B. Zuck, ed., *Vital Prophetic Issues: Examining Promises and Problems in Eschatology* (Grand Rapids: Kregal, 1995), ch. 8.

2. The English word "dominion" is derived from the Latin *dominus,* "lord."

The disciples were commissioned to evangelize the world *before* Christ's second coming; not merely to preach the Gospel, 'for a *witness*,' to a world that would not receive it till he came again . . . but to accomplish, instrumentally, the actual *'discipleship of all nations*,' to baptize them when gathered in, and to train them up as professed Christians in the knowledge and obedience of the truth, for glory – all before his second coming. In the doing of this, He promises to be with them – not merely to stand by them while preaching a rejected Gospel, and to note their fidelity, but clearly to prosper the work of their hands unto the actual evangelization of the world at large, *before* his coming.[3]

Sixty-five years later postmillennialist O. T. Allis cited the Great Commission and commented: "There is no room for pessimism or defeatism in these words. The Captain of our salvation is an invincible commander. His triumph is sure and assured."[4]

Dispensationalists scoff at postmillennialists because the latter "believe that the Great Commission will be fulfilled."[5] Amillennialists also note the postmillennial reliance upon the Great Commission.[6] But the postmillennial case, based (in part) on the Great Commission, is not so easily dismissed.

In the last chapter I briefly dealt with the Great Commission as evidence in *Christ's kingly authority*. Here I mention it as New Testament evidence for *Christianity's victorious future*.

The Great Commission reads:

Then Jesus came and spoke to them, saying, "All authority has been given to Me in heaven and on earth. Go therefore and make disciples of all the nations, baptizing them in the name of

3. David Brown, *Christ's Second Coming: Will It Be Premillennial* (Edmonton, Alberta: Still Waters Revival Books, [1882] 1990), p. 298.

4. O. T. Allis, "The Parable of the Leaven," *Evangelical Quarterly* 19:4 (Oct. 1947) 272.

5. Charles C. Ryrie, *Basic Theology* (Wheaton, IL: Victor, 1986), p. 441. See also: Lindsey, *Road to Holocaust*, p. 49; House and Ice, *Dominion Theology*, pp. 139-160.

6. Anthony A. Hoekema, *The Bible and the Future* (Grand Rapids: Eerdmans, 1979), p. 177.

the Father and of the Son and of the Holy Spirit, teaching them
to observe all things that I have commanded you; and lo, I am
with you always, even to the end of the age. Amen." (Matt.
28:18-20)

Here are the disciples, just days after the government of
Rome oversees the cruel crucifixion of their Lord. Christ confronts the little group, who had all forsaken Him and fled
(Matt. 26:56) in fear of the Jews (John 20:19). Though earlier
He confines their ministry to Israel (Matt. 10:5-6; 15:24), He
now commissions them to disciple "all the nations." The nascent
progress of the gospel among the nations is traced in Acts,
which takes up the history of the Christian faith where the
Gospels leave off. Acts opens with the commission given to the
same few disciples to promote the message of Christ in "Jerusalem, and in all Judea and Samaria, and to the end of the earth"
(Acts 1:8) and ends in Acts 28 with Paul in Rome (Acts 28:16).
This progress from Jerusalem to Rome witnesses thousands of
conversions, testifying to the dramatic spread of Christianity.[7]

It is only after claiming possession of the unbounded authority of the Lord God over heaven and earth (cf. Matt. 11:25) that
Christ commissions His disciples. With these words He does not
merely send "forth his disciples *into* all nations" (Adams) to be
a "witness" (Feinberg), providing a "testimony" that "calls for a
decision" (Hoekema). Nor does He simply commission them "to
proclaim a message to the ends of the earth" (Pentecost) or "to
preach the gospel unto all nations" (denHartog) or "to urge
universal proclamation of the gospel" (Hoyt) in order to draw
"out a people from among the peoples or nations of the world"
(Ice).[8] According to the clear words of the Commission, Christ

7. Acts 2:41; 4:4; 5:14; 9:35, 42; 11:24-26; 17:2; 18:8, 10; 19:18, 26.

8. Jay E. Adams, *The Time Is at Hand* (n.p.: Presbyterian & Reformed, 1966), p.
44 (emphasis mine). Charles Lee Feinberg, "The Jew After the Rapture," *Prophecy and
the Seventies*, Feinberg, ed. (Chicago: Moody Press, 1971), p. 182. Hoekema, *Bible and
the Future*, p. 138. J. Dwight Pentecost, *Thy Kingdom Come* (Wheaton, IL: Victor,

commands His disciples to *make disciples* of *all the nations*. Understand what this means. God's disciples are *under God's authority*. They are *under His law*. They are *under His sanctions*. Therefore, they *inherit the earth*. In this case, those who are to be made disciples *in history* are clearly identified as corporate entities: nations.

Christ certainly has the authority to command and effect such, as Matthew 28:18 testifies. A great number of scholars recognize that the Great Commission "is a clear reference to the prophecy in Daniel 7:14, not only as to the fact but in the words themselves."[9] Daniel's passage clearly provides that after He ascends to the Ancient of Days (Dan. 7:13), "to Him was given dominion and glory and a kingdom, that all peoples, nations, and languages should serve Him" (Dan. 7:14). This is precisely what the Great Commission expects: all nations will be discipled under His universal authority, with the result that they will be baptized into the glorious Name of the Triune God. Though His disciples were fearful and fumbling, Christ promises that He will be with them (and all His people) "throughout all the days" (*pasas tas hemeras*) until the end (Matt. 28:20) to see that the task is successfully completed.

Clearly pessimistic assessments of the Great Commission, such as the following, are without warrant: "We do not imagine

1990), p. 221. Arie denHartog, "Hope and the Protestant Reformed Churches' Mission Calling," *Standard Bearer* 66:7 (Jan. 1, 1990) 166. Herman A. Hoyt, "A Dispensational Premillennial Response" (to postmillennialism), *The Millennium: Four Views*, Robert G. Clouse, ed. (Grand Rapids: Eerdmans, 1977), p. 145. House and Ice, *Dominion Theology*, p. 159.

9. Herman Ridderbos, *The Coming of the Kingdom* (Philadelphia: Presbyterian & Reformed, 1962), p. 467. Gaston writes that Matthew 28:18-20 "has been formulated quite consciously in terms of" Daniel 7:13-14. Lloyd Gaston, *No Stone on Another: Studies in the Significance of the Fall of Jerusalem in the Synoptic Gospels* (Leiden: Brill, 1970), p. 385. See for example the comments of the following scholars: D. A. Carson, Frank E. Gaebelein, Henry Alford, R. T. France, W. F. Albright, C. S. Mann, B. T. D. Smith, Frank Stagg, R. H. Fuller, W. C. Allen, John A. Broadus. For bibliographic data, see: Gentry, *The Greatness of the Great Commission: The Christian Enterprise in a Fallen World* (Tyler, TX: Institute for Christian Economics, 1990), p. 44, note 15.

that there will be a worldwide conversion of all or even of the majority of peoples on the earth. The Lord gathers unto Himself a remnant according to the election of His grace."[10] The Great Commission strongly supports the postmillennial eschatology, commanding God's people to seek the *discipling* of all the nations.

Dominion Assured

The Great Commission command from Christ is given on the basis of His prior eschatological teachings. We must consider briefly a few of the important passages in this regard.

Matthew 13

In Matthew 13 the Kingdom Parables sketch some of the basic aspects of the spiritual kingdom Christ is establishing. The *Parable of the Sower* (Matt. 13:3-23) identifies those who are the righteous citizens of the kingdom: those who rightly receive the word of God (by the sovereign grace of God, of course). Their numbers will greatly increase, thirty-fold, sixty-fold, and a hundred-fold.

The *Parable of the Tares* (Matt. 13:24-30, 36:43) and the *Parable of the Net* (Matt. 13:47-50) point out that despite the growth of the righteous, the kingdom will include a mixture of the righteous and the unrighteous. These will not be separated absolutely until the resurrection.

The *Parable of the Hidden Treasure* (Matt. 13:44) and the *Parable of the Pearl of Great Price* (Matt. 13:45-46) speak of the priceless value and blessings of the kingdom. The *Parable of the Mustard Seed* (Matt. 13:31-32) and the *Parable of the Leaven* (Matt. 13:33) instruct us as to the gradual development and ultimate outcome of the kingdom. Let us consider a little more

---

10. A. denHartog, "Hope and the Protestant Reformed Churches' Mission Calling," 166.

closely the outcome of the kingdom, as spoken of in the last two parables mentioned.

The *Parable of the Mustard Seed* reads: "The kingdom of heaven is like a mustard seed, which a man took and sowed in his field, which indeed is the least of all the seeds; but when it is grown it is greater than the herbs and becomes a tree, so that the birds of the air come and nest in its branches" (Matt. 13:31-32).[11] The imagery is unquestionably of something magnificent beyond expectation: a minuscule mustard seed gives rise to a tree. To this tree flock the birds of the air in order to build their nests for their young. The Old Testament imagery involved here is interesting. Birds singing among the branches is a picture of *peaceful serenity and divine provision* (Psa. 104:12, 17). In Daniel 4:12 and Ezekiel 31:3, 6, Babylon and Assyria (which God providentially prospered, Jer. 27:5-8; Ezek. 31:3, 9[12]) are portrayed as massive kingdoms to which birds flocked to nest in their branches. Daniel 4:12 indicates that this speaks of a lovely provision of food for all; Ezekiel 31 shows that this symbolizes the kingdom's fairness, greatness, and provision for all great nations. That is, they were great kingdoms which for a time secured provisions and shelter for men.

But God has a kingdom that also will become a great tree providing a nesting place for the birds and their young. Ezekiel 17:22-24 reads: "I will also take of the highest branch of the high cedar, and will set it; I will crop off from the top of his young twigs a tender one, and will plant it upon an high mountain. In the mountain of the height of Israel will I plant it: and it shall bring forth boughs, and bear fruit, and be a goodly cedar: and under it shall dwell all fowl of every wing; in the shadow of the branches thereof shall they dwell. And all the trees of the field shall know that I the Lord have brought down

---

11. An excellent exposition of this parable may be found in Richard C. Trench, *Notes on the Miracles and the Parables of Our Lord*, 2 vols. in 1 (Old Tappan, NJ: Revell, [n.d.] 1953), 2:109-115.

12. Cf. Psa. 75:6-7; Dan. 2:21; 4:17, 32; Job 12:23.

the high tree, have exalted the low tree." The portrayal here is of a universal magnificence and exaltation of the kingdom of heaven, which will graciously provide shelter for all when it comes to full fruition. This seems to provide the specific backdrop of Christ's parable, which he adapted to mustard seed imagery. Both point to the dominance of Christ's kingdom: the twig is planted on a high mountain above all the trees; the mustard seed becomes the largest plant in the garden. The Mustard Seed Parable speaks of the extension of the kingdom in the world.

The *Parable of the Leaven* reads: "The kingdom of heaven is like leaven, which a woman took and hid in three measures of meal till it was all leavened" (Matt. 13:33).[13] This parable doubtless speaks of the kingdom's *intensive* progress in the world. Leaven is a penetrative agent that diffuses itself throughout its host from within (cf. Luke 17:20-21). The emphatic statement is that the whole of that into which the leaven is put (the world, cf. Matt. 13:38) will be thoroughly penetrated. The leaven parable, then, parallels in sentiment the glorious expectation for the kingdom of heaven in the other parables. The kingdom will *penetrate all* (Matt. 13:33). It will produce up to *a hundred-fold return* (Matt. 13:8). It will grow to *great stature* (Matt. 13:31-32). It will *dominate the field/world* (having sown the wheat seed in the world, that world to which Christ returns will be a wheat field, not a tare field, Matt. 13:30).[14]

The Kingdom Parables, then, comport well with the victorious expectation of the Old Testament. The kingdom of the God of heaven (Dan. 2:44) will grow to dominance in the world. It will manifest itself progressively as a true civilization, encompassing every aspect of cultural life.

---

13. For an excellent treatment of this parable, see: Allis, "The Parable of the Leaven," *Evangelical Quarterly*, 254-273.

14. Cf. ch. 20 below for a response to amillennialism's view of the Parable of the Tares.

Dispensational Objections

But there are objections. Dispensationalists resist the employ-ment of the Kingdom Parables as evidence for a desirable grad-ualistic growth of the kingdom. Consider, for example, J. Dwight Pentecost's treatment of three of the parables: "During the course of the age there will be a decreasing response to the sowing of the seed, from 'a hundredfold' to 'sixty' to 'thirty.' Such is the course of the age. Mark 4:13 reveals that this para-ble, with the revelation of the program which it makes, is basic to the understanding of the other parables in the discourse."[15]

Two objections may be urged against this severe misreading: First, the parable obviously is speaking of a wondrous *multiplica-tion* of effect. Even a mere (!) thirty-fold increase in an invest-ment should be considered glorious. The Lord is not informing His disciples of the *decline* of gospel influence, but of its *increase*. As such, *it is akin to the Abrahamic Covenant*, which promises that Abraham's seed will become as the sands of the sea and the stars of heaven for multitude.[16] After all, Abraham is associ-ated in the Gospels with the kingdom of heaven (Matt. 8:11; Luke 13:28).

Second, in the Gospel records of Christ's references to the increase, the *order* has absolutely *no* intended bearing on the interpretation of the parable, despite Pentecost's assertion. This

---

15. J. Dwight Pentecost, *Things to Come* (Grand Rapids: Zondervan, 1958), p. 146. Apparently Pentecost's views on this parable have changed as later printings of this work indicate. Nevertheless, his older comments are still representative of many dispensationalists: See also: John F. Walvoord, *Prophecy Knowledge Handbook* (Wheat-on, IL: Victor, 1990), pp. 374-376). Louis J. Barbieri, Jr., "Matthew," *The Bible Knowledge Commentary: New Testament*, John F. Walvoord and Roy B. Zuck, eds. (Wheaton, IL: Victor, 1983), p. 51. Edward E. Hindson, "The Gospel According to Matthew," *Liberty Commentary on the New Testament*, E. E. Hindson and Woodrow Michael Kroll, eds. (Lynchburg, VA: Liberty, 1978), p. 52. Warren W. Wiersbe, *The Bible Exposition Commentary* (Wheaton, IL: Victor, 1989), 1:46. Historic premillennialist Ladd argues that the parable merely contrasts the beginning of the kingdom with the final apocalyptic transformation, without any idea of "gradual permeation." George Eldon Ladd, *A Theology of the New Testament* (Grand Rapids: Eerdmans, 1974), p. 99.

16. Gen. 15:5; 22:17; 26:4; 32:12; Exo. 32:13; Deut. 1:10; 10:22; Neh. 9:23.

should be obvious when Matthew 13:3-9 is laid alongside Mark 4:3-8. These two records of the parable are virtually identical, except for the *order* of increase. Consequently, we must assume that the order of listing is eschatologically unimportant.

Consider Pentecost's teaching on the Mustard Seed Parable, which is representative of dispensationalism. "As the age progresses several facts are to be observed. (1) The age is characterized by an abnormal external growth. That which was to be an herb has become a tree – it has developed into a monstrosity. (2) This monstrosity has become the resting place for birds. In the first parable the birds represented that which was antagonistic to the program of God and consistency would demand that they be so interpreted here. . . . The parable teaches that the enlarged sphere of profession has become inwardly corrupt. That is the characterization of this age."[17]

This interpretation is patently erroneous as is obvious from the parable's opening words: "The kingdom of heaven is like a mustard seed." Is Jesus saying "The kingdom of heaven is like a monstrosity"? Furthermore, birds are not necessarily types of evil in Scripture.[18] Similarly, the lion is not necessarily a type of evil (1 Pet. 5:8; cf. Rev. 5:5). It would seem less disruptive of Christ's teaching to note that the birds, which originally sought to destroy the seed of the kingdom in the ground (Matt. 13:4, 19), finally convert under the influence of the seed grown to be a great plant (Matt. 13:32). After all, each of Christ's converts was at one time His enemy.[19]

Regarding the Parable of the Leaven (Matt. 13:33), Pentecost comments: "The progress of the age is marked, according to this parable, (1) by the ministry of the woman. This evidently refers to the work of a false religious system (Rev. 2:20; 17:1-8). . . . (2) The age is marked by the introduction of the leaven.

---

17. Pentecost, *Things to Come*, p. 147.
18. Gen. 1:20; Deut. 14:20; Isa. 31:5; Matt. 6:26.
19. Rom. 5:10; Eph. 2:1-4; 1 Tim. 1:15.

This figure is used in Scripture to portray that which is evil in character (Exo. 12:15; Lev. 2:11; 6:17; 10:12; Matt. 16:6; Mark 8:15; 1 Cor. 5:6, 8; Gal. 5:9). . . . There is a different emphasis in the parables of the mustard seed and the leaven. The mustard seed refers to the perversion of God's purpose in this age, while the leaven refers to a corruption of the divine agency, the Word, through which this purpose is realized."[20]

This distorts Christ's teaching on the kingdom of heaven. Christ clearly states: "The kingdom of heaven is like leaven." Is He saying, "The kingdom of heaven is like evil?" Furthermore, women are not *necessarily* types of evil in Scripture.[21] Jesus employs them in a good sense in His parables (Matt. 25:1-2; Luke 15:8). It just so happens that women normally bake bread (Lev. 26:26; 1 Sam. 28:24), much like the three measures being an amount which would be normal (Gen. 18:6; Jdgs. 6:19; 1 Sam. 1:24). The woman *imports* the leaven *into* the meal, as Christ's kingdom comes from *without* (John 18:36; Rev. 21:2) and works *within* (Luke 17:20-21; Rom. 14:17).

Pentecost's Scriptural evidences for his view are not convincing. Leaven does not *always* represent evil, for it is found in offerings in Leviticus 7:13 and 23:7. Exodus 12:15 forbids leaven in the Passover because the people are to portray the *haste* with which God removes them from Egypt (Exo. 12:11). Some offerings in Leviticus do forbid leaven, but do not tie this prohibition to leaven's evil symbolism. Even honey is forbidden, despite its symbolizing the Promised Land.[22] In Matthew 16:6; Mark 8:15; and 1 Corinthians 5:6, 8, the leaven references are all modified by such phrases as: "of the Pharisees" and "of malice." In Galatians 5:9 Paul happens to be speaking of the danger of false doctrine when he alludes to a general maxim,

---

20. Pentecost, *Things to Come*, p. 148. Cf. *The New Scofield Reference Bible* (New York: Oxford University Press, 1967), p. 1015.

21. Prov. 9:1-3; 2 Cor. 11:2; Rev. 12:1, 2; 21:2.

22. Exo. 3:8; Lev. 20:24; Num. 13:27; Deut. 6:3; Josh. 5:6.

that can be used in either a good or an evil sense: "A little leaven leavens the whole lump." Actually, the subtle penetrative power of leaven is the source of its legendary interest. When used in analogy it can be used of the penetrative influence of *either* good or evil.

Contrary to dispensationalists the kingdom of heaven is neither grotesque nor a perversion of the work of God. The Gospels present Jesus preaching the "kingdom of heaven" or "of God."[23] He urgently preaches: "Repent, for the kingdom of heaven is at hand" (Matt. 4:17; Mark 1:15). The kingdom is so spiritually glorious that those who are "poor in spirit" and "persecuted for righteousness sake" are given it (Matt. 5:3, 10; Luke 6:20). To enter that kingdom men "must be converted and become as little children" (Matt. 18:3; Mark 10:15; Luke 18:17), by the new birth via God's Holy Spirit (John 3:3, 5). He warns that to enter this kingdom it is necessary to "do the will of my Father" (Matt. 7:21). Those who do so will share with the patriarchs in the kingdom's glory (Matt. 8:11; Luke 13:29). It is so glorious that even John Baptist will be surpassed by the "least" in it (Matt. 11:11; Luke 7:28). Consequently, Christ compares the kingdom of heaven to "a treasure" that brings such "joy" that a man would "sell all that he has" to attain it (Matt. 13:44). Indeed, the kingdom of heaven is like a "goodly pearl" (Matt. 13:45). Truly the "kingdom of heaven" is majestic.

---

23. There is no internal Scriptural evidence that the kingdom of heaven (the term used in Matthew) is different from the kingdom of God (the term used in the other three Gospels). C. I. Scofield made this distinction foundational to his dispensational system, defining the kingdom of heaven as signifying "the Messianic earth rule of Jesus Christ, the Son of David." *The Scofield Reference Bible* (New York: Oxford University Press, 1909), p. 996, note 1: Matthew 3:2. This unsustainable interpretation was quietly abandoned by the editors of the *New Scofield Reference Bible*. They argue that the kingdom of heaven refers to the earthly manifestation of God's kingdom among men, while the kingdom of God sometimes includes angels. They admit that "The kingdom of heaven is similar in many respects to the kingdom of God and is often used synonymously with it, though emphasizing certain features of the divine government." *New Scofield Reference Bible*, p. 994, note 3.

John 12:31-32

In these verses Christ powerfully and confidently asserts: "Now is the judgment of this world; now the ruler of this world will be cast out. And I, if I am lifted up from the earth, will draw all men to Myself."

The moment of His greatest weakness (His crucifixion) will unleash His great strength, securing the "judgment" of the world, the casting out of Satan, and the drawing of all men. And this is about to occur, for He says it "now is." Calvin's comments on the word *judgment* (*krisis*) used here are helpful:

> The word *judgment* is taken as "reformation" by some and "condemnation" by others. I agree rather with the former, who expound it that the world must be restored to due order. For the Hebrew word *mishpat* which is translated as *judgment* means a well-ordered constitution. . . . Now we know that outside Christ there is nothing but confusion in the world. And although Christ had already begun to set up the kingdom of God, it was His death that was the true beginning of a properly-ordered state and the complete restoration of the world.[24]

The *chaos and evil* that Adam's submission to Satan brings into the world are about to be definitively corrected. Tasker writes: "By His own forthcoming conflict with evil in His passion, the situation created by the fall of Adam will be reversed. It was because of disobedience that man was driven by God out of the garden of Eden for having submitted to *the prince of this world* (31); now by the perfect obedience of Jesus on the cross the prince of this world will be deposed from his present ascendancy."[25]

---

24. John Calvin, *The Gospel According to St. John* (1553), *Calvin's New Testament Commentaries*, David W. Torrance and Thomas F. Torrance, eds. (Grand Rapids: Eerdmans, 1961), 2:42.

25. R. V. G. Tasker, *The Gospel According to St. John* (*Tyndale New Testament Commentaries*) (Grand Rapids: Eerdmans, 1960), p. 150.

The means of the restoration is immediately appended: He will cast out the great hinderer of men, Satan,[26] and will begin redemptively drawing all men to Himself. The same word for "draw" (*elkuo*) here is used in John 6:44. It speaks of the *spiritual* drawing power of the Holy Spirit. It implies a certain amount of resistance that is ultimately overcome. This is evident in its usage in John 21:11, where Peter by himself "draws" to shore a heavy-laden net full of large fishes.

The massive influence of Christ's death comes in history through the drawing of all men so that the world as a system[27] might be moved back to God. This is not to be accomplished by political imposition, but spiritual transformation. The final result, however, is not an each-and-every universalism of salvation. Rather, it is a massive, systemic conversion of the vast majority of men, who then progressively transform the world.

1 Corinthians 15:20-28

Here we come to one of the strongest New Testament passages supportive of postmillennialism. Paul here teaches not only that Christ is presently enthroned, but also that He is enthroned and ruling with a confident view to the subduing of His enemies. (I will employ the New International Version as our basic English translation.)

In 1 Corinthians 15:20-22 Paul speaks of the resurrection order: Christ is resurrected as a first-fruits promise of our resurrection. In verses 23-24 we read further of the order of and events associated with the resurrection: "But each in his own turn:[28] Christ the first fruits; then, when he comes, those who belong to him. Then the end will come." With Paul we are

---

26. For the demise of Satan, see discussion later in this chapter.

27. See the discussion of *kosmos*, see discussion later in this chapter.

28. For a discussion of the Greek word *tagma* ("turn") – often confused by dispensationalists – see B. B. Warfield, "The Prophecies of St. Paul" (1886), *Biblical and Theological Studies* (Philadelphia: Presbyterian & Reformed, 1952), p. 484.

now in the era awaiting the end-time coming of Christ, when all believers will be resurrected in glory. When Christ comes this will be "the end"![29] There will be no millennial age to follow.[30]

But notice what will precede the end. Verse 24 says: "the end will come, when he hands over the kingdom to God the Father." The end of earth history comes "whenever"[31] Christ "hands over" the kingdom to the Father. In the syntactical construction before us, the "handing over" (NIV) or "delivering up" (KJV) of the kingdom must occur in conjunction with "the end."[32] Here the contingency is the date: "whenever" it may be that He delivers up the kingdom, *then* the end will come. Associated with the predestined end here is the prophecy that the kingdom of Christ will be delivered up to the Father only "*after* he has destroyed all dominion, authority and power."[33]

Gathering these exegetical data together, we see that *the end is contingent:* it will come when He delivers up the kingdom to His Father. But this will not occur until "after He has destroyed all dominion, authority and power." Consequently, the end will

---

29. The Scripture is clear that the resurrection is a "general resurrection" of both the righteous and unrighteous (Dan. 12:2; John 5:28-29; Acts 24:15), which will occur on the "*last* day" (John 6:39-40, 44, 54; 11:24; 12:48). See Chapter 13, below.

30. For helpful discussions of this prohibition against an intervening kingdom (*Zwischenreich*) era prior to the end, see: C. K. Barrett, *From First Adam to Last* (London: Black, 1962), p. 101; Geerhardus Vos, *The Pauline Eschatology* (Phillipsburg, NJ: Presbyterian & Reformed, [1930] 1991), pp. 238-258; Herman Ridderbos, *Paul: An Outline of His Theology* (Grand Rapids: Eerdmans, 1975), pp. 556-559; W. D. Davies, *Paul and Rabbinic Judaism* (New York: Harper, 1967), pp. 291-298. See also: A. T. Robertson, *Word Pictures in the New Testament*, 6 vols. (Nashville: Broadman, 1930), 4:191.

31. A better translation of *hotan* is "whenever." We know not "when" this will be, Matt. 24:36; Acts 1:7; 2 Pet. 3:10.

32. The Greek for "hands over" here is *paradidoi*, which is in the present tense and subjunctive mode. When *hotan* is followed by the present subjunctive it indicates a present contingency that occurs in conjunction with the main clause: here the coming of the end. Arndt-Gingrich, *Lexicon*, p. 592.

33. In the Greek text the *hotan* is here followed by the aorist subjunctive, *katargese*. Such a construction indicates that the action of the subordinate clause precedes the action of the main clause. Arndt-Gingrich, *Lexicon*, p. 592.

not occur, and Christ will not turn the kingdom over to the Father, until *after He has abolished all opposition.* Here again is the gospel victory motif in the New Testament in a way co-ordinate with Old Testament covenantal and prophetic expectations.

Notice further: Verse 25 demands that "He must [*dei*] reign until He has put all His enemies under His feet." Here the present infinitive ("reign") indicates the continuance of His reign. We have already seen in Chapter 11 that *He is presently reigning, and has been so since His ascension.* References elsewhere to the Psalm 110 passage specifically mention His sitting at God's right hand. Sitting at the right hand entails active ruling and reigning, not passive resignation. He is now actively "the ruler over the kings of the earth" and "has made us kings and priests to His God and Father, to Him be glory and dominion forever and ever" (Rev. 1:5).[34] Here in 1 Corinthians 15:25 we learn that He must continue to reign, putting His enemies under His feet. Until when? The answer is identical to that which has already been concluded: His reign from heaven extends to the *end of history.* Earlier, it was awaiting the *definitive* abolition of all rival rule, authority and power (Matt. 28:18). His bodily return is delayed until *progressively* "He has put all His enemies under His feet." This repetition of His sure conquest before the end is significant. Furthermore, the last enemy

---

34. R. C. H. Lenski, *The Interpretation of Paul's First and Second Letters to the Corinthians* (Minneapolis: Augsburg, 1961), p. 672. F. F. Bruce, *I & II Corinthians (New Century Bible Commentary)* (Grand Rapids: Eerdmans, 1971), p. 147. W. R. G. Loader, "Christ at the Right Hand – Ps. 110:1 in the New Testament," *New Testament Studies* 24 (1978) 208. J. Lambrecht, "Paul's Christological Use of Scripture in 1 Cor. 15:20-28," *New Testament Studies* 28 (1982) 506. This is contrary to how dispensationalist MacLeod sees Psalm 110 used in Hebrews: He admits that Psalm 110 employs tokens of kingship (vv. 3, 8-9, 13): Christ's "throne, scepter, and kingdom – all tokens of power and dominion are mentioned." Yet he goes on to comment on the use of Psalm 110:3 in Hebrews: "Closer examination, however, reveals that Hebrews has no emphasis 'on Christ as present ruler of the world. . . .' The expression 'He sat down' carries the sense of a finished work of sacrifice (10:12) rather than that of a present reign as King. . . . At the present time Christ sits at God's right hand waiting for the day when He shall return to earth to reign (1:6, 13; 10:13)." David J. MacLeod, "The Present Work of Christ in Hebrews," *Bibliotheca Sacra* 148 (April/June 1991) 199.

that will be subdued is death, which is subdued in conjunction with the final resurrection that occurs at His coming.[35] The progressive subduing of His other enemies in history occurs before this final resurrection.

In verse 27 it is clear that *He has the legal title to rule*, for the Father "has put everything under His feet." This is the Pauline expression (borrowed from Psa. 8:6) that is equivalent to Christ's declaration that "all authority has been given Me." Christ has the *promise* of victory, and He has the *right* to victory. Psalm 110, especially as expounded by Paul in 1 Corinthians 15, shows that He will have the *historical, pre-consummation victory* as His own before His Second Advent. This verse from Psalm 110 is one of the most frequently referred to Old Testament promises to appear in the New Testament. The expectation of comprehensive victory is a frequently recurring theme.

Other Passages

There are numerous other passages in the New Testament that we could cite to fill out the victory motif. Ephesians 1:19-23 praises the "mighty power" of God in Christ's resurrection as a stepping stone to Christ's being raised "far above all principality and power and might and dominion, and every name that is named." Because of this we may rest assured that God "put all things under His feet, and gave Him to be head over all things to the church" (Eph. 1:22). The Church, which is His body, has as its head the exalted Christ. How can there be historical failure under such a glorious One? The Head of the Church, which has been given the task of baptizing all nations (Matt. 28:19), is a sovereign Lord.

Hebrews contrasts the Old Covenant and the New Covenant (Heb. 12:18-24), pointing out that the recipients of the New

---

35. Contrary to dispensationalist confusion, the resurrection of the lost is not mentioned here only because his primary concern (as in 1 Thess. 4:13) is with Christians and their ethical actions.

Covenant are in the very process of receiving (*paralambanontes*) "a kingdom which cannot be shaken" (Heb. 12:28).[36] This kingdom will "remain" after God shakes the Old Covenant order in the destruction of the Temple in A.D. 70 (Heb. 12:26-27). In Hebrews 1:3, 13 we learn, as in 1 Corinthians 15, that "when He had by Himself purged our sins" He then "sat down at the right hand of the Majesty on high," anticipating His enemies becoming His footstool (cf. Heb. 10:13). The kingdom, which He receives in history, is unshakable and will "remain" until the last enemy is vanquished (cp. Matt. 16:18).

Extension Guaranteed

The Principle of Gradualism

A proper understanding of the eschatological victory set forth in Scripture requires the recognition of an important redemptive-historical method of divine operation: gradualism – "here a little; there a little" gradualism (Isa. 28:10). This principle expects the developmental expansion of the kingdom over time. Contrary to postmillennialism the dispensationalist and premillennialist operate on the basis of *catastrophism*. In their theological systems the kingdom of Christ in all of its attendant glory will invade history as a great catastrophe. It will be introduced by wars and rumors of wars, as it is suddenly imposed on a recalcitrant world. The postmillennial principle of gradualism, however, is well-grounded in Scripture.

---

36. For some reason Hanko states: "So far as I have noticed, no postmillennialist would ever say that the kingdom of Christ to be realized here upon this earth is brought about by 'the removing of those things that are shaken' (which, according to vs. 26, refers to heaven and earth); nor that even this glorious kingdom to be realized here on earth is a 'kingdom which cannot be moved.' Even an ardent Calvinistic postmillennialist believes, I think, that this earthly kingdom, as glorious as it is, shall be moved when Christ comes again." Herman Hanko, "Response to 'The "Other Side" of Postmillennialism,' " *Standard Bearer* 66:8 (Apr. 1, 1990) 297. The kingdom of Christ will *not* "be moved when Christ comes again," for "then comes the end, when He *delivers the kingdom to God the Father*, when He puts an end to all rule and all authority and power" (1 Cor. 15:24).

A careful survey of Scripture shows that gradualism is a common divine *modus operandi* apparent throughout biblical revelation. *Creation:* Even the creation of the universe proceeds upon a gradualistic principle – an accelerated gradualism, to be sure, but gradual nonetheless. God creates the world *ex nihilo*, but He does not create the world as a complete system by one divine fiat – though He could easily have done so. He employs a series of successive divine fiats stretched out over a period of six days (Gen. 1; Exo. 20:11).[37] *Redemption:* God promises redemption just after the entry of sin into the human race in Eden (Gen. 3:15). Yet its accomplishment follows thousands of years after Adam (Gal. 4:4; Eph. 1:10). *Revelation:* Rather than giving His total special revelation of Himself and His will all at once, He gradually unfolds His Word to men over a period of 1,500 years (Heb. 1:1, 2; 1 Pet. 1:10-12). *Sanctification:* Even in salvation, justification, a once-for-all act (Rom. 4:2-3; 5:1), gives rise to sanctification, which comes by process (Phil. 2:12-13; 1 Pet. 2:2).

The Experience of Gradualism

It is likewise with His redemptive kingdom: it develops along gradualistic lines. It comes incrementally through history, progressing from a small, imperceptible beginning to a glorious, universal conclusion. Let us survey several relevant passages in this regard.

An historical indicator of a gradualistic development of the kingdom is found in the conquest of the Promised Land. In this we see specifically stated why God operates gradualistically in that situation; in other words, it is not just "a matter of natural course." In Deuteronomy 7:22 the principle is enunciated: "And the Lord your God will clear away these nations before you little by little; you will not be able to put an end to them

---

37. Kenneth L. Gentry, Jr., "Reformed Theology and Six Day Creationism," *Christianity & Society*, 5:4 (October, 1995): 25ff.

quickly, lest the wild beasts grow too numerous for you." The gradualistic principle is for the good of God's people, allowing them to conquer where they could maintain control.

In Daniel 2:31-45 the kingdom of Christ comes down to the earth as a stone smiting the world kingdom, which exists under a fourth imperial rule. As we read through the passage we learn that the kingdom grows to become a great mountain in the earth: "You watched while a stone was cut out without hands, which struck the image on its feet of iron and clay, and broke them in pieces . . . . And the *stone* that struck the image *became a great mountain* and filled the whole earth. And in the days of these kings the God of heaven will set up a kingdom which shall never be destroyed; and the kingdom shall not be left to other people; it shall break in pieces and consume all these kingdoms, and it shall stand forever" (Dan. 2:34-35, 44).

In this imagery we have both linear continuity over time and remarkable upwardly progressive development: the stone *grows* to become a "great mountain." We also witness struggle and resistance: the stone eventually smashes the image. Finally, we rejoice in its fortunes: the God-defying image is thoroughly crushed. This gradual progress to victory against opposition is portrayed also in Daniel 7:26, where we witness victory as "the result of *many* blows rather than of *one*."[38] This process manifests progressive corporate sanctification in history.

In Ezekiel 17:22-24 God promises to establish the kingdom as a small "sprig from the lofty top of the cedar." Then He will nurture it until it becomes "a stately cedar."

In Ezekiel 47:1-9 redemption flowing forth from the temple of God is stated to come in stages. The waters of life coming out from under the altar come first "to the ankles" (v. 3), then to the knees (v. 4a), then to the loins (v. 4b), then it "was a river

---

38. David Brown, *Christ's Second Coming: Will It Be Premillennial?* (Edmondton, AB: Still Waters Revival, [1882] 1990), p. 334.

that I could not ford" (v. 5). This is the river of life (v. 9).[39] Davis suggests that in John 7:38 Christ is presenting Himself as the fulfillment of Ezekiel 47.[40] This is quite consistent with Christ's presenting Himself as the True Temple (John 2:19-21). John 7:38 reads: "He who believes in Me, as the Scripture has said, out of his heart will flow rivers of living water." At Pentecost the torrential flow of the living water begins in earnest (Acts 2:33).

In Matthew 13 the parables of the kingdom speak of its increase in size and transformational influence. Matthew 13:3-9 portrays the kingdom as the scattering of seed that gradually grows to bear abundant fruit. Matthew 13:31-33 speaks of its growth as that of a mustard seed to a great plant and as a little leaven that leavens three bushels of meal. In Mark 4:26-29, the kingdom of God is said to begin as mere seed (v. 26), then it puts forth the blade, then the head, the mature grain (v. 27).

In Romans 13:11-14 and 1 John 2:8, the apostles see the kingdom light as already shining, ready to dispel the darkness. "The manifestation of the Messiah is regularly termed by the ancient Jews *yom*, *day*, because previously to this all is *night*." "The apostle considers the state of the *Gentiles* under the notion of *night*, a time of darkness and a time of evil practices. . . ."[41] He considers the Gospel as now visiting the Gentiles, and the *light* of a glorious *day* about to shine forth on them."[42]

The progress and growth of the kingdom will not be thwarted by Satan. The "gates of hell will not be able to prevail

39. Cf. living water in Joel 3:18; Zech. 14:8; John 4:10-11; Rev. 21:6; 22:1, 17.

40. John J. Davis, *Christ's Victorious Kingdom: Postmillennialism Reconsidered* (Grand Rapids: Baker, 1986), p. 40 and Holwerda, *Jesus and Israel*, pp. 74-79. For a helpful treatment of John 7:38, see: William Hendriksen, *The Gospel of John* (*New Testament Commentary*) (Grand Rapids: Baker, 1953), pp. 21-26.

41. Gentiles walk in darkness (Eph. 5:8). The Church is to bring light to the world (Matt. 5:14) and must expose the works of darkness (Eph. 5:11). Christians are "children of light" (John 12:36; Eph. 5:8; 1 Thess. 5:5) and ought to "walk in the light" (1 John 1:7).

42. Adam Clarke, *Clarke's Commentary* (Nashville: Abingdon, n.d.), 6:149.

against it" (Matt. 16:18). Though slow, it will advance in God's good time.

Vastness, Not Universalism

It is sometimes mistakenly supposed that postmillennialism implies either the ultimate salvation of all men or at least a form of temporal universalism. Evangelical postmillennialism teaches, rather, that "the greater part" of men will have been saved at the outcome of history.[43] This is quite contrary to amillennialism, which leaves the vast majority of men lost, and the remnant of the saved only a minority. Premillennialism and dispensationalism, though, may suggest that after the 1,000-year earthly kingdom, with its enhanced fecundity, the ranks of the saved may outstrip those of the lost.

But neither is it the case at any given point in history that all men will be born-again Christians. Brown comments: "Have we not evidence that *during* that bright period the world's subjection to the scepter of Christ will not be quite absolute?"[44] Campbell writes that the phrase "Christianized world" "does not mean that every living person will then be a Christian, or that every Christian will be a perfect Christian. It does surely mean that the righteous rule and authority of Christ the King will be recognized over all the earth."[45] Boettner observes only that "evil in all its many forms eventually will be reduced to negligible proportions, that Christian principles will be the rule, not the exception, and that Christ will return to a truly Christianized world."[46]

The Scriptural evidence, though clearly expecting Christ's dominion throughout the world, also allows that there will be a

---

43. Loraine Boettner, *The Millennium* (Philadelphia: Presbyterian & Reformed, 1958), p. 30.

44. Brown, *Christ's Second Coming*, p. 145.

45. Roderick Campbell, *Israel and the New Covenant* (Tyler, TX: Geneva Divinity School Press, [1954] 1981), p. 298.

46. Boettner, *Millennium*, p. 14.

262 HE SHALL HAVE DOMINION

minority who will not be converted to Him. Evidence for this exists in the events associated with Christ's return, which include a brief rebellion, as indicated in 2 Thessalonians 1:7-10 and Revelation 20:7-9. There will always be tares in the wheat field (Matt. 13:39-43). Likewise, though Israel truly possessed the land (Josh. 21:43), there remained pockets of resistance (Jdgs. 1:27ff).[47]

Some suggest,[48] and I tend to agree, that Isaiah 19:18 symbolically implies a five-to-one ratio for Christians over non-Christians at the height of the millennial glory: "In that day five cities in the land of Egypt will speak the language of Canaan and swear by the LORD of hosts; one will be called the City of Destruction." To speak the language of God's people seems to indicate salvation. Language plays an important role in Scripture: if it is the language of God's people, it evidences His favor;[49] if not, it symbolizes His curse.[50]

In point of fact the progress of redemption not only grows imperceptibly, but oftentimes sporadically. Its historical prog-

---

47. The Canaanites' successful resistance was based on the incomplete covenantal obedience of Israel. Jordan writes: "However they are termed, Israel had been forbidden to enter into any treaties or covenants with the Canaanites (Ex. 23:32). Thus, what we have here is almost certainly not only a failure to follow out God's commands, but a direct violation of them." James B. Jordan, *Judges: God's War Against Humanism* (Tyler, TX: Geneva Ministries, 1985), p. 18.

48. Alexander holds this view and notes it was Calvin's position, J. A. Alexander, *Commentary on the Prophecies of Isaiah* (Grand Rapids: Zondervan, [1875] 1977), 1:355-356. Matthew Henry leans to this interpretation. Henry, *Matthew Henry's Commentary* (Old Tappan, NJ: Revell, [1712] n.d.), 4:108.

49. Isa. 19:18; 57:19; Zeph. 3:9.

50. Deut. 28:49; Psa. 81:5; 114:1; Jer. 5:15; Ezek. 3:5-6. See the function of tongues as a sign of judgment-curse on Israel, Acts 2:4-40; 1 Cor. 14:20-21. See: Kenneth L. Gentry, Jr., "Crucial Issues Regarding Tongues," *Counsel of Chalcedon* (Oct.-Dec., 1981); O. Palmer Robertson, *The Final Word: A Biblical Response to the Case for Tongues and Prophecy Today* (Edinburgh: Banner of Truth, 1993), pp. 41-50. Richard B. Gaffin, Jr., *Perspectives on Pentecost: New Testament Teaching on the Gifts of the Spirit* (Phillipsburg, N.J.: Presbyterian and Reformed, 1979), pp. 102-109. Leonard J. Coppes, *Whatever Happened to Biblical Tongues?* (Chattanooga, TN: Pilgrim, 1977), pp. 48-52. Ronald E. Baxter, *Charismatic Gift of Tongues* (Grand Rapids: Kregal, 1981), pp. 51-54.

ress is often intermittent, being intermingled with eras of divine pruning (John 15:5-6) in anticipation of the final harvest. Such pruning is certainly true with Israel of the Old Testament (Isa. 6:9-13). At one point God offers to do away with Israel and establish a new people from Moses (Exo. 32:10). Of course, by the New Covenant era, this has long been Israel's experience (Matt. 3:9-12; Rom. 11:16-24). Such pruning can leave a region, once strongly influenced by Christianity, wholly without a Christian witness – for a time. In a sense it is like seed, which is planted and grows and produces other seed (Matt. 13:3-9, 23). Thus, we can expect it to grow in certain areas and perhaps even to die, but eventually to come back because the productivity of seed involves its death and renewal (John 12:24; 1 Cor. 15:36). Ultimately, it is God that gives the increase (1 Cor. 3:6-7) when and where He pleases (cf. Isa. 55:9-11; John 3:8).

Cultivation Encouraged

The Messianic kingdom is established in the first century through the redemptive labors of King Jesus. It is His glorious kingdom established by His mighty power and for the majesty of the His glorious Name. But by His providence, His kingdom work is carried out by His redeemed people. The world-encompassing Great Commission is no command to make bricks without straw (cf. Exo. 5:7, 8). Christ does the initial and definitive work as the Son of Man; but we who are in union with Him and under His providential governance work to promote His kingdom rule in history. Being joint-heirs with Christ (Luke 12:32; 22:29; Rom. 8:17), we presently reign with Him in this world: He has "raised us up together, and made us sit together in the heavenly places in Christ Jesus" (Eph. 2:6).[51]

---

51. Rom. 5:17; 1 Cor. 4:8; 2 Cor. 5:20; Col. 3:1-3; 2 Tim. 2:12; 1 Pet. 2:9; Rev. 1:6; 3:21.

Warfield writes: "Christians are His soldiers in this holy war, and it is through our victory that His victory is known."[52] "There is the church struggling here below – the 'militant church' we may call it; the triumphing church he would rather teach us to call it, for the essence of his presentation is not that there is continual strife here to be endured, but that there is continuous victory here to be won."[53] He writes further: "It is the distinction of Christianity that it has come into the world clothed with the mission to *reason* its way to its dominion. . . . And it is solely by reasoning that it will put all its enemies under its feet."[54]

The richness of the gracious gifts of God to His people is of surpassing greatness; those gifts are well suited to promoting His kingdom in the world. Christ commanded His disciples to wait in Jerusalem "for power on high" (Luke 24:46-49) – i.e., the Holy Spirit (Acts 2) – in order to equip them for the world-transforming task. He says that their faith, which overcomes the world,[55] is such that it can remove mountains.[56] We know that the apostles greatly rejoice in the super-abundant grace of God and unsearchable riches of Christ,[57] declaring that God blesses us with "all spiritual blessings" (Eph. 1:3) because of Christ's ascension and pouring out of His wondrous gifts upon His people (Eph. 4:8-11). They are convinced they can do "all things" through Christ and that God will supply all they need "according to his riches in glory by Christ Jesus" (Phil. 4:13,

---

52. Warfield, *Biblical and Theological Studies*, p. 493.

53. Warfield, "The Gospel and the Second Coming" (1915), *Selected Shorter Writings of Benjamin B. Warfield*, John E. Meeter, ed., 2 vols. (Nutley, New Jersey: Presbyterian & Reformed, 1970), 1:348.

54. *Ibid.*, 2:99-100.

55. 1 John 2:12-14; 3:8; 5:3, 4.

56. Matt. 17:20; 21:21; Mark 11:23; 1 Cor. 13:2.

57. Rom. 5:17; Acts 4:33; 1 Pet. 4:10; Eph. 1:7, 18; 2:7; 3:8.

19). Since they are "more than conquerors" (Rom. 8:37), they are certain that "with God nothing shall be impossible."[58]

The Church has ample gifts and graces to get the job done, in obedience to the Great Commission – a covenantal obligation upon God's people.[59] *First*, we have the very presence of the Risen Christ with us.[60] The Great Commission specifically promises His authoritative presence (Matt. 28:20) in the context of commanding that we "disciple all nations, baptizing them" (Matt. 28:19). He who will never leave nor forsake us (Heb. 13:5), has "all things under His feet" and is "head over all things to the church" (Eph. 1:22).

Second, since the ascension of Christ, we have the indwelling of the Holy Spirit,[61] who will convict the *world* of sin, righteousness, and judgment (John 16:7-15). In fact, it is "expedient" for us that Christ goes away in His temporal body, so that we might have His spiritual presence in the Person of the Holy Spirit.[62] The Holy Spirit's coming is glorious in every respect. God accomplishes His will through the Spirit's working: " 'Not by might nor by power, but by My Spirit,' says the LORD of hosts" (Zech. 4:6b).

Third, it is the Father's delight to save sinners.[63] He sovereignly and graciously saves unworthy sinners for His own glory.[64] He sends Christ to "reconcile the *world* to Himself" (John 3:17; Rom. 11:15; 2 Cor. 5:19). I will return to this theme of world reconciliation below.

---

58. Luke 1:37; Matt. 17:20; 19:26; 18:27; Mark 9:23; 10:27.

59. Gentry, *Great Commission*, ch. 2.

60. John 6:56; 14:16-20, 23; 15:4-5; 17:23, 26; Rom. 8:10; Gal. 2:20; 4:19; Eph. 3:17; Col. 1:27; 1 John 4:4.

61. John 7:39; 14:16-18; 1 Cor. 3:16; 2 Cor. 6:16.

62. John 7:39; 14:27-28; 16:7; Acts 2:33.

63. Ezek. 18:23; 33:11; Luke 15:10; 2 Cor. 5:19; 1 Tim. 1:15; 2:5.

64. Rom. 5:10ff; Eph. 1:3-11; 2 Tim. 1:9.

Fourth, we have the gospel, which is the very power of God[65] and we employ the Word of God as our spiritual weapon of victory.[66] "Though we walk in the flesh, we do not war according to the flesh. For the weapons of our warfare are not carnal but mighty in God for pulling down strongholds, casting down arguments and *every* high thing that exalts itself against the knowledge of God, bringing *every* thought into captivity to the obedience of Christ" (2 Cor. 10:3-5).

Fifth, we have full access to God through Jesus' name,[67] in prayer[68] by which we shall do even greater works than Christ did on earth (Matt. 21:21; John 14:12). Prayer opens to us the full resources of heaven (John 14:13; Jms. 4:15; 1 John 5:14). The Lord's Prayer even directs us faithfully to pray, "Your kingdom come. Your will be done on earth as it is in heaven" (Matt. 6:10). As Calvin comments: "So in this prayer we ask that, with all impediment removed, He may bring all mortals under His command, and lead them to consider the life of heaven. . . . So we pray that . . . the whole world may willingly come over to Him. . . . And now, as the Kingdom of God increases, stage upon stage, to the end of the world, we must every day pray for its coming. As far as iniquity holds the world in sway, so far is the Kingdom of God absent, for complete righteousness must come in its train."[69]

Sixth, in His ministry Christ witnesses the falling of Satan's kingdom as His followers exercise authority over demoniacs (Luke 17:10; cf. Rev. 12:9). In fact, Satan is cast down (John 12:31) and bound by Christ in order that Christ might "spoil

---

65. Rom. 1:16; 15:19; 16:25; 1 Cor. 1:18, 24; 1 Thess. 1:5.

66. 2 Cor. 6:7; Eph. 6:17; 1 Thess. 2:13; Heb. 4:12.

67. John 14:13, 14; 15:7, 16; 16:23, 24, 26; 1 John 3:22; 5:14, 15.

68. Matt. 7:7-11; 21:22; Eph. 2:18; Phil. 4:6; Heb. 4:16; 10:19-22; 1 John 3:22; 5:14-15.

69. Calvin, *Synoptics*, 1:207-8. Cf. Thomas Scott, *Holy Bible Containing the Old and New Testaments with Explanatory Notes*, 3 vols. (Philadelphia: Lippencott, 1868), 3:28.

his goods."[70] Christ specifically comes that He might "destroy" Satan (Heb. 2:14) and his "works" (1 John 3:8), making a show of him, openly triumphing over him (Col. 2:15; Eph. 4:8-11[71]), having judged him (John 16:11). Consequently, his people might not only resist the devil so that he will flee from them (Jms. 4:7; 1 Pet. 5:9), but also expect to "bruise Satan under" their feet (Rom. 16:20), "because greater is he that is in you, than he that is in the world" (1 John 4:4). Because of all this, the gospel has the power to "open their eyes, and to turn them from darkness to light, and from the power of Satan unto God" (Acts 26:18). In the Lord's Prayer there is a strong relationship between the petitions "Thy kingdom come" and "deliver us from the Evil One."[72]

Elisha's servant is made bold by the vision of the mountains filled with angelic chariots (2 Kgs. 6:17). Zechariah is strengthened by the vision of the angels of God roving the earth (Zech. 1:7-11). We should be even more confident in the power of the New Covenant, which has "Christ in you the hope of glory" (Col. 1:27). Do we not have Christ walking among His churches (Rev. 1:10-13; Matt. 28:20)? Does Christ build His Church upon sand (Matt. 7:26-27)? Will the "gates of hell" prevail against the Church?[73]

---

70. Matt. 12:28-29; 2 Tim. 2:26; cf. Rev. 20:2-3.

71. See: Charles Hodge, *Ephesians*, pp. 213-214 and Vos, *Pauline Eschatology*, p. 281ff. The word "triumphing" "is derived from *thriambos*, a hymn sung in festal procession and is kin to the Latin *triumphus* (our triumph), a triumphal procession of victorious Roman generals." Robertson, *Word Pictures*, 4:495. An example of a victor leading captives may be found in Titus' treatment of John of Gischala and Simon, Josephus, *Wars* 7:5:7. Examples are also found in *The Acts of Paul and Peter* 33; and Taitian, *Graece* 26.

72. Ridderbos, *Coming of the Kingdom*, p. 108.

73. "The expression *Gates of Hades* is an orientalism for the court, throne, power, and dignity of the infernal kingdom. Hades is contemplated as a mighty city, with formidable, frowning portals." Marvin R. Vincent, *Word Studies in the New Testament*, 4 vols. (Grand Rapids: Eerdmans, [1887] 1946), 1:96. Satan has the power of death (Heb. 2:14).

Function Specified

Postmillennialists believe that evangelism is the absolute pre-condition to worldwide, postmillennial, theocratic success.[74] Postmillennialism strongly promotes the *"gospel* of the kingdom."[75] Cultural influence and change are to be promoted by God's people – who are saved by grace alone (Eph. 2:8-10) – at large in their callings, not by the institutional Church as such.

Thus, postmillennialism seeks the Christianization of the world *by the spread of the gospel of Jesus Christ.* Evangelism has priority in Christianization. In Matthew 28:19-20, the Great Commission requires baptism – the sacramental seal of entry into the covenant. Postmillennialism strongly asserts that "apart from [Christ] you can do nothing" (John 15:5), but that we "can do all things through Christ which strengtheneth me," because "God shall supply all our need according to his riches in glory by Christ Jesus" (Phil. 4:13, 19). This leads us to "work out [our] own salvation [i.e., in all of life] with fear and trembling. For it is God which worketh in [us] both to will and to do of his good pleasure" (Phil. 2:12,13). All of this hope has but one foundation: the gospel of the resurrected Christ (Acts 4:12; 1 Cor. 3:11). Hence Paul's testimony regarding his approach: "I determined not to know any thing among you, save Jesus Christ, and him crucified" (1 Cor. 2:2).[76]

---

74. The definition of "theocracy" is "God's rule," not rule by Ayatollah Khomeini types. It must be understood as fundamentally different from any "ecclesiocracy," which would be an Erastian church-dominated government. Two of the most prolific writers calling for Christian cultural transformation along theocratic lines are Rousas J. Rushdoony and Gary North. In the writings of both, regeneration is frequently set forth as the pre-condition to success in the endeavor. For example see: R. J. Rushdoony, *Institutes of Biblical Law* (Nutley, NJ: Craig, 1973), pp. 113, 122, 147, 308, 413, 627, 780. Gary North, *Political Polytheism: The Myth of Pluralism* (Tyler, TX: Institute for Christian Economics, 1989), pp. 133, 157, 585-586, 611.

75. Matt. 4:23; 9:35; 24:14; Mark 1:14-15.

76. By this he obviously did not mean that he only taught about the gospel details, for he taught them about church divisions (1 Cor. 1-2), church discipline (ch. 5), marriage (ch. 7), etc., not to mention all the other things he taught to them and others.

The Full-Orbed Character of Redemption

Too many Christians restrict the focus and effects of Christ's redemption in history. We are told, for instance, that "the purpose of the church in this present age [is] that of a *witness*."[77] The words of the Great Commission "refer exclusively to Christian evangelism and soteriological salvation,"[78] by which is meant the salvation of individuals. "Nothing could be plainer in the New Testament than that in this age of grace God uses the church, members of the body of Christ, to be witnesses throughout the earth (Mt 28:18-20; Ac 1:8)."[79]

Though I have dealt with the Great Commission before, let me consider some additional implications that may be drawn from it. Clearly the initial focus of the Great Commission (Matt. 28:18-20) is evangelism, for the result of our going forth is the baptism of converts.[80] The other, supplemental commissionings of Christ recorded in Mark 16:15 and Luke 24:47-49 emphasize the salvation of men, as well. Yet the Great Commission speaks to the Christianization of every area of life, as men submit to the rule of Christ in salvation.[81]

It is important to understand that the "all" in the "all authority" granted to Christ (Matt. 28:18) is used in the distributive[82] sense. It speaks of *every* form of authority being at His command, whether in heaven or on earth. This is the authority

---

77. House and Ice, *Dominion Theology*, p. 165.

78. *Ibid.*, p. 151.

79. Feinberg, "The Jew After the Rapture," in *Prophecy and the Seventies*, p. 182.

80. Acts 2:38; 8:12, 36; 9:18; 10:47; 16:15, 33; 18:8.

81. An important corollary point that we do not have room to pursue is that in salvation, the convert bows to the authority of Christ as Lord. This truth is denied by most dispensationalists, John MacArthur being a notable exception. See: John MacArthur, *The Gospel According to Jesus* (Grand Rapids: Zondervan, 1988). See my book, *Lord of the Saved: Getting to the Heart of the Lordship Debate* (Phillipsburg, NJ: Presbyterian & Reformed, 1992).

82. A. B. Bruce, "Matthew," in W. Robertson Nicoll, *The Expositor's Greek New Testament*, vol. 1 (Grand Rapids: Eerdmans, 1951), p. 339.

of God Almighty,[83] and it is not limited to the authority of spiritual and moral persuasion among individuals and in the inter-personal realm. He also has authority in the ecclesiastic and familial realms, as well as the societal, political, economical, and so forth. As Revelation 1:5 says of Him *in the days when John wrote*, He *is* "the ruler of the kings of the earth." He *now* has a Name above *every* name.[84]

Following this claim to universal authority, He delivers to His few followers the obligation and plan for world conquest: "Go therefore and make disciples of all the nations, baptizing them in the name of the Father and the Son and the Holy Spirit, teaching them to observe all that I commanded you" (vv. 19-20). The command of the resurrected Christ who possesses "all authority" is for His followers to bring all nations to conversion and baptism. This is precisely the expectation of so many of the Old Testament prophecies, which foresee all nations flowing to Mount Zion (e.g., Isa. 2:1-4; Mic. 4:1-4) and anticipate "no more shall any man teach his neighbor, 'Know the Lord, for they shall all know the Lord' " (Jer. 31:34; cf. Isa. 11:9).

In addition the Commission urges our "teaching them to observe *all* things whatsoever I have commanded you." He has given His people instruction for all of life (cf. 2 Tim. 3:16-17). Involved in the proclamation of the gospel is the call for repentance. Should not the "repentance for forgiveness of sins" (Luke 24:47) that we are to preach be particular and detailed rather than general and vague? That is, should not repentance be a "change of mind"[85] regarding the *particulars* of our conduct in *all* of life, so that we strive to live differently (i.e., Christianly)?

---

83. Matt. 11:25; Amos 1:3-2:3; Oba. 1; Isa. 10:5-34.

84. See: Gen. 14:22; 24:3; Deut. 4:39; 10:14; Josh. 2:11; 2 Kgs. 19:15; 1 Chr. 29:11; Matt. 11:27; Luke 10:21; Acts 14:27. Christ has been given this authority: John 3:35; 13:3; Rom. 14:11; Eph. 1:20ff; Phil. 2:9; Col. 1:18; 1 Pet. 3:22; Rev. 17:14; 19:16.

85. The Greek term *metanoia* means a "change of mind."

According to Luke 3 should not we then bring forth particular fruits worthy of repentance (Luke 3:8), such as: Changing our external behavior by being transformed by God rather than conformed to the world (Rom. 12:1-2)? Displaying a care for the poor (Matt. 25:31-46; Luke 3:11; 16:19-25; 2 Cor. 8:13ff)? Being honest governmental officials (Luke 3:12-14)? Developing godly employer-employee relationships (Eph. 6:5-9; Luke 10:17)? Promoting honest wages (1 Tim. 5:18; Luke 10:7)? Securing free-market bargaining (Matt. 20:1-15)? Defending private property rights (Acts 5:4)? Urging godly citizenship and the proper function of the state (Rom. 13:1-7; 1 Pet. 2:13-17)? Encouraging the family as the primary agency of welfare (1 Tim. 5:8)? Cultivating a proper use of finances (Matt. 15:14ff)? Warning against the dangers of excessive indebtedness (Rom. 13:8)? Instructing in the morality of investment (Matt. 25:14-30)? Supporting the leaving of an inheritance (2 Cor. 12:14)? Demanding penal restraints upon criminals (Rom. 13:4; 1 Tim. 1:8-10), lawsuits (1 Cor. 6:1-8), and more?

Should not the Christian realize that "the weapons of our warfare are not carnal, but mighty through God to the pulling down of strong holds; casting down imaginations, and every high thing that exalteth itself against the knowledge of God, and bringing into captivity every thought to the obedience of Christ" (2 Cor. 10:4-5)? If we cast down "every high thing that exalteth itself against the knowledge of God" and bring "into captivity every thought to the obedience of Christ," will we not be engaging in culture-transforming change? If we are going to "witness" to the people of the world how they are to behave, should we not behave ourselves according to our witness and strive to lead *them* to live according to our witness, by the grace of God? Should not we do all things – whether eating or drinking or whatever we do in word or deed – to the glory of God (1 Cor. 10:31; Col 3:17)? Especially since we will give account of every word and deed before Christ (2 Cor. 10:5; Matt. 12:36; Rom. 14:12)? In other words, should not redemption affect *all of life?* May not redemption involve the turning from sin in all of life, even to the point of issuing forth in a distinctive socio-political culture, since Israel's "redemption" did such?[86]

The Breadth of Redemption

All of this discussion regarding the kingdom enterprise comes home to the eschatological argument when we consider the biblical expectations regarding redemption. But first, a word study of the Greek word *kosmos* ("world") will prove helpful.

The nominal form of the word originally meant "order, adornment." The verbal form meant "to put in order, to adorn." The verbal idea of "put in order" is evident in Matthew 12:44 where the demon that is cast out returns to his former "house" and finds it "clean, swept, and *put in order.*" The noun originally had to do with building something from individual parts to form a whole. It came to be applied to relations between men, as in the case of ordering soldiers in armies and governments in matters of state. Eventually *kosmos* came to speak of the well-ordered universe, and was an important term in Greek philosophy. In the New Testament the word *kosmos* frequently speaks of the sum of all created being. Acts 17:24 speaks of God creating the "world and all that is in it"; it signifies the universe and all that it contains.

The word "world" as employed in the passages below refers to *the world as the orderly system of men and things.* That is, the world that God created and loves is His creation *as it was designed to be*: a world system in subjection to man, who in turn is in subjection to God. Thus, God loves His created order of men and things, not for what it has become (sinful and corrupted), but for what He intended. This world order is designed to have

---

86. Gary North, *Millennialism and Social Theory* (Tyler, Tex.: Institute for Christian Economics, 1990). See also North's ongoing, multi-volume Economic Commentary on the Bible.

man set over it, to the glory of God (Psa. 8; 115:16; Heb. 2:6-8). This is why at the very beginning of human history man was a cultural creature: Adam was to "cultivate" the world (Gen. 1:26-28), beginning in Eden (Gen. 2:15).

The New Testament often speaks of the redemption of the "world" – the very system of men and things of which I have been speaking. There are several passages which speak of the world-wide scope of redemption. These passages are quite instructive in their eschatological data. They clearly present Christ in His redemptive labors; just as explicitly they speak of the divinely assured world-wide effect of His redemption.[87] In 1 John 4:14 we discover the divinely covenanted goal of the sending of the Son: He is, in fact, to be the "Savior of the *world*." Thus, John 3:17 sets forth very explicitly that "God did not send the Son into the world to judge the world; but that the *world* should be saved through Him." John 1:29 views Him as in process of actually saving the world: "the Lamb of God who takes away the sin of the *world*." Even more strongly put is 1 John 2:2 where it is said that Jesus Christ is "the propitiation for our sins; and not for ours only, but also for those of the *whole world*." Paul, too, applies the reconciling work of Christ to the world (Rom. 11:15; 2 Cor. 5:19).

Undeniably these verses speak of a redemption that has the world in view. Consider John 1:29. Here Christ is *presently in process* of "taking away" sin. "Taking away" here is the translation of a participle based on the verb *airo*. The idea is to actually "take away, remove, lift up and carry off." First John 3:5 states that Jesus is *manifested for the very purpose* of bearing away His people's sins. There is no suggestion of a mere possibility or offer; there is no restriction of the force of the statement by use of an "if." And if the Son Whom the Father sanctifies and

---

87. See Warfield, "Jesus Christ the Propitiation for the Sins of the Whole World" (1921), *Selected Shorter Writings – I*, ch. 23.

sends into the world is endeavoring to bear away sin, we may rest assured that sin will be borne away.

In John 3:17 the inspired representation of the incarnational motive is that "God did not send the Son into the world to judge the world; but that the world should be saved through Him." In the syntactical construction of this verse we have the conjunction of purpose *hina* followed by the aorist, subjunctive verb *sozo*. Such grammatical structure is a purpose clause. And when used of God's actions they signify His divine intent (cf. John 1:7; 1 John 5:20; Rev. 20:3), a divine intent that is by the very nature of the case unthwartable (Isa. 46:10; 55:11; Dan. 4:35). As a matter of fact, this very construction occurs in John 3:16 where we read: "He gave His only begotten Son that [*hina*] whoever believes in Him should not perish" [aorist subjunctive]. May we suggest that there are those who truly believe in Him who will perish? Syntactically the certainty of accomplishment of the purpose is expected; historically it is assured by the force of the divine will.

First John 4:14 does not use the purpose clause, but does speak of Christ being sent by God to be the *soter* ("savior") of the world. He is not to be a helper toward salvation, or to offer Himself as the potential or conditional Savior *if*. . . . Conditional constructions are available to John. He could use *ean* plus the subjunctive – suggesting the idea of a "more probable future condition" and indicating that some uncertainty is implied. Or he could employ *ei* and the indicative – suggesting the idea of "simple condition" and expressing a wish. Though these are available he does not employ them in 1 John 4:14.

In 1 John 2:2 the force of the teaching does not depend on syntactical features such as purpose clauses, but upon strong redemptive terminology: "He Himself is *the propitiation* for our sins; and not for ours only, but also for those of the whole world." The word "propitiation" (*hilasmos*) is one of the more potent redemptive terms available in Scripture.

In 2 Corinthians 5:19 another significant redemptive term is employed: "reconciliation." Reconciliation has to do with the bringing back of a favorable relationship between God and man. It speaks of actual relief from the consequence of sin (vv. 19, 21). Notice the emphasis on God's action: "All these things were from God, who reconciled us . . . namely, that God was in Christ *reconciling* the world to Himself" (vv. 18-20). Later verse 21 states: "He made Him that knew no sin to be sin on our behalf."

This idea is also clearly represented in Romans 11:15: "For if their being cast away is the reconciling of the world, what will their acceptance be but life from the dead?" The argument Paul is presenting in Romans 9-11 has to do with the racial Jews' place in the plan of God in light of God's calling of the Gentiles. At this juncture Paul points to their casting away by the judicial sentence of God. Though this judgment is lamentable to the Jews at present, says Paul, it is necessary in order to effect "the reconciliation of the world." And *"the reconciliation of the world*, implies, of course, the conversion of multitudes of men, and the prevalence of true religion."[88]

Thus, in each of the passages passing under our scrutiny, we have reference to the sure provision of full and free salvation. Scripture employs a variety of significant redemptive terms in order to underscore the serious nature of the salvation provided. Consequently, when these verses speak of God's actions in Christ as being in process of "taking away the sin of the world" (John 1:29), as setting forth Christ as "the Savior of the world"

---

88. Charles Hodge, *Commentary on the Epistle to the Romans* (Grand Rapids: Eerdmans, [1886]), p. 365. Some amillennialists mistakenly complain that postmillennialism's view of Romans 11 claims "that the Jews will be saved as *Jews*." They feel the postmillennial view "neglects[s] the New Testament truth that Jews who are saved lose their national identity." Herman Hanko, "An Exegetical Refutation of Postmillennialism" (unpublished conference paper: South Holland, IL: South Holland Protestant Reformed Church, 1978), pp. 12, 17. This is simply not true. The argument confuses the Jew as a racial entity with the Jew as religiously committed. Racial Jews will be saved, when they forsake Judaism and become Christians.

(1 John 4:14), as not intended to "condemn the world" but to "save" it (John 3:17), as being "the propitiation for the sins of the world" (1 John 2:2), as "reconciling the world to Himself" (2 Cor. 5:19), the idea must protensive. That is, Christ's redemptive labors will eventually effect the redemption of the created order of men and things. And that redemptive activity extends out into the future. There is coming a day when the accomplished result of Christ's labors will be evident in a world redeemed by gospel forces already long operative.

Though these passages do not teach an "each-and-every universalism," as in liberal thought, they do set forth the certain, divinely assured prospect of a coming day in which the world *as a system* (a *kosmos*) of men and things, and their relationships, will be redeemed. A day in which the world will operate systematically upon a Christian ethico-redemptive basis. Christ's redemptive labors will have gradually brought in the era of universal worship, peace, and prosperity looked for by the prophets of the Old Testament. As John puts it to the first - century Christians who are undergoing various tribulations: Christ is the propitiation not for their sins only, they being few in number (a little flock, Luke 12:32), but for the sins of the world as such. There is coming a day, in other words, in which Christ will have sought and have found that which was lost (Luke 19:10): the world. Hence, the Great Commission command to baptize "all nations" (Matt. 28:19).

The Drawing of All Men

Another class of passages having an identical import speaks of Christ's labors having fruition among "all men." Particularly relevant are two passages: John 12:32 and 1 Timothy 2:6. In John 12:32 Jesus is comforting His disciples while in the shadow of the cross: "And I, if I be lifted up from the earth, will draw all men to Myself." In 1 Timothy 2:6, Paul is encouraging Christians to effectual fervent prayer for all men (1 Tim. 2:1) because: Christ "gave himself a ransom for all, the testimony borne at the proper time." We will only briefly deal with these two passages, in that the idea is basically the same as that already presented in the passages that make reference to the "world."

In John 12:32 Christ teaches: "If I be lifted up from the earth, I will draw all men unto me." The condition set forth in the protasis is: "If I be lifted up from the earth." The apodosis sets forth the result: "I will draw all men to Myself." The condition is not founded upon the action of the creature – a fallen creature, at that. Rather, it is firmly established upon His own divine plan and action.

Paul's statement in 1 Timothy 2:6 is no less clear. He employs strong redemptive language when he says Christ "gave Himself a ransom for all." Christ's "ransom" (*antilutron*) is given "in behalf of" (*huper*) "all" (*panton*). Then he reminds us that this fact will be testified in due time. That is, the day for its accomplishment will come. Paul, with John, looks to the eventual outcome of Christ's redemptive labor: "all" the world will one day be ransomed. After all, that is why "God was in Christ reconciling the world to Himself."

Conclusion

Thus, we are to "love the Lord thy God with all [our] heart, and with all [our] soul, and with all [our] mind, and with all [our] strength" (Mark 12:30). We are not to be concerned just with the "inner spiritual life," but with the totality of life, even engaging our strength (labor) to promoting the will of God. Warfield comments:

[T]he Scriptures teach an eschatological universalism, not an each-and-every universalism. When the Scriptures say that Christ came to save the world, that he does save the world, and that the world shall be saved by him, they do not mean that there is no human being whom he did not come to save, whom he does not save, who is not saved by him. They mean that he came to save and does save the human race; and that the human race is being led by God into a racial salvation: that in the age-long development of the race of men, it will attain at last to a complete salvation, and our eyes will be greeted with the glorious spectacle of a saved world. Thus the human race attains the goal for which it was created, and sin does not snatch it out of God's hands: the primal purpose of God with it is fulfilled.[89]

Perfection, personal or cultural, is not attainable in history, as Warfield always insists.[90] Those amillennialists and premillennialists who use such phrases as "utopian perfection" when dismissing postmillennialism's vision of the future of society are substituting rhetoric for scholarly analysis. Theonomic postmillennialism, like the traditional Calvinistic postmillennialism that preceded it, does not predict heaven's full arrival on earth, but it does predict that the Lord's Prayer will be answered progressively as time goes on: "Thy kingdom come, thy will be done, in earth as it is in heaven." This will be achieved in history, contrary to amillennialism, and prior to the bodily return of Christ, contrary to premillennialism.

---

89. Benjamin B. Warfield, *The Plan of Salvation* (Grand Rapids: Eerdmans, [n.d.] 1970), pp. 102-103.

90. Warfield, *Perfectionism* (Philadelphia: Presbyterian & Reformed, 1958). This is a much-shortened version of his 1,000-page, two-volume study that was published in the Oxford University Press version of his works.

13

CONSUMMATION

But each in his own turn: Christ, the firstfruits; then, when he comes, those who belong to him. Then the end will come, when he hands over the kingdom to God the Father after he has destroyed all dominion, authority and power. (1 Corinthians 15:24)

Postmillennialism is quite close to amillennialism in its understanding of the events associated with the final consummation. As such, it is in harmony with the historic creeds of the Church, which know nothing of a millennial era in redemptive history, nor allow for more than one resurrection and judgment.[1] Consequently, regarding consummational events, postmillennialism stands in direct opposition to all forms of premillennialism, whether historic (e.g., George E. Ladd and Robert Mounce), dispensational (e.g., Charles Ryrie and John F. Walvoord), or cultic (e.g., Jehovah's Witnesses and Latter-day Saints [Mormons]).

The balanced postmillennial preterism[2] promoted in this work is set in partial contrast, as well, to the radical preterism of a few writers, who see the second advent (including the

---

1. See: Philip Schaff, ed., *The Creeds of Christendom*, 3 vols. (New York: Harper & Bros., 1919). Reprinted by Baker Book House, Grand Rapids, 1990.

2. For "preterism" see Chapter 8: "Interpretation"; Chapter 15: "Features"; and Chapter 17: "Revelation."

"rapture," resurrection, and judgment) as occurring in A.D. 70.[3] The preteristic approach taken herein is fully orthodox.[4] In demonstration of this, my focus will be on the Second Advent, the resurrection, the final judgment, and the eternal state. Because the purpose of this work is to set forth the optimistic distinctives of postmillennial eschatology, certain relatively non-controversial areas of these matters will be given only brief treatment.

Second Advent

A common error regarding the Bible's view of Christ's coming is: too many expositors overlook the different ways in which Christ "comes."[5] Such error is especially rampant among eschatological populists, particularly those of the dispensational school. Not all references to His *coming* are to the second advent at the close of history. This is an important qualification to prophecies of His "coming" that needs to be understood before I consider the Second Advent itself.[6]

---

3. See especially the masterfully written book by J. Stuart Russell, entitled *The Parousia: A Study of the New Testament Doctrine of Our Lord's Second Coming* (Grand Rapids: Baker, [1887] 1983). See also: Milton S. Terry, *Biblical Hermeneutics: Treatise on the Interpretation of the Old and New Testaments* (Grand Rapids: Zondervan, [n.d.] 1983). For more recent works see: Max R. King, *The Spirit of Prophecy* (Warren, OH: Author, 1971) and *Cross and the Parousia: Two Dimensions of One Age-Changing Eschaton* (Warren, OH: Parkman Road Church of Christ, 1987); Ed Stevens, *What Happened in 70 A.D.: A Study in Bible Prophecy* (Bradford, PA: Author, 1988).

4. For a succinct analysis of some of the problems in the preterism of the authors mentioned in the previous footnote, see Appendix C: Brief Critique of Hyper-Preterism.

5. For additional help on the various ways Christ comes, see: David Brown, *Christ's Second Coming: Will It Be Premillennial?* (Edmonton, Alb.: Still Waters Revival, 1990 [rep. 1882]), ch. 1. O. T. Allis, *Prophecy and the Church* (Phillipsburg, N.J.: Presbyterian and Reformed, 1945), 176-180. Roderick Campbell, *Israel and the New Covenant* (Phillipsburg, N.J.: Presbyterian and Reformed, 1954), ch. 8. Loraine Boettner, *The Millennium* (Phillipsburg, N.J.: Presbyterian and Reformed, 1957), Part III, ch. 9.

6. We should recognize also that *parousia* is not a technical term for the Second Advent. There are several passages in which Paul speaks of his own parousia or that of his fellow-laborers in the ministry: 1 Cor 16:7; 2 Cor. 7:6,7; 10:10; Phil. 1:26; 2:12.

The Various Comings of Christ

Christ comes spiritually to the believer *in the ministry of the Holy Spirit*. He expressly teaches this when He says: "I will pray the Father, and He will give you another Helper, that He may abide with you forever. . . . I will not leave you orphans; I will *come* to you" (John 14:16, 18, cf. vv. 23, 28). Since Pentecost this is His coming in soteric *regeneration*. Those who are not saved by the grace of God are, by definition "without Christ" (Eph. 2:12).[7] Salvation, then, requires a "coming" of Christ into their lives to save them.

Christ comes spiritually to believers *in fellowship*, as they worship and serve Him. "Behold, I stand at the door and knock. If anyone hears My voice and opens the door, I will *come* in to him and dine with him, and he with Me" (Rev. 3:20). The spiritual implications of Christian fellowship, thus considered, are far deeper than any human friendship relations (cf. 1 Cor. 12:13ff).

He comes among His people spiritually *when they worship together before Him*. "For where two or three are gathered together in My name, I am there in the midst of them" (Matt. 18:20). Though the word "come" does not appear in this reference, the implication of a coming is very clear. For wherever two or three are *not* gathered together in His name, He is not present in this sense. There is a special, holy, covenantal sense in which Christ comes into the worship service of the saints that is different from His coming in salvation and fellowship. This, of course, heightens the spirituality and seriousness of worship, when fully realized.

He comes spiritually to *believers at death*. "And if I go and prepare a place for you, I will *come* again and receive you to

---

Geerhardus Vos, *The Pauline Eschatology* (Phillipsburg, NJ: Presbyterian & Reformed, [1930] 1991), p. 74.

7. Mark 4:11; 1 Cor. 5:12-13; Col. 4:5; 1 Thess. 4:12; 1 Tim. 3:7; cf. John 15:1-7.

Myself; that where I am, there you may be also" (John 14:3).[8]
We know that the disciples (and other believers) are with the
Lord in heaven since their deaths (Phil. 1:21-23; 2 Cor. 5:6-9).
Hence, this statement must mean He comes to them at their
deaths. Though Stephen's death is unique in Scripture, it may
indicate something of Christ's personal involvement in the
deaths of all His saints (Acts 7:59). Are we left to find our way
to heaven? Or does Christ personally receive His own into the
presence of the Father? After all, Jesus said, "I am the way, the
truth, and the life. No one comes to the Father except through
Me" (John 14:6).

He comes into the presence of the Father *at His ascension*, in
order to receive His kingdom. "I was watching in the night
visions, and behold, One like the Son of Man, coming with the
clouds of heaven! He *came to* the Ancient of Days, and they
brought Him near before Him" (Dan. 7:13). He leaves the
world so that He may "come" to the Father: "Now I am no
longer in the world, but these are in the world, and I *come* to
You. . . . Now I *come* to You, and these things I speak in the
world" (John 17:11, 13a).[9]

Beyond these spiritual comings and in addition to the bodily
second advent, there is another sort of coming. This is a providential coming of Christ in *historical judgments upon men*. In the
Old Testament clouds are frequently employed as symbols of
divine wrath and judgment. Often God is seen surrounded with
foreboding clouds which express His unapproachable holiness
and righteousness.[10] Thus, God is poetically portrayed in certain judgment scenes as *coming in the clouds* to wreak historical

8. W. G. T. Shedd, *Dogmatic Theology* (Nashville: Thomas Nelson, [1894] n.d.),
2:654. A. M. Hills, *Fundamental Christian Theology: A Systematic Theology* (Salem, OH:
Schmul, 1980), 2:356. Even premillennialist J. Barton Payne interprets John 14:3 as
a reference to Christ's coming in the believer's death. Payne, *Encyclopedia of Biblical
Prophecy* (Grand Rapids: Baker, 1973), p. 561.

9. See: Luke 9:51; 24:51; John 8:14; 13:1, 3; 14:28; 16:28; Acts 1:10.

10. Gen. 15:17; Exo. 13:21-22; 14:19-20; 19:9, 16-19; Deut. 4:11; Job 22:14; Psa.
18:8ff; 97:2; 104:3; Isa. 19:1; Ezek. 32:7-8.

vengeance upon His enemies. For example: "The burden against Egypt. Behold, the LORD rides on a swift cloud, and will come into Egypt; the idols of Egypt will totter at His presence, and the heart of Egypt will melt in its midst" (Isa. 19:1).[11] This occurs in the Old Testament era when the Assyrian king Esarhaddon conquers Egypt in 671 B.C. Obviously it does not imply a literal riding upon a cloud, any more so than Psalm 68:4: "Sing to God, sing praises to His name; Extol Him who rides on the clouds, By His name YAH, And rejoice before Him."[12]

The New Testament picks up this apocalyptic judgment imagery when it speaks of Christ's coming in clouds of judgment *during history.* Matthew 26:64, for instance, must be understood as some sort of first century "coming to judge." Christ says this will be witnessed by His accusers in the Sanhedrin: "Nevertheless, I say *to you,* hereafter *you* will see the Son of Man sitting at the right hand of the Power, and coming on the clouds of heaven" (Matt. 26:64). According to Matthew 24:30 the Jews of "this generation" (Matt. 23:36; 24:34) would see a sign that the Son of Man is in heaven: "Then will appear the sign of the Son of man in heaven."[13] The sign that the Son of Man is in heaven is the smoking rubble of Jerusalem, which He prophesies beforehand (Matt. 24:2, 15-21; cf. Acts 2:16-22, 36-40).[14]

---

11. 2 Sam. 22:8, 10; Psa. 18:7-15; 68:4, 33; 97:2-39; 104:3; Isa. 13:9; 26:21; 30:27; Joel 2:1, 2; Mic. 1:3; Nah. 1:2ff; Zeph. 1:14-15.

12. See even the dispensational commentary: John A. Martin, "Isaiah," *Bible Knowledge Commentary,* John F. Walvoord and Roy B. Zuck, eds., 2 vols. (Wheaton: Victor, 1983), 1:1066.

13. Alfred Marshall, *The Interlinear Greek-English New Testament* (2nd ed.; Grand Rapids: Zondervan, 1959), p. 108. The Greek word order is important here. The New American Standard Bible alters that word order thus confusing the reader. This may be related to the premillennial commitment of the translators, which commitments are evident in paragraph headings also.

14. In Scripture the bellowing of smoke clouds from a scene of judgment often serve as evidence of that judgment (Gen. 19:28; Josh. 18:20; 20:40; Psa. 37:20; Isa. 14:31; 34:10; Rev. 14:11; 18:9).

God's judgment on Israel is taught in parabolic form in Matthew 21:40. There the Lord asks: "Therefore, when the owner of the vineyard *comes*, what will he do to those vinedressers?" The interpretation is evident even to many premillennialists. Henry Alford, for instance, makes the following important observation: "We may observe that our Lord makes 'when the Lord cometh' *coincide with the destruction of Jerusalem,* which is incontestably the overthrow of the wicked husbandmen. This passage therefore forms an important key to our Lord's prophecies, and a decisive justification for those who like myself, firmly hold that *the coming of the Lord* is, in many places, to be identified, primarily, with that overthrow."[15]

The Second Advent

In Chapter 1 I point out that the Christian conception of history is linear. Because of this, God-governed history has a beginning and it will have a conclusion. The Scripture not only informs us of the world's beginning, but also of its end. That end will be brought about by the personal, sovereign intervention of the Lord Jesus Christ in power and great glory. The universe will not suffer a naturalistic heat death under random atomic forces, as per secular scenarios. It will be a heat renovation brought about through supernatural intervention at the pre-ordained time (2 Thess. 1:7ff; 2 Pet. 3:10ff).

That there is a personal, visible, glorious return of Christ is evident in Scripture.

> Now when He had spoken these things, while they watched, He was taken up, and a cloud received Him out of their sight. And while they looked steadfastly toward heaven as He went up, behold, two men stood by them in white apparel, who also said, "Men of Galilee, why do you stand gazing up into heaven? This

---

15. Henry Alford, *The Greek New Testament,* 4 vols. (Chicago: Moody Press, [1849-1861] 1958), 1:216 (emphasis his).

same Jesus, who was taken up from you into heaven, will so come in like manner as you saw Him go into heaven." (Acts 1:9-11)

Here we have a clear and compelling reference to the second advent. Let us briefly consider this passage.

Luke is careful to say the disciples are "beholding" (*bleponton*, present participle, Acts 1:9a) Him as He ascends; He is received "from the eyes of them" (*apo ton ophthalmon auton*, v. 9b); they are "gazing" (*atenizontes*[16]) as He is "going" (v. 10); they are "looking" (*blepontes*, v. 11); they "beheld" (*etheasasthe*, from *theaomai*[17]). Clearly His ascension is a visible and glorious phenomenon involving His tangible resurrected body.[18] And there is an actual visible cloud associated with it (v. 10). This cloud "is probably to be interpreted as the cloud of the Shekhinah," the same cloud witnessed at the transfiguration.[19]

The angelic messengers resolutely declare that "this same Jesus" (i.e., the Jesus they knew for over three years, who is now in a tangible resurrected body) will "so come *in like manner* as you saw Him go into heaven" (v. 11). The Greek *on tropon* literally means "what manner." The Greek phrase "never indicates mere certainty or vague resemblance; but wherever it occurs in the New Testament, denotes identity of mode or manner"[20] (e.g., Acts 7:28; 2 Tim. 3:8). Consequently, we have

---

16. "The Greek verb strictly denotes tension or straining of the eyes." J. A. Alexander, *The Acts of the Apostles Explained*, 2 vols. (3rd ed.; Grand Rapids: Zondervan, [1875] 1956), 1:14.

17. This is the word from which we derive the English "theater." It speaks of contemplative observing, not casual noticing. See the emphasis on the careful contemplation of the physical nature of Christ in 1 John 1:1.

18. For a discussion as to the nature of His resurrected body, see the next major section below: "The Resurrection," pp. 281ff.

19. F. F. Bruce, *The Book of the Acts* (New International Commentary on the New Testament) (Grand Rapids: Eerdmans, n.d.), p. 41. A. M. Ramsey, "What was the Ascension?" *Studiorum Novi Testamenti Societas*, Bulletin II, Oxford, 1951, pp. 43ff. See: Exo. 16:10; 19:16; 24:15; 40:34-38; Matt. 17:5.

20. Alexander, *Acts*, p. 16.

express biblical warrant to expect a visible, bodily, glorious return of Christ paralleling in kind the ascension. This glorious event is mentioned in a number of Scripture passages.[21]

When the Lord returns at His second advent, this will signal the end of history. Paul notes that when Christ returns, the end will come. "Christ the firstfruits, afterward those who are Christ's at His coming. Then comes the end, when He delivers the kingdom to God the Father" (1 Cor. 15:23-24a). This is why the era we have been living in since the coming of Christ is known as "the last days" (Heb. 1:1-2). There are no other days to follow.[22] The resurrection occurs at the "last trump" (1 Cor. 15:52). Christ's coming does not open a whole new era of re-demptive history, known as the millennium. Rather, it con-cludes history.

Consequently, just as Christ is involved in the beginning of history (John 1:3; Col. 1:16), so will He be gloriously involved in the conclusion of history (1 Cor. 15:23-24). He is the "Alpha and the Omega, the Beginning and the End" (Rev 1:8; cf. 1:11; 21:6; 22:13). (Below I will survey a few of the major concomi-tant events associated with His second advent.)

A Dispensational Distortion

Scripture teaches that Christ's eschatological return is a singular, visible, glorious event. Dispensationalism, with its systemic pandemonium, however, teaches multiple literal com-ings of Christ from heaven to earth, with the initial one (the "rapture") being a secret coming: First Corinthians 15:51-52 "cannot refer to the Second Coming of Christ because that event was not a mystery unrevealed in the Old Testament. The reference is to something distinct, that is, the rapture of the Church before the tribulation." First Thessalonians 4:13-18

---

21. For example, to list but a few: Matt. 13:30, 39-43; 24:36-24:56; 1 Cor. 11:26; 15:23-24, 51-52; Phil. 3:20-21; Col. 3:4; 1 Thess. 4:13-17; Titus 2:13; Rev. 20:9.

22. See next chapter for a discussion of the last days.

"speaks of the same event."[23] "The rapture as expressed in 1 Thessalonians 4 seems to be a private event involving the church only, and unseen and unknown to the world. . . . The actual event seems to be a secret experienced only by the church." "First He comes secretly to rapture away His bride."[24] "There is no indication, however, that residents of earth will be able to see the church thus raptured."[25] The rapture "will be a secret appearing, and only the believers will know about it."[26]

Thus there are in the dispensational view at least *two* more literal eschatological comings of Christ: a *second* coming and a *third* coming. What is more, some dispensationalists teach that "the second coming of Christ involves several stages."[27] But this semantic ploy is unworkable. In the first place, most leading dispensationalists admit to two distinct eschatological comings. Chafer dogmatically asserts of the distinction between the rapture and the second advent: "The first event is in no way whatsoever a part of the second event."[28] Walvoord disagrees with those who make "the Rapture a phase of the second coming of Christ" or who teach "the Rapture will be a part of the

---

23. Charles C. Ryrie, *The Basis of the Premillennial Faith* (Neptune, NJ: Loizeaux Bros., 1953), p. 133. Other dispensationalists agree: John F. Walvoord, *Prophecy Knowledge Handbook* (Grand Rapids: Eerdmans, 1990), p. 481. J. Dwight Pentecost, *Thy Kingdom Come* (Wheaton, IL: Victor, 1990), pp. 248-249 and *Things to Come* (Grand Rapids: Zondervan, 1958), pp. 206-207. Thomas L. Constable, "1 Thessalonians," *Bible Knowledge Commentary*, 2:704. Benjamin C. Chapman, "1 Thessalonians," *Liberty Commentary: New Testament*, Edward E. Hindson and Woodrow Michael Kroll, eds. (Lynchburg: Liberty Press, 1978), p. 586.

24. Dave Hunt, *Whatever Happened to Heaven?* (Eugene, OR: Harvest House, 1989), pp. 303, 304.

25. John F. Walvoord, *The Nations, Israel, and the Church in Prophecy*, 3 vols. in 1 (Grand Rapids: Zondervan, 1988), 3:83.

26. Herschel W. Ford, *Seven Simple Sermons on the Second Coming* (Grand Rapids: Zondervan, 1946), p. 51.

27. See discussion in Charles C. Ryrie, *Basic Theology* (Wheaton, IL: Victor, 1986), p. 478.

28. Lewis Sperry Chafer, *Systematic Theology*, 8 vols. (Dallas, TX: Dallas Theological Seminary Press, 1948), 5:288.

Second Coming."[29] Pentecost and Ryrie say that these are separate "events."[30] Also, in that these two events are separated
by seven years, involve different peoples (the Church vs. Tribulation saints), and two different purposes (removal of the
Church from history vs. the establishment of the new era of the
millennium in history), it is impossible to make such a qualification.

The Bible, however, speaks only of a "second" eschatological
coming. Hebrews 9:28 says: "So Christ was once offered to bear
the sins of many; and unto them that look for him shall he
appear the *second* time without sin unto salvation." In regard to
His physical coming to earth, the Bible speaks of His coming
again (Acts 1:11), not of His "comings" or His "coming again
and again" or of a "third coming."

But let us note just one of dispensationalism's major proof-
texts: 1 Thessalonians 4:13-18. Walvoord feels that "a careful
study of this passage in 1 Thessalonians will do much to set the
matter in its proper biblical revelation," demonstrating "the
difference between the Rapture of the church and Christ's
second coming to judge and rule over the earth."[31] Another
dispensationalist author comments that "this is undoubtedly the
primary passage on the Rapture of the Church."[32] As a postmillennialist I believe that this passage refers to the visible,
glorious, second advent to conclude history, not an invisible
rapture to remove believers in preparation for the setting up of
another era of redemptive history (the millennium).

On the very surface it is remarkable that one of the noisiest
verses in Scripture is said to picture the secret rapture. Paul
says: "For the Lord Himself will descend from heaven with a

29. Walvoord, *Prophecy Knowledge Handbook*, p. 494.

30. Pentecost, *Things to Come*, p. 206. Charles C. Ryrie, *The Basis of the Premillen-nial Faith*, p. 133.

31. Walvoord, *Prophecy Knowledge Handbook*, p. 481.

32. Gerald B. Stanton, "Biblical Evidence for the Pretribulational Rapture," *Biblical Perspectives* 4:4 (July/Aug. 1991) 2.

shout, with the *voice of an archangel*, and with the *trumpet of God.* And the dead in Christ will rise first" (1 Thess. 4:16). By all appearance, this seems emphatically to be a very public event, even if we do not take these elements as literal trumpets and shouts.[33] Besides, this event involves millions of resurrections (on the order of Christ's) and the transformation of millions of living believers and their removal from the world. This has to have a public impact.

In addition the passage teaches that "so shall we ever be with the Lord." It says nothing of Christians going with Him to heaven for seven years, then returning to the earth to rule in a thousand-year millennium, then returning back to heaven. Some (not all) dispensationalists hold that: "The locale of their future is not permanent as they will be in heaven during the time preceding the Second Coming [i.e., during the seven-year Great Tribulation]. They will be on earth during the millennial kingdom. . . ."[34] If this is such a "significant" passage for the dispensational view, why are not the dispensational distinctives found here?

That there is no mention of the resurrection of the wicked here is no indicator of two resurrections, and thus of two distinct comings of Christ. Two important reasons forbid such: (1) The resurrection of the righteous and that of the wicked operate on different principles. The righteous are in Christ; their resurrection is to glory. It is not so for the unrighteous. (2) The purpose of the passage is not so much to deal with the total implications of the resurrection. Rather, as Walvoord himself admits: "Though this passage is more informative concerning the nature of the Rapture, it is designed to be an encouragement to those who are living for Christ."[35] Paul is comforting

---

33. Remarkably, Walvoord, a dispensational literalist, even allows the possibility that the "clouds" may be figurative allusions to the great numbers of saints involved! Walvoord, *Prophecy Knowledge Handbook*, p. 484.

34. *Ibid.*

35. *Ibid.*

Christians regarding their deceased love ones. If there were a millennium in which they would be ruling and reigning, it would seem that mention of it here would serve as a word of comfort. But, rather than that, Paul places all believers in the presence of the Lord – forever.

Walvoord's main argument for distinguishing this event from the second advent is: "Most significant in this passage is the fact that there are no preceding events, that is, there are no world-shaking events described as leading up to this event. As a matter of fact, the church down through the centuries could expect momentarily the Rapture of the church, which hope continues today. By contrast the second coming of Christ will be preceded by divine judgments on the world. . . ."[36]

But how can this prove a distinction between the rapture and the second advent? Does not Walvoord admit a limited design for the passage: to comfort Christians concerning the resurrection of deceased loved ones? Why would Paul have to provide the whole complex of eschatological phenomena? The dispensational argument is one from silence, based on a pre-conceived theory. In addition, this is the very same Walvoord who teaches that the seven churches of Revelation portray long ages of church history leading up to our own time (he is not alone in this contradiction)![37]   If these ages *had* to occur by prophetic portrayal, how could the rapture be deemed imminent or momentary, with no intervening events expected? How could it be an "any-moment rapture"?

This leads naturally to a consideration of:

36. *Ibid.*

37. Walvoord, *The Revelation of Jesus Christ* (Chicago: Moody Press, 1966), p. 52. Hal Lindsey, *There's a New World Coming* (Santa Ana, CA: Vision House, 1973), pp. 38ff. C. I. Scofield, *The Scofield Reference Bible* (New York: Oxford University Press, [1909] 1945), pp. 1331-2. *The New Scofield Reference Bible* (New York: Oxford University Press, 1967), p. 1353. Charles C. Ryrie, *Revelation* (*Everyman's Bible Commentary*) (Chicago: Moody Press, 1965), pp. 21ff. J. Dwight Pentecost, *Things to Come*, p. 149.

The Resurrection

An important feature of the eschatological complex of events is the bodily resurrection of the dead, both of the just and the unjust. God created angels to dwell in the spiritual realm (Psa. 104:4; Heb. 1:7, 13-14) and man to dwell in the material realm (Gen. 2:7), hence the resurrection. This will be accomplished by the almighty power of God and will be one resurrection involving all men, often designated the "general resurrection." This great resurrection will not be followed by a millennial reign on earth; it is consummational, bringing to an end the temporal order.

Such a doctrine is so clear in Scripture[38] and so important to orthodoxy that it is a constant refrain in the historic creeds of the Church. This doctrine is evident in such ancient creeds as the Apostles' Creed, the Nicene Creed, the Council of Constantinople, and the Athanasian Creed. It appears as well in later creeds, including the Tetrapolitan Confession, the First and Second Confessions of Basle, the Second Helvetic Confession, the Heidelberg Catechism, the Belgic Confession, the Orthodox Confession of 1642, the Westminster Confession of Faith,[39] the Thirty-Nine Articles of the Church of England,

---

38. The Bible clearly teaches a future existence beyond the grave: Gen. 5:22, 24; 15:15; 25:8; 35:29; 37:35; Num. 20:24; 27:13; Matt. 10:28; 20:30; 22:32; 25; Luke 16:26; John 5:24; 8:51; 11:25; 12:25; 2 Cor. 5:1-10; 1 Cor. 15; Heb. 2:16; Jude 14-15. Ancient Greeks and Romans had a conception of the afterlife, but these were Platonic, denying the resurrection and calling for the immortality of the soul only (Acts 17:18, 32; 26:8). For example: Socrates' *Phaedrus* and Marcus Aurelius' *Meditations* 10; Pliny, *Natural History* 1:7; cf. Tertullian, *Apology* 48 and *Against Marcion* 5:9; Origen, *Against Celsus* 5:14; Julian *Against the Christians* (known only through Cyril, *Contra Julian* 1:7).

39. It is strange that a church as strongly committed to creedal theology as Presbyterianism would tolerate any form of premillennialism with its demand for two resurrections. The Westminster Standards are strongly anti-premillennial. See: Robert L. Dabney, *Lectures in Systematic Theology* (Grand Rapids: Zondervan, [1878] 1976), p. 839.

and the Augsburg Confession.[40] Of course, our primary concern here is with the Scriptural evidence.

I will not here engage the age-old philosophical questions
relative to the difficulty of the resurrection of long-destroyed
bodies.[41] My concern is with issues relevant to systematic theology regarding the general conception of the eschatological
resurrection.

The Nature of the Resurrection

The Scripture teaches that Christ is resurrected in the same
body in which He dies, though with certain super-added spiritual powers.[42] His resurrection is not a mere revivification of
a lifeless cadaver; nor is it a creation of a new body. His is the
resurrection of the very body in which He dies, just as He
prophesies (John 2:19-22). As such, it is a miraculous attestation
to the truth of His divine mission on earth (John 2:18-21).[43]

This is why the tomb and burial clothing are empty: His
physical body departs from them (Matt. 28:6; John 20:4-11, 15).
The gospels present the resurrected Christ in a material body
that can be touched and handled (Luke 24:39), and which still

---

40. Schaff, *Creeds of Christendom*. See: John H. Gerstner, *Wrongly Dividing the Word
of Truth: A Critique of Dispenationalism* (Brentwood, TN: Wolgemuth and Hyatt, 1991),
pp. 9, 14.

41. For brief and insightful discussions see: Dabney, *Lectures in Systematic Theology*,
pp. 834-836; Charles Hodge, *Systematic Theology*, 3 vols. (Grand Rapids: Eerdmans,
[1871-1873] 1973), 3:774-780.

42. Tragically, there is a renewed debate among evangelicals as to whether
"Christ arose from the dead in the same material body of flesh and bones in which
He died." John G. Stackhouse, Jr., "Evangelical Fratricide," *Christianity Today* 35:6
(May 27, 1991) 64-66. Norman L. Geisler, *The Battle for the Resurrection* (Nashville:
Thomas Nelson, 1991). Murray J. Harris, *From Grave to Glory: Resurrection in the New
Testament* (Grand Rapids: Zondervan, 1990). Clark Pinnock, "Toward an Evangelical
Theology of Religions," *Journal of the Evangelical Theological Society* 33:3 (Sept. 1990).
See also the liberal international "Jesus Seminar" conducted in the first half of the
1990s. Robert J. Hutchinson, "The Jesus Seminar Unmasked," *Christianity Today*
(April 29, 1996): 28ff.

43. Matt. 12:39-41; 16:1-4; Luke 11:29.

has the wounds of the cross (John 20:27; cf. Rev. 5:6). On other occasions He bids Mary Magdalene to quit clinging (*haptomai*) to Him (John 20:17). The women who meet the Lord later "held [*krateo*] him by the feet, and worshiped" (Matt. 28:9). He even eats food (Luke 24:42-43; John 21:11-14) while in His resurrection body. Any record of His friends not recognizing Him is explained either by their vision being distorted by tears (John 20:11-16) or by supernatural intervention (Luke 24:16), not by a radical morphological change.

Likewise is it with the final resurrection. The general resurrection will be a resurrection of the body (Job 19:23-27; Isa. 26:19; 1 Thess. 4:16), which is why it occurs at the place of burial (Dan. 12:2; John 5:28).[44] Scripture calls the resurrected Christ "the first-fruits of them that slept" (1 Cor. 15:23) and "the firstborn of the dead" (Col. 1:18; Rev. 1:5; cf. Rom. 8:29). Yet we know that others physically arose from the dead prior to Him, some during His own ministry.[45] Thus, His resurrection is of a different order, an order making Him a "first" in that respect. That difference distinguishes His resurrection as eschatological: unlike other resurrections (miraculous revivifications), His body possesses elevated powers of the spirit that would render it incapable of dissolution (1 Cor. 15:28, 41-42[46]), thus suited for the eternal order.

The Scripture patterns the resurrection of men after Christ's resurrection: "But if the Spirit of Him who raised Jesus from the dead dwells in you, He who raised Christ from the dead will also give life to your mortal bodies through His Spirit who dwells in you" (Rom. 8:11). Consequently, the nature of His resurrection experience is a paradigm for ours (Phil. 3:20-21; cf. John 14:19). In 1 Corinthians 15 Paul deals at length with

---

44. Dabney, *Lectures in Systematic Theology*, pp. 831-837, 845-846.

45. 1 Kgs. 17:17-23; 2 Kgs. 4:24-37; Matt. 27:52; Heb. 11:35. See Christ's miracles in Matt. 9:18-26; 10:8; Mark 5:22-23, 35-42; Luke 7:12-15; John 11:14-44.

46. For some of the unusual functions of His resurrected body, see: Luke 24:31ff; John 20:13ff; 21:7; Acts 1:9-11.

the resurrection. In verses 23 and 24 (just mentioned above), he informs us that Christ is "the firstfruits." The idea of a "first-fruits" necessarily involves a harvest of like kind: What first-fruits harvest in the agricultural realm gives rise to a wholly different crop? First Corinthians 15:47-50 affirms a glorious resurrection experience in which we return to our physical bodies, though with enhanced "glory," as did Christ: the body that is "planted" is the body that is "raised" (1 Cor. 15:37-38, 42-44). The Corinthians passage does not teach a substitution, but a transformation of the body; it teaches resurrection, not creation. In fact, the very word *anastasis* (*ana*, up; *histemi*, stand) necessarily implies that the body which falls is the same one raised, as Tertullian argued long ago.[47] The Scripture is clear that our physical bodies are raised (Rom. 8:11, 23; Phil. 3:20).

In Colossians 1:18 and Revelation 1:5 Christ is called "the first begotten from the dead." This also implies our being begotten from the dead in like manner to His resurrection. I have already noted that Christ is resurrected in a tangible body, the very body in which He died, even though it is controlled by heightened spiritual powers.[48]

But dispensationalism multiplies resurrections – as they do comings of Christ. Adams has called this phenomenon "premillennial diplopia."[49] The dispensational system gets so bound up in its conflicting programs and divergent peoples of God that it necessarily multiplies resurrections. Most prominently dispensationalism, with its mother premillennialism, emphasizes

---

47. *Against Marcion* 5:9.

48. Hence its designation as a "heavenly" and "spiritual" body (1 Cor. 15:44, 48-49). The description "spiritual body" (1 Cor. 15:4) does not indicate a non-material body, but a body more directly controlled by the spirit. The phrase "spiritual body" no more demands the body be made of spirit than the phrase "Coke bottle" demands that bottle be made of Coke. The same word *pneumatikos* is used of a Christian in 1 Cor. 2:14-15. See Geerhardus Vos, *Pauline Eschatology*, pp. 166-171. Dabney, *Systematic Theology*, pp. 832-835.

49. Jay E. Adams, *The Time Is at Hand* (n.p.: Presbyterian & Reformed, 1966), ch. 3.

two resurrections: one of the just and one of the unjust. These resurrections are separated by at least 1000 years, on the sole basis of the highly wrought symbolism found in Revelation 20:1-6. What is worse, the system requirements of dispensationalism end up with *several* resurrections.

Dispensationalists teach: "The Bible knows nothing of one future general resurrection."[50] "All bodily resurrections fall into two categories" and the first "resurrection will include several groups: the dead saints of this Church Age (1 Thes. 4:16), the dead saints of Old Testament times (Dan. 12:2), and martyrs of the Tribulation period (Rev. 20:4). These resurrections of the saints of all ages constitute the first resurrection (Rev. 20:6). . . ."[51] The first "resurrection is made up of a number of component parts" and "includes within it all who, at any time, are raised to eternal life."[52] "The important thing to discover is whether or not the first resurrection must be a simultaneous resurrection of all the just at one definite moment, or whether the first resurrection may be understood to mean the resurrection of all the just, to be sure, but in a series of two or more ascensions."[53]

But there are various angles whereby we may see that the Bible allows for only *one* eschatological resurrection at the end of history, a resurrection of both the saved and the lost.[54]

First, the resurrection is to occur on *the last day*. "And this is the Father's will which hath sent me, that of all which he hath

---

50. James L. Boyer, *For a World Like Ours: Studies in 1 Corinthians* (Grand Rapids: Baker, 1971), p. 141.

51. Ryrie, *Basic Theology*, p. 518.

52. Pentecost, *Things to Come*, p. 397.

53. E. Schuyler English, *Re-thinking the Rapture* (Neptune, NJ: Loizeaux Bros., 1954), p. 32.

54. "[I]t must be admitted that [the resurrection of the wicked] does not stand out prominently in Scripture. The soteriological aspect of the resurrection is clearly in the foreground, and this pertains to the righteous only. They, in distinction from the wicked, are the ones that profit by the resurrection." Louis Berkhof, *Systematic Theology* (4th ed.; Grand Rapids: Eerdmans, 1941), p. 723.

given me I should lose nothing, but should raise it up again at the last day. And this is the will of him that sent me, that every one which seeth the Son, and believeth on him, may have everlasting life: and I will raise him up at the last day" (John 6:39-40). He does not say, "I will raise him up 1,007 years before the last day," allowing for a millennium, tribulation, and resurrection of the unjust to follow (as per dispensational doctrine[55]). Christ says the resurrection will be simultaneously of "all who are in the graves" (John 5:28). John's gospel record is quite clear on this matter (John 6:44, 54; 11:24). The resurrection occurs in conjunction with "the end" and at the "last trump" (1 Cor. 15:23-24, 52).

The premillennial system absolutely depends on a literal interpretation of Revelation 20:1-6 in order to assert two resurrections. It is enlightening to note: (1) This fundamental passage is in the most highly figurative book in the Bible. Revelation is widely regarded as the most difficult book of Scripture by eminently qualified biblical scholars.[56] (2) The material is taken from a scene that is manifestly figurative. It involves, for instance, a chain binding a spiritual being (Satan). (3) This passage is written by the very John who speaks of the resurrection only on the *last* day, and involving both the just and the unjust simultaneously (John 5:28-29, see below).

(4) Just after the verses in question we come upon Revelation 20:11-15. "If ever language expressed the doctrine of *a*

---

55. *New Scofield Reference Bible*, p. 1131, note 1; Pentecost, *Things to Come*, p. 400. Walvoord, *Prophecy Knowledge Handbook*, p. 408.

56. B. B. Warfield, "The Book of Revelation," *A Religious Encyclopedia*, Philip Schaff, ed., 3 vols. (NY: Funk & Wagnalls, 1883), 2:80. Milton S. Terry, *Biblical Hermeneutics* (Grand Rapids: Zondervan, [n.d.] 1983), p. 466. Henry B. Swete, *Commentary on Revelation* (Grand Rapids: Kregal, [1906] 1977), p. xii. G. R. Beasley-Murray, *The Book of Revelation*, in *New Century Bible*, R. E. Clements and Matthew Black, eds. (London: Marshall, Morgan, & Scott, 1974), p. 5. George Eldon Ladd, *A Commentary on the Revelation of John* (Grand Rapids: Eerdmans, 1972), p. 10. Eduard Wilhelm Reuss, *History of the Sacred Scriptures of the New Testament* (Edinburgh: T & T Clark, 1884), p. 155. Isbon T. Beckwith, *The Apocalypse of John: Studies in Introduction* (Grand Rapids: Baker, [1919] 1967), p. 1.

simultaneous and universal resurrection, surely we have it here."[57] John is speaking of *all* men, as is evident in his language, not just of unbelievers: (a) He says the dead "small and great" will be judged. This terminology is applied at times to believers in Revelation (Rev. 11:18; 19:5). (b) The righteous are judged on the basis of their works, as those here are (Rom. 2:5-6; 14:11-12; 2 Cor. 5:10). (c) He mentions the "book of life" here (Rev. 20:12, 15), which involves the righteous.[58]

Second, the Lord's teaching in the Kingdom Parables demands a general resurrection. "But he said, 'No, lest while you gather up the tares you also uproot the wheat with them. 'Let both grow together until the harvest, and at the time of harvest I will say to the reapers, "First gather together the tares and bind them in bundles to burn them, but gather the wheat into my barn" (Matt. 13:29-30; see also vv. 49-50). If anything this parable teaches that the resurrection of the wicked *precedes* that of the righteous![59]

Third, since there is but one resurrection, there is no resurrection centuries from the end. "There will be a resurrection of the dead, both of the just and the unjust" (Acts 24:15). *"The hour* is coming in which *all* who are in the graves will hear His voice and come forth; those who have done good, to the resurrection of life, and those who have done evil, to the resurrection of condemnation" (John 5:28-29).

Premillennialists attempt to maneuver around the rocky shoals of John 5:28-29 by arguing that the *hour* "allows for its extension over a long period."[60] This permits the reference to cover the 1,007 years necessary for their position. It is true that

---

57. David Brown, *Christ's Second Coming: Will It Be Premillennial?* (Edmonton, Alberta: Still Waters Revival Books, [1882] 1990), p. 195.

58. Rev. 3:5, 8; 17:8; 21:27; 22:19; cf. Phil. 4:3.

59. The key issue here is historical continuity. This continuity from the establishment of Christ's kingdom until He returns in final judgment denies the possibility of a discontinuous Rapture that intervenes between today and the final judgment.

60. Pentecost, *Things to Come*, p. 400.

HE SHALL HAVE DOMINION

"hour" can encompass a long period of time. But to argue such here involves the dispensationalist in manifest absurdity: It allows that the "resurrection to life" occurs over the *entirety* of the 1,007 years involved. It suggests that the "shout/trump" of Christ in John 5:28-29, 1 Corinthians 15:51, and 1 Thessalonians 4:16 continues throughout the period, for this shout/trump is that which is causative to the resurrection. It also involves the system in internal contradiction: It permits the resurrection to damnation to occur over that same period, despite the assertion that it occurs at the end (and only in one phase).

Actually "It is not the *length of time* which this word 'hour' is designed to mark . . . but it is the unity of *period and action* which alone is intended. . . ."[61] That is, there is a general resurrection, which will involve both the just and unjust.

Fourth, the resurrection is that which signals the destruction of death: "But each one in his own order: Christ the firstfruits, afterward those who are Christ's at His coming. Then comes the end, when He delivers the kingdom to God the Father, when He puts an end to all rule and all authority and power. For He must reign till He has put all enemies under His feet. The last enemy that will be destroyed is death" (1 Cor. 15:23-26). Clearly the "last enemy" is destroyed at "the end," and both occur in conjunction with the resurrection.

The Final Judgment

The covenant God of Scripture deals with men legally, reckoning to them their just desserts on the basis of their infractions of His Law, which is a divine transcript of His holy character (Rom. 7:12).[62] Man desperately needs salvation because he is a covenant-breaker (Isa. 24:5; Hos. 6:2). He has transgressed God's Law (Gal. 3:10; Jms. 2:10), which calls forth God's "righteous judgment" (Rom. 1:32; 2:5; 2 Thess. 1:5). God's judg-

---

61. Brown, *Christ's Second Coming*, p. 191.
62. See discussion of the Law of God in Chapter 7 above.

ment is characteristically described by use of forensic terminology, such as *krinein* ("to judge"), *krisis* ("judgment"), and *dikaios* ("justification").

The Law of God is naturally the legal standard of judgment. Speaking of the day of judgment (Rom. 2:5), Paul says: "when Gentiles, who do not have the law, by nature do the things contained in the law, these, although not having the law, are a law to themselves, who show the work of the law written in their hearts, their conscience also bearing witness, and between themselves their thoughts accusing or else excusing them, in the day when God will judge the secrets of men by Jesus Christ, according to my gospel" (Rom. 2:14-16; cf. Matt. 7:23; 13:41; Jms. 2:10-12). Although the temporal aspects of God's justice occur in history,[63] there are complex providential factors involved in the historical process that oftentimes obscure God's blessing and judgment in the eyes of men.[64] But on judgment day men will be judged perfectly according to their every word, thought, and deed.[65]

There must be an *eternal* resolution to the sin problem in that man has broken God's eternal law (Psa. 119:142, 144). This is necessary also since man is a creature, who continues to exist forever after his being created (Eccl. 3:11; Luke 16:23).[66] He will either exist always as one made righteous at the resurrection or as one left in sin. Furthermore, this eternal resolution will be made public in front of all rational creatures and will

---

63. Lev. 26:1ff; Deut. 9:5; 28:1ff; Psa. 9:1ff; 37:28; 59:13; Prov. 11:5; 14:11; Isa. 32:16, 17; Lam. 5:7. For a discussion of God's historical sanctions, see Gary North, *Political Polytheism: The Myth of Pluralism* (Tyler, TX: Institute for Christian Economics, 1989), ch. 3.

64. Job; Psa. 73; Isa. 5:8-19; Jer. 17:15; Mal. 2:17; 3:14-15.

65. Matt. 6:4, 6, 18; 10:26; 12:36; 25:35-40; Luke 12:2; Rom. 14:10; 1 Cor. 3:8; 4:5; 2 Cor. 5:10; Eph. 6:8; 1 Tim. 5:24-25; Heb. 10:30; 1 Pet. 1:17; Rev. 20:12.

66. For a brief but insightful study of the question of the immortality of the soul, see Anthony Hoekema, *The Bible and the Future* (Grand Rapids: Eerdmans, 1979), ch. 8. "If we wish to use the word *immortality* with reference to man, let us say that man, rather than his soul, is immortal" (p. 91).

involve man in his total being, that is, in body and soul (made possible by the resurrection). The Scriptural view of man is radically different from the Platonic view, which denigrates the material aspect of man and elevates the spiritual.[67]

The consummation of history, brought about by the second advent of Christ, involves both a general resurrection (as we have seen) and a *general judgment*. This judgment has been committed to the God-man, Jesus Christ: "The Father judges no one, but has committed all judgment to the Son" (John 5:22; cf. Matt. 11:27; John 3:35). The reason for Christ's leading role in the judgment is related to His incarnational relation to the human race: "He has given Him authority to execute judgment also, because He is the Son of Man" (John 5:27). It also serves as the necessary outcome of His incarnation: "It was right that when the Lord of all condescended, in His unspeakable mercy, to assume the form of a servant, and endure the extremist indignities of His enemies, He should enjoy this highest triumph over them, in the very form and nature of His humiliation"[68] (cf. Phil 2:9-11). Christ's prominence in the final judgment is a frequent theme in the New Testament.[69]

The doctrine of the *general* judgment (i.e., of all men in one scene) may be discerned from various angles. First, there is coming a judgment "day." "He has appointed a day on which He will judge the world in righteousness by the Man whom He has ordained" (Acts 17:31a). This singular judgment day is evident in a number of Scriptures.[70] As in the case of the day

---

67. The Christian faith is concerned with the material aspect of man's being, as well as the spiritual. (1) God created the earth and man's body as material entities, and all "very good" (Gen. 1:31; 2:7). (2) Christ came in the flesh to redeem man (Rom. 1:3; 9:5; 1 John 4:1-3). And, of course, (3) the resurrection. A denial of a material resurrection would capitulate to Platonic gnosticism.

68. Dabney, *Systematic Theology*, p. 846.

69. Matt. 25:31-32; John 5:22, 27; Acts 10:42; 17:31; Rom. 2:16; 14:9-10; 2 Cor. 5:10; Phil. 2:9-11; 2 Tim. 4:1, 8.

70. Dan. 7:10; Matt. 7:22; 11:22; 12:36; Rom. 2:5; 2 Tim. 1:10-12; 4:8; 2 Pet. 3:7; 1 John 4:17.

of resurrection, this day of judgment cannot be stretched out over a 1,007-year period, as per dispensationalism (see above discussion).

Second, judgment day involves both the saved and the lost. It is at the day of resurrection that both the just and the unjust will enter into their judgment, one to life, the other to condemnation: "Do not marvel at this; for the hour is coming in which all who are in the graves will hear His voice and come forth; those who have done good, to the resurrection of life, and those who have done evil, to the resurrection of condemnation" (John 5:28-29).

Romans 2:5-8 clearly speaks of a day of judgment that will encompass both classes of men: "In accordance with your hardness and your impenitent heart you are treasuring up for yourself wrath in the day of wrath and revelation of the righteous judgment of God, who will render to each one according to his deeds: eternal life to those who by patient continuance in doing good seek for glory, honor, and immortality; but to those who are self-seeking and do not obey the truth, but obey unrighteousness; indignation and wrath."

The simultaneity of the judgment is inescapable in Matthew 25:31-46, where we read (in part): "When the Son of Man comes in His glory, and all the holy angels with Him, then He will sit on the throne of His glory. All the nations will be gathered before Him, and He will separate them one from another, as a shepherd divides his sheep from the goats" (Matt. 25:31-32). The judgment occurs when Christ returns, not hundreds of years later. This general judgment is found elsewhere in Scripture.[71]

Although the judgment is one event encompassing both the just and the unjust, there will be an order to it. It seems that

---

71. Dan. 12:2; Eccl. 12:13-14; Matt. 12:36; 13:41; Matt. 25:14-30; Acts 10:42; Rom. 3:6; 2 Cor. 5:9-11; 2 Thess. 1:6-10; 2 Tim. 4:1; Heb. 10:27-31; Jude 14-15; Rev. 20:11-15.

the wicked will be judged immediately prior to the righteous, according to the order of events in Matthew 13:30, 41, 43 and Matthew 25:46. It is "as if, in some literal sense, 'with thine eyes shalt thou behold and see the reward of the wicked' (Psalm 91:8)."[72]

Of course, the judgment of the righteous is not to condemnation, but to future reward.[73] And we should understand that "the relation between our works and our future reward ought, however, to be understood not in a mechanical but rather in an organic way. When one has studied music and has attained some proficiency in playing a musical instrument, his capacity for enjoying music has been greatly increased. In a similar way, our devotion to Christ and to service in his kingdom increases our capacity for enjoying the blessings of that kingdom, both now and in the life to come."[74]

Dispensational Distortion

As with other features of eschatology, dispensationalists multiply judgments. They attempt a partial justification of this by assembling temporal and spiritual judgments together in lists with eschatological judgments. E. S. English writes: "Among the many judgments mentioned in Scripture, seven are invested with especial significance. These are: (1) the judgment of the believer's sins in the cross of Christ . . . , (2) the believer's self-judgment. . . ; (3) the judgment of the believer's works. . . ; (4) the judgment of the individual Gentiles at the return of Christ to the earth. . . ; (5) the judgment of Israel at the return of

---

72. David Brown, "The Gospel According to S. Matthew," *A Commentary, Critical and Explanatory on the Old and New Testaments*, Robert Jamieson, A. Faussett, and David Brown, eds., 2 vols. (Hartford: S. S. Scranton, n.d.), 2:44.

73. Rom. 2:5-10; 1 Cor. 1:4-8; 3:8; 15:32, 58; 2 Cor. 4:16; 5:10; 9:6-8; Gal. 6:5-10; Phil. 1:10, 26; 2:16; Col. 1:5; 3:24; 1 Thess. 3:13; 5:23; 2 Thess. 1:7; 1 Tim. 2:18; 4:8; 5:25; 6:18-19; 2 Tim. 2:11; 4:4-16.

74. Hoekema, *Bible and the Future*, p. 264. See: Leon Morris, *The Biblical Doctrine of Judgment* (Grand Rapids: Eerdmans, 1960), p. 73ff.

Christ to the earth. . . ; (6) the judgment of angels after the 1000 years. . . ; and (7) . . . the judgment of the wicked dead with which the history of the present earth ends."[75]

This is a patently erroneous conception, however. As in the case with the resurrection, the Scriptural evidence is of a singular (Acts 17:31), unified (Rom. 2:16) episode. That event will occur at the last day: "He who rejects Me, and does not receive My words, has that which judges him; the word that I have spoken will judge him in the last day" (John 12:48). In fact, the resurrection introduces men to the judgment. "Resurrection and Judgment are the two correlated acts of the final consummation of things."[76] And since there is a general resurrection, there will be a general judgment.

The Eternal State

Temporal history comes to an end with the final judgment, but life goes on in the eternal state. The Bible does not tell us as much about that estate, particularly our glorious heavenly abode, as we might like to know. Nevertheless, it is crystal clear that there is an everlasting existence for man beyond the judgment, and that the final estate is, in keeping with the covenantal sanctions (Deut. 11:26-29; 30:1, 19), two-fold: eternal bliss for the just and everlasting wrath for the unjust.

In 1 Corinthians 15 we learn that eventually, after Christ's enemies have been put down during history and disposed of at the end of history, God the Son will turn His kingdom rule over to the Father. "Now when all things are made subject to Him, then the Son Himself will also be subject to Him who put all things under Him, that God may be all in all" (1 Cor. 15:28). This passage speaks of the kingdom's being turned over

---

75. *New Scofield Reference Bible*, p. 1375, n 1 (at Rev. 20:12).

76. Vos, *Pauline Eschatology*, p. 261.

to the Trinity, not to God the Father. The work of redemption is no longer being prosecuted by the Mediator in eternity.[77]

Heaven

The final state for the righteous will be in the glorious presence of God.[78] It will be an existence of holy perfection[79] and impeccability (1 Thess. 4:17; Heb. 4:9; 12:23). Heaven is not a state, but a place, for there reside Enoch (Gen. 5:22-24; Heb. 11:5), Elijah (2 Kgs. 2:1, 11), and Christ (Acts 1:9-10) in their bodies. Not surprisingly there are more people who believe in heaven than believe in hell. A recent Gallup poll noted that 78 percent of the American public believe in heaven; only 60 percent believe in hell. Among non-believers the disparity is similar: 46 percent believe in heaven; 34 percent believe in hell.[80] Because there is little evangelical debate on the matter of heaven, I now turn to disputed matters of the final-estate.

Hell

The doctrine of eternal punishment in hell has long been a subject of vigorous debate, occasionally even among evangelicals.[81] Consequently, the doctrine has been a prominent factor in Christian theodicies due to its terrifying nature.[82] Of

---

77. Shedd, *Dogmatic Theology*, 2:690ff.

78. John 14:1-3; cf. Job 19:27; Psa. 17:15; John 17:24.

79. Eph. 5:27; Rom. 8:21; Heb. 12:23; 1 John 3:2.

80. "Heaven and Hell: Who Will Go There and Why," *Christianity Today* 35:6 (May 27, 1991) 29.

81. *Ibid.* (May 27, 1991) 29ff. The May, 1989, meeting of the National Association of Evangelicals refused to affirm the doctrine of hell. *World* (June 3, 1989) 9. Steven H. Travis denies eternal hell in his book, *I Believe in the Second Coming of Jesus* (Grand Rapids: Eerdmans, 1982). See: J. I. Packer, "Is Hell Out of Vogue in this Modern Era?" *United Evangelical Action* 48 (Sept. 1989) 10-11. M. J. Erickson, "Is Universalistic Thinking Now Appearing Among Evangelicals?" *United Evangelical Action* 48 (Sept./Oct. 1989) 4-6.

82. For an interesting debate on the existence of God, and in which the atheist focused on the doctrine of hell as a proof God does *not* exist, see: "Does God Exist?

course, absurdities generated by its popular treatment have not helped promote the understanding of this dreadful biblical doctrine, either.[83]

The doctrine of hell has been accepted by the vast majority in orthodox circles from ancient times. Though recognizing the clear dominance of the orthodox view, Henry overstates the case, however: "[E]xcept for Origen, whose views on the subject were condemned, the entire Christian movement had remained unchallenged for more than sixteen centuries . . . in teaching eternal punishment of the impenitent wicked."[84] In fact, eternal hell was denied by Gregory of Nyssa (d. A.D. 395), Didorus of Tarsus (d. A.D. 396), Theodore of Mopsuestia (d. A.D. 429), and others. Augustine states that in his day there were "multitudes who did not believe in eternal punishment."[85] Nevertheless, the doctrine was held by such church fathers as Barnabas (*ca.* A.D. 120), Ignatius (d. A.D. 117), Justin Martyr (A.D. 110-165), Irenaeus (A.D. 130-202), Tertullian (A.D. 160-220).[86] Denial of hell was condemned by the Council of Constantinople (A.D. 543).

Basically there are three false views of the afterlife of the wicked promoted among biblical scholars: *Universalism* teaches

---

The Bahnsen-Tabasch Debate," tape set number ASTB. Available from Covenant Media Foundation, 4425 Jefferson Ave., Suite 108, Texarkana, AR 71854. Phone: 800-553-3938. Bahnsen defends the doctrine of hell while defending Christianity. See also: Robert A. Peterson, *Hell on Trial: The Case for Eternal Punishment* (Phillipsburg, N.J.: Presbyterian and Reformed, 1995). Eryl Davies, *Condemned Forever! What the Bible Teaches About Eternal Punishment* (Hertfordshire, Eng.: Evangelical, 1987).

83. Patricia Parrott, "Hell Found Under Siberia," *Biblical Archaeology Review* 16:6 (Nov./Dec. 1990) 6.

84. Carl F. H. Henry, *God, Revelation and Authority* (Waco, TX: Word, 1983), p. 278.

85. Cited in Philip Schaff, *History of the Christian Church*, 8 vols. (5th ed.; Grand Rapids: Eerdmans, [1910] 1985), 2:612.

86. Martyr, *Apology* 1:8, 21; Irenaeus, *Against Heresies* 2:28:7; 3:4:1; Barnabus, *Epistle* 20. For a list of early fathers holding to the doctrine, see: Harry Buis, "Hell," *The Zondervan Pictorial Bible Encyclopedia*, Merrill C. Tenney, ed. (Grand Rapids: Zondervan, 1976), p. 116. Hereafter cited as *ZPEB*.

that the wicked will all be saved in the afterlife. Advocacy of universalism range from Origen, "the first Christian Universalist,"[87] to modern writers such as Nels Ferré, D. P. Walker, William Barclay, Thomas B. Talbot, and John Hick.[88] F. D. E. Schleiermacher was the most influential popularizer of universalism in the nineteenth century, laying the ground work for its appearance among twentieth-century Christians, where it is experiencing "a significant resurgence in recent years."[89]

Restorationists argue that the wicked will be punished for a time and then be allowed into the body of the redeemed.[90] This is a rare view.

Annihilationists hold that the unrepentant will be punished to elimination. Arnobius (*ca.* A.D. 327) was an ancient annihilationist.[91] Modern evangelical annihilationists include Philip E. Hughes, John R. W. Stott, and Clark H. Pinnock.[92] Annihila-

---

87. Schaff, *History*, 2:611. Though many think Origen taught the final restoration of Satan, this does not seem to be the case. See: *Epistle to the Romans* 1:8:9 (*Opera* 4:634) and *Ad quosdam amicos Alexandria* (*Opera* 1:5), as cited in Schaff, 2:611, n 3. For a brief history of universalism, see: Richard J. Bauckham, "Universalism: A Historical Survey," *Evangelical Review of Theology* 15 (Jan. 1991) 22-35.

88. D. P. Walker, *The Decline of Hell* (London: Routledge & Kegan Paul, 1964). Nels Ferré, *The Christian Understanding of God* (New York: Harper, 1951), pp. 228ff. William Barclay, *A Spiritual Autobiography* (Grand Rapids: Eerdmans, 1975), pp. 60ff. Thomas B. Talbot, "The Doctrine of Everlasting Punishment," *Faith and Philosophy* 7 (Jan. 1990) 19-42. John Hick, *Evil and the God of Love* (London: Macmillan, 1966). In addition see John A. T. Robinson, *In the End God* (2nd ed.; London: Collins, 1968), chaps. 10-11. Paul Knitter holds there are more true religions than Christianity. Knitter, *No Other Name* (Maryknoll, NY: Orbis, 1985).

89. Erickson, "Is Universalistic Thinking Now Appearing Among Evangelicals?" *Action* (Sept./Oct. 1989) 4-6.

90. Hick, *Evil and the God of Love*. Hick was once an evangelical theologian.

91. Arnobius, *Against the Nations* 2:14.

92. John R. W. Stott, *Evangelical Essentials* (Downer's Grove, IL: InterVarsity Press, 1988). "John R. W. Stott on Hell: Taking a Closer Look at Eternal Torture," *World Christian* 8 (May 1989) 31-37. Philip E. Hughes, *The True Image: The Origin and Destiny of Man* (Grand Rapids: Eerdmans, 1989). Philip Edgcumbe Hughes was relieved of his duties at Westminster Theological Seminary in the late 1980s due to his denial of hell. Pinnock has recently adopted a view he calls "postmortem evangelism," which allows for a second chance salvation: Pinnock, "Fire, Then Nothing," *Christianity Today*, 20 March 1987, p. 40; Pinnock, *A Wideness in God's Mercy: The*

tionists generally argue that only believers receive immortality, as a consequence of their union with Christ.[93] A recent poll among evangelical college and seminary students showed that almost one-third agreed that "the only hope for heaven is through personal faith in Jesus Christ except for those who have never had the opportunity to hear of Jesus Christ." This has been interpreted by James Davison Hunter as agreeing with Clark Pinnock's second chance before annihilation viewpoint.[94] We should note that unbelieving thought is a species of annihilationism. Bertrand Russell, the famous atheistic philosopher, held that man is simply an accidental collection of atoms, which in the very nature of the case is annihilated.

Hell is the judicial outcome of God's covenantal curse upon rebellious man, who is created with an ever-living soul. Hell represents the final legal sanction upon all those who have rebelled against God's eternal Law, both humans and demons. As such, hell is a place of conscious torment, as the Scripture demonstrates (Luke 16:23; Rev. 14:11). This torment is of endless duration,[95] though the degree of this torment is proportioned according to the extent of one's rebellion.[96] Its horrible nature

---

Finality of Jesus Christ in World Religions (Grand Rapids: Zondervan, 1992). For more regarding Pinnock, see John H. Gerstner, *Repent or Perish* (Ligonier, PA: Soli Deo, 1990), Erickson, "Is Universalistic Thinking Now Appearing Among Evangelicals?" 6, Peterson, *Hell on Trial*, 8-11, and Ronald H. Nash, *Is Jesus the Only Savior?* (Grand Rapids: Zondervan, 1994).

93. D. A. Dean, *Resurrection: His and Ours* (Charlotte, NC: Advent Christian General Conference of America, 1977), pp. 110ff. Edward William Fudge, *The Fire That Consumes* (Houston: Providential Press, 1982).

94. Cited by Erickson, "Universalistic Thinking," 6. On the growing liberalism of evangelicalism, see: James Davison Hunter, *Evangelicalism: The Coming Generation* (Chicago: University of Chicago Press, 1988).

95. Matt. 10:28; 13:41-42, 49-50; 18:8; 25:41, 46; Mark 9:43-48; Luke 3:17; 16:22-23; Jude 7; Heb. 6:2; Rev. 14:10-11; 20:10). See also: John 5:29; Jude 13. Although many orthodox scholars, while holding to the grievous, conscious misery involved, doubt whether literal flames of fire are used in the torment of the wicked. See: A. A. Hodge, *Outlines of Theology* (Edinburgh: Banner of Truth, [1878] n.d.), p. 580. Dabney, *Systematic Theology*, pp. 853-854.

96. Matt. 10:15; Luke 12:48. This is also implied in there being books of judg-

is directly due to the withdrawal of the presence of God (Matt. 25:41, contra. v. 34).

Interestingly, despite the revulsion of some to the doctrine, "the strongest support of the doctrine of Endless Punishment is the teaching of Christ, the Redeemer of man."[97] Due to the same language of eternal duration being applied to hell as to heaven (e.g., Matt. 25:46), "We must either admit the endless misery of Hell, or give up the endless happiness of Heaven."[98] The classic study on hell is W. G. T. Shedd's, *The Doctrine of Endless Punishment* (1886).[99]

New Earth

Though not all postmillennialists agree, biblical evidence suggests a refashioning of the earth as the eternal abode of the saints. The teaching of Scripture is often distorted when the "now/not yet" understanding of the kingdom is overlooked. Just as there is a "now" aspect of the Messianic Kingdom (Matt. 12:28) as well as a "not yet" aspect (Matt. 6:10), so there is a "now" aspect of the new creation (2 Cor. 5:17), as well as a "not yet" future to it (2 Pet. 3:13). Because this present chapter is devoted to the consummational features of eschatology, I am dealing with the "not yet" aspects of the new creation. For a discussion of the *spiritual* new creation, which precedes and prepares us for the material new creation, see Chapter 15.

We may expect a renovated new earth on the following bases: First, the language in some portions of Scripture states

ment, Rev. 20:11-13.

97. Shedd, *Dogmatic Theology*, 2:675. See: C. S. Lewis, *The Problem of Pain* (New York: Macmillan, 1944). Cf. Buis, "Hell," *ZPEB*, 3:114.

98. Moses Stuart, *Several Words Relating to Eternal Punishment* (Philadelphia: Presbyterian Publishing Committee, n.d.), p. 89.

99. A helpful recent defense of the doctrine is John H. Gerstner's *Repent or Perish* (1990). See also: Robert Morey's *Death and the Afterlife* (Minneapolis, MN: Bethany House, 1984), which is a refutation of Fudge, *Fire That Consumes*. Roger Nicole, "The Punishment of the Wicked," *Christianity Today* (June 9, 1958). J. I. Packer, "The Problem of Eternal Punishment," *Crux* 26 (Sept. 1990) 18-25.

that the earth is permanent: "He built His sanctuary like the heights, Like the earth which He has established forever" (Psa. 78:69).[100] Yet at the same time there are verses indicating it will pass away: "Lift up your eyes to the heavens, and look on the earth beneath. For the heavens will vanish away like smoke, the earth will grow old like a garment" (Isa. 51:6).[101] These two statements are capable of harmonization if the earth is to be transformed, passing through the cleansing fire of judgment to renewal.

Second, we may expect a renewed earth on the analogy of the individual's transformation. Just as we receive a new body at the resurrection (Eph. 1:14), so we will inherit a renewed earth on which to dwell with that body. "For the earnest expectation of the creation eagerly waits for the revealing of the sons of God. For the creation was subjected to futility, not willingly, but because of Him who subjected it in hope; because the creation itself also will be delivered from the bondage of corruption into the glorious liberty of the children of God. For we know that the whole creation groans and labors with birth pangs together until now. And not only they, but we also who have the firstfruits of the Spirit, even we ourselves groan within ourselves, eagerly waiting for the adoption, the redemption [resurrection] of our body" (Rom. 8:19-23). The comprehensive nature of sin and redemption (involving both soul and body), demands a comprehensive new earth (spiritual and material). For what other purpose would we be returned to our bodies via resurrection, if we were to remain solely and forever in the spiritual, heavenly realm?[102]

---

100. Psa. 104:5; 119:90; Eccl. 1:4. It should be noted that *olam*, which is often translated "forever," does not necessarily indicate eternality. It is employed in other senses: of the Passover (Ex. 12:24), a slave to a master (Exo. 21:6), the lamp burning in the Tabernacle (Ex. 27:20), various levitical functions (Ex. 29:28; 30:21; Lev. 6:18, 22; 7:343, 36; 10:15; 16:29, 31; 17:7; 23:14, 21, 41; 24:3; Num. 18:8; etc.), Joshua's memorial stones (Josh. 4:7).

101. Psa. 102:26; Isa. 51:6; Heb. 1:11.

102. See: Patrick Fairbairn, *The Typology of Scripture*, 2 vols. in one (Grand

Continuity and Discontinuity

There is both a continuity and a discontinuity between the present world and the new world. Things we do righteously are patterned after God's Law and will. Of the righteous who enter the eternal realm, we read: "Then I heard a voice from heaven saying to me, 'Blessed are the dead who die in the Lord from now on. Yes,' says the Spirit, 'that they may rest from their labors, and their works follow them' " (Rev. 14:13). Our temporal labor (which is commanded of God, Gen. 1:26-30) is a training ground for eternity. The biblical concept of rewards seems to come to play in this arena: "His lord said to him, 'Well done, good and faithful servant; you were faithful over a few things [in earth history], I will make you ruler over many things [in eternity in the new earth?]. Enter into the joy of your lord' " (Matt. 25:21).

As we strive to subdue the earth in a holy and spiritual fashion we approach God's design for man. Thus, we should expect our present cultural labors to have eternal significance, for we are commanded, in light of Christ's bodily resurrection, to "be steadfast, immovable, always abounding in the work of the Lord, knowing that your labor is not in vain in the Lord" (1 Cor. 15:58). Amillennialist Hoekema goes too far in assigning obviously spiritual references (e.g., Isa. 65:17) and many kingdom victory passages (Psa. 72) to the consummate new heavens and new earth.[103] Nevertheless, he well states the significance of our present cultural labors in the light of eternity: "[W]e may firmly believe that products of science and culture produced by unbelievers may yet be found on the new earth. . . . [O]ur mission work, our attempt to further a distinctively Christian culture, will have value not only for this world but even the world to come."[104] This comports well with the postmillennial drive to cultural and spiritual activity.

2 Peter 3

The key passage for the consummate new heavens and new earth is found in 2 Peter 3. Unfortunately, this passage has been the source of a good deal of confusion. Some dispensationalists hold that it refers to the earthly millennium, while others argue that it speaks of the consummate new creation.[105] Some postmillennialists hold that it refers to the present era introduced by the destruction of Jerusalem,[106] others apply it to the consummate new heavens and new earth.[107] Many amillennialists refer the new creation concept in all of Scripture solely to the final consummate order, using this passage as determinative of the others.[108]

A part of the problem with 2 Peter 3 lies in the fact that the passage employs terminology that is sometimes used to designate the spiritual new creation and at other times is used in reference to the destruction of Jerusalem in A.D. 70. This passage, however, does not speak either of the spiritual new creation (Isa. 65:17) or the conflagration of Jerusalem (Heb. 12:25-29). It points instead to the consummate order to follow the

---

104. *Ibid.*, pp. 39-40.

105. See the brief discussion in Walvoord, *Prophecy Knowledge Handbook*, pp. 510-513, 633.

106. Roderick Campbell, *Israel and the New Covenant* (Tyler, TX: Geneva Divinity School Press, [1954] 1981), ch. 13. See also the amillennialist and preterist Cornelius Vanderwaal, *Search the Scriptures* (St. Catherines, Ontario: Paideia, 1979), pp. 52-53.

107. See: John Calvin, *Hebrews and I and II Peter* (1549), *Calvin's New Testament Commentaries*, David W. Torrance and Thomas F. Torrance, eds. (Grand Rapids: Eerdmans, 1963), pp. 363-366. Dabney, *Systematic Theology*, pp. 850-852. Shedd, *Dogmatic Theology*, 2:665.

108. See for example: Hoekema, *Bible and the Future*, ch. 20. Adams, *Time Is at Hand*, pp. 13ff. Philip Edgcumbe Hughes, *Interpreting Prophecy* (Grand Rapids: Eerdmans, 1976), pp. 131-135. G. C. Berkouwer, *The Return of Christ* (Grand Rapids: Eerdmans, 1972), ch. 7. Herman Ridderbos, *The Coming of the Kingdom* (Grand Rapids: Eerdmans, 1962), p. 274.

resurrection and final judgment, as is evident from the following considerations.

First, the thrust of the book seems to promote a spiritual *perseverance* in anticipation of the historical long run – a long run that ends up in the eternal new creation. Peter urges the perseverance of his readers (1 Pet. 1:6) and warns against short-sightedness (1:9). It is only through long-term perseverance that we may expect access to the eternal kingdom of Jesus Christ (1:11). Peter himself expects to die soon (1:13-14; as did Paul, 2 Tim. 4:6-8). Consequently, he urges his readers to recall these things after he is gone (1:15), apparently not expecting a rapture of the Church in A.D. 70 (as per radical preterists[109]).

Peter gives Noah and Lot as examples of those who persevered through hard times, like those facing the looming destruction of Jerusalem. They came out on the other end *still upon the earth* (2:5-9). The rescue of believers from the oncoming temptation (2:9a) associated with A.D. 70 (by preserving them in trial, Luke 21:18-22) is set in contrast to the reserving of the fallen angels and the ungodly until the (later) Judgment Day (2:4, 9b). While contemplating the judgment cleansing of the earth, we are urged to "holy livings" and "pieties" (Greek plurals of these words occur only here, 3:11), suggesting many acts of righteousness for the long term. The book ends with a call to perseverance, as well (3:15, 17).

Second, the mockers scoff at the promised second advent of Christ due to the long wait associated with it (2 Pet. 3:3-4, 9). Despite the trials to come soon (2:9), Peter even suggests it may be thousands of years before Christ's return, in that the delay is based on God's time rather than man's: "But, beloved, do not forget this one thing, that with the Lord one day is as a thousand years, and a thousand years as one day" (3:8). This fits well with Christ's "now/not yet" teaching elsewhere, where He contrasts the short time until the destruction of Jerusalem

---

109. Russell, *Parousia*, Preface, and pp. 126, 137, 165, 168, 199, 445, 525.

(Matt. 23:36; 24:34) with that of the long wait for the second advent to end history (Matt. 25:5, 14).[110]

Third, the longsuffering of the Lord is due to a process necessarily age-long: "The Lord is not slack concerning His promise, as some count slackness, but is longsuffering toward us, not willing that any should perish but that all should come to repentance" (2 Pet. 3:9 NKJV). "Account that the longsuffering of our Lord is salvation" (2 Pet. 3:15a). The process of calling the "all" to "repentance" unto salvation spans the entire inter-adventual era and is still continuing today. This "slowness" (*bradutes*, v. 9) of Christ's second advent is so that the postmillennial kingdom victory might continue to grow unto full fruition.[111]

In verse 12a Peter urges Christians to "hasten (*speudo*, "speed up") the coming of the day of God" (3:12). Vincent comments: "I am inclined to adopt, with Alford, Huther, Salmond, and Trench, the transitive meaning, *hastening on*; i.e., 'causing the day of the Lord to come more quickly by helping to fulfil those conditions without which it cannot come; that day being no day inexorably fixed, but one the arrival of which it is free to the church to hasten on by faith and by prayer.' "[112] This is in keeping with "the cumulative evidence from Scripture, inter-testamental literature, and Jewish sources" regarding the term *speudo*.[113] The way that we "hasten the coming of the day of God" (3:12) is by evangelistic endeavor. Hence, the earnest prayer "Thy kingdom come, thy will be done on earth as it is in heaven" (Matt. 6:10; cf. Acts 3:19ff).

---

110. See Chapter 14 below.

111. For a discussion on the gradualistic principle of the kingdom, see Chapter 12 above.

112. Marvin R. Vincent, *Word Studies in the New Testament*, 4 vols. (Grand Rapids: Eerdmans, [1887] 1985), 1:707.

113. Simon Kistemaker, *Peter and Jude* (*New Testament Commentary*) (Grand Rapids: Baker, 1987), p. 338. Cf. A. T. Robertson, *Word Pictures in the New Testament*, 6 vols. (Nashville: Broadman, 1933), 6:177.

Fourth, the reference to the unraveling and conflagration of the heavens and the earth is expressly tied to the material creation. Hence, it refers to the consummation and not to A.D. 70, despite certain similarities. Peter expressly refers to the material creation order: "from the beginning of creation" (3:4; cf. Gen. 1:1[114]); "by the word of God the heavens were of old, and the earth standing out of water and in the water" (3:5; cf. Gen. 1:2, 9[115]); "the heavens and the earth which now exist" (2 Pet. 3:7). He defines the "heavens and earth" to which he refers. He is not contemplating the destruction of the old Jewish order, but the material heavens and the earth.

Fifth, the strong detailed language of the destruction of the heavens and the earth seems to go beyond apocalyptic imagery, referring to the actual consummation: "the heavens will pass away with a great noise, and the elements will melt with fervent heat; both the earth and the works that are in it will be burned up" (2 Pet. 3:10). "The heavens will be dissolved being on fire, and the elements will melt with fervent heat" (3:12). In the apocalyptic-symbolic passages thought to parallel 2 Peter 3 we find time frame factors[116] and cultural limitations.[117] Neither does this destruction terminology appear in Isaiah 65:17ff, where the phrase "new heavens and new earth" first appears.

In conjunction with "the promise" of His coming (3:4, 9), we are to await the ultimate "new heavens and new earth" (3:13). Peter obviously employs the terminology of Isaiah 65:17 (which speaks of a spiritual event, see Chapter 15). Yet as an inspired apostle he expands on that truth, looking to the ultimate outcome of the spiritual new heavens and earth in the eternal new

---

114. The Petrine phraseology (*apo arches ktiseos*) reflects that of the Lord's when He spoke of the creation of the material universe. See: Mark 10:6 and 13:9.

115. The phraseology is reminiscent of Psalm 33:6-7 [Psa. 32:6-7 in Hebrew], which speaks of the creative act of God in making the world.

116. For example, see: Matt. 24:29, cf. v. 34; Rev. 6:13-14, cf. Rev. 1:1, 3; 6:10.

117. For example, see: Isa. 13:10, cf. 1, 14-21.

creation, just as Zechariah 12:10 may be applied by an apostle either to the crucifixion (John 19:37) or A.D. 70 (Rev. 1:7).

The new creation, then, of 2 Peter 3 is the renovated material world that will succeed the present temporal order. It will be purified by fire and refashioned by the hand of God. It is on this new earth that the saints will dwell forever.

Conclusion

As indicated in Chapter 1 Christianity provides a distinctive philosophy of history. History is linear in its movement; it has a starting point in creation and a concluding point at the Second Advent. Both the creation and the consummation are divinely ordained events. They are not brought about by naturalistic forces. The consummational events – Second Advent, resurrection, judgment, – indicate the personal involvement of the Lord God in the operation of the universe. These events also indicate the ethical nature of reality: history is moving somewhere specific; final judgment is coming.

Postmillennialism fills out the general Christian conception of linear history. Postmillennialists speak not only of linear movement, but of upward progression. The redemptive power of the work of the Lord Jesus Christ is progressively drawing men and nations to Himself. From a postmillennial perspective the Second Advent of Christ is truly consummational: it brings about the eternal resolution of the affairs of history, rather than setting up another scenario (as per premillennialism and dispensationalism). That glorious consummational day will richly evidence the mighty power of God. Not only will He catastrophically intervene to end history with a glorious display of His sovereignty, but He will do so after a long era of righteousness, which will have brought the vast majority of the human race to salvation.

PART IV

SPECIFICATION

14

TIME FRAMES

Daniel answered and said: "Blessed be the name of God forever and ever, for wisdom and might are His. And He changes the times and the seasons; He removes kings and raises up kings; He gives wisdom to the wise And knowledge to those who have understanding." (Daniel 2:20-21)

I have presented the postmillennial view of the major flow of biblical eschatology from creation to new creation. In this and the next three chapters I will survey some of the more detailed *specifics* that are often debated in eschatological discussion. Of course, the proper understanding of most of these issues depends on the *system* of eschatology already set in place by the Scriptural research I have presented. Specific questions that arise in the millennial discussion must be capable of resolution from within one's exegetically derived eschatological system. Any system of eschatology that does not provide consistent, exegetically-based resolutions should be discarded.

In this chapter I will begin with an inquiry into certain of the *prophetic time frames* that are generally well-known. The bulk of this chapter will be given over to a study of Daniel's Seventy Weeks due to its significance in the eschatological debate.

The Seventy Weeks

The chronology provided in Daniel's prophecy of the Seventy Weeks (Dan. 9:24-27) is a linchpin in the dispensational system, although it is not crucial to any of the other millennial systems. Walvoord comments that the "interpretation of Daniel 9:24-27 is of major importance to premillennialism as well as pretribulationism." Being such, it is the "key" to prophecy and, consequently, "one of the most important prophecies of the Bible." Surely Allis is correct when he observes that "the importance of the prophecy of the Seventy Weeks in Dispensational teaching can hardly be exaggerated."[1]

This dependence upon Daniel 9 is unfortunate for dispensationalism for two reasons. First, historically: Great difficulties are associated with the interpretation of this passage. J. A. Montgomery calls the prophecy "the Dismal Swamp of Old Testament criticism."[2] Young comments: "This passage . . . is one of the most difficult in all the OT, and the interpretations which have been offered are almost legion."[3]

Second, theologically: This "extremely important prophecy" is the most difficult for dispensationalists to make credible to those outside of their system. Even dispensationalist Robert Culver admits: "The difficulty of the verses that now lie before us is evident."[4] "Premillennial writers of two or three generations ago were very far apart on the details. Much of the same diversity appears in premillennial contemporary writers."[5] In

---

1. John F. Walvoord, *The Rapture Question* (Grand Rapids: Zondervan, 1957), p. 24. John F. Walvoord, *Daniel: The Key to Prophetic Revelation* (Chicago: Moody Press, 1971), pp. 201, 216. O. T. Allis, *Prophecy and the Church* (Philadelphia: Presbyterian & Reformed, 1945), p. 111. See also: Alva J. McClain, *Daniel's Prophecy of the 70 Weeks* (Grand Rapids: Zondervan, 1940), p. 9. J. Dwight Pentecost, *Things to Come* (Grand Rapids: Zondervan, 1958), p. 240. E. Schuyler English, "The Gentiles in Revelation," *Prophecy and the Seventies*, Charles Lee Feinberg, ed. (Chicago: Moody Press, 1971), p. 242.

2. J. A. Montgomery, *A Critical and Exegetical Commentary on the Book of Daniel* (*International Critical Commentary*) (New York: Scribner's, 1927), p. 400.

3. E. J. Young, *The Prophecy of Daniel* (Grand Rapids: Eerdmans, [1949] 1977), p. 191.

4. Robert Duncan Culver, *Daniel and the Latter Days* (2nd ed.; Chicago: Moody Press, 1977), p. 144.

5. *Ibid.*, p. 144.

fact, Daniel's Seventy Weeks prophecy leads dispensationalism into one of its most strained peculiarities: the doctrine of the gap theory of the Church Age.[6] I will consider this later.

Covenantal Structure

As we get started it is crucial to grasp the structure of the prophecy. Meredith Kline provides a thorough presentation of the strongly covenantal cast of Daniel 9 which leads up to the prophecy, noting that it is "saturated with formulaic expressions drawn from the Mosaic treaties, particularly from the Deuteronomic treaty" (cf. Dan. 9:4-6, 10-15).[7] This prayer regarding covenant loyalty (*hesed*, 9:4) is answered in terms of the covenantal sabbath pattern of the seventy weeks (9:24-27), which results in the confirmation of the covenant (9:27). Daniel 9 is the only chapter in Daniel to use God's special covenant name, *YHWH* (vv. 2, 4, 10, 13, 14, 20; cf. Exo. 6:2-4).

Recognizing the covenantal framework of the Seventy Weeks is crucial to its proper interpretation. It virtually demands a focus on the fulfillment of covenantal redemption in the ministry of Christ. Let us see why this is so.

The prophecy of the Seventy Weeks is clearly framed in terms of *sabbatic chronology*. The first phase of the Seventy Weeks is "seven weeks," or (literally) "seven sevens" (Dan. 9:25), which results in a value of forty-nine. This reflects the time frame leading up to the redemptively significant Year of Jubilee (Lev. 25:8ff). The total period of *"seventy* sevens" is also covenantal. Seventy represents ten seven-week periods: ten jubilees.

---

6. Allis mentions this teaching flowing out of the dispensational approach to Daniel 9:24-27 as "one of the clearest proofs of the novelty of that doctrine as well as of its revolutionary nature." Allis, *Prophecy and the Church*, p. 109. Kline's analysis of Daniel 9 leads him to call dispensationalism an "evangelical heresy." Meredith Kline, "Covenant of the Seventieth Week," *The Law and the Prophets: Old Testament Studies in Honor of Oswald T. Allis*, John H. Skilton, ed. (n.p.: Presbyterian & Reformed, 1974), p. 452.

7. Kline, "The Covenant of the Seventieth Week," p. 456.

The seventy sevens (weeks) appear to point to a *completed* redemptive Jubilee. This appropriately points to Christ who brings in that ultimate Jubilee (cf. Luke 4:17-21; Isa. 61:1-3; Matt. 24:31), and who is the leading character in Daniel's prophecy. Consequently, the time frame revealed to Daniel demarcates the period in which "the Messianic redemption was to be accomplished."[8]

Chronological Value

The seventy weeks represent a period of seventy times seven *years*, or 490 years: (1) In the preceding context, the original seventy *years* of Jeremiah's prophecy is in Daniel's mind (Dan. 9:2). Years are suggested, then, by the prior reference which is crucial to the historical context. (2) The sabbath *year* (the seventh year of the sabbath period) is frequently referred to simply as "the sabbath."[9] Thus, a "sabbath day" (Gen. 2:2; Exo. 20:11) is expanded to cover a year. (3) There is Scriptural warrant for measuring days in terms of years in certain passages (Gen. 29:27-28; Num. 14:34; Deut. 14:28; 1 Sam. 2:19; Eze. 4:6; Amos 4:4). (4) Daniel seems to shift gears and even notify the reader of the change in Daniel 10:2, where he qualifies his situation by saying he mourned "three weeks of days" (Heb.).

The "command" in Daniel 9:25 is: "Know therefore and understand, that from the going forth of the command to restore and build Jerusalem. . . ." At first appearance it would seem to refer to Cyrus' decree to rebuild the Temple in 538 B.C. This command is mentioned in 2 Chronicles 36:22-23 and in Ezra 1:1-4; 5:13, 17, 6:3. Daniel, however, specifically speaks of the command to "*restore* and build *Jerusalem*," which is an important qualification.[10]

---

8. E. J. Young, "Daniel," *Eerdmans Bible Commentary*, Donald Guthrie and J. Motyer, eds. (Grand Rapids: Eerdmans, 1970), p. 698.

9. Lev. 25:2-5; 26:34, 35, 43; 2 Chr. 36:21; etc.

10. E. W. Hengstenberg, *Christology of the Old Testament*, 2 vols. (McLean, VA:

Though half-hearted efforts are made to rebuild Jerusalem after Cyrus' decree, for a long time Jerusalem is little more than a sparsely populated, unwalled village. Daniel speaks of the command to "restore" (*shub*, return) Jerusalem (Dan. 9:25). This requires that it be returned to its original integrity and grandeur "*as at the first*" (Jer. 33:7). It was not until the middle of the fifth century B.C. that this is undertaken seriously.[11]

The first period of seven weeks must indicate something, for it is set off from the two other periods. Were it not significant Daniel could speak of the sixty-nine weeks, rather than the "seven weeks and sixty-two weeks" (Dan. 9:25). This seven weeks (or forty-nine years) apparently witnesses the successful conclusion of the rebuilding of Jerusalem.[12]

The second period of sixty-two weeks extends from the conclusion of the rebuilding of Jerusalem to the introduction of Israel's Messiah at His baptism when He begins His public ministry (Dan. 9:25), sometime around A.D. 26. This interpretation is quite widely agreed upon by conservative scholars, being virtually "universal among Christian exegetes"[13] – excluding dispensationalists. The third period of one week is the subject of intense controversy between dispensationalism and other conservative scholarship. I will turn to this shortly.

Interpretation of Daniel 9:24

In Daniel 9:24 the overriding, glorious expectation of the prophecy is stated: "Seventy weeks are determined for your people and for your holy city, to finish the transgression, to make an end of sins, to make reconciliation for iniquity, to

---

MacDonald, [1854] n.d.), 2:884ff.

11. *Ibid.*, 2:884-911. J. Barton Payne, *Encyclopedia of Biblical Prophecy* (New York: Harper & Row, 1973), pp. 388ff. C. Boutflower, *In and Around the Book of Daniel* (London: SPCK, 1923), pp. 195ff.

12. Hengstenberg, *Christology of the Old Testament*, 2:894ff.

13. Montgomery, *Daniel*, p. 332.

bring in everlasting righteousness, to seal up vision and prophecy, and to anoint the Most Holy."

The six infinitival phrases of verse 24 should be understood as three *couplets* (Payne, Terry, Maurer, Hitzig, and the Massoretes), rather than as two triplets (Keil and Young).[14] These six results are the main point of the prophecy, serving as the heading of the explication to follow. The "know therefore and understand" statement in verse 25 begins that explication.

The general view of Daniel 9:24 among non-dispensational evangelicals is that "the six items presented . . . settle the *terminus ad quem* of the prophecy,"[15] that is, they have to do with the First Advent. Dispensationalists, however, hold that these events are "not to be found in any event near the earthly lifetime of our Lord."[16] Rather they teach that "God will once again turn His attention in a special way to His people the Jews and to His holy city Jerusalem, as outlined in Daniel 9:24."[17] The dispensationalist takes a decidedly futurist approach to the prophecy — when he gets past the first sixty-nine weeks.

Let us notice, first, that the Seventy Weeks will witness the *finishing of the transgression.* As just noted Daniel's prayer of confession was regarding Israel's sins (Dan. 9:4ff) and the prophecy's focus is on Israel (Dan. 9:24a). Consequently, this *finishing (kala) the transgression* has to do with Israel's finishing, i.e., completing, her transgression against God. The finishing of that

---

14. For couplet view, see: J. Barton Payne, "The Goal of Daniel's Seventy Weeks," *Journal of the Evangelical Theological Society* 21:2 (June, 1978) 111; Milton Terry, *Biblical Apocalyptics: A Study of the Most Notable Revelations of God and of Christ* (Grand Rapids: Baker, [1898] 1988), p. 200. Young lists the other two: F. Maurer, *Commentarius grammaticus criticus in Vetus Testamentum*, vol. 2 (Leipzig: 1838); F. Hitzig, *Das Buch Daniel* (1850). For the triplet view, see: C. F. Keil, "The Book of Daniel," *Commentary on the Old Testament*, C. F. Keil and Franz Delitzsch, eds. (Grand Rapids: Eerdmans, [1877] 1975), p. 341. E. J. Young, *Prophecy of Daniel*, p. 197.

15. Keil and Delitzsch, "Daniel," p. 201.

16. Robert Duncan Culver, *Daniel and the Latter Days* (Westwood, NJ: Revell, 1954), p. 155.

17. Charles C. Ryrie, *Basic Theology* (Wheaton, IL: Victor, 1986), p. 465.

transgression occurs in the ministry of Christ, when Israel culminates her resistance to God by rejecting His Son and having Him crucified (Matt. 21:37-38; cf. 21:33-45; Acts 7:51-52).[18]

The second part of the couplet is directly related to the first: Having finished the transgression against God in the rejection of the Messiah, now the *sins are sealed up* (NASB marg.; *chatham*). The idea here is, as Payne observes, to seal or to "reserve sins for punishment."[19] Because of Israel's rejection of Messiah, God reserves punishment for her: the final, conclusive destruction of the temple, which was reserved from the time of Jesus' ministry until A.D. 70 (Matt. 24:2, 34). The sealing or reserving of the sins indicates that *within* the "Seventy Weeks" Israel will complete her transgression, *and* with the completing of her sin by crucifying Christ, God will act to reserve (*beyond the seventy weeks*) her sins for judgment.

The third result (beginning the second couplet) has to do with the provision of *"reconciliation for iniquity."*[20] The Hebrew word *kaphar* is the word for "atonement," i.e., a covering of sin. It clearly speaks of Christ's atoning death, which is the ultimate atonement to which all temple rituals looked (Heb. 9:26[21]). This also occurred during His earthly ministry – at His death. The dispensationalist here prefers to interpret this result as *application* rather than *effecting*. He sees it as subjective appropriation instead of objective accomplishment: "[T]he actual application of it is again associated with the second advent as far as Israel is concerned."[22] But on the basis of the Hebrew

---

18. Matt. 20:18-19; 23:37-38; 27:11-25; Mark 10:33; 15:1; Luke 18:32; 23:1-2; John 18:28-31; 19:12, 15; Acts 2:22-23; 3:13-15a; 4:26-27; 5:30; 7:52.

19. Payne, "Goal of Daniel's Seventy Weeks," p. 111.

20. The definite article, which occurred before "transgression" and "sins," is lacking here. There it referred to the particular situation of Israel. Here it considers the more general predicament of mankind.

21. Heb. 1:3; 7:27; 9:7-12, 26, 28; 10:9-10. See also: John 1:29; Rom. 3:25; 2 Cor. 5:19; 1 Pet. 2:24; 1 John 2:2.

22. Walvoord, *Daniel*, p. 222.

verb, the passage clearly speaks of the actual *making reconciliation* (or *atonement*).

Because of this atonement to cover sin the fourth result is that *everlasting righteousness* is effected. That is, the final, complete atonement establishes righteousness. This speaks of the objective accomplishment, not the subjective appropriation of righteousness. This was effected by Christ within the seventy-week period, as well (Rom. 3:21-22a).

The fifth result (the first portion of the third couplet) has to do with the ministry of Christ on earth, which is introduced at His baptism: He comes "*to seal up vision and prophecy.*" By this is meant that Christ fulfills (and thereby confirms) the prophecy (Luke 18:31; cf. Luke 24:44; Acts 3:18).[23]

Finally, the seventy years are for the following goal: "*to anoint the Most Holy.*" This anointing [*mashach*] speaks of the Christ's baptismal anointing for the following reasons: (1) The overriding concern of Daniel 9:24-27 is Messianic. The temple that is built after the Babylonian Captivity is to be destroyed after the seventy weeks (v. 27), with no further mention made of it. (2) In the following verses the Messiah (*mashiyach*, "Christ," "Anointed One") is specifically named twice (vv. 25, 26). (3) The "most holy" phraseology speaks of the Messiah, who is "that Holy One who is to be born."[24] It is of Christ that the ultimate redemptive Jubilee is prophesied by Isaiah (Isa. 61:1-2a; cf. Luke 4:17-21). It was at His baptismal anointing that the Spirit came upon Him (Mark 1:9-11). This was introductory to His ministry, of which we read three verses later: "Jesus came to

---

23. Walvoord slips by allowing this prophecy to cover "the cessation of the New Testament prophetic gift seen both in oral prophecy and in the writing of the Scriptures." Walvoord, *Daniel*, p. 222. This, however, does not occur in either the first sixty-nine weeks (up to "just before the time of Christ's crucifixion") or in the seventieth week (the future Great Tribulation), the periods which he claims involve the 490 years. Walvoord, *Prophecy Knowledge Handbook*, p. 258. Yet he specifically says that the "six major events characterize the 490 years"! *Ibid.*, p. 251.

24. Luke 1:35; cf. 4:34, 41. See also: Mark 1:24; Acts 3:14; 4:27, 30; 1 John 2:20; Rev. 3:7; He is called the "anointed one" (Psa. 2:2; Isa. 42:1; Acts 10:38).

Galilee, preaching the gospel of the kingdom of God, and saying, '*The time* is *fulfilled* [the Sixty-ninth week?[25]], and the kingdom of God is at hand. Repent, and believe in the gospel" (Mark 1:14-15). Christ is pre-eminently *the* Anointed One.[26]

The Seventieth Week

The Messiah now experiences something "after the sixty-two weeks" (Dan. 9:26), which follow the preceding "seven weeks" (v. 25). This is to occur, then, sometime *after* the sixty-ninth week. A natural reading of the text shows this is in the seventieth week, for that is the only time frame remaining for the accomplishment of the goal of the prophecy listed in verse 24. That which occurs at this time is: "Messiah shall be *cut off*." The Hebrew word translated "cut off" here (*karath*) "is used of the death penalty, Lev. 7:20; and refers to a violent death,"[27] i.e, the death of Christ on the cross.

Given the Hebraic pattern of repetition, we may easily discern a parallel between verses 26 and 27; verse 27 gives an

---

25. Interestingly, there was a current and widely held belief that a ruler from within Israel was to arise "at that very time," i.e., during the Jewish War. Tacitus, *Histories* 5:13: "The majority were convinced that the ancient scriptures of their priests alluded to *the present as the very time* when the Orient would triumph and from Judaea would go forth men destined to rule the world. This mysterious prophecy really referred to Vespasian and Titus. . . ." Suetonius, *Vespasian* 4: "An ancient superstition was current in the East, that out of Judaea at this time would come the rulers of the world. This prediction, as the event later proved, referred to a Roman Emperor. . . ." Josephus even picks up on this idea, when he ingratiates himself to Vespasian by declaring he was the one to rule (*Wars* 3:8:9). The only prophecy regarding Israel that actually dates Messianic era events is Daniel 9:24-27. Josephus also applies the Daniel 9 passage to the rule of the Romans in another context: "In the very same manner Daniel also wrote concerning the Roman government, and that our country should be made desolate by them. All these things did this man leave in writing, as God had shewed them to him. . . " (*Ant.* 10:11:7).

26. Psa. 2:2; 132:10; Isa. 11:2; 42:1; Hab. 3:13; Acts 4:27; 10:38; Heb. 1:9. Vanderwaal denies the Messianic referent of this passage, preferring a Maccabean priestly referent. Cornelius Vanderwaal, *Hal Lindsey and Biblical Prophecy* (St. Catherines, Ontario: Paideia, 1978), p. 37.

27. Young, *Daniel*, p. 206.

expansion of verse 26. Negatively, Messiah's *cutting off* in verse 26 is the result of Israel's completing her transgression and bringing it to a culmination (v. 24) by crucifying the Messiah.[28] Positively, verse 27 states this same event: "He shall *confirm a covenant* with many for one week; but in the middle of the week He shall bring an end to sacrifice and offering." Considered from its positive effect, this confirming of the covenant with many makes reconciliation and brings in everlasting righteousness (v. 24). The *confirming of a covenant* (v. 27) refers to the prophesied covenantal actions of verse 24, which come about as the result of the Perfect Covenantal Jubilee (Seventy Weeks) and are mentioned as a result of Daniel's covenantal prayer (cf. v. 4). The covenant mentioned, then, is the *divine* covenant of God's redemptive grace.[29] Messiah came to *confirm* the covenantal promises (Luke 1:72; Eph. 2:12). He confirmed the covenant by His death on the cross (Heb. 7:22b).[30]

The word translated "confirm" (*higbir*) is related to the angel Gabriel's name, who brought Daniel the revelation of the Seventy Weeks (and who later brings the revelation of Christ's birth [Luke 1:19, 26]). "Gabriel" is based on the Hebrew *gibbor*, "strong one," a concept frequently associated with the covenant God.[31] The related word found in Daniel 9:27 means to "make strong, confirm."[32] This "firm covenant" brings about "*everlasting* righteousness" (Dan. 9:24) – hence its firmness.

---

28. Matt. 20:18-19; 27:11-25; Mark 10:33; 15:1; Luke 18:32; 23:1-2; John 18:28-31; 19:12, 15; Acts 2:22-23; 3:13-15a; 4:26-27; 5:30; 7:52.

29. When "covenant" is mentioned in Daniel, it is always God's covenant, see: Daniel 9:4; 11:22, 28, 30, 32. This includes even Daniel 11:22. See: J. Dwight Pentecost, "Daniel," *Bible Knowledge Commentary*, John F. Walvoord and Roy B. Zuck, eds., 2 vols. (Wheaton, IL: Victor, 1985), 1:1369. Hereafter referred to as *BKC*.

30. Matt. 26:28; Mark 14:24; Luke 22:20; 1 Cor. 11:25; 2 Cor. 3:6; Heb. 8:8, 13; 9:15; 12:24.

31. Deut. 7:9, 21; 10:17; Neh. 1:5; 9:32; Isa. 9:6; Dan. 9:4. Hengstenberg argues convincingly that the source of Daniel 9 seems to be Isaiah 10:21-23, where God is the "Mighty God" who blesses the faithful remnant.

32. Young, *Daniel*, p. 209; Allis, *Prophecy and the Church*, p. 122; Hengstenberg, *Christology of the Old Testament*, p. 856.

Daniel's prayer was particularly for Israel (Dan. 9:3ff), and it was uttered in recognition of God's promises of mercy upon those who love Him (v. 4). Therefore, the covenant will be confirmed with *many* for *one week*. The reference to the "many" speaks of the faithful in Israel. "Thus a contrast is introduced between *He* and the *Many*, a contrast which appears to reflect upon the great Messianic passage, Isaiah 52:13-53:12 and particularly 53:11. Although the entire nation will not receive salvation, the many will receive."[33]

This confirmation of God's covenant promises to the "many" of Israel will occur in the middle of the *seventieth week* (v. 27), which parallels "after the sixty-two [and seven] weeks" (v. 26), while providing more detail. We know Christ's three-and-one-half-year ministry was decidedly focused on the Jews in the first half of the seventieth week (Matt. 10:5b; cf. Matt. 15:24). For a period of three and one-half years after the crucifixion,[34] the apostles focused almost exclusively on the Jews, beginning first "in Judea" (Acts 1:8; 2:14) because "the gospel of Christ" is "for the Jew first" (Rom. 1:16; cf. 2:10; John 4:22).

Although the event that serves as the terminus of the sixty-ninth week is clearly specified, such is not the case with the terminus of the seventieth. Thus, the exact event that ends the seventieth is not so significant for us to know. *Apparently* at the stoning of Stephen, the first martyr of Christianity, the covenantal proclamation began to be turned toward the Gentiles (Acts 8:1). The apostle to the Gentiles appears on the scene at Stephen's death (Acts 7:58-8:1), as the Jewish persecution against Christianity breaks out. Paul's mission is clearly stated as exceeding the narrow Jewish focus (Acts 9:15).

This confirmation of the covenant occurs "in the middle of the week" (v. 27). I have already shown that the seventieth

---

33. Young, *Daniel*, p. 213.

34. Payne, "The Goal of Daniel's Seventy Weeks," p. 109n; Boutflower, *In and Around the Book of Daniel*, pp. 195ff; Hengstenberg, *Christology of the Old Testament*, 2:898. Young, *Daniel*, p. 213.

week *begins* with the baptismal anointing of Christ. Then, after three and one-half years of ministry – the middle of the seventieth week – Christ was crucified (Luke 13:6-9; *Eccl. Hist.* 1:10:3). Thus, the prophecy states that by His conclusive confirmation of the covenant, Messiah will "bring an end to sacrifice and offering" (v. 27) by offering up Himself as a sacrifice for sin (Heb. 9:25-26; cf. Heb. 7:11-12, 18-22). Consequently, at His death the Temple's veil was torn from top to bottom (Matt. 27:51) as evidence that the sacrificial system was *legally disestablished* in the eyes of God (cf. Matt. 23:38), for Christ is the Lamb of God (John 1:29; Acts 8:32; 1 Pet. 1:19; Rev. 5-7).

The Destruction of Jerusalem

But how are we to understand the latter portions of both verses 26 and 27? What are we to make of the destruction of the city and sanctuary (v. 26) and the abomination that causes desolation (v. 27), which most non-dispensational evangelical commentators agree occurred in A.D. 70?

In verse 26 we learn that *two* events are to occur *after* the sixty-ninth week: (1) The Messiah is to be "cut off," and (2) the city and sanctuary are to be destroyed. Verse 27a informs us that the Messiah's cutting off (v. 26a) is a confirmation of the covenant and is to occur at the half-way mark of the seventieth week. So, the Messiah's death is clearly within the time frame of the Seventy Weeks (as we expect because of His being the major figure of the fulfillment of the prophecy).

The events involving the destruction of the city and the sanctuary with war and desolation (vv. 26b, 27b) are the *consequences* of the cutting off of the Messiah and do not necessarily occur *in* the seventy weeks time frame. They are an *addendum* to the fulfillment of the focus of the prophecy, which is stated in verse 24. The destructive acts are *anticipated*, however, in the divine act of sealing up or reserving the sin of Israel for punishment. Israel's climactic sin – her completing of her transgression (v. 24) with the cutting off of Messiah (v. 26a) – results in God's act of *reserving Israel's sin until later*. Israel's judgment will not be postponed forever; it will come after the expiration of the seventy weeks. This explains the "very indefinite"[35] phrase "till the end of the war": *the "end" will not occur during the seventy weeks*. That prophesied end occurred in A.D. 70, exactly as Christ had made abundantly clear in Matthew 24:15.

The Dispensational Interpretation

The Gap in the Seventy Weeks

Dispensationalism incorporates a gap or parenthesis between the sixty-ninth and seventieth weeks. This gap spans the entirety of the Church Age from the Triumphal Entry to the Rapture.[36] The dispensational arguments for a gap of undetermined length between the sixty-ninth and seventieth weeks are not convincing. Let us consider a few of their leading arguments for a gap.

First, *the peculiar phraseology in Daniel*: Daniel places the cutting off of the Messiah "*after* the 62 'sevens,'" not in the 70th 'seven.'"[37] This is so stated to allow for a gap between the sixty-ninth and seventieth-weeks. If the cutting-off did not occur during the sixty-ninth week or during the seventieth week, there must be a gap in between wherein it does occur.

In response it is obvious that seventy occurs *after* sixty-nine, and thus fits the requirements of the prophecy. Consequently, such an argument does not prove that the "after" *requires* a gap.

---

35. Allis, *Prophecy and the Church*, p. 115.

36. Walvoord, *Prophecy Knowledge Handbook*, pp. 256-257. Ryrie, *Basic Theology*, p. 465. Pentecost, "Daniel," *BKC*, 1:161. Walvoord, *Daniel*, pp. 230-231. It is interesting to note that the early Fathers held to a non-eschatological interpretation of the Seventieth Week, applying it either to the ministry of Christ or to A.D. 70. See: Barnabas, *Epistles* 16:6; Clement of Alexandria, *Miscellanies* 1:125-26; Tertullian, *An Answer to the Jews* 8; Julius Africanus, *Chronology* 50. See: L. E. Knowles, "The Interpretation of the Seventy Weeks of Daniel in the Early Fathers," *Westminster Theological Journal* 7 (1945) 136-160.

37. Pentecost, "Daniel," *BKC*, p. 1364. See: Walvoord, *Rapture Question*, p. 25.

Besides, Daniel mentions only seventy weeks and, as LaRondelle has pointed out, Daniel most certainly does *not* say "after
sixty-nine weeks, but not in the seventieth."[38] Such an explanation is a gratuitous assumption. Since Daniel has yet to deal
with the seventieth week, and since he has clearly dealt with the
preceding sixty-nine weeks (v. 25), it is quite natural to assume
this cutting off of the Messiah must be sometime *within* the
seven-year period covered by the seventieth week.

Second, *a fatal admission*: "Historically the destruction of
Jerusalem occurred in A.D. 70 almost forty years after the
death of Christ."[39] Since this was given in Daniel's prophecy
and was to occur within the seventy weeks, "the continuous
fulfillment theory [is] left without any explanation adequate for
interposing an event as occurring after the sixty-ninth seven by
some thirty-eight years."[40]

I have already explained the relation of the seventy weeks to
the destruction of the Temple in A.D. 70 (see above). The goal
of the Seventy Weeks is *not* the A.D. 70 destruction of the Temple, which is not mentioned in verse 24. That destruction is a
later consequence of certain events brought to fulfillment within
the seventy weeks. The actual act of God's reserving judgment
(v. 24) occurred within the seventy weeks; the later removal of
that *reservation* did not. There is no necessity at all for a gap.

Third, *the general tendency in prophecy*: Walvoord writes:
"Nothing should be plainer to one reading the Old Testament
than that the foreview therein provided did not describe the
period of time between the two advents. This very fact confused
even the prophets (cf. 1 Pet. 1:10-12)."[41] His argument then
is: Old Testament prophecy can merge the First and Second
Advents into one scene, though separated by thousands of

---

38. Hans K. LaRondelle, *The Israel of God in Prophecy* (Berried Springs, MI:
Andrews University, 1983), p. 173.

39. Walvoord, *Daniel*, p. 230.

40. *Ibid.*, p. 230.

41. Walvoord, *Rapture Question*, p. 25.

years. Consequently, we have biblical warrant for understanding the sixty-ninth and seventieth weeks as merged into one scene, although separated by a gap of thousands of years.

This argument is wholly without merit. The Seventy Weeks are considered as a unit, though sub-divided into three unequal parts: (1) It is *one* period of seventy weeks that must transpire in order to experience the events mentioned. The plural "seventy weeks" is followed by a *singular* verb "is decreed," which indicates the unity of the time period. (2) An overriding concern of the prophecy, in distinction to all other Messianic prophecies, is that it is designed as a *measuring* time frame. If the dispensational gap theory regarding the seventieth week is true, then the gap separating the seventieth from the sixty-ninth week is now almost 2000 years long, or four times the whole time period of the seventy weeks or 490 years. And who know how much longer it will continue. The concept of measuring is thus destroyed.

The Dispensational Covenant

The confirmation of the covenant mentioned in verse 27 is woefully misunderstood by dispensationalists. According to Walvoord: "[T]his refers to the coming world ruler at the beginning of the last seven years who is able to gain control over ten countries in the Middle East. He will make a covenant with Israel for a seven-year period. As Daniel 9:27 indicates, in the middle of the seven years he will break the covenant, stop the sacrifices being offered in the temple rebuilt in that period, and become their persecutor instead of their protector, fulfilling the promises of Israel's day of trouble (Jer. 30:5-7)."[42]

Several problems plague this interpretation, some of which have already been indicated in another connection: (1) The covenant here is not *made*, it is *confirmed*. This is actually the

---

42. Walvoord, *Prophecy Knowledge Handbook*, p. 257. Pentecost, "Daniel," *BKC*, p. 1364.

confirmation of a covenant already extant, i.e., the covenant of God's redemptive grace confirmed by Christ (Rom. 15:8).

(2) As noted above the term is related to the name of the angel of God who delivered the message to Daniel: Gabriel ("God is *strong*"). The lexical correspondence between the name of the strong angel of God (who reveals the seventy weeks to Daniel) and the making strong of the covenant themselves suggest the divine nature of the covenant. In addition, covenantal passages frequently employ related terms, when speaking of the strong God of the covenant.[43]

(3) The parallelism with verse 26 indicates that the death of the Messiah is directly related to the confirming of the covenant. He is "cut off" but "not for himself" (v. 26a), for He "confirms the covenant" for the "many" of Israel (v. 27a). His "cutting off" *brings* the confirmation of the covenant, for "without shedding of blood there is no remission" (Heb. 9:22).

(4) The indefinite pronoun "he" does not refer back to "the prince who is to come" of verse 26.[44] That "prince" is a subordinate noun; "the people" is the dominant noun. Thus, the "he" refers back to the last dominant individual mentioned: "Messiah" (v. 26a). The Messiah is the leading figure in the whole prophecy, so the destruction of the Temple is related to His death. In fact, the people who destroy the Temple are providentially "His armies" (Matt. 22:2-7).

The Last Days

An eschatological theme that is as widely misunderstood as it is commonly discussed in popular prophetic literature is the

43. Deut. 7:9, 21; 10:17; Neh. 1:5; 9:32; Isa. 9:6; Dan. 9:4. See earlier discussion above.

44. Kline provides interesting arguments for the reference "the prince who is to come" (v. 27) being to "Messiah the Prince" (v. 25). If this were conclusive, the "he" would then refer back to the Messiah in either view.

"last days." This factor of eschatological chronology is an important concept that requires a deep appreciation of the complexity of God's sovereign governance of history and the outworking
of His redemptive purposes. Unfortunately, the idea of the last
days is greatly abused by many.

In a popular work the writer comments about those of us
living among the "generation" (Matt. 24:34) of World War I:
"There is no question that we are living in the last days. . . .
The fact that we are the generation that will be on the earth
when our Lord comes certainly should not depress us."[45]

The average Christian believes his is the very last times, that
he is living in the shadow of the Second Coming. Consider
some representative statements pointing in alarm to the imminence of the end in the "last days": (1) The Antichrist "is now
close at hand." (2) "The world is failing, passing away, and it
witnesses to its ruin, not now by the age, but by the end of
things." Because of this the Christian should know (3) that "still
more terrible things are imminent." Indeed, (4) "Already the
heavenly fire is giving birth, already the approach of divine
punishment is manifest, already the doom of coming disaster is
heralded." (5) Because of world circumstances the plea is:
"Consider, I beg you, whether the age can bear this for long?"
(6) "All creation now waits in suspense for his arrival. . . . The
world, which must be transformed anew, is already pregnant
with the end that is to come on the final day." How often have
we heard such cries of the end? Are not these the concerns of
so many of the current crop of prophetic studies so wildly
popular in our time?

I should confess to the reader, though, that I have not been
entirely up front. All of the statements in the immediately preceding paragraph were made, not by contemporary prophetic

---

45. Tim LaHaye, *The Beginning of the End* (Wheaton, IL: Tyndale, 1972), pp.
171-172. See also Charles H. Dyer, *The Rise of Babylon: Sign of the End Times* (Wheaton, IL: Tyndale, 1991). The latter book has to do with Saddam Hussein in contemporary Iraq.

writers, but by Christians living well over a thousand years ago. The following is a list of the sources: Number (1) is from Tertullian (160-220), *De Fuga* 12. Numbers (2) and (3) are from Cyprian (A.D. 195-258), *De Mort* 25. Number (4) is from Firmicus Maternus (*ca.* A.D. 346), *De Errore Profanarum Religionum* 25:3. Number (5) is from Evodius of Uzala (*ca.* A.D. 412). Number (6) is from Paulinus of Nola (A.D. 353-431).[46] Too many have misunderstood the eschatology of Scripture and the function of the "last days" in eschatology — and that for untold hundreds of years.

Properly understood the idea of the *last days* is focused on the most important episode of history: *the life of Jesus Christ lived out in fulfillment of divine prophecy and of redemptive history. Christ is the focal point of all Scripture.* He is anticipated in the Old Testament revelation and realized in the New: "You search the Scriptures, for in them you think you have eternal life; and these are they which testify of Me" (John 5:39).[47] As such He stands as history's dividing line – hence the historical appropriateness and theological significance of dividing history between B.C. and A.D.[48]

There are many prophetic references looking forward to the "Messianic age of consummation" introduced by Christ.[49] This era is frequently deemed "the last days" or "the latter days."[50] "The expression then properly denoted *the future times* in general; but, as the coming of the Messiah was to the eye of a Jew the

---

46. For references, see: Brian E. Daley, *The Hope of the Early Church: A Handbook of Patristic Eschatology* (Cambridge: University Press, 1991).

47. Luke 24:25-27; John 1:45; 5:39, 46; Acts 3:24; 10:43; 2 Cor. 1:20; Rev. 19:10.

48. Oscar Cullmann, *Christ and Time: The Primitive Christian Conception of Time and History*, trans. by Floyd V. Filson (3rd ed.; Philadelphia: Westminster, 1964), pp. 18-19.

49. C. F. Keil and Franz Delitzsch, *The Pentateuch*, in *Commentary on the Old Testament* (Grand Rapids: Eerdmans, [n.d.] 1975), 1:387.

50. Gen. 49:1, 10; Num. 24:14; Deut. 4:30; 31:29; Isa. 2:2; Jer. 23:20; 30:24; 48:47; 49:39; Dan. 2:28; Hos. 3:4; Mic. 4:1.

most important event in the coming ages, the great, glorious, and crowning scene in all that vast futurity, the phrase came to be regarded as properly expressive of that. . . . It was a phrase in contrast with the days of the patriarchs, the kings, the prophets, etc. The *last days*, or the closing period of the world, were the days of the Messiah."[51] His coming was "nothing less than the beginning of the great *eschaton* of history."[52]

It is when Christ came that "the fullness of times" was realized: "The phrase *pleroma tou chronou*, Gal. iv. 4, implies an orderly unrolling of the preceding stages of world-history towards a fixed end."[53] Hence, the preparatory preaching at the beginning of His ministry: "[T]he time is fulfilled, the kingdom of God is at hand" (Mark 1:15; Matt. 4:17). Prior to this, the Old Testament era was typological and anticipatory. The Old Testament era served as the "former days" (Mal. 3:4)[54] that gave way to the "last days," the times initiated by Christ's coming: "God, who at various times and in different ways spoke in time past to the fathers by the prophets has in these *last days* spoken to us by His Son, whom He has appointed heir of all things" (Heb. 1:1-2).

Thus, we find frequent references to the presence of the last days during the New Testament time. The last days are initiated by the appearance of the Son (Heb. 1:2; 1 Pet. 1:20) to effect redemption (Heb. 9:26) and by His pouring out of the Spirit (Acts 2:16, 17, 24; cf. Isa. 32:15; Zech. 12:10). The "ends of the ages" comes during the apostolic era (1 Cor. 10:11). These will run until "the last day," when the resurrection/judgment occurs to end history (John 6:39; 11:24; 12:48). But before the final

---

51. Albert Barnes, *Barnes' Notes on the New Testament*, 1 vol. edition (Grand Rapids: Kregal, [n.d.] 1962), p. 381.

52. Herman Ridderbos, *The Coming of the Kingdom* (Philadelphia: Presbyterian & Reformed, 1962), p. 36.

53. Geerhardus Vos, *The Pauline Eschatology* (Phillipsburg, NJ: Presbyterian & Reformed, [1930] 1991), p. 83.

54. See: Jer. 46:26; Lam. 1:7; Amos 9:11; Mic. 7:14, 20.

end point is reached, perilous times will punctuate the era of the end (2 Tim. 3:1) and mockers will arise (2 Pet. 3:3).

The last days of Old Testament prophecy anticipated the establishment of Mount Zion/Jerusalem as the enduring spiritual and cultural influence through the era.[55] This came in the first century with the establishment of the New Covenant phase of the Church, the focal point of the kingdom of Christ (cf. Joel 2 with Acts 2:16ff; Heb. 12:18-27).

Because the last days have been with us since the first-century coming of Christ,[56] there are no days to follow. There is no millennium that will introduce another grand redemptive era in man's history (see discussion of "Millennium" below). With the coming of Christ, earth history reached "epochal finality."[57] The idea of the appearance of Christ as the "Last Adam" (1 Cor. 15:45) is indicative that there is no different historical age to follow. The finality has come, though it has undergone continuous development since its arrival in the ministry of Christ.[58]

It is primarily in the dispensational literature of the millennial discussion that reference to the "last days" generates erroneous conclusions. Dispensationalists point to contemporary international social decline as indicative of the onset of the "last days": "The key that would unlock the prophetic book would be the current events that would begin to fit into the predicted pattern."[59] "The conflicts that we see in our world today are

---

55. Isa. 2:2; 24:23; 37:32; Joel 2:32; Oba. 1:17, 21; Mic. 4:7.

56. The last day resurrection has yet to occur (Matt. 13:39-40, 49). The Great Commission is still in effect (Matt. 28:20).

57. Vos, *Pauline Eschatology*, p. 28.

58. Contrary to Richard B. Gaffin, "Theonomy and Eschatology: Reflections of Postmillennialism," *Theonomy: A Reformed Critique*, William S. Barker and W. Robert Godfrey, eds. (Grand Rapids: Zondervan, 1990), ch. 9. See my response to Gaffin: "Whose Victory in History?" *Theonomy: An Informed Response*, Gary North, ed. (Tyler, TX: Institute for Christian Economics, 1991), ch. 8.

59. Hal Lindsey, *The Late Great Planet Earth* (Grand Rapids: Zondervan, 1970), p. 181. Pentecost, *Things to Come*, pp. 154ff.

symptoms of the day in which we live. They may be symptoms of the last days. . . ."[60] Such observations overlook the biblical function of the "last days" in regard to the grand sweep of redemptive history. The "last days" of postmillennialism comprise the great era of redemptive history that gradually will issue forth in historical victory for the Church of Jesus Christ; the "last days" of dispensationalism introduce the collapsing of culture as the Great Tribulation looms (after which will follow the discontinuous personal reign of Christ on earth).

Imminence

One of the remarkable features of prophetic interest is the Christian market's conviction that we are living in the shadow of the Second Coming.[61] In conjunction with a radical misunderstanding of the last days is often found the doctrine of the *imminent return of Christ,* among dispensationalists, premillennialists, and amillennialists.[62]

The doctrine of imminency is explained by John Walvoord: "The hope of the return of Christ to take the saints to heaven is presented in John 14 as an imminent hope. There is no teaching of any intervening event. The prospect of being taken to heaven at the coming of Christ is not qualified by description of any signs or prerequisite events."[63]

Strangely, this is held quite inconsistently among dispensationalists, who are also convinced that the entirety of the Church Age up into the 1900s is outlined in the Letters to the

---

60. John F. Walvoord, "Why Are the Nations in Turmoil?" *Prophecy and the Seventies,* pp. 211-212.

61. Timothy P. Weber, *Living in the Shadow of the Second Coming: American Premillennialism, 1875-1925* (New York: Oxford University Press, 1979).

62. Even amillennialists can sound like dispensationalists when they cry the alarm: "The year 1990 and the decade it initiates will bring that tribulation ever closer." Dale Kuiper, "The Illusory Hope of the Rapture," *Standard Bearer* 66:7 (Jan. 1, 1990) 155.

63. Walvoord, *The Rapture Question,* pp. 78-79.

Seven Churches in Revelation 2 and 3.[64] How could the return of Christ have been imminent *before* the 1900s, if the 1900s are foreshadowed in Revelation 2-3? Often dispensationalists try to distinguish between the *imminence* of Christ's return and its being *soon*. This is an attempt to protect them against charges of date-setting. The attempt never succeeds to protect from the charge, however, because it is inconsistently held. In a letter to me dated June 1, 1994, from Thomas D. Ice, Executive Director of the Pre-Trib Research Center, Ice writes: "We distinguish between imminent and soon in the sense that soon would require a near coming, while imminent would allow, but not require a soon coming." Bundled in that very letter was his first newsletter entitled: "The Pre-Trib Research Center: A New Beginning."[65] The first sentence of the newsletter (once past the headings) was: "Our purpose is to awaken in the Body of Christ a new awareness of the soon coming of Jesus." The system giveth and taketh away.

An irony is that due to this dispensational doctrine of perpetual imminence, dispensationalists should be the last people to seek signs of the approaching end. Such a quest undermines their most distinctive doctrine: the ever-imminent, sign-less, secret rapture. Yet, date-setting has long been a problem associated with premillennialism, especially dispensationalism.[66] The

---

64. John F. Walvoord, *The Revelation of Jesus Christ* (Chicago: Moody Press, 1966), p. 52; Pentecost, *Things to Come*, p. 149; Charles C. Ryrie, *Revelation* (Chicago: Moody Press, 1968), pp. 24ff; James L. Boyer, "Are the Seven Letters of Revelation 2-3 Prophetic?" *Grace Theological Journal* 6:2 (Fall 1985) 267-273; Hal Lindsey, *There's a New World Coming* (Santa Ana, CA: Vision House, 1973), pp. 38ff; *The Scofield Reference Bible* (New York: Oxford University Press, [1909] 1945), pp. 1331-2; *The New Scofield Reference Bible* (New York: Oxford University Press, 1967), p. 1353.

65. Dr. Tim LaHaye, "The Pre-Trib Research Center: A New Beginning," in *Pre-Trib Perspectives*, 1:1 (May, 1994): 1.

66. See the classic historical study on the problem: Dwight L. Wilson, *Armageddon Now! The Premillenarian Response to Russia and Israel Since 1917* (Tyler, TX: Institute for Christian Economics, [1977] 1991). For an exegetical study of the error, see: Gary DeMar, *Last Days Madness: The Folly of Trying to Predict When Christ Will Return* (Brentwood, TN: Wolgemuth & Hyatt, 1991). The problem is indicated in the following

last twenty years have been particularly rife with cries of the approaching end. Alden Gannet (1971): "While many of God's people through the centuries have looked for Christ's imminent return, it is only in our generation that the events of Ezekiel 37 are *beginning* to come to pass." Charles Ryrie (1976): "[T]ake a good look again at current events. . . . How do you account for these unusual events converging in our present day? Jesus said: 'Even so, when you see all these things, you know that it is near, right at the door' (Matthew 24:33 NIV)." Herman Hoyt (1977): "The movement of events in our day suggests that the establishment of the kingdom is not far away."[67] Hal Lindsey (1980): "The decade of the 1980's could very well be the last decade of history as we know it." Dave Hunt (1983): "This is strong evidence indeed that the Antichrist could appear very soon – which means that the rapture may be imminent." In 1988 Edgar C. Whisenant created an uproar among expectant dispensationalists, when he published his *88 Reasons Why the Rapture Could Be in 1988*. Richard Ruhling (1989): "Dr. Ruhling says the 50th jubilee in 1994 correlates with Usher's Chronology that our world will be 6,000 years old in 1996. . . . The

---

popular dispensational titles: Hal Lindsey, *Planet Earth – 2000: Will Mankind Survive?* (Palos Verdes, Calif.: Western Front, 1994). Lester Sumrall, *I Predict 2000* (South Bend: LeSea, 1987). David Allen Lewis, *Prophecy 2000: Rushing to Armageddon* (Green Forest, Ark.: Green Leaf, 1990). Steve Terrell, *The 90's: Decade of the Apocalypse* (S. Plainfield, N.J.: Bridge, 1992). Dave Hunt, *How Close Are We?: Compelling Evidence for the Soon Return of Christ* (Eugene, Ore.: Harvest, 1993). Billy Graham, *Storm Warning* (Dallas: Word, 1992). Charles C. Ryrie, *The Final Countdown* (Wheaton, Ill.: Victor, rep. 1991). Grant R. Jeffries, *Armageddon: Appointment with Destiny* (Toronto: Frontier Research, 1988). James McKeever, *The Rapture Book: Victory in the End Times* (Medford, Ore.: Omega, 1987). Don McAlvanny, *et al.*, *Earth's Final Days* (Green Forest, Ariz.: New Leaf, 1994). Texe Marrs, *et al.*, *Storming Toward Armageddon: Essays in Apocalypse* (Green Forest, Ariz.: New Leaf, 1992). Roberts Liardon, *Final Approach: The Opportunity and Adventure of End-Times Living* (Orlando: Creation House, 1993). David Webber and Noah Hutchins, *Is This the Last Century?* (Nashville: Thomas Nelson, 1979).

67. It is ironical that his niece, a postmillennialist, was one of the proofreaders of my manuscript.

seventh millennium" will begin shortly thereafter.[68] Grant Jeffrey suggests that "the year A.D. 2000 is a probable termination date for the 'last days.' "[69]

In 1990-91 needless American fears over the 30-day Gulf War – Iraq's great tribulation – fueled the flames of date-setting, much like in World War I.[70] Lindsey writes: "At the time of this writing, virtually the entire world may be plunged into a war in which this city [Babylon] may emerge with a role and destiny that few have any inkling of." Later he sums up: "This is the most exciting time to be alive in all of human history. We are about to witness the climax of God's dealing with man."[71] Even noted dispensational theologians are becoming involved in date-setting. Ironically, in the summer of 1990, as the Gulf's

---

68. Dave Hunt, *Peace Prosperity and the Coming Holocaust* (Eugene, OR: Harvest House, 1983), pp. 255-256; Hal Lindsey, *The 1980's: Countdown to Armageddon* (New York: Bantam, 1980), p. 8; Herman A. Hoyt, "Dispensational Premillennialism," *The Meaning of the Millennium: Four Views*, Robert G. Clouse, ed. (Downer's Grove, IL: InterVarsity Press, 1977), p. 63; Charles C. Ryrie, *The Living End* (Old Tappan, NJ: Revell, 1976), pp. 128-129; Alden A. Gannett, "Dry Bones Coming Alive," *Prophecy and the Seventies*, pp. 178-179; Edgar C. Whisenant, *88 Reasons Why the Rapture Could Be in 1988* (Nashville: World Bible Society, 1988); Review of Richard Ruhling, M.D., *Sword Over America*, in *Chattanooga News – Free Press* (Oct. 21, 1989).

69. Grant R. Jeffrey, *Armageddon: Appointment with Destiny* (Toronto: Frontier Research, 1989). Walvoord, at age eighty, "expects the Rapture to occur in his own lifetime." Kenneth L. Woodward, "The Final Days Are Here Again," *Newsweek* (March 18, 1991) 55.

70. Arthur Pink wrote: "Brethren, the end of the Age is upon us. All over the world, reflecting minds are discerning the fact that we are on the very eve of another of those far-reaching crises which make the history of our race. . . . Those who look out on present conditions are forced to conclude that the consummation of the dispensation is at hand. . . . The sands in the hour glass of this Day of Salvation have almost run out. The signs of the Times demonstrate it. . . . [T]he Signs are so plain they cannot be mis-read, though the foolish may close their eyes and refuse to examine them." Arthur W. Pink, *The Redeemer's Return* (Ashland, KY: Calvary Baptist Church, [1918] n.d.), pp. 318-19. As the Foreword to the reprint of this book indicates, he later renounced this view.

71. Hal Lindsey, "The Rise of Babylon and the Persian Gulf Crisis: A Special Report" (Palos Verdes, CA: Hal Lindsey Ministries, 1991), pp. 2, 51. See also: Betty Lynn, "The Gulf War and the Coming Fall of Babylon," *Christian World Report* 3:2 (Feb. 1991) 1.

war clouds loomed, Walvoord's book review appeared in which he wrote disparagingly of my insistence that dispensationalists are date-setters: "So premillennialism and dispensationalism have been derided as a date-setting system of doctrine, even though very few of its adherents indulge in this procedure."[72] By the time this review was published, Walvoord's clock of prophecy was ticking audibly in his ears.[73]

The New Testament teaches, however, that the Lord's glorious, bodily return will be in the *distant* and *unknowable* future. It has not been *imminent* and will not be *datable*. Theologically "distinctive to [postmillennialism] is the *denial* of the imminent physical return" of Christ.[74]

His return has not been imminent since the Ascension. Jesus clearly taught: "While the bridegroom was *delayed*, they all slumbered and slept" (Matt. 25:5). "For the kingdom of heaven is like a man traveling to a *far* country, who called his own servants and delivered his goods to them. . . . After a *long* time the lord of those servants came and settled accounts with them" (Matt. 25:14, 19). There is no expectation here of an *any-moment* return – there is quite the opposite.

---

72. John F. Walvoord, "Review of *House Divided*," *Bibliotheca Sacra* 147:587 (July/Sept. 1990) 372. Even as I write these words, on this very day, I have received in the mail a leaflet sent to me on "Christ's Second Coming." The author, Thomas W. Staggs of Wichita, Kansas, announces: "Russia attempts to invade Israel. *Ezk. 38-39.*" Beside this statement the author wrote: "Soon. Watchman let your people know." On the top of the leaflet, he wrote: "The Truth." The envelope is postmarked: December 3, 1991.

73. Barbara Reynolds, "Prophecy clock is ticking in Mideast" (interview with John F. Walvoord), *U. S. A. Today*, Inquiry section, January 19, 1991. A spate of dispensational prophetic best-sellers were generated by the Gulf War. See: Joe Maxwell, "Prophecy Books Become Big Sellers," *Christianity Today*, 34:3 (March 11, 1991) 60. One of them was Walvoord's hastily revised 1974 book, *Armageddon, Oil and the Middle East Crisis: What the Bible says about the future of the Middle East and the end of Western Civilization* (Grand Rapids: Zondervan, 1990). Within months, it had sold a million and a half copies. *Time* (Feb. 11, 1991).

74. Greg L. Bahnsen, "The *Prima Facie* Acceptability of Postmillennialism," *Journal of Christian Reconstruction* 3:2 (Winter 1976) 60. Cf. Allis, *Prophecy and the Church*, pp. 173-174.

HE SHALL HAVE DOMINION

Just before His ascension Christ had to deal with the problem of imminence among His often-confused disciples: "They asked Him, saying, 'Lord, will You at *this time* restore the kingdom to Israel?' And He said to them, 'It is not for you to know *times* [*chronos*] or seasons which the Father has put in His own authority" (Acts 1:7). The *chronos* time-reference in Christ's answer indicates a long period of time of uncertain duration. In fact, it is found in the plural, which indicates "a rather long period of time composed of several shorter ones."[75] According to Urwick, "the only errors mentioned in the New Testament respecting the time of our Lord's coming, all consist in dating it too early."[76] This is indicated in the passages already cited, as well as in the famous passages: 2 Thessalonians 2:1-3 and 2 Peter 3:3-4.

Matthew 28:20 says that the Great Commission will stretch through "all the days" (literal translation of the Greek). This indicates a great many days before the end. The parables of the mustard seed and leaven set forth gradualistic growth and development for the kingdom until it dominates the world's landscape and penetrates all of the world's cultures. This surely is suggestive of the passage of a long period of time. As I showed in Chapter 13, 2 Peter 3 allows a long delay in His coming as evidence of the "longsuffering" of God. This fits well with postmillennial eschatology, for it allows time for the advancement and victory of Christ's kingdom in the world and encourages a future-orientation to the labors of God's people.

Neither will His return be datable. Rather than giving specific signs that allow even generalized date-setting, the Scripture forthrightly states: "of that day and hour no one knows, no, not even the angels of heaven, but My Father only" (Matt. 24:36). This is why there is a danger that some who claim to be His

---

75. William F. Arndt and F. W. Gingrich, *A Greek-English Lexicon of the New Testament* (Chicago: University of Chicago Press, 1957), p. 896.

76. Quoted in David Brown, *Christ's Second Coming: Will It Be Premillennial?* (Edmonton, Alberta: Still Waters Revival, [1882] 1990), p. 41n.

people will be caught unawares: they will let down the guard because the date is unknowable (Matt. 25:1ff). Although prophecy portrays a long era in history in which Christianity will reign supreme, it never gives information that allows the determination of the temporal end of His kingdom. The glorious rule of Christ through his covenant people will be for a long time before He returns in judgment, but for how long, no man knows.

The Millennium

As indicated in Chapter 3 a time frame that has played a far greater role in the eschatological debate than it warranted is the millennium, or the thousand years, in Revelation 20:1-6. It is almost incredible that the various eschatological schools have been denominated "millennial" schools on the basis of this passage. Amillennialist William Cox writes: "Most millennial thinking begins with Revelation 20, since this is the only place in the entire Bible where the thousand years is mentioned. We feel that Revelation 20 ought to be our last stop, not our first."[77] Indeed, "this is one of the most hotly debated issues in the whole field of eschatology."[78]

The role of Revelation 20 in the debate, which is absolutely essential to premillennialism, is surprising for at least two major reasons. First, the *only* place in all of Scripture that associates "one thousand years" with the reign of Christ is in the first six verses of this one chapter. Against such a complaint, premillennialist Ladd comments: "the fact that the New Testament in only *one* place teaches an interim kingdom, between this age and the Age to Come is no reason for rejecting it."[79] Yet the

---

77. William E. Cox, *Biblical Studies in Final Things* (Nutley, NJ: Presbyterian & Reformed, 1966), p. 174.

78. Bruce Milne, *Know the Truth: A Handbook of Christian Belief* (Downer's Grove, IL: InterVarsity Press, 1982), p. 262.

79. Ladd, "A Historic Premillennial Response," *Meaning of the Millennium*, p. 190.

postmillennial complaint is well-justified. If a literal earthly millennium is so prominent in Scripture and such an important era in redemptive history (as premillennialists and dispensationalists argue), then why should we not expect that a reference to the thousand years should appear in more than *one* passage?

This is even more difficult to conceive of in light of our second observation: the mention of the thousand-year reign occurs in the most figurative and difficult book in all of Scripture. If it is a literal time frame, why is it that it is only mentioned in this highly symbolic book? It is a bit odd, too, that this time frame is so perfectly rounded and exact, which seems more compatible with a figurative view. Warfield is surely correct when he comments: "we must not permit ourselves to forget that there is a sense in which it is proper to permit our understanding of so obscure a portion of Scripture to be affected by the clearer teaching of its more didactic parts. . . . [T]he order of investigation should be from the clearer to the more obscure." But this hermeneutical principle has not often been honored. "Nothing, indeed, seems to have been more common in all ages of the Church than to frame an eschatological scheme from this passage, imperfectly understood, and then to impose this scheme on the rest of Scripture *vi et armis*."[80]

Clouse well notes: "These categories [amillennial, premillennial, postmillennial], although helpful and widely accepted, are in certain respects unfortunate as the distinctions involve a great deal more than the time of Christ's return."[81] Nevertheless, postmillennialist Boettner is scolded by *amillennialist* Hoekema for not giving exposition to Revelation 20:1-6 in his presentation of the postmillennial conception of the kingdom[82]

80. B. B. Warfield, "The Millennium and the Apocalypse," *Princeton Theological Review*, 2 (Oct. 1904) 599.

81. Clouse, "Introduction," *Meaning of the Millennium*, p. 7.

82. Anthony Hoekema, "An Amillennial Response," *ibid.*, p. 150.

The proper understanding of the thousand-year time frame in Revelation 20 is that it represents a long and glorious era and is not limited to a literal 365,000 days. The figure represents *a perfect cube of ten*, which is the number of quantitative perfection.[83] The thousand here is no more literal than that which affirms God's ownership of the cattle on a thousand hills (Psa. 50:10), or promises Israel will be a thousand times more numerous (Deut. 1:11), or measures God's love to a thousand generations (Deut. 7:9), or expresses the desire for a thousand years in God's courts (Psa. 84:10), or compares a thousand years of our time to one of God's days (Psa. 90:4).

The millennial designation, then, is John's visionary portrayal of the kingdom of Christ, which was established at Christ's first coming. Revelation 20:1 clearly establishes the passage as a *vision*; John opens with: "and I saw" (Rev. 20:1a). This is strongly suggestive of its symbolic import and is evidence against a strictly literal interpretation of the one thousand years. In addition, the first event seen in the vision is the binding of the angel Satan with a chain, which surely is not literal (especially since His binding is shown to be spiritual elsewhere: Matt. 12:29[84]). Revelation 20:4-6 speaks of the saints living and reigning with Christ, which is elsewhere presented as a spiritual reality in the present experience of God's people (1 Cor. 3:21-22; Eph. 1:3; 2:6; Col. 3:1-2). This reigning of the saints with Christ on thrones pictures the kingdom of Christ,

---

83. Perhaps the figure's symbolic importance is partially due to the fact that it is a period of time beyond man's reach. The oldest living man ever, Methusaleh, fell short of this perfect number. He lived only to be 969 years old (Gen. 5:27). I take the historical account of Methusaleh to be literal. When the names and ages of the genealogies in Genesis 5 and 10 are set forth, it is obvious that long life spans were consistent before the Flood of Noah's day, but dropped off quickly thereafter.

84. The binding of Satan during Christ's earthly ministry and until His Second Advent was known in ancient times. See: *Acts of Pilate* 22:2.

which is already established (cf. Chapter 11).[85] His kingdom, then, is defined chronologically as *a complete and perfect time*.

Besides, elsewhere the Second Coming of Christ is associated with "the end" (1 Cor. 15:23-24) and brings in "the last day": *resurrection* (John 6:39, 40, 44, 54). "Therefore, in view of the total absence of supporting evidence from the New Testament, it is exceedingly hazardous to claim that a thousand years intervene between Christ's coming and the end of the world on the grounds that Revelation 20 teaches a millennium."[86]

The millennial era has already turned out to be almost 2,000 years; it may continue another 10,000 or more for all we know. It is the perfect time of Christ's rule in His kingdom (Rev. 1:5) – a time that shall eventually result in the subduing of all nations.[87]

Conclusion

Christianity is an historical faith: it is intimately intertwined with objective reality. Our God not only originated history (creation) but governs it (providence), speaks in it (revelation), and involves Himself in it (incarnation). Consequently, the issues of time are relevant to Christianity as it operates in the temporal realm.

There are a number of prophetically significant time frames established in Scripture. I have only dealt with a few of the more prominent ones. God is governing history on the basis of His redemptive plan. The time frames dealt with above demonstrate the temporal impact of God's comprehensively redemp-

85. Older postmillennialists and some more recent ones hold that the millennium is a distinct final stage in the advance of Christ's kingdom. See: David Brown (1800s) and Steve Schlissel (1990), *Hal Lindsey and the Restoration of the Jews* (Edmonton, ALB: Still Waters Revival, 1990).

86. Iain Murray, *The Puritan Hope: Revival and the Interpretation of Prophecy* (Edinburgh: Banner of Truth, 1971), pp. xvii-xviii.

87. For more information see my contribution to H. Marvin Pate, ed., *Four Views of Revelation* (Grand Rapids: Zondervan, 1997).

tive action in history.

15

FEATURES

Now as He sat on the Mount of Olives, the disciples came to Him privately, saying, "Tell us, when will these things be? And what will be the sign of Your coming, and of the end of the age?" (Matthew 24:3)

In this chapter I will consider three of the familiar features of the eschatological debate which I have not considered in detail so far: the Great Tribulation, the rebuilding of the Temple, and the New Creation.

It is odd that the biggest-selling prophetic studies published today deal with the horrible Great Tribulation.[1] Despite the prominence of the glorious millennium in the eschatological debate, it seems that the Christian public has more interest in the tribulational woes than in the millennial glory. What is worse, the Great Tribulation is greatly misinterpreted – even being placed at the wrong end of history.

Space does not permit a thorough analysis of the Great Tribulation.[2] A truly preteristic approach to the Great Tribulation is denied by all premillennialists and by many amillennial-

---

1. Hal Lindsey's *The Late Great Planet Earth* (Grand Rapids: Zondervan, 1970) has sold over 35 million copies in fifty-four languages. Recent books on the Gulf War and the supposed looming Great Tribulation have sold millions.

2. For more detail, see: Thomas D. Ice and Kenneth L. Gentry, Jr., *The Great Tribulation: Past or Future?* (Grand Rapids: Kregal, 1997).

ists.[3] In the next few pages I will sketch the general argument for a preterist understanding of the Great Tribulation. My focus will be on its presentation in Matthew 24 (which was briefly mentioned in Chapter 8).

Matthew 24: Interpretations

Matthew 24 is held by some to be contra-indicative to post-millennialism: "Postmillenarians have a different problem in that they want to support their view that the world is going to get better and better as the Gospel gradually triumphs; but this passage of Scripture does not support this and, in fact, predicts increasing evil with the climax at the Second Coming."[4] Post-millennialism "stands in sharp contrast with that whole body of biblical data which describes the days prior to the coming of Christ as days in which lawlessness abounds (Matthew 24:12)" and "Matthew 24 itself is strong proof of all this."[5]

Due to the prominence afforded the Great Tribulation in popular study, I have allotted more space to it than to the other features to be considered. It is the key to the preterist interpretation. If the Great Tribulation refers to the fall of Jerusalem in A.D. 70, all "futurist" interpretations collapse. So does the pessimism created by an eschatology of predestined defeat.

---

3. Amillennialists Anthony Hoekema (*The Bible and the Future* [Grand Rapids: Eerdmans, 1979], pp. 112-117, 178) and Herman Ridderbos (*The Coming of the Kingdom* [Philadelphia: Presbyterian & Reformed, 1962], pp. 498ff) deny the preterist view. Amillennialists Jay Adams (*The Time Is at Hand* [n.p.: Presbyterian & Reformed, 1966], Appendix B) and George Murray (*Millennial Studies: A Search for Truth* [Grand Rapids: Baker, 1948], pp. 110ff) affirm it.

4. John F. Walvoord, *Prophecy Knowledge Handbook* (Wheaton, IL: Victor, 1990), p. 381.

5. Herman Hanko, "The Illusory Hope of Postmillennialism," *Standard Bearer* 66:7 (Jan. 1, 1990) 158. Hanko, "An Exegetical Refutation of Postmillennialism" (unpublished conference paper: South Holland, IL: South Holland Protestant Reformed Church, 1978), p. 27.

The Key Text

As I noted in Chapter 8 the key to understanding the Great Tribulation in Matthew 24 is the *time statement* in verse 34: "Assuredly, I say to you, this generation will by no means pass away till all these things are fulfilled." This is *the* statement that must be reckoned with by the futurist or historicist viewpoints. Some point to Matthew 24:34 and such verses as "difficult texts" requiring that we "look at them carefully."[6] The difficulty is generally held to be due to two problems. (1) The necessity of reconciling the nearness statement of verse 34 with verse 36, which reads: "But of that day and hour no one knows, no, not even the angels of heaven, but My Father only." (2) How to understand the reference to "*all* these things," when many of these seem to be of worldwide effect and/or are consummational and incapable of application to the first century (e.g., Matt. 24:14, 21, 27, 29-30).

Amillennialist theologian Anthony Hoekema holds that "this generation" is used in a qualitative sense, as of an "evil" (Matt. 12:45), "adulterous" (Mark 8:38), or "perverse" (Matt. 17:17) generation. "By 'this generation,' then, Jesus means the rebellious, apostate, unbelieving Jewish people, as they have revealed themselves in the past, are revealing themselves in the present, and will continue to reveal themselves in the future."[7]

Ridderbos' amillennial view is similar to Hoekema's, but is somewhat broader. With Hoekema, he sees in "all these things" *a compaction of two events:* the A.D. 70 destruction of the Temple *and* the consummative Return of Christ.[8] Consequently, "all

---

6. Hoekema, *Bible and the Future*, p. 113.

7. *Ibid.* F. Büchsel, "*genea*," *Theological Dictionary of the New Testament*, Gerhard Kittel, ed., 10 vols. (Grand Rapids: Eerdmans, 1964), 1:663. For a literary critical perspective by a dispensationalist arguing the same, see: Neil Nelson, Jr., " 'This Generation' in Matt 24:34: A Literary Critical Perspective," *The Journal of the Evangelical Theological Society*, 38:3 (September 1995): 369-386.

8. Ridderbos, *Coming of the Kingdom*, p. 502. Hoekema, *Bible and the Future*, p. 178.

these things" are to occur upon "this generation," which in his understanding refers not just to the Jewish race, but to all "people of this particular disposition and frame of mind who are averse to Jesus and his words." Matthew 24:34, then, serves as "a pronouncement upon the certainty of the fulfillment, without any further limitation of the time."[9]

Some dispensationalists hold that "this generation" means "this race," i.e., *generic Israel*. This was the view of Pentecost in the 1950s: "[T]he word generation is to be taken in its basic usage of 'race, kindred, family, stock, breed,' so that the Lord is here promising that the nation Israel shall be preserved until the consummation of her program at the second advent."[10] So, "this generation" = Israel throughout the ages. But. . . .

Other dispensationalists hold Pentecost's current view: "Since these signs will all occur in the seven years of Daniel's seventieth week, the generation that sees the beginning of these signs will 'not pass away until all these things happened' (v. 34), for they all will fall within a brief span of time. . . . [T]hese signs will be given to a generation that cannot begin until after the church has been translated."[11] So, "this generation" = Israel during the post-Rapture Great Tribulation. It would be helpful if the commentators, including Pentecost, would go into greater detail about why there was a need for this new interpretation.

The proper view is much simpler, as we shall see. I shall present arguments that undermine all of the previously men-

---

9. Ridderbos, *Coming of the Kingdom*, p. 502.

10. J. Dwight Pentecost, *Things to Come* (Grand Rapids: Zondervan, 1958), p. 281. Cf. L. S. Chafer, *Systematic Theology*, 8 vols. (Dallas, TX: Dallas Theological Seminary, 1948), 4:316. C. I. Scofield, *Scofield Reference Bible* (New York: Oxford University Press, [1909] 1945), p. 1034. E. Schuyler English, *Studies in the Gospel According to Matthew* (New York: Revell, 1935), p. 179. William Kelly, *Lectures on the Gospel of Matthew* (New York: Loizeaux Bros., 1911), pp. 451-453.

11. Pentecost, *Thy Kingdom Come* (Wheaton, IL: Victor, 1990), p. 256. See also: Warren W. Wiersbe, *The Bible Exposition Commentary* p. 89. H. Wayne House and Thomas D. Ice, *Dominion Theology: Blessing or Curse?* (Portland, OR: Multnomah, 1988), pp. 286-287. Walvoord, *Prophecy Knowledge Handbook*, pp. 391ff.

tioned views. First, however, I need to point out specific difficulties in the other interpretive suggestions.

Responses

Regarding Hoekema's view that "this generation" is a qualitative pronouncement, this does not crowd out the more obvious view that He speaks of His contemporary generation. In
fact, it harmonizes with it. The Jews of that very era are a rebellious generation. Theirs is a most heinous transgression ("*the*
transgression," Rom. 11:11-12, in the Greek): the crucifixion of
Christ the Lord (John 19:4-16[12]), an unrepeatably horrible act
(Matt. 21:33-45). It is *because* the Jews *of that era* reject the Son
of God that they are deemed by God an adulterous, perverse,
evil *generation*. God's judgment fell on them.

Ridderbos' view that Matthew 24:34 simply means these
events are certain to transpire upon people of that "frame of
mind" fares no better. We must note that if this speaks of both
the A.D. 70 event and an end time Great Tribulation (as he argues), then these events do *not* occur to all people "who are
averse to Jesus and his words." The negative sanctions fall only
upon those living when "all these things" occur, which in his
view *was* in A.D. 70 and *will be* at the Return of Christ.

Pentecost's 1958 view says that "this generation" means "the
race of Israel." Ridderbos correctly notes that such a view ends
up as a mere truism if "this generation" simply means "Israel as
a nation."[13] It would mean that Israel will not pass away until
all these things happen to Israel. But in the dispensational
view, Israel will never pass away. So the statement would be
irrelevant as a means of identifying any prophetic time context.

---

12. Matt. 20:18-19; 27:11-25; Mark 10:33; 15:1; Luke 18:32; 23:1-2; John 18:28-
31; 19:12, 15; Acts 2:22-23; 3:13-15a; 4:26-27; 5:30; 7:52; 1 Thess. 2:14-15.

13. H. N. Ridderbos, *Commentary on Matthew* (Grand Rapids: Zondervan, 1987),
p. 450.

What about Pentecost's 1990 view that "this generation" refers to a distantly future generation that will see the outbreak of "all these things"? The Lord was speaking to His present disciples who had just pointed out the stones of the historical Temple (Matt. 24:1). It was *that* Temple which was to be destroyed (v. 2). It was His statement regarding *that* Temple's coming destruction which gave rise to His entire discourse (v. 3). The signs were identified by Jesus as things that *they* would experience: "Let no one deceive *you*" (v. 4), "they will deliver *you* up to tribulation" (v. 9), "when *you* see the abomination" (v. 15), and "when *you* see all these things" (v. 33).

The Proper View

The proper view is that "this generation" means the contemporary hearers of Christ, *the very Jews of the era who reject Him*. This view is defensible from a number of angles. First, although the Greek *genea* ("generation") is commonly used in Matthew, it is only employed of a contemporary generation of people. Matthew 1:14 illustrates the *temporal generation* view: "So all the generations from Abraham to David are fourteen generations, from David until the captivity in Babylon are fourteen generations, and from the captivity in Babylon until the Christ are fourteen generations."[14] Here one generation follows upon another. A generation comes; then it goes.

Second, in the five other instances in Matthew where the word *genea* is coupled with the near demonstrative to read "this generation," it clearly refers to the generation *then living* (Matt. 11:16; 12:41, 42, 45; and 23:36). In Scripture, the idea of a "generation" of people involves roughly twenty-five to forty years (Num. 32:13; Psa. 95:10).

Third, the phrase "this generation" appears in the very context intimately related to and leading into Matthew 24 (cf.

---

14. See also: Matt. 11:16; 12:39-45; 16:4; 17:17; and 23:36.

23:36-38 with 24:1-2). In Matthew 23:36 "this generation" unquestionably speaks of Jesus' contemporaries, as even dispensationalists are forced to admit.[15] Here Jesus is condemning His contemporary adversaries, the scribes and Pharisees (23:2, 13-16, 23-29). He says that they will "fill up the measure of the guilt" of the generations preceding them (23:32). They will do this by persecuting Jesus' followers (23:34), so that "upon you [scribes and Pharisees] may fall the guilt of all the righteous blood shed" (23:35). He concludes: "Verily I say unto you, All these things shall come upon this generation." This employs the same crucial terms as Matthew 24:34.

A Survey of Matthew 24:1-36

Precursory signs. The approaching destruction of the Temple to be experienced by "this generation" is preceded by certain signs. Jesus did not want His disciples to become confused by these (24:4ff). The first few mentioned are but pre-indicators of the final judgment on the Temple (24:8). This point is significant because later He turns to instruct the disciples regarding His glorious Second Advent (24:36ff). He specifically says of "that"[16] distant event there will be no such signs (24:36-44).

He warns His disciples that false Christs will arise and mislead many (24:5). There are a number of examples of great pretenders who almost certainly made Messianic claims, such as Simon Magus (Acts 8:9, 10). Justin Martyr mentions him and others: "[A]fter Christ's ascension into heaven the devils put forward certain men who said that they themselves were gods" (*First Apology* 26). Josephus, who witnessed the fall of Jerusalem,

---

15. Louis A. Barbieri, Jr., "Matthew," *The Bible Knowledge Commentary: New Testament*, John F. Walvoord and Roy B. Zuck, eds. (Wheaton, IL: Victor, 1983), p. 75. John F. Walvoord, *The Nations, Israel, and the Church in Prophecy*, 3 vols. in 1 (Grand Rapids: Zondervan, 1988), 2:106. Edward E. Hindson, "Matthew," *Liberty Commentary on the New Testament*, Edward E. Hindson and Woodrow Michael Kroll, eds. (Lynchburg, VA: Liberty Commentary, 1978), p. 77.

16. A far demonstrative, in contrast to the near demonstrative "this" in v. 34.

mentions the "deceivers and impostors, who under the pretence of divine inspiration fostering revolutionary changes" (*Wars* 2:13:4) and "the Egyptian false prophet" (*Wars* 2:13:5; cf. Acts 21:38) who even operated at the Mount of Olives.

We read in the next verses of "wars and rumors of wars" (Matt. 24:6-7a). These serve as signs of the end of the Temple because of the dramatically successful *Pax Romana*. Origen (A.D. 185-254) speaks of the "abundance of peace that began at the birth of Christ" (Origen, *Romans* 1:3). Historians observe that "in the Roman Empire proper, this period of peace remained comparatively undisturbed *until the time of Nero*."[17] It was ruptured with the outbreak of the Jewish War and the Roman Civil Wars in the violent Year of Four Emperors (A.D. 68-69), which for Rome "was almost the end" (Tacitus, *Histories* 1:11).

In Matthew 24:7-11 many woes are prophesied. All of these woes are abundantly accounted for in the events of the era leading up to the crisis of A.D. 70: famines,[18] pestilences,[19] earthquakes,[20] persecution,[21] apostasy, and false prophets.[22]

The "world" witness. In verse 14 we read: "And this gospel of the kingdom will be preached in all the world as a witness to all the nations, and then the end will come." The word "world"

---

17. Bo Reicke, *The New Testament Era: The World of the Bible from 500 B.C. to A.D. 100* (Philadelphia: Fortress, 1968), p. 110.

18. Acts 11:28; Josephus, *Ant.* 20:2:5; *Wars* 5:10:2-5; Tacitus, *Annals* 12:43; Suetonius, *Life of Claudius* 18:2; Dio Cassius, *History* 60:11; Eusebius, *Chronicle*, Year of Abraham 2065; Orosius, *History* 7:6:17.

19. *Annals* 16:13; Suetonius, *Nero* 39.

20. *Wars* 4:4:5; Tacitus, *Annals* 2:47; 12:58 14:27; 15:22; Pliny, *Natural History* 2:86; Suetonius, *Nero* 48; *Galba* 18; Philostratus, *Life of Apollon* 4:11; Orosius 7:7; Seneca, *Epistles* 91.

21. Acts 4:3; 5:18-33; 6:12; 7:54-60; 8:1ff; 9:1-4, 13, 23; 11:19; 12:1-3; 13:45-50; 14:2-5, 19; 16:23; 17:5-13; 18:12; 20:3, 19; 21:11, 27; 22:30; 23:12, 20, 27, 30; 24:5-9; 25:2-15; 25:24; 26:21; 2 Cor. 11:24; 2 Thess. 2:14-15; Heb. 10:32-34; Rev. 2:9; 3:9. This was followed by the Neronic Persecution (A.D. 64-68) just preceding the Temple's destruction (A.D. 67-70): Tacitus, *Annals* 15:44.

22. Acts 13:6; 20:29; Rom. 16:17,18; 2 Cor. 11:13, 26; Gal. 2:4; 1 Tim. 4:1; 2 Pet. 2:1; 1 John 4:1; Josephus, *Wars* 6:5:2-3.

(*oikumene*) often stands for the Roman Empire (Luke 2:1; Acts 11:28; 24:15). The phrase "all the nations" is epexegetical, referring to those nations that are subsumed under the imperial authority of Rome. The world to which the "gospel of the kingdom was preached" is provided a witness: "the gospel which has come to you, as it has also in all the world. . . . [T]he gospel which you heard, which was preached to every creature under heaven" (Col 1:6, 23; cf. Acts 2:5; Rom. 1:8; 10:18).

The Abomination of Desolation. Jesus warns: "Therefore when you see the 'abomination of desolation,' spoken of by Daniel the prophet, standing in the holy place (whoever reads, let him understand)" (Matt. 24:15). This refers to the A.D. 70 event, as we may discern from several angles: (1) The Temple is then standing in the "holy city" (Jerusalem, Matt. 4:5; 27:53). (2) That Temple has just been pointed to by the disciples (Matt. 24:1), giving rise to this very discourse (Matt. 23:38-24:3). (3) Christ points to that particular Temple to speak of its destruction (Matt. 24:2). (4) The specific time frame demands an A.D. 70 reference for the "abomination" (Matt. 24:34).

The "abomination of desolation," so dreaded as to give rise to desperate flight from the area (Matt. 24:16-20), was to occur "in the holy place." Surely the Temple is involved here, but the reference is broader, speaking of both the city and the Temple. Two problems present themselves to the Temple-only view: (1) Luke 21:20 interprets the phrase as the surrounding of the city, which did indeed happen (Josephus, *Wars* 5:12:1). Jerusalem was considered a holy place, being the capital of the "holy land" (Zech. 2:12).[23] (2) The original Old Testament context mentions both "the city and the sanctuary" (Dan. 9:26).

The events leading up to the destruction of Jerusalem and the Temple by the Roman armies are summarily designated by

---

23. Jerusalem is a holy place: Neh. 11:1, 18; Isa. 48:2; 52:1; 66:20; Dan. 9:16, 24; Joel 3:17. For Jewish references to Israel as the "holy land," see: 2 Baruch 63:10; 4 Ezra 13:48; 2 Maccabees 1:7.

the Lord by citing Daniel's phrase, the "abomination of desolation." During the days leading up to Jerusalem's final destruction, revolution is stirred within the city which results in "the outer Temple [being] all of it overflowed with blood" (*Wars* 4:5:1; cf. 5:1:1-3; 5:13:6).

Ultimately, of course, Titus' victory is completed. Upon that victory the Romans burn "the holy house itself, and all the buildings lying round about it, brought their ensigns to the Temple, and set them over against its eastern gate; and there did they offer sacrifices to them" (*Wars* 6:6:1). It is particularly distressing to the Jew that the abominable Gentile (Acts 10:28; 11:2-3; cf. Eph. 2:14[24]) would ultimately enter into the Temple of God. The "abomination of desolation" involves the destruction of Jerusalem (beginning with its encircling) and culminates in this final abominable act.

The eagles and lightning. This very conclusion seems to be in Christ's mind, when Christ states: "For wherever the carcass is, there the *eagles* [*aetos*] will be gathered together" (Matt. 24:28 NKJV). The Roman ensigns set up by Titus in the holy of holies in the Temple were *eagles* (*Wars* 3:6:2). According to verse 27, the coming of the Roman armies under the direction of Christ (Matt. 22:7) is a death-dealing, destructive judgment coming on Israel "like lightning."[25]

Great tribulation. Matthew 24:21 is often brought forth to overthrow the broad-based argument for a preterist interpretation of Matthew 24:1-34. Dispensationalist Walvoord states that: "Interpreted literally, the tribulation clearly eclipses anything

---

24. "If a man went through the country of the gentiles in hilly or rocky country, he becomes unclean" (Oholoth 17:6). "The dwelling-places of gentiles are unclean" (Oholoth 17:7).

25. Lightning is a frequent symbol of destructive power: 2 Sam. 22:15; Job 36:32; Psa. 18:14; 78:48-49; 140:6; Ezek. 19:16; 20:18; 21:10; Zech. 9:14; Rev. 11:19; 16:18.

that the world has ever known by way of destruction."[26] Amillennialist Hoekema agrees.[27]

But against such comments I would argue: First, the *covenantal significance* of the loss of the Temple stands as the most dramatic redemptive-historical outcome of the Jewish War. Because of the carnage, Josephus laments the destruction of Jerusalem in words similar to our Lord's: "[T]he war which the Jews made with the Romans hath been the greatest of all those, not only that have been in our times, but, in a manner, of those that ever were heard of" (*Wars*, Preface, 1, 4; cf. 5:10-5).

Second, the events must be regarded as the *holy judgment* of God for the wicked crucifixion of His Son by the Jews.[28] This is clear in the Parable of the Vineyard (Matt. 21:37-41) and in Christ's lament (Luke 19:41-44).

Third, just a few verses after Matthew 24:21-22, the Lord mentions the Noahic Flood (vv. 38-39), which *actually did* destroy the *entire* world, except for one family. Even the futurists see their Great Tribulation as stopping far short of leaving only *one family* alive (dispensationalists leave one-third of the Jewish race alive at the end of the Great Tribulation[29]). The issue was therefore the magnitude of the covenantal transformation, not the magnitude of the death toll.

Fourth, Christ's language is *apocalyptic hyperbole*, well justified by the gravity of the situation. Such apocalyptic language was

---

26. Walvoord, *The Nations, Israel, and the Church in Prophecy*, 3:129. See also: David L. Turner, "Structure and Sequence of Matthew 24:1-41: Interaction with Evangelical Treatments," *Grace Theological Journal* 10:1 (Spring 1989) 13.

27. Hoekema, *Bible and the Future*, p. 178.

28. So emphasized in the New Testament. The Jews were responsible: Acts 2:22-23; 3:13-15a; 4:26-27; 5:30; 7:52; 1 Thess. 2:14-15. They demanded that the Romans crucify Him: Rev. 17; Matt. 20:18-19; 27:11-25; Mark 10:33; 15:1; Luke 18:32; 23:1-2; John 18:28-31; 19:12, 15.

29. For evidence of this see dispensational writings such as: Regald E. Showers, "Further Evaluation of Christian Reconstructionism," *Israel My Glory*, 49:4 (Aug./Sept., 1991), p. 19. John F. Walvoord, *The Revelation of Jesus Christ* (Chicago: Moody, 1966), p. 195.

stock-in-trade terminology in the Bible's prophetic writing. It was applied to the tenth plague on Egypt (Exo. 11:6) and the Babylonian captivity (Ezek. 5:9). Both of these were covenantal judgments in history: radical changes in legal and social life.

Astronomical signs. In Matthew 24:29-30 we read: "Immediately after the tribulation of those days the sun will be darkened, and the moon will not give its light; the stars will fall from heaven, and the powers of the heavens will be shaken. Then will appear the sign of the Son of Man in heaven, and then all the tribes of the earth will mourn, and they will see the Son of Man coming on the clouds of heaven with power and great glory." Futurists see these verses as "of particular importance" in demonstrating the error of preterism,[30] showing that "this approach to 24:29-31 cannot be sustained."[31]

The darkening of the sun and moon is common apocalyptic language for the collapse of nations, such as in Old Testament judgments on Babylon (Isa. 13:1, 10, 19), Idumea (Isa. 34:3-5), Israel (Jer. 4:14, 16, 23ff; Joel. 2:10-11), and Egypt (Ezek. 32:2, 7-8, 11-12).[32] This interpretation of the apocalyptic language of these passages is not exceptional. Even allegedly literalistic dispensationalists can write of Isaiah 13:10: "The statements in 13:10 about the heavenly bodies . . . no longer function may figuratively describe the total turnaround of the political structure of the Near East. The same would be true of *the heavens* trembling *and the earth* shaking (v. 13), figures of speech suggesting all-encompassing destruction."[33]

The final collapse of Jerusalem and the Temple will be the sign that the Son of Man, whom the Jews rejected and cruci-

---

30. Hoekema, *Bible and the Future*, p. 178.

31. Turner, "Structure and Sequence of Matthew 24:1-41," p. 19.

32. See: David Chilton, *Paradise Restored: A Biblical Theology of Dominion* (Ft. Worth, TX: Dominion Press, 1985), pp. 98-100.

33. John A. Martin, "Isaiah," *Bible Knowledge Commentary: Old Testament*, p. 1059. See also: comments at Isa. 34:2-4 (p. 1084); Jer. 4:23-28 (p. 1136); Joel 2:2a, 10-11 (pp. 1415-1417).

fied, is in heaven (Matt. 24:30).[34] The fulfillment of His judgment word demonstrates His heavenly position and power. This causes the Jewish tribes of the Land (*ge*) to mourn (*kopto*, cf. Luke 23:27-28). Through these events the Jews were to "see" the Son of Man in His judgment-coming in terrifying cloud-glory: clouds are symbols of divine majesty often entailing stormy destruction (Isa. 19:1; cf. Psa. 18:10-14; Lam. 2:1; Ezek. 30:3-5). The members of the Sanhedrim and others would experience such in their life times (Matt. 26:64; Mark 9:1; cf. Rev. 1:7 with Rev. 1:1, 3).

The trumpet gathering. Matthew 24:31 portrays the ultimate Jubilee of salvation, decorated with imagery from Leviticus 25. Following upon the collapse of the Temple order, Christ's "messengers"[35] will go forth powerfully trumpeting the gospel of salvific liberation (Luke 4:16-21; Isa. 61:1-3; cf. Lev. 25:9-10). Through gospel preaching the elect are gathered into the kingdom of God from the four corners of the world, from horizon to horizon.[36]

The remainder of the Olivet Discourse (Matt. 24:36-25:46) looks beyond the signs for "this generation" (near demonstrative) to "that" (far demonstrative) *sign-less* day and hour (Matt. 24:34-36). Thus, the Lord's attention turns from the imminent events of that generation to His Second Advent at the end of history.

There is abundant, clear evidence that the Great Tribulation was an event of the first century. It punctuated the end of the Jewish era and the Old Covenant: the separation of Christianity from its Jewish mother, as by "birth pangs" (Matt. 24:8).

---

34. Chilton, *Paradise Restored*, pp. 100-101.

35. "Angels" (*aggeloi*) should be understood here as "messengers," as in Matt. 11:10; Mark 1:2; Luke 7:24, 27; 9:52. Chilton, *Paradise Restored*, pp. 103-105.

36. For the phrase "one end of heaven to the other," see: Deut. 30:4; Neh. 1:9. The proclamation of the gospel is to be worldwide, Isa. 45:22; Psa. 22:27; Luke 13:29; Acts 13:39.

The Rebuilding of the Temple

There are a few prophecies in the Old Testament that seem on first reading to predict a rebuilding of the Temple of Israel at some time in the future, i.e., the New Covenant era. Among the passages so understood are: Isaiah 56:7; 66:20-23; Jeremiah 33:18; Zechariah 14:16-21; and Malachi 3:3-4.

The concept of the Jews returning to their Land so that the returned Messiah can rule over an exalted Jewish kingdom, complete with a re-established Jewish Temple and the sacrificial system, has long been attractive to dispensationalists. Some even hold such teachings to be cardinal Scriptural truths.[37] John Walvoord freely admits that "most thoroughgoing students of premillennialism [i.e., dispensationalism] who evince understanding of the relation of literal interpretation to premillennial doctrine usually embrace the concept of a literal temple and literal sacrifices."[38] Grace Theological Seminary professor John Whitcomb has put it even more strongly: "[C]onsistent dispensationalism must teach the practice of animal sacrifices for a restored and regenerated Israel in the Millennium."[39]

A recent work entitled *The Coming Temple: Center Stage for the Final Countdown* clearly reveals this dispensational longing: "How can we be so sure that the Temple will really be rebuilt? Because the Bible says so." The book shows that there are Christians today who are raising money for this rebuilding.[40]

---

37. Hal Lindsey, *The Road to Holocaust* (New York: Bantam, 1989); Dave Hunt, *Whatever Happened to Heaven?* (Eugene, OR: Harvest House, 1988); Don Stewart and Chuck Missler, *The Coming Temple: Center Stage for the Final Countdown* (Orange, CA: Dart, 1991), especially p. 188. See: Ken Sidey, "For the Love of Zion," *Christianity Today* 36:3 (March 9, 1992) 46-50.

38. John F. Walvoord, *The Millennial Kingdom* (Findlay, OH: Dunham, 1959), p. 315. See also: Thomas D. Ice and Randall Price, *Ready to Rebuild: The Imminent Plan to Rebuild the Last Days Temple* (Eugene, OR: Harvest House, 1992); David Allen Lewis, *Prophecy 2000: Rushing to Armageddon* (Green Forest, AR: New Leaf, 1990), pp. 130ff.

39. John C. Whitcomb, "Christ's Atonement and Animal Sacrifices," *Grace Theological Journal* 6:2 (1985) 215.

40. Stewart and Missler, *Coming Temple*, p. 171. The book is dedicated: "To our

The fundamental passage upon which this view is based is the extensive description in Ezekiel 40-48. According to dispensationalists: "the land will be redistributed among the twelve tribes, and the Temple will be rebuilt with the sacrifices, as memorials, reinstituted (Ezek. 40-48)."[41] "Ezekiel's temple is a literal future sanctuary to be constructed in Palestine as outlined during the millennium."[42]

The doctrine of a rebuilt Temple is so patently erroneous, both theologically and exegetically, that it is called by some the "Achilles' heel of the Dispensational system of interpretation."[43] Even dispensationalists recognize that "the future function of the millennial temple (Ezekiel 40-48) has long been problematic for dispensationalists."[44]

The Dispensational View

Walvoord presents the dispensational position on Ezekiel's millennial Temple: "In the Millennium, apparently, sacrifices will also be offered, though somewhat different than those required under the Mosaic Law, but this time the sacrifices will be memorial, much as the Lord's Supper is a memorial in the Church Age for the death of Christ."[45]

---

wonderful friends in Israel this book is lovingly dedicated." A major group working to this end is the Jerusalem Temple Foundation in Los Angeles, California (p. 189).

41. Charles L. Feinberg, *Millennialism: The Two Major Views* (3rd ed.; Chicago: Moody Press, 1980), p. 186.

42. Merrill F. Unger, "The Temple Vision of Ezekiel," *Bibliotheca Sacra* 105 (Oct. 1948) 423. See also: A. C. Gaebelein, *The Prophet Ezekiel* (New York: Our Hope, 1918), p. 312; Pentecost, *Things to Come*, p. 514; Walvoord, *Prophecy Knowledge Handbook*, pp. 198ff; Stewart and Missler, *Coming Temple*, p. 225.

43. O. T. Allis, *Prophecy and the Church* (Philadelphia: Presbyterian & Reformed, 1945), p. 248.

44. John C. Whitcomb, "Christ's Atonement and Animal Sacrifices in Israel," 201.

45. Walvoord, *Prophecy Knowledge Handbook*, p. 202. Fellow dispensationalist Whitcomb disagrees that the sacrifices will be memorial: "[F]uture animal sacrifices will be 'efficacious' and 'expiatory' only in terms of the strict provision for ceremonial (and thus temporal) forgiveness within the theocracy of Israel." Whitcomb, "Christ's

The argument for such a Temple is ultimately due to the literalistic hermeneutic employed by dispensationalists. It is maintained that a symbolic interpretation of Ezekiel's revelation is hermeneutically flawed in that it leaves "unanswered why such specific details were revealed" to Ezekiel. Furthermore, Walvoord admits, "those who adopt the figurative interpretation have not agreed as to the meaning of this temple"[46] (as if differences of opinion were absent in dispensational discussions of this issue[47]). Here is his rationale for a rebuilt Temple: "Though it is objectionable to some to have animal sacrifices in the millennial scene, actually, they will be needed there because the very ideal circumstances in which millennial saints will live will tend to gloss over the awfulness of sin and the need for bloody sacrifice. The sacrifices offered will therefore be a reminder that only by the shedding of blood and, more specifically, the blood of Christ, can sin be taken away."[48]

Problems with the Dispensational View

First, the dispensational view is hermeneutically flawed. We have already commented on the error of the literalism of dispensationalism as a basic hermeneutic (Chapter 8). What is more, in Ezekiel we have a *vision.* This fact could easily militate against literalism, because spiritual truths in the Bible are often conceptualized ideally in visions. This approach matches well the tendency in earlier visionary chapters in Ezekiel, where

Atonement and Animal Sacrifices," p. 210. But Walvoord's view is the predominant view in dispensationalism, as is demonstrated by John L. Mitchell, "The Question of Millennial Sacrifices," *Bibliotheca Sacra* 110 (1953) 248ff.

46. Walvoord, *Prophecy Knowledge Handbook*, p. 202. Cf. Stewart and Missler, *The Coming Temple*, pp. 227ff.

47. Two prominent dispensationalists who deny a future Temple are: H. A. Ironside, *Ezekiel the Prophet* (New York: Loizeaux Bros., 1949), pp. 284ff; J. Sidlow Baxter, *Explore the Book* (Grand Rapids: Zondervan, 1960), p. 32ff. Some such as Whitcomb have disputed the common explanation of the sacrifices as "memorials." Whitcomb, "Christ's Atonement and Animal Sacrifices in Israel," pp. 201-217.

48. Walvoord, *Prophecy Knowledge Handbook*, p. 202

spiritual truths are framed in terms of concrete realities. See particularly Ezekiel 1-3 and 8-11 (cf. the distinction between a vision
and direct revelation in Num. 12:6).

In fact, there clearly are aspects of the vision that cannot be
taken literally: (1) The site of the Temple is on a "very high
mountain" (Ezek. 40:2), although there is no "very high mountain" in the area of Jerusalem. (2) The source and flow of the
river is incredible – flowing from under the threshold of the
Temple it becomes a great river (Ezek. 47:1-2). (3) The function
of the river in making the Dead Sea fresh and bringing life to
all that it touches (Ezek. 47:6-12) is surely symbolism. (4) The
Twelve Tribes are provided parallel tracts of land, which would
be awkward in real geography (Ezek. 47:13ff). The exegetical
pressures against the dispensational view of future sacrifices are
just too great. The *New Scofield Reference Bible* (1967) notes of
the *sin offering* sacrifices in Ezekiel 43:19: "the reference to
sacrifices is not to be taken literally."[49] This is a major conces-
sion to the critics of dispensationalism.

The "problem" with particular details militating against an
ideal portrayal is no problem, as Fairbairn demonstrated in
1851.[50] This is quite common in Ezekiel. When Isaiah speaks
of the king of Tyre, he does so in a few verses in brief, general
terms (Isa. 23:1-17). But Ezekiel provides many details in three
chapters dealing with the greatness and the fall of that king
(Ezek. 26-28). The same sort of detailed portrayal occurs in
Ezekiel in regard to judgments upon Egypt and Jerusalem.

The special details of the Temple vision flow from the fact of
Ezekiel's being a priest (Ezek. 1:3). He even characterizes the
sin of Israel as centered in the Temple (Ezek. 8-11). We must
remember that even Solomon's Temple was a material symbol
of heavenly and spiritual truths that were important in its con-

49. *New Scofield Reference Bible*, p. 888, note 1.
50. See: Patrick Fairbairn, *An Exposition of Ezekiel* (Minneapolis: Klock & Klock,
[1851] 1979), pp. 431-450.

struction. So why should not a vision allow for such detail in portrayal of spiritual truth?

Furthermore, John's vision of the New Jerusalem obviously reflects back in some ways upon Ezekiel's vision. John seems to have adapted Ezekiel's vision as a portrayal of the kingdom of God in history.[51] But John's is manifestly a symbolic portrayal, for the city's size is a 1,342-mile cube. This would cause the top of the city to extend 1000 miles beyond the orbit of today's Space Shuttle! Like John's vision, Ezekiel's is an ideal symbol, not a prophecy of a literal city.

Second, the dispensational view is redemptively retrogressive. As David Brown complained over a century ago: Such a position is guilty of "Judaizing our Christianity, instead of Christianizing the adherents of Judaism."[52]

Ezekiel's Temple vision, if interpreted literally, would reimpose *circumcision* and displace baptism (at least for males): "No foreigner, uncircumcised in heart or uncircumcised in flesh, shall enter My sanctuary, including any foreigner who is among the children of Israel" (Ezek. 44:9). This re-establishes that which has forever been done away with, according to the clear teaching of the New Testament.[53] The circumcisional separating "partition" between Jew and Gentile has been permanently broken down, according to the New Testament (Eph. 2:11-21).

A literalistic approach to Ezekiel's vision would re-institute *redemptive* sacrifices, despite their fulfillment and removal in the New Testament (Heb. 7:27; 9:26; 10:1-14). It re-institutes "the burnt offering, the sin offering, and the trespass offering" (Ezek. 40:39; cf. 43:21), though these were taken away in Christ (Heb. 10:5, 9, 18). Why would the Lord return again to the

---

51. G. R. Beasley-Murray, "Ezekiel," *The Eerdmans Bible Commentary*, Donald Guthrie and J. A. Motyer, eds. (3rd ed.; Grand Rapids: Eerdmans, 1970), p. 684.

52. David Brown, *Christ's Second Coming: Will It Be Premillennial?* (Edmonton, Alberta: Still Waters Revival, [1882] 1990), p. 352.

53. Acts 15; Rom. 2:26-29; 4:9-12; 1 Cor. 7:18-19; Gal. 5:2-6; 6:12-15; Phil. 3:3; Col. 2:11; 3:11.

"weak and beggarly elements" of the ceremonial law (Gal. 4:9)? These are the redemptive sacrifices of the *Levitical* priesthood performed by the sons of Zadok (Ezek. 40:46; 43:19; 44:15; 48:11), despite the existence of a new order of priest: Jesus Christ who is the Melchizedekan priest (Heb. 5:5-10; 6:20; 7:11-21).[54]

John 4:21 anticipates the removal of the Temple order: "The hour is coming when you will neither on this mountain, nor in Jerusalem, worship the Father." Various other Old Testament prophecies are found to transcend the Mosaic pattern of worship in the Temple environs (Isa. 19:19; Jer. 3:16; Zech. 14:21; Mal. 1:11). Which shall we follow? References that transcend Temple worship or those that reintroduce it? Obviously, we are dealing with symbolic language. There is no contradiction between the two sorts of references, when properly interpreted.

It is important to note that there is absolutely *no hint* that these sacrifices will be "memorial," as per dispensationalists (and contrary to their literalism). Dispensationalist Whitcomb writes: "Ezekiel, however, does not say that animals will be offered for a 'memorial' of Messiah's death. Rather, they will be for 'atonement' (45:15, 17, 20; cf. 43:20, 26)."[55] He is correct. The Ezekelian sacrifices are those established by Moses in the Levitical system – for these sacrifices *are* those sacrifices renewed, if literally conceived. The Scripture clearly speaks of their legal function in the Old Testament as *actually making reconciliation*. In fact, in Ezekiel 45:15, 17, 20 the sacrifices to be offered in the alleged future Temple are specifically said to "make reconciliation" or "atonement." They are *not* memorials. The

---

54. Clowney offers an interesting paradox of the re-establishing of the Levitical priesthood, given the fact that Jesus was of the tribe of Judah (Heb. 7:14): "Imagine . . . a rebuilt temple in Jerusalem where the Risen Lord, returning to rule, would be barred from the sanctuary while sons of Levi mediated between him and the Father!" Edmund Clowney, "The Final Temple," in *Studying the New Testament Today* (n.p.: Presbyterian & Reformed, 1974), p. 111.

55. Whitcomb, "Christ's Atonement and Animal Sacrifices in Israel," p. 211.

phraseology used here – the piel form of *kaphar* – is identical to that employed in Leviticus and Numbers.[56]

How could the "millennial scene" require bloody sacrifices "because the very ideal circumstances in which millennial saints will live will tend to gloss over the awfulness of sin and the need for bloody sacrifice"? Does this mean that the universal prevalence of the righteous knowledge of God (Isa. 11:9) under the direct administration of Christ "glosses over the awfulness of sin" in the dispensational millennium? Would not such universal, deeply rooted righteousness make sin all the more heinous and conspicuous? And does not the Lord want us today deeply to recognize the awfulness of sin? Why then did not the sacrificial system continue in the present? Do not the words in the administration of the Lord's Supper point to the awful fact of sin, without animal sacrifices (1 Cor. 11:23-32)?

The Postmillennial View

To understand the significance of Ezekiel's visionary Temple, we must keep in mind the conceptual idea embodied in the Temple structure and services. The essence of the Temple is its standing as a symbol. That is, it is symbolic of the *covenantal relationship* of God with His people. The essence of the covenant is contained in that most important promise: "I will be your God, you will be My people."[57] The Temple was the special place where God dwelt among His people (1 Kgs. 6:12-13; Jer. 7:4-7), as He did in the Tabernacle preceding it (Exo. 29:42; 25:22; 30:36). The glory of God was especially present in His sanctuary (1 Kgs. 8:11; 2 Chr. 7:1-2), although no Temple

---

56. Lev. 6:30; 8:15; 16:6, 11, 24, 30; Num. 5:8; 15:28; 29:5.

57. See earlier discussion in Chapter 6. See: Gen. 17:7; Exo. 5:2; 6:7; 29:45; Lev. 11:45; 26:12,45; Deut. 4:20; Deut. 7:9; 29:14-15; 2 Sam. 7:24; Psa. 105:9; Isa. 43:6; Jer. 24:7; 31:33; 32:38; Ezek. 11:20; 34:24; 36:28; 37:23; Hos. 1:10; Zech. 8:8; 13:9; 2 Cor. 6:18; Rev. 21:3, 7.

could contain His immense being (1 Kgs. 8:27; Isa. 66:1; Jer. 23:24).

This idea is clearly related to Ezekiel's Temple vision in 48:35: "The name of the city from that day shall be: The Lord is There." That visionary Temple is symbolic of the glorious presence of God in the Kingdom of Christ coming in the New Covenant era. And it is so because even further defined, it is symbolic of Christ Himself. *Christ is the true presence of God* which could only be hinted at in the temple construction. "Ezekiel's vision of the new temple is part of this prophetic pattern of a restoration so total that it sublimates the ceremonial structure in glory. Ezekiel's restoration returns David to the throne, and sees a temple that is a sanctuary of Paradise, where the river of life flows from God's throne past trees whose leaves are for the healing of the nations."[58]

One of the closing prophecies of the Old Testament is Malachi 3:1: "And the Lord, whom you seek, will suddenly come to His temple, even the Messenger of the covenant, in whom you delight." This coming is the message of the New Testament: the Lord has come to "tabernacle" among us (John 1:14, Greek; cf. John 1:1; 1 John 1:1-3). When He came, He was first visited by shepherds, who had been out in the fields keeping *sacrificial sheep* destined for the Temple.[59] When presented forty days later in the Temple, He was praised as the "glory of Your people Israel" (Luke 2:32) – language reflecting the Shekinah glory of God, which evidenced God's presence in the Temple (Exo. 40:34, 35; 1 Sam. 4:21-22).

He so stands as the glorious realization of the meaning of the Temple that he who had seen Him had seen the Father (John 14:9), for "in Him dwells all the fullness of the Godhead

---

58. Clowney, "The Final Temple," p. 106. I am indebted to Clowney for his insights presented in this article, several of which I relate below.

59. William Hendriksen, *The Gospel of Luke* (*NTC*) (Grand Rapids: Baker, 1978), p. 150. The presence of shepherds in the fields in winter months was indicative of the tending of sacrificial sheep.

bodily" (Col. 2:9). He even was transfigured in a glorious display of His true identity (Matt. 17:1-8; Mark 9:2-8). Consequently, He justly claims to be *greater than the Temple* (Matt. 12:6), for He is its fulfillment, being the very presence of God. In fact, He is "the stone which the builders rejected" which "has become the chief cornerstone" of God's new Temple (Matt. 21:42).[60]

Consequently, as His prophetic ministry opens, He stands in the shadow of the earthly Temple and informs Jerusalem of this glorious truth: "Destroy this temple, and in three days I will raise it up," by which "He was speaking of the temple of His body" (John 2:19, 21), a Temple "not made with hands" (Mark 14:58). Therefore, He offers Himself to men as the heavenly manna, which was once housed in the Ark of the Covenant in the Temple.[61] He offers the living waters of Ezekiel's Temple (Ezek. 47; cf. Joel 3:18; Zech. 14:8) to His hearers (John 4:10-15; 7:38-39). He is the sacrificial "Lamb of God" destined for Temple service (John 1:29). As He establishes the New Covenant (Luke 22:20), He impresses upon the hearts of His followers the Law of God (Jer. 31:31-34; 2 Cor. 4:3, 6; Heb. 8:8-11), which was formerly kept on tables of stone in the Holy of holies (Exo. 25:21; Deut. 10:5; Heb. 9:4). Thus, when He dies, the Temple era is formally ended with the rending of the veil (Matt. 27:51). When He speaks of the absolute destruction of the physical Temple in A.D. 70, He leaves no intimation of its God-endorsed rebuilding (Matt. 24[62]), nor of the return of the Temple *mount* to holy status (John 4:21-24).

---

60. See R. J. McKelvey, "Christ the Cornerstone," *The New Temple*, Alan Cole, ed. (London: Tyndale, 1950), pp. 195-204. Joachim Jeremias, *"lithos," Theological Dictionary of the New Testament*, 4:268ff.

61. John 6:49-58; Rev. 2:17; cf. Exo. 16:33-34; Heb. 9:4.

62. Compare our study of Daniel 9:24-27 in the preceding chapter with the Great Tribulation study above (particularly Matt. 24:15; Dan. 9:27). The Temple is to be finally destroyed, never to be endorsed by God again.

Christ, then, is the True Temple. In fact, many commentators note John's demonstrating Jesus' fulfillment of the Temple (John 2) as one of the purposes of his Gospel, as well as His fulfilling the sabbath (John 5), the Passover (John 6), the Feast of Tabernacles (John 7).[63] And His people in mystical union with Him are called His "body" (Rom. 12:5; 1 Cor. 12:27; Eph. 4:12). Consequently, we who are His people are also designated a "temple."[64] This is due to His indwelling presence among His people, so that we, having the True Temple within, may be called a temple. Christ in us is the hope of glory (Col. 1:27). Not only is He Who is the True Temple in us, but we are also spoken of as being "in Christ."[65]

Thus, the prophetic notion of the rebuilding of the Temple (when not making reference to Zerubbabel's Temple) speaks of Christ and the building of His Church (Matt. 16:18; cf. Zech. 6:12-13). He Himself is the foundation and cornerstone (1 Cor. 3:11, 16-17; Eph. 2:20). As Christ's people we are *priests* (Rom. 15:16; 1 Pet. 2:5, 9; Rev. 1:6) who offer our bodies as *living sacrifices* (Rom. 12:1-2) and our service as acceptable *sweet smell offerings* (2 Cor. 2:14-16; Phil. 4:18; Hcb. 13:15-16; 1 Pet. 2:5). Thus, "we have an *altar* from which those who serve the tabernacle have no right to eat" (Heb. 13:10). As more people are converted by His sovereign grace, His New Covenant Temple grows stone by stone (Eph. 2:21; 4:12, 16; 1 Pet. 2:5,9). As a master builder Paul labored in that Temple (1 Cor. 3:9-17).

Through a series of Old Testament Temple and ritual allusions, Paul points to *the New Temple of God:* "And what agree-

---

63. See David E. Holwerda, *Jesus and Israel: One Covenant or Two?* (Grand Rapids: Eerdmans, 1995), p. 77. Commentators noting this include: C. H. Dodd, Raymond Brown, R. Schnackenburg, B. Lindars, C. K. Barrett, and Leon Morris.

64. 1 Cor. 3:16-17; 6:19; 2 Cor. 6:16; Eph. 2:19-20; 1 Pet. 2:5-9.

65. Rom. 3:24; 6:11, 23; 8:1, 2; 39; 9:1; 12:5; 15:17; 16:3, 7, 9,10; 1 Cor. 1:2, 30; 3:1; 4:10, 15, 17; 15:18, 19, 22, 31; 16:24 2 Cor. 1:21; 2:14, 17; 3:14; 5:17, 19; 11:3; 12:2, 19; Gal. 1:22; 2:4, 16; 3:14, 17, 26, 28; 5:6; 6:15; Eph. 1:1, 3, 10, 12, 20; 2:6, 7, 10, 13; 3:11; 4:32; Phil. 1:1, 13; 2:1, 5; 3:3, 9, 14; 4:21; Col. 1:2, 4, 28; 2:5; 1 Thess. 2:14; 4:16; 5:18; 1 Tim. 1:14; 2:7; 3:13; 2 Tim. 1:1, 9, 13; 2:1, 10; 3:12, 15.

ment has the temple of God with idols? For you are the temple of the living God. As God has said: 'I will dwell in them and walk among them. I will be their God, and they shall be My people.' Therefore 'Come out from among them and be separate, says the Lord. Do not touch what is unclean, and I will receive you. I will be a Father to you, and you shall be My sons and daughters, says the LORD Almighty.' Therefore, having these promises, beloved, let us cleanse ourselves from all filthiness of the flesh and spirit, perfecting holiness in the fear of God" (2 Cor. 6:16-7:1). So, as Clowney well notes, "we must recognize that this is not spiritualization in our usual sense of the word, but the very opposite. In Christ is realization. It is not so much that Christ fulfills what the temple means; rather Christ is the meaning for which the temple existed."[66]

Taylor well distills the basic ideas in Ezekiel's complex Temple vision: (1) The immaculate symmetry of the building portrays the perfection of God's plan for His people. (2) The meticulous detail of the rites indicates the centrality of worship in the New Covenant era. (3) The central idea of the Temple points to the abiding presence of God with His redeemed community. (4) The waters of life flowing from the Temple express the life-giving operation of the Holy Spirit in the new age. (5) The careful allocation of levitical duties and land apportionment speak of the duties and privileges of God's people in the future.[67]

New Creation

In Chapter 13 I made reference to the new creation. There I focused on the *consummational* New Heavens and New Earth. In this chapter I will concentrate on the *pre-consummational* new creation which I only briefly alluded to earlier.

66. Clowney, "The Final Temple," p. 119.

67. John B. Taylor, *Ezekiel: An Introduction and Commentary* (*Tyndale*) (Downer's Grove, IL: InterVarsity Press, 1969), pp. 253-254.

Oftentimes the tremendous redemptive historical transformation initiated by Christ in His incarnation is not fully appreciated in non-postmillennial eschatologies. Premillennial eschatologies tend to postpone the radical transformation to the end of history, after the historically discontinuous Second Advent.[68] Amillennial eschatology tends to remove the transformational blessings above or beyond history, either to heaven or to the consummational New Earth.[69] Postmillennialism, however, expects the redemptive labor of Christ to have a transformational effect in time and on earth, continuous with present spiritual realities already set in motion by Christ.

The major passage setting forth the spiritual conception of the change wrought by Christ in history is Isaiah 65:17-25. In that vast scene we have a sweeping picture of the full extent of the coming gospel economy, a reality established by Christ at His first coming. This economy will develop through "a multistage process that culminates at the final judgment."[70] This is a *redemptive* economy that will gradually so transform the world ethically and spiritually that it is here portrayed as a "new heavens and a new earth" of which "the former shall not be remembered or come to mind" (Isa. 65:17).

This Isaianic vision is in the background of Paul's statement in 2 Corinthians 5:17, which refers to contemporary spiritual realities: "Therefore, if anyone is in Christ, he is a new creation; old things have passed away; behold, all things have become new."[71] According to New Testament theology, the Second

68. See: Gary North, *Millennialism and Social Theory* (Tyler, Texas: Institute for Christian Economics, 1990).

69. See my response to amillennialist Richard B. Gaffin's article "Theonomy and Eschatology: Reflections on Postmillennialism": Gentry, "Whose Victory in History?" *Theonomy: An Informed Response*, Gary North, ed. (Tyler, TX: Institute for Christian Economics, 1991), pp. 207-230. See also: North, *Millennialism and Social Theory*, ch. 5.

70. North, *Millennialism and Social Theory*, p. 104.

71. See: John Calvin, *The Second Epistle of Paul to the Corinthians, and the Epistles to Timothy, Titus and Philemon* (1577), David W. Torrance and Thomas F. Torrance, eds., trans. by T. A. Smail (Grand Rapids: Eerdmans, 1964), pp. 75-76. F. F. Bruce,

Adam, Christ, stands at the head of a new creation (Rom. 5:14; 1 Cor. 15:22, 45).

Calvin viewed Isaiah 65:17-25 as a New Covenant blessing that resulted from a change in covenantal administration:

> By these metaphors he promises a remarkable change of affairs; as if God had said that he has both the inclination and the power not only to restore his Church, but to restore it in such a manner that it shall appear to gain new life and to dwell in a new world. These are exaggerated modes of expression; but the greatness of such a blessing, which was to be manifested at the coming of Christ, could not be described in any other way. Nor does he mean only the first coming, but the whole reign, which must be extended as far as to the last coming.[72]

The transformational effect of the gospel kingdom is such that those who are newly born of its power[73] are thereby constituted *new creatures*, so that "in Christ Jesus neither circumcision nor uncircumcision avails anything, but a new creation" (Gal. 6:15). The transforming power of the gospel creates a "new man" of two warring factions, Jew and Gentile (Eph. 2:15-18). Gospel-transformed new creatures are to lay aside the old self and take on the new (Eph. 4:22-23), which is "created according to God, in righteousness and true holiness" (Eph. 4:24; cf. Col. 3:9-11). This is because they are "His workmanship, created in Christ Jesus for good works, which God prepared beforehand that we should walk in them" (Eph. 2:10).

This glorious conception involves both a re-created "Jerusalem" and "people" (Isa. 65:18-19). Interestingly, in Galatians 6 Paul speaks of the new creation in the context of a transformed

---

I & II Corinthians (*New Century Bible Commentary*) (Grand Rapids: Eerdmans, 1971), p. 209. See also: Geerhardus Vos, *The Pauline Eschatology* (Phillipsburg, NJ: Presbyterian & Reformed, [1930] 1991), pp. 48-49.

72. John Calvin, *Commentary on the Book of the Prophet Isaiah* (1559), trans. by William Pringle, 4 vols. (Grand Rapids: Baker, [n.d.] 1979), 4:397-398.

73. John 3:3; Jms. 1:18; 1 Pet. 1:23; 1 John 2:29; 3:9; 5:1, 18.

"Israel of God" existing in his day: "For in Christ Jesus neither circumcision nor uncircumcision avails anything, but a *new creation*. And as many as walk according to this rule, peace and mercy be upon them, even upon *the Israel of God*" (Gal. 6:15-16; cf. Rom. 2:28-29).[74] In that same epistle, he urges a commitment to the "Jerusalem above" (the heavenly Jerusalem, Heb. 12:22) rather than to the cast out Jerusalem that now is (the historical capital city of Israel, Gal. 4:25-26).

The *heavenly Jerusalem* is the *bride of Christ* that came down from God to replace the earthly Jerusalem (Rev. 21:2-5) in the first century (Rev. 1:1, 3; 22:6, 10). With the shaking and destruction of the old Jerusalem in A.D. 70, the heavenly (re-created) Jerusalem replaced her: His "voice then shook the earth; but now He has promised, saying, 'Yet once more I shake not only the earth, but also heaven.' Now this, 'Yet once more,' indicates the removal of those things that are being shaken, as of things that are made [i.e., the Levitical ritual system[75]], that the things which cannot be shaken may remain. Therefore, since we *are receiving* a kingdom which cannot be shaken, let us have grace, by which we may serve God acceptably with reverence and godly fear" (Heb. 12:26-28).

Contrary to amillennialism there is no reason, neither is there "substantial evidence . . . for identifying [Isaiah 65:17ff] with the perfect eternal state."[76] Isaiah speaks of glorious elevated conditions, but conditions still continuous with the present. This is evident in the experiencing of birth, aging, death, time, sin, and curse: "No more shall an *infant* ['ol, "suckling"] from there live but a few days, nor an *old man* who has not

---

74. See previous discussion of this passage in Chapter 8.

75. Heb. 9:11 (cf. vv. 2, 8, 24) reads: "Christ came as High Priest of the good things to come, with the greater and more perfect tabernacle not *made with hands*, that is, not of *this creation*." The old Tabernacle/Temple system was "made with hands" (Heb. 9:24, cf. 2, 11) and was of "this creation," whereas the new is heavenly (8:5; 9:23). Notice the contextual contrast between Mt. Sinai, where the ceremonial system was received, (12:18-21) and heavenly Mt. Zion (12:22-25).

76. Adams, *Time Is at Hand*, p. 15.

fulfilled his days; for the child shall *die* one *hundred years old*, but the *sinner* being one hundred years old shall be *accursed*" (Isa. 65:20). Sinners will not be in the post-resurrection perfect state.

Adams defends the amillennial interpretation of these elements with a rhetorical question: "How else can perfection be described in words which have imperfect objects and concepts as referents?"[77] The answer is: Easily! Surely it is not impossible to think of post-resurrection perfection without mentioning six elements of temporal imperfection in the same sentence.

Fellow amillennialist Hoekema also deals with the passage rhetorically by reference to Isaiah 65:19: "Can one imagine death without weeping?"[78] This is surely less difficult than imagining death without death (cf. 65:20). But in the context, the reference is to be understood *culturally*: when God's blessings come upon His city and people, the "old things" (65:17) of cultural judgment, devastation, and sorrow due to sinful rebellion (65:2-8, 11-12) will pass away. In Isaiah's day the Lord noted: "Behold, My servants shall sing for joy of heart, but you shall cry for sorrow of heart, and wail for grief of spirit" (Isa. 65:14). The rejoicing of God in His people *collectively considered* will lead to the relief of their sorrow caused by His past displeasure and cultural wrath (cf. Deut. 28:15ff; Psa. 137). No longer will the "cry of distress" be heard from His people (cf. 2 Sam. 22:7; Psa. 18:6; Isa. 19:20), because the world will be dominated by them and not by the oppressor (65:25).

The covenantal language here shows that *culture-wide disinheritance* caused by rebellion will be *a thing of the past*. Instead, covenantal inheritance will prevail: "They shall build houses and inhabit them; they shall plant vineyards and eat their fruit. They shall not build and another inhabit; they shall not plant and another eat; for as the days of a tree, so shall be the days of My people, and My elect shall long enjoy the work of their

---

77. *Ibid.*
78. Hoekema, *Bible and the Future*, p. 202.

hands" (Isa. 65:21-22). This reverses covenantal curse language (which Isaiah spoke so much about): "You shall betroth a wife, but another man shall lie with her; you shall build a house, but you shall not dwell in it; you shall plant a vineyard, but shall not gather its grapes" (Deut. 28:30; cf. Zeph. 1:13; Mic. 6:15).

The New Heavens and New Earth here (and many places elsewhere) has reference to the New Covenant era. It characterizes the system-wide transformation that will occur with the spread of the gospel.

Conclusion

Although one's millennial view should flow out of a comprehensive understanding of Scripture, often a few particular biblical features play an inordinately significant role in millennial debate. A misapprehension of these discrete features can distort the overall system of biblical eschatology.

I have surveyed several prominent features of God's prophetic Word to show how they are understood within the postmillennial framework. Though some of these aspects of biblical revelation are thought to be contra-indicative of postmillennialism (e.g., the Great Tribulation, the rebuilding of the Temple), they are perfectly accounted for in the postmillennial system. The Great Tribulation was the fall of Jerusalem in A.D. 70. The rebuilt Temple is the bride of Christ, His body, the Church.

Dealing with the New Heaven and New Earth language in Isaiah 65 poses no problem for the postmillennialist, nor should it pose a problem for the premillennialist. That a period of unprecedented, literal blessings is in store for mankind prior to the resurrection and the final judgment is not a hermeneutical problem for either system of interpretation. It is, however, a decided problem for the amillennialist.

16

CHARACTERS

He who is not with Me is against Me, and he who does not gather with Me scatters abroad. (Matthew 12:30)

As in the last chapter, I consider some stray issues that are often associated with eschatological studies. In this chapter I turn to various eschatologically significant characters.

Elijah the Prophet

In Malachi 4:5, the last word spoken by God to Israel before the coming of Christ, there is a short reference of eschatological significance that has caused a good deal of debate between dispensationalists and other evangelicals. That brief reference reads: "Behold, I will send you Elijah the prophet before the coming of the great and dreadful day of the LORD" (Mal. 4:5).

The Significance of Malachi 4:5

The significance of this reference to Elijah is two-fold. First, because of it there was a widespread anticipation among the Jews that the literal Elijah would appear before the end. The great student of the Talmud John Lightfoot noted: "It would be an infinite task to produce all the passages out of the Jewish writings which one might concerning the expected coming of

Elias."[1] Consequently, Elijah was deemed by the Jews "the loftiest prophet of the OT," so that "no OT hero fills a larger place in Jewish tradition."[2] No other Old Testament prophet is named so many times as Elijah in the New Testament (thirty).

Second, Elijah and this reference are even alluded to several times in conjunction with the ministry of Christ. Due to the Malachi 4:5 reference, the Jews held that Elijah was to come before the great Day of the Lord (Matt. 17:10-12; Mark 9:11-12). Consequently, during John Baptist's ministry, he was thought to be Elijah returned (John 1:21-25), because he preached in the spirit and power of Elijah (Luke 1:17). When John denied he was Elijah returned, many thought Jesus might be (Matt. 16:13-14; Mark 8:27-28; Luke 9:7-8, 18-19). As Christ was dying, some mistakenly thought He was calling for Elijah from the cross (Matt. 27:47-49; Mark 15:35-36). There is a literal sense in which Elijah *did* come during the ministry of Christ, for He appeared with Moses when the Lord was transfigured (Matt. 17:3-4; Mark 9:4-5; Luke 9:30-33). Two of these references note that this event brought the Malachi 4 reference to the mind of the three disciples who witnessed it (Matt. 17:11-13; Mark 9:12-13).

The Fulfillment of Malachi 4:5

The evidence is really quite clear that Malachi's Elijianic prophecy was fulfilled during the ministry of Christ. This fulfillment is counter-indicative to both dispensationalism's hermeneutic and its eschatology, as well as being supportive of the preteristic hermeneutic and postmillennial eschatology.

---

1. John Lightfoot, *A Commentary on the New Testament from the Talmud and Hebraica*, 4 vols. (Peabody, MA: [1658] 1989), 2:243.

2. J. Strachan, "Elijah," *A Dictionary of the Bible*, James Hastings, ed., 5 vols. (Peabody, MA: Hendrikson, [1898] 1988), 1:687, 691. See: Sirach 48:1ff.

In Matthew 17:10-13 we read: "And His disciples asked Him, saying, 'Why then do the scribes say that Elijah must come first?' Then Jesus answered and said to them, 'Elijah truly is coming first and will restore all things. But I say to you that Elijah has come already, and they did not know him but did to him whatever they wished. . . .' Then the disciples understood that He spoke to them of John the Baptist."

Here Christ dogmatically teaches His disciples that John Baptist had fulfilled the Malachi prophecy *covenantally*, which the Jews did not understand. John had introduced the restoration of all things, i.e., the coming of the final phase of redemptive history through the kingdom of Christ, with its power progressively to bring the world to salvation (as per postmillennialism, Matt. 13:31-33; John 3:17; Rom. 11:15). Christ established the kingdom and then returned to heaven to await the historical conquest of all His enemies (Acts 2:33-35; 1 Cor. 15:21-27; cf. Matt. 28:18-20). He will not return until all things have been restored under His providential rule (Acts 3:21; 1 Cor. 15:25).

Objections to the Fulfillment of Malachi 4:5

Dispensational objections sometimes approach desperation. Some commentators even forsake their literalism and allow that John did fulfill the passage. Pentecost writes: "The prophecy is interpreted by the Lord as being fulfilled, *not in literal Elijah*, but in one who comes in Elijah's spirit and power."[3]

Others focus in on (and misinterpret) a reference similar to Matthew 17. In a critique of postmillennialist Loraine Boettner, dispensationalist Herman Hoyt writes: "When citing a prophecy from Malachi 4:5 and the New Testament reference to it, Boettner erred in ignoring part of the text in Matthew (11:14). Christ said that John the Baptist would have stood for Elijah if

---

3. J. Dwight Pentecost, *Things to Come* (Grand Rapids: Zondervan, 1958), p. 312 (emphasis mine); cf. E. S. English, "The Two Witnesses," *Our Hope* 47 (April 1941) 666.

they would receive him. But they did not, which must mean that Elijah is yet to come. The reason Christ could make reference to John the Baptist as he did was that John the Baptist came in the spirit and power of Elijah (Luke 1:17). It therefore seems obvious that there was a principle in relation to Elijah which was also true of John the Baptist, and the reference made by Christ was by way of application and not interpretation."[4] In short, John might have been Elijah, but was not.

But Matthew 17 is unambiguously clear. In Matthew 11 Christ is rebuking the spiritual obstinacy (11:16ff) of the crowds that came to hear Him (11:7). He urges them to hear and understand (11:15). He does not fear that they will derail prophetic fulfillment by their unbelief! When He says, "He who has ears to hear" (11:15), He does not imply the possible invalidity of His observations on John, but alludes to the spiritual dullness of those hearers who reject those observations (Matt. 13:9, 43; Mark 4:9; Luke 8:8; 14:35). The reason why John comes in the "spirit and power of Elijah" (Luke 1:17), and why he should be received as "Elijah who was to come" (Matt. 11:14), is because he is the fulfillment of the Elijah prophecy.

Neither may John Baptist's denial of being Elijah (John 1:21) be inimical to his fulfilling the prophecy.[5] His denial is with regard to his being the actual *corporeal* return of Elijah from heaven which is widely anticipated among the first century Jews. At one place in the Talmud it is written: "But when God shall bring [Elijah] to life in the body, he shall send him to Israel before the day of judgment."[6]

---

4. Herman Hoyt, "A Dispensational Response," *The Meaning of the Millennium: Four Views*, Robert G. Clouse, ed. (Downer's Grove, IL: InterVarsity Press, 1977), pp. 147-148. Cf. Louis A. Barbieri, Jr., "Matthew," *The Bible Knowledge Commentary: New Testament*, John F. Walvoord and Roy B. Zuck, eds. (Wheaton: Victor, 1983), p. 60.

5. John F. Walvoord, *Prophecy Knowledge Handbook* (Wheaton, IL: Victor, 1990), p. 339.

6. See sampling of Talmudic references in: Lightfoot, *Commentary on the New Testament from the Talmud and Hebraica*, 2:243-247.

The Antichrist

Perhaps more than any other evil figure in Scripture, the Antichrist is the most feared. Many dispensationalists are convinced that he is alive today. In an interview in *Eternity* magazine in 1977 Hal Lindsey responded to a question regarding the Antichrist: "[I]n my personal opinion, he's alive somewhere now."[7] This reminds us of Tertullian's statement in 1700 years ago that Antichrist "is now close at hand."[8] One poorly timed 1988 book was *Gorbachev: Has the Real Antichrist Come?*[9] Of course, this sort of belief has for generations been the tendency among dispensationalists, who have pointed out a number of possible Antichrist candidates.[10] One best-selling dispensationalist writes that there "is strong evidence indeed that the Antichrist could appear very soon – which means that the rapture may be imminent."[11] He is convinced that "somewhere, at this very moment, on planet Earth, the Antichrist is almost certainly alive."[12]

Ironically, the least helpful verses for developing the dispensational, premillennial, and amillennial view of the Antichrist are the *only* ones that expressly mention him. "Antichrist" ap-

7. Hal Lindsey interview, "The Great Cosmic Countdown: Hal Lindsey on the Future," *Eternity* (Jan. 1977) 80.

8. Tertullian *De Fuga* 12.

9. Robert W. Faid, *Gorbachev: Has the Real Antichrist Come?* (Tulsa, OK: Victory House, 1988).

10. Dwight Wilson, *Armageddon Now!: The Premillennial Response to Russia and Israel Since 1917* (Tyler, TX: Institute for Christian Economics, [1977] 1991). Gary DeMar, *Last Days Madness: The Folly of Trying to Predict When Christ Will Return* (Brentwood, TN: Wolgemuth & Hyatt, 1991). Gary North, *Rapture Fever: Why Dispensationalism is Paralyzed* (Tyler, Tex.: Institute for Christian Economics, 1993). See especially a dispensational analysis of the problem which adopts a modified preterism: C. Marvin Pate and Calvin B. Haines, Jr., *Doomsday Delusions: What's Wrong with Predictions About the End of the World* (Downer's Grove, Ill.: Inter-Varsity, 1995).

11. Dave Hunt, *Peace, Prosperity, and the Coming Holocaust* (Eugene, OR: Harvest House, 1983), p. 256. Commas were not in the original title.

12. Dave Hunt, *Global Peace and the Rise of Antichrist* (Eugene, OR: Harvest House, 1990), p. 5.

pears only four times in all of Scripture: 1 John 2:18, 22; 4:3; and 2 John 7. (Walvoord in his comprehensive *Prophecy Knowledge Handbook* does not even mention these verses in his treatment of "Prophecy in 1, 2, and 3 John and the Epistle of Jude" – or anywhere else in his 800-page work.)[13]

Often other figures, such as Daniel's Little Horn, Paul's Man of Sin, and John's Beast, are deemed to be references to Antichrist: The "organic development of sin finally culminates in the 'man of sin' (II Thessalonians 2:3-12). That is the kingdom of Antichrist."[14] "Plainly the idea [in Rev. 13:18] is that the world . . . ultimately will bring forth the antichrist, who is here called the beast."[15] But such do not appear to be so. None of these is called "Antichrist" – not even the Beast, who appears in the writings of the one who does employ the word "antichrist" elsewhere, John.[16]

The origin of the doctrine of Antichrist in the first century is obscure. It does seem that the Antichrist was thought to be a particular individual: "You have heard that the Antichrist is coming" (1 John 2:18b). John's point in mentioning him, however, is due to what his readers are hearing – and he sets out to correct the false views current on the notion. This is certainly a worthy task in our own time. Many things were heard among

---

13. Walvoord, *Prophecy Knowledge Handbook*, pp. 513ff. On the cover and beneath the title of this massive work we read: "All the prophecies of Scripture explained in one volume." Pentecost cites 1 John 4:2-3 once, but does not explain it or allude to the other verses in his treatment of "Antichrist" in his recent 350-page work. J. Dwight Pentecost, *Thy Kingdom Come* (Wheaton, IL: Victor, 1990), pp. 302ff.

14. Herman Hanko, "Response to 'The "Other Side" of Postmillennialism'," *Standard Bearer*, 66:8 (Apr. 1, 1990) 298.

15. John Heys, "Our Hope for Our Savior's Return," *ibid.* 66:7 (Jan. 1, 1990) 152.

16. Dispensationalist Walvoord mentions Antichrist in his discussion of the Little Horn in Daniel 8, which he also draws into his treatment of the Man of Lawlessness and the Beast. Walvoord, *Prophecy Knowledge Handbook*, pp. 240, 493. Amillennialist Anthony A. Hoekema and premillennialist George Eldon Ladd do, as well: Hoekema, *The Bible and the Future* (Grand Rapids: Eerdmans, 1979), pp. 154-162; Ladd, *The Last Things* (Grand Rapids: Eerdmans, 1978), ch. 6.

the early Christians, but were not properly understood. John even corrects a false notion regarding his living until Christ's return (John 21:22-23). Paul uses a false teaching regarding baptism for the dead to drive a point home regarding the resurrection (1 Cor. 15:29). Paul often urges his followers to hear him and preserve those things he teaches (Phil. 4:9; 1 Thess. 2:13; 2 Tim. 1:13; 2:2).

It is terribly important to observe that in John's correcting of the Antichrist notion "he makes three declarations concerning Antichrist which appear to traverse its implications. He transposes Antichrist from the future to the present. He expands him from an individual to a multitude. He reduces him from a person to a heresy."[17] With these three observations the bulk of modern Antichrist discussion is wholly undermined.

Antichrist's Time

John's readers had heard Antichrist was not yet on the scene but rather "is coming." John informs them that this "antichrist" "is *now* already in the world" (1 John 4:3). As Warfield notes "that post-posited 'already' [carries] with it the utmost strength of assertion."[18] "And this is the spirit of the Antichrist, which you have heard was coming, and is now already in the world" (1 John 4:3b). That which they "heard was coming" is expressly that which "is now already in the world." In addition, John remarks: "As you have heard that the Antichrist is coming, *even now* many antichrists have come" (1 John 2:18). Because of the appearance of these Antichrists, they were to know that "it is the last hour" (2:18). The appearance of these antichrists was not a harbinger of a future coming Antichrist, for their presence was the signal that "the last hour" had already "come"

---

17. Benjamin B. Warfield, "Antichrist" (1921), *The Selected Shorter Writings of Benjamin B. Warfield*, John E. Meeter, ed., 2 vols. (Nutley, NJ: Presbyterian & Reformed, 1970), 1:358.

18. *Ibid.*

(*gegonasin*). The "even now" emphasizes the presence of that which they feared ("as you heard").

An objection from one amillennialist theologian against post-millennialism is postmillennialism's removal of the antichrist not only from our future expectation but from the very center of time! "More and more that kingdom of darkness comes to manifestation as time progresses. At the very center of time therefore, stands the development of the Antichristian world power. Really, postmillennialism has no room for Antichrist in its thinking. . . . Antichrist cannot be taken seriously."[19]

Antichrist's Impersonality

In redirecting his readers' focus from the futurity of the Antichrist to his contemporary existence, John points out that the Antichrist is a *movement*, rather than an individual. In dealing with the idea of "the Antichrist," John writes: "even now many antichrists have come" (1 John 2:18). In fact, Antichrist is a "spirit" (1 John 4:3) that pervades these many "antichrists" (1 John 2:18), which are represented as "many deceivers" (2 John 7). Such views as Hoekema's are surely mistaken: "[T]he New Testament also teaches us to look for a single, final antichrist in the future (see 2 Thess. 2:3-4)."[20]

Antichrist's Tendency

Thus, Antichrist really is not a multitude of people, but rather the "spirit" (1 John 4:3) among them that would promote deception (2 John 7) regarding Christ. "Who is a liar but he who denies that Jesus is the Christ? He is antichrist who

---

19. Herman C. Hanko, "An Exegetical Refutation of Postmillennialism" (unpublished conference paper: South Holland, IL: South Holland Protestant Reformed Church, 1978), pp. 25-26.

20. Hoekema, *Bible and the Future*, p. 70. See discussion of 2 Thessalonians 2 below. For further detail, see: Kenneth L. Gentry, Jr, *Perilous Times: A Study in Eschatological Evil* (forthcoming).

denies the Father and the Son" (1 John 2:22). John clearly applies the conception of the one Antichrist (*ho antichristos*) to the generic tendency to promote lies about the identity of Christ. He repeats this point in his second letter: "For many deceivers have gone out into the world who do not confess Jesus Christ as coming in the flesh. This is a deceiver and the antichrist [*ho antichristos*]" (2 John 1:7).

On the basis of these four references we may learn that Antichrist is not an individual, malevolent ruler looming in our future. Rather, *Antichrist was a contemporary heretical tendency* regarding the person of Christ that was current among many in John's day. Hoekema is mistaken when he writes: "Yet it would not be correct to say that John had no room in his thinking for a personal antichrist, since he still looks for an antichrist who is coming."[21] As we shall see below, the Beast of Revelation and the Man of Lawlessness were also contemporary realities in the first century – though distinct from Antichrist.

The Beast of Revelation

Next to Antichrist the Beast of Revelation is probably one of the best-known eschatological images in Scripture.[22] Much has been written about him – much of it is worthless because a fundamental element necessary to properly identifying the Beast is often glossed over. That element is the exegetical determination of John's own expectations regarding the timing of the events of Revelation.

The Beast's Time

As I showed in Chapter 8 John clearly expected the events to occur in his day. Revelation opens and closes with anticipation of the imminent occurrence of the events specified within.

---

21. *Ibid.*, p. 158.

22. For a more detailed argument see my book, *The Beast of Revelation* (Tyler, TX: Institute for Christian Economics, 1989).

HE SHALL HAVE DOMINION

Revelation 1:1a reads: "The Revelation of Jesus Christ, which God gave Him to show His servants; things which must shortly take place." Revelation 22:10 warns: "Do not seal the words of the prophecy of this book, for the time is at hand."

In light of the original significance of Revelation to its first-century audience (Rev. 1:4, 11; 2-3), the Beast must be someone of relevance to that audience. Revelation 13 portrays him as a horrible and powerful foe of God's people and of all righteousness.

The Beast's Identity

Most commentators agree that the Beast imagery in Revelation shifts between the generic and the specific.[23] That is, sometimes the Beast seems to picture a kingdom, sometimes an individual leader of that kingdom. At some places the Beast has seven heads, which are seven kings collectively considered. In Revelation 13:1 John notes that he "saw *a beast* coming up out of the sea, having ten horns and *seven heads*." Revelation 17:10 specifically notes that the seven heads represent "seven kings." Thus, the *Beast* is generically portrayed as a *kingdom*. Kingdoms, however, have representatives. This is why, in the same contexts the Beast is also spoken of as an individual. John urges his readers to "calculate the number of the beast, for the number is that of *a man*" (Rev. 13:18). In Revelation 17:11 the interpretive angel tells John and his readers "the beast which was and is not, is himself also an eighth, and *is one of the seven*." This frustrating feature is recognized by many commentators of various schools of interpretation.

---

23. Walvoord, *Prophecy Knowledge Handbook*, p. 582. See also: Leon Morris, *The Revelation of St. John* (Grand Rapids: Eerdmans, 1969), pp. 210-211; R. H. Charles, *A Critical and Exegetical Commentary on the Revelation of St. John*, 2 vols. (Edinburgh: T. & T. Clark, 1920), 1:349; Philip Mauro, *Things Which Soon Must Come to Pass* (rev. ed.: Swengel, PA: Reiner Publications, [1925] 1984), p. 402; Pentecost, *Thy Kingdom Come*, pp. 306-307.

His Generic Identity. The generic identity of the Beast is the ancient Roman Empire of the first century. According to Revelation 17:9 the seven heads of the Beast represent "seven mountains." Perhaps no point is more obvious in Revelation than this: Rome is here symbolized by the seven mountains. After all, *Rome* is the one city in history distinguished by and recognized for its seven mountains.[24] The referent is virtually beyond doubt: the very Rome existing in the day of the Seven Churches of Revelation 2-3 – *not* a "revived Roman Empire," as per dispensationalism.

His Specific Identity. But who is the Beast *individually* considered? John tells us that the Beast imagery is also of "a man." The Beast in his personal incarnation is Nero Caesar. He and he alone fits the bill as the specific or personal expression of the Beast. This vile character fulfills all the requirements of the principles derived from the very text of Revelation. Notice the following:

First, the *number of the Beast.* In Revelation 13:18 the number of the beast is the number of "a man." That famous number is "666." The usefulness of this number lies in the fact that in ancient days alphabets served as both phonetic symbols and arithmetical values.[25] It is quite relevant that a *Hebrew* spelling of his name was *Nrwn Qsr*, which provides the numerical sum

24. See pagans writers: Ovid, *De Tristia* 1:5:69 and *Elegiae* 4; Claudian, *In Praise of Stilicon* 3:135; Statius, *Sylvae* 1; 2:191; Pliny, *Natural History* 3:5, 9; Virgil, *Aeneid* 6:782 and *Georgics* 2:535; Horace, *Carmen Secularae* 7; Propertius 3:10, 57; Martial 4:64; Cicero, *Ad Atticum* 6:5. Christians: Tertullian, *Apology* 35; Jerome, *Letter to Marcella*; and *Sibylline Oracles* 2:18; 11:114; 13:45; 14:108.

25. For the Hebrew values of the alphabet see: For Hebrew see: *Gesenius' Hebrew Grammar*, E. Kautzsch, ed., A. E. Cowley, trans. (28th ed.; Oxford: Clarendon, 1946), p. 30. Or see the appropriate letters at their entries in *A Hebrew and English Lexicon of the Old Testament*, Francis Brown, S. R. Driver, and Charles A. Briggs, eds. (Oxford: Clarendon, 1972).

666.[26] Hebrew would not have been widely known by non-Jewish, Greek-speaking Roman informers.

Second, the *textual variant*. The number 666 in some ancient manuscripts of Scripture is actually changed to 616. The difference surely is no accident of sight made by an early copyist. The numbers 666 and 616 are not similar in appearance in the original Greek – whether spelled out in words or written out as numerals. Textual scholars agree: it must be intentional.[27]

Although we cannot be absolutely certain, a strong and most reasonable case may be made for the following conjecture. John, a Jew, used a Hebrew spelling of Nero's name in order to arrive at the figure 666. But when Revelation began circulating among those less acquainted with Hebrew, a well-meaning copyist who knew the meaning of 666 might have intended to make its deciphering easier by altering it to 616. It surely is no mere coincidence that 616 is the numerical value of "Nero Caesar," when spelled in Hebrew by transliterating it from its more common Latin spelling.

Third, the *beastly image*. In Revelation 13, the one behind the 666 riddle is both called and portrayed as a "beast." Because of its natural association, the term "beast" is often used figuratively of persons with a bestial nature. It is almost universally agreed that Nero possessed a bestial nature. Nero was even feared and hated by his own countrymen, as ancient Roman historians agree.[28] The pagan writer Apollinius of Tyana, a contempo-

---

26. D. R. Hillers, "Revelation 13:18 and A Scroll from Murabba'at," *Bulletin of the American Schools of Oriental Research* 170 (April 1963) 65. Marcus Jastrow, *A Dictionary of the Targumim, the Talmud Babli and Yerushalmi, and the Midrashic Literature* (London: 1903). For a description of how this works, see ch. 17 below.

27. Bruce M. Metzger, *A Textual Commentary on the Greek New Testament* (London: United Bible Societies, 1971), pp. 751-752. David H. Van Daalen, "Six Hundred Sixty-six," in Bruce M. Metzger and Michael D. Coogan, eds., *The Oxford Companion to the Bible* (New York: Oxford University Press, 1993), pp. 699-700.

28. Suetonius, *Nero* 7:1; 27:1; 12:1; 28-29; 33-35; Tacitus, *Histories* 4:7; 4:8; Pliny, *Natural History* 7:45; 22:92; Juvenal, *Satire* 7:225; 10:306ff; See also: Dio, *Roman History* 61:1:2; *Ascension of Isaiah* 4:1; *Sibylline Oracles* 5:30; 12:82.

rary of Nero, specifically mentions that Nero was called a "beast."[29]

Fourth, the *war with the saints*. The Beast is said to "make war with the saints and to overcome them" (Rev. 13:7). In fact, he is said to conduct such blasphemous warfare for a specific period of time: 42 months (Rev. 13:5). The Neronic persecution initiated by Nero in A.D. 64[30] is the first ever *Roman* assault on Christianity, as noted by Church fathers Eusebius, Tertullian, Paulus Orosius, and Sulpicius Severus, as well as by Roman historians Tacitus and Suetonius.[31] The persecution finally ended when Nero died on June 8, A.D. 68, forty-two months later, but for a few days.[32] Nero's own end even came with a sword, as per Revelation 13:14.[33]

The Great Harlot

In Revelation 17:3-6 John views a horrifying sight. Seated upon the dreadful Beast is the sinful Harlot:

> I saw a woman sit upon a scarlet coloured beast, full of names of blasphemy, having seven heads and ten horns. And the woman was arrayed in purple and scarlet colour, and decked with gold and precious stones and pearls, having a golden cup in her hand full of abominations and filthiness of her fornication: And upon her forehead [was] a name written, MYSTERY, BABYLON THE GREAT, THE MOTHER OF HARLOTS AND ABOMINA-

29. Philostratus, *Life of Apollonius* 4:38.

30. Herbert B. Workman, *Persecution in the Early Church* (Oxford: Oxford University Press, [1906] 1980), p. 22; Philip Schaff, *History of the Christian Church*, 8 vols. (3rd. ed.; Grand Rapids: Eerdmans, [1910] 1950), 1:379.

31. Eusebius, *Ecclesiastical History* 2:25:3; Sulpicius Severus, *Sacred History* 2:28; Tertullian (A.D. 160-220), *On the Mantle* 4; *Apology* 5; Paulus Orosius (A.D. 385-415), *The Seven Books of History Against the Pagans*, 7:7; Tacitus, *Annals* 15:44; Suetonius, *Nero* 16.

32. Justo L. Gonzalez, *The Early Church to the Dawn of the Reformation* (San Francisco: Harper & Row, 1984), p. 36; John Laurence von Mosheim, *History of Christianity in the First Three Centuries*, 2 vols. (New York: Converse, 1854), 1:138-139.

33. Suetonius, *Nero* 49.

HE SHALL HAVE DOMINION

TIONS OF THE EARTH. And I saw the woman drunken with the blood of the saints, and with the blood of the martyrs of Jesus: and when I saw her, I wondered with great admiration.

Since the woman is seated upon the seven-headed Beast, some have thought that she is representative of the city of Rome. She is resting upon the seven hills of Rome and she is called "Babylon," the Old Testament oppressor of God's people, which seems to refer to her New Testament oppressor, Rome. But since the Beast itself represents Rome, it would seem redundant to have the woman representing the same. Also, the name "Babylon" does not historically belong either to Rome or Jerusalem, and thus cannot be proof that the city is Rome rather than Jerusalem.[34] I am convinced beyond any doubt that this Harlot is first-century Jerusalem. The evidence for so identifying Jerusalem is based on the following considerations.

First, in Revelation 14:8 "Babylon" is called "the great city." But in the first mention of "the great city" in Revelation 11:8, the reference indisputably pointed to Jerusalem, "where also our Lord was crucified" (cf. Luke 9:31; 13:33-34; 18:31; 24:18-20). This greatness is especially in regard to her *covenantal status* in the Old Testament.[35] Even pagan writers spoke highly of Jerusalem. Tacitus called it "a famous city." Pliny the Elder said of Jerusalem that it was "by far the most famous city of the ancient Orient." Appian, a Roman lawyer and writer (*ca.* A.D.

---

34. Most commentators, even dispensationalists, recognize the term "Babylon" as symbolic. See: John F. Walvoord, *The Revelation of Jesus Christ* (Chicago: Moody Press, 1966), p. 218. Charles Dyer has recently (and wrongly, I believe) suggested it may be ancient Babylon that is actually rebuilt in his *The Rise of Babylon: Sign of the End Times* (Wheaton, IL: Tyndale, 1991). This book became a best-seller during the Persian Gulf crisis: August, 1990, to February, 1991.

35. The adjective "great" is applied to Jerusalem in ancient Jewish writings: "In opposition to her rival Alexandria, which was designated 'the little,' Jerusalem was called 'the great.' " Alfred Edersheim, *Sketches of Jewish Social Life in the Days of Christ* (Grand Rapids: Eerdmans, [1876] 1970), p. 82.

160) called it "the great city Jerusalem."[36] The Sibylline Oracles, Josephus, and the Talmud concur in calling Jerusalem "a great city."[37] Thus, the first interpretive clue to the identity of Babylon points to Jerusalem: the great city.

Second, the Harlot is filled with the blood of the saints according to Revelation 16:6; 17:6; 18:21, 24. Of course, with the outbreak of the Neronic persecution, which had just commenced when John wrote Revelation,[38] Rome was stained with the blood of the saints. But Rome had only recently entered the persecuting ranks of God's enemies. Throughout Acts *Jerusalem* is portrayed as the *persecutor* and Rome as the protector of Christianity.[39] Interestingly, in the Olivet Discourse context Jesus reproaches Jerusalem: "Therefore, indeed, I send you prophets, wise men, and scribes: some of them you will kill and crucify, and some of them you will scourge in your synagogues and persecute from city to city, that on you may come all the righteous blood shed on the earth, from the blood of righteous Abel to the blood of Zechariah, son of Berechiah, whom you murdered between the temple and the altar. . . . Jerusalem, Jerusalem, the one who kills the prophets and stones those who are sent to her! How often I wanted to gather your children together, as a hen gathers her chicks under her wings, but you were not willing!" (Matt. 23:34-35, 37). Before his stoning Stephen rebukes Jerusalem: "Which of the prophets have not your fathers persecuted? And they have slain them who showed

---

36. Tacitus, *Histories* 5:2; *Fragments of the Histories* 1; Pliny, *Natural History* 5:14:70; Appian, *The Syrian Wars* 50.

37. *Sibylline Oracles* 5:150-154, 408-413; Josephus, *Wars* 7:1:1; 7:8:7. For Talmudic references, see: Edersheim, *Sketches of Jewish Social Life*, p. 82. For a discussion of this issue, see my *Before Jerusalem Fell: Dating the Book of Revelation* (Tyler, TX: Institute for Christian Economics, 1989), pp. 169ff.

38. Gentry, *Before Jerusalem Fell*.

39. See for example: Acts 4:3; 5:18-33; 6:12; 7:54-60; 8:1ff; 9:1-4, 13, 23; 11:19; 12:1-3; 13:45-50; 14:2-5, 19; 16:23; 17:5-13; 18:12; 20:3, 19; 21:11, 27; 22:30; 23:12, 20, 27, 30; 24:5-9; 25:2-15; 25:24; 26:21. See also: 2 Cor. 11:24; 2 Thess. 2:14-15; Heb. 10:32-34; Rev. 2:9; 3:9; etc.

before of the coming of the Just One, of whom ye have been now the betrayers and murderers" (Acts 7:51-52).

Paul warns of Jewish persecution: "For you, brethren, became imitators of the churches of God which are in Judea in Christ Jesus. For you also suffered the same things from your own countrymen, just as they did from the Jews, who killed both the Lord Jesus and their own prophets, and have persecuted us; and they do not please God and are contrary to all men, forbidding us to speak to the Gentiles that they may be saved, so as always to fill up the measure of their sins; but wrath has come upon them to the uttermost" (1 Thess. 2:14-16).

Third, the Harlot is arrayed in *Jewish priestly colors* of scarlet, purple, and gold (Exo. 28).[40] She has a blasphemous tiara on her forehead, which reads: "Mystery, Babylon the Great, the Mother of Harlots and of the Abominations of the Earth" (Rev. 17:5). This gives a negative portrayal of the holy tiara that the Jewish high priest wore, which said "Holy to the Lord" (Exo. 28:36-38). Also, the Harlot has a gold cup in her hand, as did the high priest on the Day of Atonement, according to the Jewish Talmud.[41]

Fourth, Rome could not commit adultery against God, for she had never been God's wife. But Jerusalem was God's wife (Jer. 31:31), and she is often said to commit adultery against Him.[42] The imagery of the Harlot better suits an adulterous wife, and the biblical record points to Jerusalem as that adulterous wife.

Fifth, there is an obvious *literary contrast* between the Harlot and the chaste bride, suggesting an intentional contrast with the

---

40. Cf. Rev. 17:4-5 with Exo. 25:2, 4; 26:1, 31, 36; 27:16; 28:1-2, 5-12, 15, 17-23, 33.

41. Golden vessels are common on the Day of Atonement. The fire-pan for scooping cinders was gold, Yoma 4:4. "The High Priest always sanctified his hands and his feet from a golden jug," Yoma 4:5.

42. Isa. 1:21; 57:8; Jer. 2:2, 20; 3:1-20; 4:30; 11:15; 13:27; Ezek. 16; Hos. 2:5; 3:3; 4:15.

Jerusalem below and the *Jerusalem above* (Rev. 21:2; cf. Gal. 4:24ff.; Heb. 12:18ff.). In Revelation 17:2-5 and Revelation 21:1ff the contrast is remarkable and exact. We must remember that the bride is specifically called the "New Jerusalem" from heaven. We see five contrasts:

(1) Notice how John is *introduced* to the Harlot: "Then one of the seven angels who had the seven bowls came and talked with me, saying to me, 'Come, I will show you the judgment of the great harlot who sits on many waters' " (Rev. 17:1). Then notice how he is introduced to the bride: "Then one of the seven angels who had the seven bowls filled with the seven last plagues came to me and talked with me, saying, 'Come, I will show you the bride, the Lamb's wife' " (Rev. 21:9).

(2) The two women are contrasted as to *character:* "Come, I will show you the judgment of the great harlot who sits on many waters" (Rev. 17:1). "Come, I will show you the bride, the Lamb's wife" (Rev. 21:9).

(3) The two women are seen in *contrasting environments* to which John is carried by the angel. "So he carried me away in the Spirit into the wilderness. And I saw a woman sitting on a scarlet beast" (Rev. 17:3). "And he carried me away in the Spirit to a great and high mountain, and showed me the great city, the holy Jerusalem, descending out of heaven from God" (Rev. 21:10).

(4) The *dress* of each is detailed and contrasted: "The woman was arrayed in purple and scarlet, and adorned with gold and precious stones and pearls, having in her hand a golden cup full of abominations and the filthiness of her fornication" (Rev. 17:4). "And to her it was granted to be arrayed in fine linen, clean and bright, for the fine linen is the righteous acts of the saints . . . having the glory of God. And her light was like a most precious stone, like a jasper stone, clear as crystal" (Rev. 19:8; 21:11).

(5) The *names* are contrasted. Jerusalem had previously been called by pagan names quite compatible with the designation

"Babylon." In Revelation 11:8 she is called "spiritually Sodom and Egypt." In an earlier day Isaiah identifies Jerusalem as Sodom and Gomorrah (Isa. 1). The idea is that rather than conducting herself as the wife of God, she has become one of God's enemies, like Sodom, Egypt, and Babylon.

The fact that the Harlot is seated on the seven-headed Beast (representing Rome, as shown above) indicates not her *identity* with Rome, but her *alliance* with Rome against Christianity. The Jews demanded Christ's crucifixion and constantly stirred up the Romans against the Christians (cf. Matt. 23:37ff.; Acts 8:1; 12:1-3; 17:5-7; 1 Thess. 2:14-17).

The evidence proves that the Harlot is Jerusalem.[43] John's Revelation contrasts the Jerusalem below with the Jerusalem above, as in Hebrews 12:22 and Galatians 4:25-26. The Jerusalem below has forsaken her husband in denying the Messiah.

The Man of Lawlessness

We come now to another of those very difficult passages of Scripture, one rivaling Daniel 9 in the intensity of interpretive controversy: 2 Thessalonians 2. This famous eschatological reference contains Paul's reference to the "Man of Lawlessness" (Nestle's Text) or "Man of Sin" (Majority Text).

The passage is noted for its exceptional difficulty. The noted church father Augustine writes of a certain portion of the passage: "I confess that I am entirely ignorant of what he means to say." New Testament Greek scholar Vincent omits interpreting the passage in his four volume lexical commentary: "I attempt no interpretation of this passage as a whole, which I do not understand." Renowned Greek linguist Robertson despairs of the task of interpreting this passage because it is "in such vague form that we can hardly clear it up." Morris urges "care" in handling this "notoriously difficult passage." Bruce notes that

---

43. Joseph Balyeat, *Babylon, The Great City of Revelation* (Sevierville, TN: Onward Press, 1991).

"there are few New Testament passages which can boast such a variety of interpretations as this."[44] There are even some dispensationalists who admit that it is an "extremely puzzling passage of Scripture that has been a thorn in the flesh of many an expositor."[45]

As with the hotly debated Daniel 9:24-27 passage, so it is here: An exceedingly difficult prophecy becomes a key text for dispensationalism. Note the following comments by dispensationalists. Constable observes that "this section of verses contain truths found nowhere else in the Bible. It is key to understanding future events and it is central to this epistle." According to Walvoord, the Man of Lawlessness revealed here is "the key to the whole program of the Day of the Lord." Of 2 Thessalonians 2 Chafer notes: "though but one passage is found bearing upon the restraining work of the Holy Spirit, the scope of the issues involved is such as to command the utmost consideration." Ryrie and Feinberg employ 2 Thessalonians 2:4 as one of the few passages used "to clinch the argument" for the rebuilding of the Temple.[46] There is no doubt that anti-postmillennial commentators place considerable weight on this passage.

Because of its enormous difficulties, 2 Thessalonians 2 has generated lively debate in eschatological studies. The pessimistic eschatologies of amillennialism, premillennialism, and dispensationalism frequently employ this passage as evidence of worsen-

---

44. Augustine is cited in Henry Alford, *The Greek New Testament*, 4 vols. (Chicago: Moody Press [n.d.] 1958), 2:82. Marvin R. Vincent, *Word Studies in the New Testament*, 4 vols. (Grand Rapids: Eerdmans, [1887] 1985), 4:67. A. T. Robertson, *Word Pictures in the New Testament*, 6 vols. (Nashville: Broadman, 1930), 4:51. Leon Morris, *The First and Second Epistles to the Thessalonians* (*NICNT*) (Grand Rapids: Eerdmans, 1959), p. 213. F. F. Bruce, *New Testament History* (Garden City, NY: Anchor, 1969), p. 309.

45. E. S. English, *Rethinking the Rapture* (Neptune, NJ: Loizeaux, 1954), p. 72.

46. Thomas L. Constable, "2 Thessalonians," *Bible Knowledge Commentary: New Testament*, p. 717. Walvoord, *Prophecy Knowledge Handbook*, p. 493. Lewis Sperry Chafer, *Systematic Theology*, 8 vols. (Dallas: Dallas Theological Seminary, 1948), 6:85. Charles C. Ryrie, *The Basis of the Premillennial Faith* (Neptune, NJ: Loizeaux Bros., 1953), p. 151. See also: Charles Lee Feinberg, "The Jew After the Rapture," *Prophecy and the Seventies*, Feinberg, ed. (Chicago: Moody Press, 1971), p. 181.

ing world conditions until the final apostasy. When setting forth objections against postmillennialism, amillennialist Hoekema makes but a cursory reference to this passage in a mere two sentences, confident that it offers a self-evident refutation of postmillennialism.[47] Though a perplexing passage requiring caution, there are sufficient data in it to remove it at least as an objection to postmillennialism.

The Historical Setting

During Paul's visit to Thessalonica he preached to the Jews that Jesus was the Messiah (Acts 17:1-3). Though some Jews believed Paul, others were riled to mob action regarding the Christian message (17:4-5). They dragged "some of the brethren to the rulers of the city" complaining: "These who have turned the world upside down have come here too. Jason has harbored them, and these are all acting contrary to the decrees of Caesar, saying there is another king – Jesus" (17:6-7). After taking security from Jason and the others, the civil rulers let them go (17:9). This allowed Paul to depart safely to Berea. The Jews were not so easily quieted, however, for "when the Jews from Thessalonica learned that the word of God was preached by Paul at Berea, they came there also and stirred up the crowds" (17:13). This resulted in the immediate sending away of Paul to Athens (17:14-15).

This explains the strong language against the Jews in the Thessalonian epistles, and helps uncover some of the more subtle concerns therein. In his first letter he writes: "For you, brethren, became imitators of the churches of God which are in Judea in Christ Jesus. For you also suffered the same things from your own countrymen, just as they did from the Jews, who killed both the Lord Jesus and their own prophets, and have persecuted us; and they do not please God and are con-

---

47. Hoekema, *Bible and the Future*, p. 178. See also: Hanko, "An Exegetical Refutation of Postmillennialism," p. 26.

trary to all men, forbidding us to speak to the Gentiles that they may be saved, so as always to fill up the measure of their sins; but wrath has come upon them to the uttermost" (1 Thess. 2:14-16).

This Jewish context is important for grasping the situation Paul confronts. I show in the exposition to follow that there are a number of allusions to the Olivet Discourse. The Olivet Discourse speaks of the destruction of the Temple and the judgment of the Jews for rejecting Jesus as the Messiah (cf. Matt. 23:35-24:2; cf. Acts 17:3; 18:5).[48]

Exposition of the Text

Verses 1-2. Paul's reference "concerning the coming of our Lord Jesus Christ and our gathering together to Him" (2 Thess. 2:1) is the *crux interpretum* of this passage. Paul is here speaking of the A.D. 70 judgment on the Jews – the very judgment given emphasis in the first portion of the Olivet Discourse, the Book of Revelation, and several other passages of Scripture.

Though he speaks of the Second Advent just a few verses before (1:10), he is not dealing with that issue here. In 2 Thessalonians 1:10 Paul even employs a different word for the *coming* of Christ (*elthe*) from what he uses in 2:1 (*parousia*). There the Second Adventent judgment brings "everlasting destruction from the presence of the Lord" (1:9); here a temporal "destruction" (2:8). There the Second Advent includes "his mighty angels" (1:7); here the temporal judgment makes no mention of these mighty angels (2:1-12). Thus, the *Second Advent* provides an *eternal resolution* to their suffering; the *A.D. 70* Day of the Lord affords *temporal resolution* (cf. Rev. 6:10).

---

48. Page attempts to draw the parallel with Revelation 20, comparing the restraint and deception of Satan and the flaming coming of Christ there with the deception, restraint, and coming here. Sydney H. T. Page, "Revelation 20 and Pauline Eschatology," *Journal of the Evangelical Theological Society* 23:1 (March 1980) 31-44.

Furthermore, the "gathering together to Him" mentioned by Paul in 2 Thessalonians 2:1 picks up on the reference of our Lord in Matthew 24:31. The word translated "gather together" here is *episunagoge*. Its cognate verb form is found in Matthew 24:31, where the *gathering* is tied to "this generation" (Matt. 24:34) and signifies the calling out of the elect into the body of Christ with the *trumpeting in* of the archetypical Great Jubilee (cf. 2 Thess. 1:11; 2:14).[49] Here it functions the same way. With the coming destruction of Jerusalem and the Temple, Christians would henceforth be "gathered together" in a *separate* and *distinct* "assembly" (*episunagoge*; the Church is called a *sunagoge* in James 2:2). After the Temple's destruction, God would no longer tolerate going up to the Temple to worship (it would be impossible!), as Christians frequently did prior to A.D. 70.[50]

Paul consoles them by denying the false report that "the day of Christ had come" (2 Thess. 2:2). Apparently, the very reason for this epistle, written so soon after the first one, is that some unscrupulous deceivers had forged letters from Paul and had claimed erroneous charismatic insights relevant to eschatological concerns. In his earlier letter, he had to correct their grief over loved ones who had died in the Lord, as if this precluded their sharing in the resurrection (1 Thess. 4:13-17). Now new eschatological deceptions were troubling the young church (2 Thess. 2:1-3a): Some thought that the Day of the Lord had come[51] and, consequently, they quit working (2 Thess. 3:6-12).

---

49. See: pp. 333-349, above, for a discussion of the Great Tribulation passage in Matthew 24. Cf. J. Marcellus Kik, *An Eschatology of Victory* (n.p.: Presbyterian & Reformed, 1971), pp. 144-150. David Chilton, *The Great Tribulation* (Ft. Worth, TX: Dominion Press, 1987), pp. 25-28.

50. Acts 1:4; 1:8; 18:21; 20:16; 24:11. Even in this early post-commission Christianity, believers continued to gravitate toward the Jews: engaging in Jewish worship observances (Acts 2:1ff.; 21:26; 24:11), focusing on and radiating their ministry from Jerusalem (Acts 2-5), frequenting the Temple (Acts 2:46; 3:1ff.; 4:1; 5:21ff.; 21:26; 26:21), and attending the synagogues (13:5, 14; 14:1; 15:21; 17:1ff.; 18:4, 7, 19, 26; 19:8; 22:19; 24:12; 26:11).

51. Greek: *enesteken*. A. M. G. Stephenson, "On the meaning of *enesteken he hemera*

The word "trouble" (*throeo*; 2:2) is in the present infinitive form, which signifies a continued state of agitation. It is the same word used elsewhere only in the Olivet Discourse (Mark 13:7; Matt. 24:6). There it is even found in the same sort of theological context: one warning of *deception* and *trouble* regarding the *coming* of the Day of Christ (Mark 13:5-7).

Verses 3-7. Paul is quite concerned about the deception being promoted (v. 3a). To avoid the deception and to clarify the true beginning of the Day of the Lord upon Jerusalem, Paul informs them that "that Day will not come unless the falling away comes first, and the man of sin is revealed, the son of perdition" (2 Thess. 2:3). Before they could say the Day of the Lord "is come," then, there must first (see RSV) be the falling away and the revelation of the man of lawlessness, who is also called "the son of perdition." (These do not have to occur in the chronological order presented, as even dispensationalists admit.[52] Verse nine is clearly out of order and should occur in the midst of verse eight, if strict chronology were important.)

The word "falling away" is *apostasia*, which occurs in the New Testament only here and in Acts 21:21. Historically, the word can apply to a *revolt*: either political or religious.[53] But to which does it refer here? Does it refer to a future worldwide apostasy from the Christian faith, as per pessimistic eschatologies? Amillennialist William Hendriksen writes that this teaches

---

tou kuriou in 2 Thessalonians 2:2," *Texte und Untersuchungen zur Geschichte der altchristlichen Literatur* 102 (1968) 442-451. W. F. Arndt and F. W. Gingrich, *A Greek-English Lexicon of the New Testament* (Chicago: University of Chicago Press, 1957), p. 266. See: Morris, *1 and 2 Thessalonians*, p. 215. Note the agreement among the following translations: NASB, NKJV, NEB, TEV, Moffatt's New Translation, Weymouth, Williams, Beck.

52. Constable, "2 Thessalonians," p. 718. Non-dispensationalist Marshall comments: "The argument is difficult to follow, partly because of the way in which Paul tackles the theme in a non-chronological manner." I. Howard Marshall, *1 and 2 Thessalonians* (Grand Rapids: Eerdmans, 1983), p. 185.

53. For political *apostasia* see the Septuagint at Ezra 4:12, 15, 19; Neh. 2:19; 6:6. For religious *apostasia*, see: Septuagint at Josh. 22:22; 2 Chr. 29:19; and 33:19, and in the New Testament Acts 21:21.

that "by and large, the visible Church will forsake the true faith." Dispensationalist Constable comments: "This rebellion, which will take place within the professing church, will be a departure from the truth that God has revealed in His Word."[54] Or does the *apostasia* refer to a political rebellion of some sort?

A good case can be made that it speaks of the Jewish apostasy/rebellion against Rome. Josephus certainly speaks of the Jewish War as an *apostasia* against the Romans (Josephus, *Life* 4). Probably Paul merges the two concepts of religious and political apostasy here, although emphasizing the outbreak of the Jewish War, which was the result of their apostasy against God. The emphasis must be on the revolt against Rome because it is *future and datable*, whereas the revolt against God is ongoing and cumulative. Such is necessary to dispel the deception that Paul was concerned with. In conjunction with this final apostasy and the consequent destruction of Jerusalem, Christianity and Judaism were forever separated and both were exposed to the wrath of Rome.[55]

The Man of Lawlessness is Nero Caesar, who also is the Beast of Revelation, as a number of Church Fathers believed.[56] The difficulty of this passage lies in the fact that Paul "describes the Man of Sin with a certain reserve" (Origen, *Celsus* 6:45) for fear of incurring "the charge of calumny for having spoken evil of the Roman emperor" (Augustine, *City of God* 20:19). Paul and his associates had already suffered at the hands of the Thessalonian Jews for "acting contrary to the decrees of Caesar, saying there is another king – Jesus" (Acts

---

54. Hendriksen, *I and II Thessalonians* (*NTC*) (Grand Rapids: Baker, 1955), p. 170. Constable, "2 Thessalonians," p. 718.

55. See: Gentry, *Before Jerusalem Fell*, pp. 293-298. Warfield, "The Prophecies of St. Paul," *Selected Shorter Writings*, 1:473-475.

56. For example: Augustine, *City of God* 20:19; Chrysostom cited in Alford, *Greek Testament*, 2:80. If we are correct in equating him with the Beast, we could add: Victorinus, *Apocalypse* 17:16; Lactantius, *On the Death of the Persecutors* 2; Sulpicius Severus, *Sacred History* 2:28, 29. See my book, *Beast of Revelation*.

17:7). Wisdom demanded discreetness in referring to imperial authority; his recent (1 Thess. 2:17) personal ministry among them allowed it: they were to "remember" that while with them he "told [them] these things" (2:5).

It is at least clear from Paul that something is presently (*ca.* A.D. 52) "restraining" (present participle) the Man of Sin "that he may be revealed in his own time" (2:6). The Man of Lawlessness was alive and waiting to be "revealed." This implies that for the time being, Christians could expect at least some protection from the Roman government: the Roman laws regarding *religio licita* were currently in Christianity's favor, while it was considered a sect of Judaism but before the malevolent Nero ascended the throne. Paul certainly was protected by the Roman judicial apparatus (Acts 18:12ff) and made important use of these laws in A.D. 59 (Acts 25:11-12; 28:19) as protection from the malignancy of the Jews. He expressed no ill-feelings against Rome when writing Romans 13 in A.D. 57-59: during the early reign of Nero, the famous *Quinquennium Neronis*.[57]

When Paul wrote 2 Thessalonians 2, he was under the reign of Claudius Caesar. It may be that he employs a word play on Claudius' name. The Latin word for "restraint" is *claudere*, which is similar to "Claudius."[58] It is interesting that Paul shifts between the neuter and masculine forms of "the restrainer" (2 Thess. 2:6, 7). This may indicate he includes both the imperial law and the present emperor in his designation "restrainer." While Claudius lived, Nero, the Man of Lawlessness, was without power to commit public lawlessness. Christianity was free from the imperial sword until the Neronic persecution began in November, A.D 64.

Remarkably, the Jews were kept so in check by imperial law that they did not kill James the Just in Jerusalem until about

---

57. Trajan, *Epistle* 5; cf. Suetonius, *Nero* 19. See: B. W. Henderson, *The Life and Principate of the Emperor Nero* (London: Methuen, 1903), ch. 3.

58. Bruce, *New Testament History*, p. 310.

A.D. 62, after the death of the Roman procurator Festus and before the arrival of Albinus (Josephus, *Ant.* 20:9:1). With these events the "*mystery* of lawlessness" was being uncovered as the "*revelation* of the Man of Lawlessness" (the transformation of the Roman imperial line into a persecuting power in the person of Nero) was occurring.

The evil "mystery of lawlessness" was "already working," though restrained in Claudius' day (2 Thess. 2:7). This is perhaps a reference to the evil conniving and plotting of Nero's mother, Agrippina, who may have poisoned Claudius so that Nero could ascend to the purple (Tacitus, *Annals* 12:62ff; Suetonius, *Claudius* 44). The Roman emperor, according to Paul, "exalts himself above all that is called God or that is worshiped" (2 Thess. 2:4a). The evil potential of emperor worship was publicly exhibited just a few years before, when the emperor Caligula (a.k.a. Gaius, sometimes spelled: Caius) attempted to put his image in the Temple in Jerusalem (Josephus, *Ant.* 18:8:2-3).

The phrase "so that he sits as God in the temple of God, showing himself that he is God" is interesting. When *hoste* ("so that") is followed by an infinitive (*kathisai*, "to sit"), it indicates a *purpose* intended, not necessarily a *purpose accomplished*.[59] It was Caligula's *intention* to sit in "the temple of God" in Jerusalem; it was the emperor's desire to "show himself that he is God." In fact, Philo tells us that "so great was the caprice of Caius [Caligula] in his conduct toward all, and especially toward the nation of the Jews. The latter he so bitterly hated that he appropriated to himself their places of worship in the other cities, and beginning with Alexandria he filled them with images and statues of himself."[60]

---

59. As in Luke 4:29, where the Jews led Jesus to a hill "so as to cast him down (*hoste katakremnisai auton*)." E. Best, *Commentary on First and Second Thessalonians* (London: Black, 1977), pp. 286-290. H. E. Dana and Julius R. Mantey, *A Manual Grammar of the Greek New Testament* (Toronto: Macmillan, 1955), p. 214.

60. Philo, *Legatio ad Caium* 43, as cited by Eusebius, *Ecclesiastical History* 2:6:2.

This was for all intents and purposes accomplished by future emperor Titus, who concluded the devastation of Jerusalem set in motion by Nero. Titus actually invaded the Temple in A.D. 70 (Josephus, *Wars* 6:6:1). This parallels Matthew 24:15 and functions as *Paul's abomination of desolation*, which was to occur in "this generation" (Matt. 24:34).

Not only so but in Nero the imperial line eventually openly "opposed" (2 Thess. 2:4) Christ by persecuting His followers. Nero even began the persecution of Christians when he presented himself in a chariot as the sun god Apollo, while burning Christians in order to illuminate his self-glorifying party.[61]

Verses 8-9. Verses 8 and 9 read: "And then the lawless one will be revealed, whom the Lord will consume with the breath of His mouth and destroy with the brightness of His coming. The coming of the lawless one is according to the working of Satan, with all power, signs, and lying wonders."[62] As indicated, the lawless one was eventually openly revealed. The mystery form of his character gave way to a revelation of his lawlessness in Nero's wicked acts. This occurred after the restrainer [Claudius] was "taken out of the way," allowing Nero the public stage upon which he could act out his horrendous lawlessness.

In that judgment-coming against Jerusalem, there is also judgment for the Man of Lawlessness, Nero. There is hope and comfort in the promised relief from the opposition of the Jews and Nero (2 Thess. 2:15-17). Not only was Jerusalem destroyed within twenty years, but Nero himself died a violent death in the midst of the Jewish War (June 8, A.D. 68). His death, then, would occur in the Day of the Lord in conjunction with the judgment-coming of Christ. He would be destroyed by the breath of Christ, much like Assyria was destroyed with the

---

61. Gentry, *Before Jerusalem Fell*, pp. 279-284. Tacitus, *Annals* 15:44.

62. Such imperial arrogance would produce alleged miracles as confirmation. Vespasian is called "the miracle worker, because by him "many miracles occurred." Tacitus, *Histories* 4:81; Suetonius, *Vespasian* 7.

coming and breath of the LORD in the Old Testament (Isa. 30:27-31) and like Israel was crushed by Babylon (Mic. 1:3-5).

Conclusion

There are a number of prominent characters who dot the prophetic Scriptures. Often it seems that these are better known than the general flow of eschatology itself. What contemporary evangelical Christian has not heard and spoken about the Beast and the Antichrist? So many of these characters are evil minions of Satan and are thought by adherents to pessimistic eschatologies to be inimical to the postmillennial hope. We have seen that this pessimistic concern regarding the persecutors prophesied in the New Testament is no longer legitimate. When the characters highlighted above are carefully studied in terms of their historical context, the prophecies concerning their imminent appearance are shown to mesh well with postmillennialism. This is largely due to the preteristic conception of these characters – good (Elijah) and bad (the Harlot) – in terms of a proper biblical hermeneutic. The historical Elijah had gone to his reward long before Jesus appeared; he will not be back. The covenantal, baptizing Elijah has done the same. So has the Harlot Jerusalem, being destroyed in A.D. 70 by the corporate Beast Rome. The personal Beast Nero had gone to his reward the year before.

17

REVELATION

Then he said to me, "These words are faithful and true." And the Lord God of the holy prophets sent His angel to show His servants the things which must shortly take place. (Revelation 22:6)

Introduction

Revelation stands apart from all other New Testament books as the one pre-eminently concerned with prophetic questions. A substantially wrong view of this capstone of biblical prophecy is therefore inimical to any hope for a truly biblical eschatology. Indeed, non-postmillennial scholars often point to the woes of Revelation as contra-indicative to postmillennialism.[1] Although we cannot delve deeply into Revelation, it is important that we at least grasp its fundamental drift and major features.[2] The vantage point from which I approach Revelation is that of preterism,[3] which I introduced briefly in Chapter 8. Despite

---

1. For example, Floyd E. Hamilton, *The Basis of the Millennial Faith* (Grand Rapids: Eerdmans, 1942), p. 33; Bruce Milne, *What The Bible Teaches About the End of the World* (Wheaton, IL: Tyndale, 1979), pp. 80-81.

2. For more information see my: *The Divorce of Israel: A Commentary on Revelation* (forthcoming) and David Chilton, *The Days of Vengeance: An Exposition of the Book of Revelation* (Ft. Worth, TX: Dominion Press, 1987).

3. For a comparison of the four basic approaches to Revelation, see C. Marvin Pate, ed., *Four Views of the Book of Revelation*, which includes my detailed defense of the preterist view.

popular opinion, Revelation is a prophetic work that has largely been fulfilled in the past. After introducing several interpretively significant aspects of Revelation, I will survey its prophetic flow.

Original Audience

When interpreting any book of the Bible it is important to understand the audience to which it was originally directed. The concern of the evangelical interpreter is to understand the grammar of a passage in light of its historic context, not despite that context. There are at least three factors in Revelation that emphasize the original audience and their circumstances. These are strongly supportive of a preterist position. When these are combined with the matter of the *expectation* of Revelation, the preterist approach becomes justified on the basis of sound hermeneutical principle.

First, in Revelation John was writing to particular, historic, individual churches that existed in his day. Revelation 1:4 provides a common epistolary opening: "John to the seven churches which are in Asia: Grace [be] unto you, and peace, from him which is, and which was, and which is to come." In verse 11, he specifically names the seven churches to whom he writes: Ephesus, Smyrna, Pergamos, Thyatira, Sardis, Philadelphia, and Laodicea. We know these cities as historical cities containing actual churches.

In Revelation 2 and 3 these seven churches are addressed with individual exhortations and warnings. Interestingly, a number of the historical, geographical, and political allusions contained in the letters show that John did, in fact, have in view the specific churches addressed.[4]

---

4. See: William Ramsey, *The Letters to the Seven Churches* (Grand Rapids: Baker, [1904] 1963); Robert H. Mounce, *The Book of Revelation* (*New International Commentary*) (Grand Rapids: Eerdmans, 1977), chaps. 3 and 4.

Second, we learn that John wrote to those churches in order to be *understood*. The first sentence of John's work has become the title of the work. And from that title we know John fully intended that his work be a "revelation." The Greek word for "revelation" is *apokalupsis*, which means an "opening up, uncovering." John intended his book to be an opening up of divine truth for his original audience.

Furthermore, in Revelation 1:3 we read: "Blessed is he who reads and those who hear the words of this prophecy, and keep those things which are written in it; for the time is near." The members of the churches to whom Revelation was addressed are expected to hear, *understand*, and keep the directives in Revelation. Revelation calls upon each church to give careful, spiritual attention to its words.[5]

Third, in Revelation John notes that he and the seven churches have already entered "tribulation," which is the harbinger of the major focus of the book: the "Great Tribulation" (Rev. 7:14). "I John, who also am your brother, and companion in the tribulation" (Rev. 1:9a). Revelation 2 and 3 contain allusions to greater problems brewing on the world scene.[6]

John is clearly writing to particular historical churches about their current, grave, and worsening circumstances. The original audience factor cannot be overlooked; the message of Revelation must be relevant to them.

Contemporary Expectation

As mentioned in Chapter 8, one of the most obvious, yet most overlooked features of Revelation is John's expectancy. The expectation of the events in Revelation is urgent and impending. The "time is at hand"; the events "must shortly come to pass." This temporal expectation is strategically placed: it appears three times in the opening, introductory chapter (Rev.

---

5. Rev. 2:7, 11, 17, 29; 3:6, 13, 22.
6. Rev. 2:10, 22-23, 25; 3:9-11.

1:1, 3, 19) and four times in the final, concluding chapter (Rev. 22:6, 7, 12, 20). Its appearance in both of these chapters is significant because these bracket the highly wrought symbolism of the prophetic body of the book which is contained in the section from Revelation 4:1 through 22:6. The portions of Revelation in which the time indicators are embedded are generally of a more historical than prophetic character; they are more didactic than symbolic.

With the particularity of the audience emphasized and the imminent expectation of its events, I do not see how a preterism of some sort can be escaped. Nevertheless, many attempt to escape such logic.

Some commentators, such as John Walvoord, understand these terms as indicating that whenever the events do start coming to pass, they will occur with *great speed*, following one upon the other with great rapidity. Others, such as Robert Mounce, view them as indicating such events are *always imminent*. That is, the events are always ready to occur, though they may not actually occur until thousands of years later. Still others, such as Leon Morris, see John's references as a measure of *God's time, not man's*. That is, John is saying that these events will come to pass "shortly" from God's perspective. But, then, we must remember that "a day with the Lord is as a thousand years" (2 Pet. 3:8).[7]

But are these attempts capable of overthrowing our evidence? We must remember that John was writing to historical churches existing in his own day. He and they had *already* entered the earliest stages of "tribulation" (Rev. 1:9a). It would be a cruel mockery of their circumstances for John to tell them that when help comes, it will come with swiftness – even though it may not come until two or three thousand years later. Or to

---

7. John F. Walvoord, *The Revelation of Jesus Christ* (Chicago: Moody Press, 1966), p. 35. Mounce, *Revelation*, pp. 64-65. Leon Morris, *The Revelation of St. John* (Grand Rapids: Eerdmans, 1969), p. 45.

tell them that the events are always imminent – even though the readers of his letter may never experience them. Or that God will send help soon – according to the way the Eternal God measures time.

In addition, each of these approaches is destroyed by the very fact that John repeats and varies his terms as if to dispel any confusion. Think of it: If these words in these verses do not indicate that John expected the events to occur soon, *what words could John have used to express such?* How could he have said it more plainly?

Date of Writing

The date of the writing of the Book of Revelation is certainly pre-A.D. 70, and probably as early as A.D. 65-66. I will not rehearse here the argument for this "early date" (as opposed to A.D. 95-96), because I have dealt with this in depth in another place.[8] Suffice it to say that when John writes, the Temple is still standing in Jerusalem (Rev. 11:1-8) and the sixth emperor of Rome (Nero) is still ruling (Rev. 17:9-10). We do need to keep this in mind because a large portion of the prophecies in Revelation find fulfillment in the era leading up to the destruction of the Temple, as I will show.

Revelational Theme

The theme of Revelation is set forth in Revelation 1:7: "Behold, He is coming with the clouds, and every eye will see Him, even those who pierced Him; and all the tribes of the earth will mourn over Him." This theme is easily applicable to Christ's judgment-coming on first-century Israel.[9] This cloud-coming of

---

8. Kenneth L. Gentry, Jr., *Before Jerusalem Fell: Dating the Book of Revelation* (Bethesda, MD: International Scholars Publications, rep. 1996). Some dispensationalists are even accepting the early date: C. Marvin Pate and Calvin B. Haines, Jr., *Doomsday Delusions: What's Wrong with Predictions About the End of the World* (Downer's Grove, Ill.: Inter-varsity, 1995), p. 40.

9. For the different ways in which Christ is said to "come" in Scripture, see ch.

Christ in judgment is reminiscent of Old Testament cloud-comings of God in judgment upon ancient historical people and nations. God "comes" upon Israel's enemies in general (Psa. 18:7-15; 104:3), upon Egypt (Isa. 19:1), upon disobedient Israel in the Old Testament (Joel 2:1, 2), and so forth. It is not necessary that it refer to His final, Second Advental coming to end history. This is so for the following reasons.

(1) The coming will be *witnessed* by "those who pierced him." The New Testament clearly emphasizes the guilt of the Jews of the first century in killing Christ.[10] (2) The reference to those who pierced him is reinforced by the designation of the *mourners*. They are called "all the tribes of the earth." Here the "earth" (*ge*) should most probably be translated "land," i.e. the Promised Land (see discussion below). The "tribes" in Revelation are Israel's Twelve Tribes (Rev. 7:1ff). Whenever "tribes" is applied beyond Israel, the application adds the notion of "every tongue and kindred." Furthermore, Christ teaches that the focus of the "Great Tribulation" (Rev. 7:14) is Judea (Matt. 24:16, 21). (3) This coming is expected *soon* by an inspired writer (see previous discussion). The Second Advent has not occurred yet, while over 1,900 years have transpired since the time in which *this* coming was expected "quickly" (Rev. 22:7, 12, 20).

In regard to the Jews, the Jewish War with Rome from A.D. 67 to 70 brought about the deaths of tens of thousands of the Jews in Judea, and the enslavement of thousands upon thousands more. The Jewish historian Josephus, who was an eye-witness, records that 1,100,000 Jews perished in the siege of Jerusalem, though this figure is disputed. J. L. von Mosheim, the great ecclesiastical historian, wrote that "throughout the whole history of the human race, we meet with but few, if any,

---

13, above.

10. See: Acts 2:22, 23, 36; 3:14, 15; 4:8-10; 5:30; Matthew 21:33-35; 23:29-34:2; Luke 23:27-31; John 19:5-15; 1 Thess. 2:14-16.

instances of slaughter and devastation at all to be compared with this."[11]

But as awful as the Jewish loss of life was, the utter devastation of Jerusalem, the final destruction of the Temple, and the conclusive cessation of the sacrificial system were lamented even more. The *covenantal significance* of the loss of the Temple stands as the most dramatic outcome of the War. Hence, any Jewish calamity after A.D. 70 would pale in comparison to the redemptive-historical significance of the loss of the Temple.

So then, the expectation of a judgment-coming of Christ in the first century is easily explicable in terms of the biblical and historical record. Hence, John clearly expects the imminent occurring of the events of Revelation.

Primary Focus

One of the very common terms of significance in Revelation is the Greek word *ge*. It occurs eighty-two times in the twenty-two chapters of Revelation. This word may be translated in two ways: (1) "earth" (indicating the entire globe) or (2) "land" (referring to a particular portion of the earth, such as the Promised Land). The overwhelming majority of occurrences of this term in Revelation suggest it refers to "the Land," I. e., the famous and beloved Promised Land.[12] The reasons justifying such a translation are as follows:

The very Jewish nature of Revelation suggests the plausibility of such a translation. The lexical and syntactical peculiarities of Revelation are extremely Hebraic.[13] Furthermore, the first

---

11. John Laurence von Mosheim, *History of Christianity in the First Three Centuries*, 3 vols. (New York: Converse, 1854) 1:125.

12. "Palestine was to the Rabbis simply 'the land', all other countries being summed up under the designation of 'outside the land.' " Alfred Edersheim, *Sketches of Jewish Social Life* (Grand Rapids: Eerdmans, [1876] n.d.), p. 14. In the Mishnah at Kelim 1:6, we read: "There are ten degrees of holiness. The Land of Israel is holier than any other land."

13. See R. H. Charles, *The Revelation of St. John*, 2 vols. (Edinburgh: T. & T.

occurrence of the term appears in the theme verse in Revelation 1:7 and must mean the Promised Land (see previous argument). In addition, it is used later in ways strongly suggestive of a Palestinian reference. It is sometimes set against the "world" (Rev. 3:10) or "every nation" (Rev. 11:9,10; 13:7, 8; 14:6). In Revelation the devastation on the "land" awaits the sealing of 144,000 Jews representing all twelve tribes (cf. Rev. 7; 14:3).

Having now considered these interpretive factors, we will survey Revelation itself.

Preparation for Judgment

In the first part of Revelation (Rev. 1-5) John and his audience are prepared for the terrifying judgment scenes to follow. Despite the turmoil Christ appears among the seven churches as their Defender (Rev. 1:12ff). He knows their tribulation and will cut it short for the faithful (Rev. 2-3; especially: 2:10; 3:10; 6:10).

Then John and his readers are steeled against the storm of God's Judgment by a vision of the heavenly role in the upheaval and devastation. Almighty God is seen in glorious, serene, sovereign control seated upon a throne of judgment (Rev. 4). The Lord Jesus Christ is seen as the Judge of Israel (Rev. 5; cf. Matt. 26:64). The scroll that Christ is given represents God's divorce decree against Israel.

The Divorce of Israel

The Seven-Sealed Scroll

In Revelation 6-19 the judgment of Israel is portrayed in cyclical fashion. The Seven-Sealed Scroll seems quite certainly to represent God's "bill of divorcement" handed down by the Judge on the throne against Israel. It is known that divorce

Clark, 1920), 1:cxvii-clix.

decrees were written out among the Jews in the biblical era.[14] It is equally certain that marriage was based on a covenant contract.[15] That the scroll in Revelation 6 would be *a bill of divorcement* is suggested on the following considerations.

First, in Revelation we have prominent emphases on two particular women, two women who obviously correspond as opposites to one another. The two women are the wicked harlot on the beast (Rev. 17-18) and the pure bride of Christ (Rev. 21). They correspond with the *earthly Jerusalem*, which was the scene of Christ's crucifixion (Rev. 11:8), and the *heavenly Jerusalem*, which is holy (Rev. 21:10), as I will show below. The flow and drift of the book is the revelation and execution of the legal (Rev. 15:3; 16:5-7) judgment on the fornicating harlot (Rev. 17-19) and the coming of a virginal bride (Rev. 21), obviously to take the harlot's place after a marriage supper (Rev. 19).

Second, the apparent Old Testament background for this imagery is found in Ezekiel. In Ezekiel 2:9-10 Israel's judgment is portrayed as written on a scroll on the front and back and given to Ezekiel. This corresponds perfectly with Revelation 5:1. In Ezekiel chapters 2 and following the devastation of Israel is outlined, which corresponds with Revelation 6ff. In Ezekiel 16 Israel is viewed as God's covenant wife who became a harlot (see also Jer. 3:1-8; Isa. 50:1) who trusted in her beauty and committed fornication, just as Jerusalem-Babylon of Revelation (Rev. 18). She is cast out and judged for this evil conduct.

Third, following the "divorce" and judgments associated with them, John turns to see the coming of a new "bride" out of heaven (Rev. 21-22). It would seem that the new bride could

---

14. Deut. 24:1, 3; Isa. 50:1; Jer. 3:8; Matt. 5:31; 19:7; Mark 10:4. See: Gittin in the Mishnah. *Git* "literally 'writ' [of separation]" (Herbert Danby, *The Mishnah: Translated from the Hebrew with Introduction and Brief Explanatory Notes* [Oxford: University Press, 1933], p. 307). Also: Mendell Lewittes, *Jewish Marriage: Rabbinic Law, Legend, and Custom* (Northvale, NJ: Jason Aronson, 1994), ch. 10: "The *Get*."

15. Prov. 2:17; Ezek. 16:8; Mal. 2:14.

not be taken until the harlotrous wife should first be dealt with legally. John imports the imagery of the harlot, bride, and marriage feast — this is not being read into the text exegetically. Thus, the imagery of divorce fits the dramatic flow of the work.

The judgment of the fornicating harlot is begun when Christ begins opening the seven seals on the scroll: God the Father turns over the judgment to Christ, who will open the scroll, thus having judgment authority committed to Him (John 5:22; cf. Rev. 5:4-7). Jesus tells Caiaphas and those later associated with him in the crucifixion, that they shall see the "Son of Man coming with the clouds of heaven" (Matt. 26:64). This fits well with the Pauline imagery of the casting out of the one wife (Hagar who is representative of the Jerusalem below) and the taking of the other wife (Sara who is representative of the Jerusalem above) in Galatians 4:24ff.

As the seals are opened the judgments begin. At the opening of the *first seal* (the white horse) we have a picture of the Roman army victoriously entering Israel toward Jerusalem (Rev. 6:1-2). This cannot be Christ because: (1) The white horse is the only similarity with Revelation 19:11. (2) Christ is the One opening the seals in heaven (Rev. 5:5, 9; 6:1, 3, 5, 7). (3) It would seem most inappropriate for the Living Creatures (who had just fallen before Christ in praise, Rev. 5) to command Christ the Lord: "Come!" This horseman is God's "avenger" upon Israel. The white horse indicates victory, not holiness. God often uses the unjust to bring His judgments in history.[16]

The *second seal* (the red horse) speaks of the eruption of Jewish civil war (Rev. 6:3-4). In Greek "the peace" is emphasized. It refers to the famous *Pax Romana* covering the Roman Empire.[17] Hence, the significance of "rumors of wars" (Matt.

---

16. Deut. 28:15,49; Isa. 10:5-6; 44:18-45:4.

17. "Building on the foundations laid by his uncle, Julius Caesar, [Augustus] brought peace. . . . The internal peace and order which Augustus achieved endured, with occasional interruptions, for about two centuries. Never before had all the shores of the Mediterranean been under one rule and never had they enjoyed such

24:6) in such a peaceful era. Josephus notes that the civil war in the Land was worse than the carnage wrought by the Romans themselves.[18] The *third seal* (black horse) portrays famine plaguing Israel (Rev. 6:5-6). Black symbolizes famine (Lam 4:8; 5:10). One of the most horrible aspects of Jerusalem's woes was the famine caused by civil strife.[19] The *fourth seal* (pale horse) witnesses the death of one-fourth of Israel (Rev. 6:7-8). The pale horse is death personified. The animals devouring the dead indicate covenantal curse (Deut. 28:15, 26).

With the opening of the *fifth seal* we get another look into heaven. We see the altar in heaven and hear vindication promised Christian martyrs (Rev. 6:9-11). This vindication will occur in "a little while" (Rev. 6:10). It comes in the final collapse of Israel.

The *sixth seal* (stellar phenomena) symbolizes the fall of Israel's government (Rev. 6:12-17). Such symbolic phenomena are often associated with the collapse of governments: Babylon (Isa. 13:1, 10, 19); Egypt (Ezek. 32:2, 7-8, 16, 18); Idumea (Isa. 34:3-5); Judah (Jer. 4:14, 23-24). Josephus mentions that the Jews actually sought refuge underground during the A.D. 67-70 war, as per the symbolic imagery.[20] Christ warns that this would happen to His generation (Luke 23:27-30).

At Revelation 7:1 there is a gracious interlude between seals (Rev. 7:1-8). The "four angels" temporarily hold back the "winds" (of destruction[21]) and counter the four destroying horsemen. This providential halt in the judgments allows the minority population of Jewish Christians in Jerusalem to flee as the Roman General Vespasian is distracted (with the fall of

---

prosperity. The *pax Romana* made for the spread of ideas and religions over the area where it prevailed." Kenneth Scott Latourette, *A History of Christianity*, 2 vols. (2nd ed.; San Francisco: Harper & Row, 1975), 1:21.

18. Josephus, *Wars* 4:3:2; 5:1:1, 5.

19. *Ibid.*, 5:10:2-5.

20. *Ibid.*, 6:7:3 (cf. 7:2:1).

21. Jer. 49:36, 37; 51:1, 2; Dan. 7:2; Matt. 7:24ff.

Nero and the Roman Civil Wars) before he reaches Jerusalem.[22] There is a prophecy (Luke 21:20-22) and an historical record[23] that Christians would be preserved through Jerusalem's tribulation.

Here we are introduced to the 144,000 sealed saints of God. It should be noted initially that the figure "144,000" is a perfect number composed of exactly twelve squared times 1,000. The numerical figure itself is obviously stylized symbolism. But of what?

The 144,000 saints seem to be representative of *Jewish converts to Christianity* who dwelt in Israel, for the following reasons: (1) The particular reference to the Twelve Tribes and the fact that they are the "first fruits" (Rev. 14:4). Christianity's first converts were from Jerusalem (Acts 2). (2) Their distinction from the great multitude from every nation (Rev. 7:9). (3) The Old Testament background in Ezekiel 9:4 clearly specifies their habitation at Jerusalem. (4) They are protected by God in "the Land" (*ge*), which is being judged (Rev. 7:1-3). This fits well with the forgoing action as being in Israel. (5) Such a designation is compatible with Christ's warning His followers to flee Jerusalem before its final overthrow (Matt. 24:15-16; Luke 21:20-24). He promised that His followers who heeded His prophecy would be protected (Luke 21:18-19). (6) The events of Revelation are spoken in anticipation of their soon occurring. This fits perfectly the historical outcome of the flight of the Christians from Jerusalem prior to her fall.

The Seven Trumpets

With the opening of the *seventh seal* we hear the sounding of the seven trumpets (Rev. 8:1-6). The first four trumpets show judgments upon things, the last three upon men. They review and intensify the chaos of the seals: destruction increases from

---

22. Josephus, *Wars* 4:9:2; 4:11:5.
23. Eusebius, *Ecclesiastical History* 3:5.

one-fourth (Rev. 6:8) to one-third (Rev. 8:7-12). Regarding earthquakes and eruptions, James Moffatt writes: "Portents of this abnormal nature are recorded for the seventh decade of the first century by Roman historians. . . . Volcanic phenomena . . . in the Egean archipelago . . . are in the background of this description, and of others throughout the book; features such as the disturbance of islands and the mainland, showers of stones, earthquakes, the sun obscured by a black mist of ashes, and the moon reddened by volcanic dust, were the natural consequences of eruption in some marine volcano, and there – adjoining Patmos – was in a state of more or less severe eruption during the first century."[24] W. Boyd Carpenter writes: "Perhaps no period in the world's history has ever been so marked by these convulsions as that which intervenes between the Crucifixion and the destruction of Jerusalem. Josephus records one in Judea (*Wars* 4:4:5); Tacitus tells of them in Crete, Rome, Apamea, Phrygia, Campania (*Ann.* 12:58; 14:27; 15:22); Seneca (*Ep.* 91), in A.D. 58, speaks of them as extending their devastations over Asia (the proconsular providence, not the continent), Achaia, Syria, and Macedonia."[25]

These judgments reflect the plagues upon Egypt at the Exodus.[26] Jerusalem has become the equivalent of Egypt (see Rev. 11:8). She and other cities in Israel are worse than Nineveh (Matt. 12:41), Tyre, Sidon, and Sodom (Matt. 11:21-23). She has become a "synagogue of Satan" (Rev. 2:9; 3:9).

With the fifth trumpet, we witness an outbreak of demonic torment (Rev. 9:1-21). The fallen star here is Satan, "the angel" of the pit (v. 11). The demons confined to the pit (2 Pet. 2:4;

---

24. James Moffatt, *Revelation*, in W. R. Nicoll, *The Expositor's Greek Testament*, 5 vols. (Grand Rapids: Eerdmans, [n.d.] 1980), 5:404. See: Seneca, *Lucilius* 91; Tacitus, *Histories* 1:2-3 and *Annals* 12:58; 14:27; 15:22.

25. W. Boyd Carpenter, "The Gospel According to Matthew," *Ellicott's Commentary on the Whole Bible*, John C. Ellicott, ed., 8 vols. (Grand Rapids: Zondervan, n.d.), 6:146.

26. Cf. Rev. 8:5 with Exo. 19:16f, Rev. 8:7 with Exo. 9:18ff; 8:8-9 with Exo. 7:20f; 8:11 with Exo. 10:21. Cf. Deut. 28:15, 60ff.

Jude 6; Luke 8:31) are loosed to torment Israel (vv. 2, 3; cf. Rev. 18:2), just as Christ warned (Matt. 12:43f). The period of torment is "five months," which indicates the final siege of Jerusalem by Titus, when the Jews were driven mad as they were hopelessly trapped.[27] This siege lasted five months: "Titus began the siege of Jerusalem in April, 70. The defenders held out desperately for five months, but by the end of August the Temple area was occupied and the holy house burned down, and by the end of September all resistance in the city had come to an end."[28]

At the sixth trumpet Roman reinforcements are sent (Rev. 9:12-21). The four angels are destroying "angels" loosed upon Israel in fury. They represent the four Roman legions kept at the Euphrates.[29]

The Mighty Angel

In Revelation 10:1-11 we see a mighty angel standing astride land and sea. The angel is clearly Christ, as a comparison of Revelation 10:1 with 1:13-16 demonstrates. He declares that Israel's time is up: "[T]here should be no more delay." This is in answer to the plea from the souls at the altar (Rev. 6:10).

As He does so He proclaims that "the mystery of God is finished." By this is meant that the Gentiles are fully accepted by God[30] as the Temple (with its "separating wall," Eph 2:14) is about to be removed (Rev. 11). The end of the Temple economy and national Israel is near (1 Cor 10:11; 1 Thess. 2:16; Heb. 1:2; 9:26; 12:26-27; 1 John 2:18).

---

27. Josephus, *Wars* 5:1:1, 5.

28. F. F. Bruce, *New Testament History* (Garden City, NY: Anchor Books, 1969), p. 382.

29. W. J. Coneybeare and J. S. Howson, *The Life and Epistles of St. Paul* (New York: Scribner's, 1894), p. 76.

30. Eph. 2:12,19; 3:3-6; Rom. 16:25; Col 1:25ff.

The Temple and the Two Prophets

In Revelation 11 John is commanded to measure the *inner Temple* in the "holy city" (Jerusalem),[31] where the Lord was crucified (Rev. 11:8).[32] This measuring signifies the *preservation* (cf. Zech. 2:1-5; Rev. 21:15) of the inner court of the Temple. But the *outer Temple court* is left unmeasured; thus, it is destined for *destruction* (Rev. 11:1, 2).

The inner Temple represents the true essence of the Temple that continues in Christianity. Christians are called "temples" by use of this very Greek term, *naos*.[33] As in the Epistle to the Hebrews, the Temple/tabernacle here receives a heavenly replacement (Rev. 11:19). The outer court speaks of the physical Temple, which is to be destroyed (Matt. 24:1-2). History records that Jerusalem's wall "was so thoroughly laid even with the ground by those that dug it up to the foundation, that there was left nothing to make those that came thither believe it had ever been inhabited. This was the end which Jerusalem came to."[34]

The "forty-two months" (v. 2) or "1260 days" (v. 3) indicates the period of the Jewish War with Rome from its formal engagement until the Temple was destroyed. "When Vespasian arrived the following Spring [A.D. 67] to take charge of operations, he steadily reduced Galilee, Peraea. . . . Titus [Vespasian's son] began the siege of Jerusalem in April, 70. . . . By the end of August the Temple area was occupied and the holy house burned down. . . ."[35] From Spring A.D. 67 to August/September A.D. 70 is a period of forty-two months.

The "two prophets" probably represent a small body of Christians who remained in Jerusalem to testify against it. They

---

31. Isa. 48:2; 52:1; Neh. 11:1-18; Matt. 4:5; 27:53.
32. Luke 9:22; 13:32; 17:11; 19:28.
33. 1 Cor. 3:16-17; 2 Cor. 6:16; Eph. 2:19ff; 1 Pet. 2:5.
34. Josephus, *Wars* 7:1:1.
35. Bruce, *New Testament History*, pp. 381-382.

are portrayed as *two*, in that they are legal witnesses to the covenant curses.[36]

The Jerusalem Church Protected

In Revelation 12 John backs up chronologically in order to show the "mother" church in Jerusalem, which was being protected from Satan-inspired resistance. This would cover the time frame from Christ's ministry through the Book of Acts up until the destruction of Jerusalem.

The Persecution by the Beast

In Revelation 13 the "first beast" must be considered both generically and specifically. This is not unusual in Scripture: Christ's body is generic (the Church) and specific (Jesus); Adam is generic (man) and specific (Adam). Generically the "Beast" is Rome; specifically it is Nero Caesar, the head of the Roman Empire of the day.[37]

The rationale for the generic identity is as follows. The time frame of the book is supportive of the identification (see earlier argumentation). The Beast rises from the sea, which suggests the Italian peninsula where Rome is located, when considered from the vantage of either Patmos or Israel (across the Mediterranean Sea). It has "seven heads" (Rev. 13:1; 17:3) that are "seven mountains" (Rev. 17:8,9); Rome is famous for its "Seven Hills." The Beast's number is an exercise in Hebrew gematria: converting letters into numbers. An ancient Hebrew spelling of Nero Caesar perfectly fits the value: *"Nrwn Qsr"* (Rev. 13:18): n [50] r [200] w [6] n [50] q [100] s [60] r [200]. Its evil and blasphemous character suggests Nero specifically, and the emperors

---

36. Deut. 17:6; 19:5; Matt. 18:16; 2 Cor. 13:1; 1 Tim. 5:19; Heb. 10:28.

37. See the beast study in ch. 16 above. For more detailed information, see: Gentry, *The Beast of Revelation* (Tyler, TX: Institute for Christian Economics, 1989) and Gary DeMar's three-part series in *Biblical Worldview* (June-Aug. 1991), published by American Vision, Atlanta.

generically: Since Julius Caesar the emperors were often considered divine. Roman historian Dio Cassius records of Nero's return to Rome from Greece: "The people cried out: 'Thou August, August! To Nero, the Hercules! To Nero, the Apollo! The Eternal One! Thou August! Sacred voice! Happy those who hear thee!' "[38] In addition, Nero was the first emperor to persecute Christianity (13:7), and he did so for a period of forty-two months (Nov. A.D. 64 to June A.D. 68, Rev. 13:5).

The deadly wound which is healed suggests the revival of Rome after the Roman Civil Wars of A.D. 68-69, which were caused by Nero's suicide with his own sword. Roman historian Tacitus reported of the Roman Civil Wars: "This was the condition of the Roman state when Servius Galba . . . entered upon the year that was to be for Galba his last and for the state almost the end."[39] Roman historian Suetonius wrote of the outcome of the Civil Wars two years later: "[T]he empire, which for a long time had been unsettled and, as it were, drifting through the usurpation and violent death of three emperors, was at last taken in and given stability by the Flavian family."[40] Josephus, the Jewish court historian to the Flavians, agrees: "So upon this confirmation of Vespasian's entire government, which was now settled, and upon the unexpected deliverance of the public affairs of the Romans from ruin. . . ."[41]

The "second beast" is a minion of the first beast (Rev. 13:11-12). He arises from "the land" (*tes ges*), i.e., from within Palestine. This is probably Gessius Florus, the Roman Procurator over Israel, who caused the Jewish War.[42]

---

38. Dio, *Roman History* 62:20:5.

39. *Histories* 1:2, 11.

40. *Vespasian* 1:1.

41. Josephus, *Wars* 4:11:5.

42. J. Stuart Russell, *The Parousia: A Study of the New Testament Doctrine of Our Lord's Second Coming* (Grand Rapids: Baker, [1887] 1983), pp. 465ff.

The Angelic Proclamation

In Revelation 14:6-8 we read the angelic proclamation of "Babylon's" destruction: "Then I saw another angel flying in the midst of heaven, having the everlasting gospel to preach to those who dwell on the earth; to every nation, tribe, tongue, and people; saying with a loud voice, 'Fear God and give glory to Him, for the hour of His judgment has come; and worship Him who made heaven and earth, the sea and springs of water.' And another angel followed, saying, 'Babylon is fallen, is fallen, that great city, because she has made all nations drink of the wine of the wrath of her fornication.' " As noted in the preceding chapter, "Babylon" stands for Jerusalem.

In Revelation 14:14ff Israel is "harvested" in judgment. In the days of Christ and the apostles Israel becomes ripe for judgment (Matt. 23:31-36; 1 Thess 2:16). The gruesome action taking place here is spoken of as "outside the city," i.e., outside Jerusalem. This corresponds to Christ's crucifixion "outside" the gate or the city (Heb. 13:12-13; John 19:17). It also clearly relates the scene to the area surrounding Jerusalem, i.e., the land of Israel. The land of Israel as a Roman province stretched from the Leontes River to Wadi el Arish, a distance of 1,600 furlongs, or about 200 miles (Rev. 14:20).

The blood flowing up to the horses' bridles seems to be a poetic description of the blood that covered the lakes and rivers during several dramatic battles between the Romans and the Jews. We have confirming evidence of this in the language adopted by Josephus to describe warfare: "But as many of these were repulsed when they were getting ashore as were killed by the darts upon the lake; one might then see the lake all bloody, and full of dead bodies, for not one of them escaped. And a terrible stink . . . as for the shores, they were full of shipwrecks, and of dead bodies all swelled."[43]

---

43. Josephus, *Wars* 3:10:9; 4:7:5-6; 6:8:5.

The Seven Vials of Wrath

In Revelation 15 we have a vision of the saints in heaven just preceding the pouring out of the vials of wrath. Again, the saints' prayers of Revelation 6 are being answered.

These vials bring increasing woe (Rev. 16). The Roman armies come with ease from the Euphrates (Rev. 16:12). Josephus notes that "there followed [Titus] also three thousand, drawn from those that guarded the river Euphrates" (*Wars* 5:1:6). The Roman soldiers were supplemented with troops provided by auxiliary kings from the east (Rev. 16:12; *Wars* 3:4:2; 5:1:6). With the convergence of so many trained soldiers, Jerusalem divides into three bickering factions (Rev. 16:19).[44] The Roman legions pummel the city with talent-weight stones (Rev. 16:21): "The catapults, that all the legions had ready prepared for them, were admirably contrived; but still more extraordinary ones belonged to the tenth legion: those that threw darts and those that threw stones, were more forcible and larger than the rest. . . . Now, the stones that were cast, were of the weight of a talent, and were carried two furlongs and further. . . . As for the Jews, they at first watched the coming of the stone, for it was of a white colour. . . ."[45]

The Final Collapse of Babylon/Jerusalem

Revelation 17-19 contains a highly wrought description of the collapse of Jerusalem. She is satisfied that she is beautiful and has all that she needs and is not bereft of a "husband" (Rev. 18:7). " 'Ten measures of beauty,' say the Rabbis, 'hath God bestowed upon the world, and nine of these fall to the lot of Jerusalem' – and again, 'A city, the fame of which has gone

---

44. *Ibid*. 5:1:1: "It so happened that the sedition at Jerusalem was revived, and parted into three factions, and that one faction fought against the other." Elsewhere Josephus designates the leaders of the faction by the names John, Eleazar, and Simon.

45. *Ibid*. 5:6:3.

out from one end of the world to the other.' 'Thine, O lord, is the greatness, the power, the glory, and eternity.' This – explains the Talmud – 'is Jerusalem.' "[46]

The beast's *seven heads* are seven mountains (Rev. 17:9) representing the seven hills of Rome. These seven heads also represent seven kings, or the *first seven emperors* of Rome (Rev. 17:9-10). The sixth king[47] (Nero) is in power at the writing of Revelation. The seventh will soon be ruling, but only for a short while (Galba ruled from June 8, A.D. 68 to January 15, A.D. 69). The ten horns (Rev. 17:12) apparently represent the ten major Roman provinces: Italy, Achaia, Asia, Syria, Egypt, Africa, Spain, Gaul, Britain, and Germany.[48] The beast fails to destroy Christianity, but destroys Jerusalem (Rev. 17:14-18:24). The destruction of Jerusalem (and of Nero, the beast) is attributed to the providence of Christ (Rev. 19:11ff).

The Glory of Christ's Bride

In Revelation 20-22 we are presented the bride of Christ, in contrast to the adulterous harlot. The heavenly rule of Christ with His saints (both those in heaven and those on the earth) is portrayed in Revelation 20:1-6. This passage with its 1,000 years, though beginning in John's era, necessarily extends out into the future beyond the short time frame restrictions common to Revelation. The whole of Revelation 20 is a unique section that projects the reader beyond the limited time frame.

I have already dealt with the *length* of the "millennium" in Chapter 14. The "thousand years" is symbolic of a great extensive period of time, and is not to be understood literally. I have also explained the binding of Satan in Chapter 12. I will not re-

---

46. Edersheim, *Sketches of Jewish Social Life*, p. 82.

47. Notice the enumeration of the emperors in Josephus, *Ant.* 18-19; 4 Ezra 11 and 12; Sibylline Oracles 5; 8; Barnabas 4; Suetonius, *Lives of the Twelve Caesars*, and Dio Cassius, *Roman History* 5.

48. F. W. Farrar, *The Early Days of Christianity* (London: Cassell, 1884), 464, n 1.

hearse the argument for the figurative use of "one thousand" here. I will, however, briefly reflect on the binding of Satan to fill out the picture of the kingdom. At this juncture I will provide a brief exposition of Christ's "millennial" reign as presented here, while mentioning the various elements included by John.

The Binding of Satan

Revelation 20 opens with a reference to "an angel coming down from heaven." This angel, who possesses "the key to the bottomless pit," binds Satan for a "thousand years." This angelic figure seems clearly to be Christ Himself, for the following reasons: (1) Christ appears as "the angel of the Lord" in the Old Testament.[49] Thus, there is no *a priori* difficulty with His appearing as an angel here. (2) Christ appears under angelic guise elsewhere in Revelation (cf. Rev. 10:1 with 1:13-15). (3) As here, Christ is seen holding "keys" in Revelation 1:18. (4) The struggle of the ages is ultimately between Satan and Christ (Gen. 3:15; Matt. 4:1-11). Appropriately, the sovereign work of Christ debilitates Satan in this passage (cf. Heb. 2:14; 1 John 3:8). In fact, in Matthew 12:28-29 the "binding" [*deo*] of Satan is attributed to Christ.

As I indicated in Chapter 12 the "chain" here must be a *spiritual* chain that spiritually "binds" this spiritual being, Satan. The same is true of its corollaries: the "seal" (cf. Rev. 7:2-8) and the "bottomless pit/abyss." The binding of Satan began in the first century. It was initiated during the ministry of Christ (Matt. 12:24-29), secured in legal fact at Christ's death and resurrection (Luke 10:17; John 12:31-32; Col. 2:15; Heb. 2:14-15), and dramatically evidenced in the collapse of Christianity's first foe, Judaism (Rev. 12; 17-18[50]). The collapse of Jerusalem

---

49. Gen. 16:7-14; 22:11-18; 31:11, 13; Exo. 3:2-5; Num. 22:22-35; Jdgs. 6:11-23; 13:2-25; 1 Chron. 21:15-17; 1 Kgs. 19:5-7.

50. The demise of the Great Harlot is the demise of Jerusalem. See ch. 16 above.

HE SHALL HAVE DOMINION

is significant because the Satanic resistance to Christ's kingdom came to expression in the Jewish persecution of Christ and Christianity.[51]

The binding of Satan continues throughout the Christian era (i.e., the "one thousand years"), except for a brief period just prior to the Second Advent (Rev. 20:2-3, 7-9). This binding does *not* result in the *total inactivity* of Satan; rather it enforces a complete control of his power by Christ. The same restriction is true of the demons who are bound (Jude 6; 2 Pet. 2:4; cf. Luke 8:31). The purpose of this binding is specifically qualified: it is "in order that" (*hina*) Satan not "deceive the nations."

The implications of this binding are enormous. Before the coming of Christ, all nations beyond the borders of Israel were under the dominion of Satan.[52] Israel alone of all the peoples of the earth was an oasis where the true God and His salvation were known.[53] But with the coming of Christ and the spread of "the gospel of the kingdom," Satan's dominion over the Gentiles is severely restricted. In the years between Christ's ministry upon earth until the destruction of the Temple, there was massive demonic activity as Satan resisted the binding of God and the establishing of the kingdom of Christ. Consequently, where Christianity spread, idolatry withered in its presence.[54]

---

51. The Scriptures speak of Satan's involvement in the Jewish apostasy (Matt. 12:43-45; John 8:44; Rev. 2:9; 3:9). Because of this, the Jews prompted Christ's crucifixion (Matt. 20:18-19; 27:11-25; Mark 10:33; 15:1; Luke 18:32; 23:1-2; John 18:28-31; 19:12, 15; Acts 2:22-23; 3:13; 4:26-27; 5:28, 30; 7:52; 1 Thess. 2:14-15), and Israel became the first persecutor of the Church (Matt. 23:37ff.; Acts 8:1; 12:1-3; 17:5-7; 1 Thess. 2:14-17).

52. 2 Kgs. 17:29; Psa. 96:3-5 [cf. 1 Cor. 10:20]; Luke 4:6; Acts 14:16; 17:30; 26:17-18.

53. Deut. 7:6ff; Psa. 147:19-20; Amos 3:2; Rom. 3:1-2.

54. "All heathen at any rate from every region, abjuring their hereditary tradition and the impiety of idols, are now placing their hope in Christ, and enrolling themselves under Him." Athanasius, *Incarnation* 37:5. See also: Sections 30:4, 6-7; 31:2-3.

The Millennial Reign and Resurrection

Concurrent with the binding of Satan is the spreading rule of the righteous (Rev. 20:4-6). Although the vast majority of Revelation focuses on events that will occur "soon" (Rev. 1:1, 3), this section on the thousand years *begins*, but is not completed, in the first century. It projects itself into the distant future, allowing a glimpse of the end result of the events begun in the apostolic era.

While Satan is bound some participate in the rule of Christ (Rev. 20:4). These participants include both the martyred saints in heaven ("the souls of those who had been beheaded for their witness") and the persevering saints on earth ("and those who [*oitines*] had not worshiped the beast"[55]). Given the time frame concern of John (cf. Rev. 1:3, 9), his focus is particularly on those martyrs[56] and other saints[57] of the first-century era. But it also involves all those who are martyred for Christ and those who live for Him apart from being martyred, for the blessings spread throughout the millennial era.

In Revelation 20:1-3 John explicates the first phase of Christ's triumph over Satan: he is *spiritually bound*, being restricted from successfully accomplishing his evil design in history. In Revelation 20:7-10 we witness the second and conclusive phase of Christ's triumph over him: Satan is *physically punished*, being tormented in the eternal flames of the Lake of Fire. This two-fold pattern of spiritual/physical, initial/conclusive is employed in the resurrection reference in Revelation 20, as well. The defender of a strict literalist hermeneutic faces the problem of the actual usage of the New Testament. *Resurrection* refers to more than the body's resurrection at the final judgment.

---

55. We must note that "*kai oitines* introduces a second class of persons, 'confessors. . . .' " Henry Barclay Swete, *Commentary on Revelation* (Grand Rapids: Kregal, [1906] 1977), p. 262.

56. Rev. 6:9-11; 7:9, 13-15; 11:7-12; 12:5; 13:7, 15; 14:13; 16:6; 17:6; 18:20, 24.

57. Rev. 5:9-10 (NASB); 7:1-4; 12:6, 13-17; 14:1-6; 16:15; 17:14; 18:4.

The "first resurrection" secures the participation of the saints (both martyred and living) in the rule of Christ (Rev. 20:4-6). As in the case of the two-fold triumph over Satan, this is the *initial, spiritual victory-resurrection.*[58] That is, it refers to the spiritual resurrection of those who are born again of the grace of God. *Salvation is spoken of as a spiritual resurrection:* "We know that we have passed from death to life, because we love the brethren. He who does not love his brother abides in death" (1 John 3:14[59]).

John, the author of Revelation, in his Gospel also parallels the spiritual resurrection of salvation with the physical resurrection of eschatology, just as he does in Revelation 20:

> Most assuredly, I say to you, he who hears My word and believes in Him who sent Me has everlasting life, and shall not come into judgment, but has passed from death into life. Most assuredly, I say to you, the hour is coming, and now is, when the dead will hear the voice of the Son of God; and those who hear will live. For as the Father has life in Himself, so He has granted the Son to have life in Himself, and has given Him authority to execute judgment also, because He is the Son of Man. Do not marvel at this; for the hour is coming in which all who are in the graves will hear His voice and come forth; those who have done good, to the resurrection of life, and those who have done evil, to the resurrection of condemnation. (John 5:24-29)

Having been spiritually resurrected, the saints (whether in heaven or on earth) are enthroned. He "has made us kings and priests to His God and Father, to Him be glory and dominion forever and ever" (Rev. 1:6). Christians are "overcomers" (cf. 1 John 2:13-14; 4:4; 5:4-5) and are seated with Christ in rule: "To him who overcomes I will grant to sit with Me on My

---

58. Milton Terry, *Biblical Apocalyptics: A Study of the Most Notable Revelations of God and of Christ* (Grand Rapids: Baker, [1898] 1988), p. 449.

59. See also: Rom. 6:8-11; Eph. 2:6; Col. 2:13-14.

throne, as I also overcame and sat down with My Father on His throne" (Rev. 3:21). As Paul puts it, Christ "raised us up together, and made us sit together in the heavenly places in Christ Jesus" (Eph. 2:6).

The "rest of the [spiritually] dead" do not participate in this spiritual resurrection. In fact, they "do not live again until the thousand years" is finished (Rev. 20:5). At that time they are physically resurrected (implied) in order to be overwhelmed by "the second death" (eternal torment), which is brought about by Judgment Day (Rev. 20:11-15).

Judgment Day

At the end of the kingdom era and just preceding Judgment Day, Satan is loosed very briefly (a "little while," Rev. 20:3) from his bondage. During this short period of time, he is allowed to gather a sizeable force of rebels, who will attempt to supplant the prevailing Christian majoritarian influence in the world (Rev. 20:7-9).[60] Under His providential rule, Christ's spiritual kingdom will have spread over the face of the earth and have dominated human life and culture for ages. But not all men are converted during any period of history. Consequently, upon Satan's brief loosing he quickly incites to war the repressed children of wrath.

No sooner does he prepare his forces than fire comes down from God out of heaven and devours them (Rev. 20:9). This figuratively portrays the Coming of Christ for what it represents to the wicked. Christ returns "in flaming fire taking vengeance on those who do not know God, and on those who do not obey the gospel of our Lord Jesus Christ" (2 Thess. 1:8). Before he can actually harm the Christian order (he merely surrounds "the camp of the saints and the beloved city," Rev. 20:9), Christ's Second Advent ends history and sweeps all evil into

---

60. See: Gary North, *Dominion and Common Grace: The Biblical Basis of Progress* (Tyler, TX: Institute for Christian Economics, 1987).

eternal judgment. At this event men enter their final, eternal abode: either the New Heavens and New Earth or the Lake of Fire (see Chapter 13, above). Here John shows that not only will the Lord vindicate His people by historical sanctions on earth, but there will be a final and conclusive judgment of the wicked and a blessed confirmation of the righteous.

The Spiritual Beauty of the Bride

The New Creation/Jerusalem of Revelation 21-22 began in the first century, although it stretches out into eternity in its ultimate consummation. The reasons for this assertion are as follows.

(1) The time frame, following closely upon the New Creation/Jerusalem description, strongly suggests it (Rev. 21:1, 2; 22:5-7). (2) The flow of Revelation intimates it. The destroyed old Jerusalem (Rev. 19) is immediately replaced by the New Jerusalem (Rev. 20-22), rather than waiting several thousand years. (3) The new creation (salvation) is realized in history before the final consummation.[61] Isaiah 65:17-25 shows that the New Creation on earth still experiences sin, aging, and death in the physical realm; thus, it cannot refer to heaven and eternity. It is from above, however.[62] (4) The New Testament anticipates the immediate change of the old era into the new.[63] (5) The New Testament speaks of the Church as Christ's bride (Eph. 5:25ff; 2 Cor. 11:2ff; John 3:29). The bride totally supplants Israel in A.D. 70.

The glory of salvation is here expressed in poetic terms. The absence of the sea (Rev. 21:1) speaks of harmony and peace within. In Scripture, the sea is often symbolic of discord and sin.[64] Christianity offers the opposite (Rom. 5:1; Eph 2:12ff;

---

61. 2 Cor. 5:17; Eph. 2:10; 4:24; Gal. 6:15. See Chapter 15.
62. Rev. 21:2; Gal. 4:22ff; Heb. 12:22; Col. 3:1,2.
63. John 4:20-24; Heb. 2:5; 12:18-29; Mark 9:1.
64. Rev. 13:1,2; Isa. 8:7ff; 23:10; 57:20; Jer. 6:23; 46:7.

Phil. 4:7,9). The bride-church is the tabernacle-temple of God (Rev. 21:3) because God dwells within and no literal Temple is needed.[65] Salvation removes grief,[66] introduces one into the family of God,[67] and brings eternal life (Rev. 21:6, 8).

The glory of the bride-church (Rev. 21:9-22:5) is also expressed poetically. She shines brilliantly like light.[68] Consequently, she is as precious to God as costly gold and jewels.[69] This beautiful bride-church has a sure foundation and impregnable walls.[70] Thus, she is destined to have a massive influence in the world.[71] She is cared for by God's provision of the water of life.[72] Thus, she brings healing to the nations by her presence.[73]

Closing Exhortations by John

In Revelation 22:6ff we find closing assurances of the veracity of the prophecies contained in Revelation. An angel declares them certain (v. 6), testifies that they come from God (v. 6), and notes that they are continuous with the Old Testament prophetic line (v. 7). Furthermore, Christ reaffirms their truth (vv. 7, 12-13, 16, 20) and John speaks by revelation (v. 8a).

The closing emphasis on the expectation of Revelation reiterates the temporal nearness of the events prophesied. The restatement of the nearness of the events harmonizes with Revelation 1:1-3 and serves as a closing bracket to the time

---

65. Rev. 21:22; cf. Eph. 2:19-22; 1 Cor. 3:16; 6:19; 2 Cor. 6:16; 1 Pet. 2:5,9.

66. Rev. 21:4; 1 Thess. 4:13; 1 Cor. 15:55-58; Jms. 1:2-4.

67. Rev. 21:7; cf. John 1:12-13; 1 John 3:1ff.

68. Rev. 21:10,11; Matt. 5:14-16; Acts 13:47; Rom. 13:12; 2 Cor. 6:14; Eph 5:8ff.

69. Rev. 21:11, 18ff; 1 Pet. 1:7; 2:4-7; 1 Cor. 3:12.

70. Rev. 21:12-21; Matt. 16:18; Acts 4:11; Eph. 2:19f; 1 Cor. 3:10ff; Isa. 26:1; 60:18.

71. Rev. 21:16, Isa. 2:2ff; Ezek. 17:22ff; 47:1-11; Dan. 2:31-35; Mic. 4:1; Matt. 13:31-32; 28:18-20; John 3:17; 1 Cor. 15:20ff; 2 Cor. 5:19.

72. Rev. 21:22; 22:1-5; John 4:14; 7:37-38; 6:32-35.

73. Rev. 22:2,3; Isa. 53:5; Ezek. 47:1-12; Matt. 13:33; Luke 4:18; John 4:14; Heb. 5:12-4; Gal. 3:10-13; 1 Pet. 2:2,24.

frame. We discover this through express declaration (Rev. 22:6), a promise of imminent divine intervention,[74] the command forbidding the sealing of the prophecies,[75] and the compelling urgency and contemporary relevance of the message to its original audience.[76]

John closes the book by giving covenantal warnings against tampering with its contents. Revelation is a covenant document from God Himself.

Conclusion

Interestingly, the Book of Revelation really does not speak to postmillennialism until its *last three chapters*. There, it holds forth the postmillennial hope of an expanding and dominating kingdom of Christ. The previous chapters, which clearly speak of chaos and devastation, and which influence today's pessimistic eschatologies, were prophetic visions of imminent events in John's day, and are therefore distant past events from our perspective today. To approach Revelation with the view that its judgment scenes still loom before us is to misunderstand Revelation in particular and biblical eschatology in general. He who has an ear to hear, let him hear.

---

74. Rev. 22:7, 12, 20; cf. Mark 9:1; Matt. 24:30, 34; 26:64.
75. Rev. 22:10 contra Dan. 8:26; 12:4,9.
76. Rev. 22:14-17; cf. Rev. 1:3,4.

PART V

OBJECTION

18

PRAGMATIC OBJECTIONS

So Jesus said to them, "Because of your unbelief; for assuredly, I say to you, if you have faith as a mustard seed, you will say to this mountain, 'Move from here to there,' and it will move; and nothing will be impossible for you." (Matthew 17:20)

In this section I respond to commonly heard objections to postmillennialism. Davis has rightly analyzed the problem: "Since postmillennialism is a position which has not been widely held in recent times, some contemporary authors in their references to it have not given an accurate representation of its true nature and claims."[1] I have arranged the objections into three basic classes: pragmatic (Ch. 18), theological (Ch. 19), and biblical (Ch. 20). Of course, many of the objections have been anticipated in the presentation of postmillennialism heretofore. Here, however, I shall give a more focused and specific response.

"Historical Decline Disproves Postmillennialism"

Perhaps the most popular objection to postmillennialism is that experience teaches that the world is in a great moral and spiritual decline that is antithetical to postmillennialism's historical optimism. Dispensational theologians are especially vigorous

---

1. John Jefferson Davis, *Christ's Victorious Kingdom: Postmillennialism Reconsidered* (Grand Rapids: Baker, 1986), p. 12.

in pressing this argument. Chafer said postmillennialism died in the 1930s: "[T]he present insane, corrupt condition of the world killed the theory by the contradiction of its own developing character." McClain scoffed that "this optimistic theory of human progress had much of its own way for the half-century ending in World War I of 1914. After that the foundations were badly shaken; prop after prop went down. . . ." Pentecost notes its "failure to fit the facts of history." Hoyt complains: "I am unable to see any comparable relation of the doctrine to the world of reality round about me." Walvoord "wonders how the writers of this [postmillennial] book can read the newspapers with their accounts of increased crime and a decaying church and come up with the idea. . . ." He also writes: "This view has largely been discarded in the 20th century, because many anti-Christian movements have prospered and the world has not progressed spiritually." Enns noted in 1989 that World Wars I and II "militated against the optimism of the doctrine."[2]

Historic premillennialists and amillennialists frequently make the same sort of observations. Premillennialist Kromminga writes (and amillennialist Hanko would agree): "In view of the present collapse of our western civilization and of the tremendous obstacles that have of late been thrown in the way of Christian missions and of the oppression to which the Christian Church is subjected in many an erstwhile Christian country to

---

2. L. S. Chafer, "Foreword," Charles Lee Feinberg, *Millennialism: The Two Major Views* (Chicago: Moody Press, [1936] 1980), p. 9. Alva J. McClain, "Premillennialism as a Philosophy of History," *Understanding the Times*, W. Culbertson and H. B. Centz, eds. (Grand Rapids: Zondervan, 1956), p. 22. J. Dwight Pentecost, *Things to Come: A Study in Biblical Eschatology* (Grand Rapids: Zondervan, 1958), pp. 386-387. Herman Hoyt, "A Dispensational Premillennial Response," *The Millennium: Four Views*, Robert G. Clouse, ed. (Downer's Grove, IL: InterVarsity Press, 1977), p. 144. John F. Walvoord, "Review of *House Divided*," *Bibliotheca Sacra* 147 (July/Sept. 1990) 372. Walvoord, "Revelation," *Bible Knowledge Commentary: New Testament*, Walvoord and Roy B. Zuck, eds. (Wheaton, IL: Victor, 1983), p. 978. Paul Enns, *The Moody Handbook of Theology* (Chicago: Moody Press, 1989), p. 384.

the point of virtual extinction, it is not at all surprising, that the postmillenarian view should at present be at low ebb."[3]

Adams notes that "the advent of two World Wars . . . virtually rang the death knell upon conservative postmillennialism as well. . . . It is spurned as highly unrealistic because it predicts a golden age around the corner in a day in which the world nervously anticipates momentary destruction by nuclear warfare." Hamilton writes: "The events of the past thirty years have revealed the fallacy of such reasoning. World War I shattered the hopes of the advocates of peace through international cooperation, in the Hague Peace Conference. The failure of the League of Nations and the breaking out of World War II, have given the final death blow to any hopes of the ushering in of an era of universal peace and joy through the interplay of forces now in action in the world." Berkhof assumes that "the experiences of the last quarter of a century" are inimical to postmillennialism. Premillennialist Erickson follows suit: One problem with postmillennialism "is its optimism concerning the conversion of the world, which seems somewhat unrealistic in the light of recent world developments."[4]

Neo-orthodox and liberal scholars also dispute postmillennialism on this basis. In analyzing the decline of postmillennialism earlier in this century, Moorhead states: ". . . postmil-

---

3. D. H. Kromminga, *The Millennium in the Church* (Grand Rapids: Eerdmans, 1945), p. 264-265. Herman Hanko, "An Exegetical Refutation of Postmillennialism" (unpublished conference paper: South Holland, IL: South Holland Protestant Reformed Church, 1978), p. 26.

4. Jay E. Adams, *The Time Is at Hand* (n.p.: Presbyterian & Reformed, 1966), p. 2. Floyd E. Hamilton, *The Basis of Millennial Faith* (Grand Rapids: Eerdmans, 1942), p. 22. Louis Berkhof, *Systematic Theology* (Grand Rapids: Eerdmans, 1941), p. 719. Millard J. Erickson, *Contemporary Options in Eschatology: A Study of the Millennium* (Grand Rapids: Baker, 1977), p. 71. See also: William E. Cox, *Biblical Studies in Final Things* (Nutley, NJ: Presbyterian & Reformed, 1966). Robert G. Gromacki, *Are These the Last Days?* (Old Tappan, NJ: Revell, 1970), p. 179. William S. LaSor, *The Truth About Armageddon* (New York: Harper & Row, 1982), p. 160. Leon J. Wood, *The Bible and Future Events* (Grand Rapids: Zondervan, 1973), p. 38. Bruce Milne, *What the Bible Teaches About the End of the World* (Wheaton, IL: Tyndale, 1979), p. 80.

lennialism looked increasingly implausible because events had stubbornly refused to follow its scenario. . . . [E]xperience simply had not sustained postmillennialism. The product of an era when evangelicalism enjoyed cultural dominance, it could not survive when that ascendance waned. It became a relic of a lost world."[5] Peters surmises: "People of the twentieth century cannot accept this naïve optimism, however. Moral progress has stopped, if not reversed. Two world wars, the conversion of 5 million Jews not into Christians but into ashes, atomic warfare. . . . all this removes any ground for belief that Christ now rules and that the devil is chained. Postmillennialism is dead. . . ."[6]

Nowhere does this objection find more vigorous expression, however, than among dispensational popularizers (whose ideas are sometimes bemoaned by professionally trained dispensational theologians[7]). Hal Lindsey writes: "There used to be a group called 'postmillennialists.' . . . World War I greatly disheartened this group and World War II virtually wiped out this viewpoint. No self-respecting scholar who looks at the world conditions and the accelerating decline of Christian influence today is a 'postmillennialist.' "[8]

Of course, a quick rhetorical response to observations based on the World Wars has at least as much merit as those objections: Who won World Wars I and II? Did the anti-Christian forces of evil overwhelm those nations wherein resided the greatest missionary forces for Christianity in the world? Was the

---

5. James H. Moorhead, "The Erosion of Postmillennialism in American Religious Thought, 1865-1925," *Church History* 53 (1984) 77.

6. Ted Peters, *Futures – Human and Divine* (Atlanta: John Knox, 1977), p. 30.

7. Craig A. Blaising attempts to distance "expositional-theological" dispensationalism from Lindsey's "popular" views. Review section of *Bibliotheca Sacra* 147 (July/Sept. 1990) 365. Robert P. Lightner, *The Last Days Handbook* (Nashville: Thomas Nelson, 1990), p. 172; Darrell L. Bock, "Charting Dispensationalism," *Christianity Today* (September 12, 1993): pp. 26-28.

8. Hal Lindsey, *The Late Great Planet Earth* (Grand Rapids: Zondervan, 1970), p. 176.

world made a more dangerous place for Christianity because of the defeat of Japan in Asia and Germany in Europe?

There are deeper responses to such objections, however. These are basically three-fold.

1. The Problem of Narrow Sampling

Such historical experience arguments involve too narrow a sample. The better question regarding historical development is: Have world circumstances and particularly conditions for the Christian Church improved *since Christianity's inception in the first century*? That is, taking into account the big picture, the historical long run: Are Christians as a class today generally better off than were Christians as a class of the first two or three centuries? Are world conditions better today in Christian-influenced areas than they were in the first century? Anyone who is cognizant of the Roman persecutions against the early Church should be quite aware that Christians today are in a much better situation in most places on earth.

In debates on the subject I point out the irony of this objection to postmillennialism in light of the circumstances of the debate: "Here we are in a free land, sitting in our comfortable Bible-believing church, dressed in our 'Sunday best,' holding one of our many personal Bibles (the world's largest selling book!) debating whether or not there has been any advance in the conditions of Christianity since its persecuted inception 2,000 years ago!" Ironically, the one who most vigorously bemoans the decline of Christianity, Hal Lindsey, is the author of a book published (before Bantam Books bought the rights) by one of the nation's largest Christian publishers, one of the largest selling books of the last twenty years, selling thirty-five million copies in fifty-four languages: *The Late Great Planet Earth.*[9] It may be the case that we have witnessed a decline in

---

9. As reported in Hal Lindsey and Chuck Missler, "The Rise of Babylon and the Persian Gulf Crisis" (Palos Verdes, CA: Hal Lindsey Ministries, 1991), p. 64.

America over the last fifty or one hundred years. (It may even be the case that the sales figures for Lindsey's book are indicative of this decline!) But has this decline completely wiped out centuries of Christian progress? The answer clearly is that it has not. Will our present slippage and decline continue and spread into total apostasy and chaos to a point beneath that of the first century? Of course, we cannot answer this today on the basis of *historical analysis*. Answering this question is the task of the Christian exegete who recognizes that God's Word "shall not return to Me void, but it shall accomplish what I please, and it shall prosper in the thing for which I sent it" (Isa. 55:11). It is the point of this book to demonstrate that God's will is for the redemption of the world as a system in the historical long-run and before the physical return of Christ in final judgment.

Of course, the postmillennialist can turn the tables on the pessimistic historical short-run argument. Consider the collapse in 1991 of Communism in Russia and Eastern Europe. As recently as 1987 anti-postmillennialists would have scoffed at the very notion of the collapse of Communism – a threat to their eschatologies. Twenty years ago dispensationalist Gannet saw the Second Advent as the only hope for the overthrow of Communism and other forms of political oppression: "What peace of mind this brings to Christians as the end time approaches. What a cause for rejoicing that righteousness, not Russia, shall ultimately triumph. This triumph of Christ over Communism emphasizes the folly of getting side-tracked in spending our time primarily in opposing Communism rather than in an all-out proclamation of the gospel of grace."[10] Also keep in mind Adams' comment, which obviously had the Communist Soviet Union in view: Postmillennialism "is spurned as highly unrealistic because it predicts a golden age around the corner in a day in which the world nervously anticipates momentary destruc-

10. Alden A. Gannet, "Will Christ or Communism Rule the World?" *Prophecy and the Seventies*, Charles Lee Feinberg, ed. (Chicago: Moody Press, 1971), pp. 64-65.

tion by nuclear warfare."[11] A book brimming with newspaper clippings of the portentous danger of Communist Russia warns: "We are on an irreversible course for world disaster."[12]

Note well: No knowledgeable postmillennialist would point to the current apparent collapsing of Communism as definitive proof of postmillennialism (although Communism everywhere will have to collapse before the final stages of the postmillennial advance of Christ's kingdom, since it is inherently anti-Christian).[13] Yet, it is encouraging to watch the freeing up of Christianity in the totalitarian lands once dominated by monolithic, atheistic Communism – despite claims by dispensationalists of irreversibly worsening world conditions. It is a heartening cause for rejoicing and continuing prayer (and surely the result of the effectual fervent prayers of persecuted Christians) to read such headlines as: "Religion Gains Momentum in Soviet Union,"[14] "Prayers and Bible Welcomed in the Kremlin,"[15] "Albania Awakes from Atheism,"[16] "Churches Gain Favor with Castro, See Spiritual Awakening,"[17] "New Law Extends Religious Freedom,"[18] and "Evangelism Finds a Place on New Soviet Agenda."[19] Who knows where all of this will lead in the near future? If "short run" arguments were valid, such headlines could just as easily be used as newspaper exegesis for the evidence of postmillennialism.

---

11. Adams, *Time Is at Hand*, p. 2.

12. Salem Kirban, *Countdown to Rapture* (Eugene, OR: Harvest House, 1977), p. 11. Cf. pp. 148-160.

13. Gary North, *Marx's Religion of Revolution: The Doctrine of Creative Destruction* (rev. ed.; Tyler, TX: Institute for Christian Economics, [1968] 1989). Francis Nigel Lee, *Communist Eschatology: A Christian Philosophical Analysis of the Views of Marx, Engels, and Lenin* (Nutley, NJ: Craig, 1974). David Chilton, *Productive Christians in an Age of Guilt Manipulators* (3rd ed.; Tyler, TX: Institute for Christian Economics, 1985).

14. New York Times release, *Greenville Piedmont* (Oct. 7, 1991) A-1.

15. Article in *Christianity Today* 35:11 (Oct. 7, 1991) 42-43.

16. Art Moore, in *Christianity Today* 35:6 (May 27, 1991) 52-54.

17. Christ Woehr, in *Christianity Today* 35:1 (Jan. 14, 1991) 46ff.

18. Ken Sidey, in *Christianity Today* 34:16 (Nov. 5, 1991) 76ff.

19. Russell Chandler, in *Christianity Today* 34:18 (Dec. 17, 1990) 39ff.

2. The Problem of Impatient Anticipation

Nothing in the postmillennial definition requires either relentlessly forward progress or a reaching of the height of postmillennial advance by any particular date. The gradualistic postmillennialism presented in this book simply teaches that *before the end* – whenever that indeterminate time might be (Matt. 24:36), it certainly has not occurred yet – the kingdom of God will have reached world-dominating proportions. In fact, there are some branches of evangelical postmillennialism – catastrophic postmillennialism – that assert the postmillennial "millennium" is entirely future and has not yet arrived.[20]

Furthermore, why has not dispensationalism and premillennialism been wholly discredited by its constant cry of "the end is at hand"? LaHaye wrote with no hesitation: "The fact that we are the generation that will be on the earth when our Lord comes certainly should not depress us. . . . [I]f you are a Christian, after reading this book you ought to know the end is near!"[21] We see the clearest examples of date setting in Hal Lindsey's *The 1980s: Countdown to Armageddon* (expected before 1990), Edgar C. Whisenant's *88 Reasons Why the Rapture Is in 1988* (expected in 1988) and *The Final Shout: Rapture Report 1989* (expected in 1989), and Richard Ruhling, M.D., *Sword Over America* (expected in early 1990s), and Grant R. Jeffrey, *Armageddon: Appointment with Destiny* (expected in A.D. 2000).[22]

Unfortunately, as the following titles indicate, the list continues to grow as the year 2000 approaches: *Planet Earth — 2000:*

20. For example: Davis, *Christ's Victorious Kingdom*; Willard Ramsey, *Zion's Glad Morning* (Simpsonville, SC: Millennium III, 1991).

21. Tim LaHaye, *The Beginning of the End* (Wheaton, IL: Tyndale, 1972), p. 172.

22. Hal Lindsey, *The 1980's: Countdown to Armageddon* (New York: Bantam, 1980): "*The decade of the 1980's could very well be the last decade of history as we know it*" (p. 8, emphasis his). Edgar C. Whisenant, *88 Reasons Why the Rapture Is in 1988* (Nashville, TN: World Bible Society, 1988). See: Jim Ashley, "Ruhling Believes 'Crisis' Events Near," *Chattanooga News – Free Press* (Oct. 7, 1989), Church News Section. Grant R. Jeffrey, *Armageddon: Appointment with Destiny* (Toronto: Frontier, 1988).

Will Mankind Survive?; *I Predict 2000*; *Prophecy 2000: Rushing to Armageddon*; *The 90's: Decade of the Apocalypse*; *How Close Are We?: Compelling Evidence for the Soon Return of Christ; Storm Warning*; *The Final Countdown; Armageddon: Appointment with Destiny; The Rapture Book: Victory in the End Times; Earth's Final Days; Storming Toward Armageddon: Essays in Apocalypse; Final Approach: The Opportunity and Adventure of End-Times Living; Is This the Last Century?*[23]

Robert Fuller's scholarly research into the naivete of date-setting shows the relentless determination by dispensationalists to identify the Antichrist.[24] Dwight Wilson's plea to fellow premillenarians is for them to quit embarrassing the viewpoint by participating in the practice known as date-setting: creating false expectations of an imminent end.[25] Marvin Pate and Calvin Haines also urge fellow dispensationalists to avoid *Doomsday Delusions*. Their warnings has not been heeded. The very argument that is employed against postmillennialism – "we see no postmillennial progress" – could be turned in another way upon premillennial Christians (and other evangelicals). Christ

---

23. Hal Lindsey, *Planet Earth – 2000: Will Mankind Survive?* (Palos Verdes, Calif.: Western Front, 1994). Lester Sumrall, *I Predict 2000* (South Bend: LeSea, 1987). David Allen Lewis, *Prophecy 2000: Rushing to Armageddon* (Green Forest, Ark.: Green Leaf, 1990). Steve Terrell, *The 90's: Decade of the Apocalypse* (S. Plainfield, N.J.: Bridge, 1992). Dave Hunt, *How Close Are We?: Compelling Evidence for the Soon Return of Christ* (Eugene, Ore.: Harvest, 1993). Billy Graham, *Storm Warning* (Dallas: Word, 1992). Charles C. Ryrie, *The Final Countdown* (Wheaton, Ill.: Victor, rep. 1991). Grant R. Jeffries, *Armageddon: Appointment with Destiny* (Toronto: Frontier Research, 1988). James McKeever, *The Rapture Book: Victory in the End Times* (Medford, Ore.: Omega, 1987). Don McAlvanny, *et al.*, *Earth's Final Days* (Green Forest, Ariz.: New Leaf, 1994). Texe Marrs, *et al.*, *Storming Toward Armageddon: Essays in Apocalypse* (Green Forest, Ariz.: New Leaf, 1992). Roberts Liardon, *Final Approach: The Opportunity and Adventure of End-Times Living* (Orlando: Creation House, 1993). David Webber and Noah Hutchins, *Is This the Last Century?* (Nashville: Thomas Nelson, 1979).

24. Robert Fuller, *Naming the Antichrist: The History of an American Obsession* (New York: Oxford, 1995).

25. Dwight Wilson, *Armageddon Now! The Premillenarian Response to Russia and Israel Since 1917* (Tyler, TX: Institute for Christian Economics, [1977] 1991). Gary DeMar, *Last Days Madness: The Folly of Trying to Predict When Christ Will Return* (Brentwood, TN: Wolgemuth & Hyatt, 1991).

said that He would come again. Since He has not come yet, and since His coming is allegedly always impending, we may assume He is not going to return at all. But surely this sort of argument is erroneous: simply because something has not happened *yet*, does not mean it cannot and will not happen *ever*.

Erikson admits of this sort of objection (which he himself makes): "This criticism, it must be admitted, may have to be qualified eventually."[26] Kromminga agrees: "But it remains doubtful, to say the least, in case through the operation of these same forces peace should once again be restored to our world, whether then postmillennial hopes will not also revive once more."[27] Even dispensationalist Culver has changed his view in this regard: "Postmillennialism is not dead. It seems probable that any period of prolonged peace in the world would provide the climate in which a revival of postmillennialism might take place."[28]

3. The Problem of Newspaper Exegesis

The eschatological debate must be resolved on the basis of biblical analysis, not newspaper exegesis. Short-cut arguments from experience may carry weight among those not theologically inclined, but they should have no bearing upon the theological argument in light of the above observations. Abram was old and childless when the Lord promised Him an innumerable seed (Gen. 15:5). He even died with only one legitimate son. Yet he believed God would perform the work promised. Could not righteous Simeon have been mocked for awaiting the consolation of Israel, since God's voice had been silent for four hundred years (Luke 2:25)? Warfield writes:

---

26. Erickson, *Contemporary Options in Eschatology*, p. 72.

27. Kromminga, *Millennium*, p. 264-265.

28. Robert D. Culver, *Daniel and the Latter Days* (2nd ed.; Chicago: Moody Press, 1977), p. 207.

The redemption of the world is similarly a process. It, too, has its stages: it, too, advances only gradually to its completion. But it, too, will ultimately be complete; and then we shall see a wholly saved world. Of course it follows, that at any stage of the process, short of completeness, the world, as the individual, must present itself to observation as incompletely saved. We can no more object the incompleteness of the salvation of the world today to the completeness of the salvation of the world, than we can object the incompleteness of our personal salvation today (the remainders of sin in us, the weakness and death of our bodies) to the completeness of our personal salvation. Everything in its own order: first the seed, then the blade, then the full corn in the ear. And as, when Christ comes, we shall each of us be like him, when we shall see him as he is, so also, when Christ comes, it will be to a fully saved world, and there shall be a new heaven and a new earth, in which dwells righteousness.[29]

In the final analysis Rushdoony is on target when he notes the *underlying modernism* of eschatological arguments that are based on current world conditions: "Such comments are in principle modernistic, in that they assess Scripture, not in terms of itself, but in terms of the times, the modern age."[30]

"Postmillennialism Undermines Watchfulness"

Because of the widespread (and false!) view of the imminency of Christ's return (see Chapter 14), some have argued that postmillennialism destroys the spirit of "watchfulness" that the Lord enjoined upon His people. This objection is frequently employed in either or both of two ways. It may allege that specific Scriptural passages encouraging watchfulness are dismissed by the postmillennial system (e.g., Matt. 24:42; 25:13).

---

29. Benjamin B. Warfield, *The Plan of Salvation* (Grand Rapids: Eerdmans, [n.d.] 1970), pp. 101-102.

30. R. J. Rushdoony, "Introduction," J. Marcellus Kik, *An Eschatology of Victory* (n.p.: Presbyterian & Reformed, 1971), p. vii.

Or it may imply that postmillennial adherence has the practical effect of dulling Christian sensitivity to the things of God by taking the believer's mind off the Second Coming of Christ to receive His Church into heaven.

Amillennialist Gaffin has reservations with regard to postmillennialism because it "deprives the church of the imminent expectation of Christ's return and so undermines the quality of watchfulness that is incumbent on the church." Amillennialist Hanko warns of the postmillennial concern for Christian victory in history: "And through it all, he no longer is mindful of his calling to watch unto the end. . . . The believer must live, in obedience to his Lord, in constant longing and expectation of the end of all things."

The best-selling dispensationalist author Dave Hunt laments postmillennialism because, he says, "there is an increasing antagonism against eagerly watching and waiting for Christ's return, which surely was the attitude of the early church." Premillennialists Demarest and Gordon write: "The objection thus impeaches the wisdom of Christ in making known to man the fact of his coming again in the clouds, and then drawing an argument for our constant WATCHING." Milne agrees.[31]

Despite many anti-postmillennial protestations, "to expect the Lord in our life-time is not a pre-requisite of true piety – this would be to base the Christian life, in most generations, upon a falsehood."[32] Those who argue for an "any moment"

---

31. Richard B. Gaffin, Jr., "Theonomy and Eschatology: Reflections on Postmillennialism," *Theonomy: A Reformed Critique*, William S. Barker and W. Robert Godfrey, eds. (Grand Rapids: Zondervan, 1990), p. 218. For a critique of Gaffin's article see: Kenneth L. Gentry, Jr., "Whose Victory in History?" *Theonomy: An Informed Response*, Gary North, ed. (Tyler, TX: Institute for Christian Economics, 1991). Hanko, "An Exegetical Refutation of Postmillennialism," p. 24. Dave Hunt, *Whatever Happened to Heaven?* (Eugene, OR: Harvest House, 1989), p. 8. John T. Demarest and William R. Gordon, *Christocracy: Essays on the Coming and Kingdom of Christ* (New York: R. Brinderhoff, 1878), p. 384. Milne, *Know the Truth*, p. 263.

32. Donald Macleod, "The Second Coming of Christ," *Banner of Truth*, Nos. 82-83 (July/Aug. 1970) 20.

view of the return of Christ as a major spur for holy living root ethical conduct in erroneous expectations.

As I pointed out in Chapter 14, the Scripture very clearly notes that *we cannot know when Christ is going to return* (Matt. 24:36). Consequently, *we must always be prepared* (Matt. 25:13), despite our ignorance as to the timing of His return. Although we cannot know its timing, if we are *obediently working* for His glory according to His Word, then that Day will not catch *Christians* as "a thief in the night" (1 Thess. 5:1ff). This is the true meaning of "watchfulness." "After all, watchfulness implies delay."[33] *We are to watch ourselves, not for "signs."*

The word "watch" in Matthew 24:42 and 25:13 is *gregoreo*. This word literally means "be awake." It implies being alert as opposed to being asleep. Being awake signifies *active spiritual service*, whereas being asleep indicates moral laxity and spiritual dereliction (1 Thess. 5:6-7). In 1 Corinthians 16:13 we find this word tied in with a series of words of ethical synonymity: "Watch, stand fast in the faith, be brave, be strong." The accent is on diligent commitment and faithful readiness to serve. The emphasis in the Scriptural employment of this term is not on literally looking out each day in anticipation of an any moment appearing of Christ, but on vibrant service. Since we cannot know when He will return, we must always be alert. *This* is the calling of the Christian. *Eschatological imminency is not mandatory for moral watchfulness.* During World War II Allis wrote:

> This argument has been stated in various ways, all of which involve the assumption that men cannot expect and watch for the coming of Christ and be stimulated and safeguarded by the thought of it unless they can believe that it may take place 'at any moment.' This argument is not valid. A mother may live in the constant, ever-present hope and expectation of seeing her absent boy, even when she knows that he is on the other side of

---

33. G. C. Berkouwer, *The Return of Christ* (Grand Rapids: Eerdmans, 1972), p. 91.

the globe. Intensity of affection disregards time and distance. Seven years was a long time for Jacob to serve for Rachel; and he had made a contract with Laban and knew that he would be held to the letter of it. Yet the years seemed to him like a 'few days' (the Hebrew might be rendered 'single days') for the love he had for her. . . . The interest men take in an objective, the effort they are willing to make to attain it, does not depend on its nearness nearly so much as on its greatness, its desirability, and the probability or certainty of its ultimate achievement. The nearness of the goal may appeal to a man's selfishness, ambition, pride, even to his indolence.[34]

Despite its employment in the debate by some, Paul's statement in Titus 2:13 does not demand imminency, when he urges our "looking for the blessed hope and glorious appearing of our great God and Savior Jesus Christ." The word "looking" (*prosdechomai*) does not demand the connotation "look for with imminent expectation." It simply means "wait for, expect." A number of translators translate the passage with the idea of "waiting."[35] Hendriksen notes that it means *"waiting for or patient looking forward to."*[36] Patience anticipates *delay*.

Though it is true that we should eagerly long for the Return of Christ, it is neither true that this entails its imminence nor that this is the only genuine spur to diligence. As far as the imminent expectation of Christ's Return goes, the Christian should deeply long for personal release from this body of sin and his entry into the glories of heaven, which comes at death. Yet he labors where God has currently placed him by His providence: in the God-created world of time and space.

---

34. O. T. Allis, *Prophecy and the Church* (Philadelphia: Presbyterian & Reformed, 1945), p. 169.

35. See: *Young's Literal Translation of the Bible*, Phillips' *New Testament in Modern English*, Moffatt's *New Translation*, Weymouth's *New Testament in Modern Speech*, *Amplified Bible*, Williams' *New Testament in the Language of the People*.

36. William Hendriksen, *I and II Timothy and Titus (NTC)* (Grand Rapids: Baker, 1957), p. 372.

Furthermore, regarding imminence as a spur to holiness we all know that we could die this very minute. We are statistically more certain that we *will* die in a relatively short time (Psa. 90:4-6, 10; 1 Pet. 1:24) than we are that Christ will return today. Upon exiting temporal life through the door of death we will find ourselves in the presence of the Lord our Judge, where we will give account (2 Cor. 5:8, 10). This ought to spur us to live for Him, as the Parable of the Rich Barn Owner (Luke 12:16-21) indicates. John Chrysostom (A.D. 347-407) wisely warns: "Is not the consummation of the world, for each of us, the end of his own life? Why are you concerned and worried about the common end?" (*In Ep I ad Thes 9:1*).

Still further, every Christian knows that he lives constantly under the moment-by-moment scrutiny of Almighty God. We cannot escape His presence during any moment of life, for "there is no creature hidden from His sight, but all things are naked and open to the eyes of Him to whom *we must give account*" (Heb. 4:13). This motivated David to live for God and to praise Him for His greatness (Psa. 139). The *certainty* of our absolute *present openness* to the Lord ought to move us to serve Him more faithfully, even more so than the *prospect* that He may possibly return today.[37]

No spur to holiness is lost by denying the imminency of Christ's Return. Besides, if anticipation of the appearing of Christ at any moment is a major New Testament theme and ethical spur, how can we account for passages that clearly expect a *delay* of His return – in the same passages (see Matthew 25:5, 14, 19 in conjunction with Matthew 24:42; 25:13)? It is interesting that in Christ's parable the *foolish* virgins expect His imminent return (Matt. 25:1-13). It is significant that the *wicked scoffer* is not prepared for the long delay of Christ's Return (2 Pet. 3:3-9).

---

37. J. A. Alexander, "The End is Not Yet," *Banner of Truth*, No. 88 (Jan. 1971) 1ff.

As Davis observes, we should understand that the call to watchfulness in regard to the Second Coming is based on its *unexpectedness*, not its calculability (Luke 12:35-40).[38]

"Postmillennialism is Rooted in Evolutionary Thought"

In this and the next two sections I will analyze inter-related objections to postmillennial eschatology. These problems point to the alleged basis (evolution), method (liberalism), and result (social gospel) of postmillennialism. Let us consider the evolutionary argument first.

Not infrequently a complaint against postmillennialism is that it is closely associated with evolutionary thought. Often both the optimism and the developmental progress inherent in evangelical postmillennialism are alleged to have been derived from evolutionary science. Because of this misperception it is not uncommon to hear the criticism that "postmillennialists have had some difficulty maintaining a genuine supernaturalism."[39] In his study of millennial views Walvoord parallels a theologically liberal, evolution-based postmillennialism with theologically orthodox, Scripture-based postmillennialism (although he allows there is some distinction between them).[40] Berkhof sharply distinguishes between evangelical, supernaturalistic postmillennialism and its naturalistic, evolutionary imitation. Yet, after citing several liberal postmillennialists, he writes: "These quotations are quite characteristic of a great deal of present day Postmillennialism, and it is no wonder that the Premillenarians react against it."[41]

Historically, this alleged association of evolutionary thought with postmillennial theology has ignored the fact that both a

---

38. Davis, *Christ's Victorious Kingdom*, p. 105.

39. Erickson, *Contemporary Options in Eschatology*, p. 72.

40. John F. Walvoord, "The Millennial Issue in Modern Thought," *Bibliotheca Sacra* 106 (Jan. 1948) 154.

41. Berkhof, *Systematic Theology*, p. 718.

developed postmillennialism (e.g., the Puritans), as well as nascent postmillennialism (e.g., Athanasius), arose well before scientific evolutionism, which is generally dated from the publication of Darwin's *Origin of Species* (1859). Historically, it may more forcibly be argued that the evolutionist stole from the postmillennial idea of progress rather than vice versa.

Interestingly, earlier in this century dispensationalists were strong advocates of Thomas Chalmers' 1814 "Gap Theory" of Genesis 1 through the influence of G. H. Pember's *Earth's Earliest Ages*. This was an attempt to accommodate Scripture to evolutionary geology. Scofield himself was very strong on this view of Genesis 1:1 and 2, as was the Pilgrim Bible (1948).[42] *The New Scofield Bible* (1967) removed the note from Genesis 1:1-2, but then placed its essence at Isaiah 45:18. Even when dispensationalists reject this viewpoint (e.g., John Whitcomb and Henry Morris), they still play into the hands of the evolutionary humanists. North points out that "there is also no doubt that the humanists have relied on the widespread fundamentalist faith in premillennialism to strengthen their hold over American life."[43] This is due to the premillennialists' retreat from cultural influence. They hand over authority to the humanists.

Is Darwinism optimistic? Not regarding the long run. The atheistic, evolutionist philosopher Bertrand Russell wrote in 1935: "There is no law of cosmic progress, but only an oscillation upward and downward, with a slow trend downward on a balance owing to the diffusion of energy. This, at least, is what science at present regards as most probable, and in our disillusioned generation it is easy to believe. From evolution, so far as our present knowledge shows, no ultimately optimistic philoso-

42. C. I. Scofield, *The Scofield Reference Bible* (New York: Oxford, [1909] 1917), see notes spanning pp. 3-4. See brief discussion in R. J. Rushdoony, *God's Plan for Victory: The Meaning of Postmillennialism* (Fairfax, VA: Thoburn Press, 1977), pp. 6-7 and Gary North, *Is the World Running Down? Crisis in the Christian Worldview* (Tyler, TX: Institute for Christian Economics, 1988), p. 270.

43. North, *Is the World Running Down?*, p. 271.

HE SHALL HAVE DOMINION

phy can be validly inferred."[44] It is difficult to see how such statements could be deemed close to postmillennialism. Indeed, North has noted similar applications of the Law of Entropy in the Scientific Creation movement and also in certain New Age philosophies and modern evolutionism.[45]

The ultimate problem with the "postmillennialism = evolutionism" argument is that *it identifies things that differ in fundamental respects*. The goals, motives, and standards of evangelical postmillennialism are clearly supernaturalistic, whereas those of secular humanism are thoroughly naturalistic. Postmillennialism's *goal* is the glorification of Jesus Christ in all areas of life; humanism's goal is the glorification of man in all areas of life. Postmillennialism's *motive* is faithfulness to the resurrected Christ; humanism's motive is faithfulness to self-sufficient man. Postmillennialism's *standard* is the written revelation of Almighty God in Scripture; humanism's standard is autonomous human reason or mystical illumination. Evangelical postmillennialism and *some* forms of evolutionism expect historical progress. Yet the nature and results of this progress are radically different.

This leads to the next objection.

"Liberal Tendencies Govern Postmillennialism"

A more popular and more simplistic exception to postmillennialism is that it contains the *seeds of liberalism* within it. Dallas Theological Seminary professor Robert Lightner writes: "[P]ostmillennialism found it almost impossible to stem the tide toward liberal theology. The nonliteral method of prophetic interpretation that both postmillennialism and amillennialism rest on, leaves the door wide open, hermeneutically at least, for the same kind of interpretation to be applied to other biblical mat-

---

44. Bertrand Russell, "Evolution," in Russell, *Religion and Science* (New York: Oxford University Press, [1935] 1972), p. 81.

45. North, *Is the World Running Down?*, *passim*.

ters, such as the deity of Christ, and the authority of the Bible."[46] Walvoord argues similarly when he complains that postmillennialism cannot resist the tendency to liberalism in that it "lends itself to liberalism with only minor adjustments."[47] Pentecost agrees that there is "the trend toward liberalism, which postmillennialism could not meet, because of its spiritualizing principle of interpretation."[48] *This argument equates theological liberalism with optimism, a very questionable assumption.* Neo-orthodox theology, existentialist to the core, was a reaction to the optimism of the older liberalism. It is nonetheless equally hostile to an orthodox view of biblical revelation.

Adams notes the temptation of this sort of argument for premillennialists, while disavowing its helpfulness: "But side-by-side with [the postmillennialists], liberals began announcing similar expectations, while attributing them to very different causes. . . . Evangelicals found it easier to attack the general idea of a world getting better and better (held by both) than to make methodological distinctions between conservative, supernaturalistic postmillennialism and liberal, naturalistic modernism."[49] Dispensationalist Culver's honesty in this regard is refreshing: "During the 'golden age' of American Protestant modernism, which came to an end with World War II, modernists adopted a kind of postmillennialism to which earlier advocates would have given no approval. . . . It was based more on the theory of evolution and humanism than on any interpretation of the Bible and need not occupy our attention here.

46. Robert P. Lightner, *The Last Days Handbook* (Nashville: Thomas Nelson, 1990), p. 84.

47. John F. Walvoord, *The Millennial Kingdom* (Grand Rapids: Zondervan, 1959), p. 35; see also p. 34. This is an incredible and indefensible assertion. Postmillennialists believe in the visible, glorious return of Christ to cause the physical resurrection of the dead and to hold the Great Judgment of all men, assigning some to heaven and others to hell. I know of no liberal theologian that holds any of these fundamental assertions.

48. Pentecost, *Things to Come*, p. 386.

49. Adams, *Time Is at Hand*, p. 1.

The present heirs of modernism, the neoorthodox and neolib-
eral people, are scarcely more optimistic about the course of the
present era than premillenarians and so are not inclined to
postmillennialism."[50]

I have already dealt briefly with the issue of hermeneutics in
Chapter 8. Virtually no evangelical scholars except dispensationalists assert that "literalism" is a protection against liberalism. Premillennialist Ladd complains against dispensationalists:

> Walvoord goes on to say that 'the diverse theological systems of
> Roman Catholic, modern liberal, and modern conservative writ-
> ers are found to be using essentially the same method.' This
> amounts to the claim that only dispensationalism, with its literal
> hermeneutic of the Old Testament, can provide a truly evangeli-
> cal theology. In my view this simply is not true. B. B. Warfield
> did not use the same 'spiritualizing' hermeneutic as the liberal.
> The liberal *admits* that the New Testament teaches the bodily
> resurrection of Christ, but his philosophical presuppositions
> make it impossible for him to accept it. On the other hand, B. B.
> Warfield was the greatest exponent of a high view of biblical
> inspiration of his day. He was prepared to accept any doctrine
> which could be proved by the Scriptures. If he 'spiritualized' the
> millennium, it was because he felt *a total biblical hermeneutic re-
> quired him to do so.* This is not liberalism.[51]

In his response to dispensationalist Hoyt, Ladd laments:

> Hoyt's essay reflects the major problem in the discussion of the
> millennium. Several times he contrasts nondispensational views
> with his own, which he labels 'the biblical view' (pp. 69-70, 84).
> If he is correct, then the other views, including my own, are
> 'unbiblical' or even heretical. This is the reason that over the

---

50. Culver, *Daniel in the Latter Days*, pp. 206-207.

51. George Eldon Ladd, "Historic Premillennialism," *Meaning of the Millennium*,
pp. 19-20.

years there has been little creative dialogue between dispensationalists and other schools of prophetic interpretation.[52]

Cox notes: "Indeed, some [dispensationalists] allow but two alternatives: their own school or liberalism. In this area of theology, especially, a label often becomes a libel."[53]

Does literalism protect against theological distortion? This sort of argument can be turned on the dispensationalist. Should it be argued that *premillennialism leads to cultism* because of the literalistic hermeneutic of such premillennial cults as: Mormonism, the Jehovah's Witnesses, Herbert W. Armstrong's Worldwide Church of God, and others?[54] Does not Pentecost himself admit that *literalism was the method applied by the Christ-rejecting Pharisees?*[55] Was not literalism a factor in the medieval cloister and self-flagellation?

Does possible misuse of a particular hermeneutic require the abandonment of that hermeneutic "for safety's sake"? Surely Pentecost is correct in his forced admission: "And yet it can not be denied that literalism was the accepted method [of rabbinism]. Misuse of the method does not militate against the method itself. It was not the method that was at fault, but rather the misapplication of it."[56] The question arises: why should postmillennialists abandon a hermeneutic method that is *vaguely* akin to that which is twisted by liberals? Why should postmillennialists not use Pentecost's argument in self-defense?

---

52. *Ibid.*, p. 93.

53. Cox, *Biblical Studies in Final Things*, p. 175. Cox is amillennial.

54. I have responded elsewhere to this fallacy of equating divergent systems by their use of similar terminology. See: Greg L. Bahnsen and Kenneth L. Gentry, Jr., *House Divided: The Break-up of Dispensational Theology* (Tyler, TX: Institute for Christian Economics, 1989), pp. 318-340.

55. Pentecost, *Things to Come*, pp. 17-19.

56. *Ibid.*, p. 19.

"Postmillennialism Results in a Social Gospel"

Due to the pietistic retreatism so characteristic of fundamentalism, there is a strong tendency among dispensationalists to equate the social concern of postmillennial eschatology with Social Gospel liberalism. The dispensationalist urges that "God didn't send me to clean the fish bowl, he sent me to fish."[57] When the Christian expresses a cultural concern for the sins of modern culture and a desire for their rooting out, the pietist moans, *Whatever Happened to Heaven?*, or frets: *Dominion Theology: Blessing or Curse?* He fears that such a concern is surely *The Road to Holocaust*.[58]

Some retreatist amillennialists fear the same. Protestant Reformed Church theologian Herman Hanko insists: "There [is] also a question raised as to whether even mild, or moderate, postmillennialism does not after all, in fact, with its view of a kingdom of Christ being realized in this present world, end up by laboring for the realization of the kingdom of Anti-Christ and develop into radical and liberal postmillennialism and social gospelism."[59] Such, then, "makes postmillennial thinking of considerable danger."[60]

---

57. Hal Lindsey in an interview, "The Great Cosmic Countdown: Hal Lindsey on the Future," *Eternity* 28 (Jan. 1977) 21.

58. Hunt, *Whatever Happened to Heaven?*; H. Wayne House and Thomas D. Ice, *Dominion Theology: Blessing or Curse?* (Portland, OR: Multnomah, 1988); Hal Lindsey, *The Road to Holocaust* (New York: Bantam, 1989). For a thorough response to these see: Bahnsen and Gentry, *House Divided*. See also: Gary DeMar, *The Debate Over Christian Reconstruction* (Tyler, TX: Institute for Christian Economics, 1988); Gary DeMar, *The Legacy of Hatred Continues: A Response to Hal Lindsey's **The Road to Holocaust*** (Tyler, TX: Institute for Christian Economics, 1989); and Gary North and Gary DeMar, *Christian Reconstruction: What It Is, What It Isn't* (Tyler, TX: Institute for Christian Economics, 1991).

59. Herman C. Hanko, "An Interesting Conference on Postmillennialism" (unpublished conference paper: South Holland, IL: South Holland Protestant Reformed Church, 1978), p. 60.

60. Herman C. Hanko, "The Illusory Hope of Postmillennialism," *Standard Bearer* 66:7 (Jan. 1, 1990) 159.

Renaissance humanism in the 1700s and 1800s held a high view of man, which led it to believe that unaided human effort could lift the human race to a higher plane of moral integrity and cultural glory. Such man-centered labor would bring in a secular millennium of abundance and peace. This teaching became known as the Social Gospel.

Just as the premillennialist would argue that the millennial cults are aberrations of the premillennial hope, so I argue that the Social Gospel is a mutation of the postmillennial vision. This has been recognized even by non-evangelical historians, when comparing evangelical postmillennialism and Social Gospel advocacy: "The concepts which had earlier clustered around a gradualist vision of the millennium in fact persisted until the end of the [1800s] and even beyond. Of course considerable changes occurred in the configuration of ideas. What had once been defined solely in terms of evangelical Protestantism was later secularized in important ways. The process of secularization entailed a partial transfer of redemptive power from religious to secular institutions."[61] This resulted in the wholesale "secularization of the eschatological vision" and a strong tendency "to divinize society."[62] Clearly, when postmillennialism is gutted of its supernaturalism and redemptive concerns it is no longer evangelical postmillennialism.

Lindsey makes one of the most astounding and groundless charges in this regard, when he asserts that postmillennialists "rejected much of the Scripture as being literal and believed in the inherent goodness of man. . . . No self-respecting scholar who looks at the world conditions and the accelerating decline of Christian influence today is a 'postmillennialist.' "[63] Because some of the leading postmillennialists have been devout Calvin-

---

61. Jean B. Quandt, "Religion and Social Thought: The Secularization of Post-millennialism," *American Quarterly* 25 (Oct. 1973) 391.

62. *Ibid.*, pp. 396, 407.

63. Lindsey, *Late Great Planet Earth*, p. 176.

ists – e.g., Charles Hodge, A. A. Hodge, B. B. Warfield, W. G. T. Shedd, R. L. Dabney, J. H. Thornwell – adhering to the doctrine of man's inherent total depravity, this claim is groundless.[64] Lightner is a bit more reluctant to tar evangelical postmillennialism with the Social Gospel brush, noting evangelical postmillennialism "needs to be distinguished."[65]

The postmillennial concern with social righteousness as well as individual holiness causes lamentation even among some non-dispensationalists. Peter Masters writes: "May the Lord keep us all dedicated wholly to the work of the Gospel, and deliver us from taking an unbiblical interest in social affairs (especially out of frustration at the poor progress of our evangelistic labours!)."[66]

Social Gospel advocacy certainly picked up elements of evangelical postmillennialism. But it reduced the supernatural transformation wrought by regeneration into mere humanistic moral effort.[67] Immanent forces replaced transcendent ones as the impetus to advance and the basis of hope. Though many of the hopes of the two views are similar – the reduction of crime, poverty, and suffering – the explanations, methodologies, and goals are vastly different.

Furthermore, as Rushdoony argues, it is erroneous to assert "that historical succession means necessary logical connection and succession."[68] Evangelical postmillennialism is a vastly different schema for history from Social Gospelism. Liberal H. Richard Niebuhr traced the development of the Social Gospel

64. For helpful discussions of God's common grace in the world in light of man's total depravity, see: Gary North, *Dominion and Common Grace: The Biblical Basis of Progress* (Tyler, TX: Institute for Christian Economics, 1987); North and DeMar, *Christian Reconstruction*, ch. 7.

65. Lightner, *The Last Days Handbook* (Nashville: Thomas Nelson, 1990), p. 84.

66. Peter Masters, "World Dominion: The High Ambition of Reconstructionism," *Sword & Trowel* (May 24, 1990) 21.

67. Jean B. Quandt, "Religion and Social Thought," p. 396.

68. R. J. Rushdoony, "Postmillennialism versus Impotent Religion," *Journal of Christian Reconstruction* 3:2 (Winter 1976-77) 123.

from: (1) Calvinistic postmillennialism, to (2) revivalistic Arminianism, to (3) statist humanism (Social Gospel).[69] Rushdoony properly notes that if Calvinistic postmillennialism is considered the cause of the Social Gospel it must also be considered the cause of its *opposite*: revivalistic Arminianism.

Conclusion

The average evangelical Christian is more likely to respond to postmillennialism with pragmatic objections than with either theological or biblical objections. After all, we live in a highly pragmatic age. What dispensational author Thomas Ice has said of premillennialists is also true of amillennialists: "Premillennialists have always been involved in the present world. And basically, they have picked up on the ethical positions of their contemporaries."[70] But when these pragmatic objections are carefully considered in terms of what the Bible says and what postmillennialists say, they quickly fade away. These objections are rooted in either a misunderstanding of the postmillennial system itself or a misreading of the historical evidence.

When postmillennialism is analyzed in terms of its systemic unity and its insistence on the long-term glory of God's work of salvation in history, it should at least be appreciated as a valid eschatological option. But it is more than that. As I have been arguing throughout this book, postmillennialism is the eschatology of Scripture.

---

69. See: H. Richard Niebuhr, *The Kingdom of God in America* (NY: Harper Torchbooks, [1937] 1959).

70. Comment during a 1988 debate: Gary North and Gary DeMar vs. Thomas Ice and Dave Hunt. Quoted by DeMar, *Debate Over Christian Reconstruction*, p. 185.

19

THEOLOGICAL OBJECTIONS

So he answered and said to me: "This is the word of the LORD to Zerubbabel: 'Not by might nor by power, but by My Spirit,' says the LORD of hosts. 'Who are you, O great mountain? Before Zerubbabel you shall become a plain! And he shall bring forth the capstone with shouts of "Grace, grace to it!" ' (Zechariah 4:6-7)

In this chapter we leave the experiential and historical objections and enter into more serious ones: those related to theological aspects of the eschatological question.

"Sin Undermines the Postmillennial Hope"

In the last chapter I alluded to the Calvinistic doctrine of the total depravity of man. It is clear that leading postmillennial scholars have held strongly to this doctrine. In this section I will consider the implications of the doctrine that the human race is composed of depraved sinners, whose sin affects every aspect of their beings. We must appraise this in light of the optimistic teaching that this world of depraved sinners will one day experience universal righteousness, peace, and prosperity *before the Second Advent of Christ.* The theological doctrine of the depravity of man is frequently urged against the prospect of postmillennial kingdom victory. In fact, this is the most common objection that I encounter when I lecture on the subject.

In Pentecost's assessment of the deficiencies of postmillennialism, his fourth objection is along these lines. He speaks of "the new trend toward realism in theology and philosophy, seen in neo-orthodoxy, which admits man is a sinner, and can not bring about the new age anticipated by postmillennialism."[1] As mentioned in the last chapter, Lindsey asserts that postmillennialism believes in "the inherent goodness of man."[2] Hanko is convinced that "from the fall on, the world develops the sin of our first parents. This development continues throughout history. . . . More and more that kingdom of darkness comes to manifestation as time progresses."[3] Indeed, postmillennialism "is a mirage, therefore, a false hope, because it fails to reckon properly with the fact of sin" and "cannot take sin as seriously as do the Scriptures."[4] The implication is clearly that his view of man's innate sinfulness is contradictory to postmillennial expectations for the future.

Regarding the question whether the depravity of man undermines the postmillennial system, we must realize that each and every convert to Christ was at one time a totally depraved sinner. And yet there are millions of Christians. Salvation comes by the gospel which is the power of God unto salvation. How can we discount the power of the gospel to save multiple millions? What God can do for one depraved sinner He can do for another. This is evident in the apostolic era (Acts 2:41; 4:4), as well as in biblical prophecy (Rev. 5:9; 7:9).

A fatal objection to postmillennialism cannot be made by pointing to the *power of sin*. The power of God to save greatly

1. J. Dwight Pentecost, *Things to Come: A Study in Biblical Eschatology* (Grand Rapids: Zondervan, 1958), p. 387.

2. Hal Lindsey, *The Late Great Planet Earth* (Grand Rapids: Zondervan, 1970), p. 176.

3. Herman C. Hanko, "An Exegetical Refutation of Postmillennialism" (unpublished conference paper: South Holland, IL: South Holland Protestant Reformed Church, 1978), p. 25.

4. Herman C. Hanko, "The Illusory Hope of Postmillennialism," *Standard Bearer* 66:7 (Jan. 1, 1990), p. 159.

overshadows the might of sin. Indeed, "with God all things are possible" (Luke 18:27). The issue is not the power of sin, but the power of God. We have seen that the Bible teaches that it is God's will to bring redemption gradually to the whole world *as a system* through the proclamation of Christ's gospel while building His Church.

In a sense it is true that the postmillennialist overlooks the depravity of man. He *over*looks it, or better: *looks over and beyond it* to see the resurrection of Jesus Christ.[5] We see the glorious reconstructive power of the resurrection of Christ as over-whelming the very real destructive power of the Fall of Adam.[6] We need to consider the *strength of grace* in comparison to the *power of sin*. The Christian should ask himself: Have I ever seen a lost man become saved? The answer is: *Yes*. This being the case, it is evident that grace is stronger than sin. Then again, he should ask: Does the Bible teach that a saved man can lose his salvation? Here the answer is: *No*. In both cases, we see the superior power of God's grace over man's sin.

"Souls that have felt the Saviour's grace know right well its matchless power. After their own conversion, they can never doubt its converting efficacy *on any scale that may be required.*"[7] To respond to Lindsey's plaint: We do not believe in the inher-ent goodness of man, but Lindsey most definitely believes in the

---

5. Chilton well states: "Like Peter walking on the Sea of Galilee, they [despairing evangelicals] looked at 'nature' rather than at the Lord Jesus Christ; like the Israelites on the border of Canaan, they looked at the 'giants in the land' instead of trusting the infallible promises of God; they were filled with fear, and took flight." David Chilton, *Paradise Restored: A Biblical Theology of Dominion* (Ft. Worth, TX: Dominion Press, 1985), p. 232.

6. Gary North, *Is the World Running Down? Crisis in the Christian Worldview* (Tyler, TX: Institute for Christian Economics, 1988). Strangely, a sentence after stating that postmillennialism "fails to reckon properly with the fact of sin," Hanko stumbles past the postmillennial resolution to the problem: "Nothing will be changed until sin is taken away. Christ did this on His cross"! Hanko, "The Illusory Hope of Postmillen-nialism," p. 159.

7. David Brown, *Christ's Second Coming: Will It Be Premillennial?* (Edmonton, AB: Still Waters Revival, [1882] 1990), pp. 302-303.

inherent weakness of the gospel, for he says man's sin success-fully resists it even to the end of present-day history. Jonah also had a concern regarding the power of the gospel. He feared its power *to save* powerful Nineveh (Jon. 1:2-3, 10; 3:2; 4:1-4).

North notes the irony of the sort of complaint that I am considering here. Anti-postmillennialists "believe that a postmil-lennial revival is inherently impossible because of the power of rebellious autonomous men. They have great faith in man – autonomous, unsaved man. He can thwart the plan of God. Autonomous man says 'no' to God, and God supposedly choos-es never to overcome this 'no.' So, it is in fact the critic of post-millennialism who has faith in autonomous man. He believes that unsaved mankind has such enormous power to do evil that God cannot or will not overcome evil in history by the Spirit-empowered gospel."[8]

Though the "heart is deceitful above all things, and desper-ately wicked" (Jer. 17:9a), the postmillennialist firmly believes that "God is greater than our heart" (1 John 3:20b). We are confident that "He who is in you is greater than he who is in the world" (1 John 4:4). Since the resurrection of Christ, the Church has received the outpouring of the Holy Spirit (John 7:39; Acts 2:33). Because of this, the postmillennialist looks to the effective empowering by the Holy Spirit in history.

This point must be emphasized: *No optimistic expectation for the future of mankind can be convincingly argued on a secular base.* This glorious postmillennial prospect is not in any way, shape, or form rooted in any humanistic effort. We cannot have a high estimation of the prospects of man's future based on man in himself, for "the mind set on the flesh is hostile toward God; for it does not subject itself to the law of God, for it is not even able to do so; and those who are in the flesh cannot please God" (Rom. 8:7-8). When left to himself, man's world is cor-

---

8. Gary North and Gary DeMar, *Christian Reconstruction: What It Is, What It Isn't* (Tyler, Texas: Institute for Christian Economics, 1991), p. 63.

rupted and destroyed – a classic illustration being in the days of Noah (Gen. 6:5). *But God refuses to leave man to himself.*

Bernard Woudenberg is a pastor in the amillennialist Calvinist denonination, the Protestant Reformed Church. This denomination's leaders have been more vociferous than any other in its rejection of theonomic postmillennialism.[9] His complaint against postmillennialism is woefully ill-conceived: "It is like the children of Israel rushing in to take the land of Canaan, but without Moses at their head (Numbers 14:40-45). Christ alone holds the right to rule, and He does (Ephesians 1:19-22), and we are never more than simply servants of His."[10] As Woudenberg notes in his self-vitiating argument, Christ *does* rule! Therefore, postmillennialists humbly bow themselves before Him and seek to employ His Law-word under His headship. Would Woudenberg dismiss authoritative church leadership? Is eldership a usurpation of the authority of Christ the Head of His Church? How, then, can he dismiss the prospect of Christian leadership in the world, as if it implied a usurpation of Christ's authority?

But neither is the hope for the progress of mankind under the gospel related to the Christian's self-generated strength, wisdom, or cleverness.[11] Left to our own efforts, we Christians

---

9. See Appendix A, "Cultural Antinomianism," for my response to the PRC's Herman Hanko. See Gary North's Preface to his book, *Sanctions and Dominion: An Economic Commentary on Numbers* (Tyler, Texas: Institute for Christian Economics, 1996), pp. 26-36, for a critique of David J. Engelsma's attack on theonomic postmillennialism. Engelsma is also a PRC leader.

10. Bernard Woudenberg, "Hope as an Incentive to Godliness," *Standard Bearer* 66:7 (Jan. 1, 1990) 161.

11. It seems that too many even among evangelicals see evangelism as a manipulative method, rather than a delivering of the message of truth. One of the great evangelists of the last century, Dwight L. Moody, is praised by one writer as "the creator of many innovations in evangelism, such as the effective use of publicity, organization, and advertising, and in so doing he 'completed the reduction of evangelism to a matter of technique and personality.' " George Dollar, *A History of Fundamentalism in America* (Greenville, SC: Bob Jones University, 1973), p. xi. Megachurch fundamentalist pastor Jack Hyles has even taught the necessity of having fresh breath when doing personal evangelism. This is because bad breath may turn

too quickly learn that "apart from Me you can do nothing" (John 15:5). Were our hope in the unaided power of man, all would be hopeless. But our hope is in the resurrected Christ. "The labor is ours; the subduing is His."[12]

"A Kingdom With the King Absent"

An objection to postmillennialism that recently has been much used grows right out of the dispensational hermeneutic of literalism. It has been asked: How can there be a kingdom without a king? Hunt radically distorts and corrupts the post-millennial vision in objecting to postmillennial doctrine: "The growing acceptance of the teaching that a Christian elite has a mandate to set up the kingdom without Christ's personal presence is genuine cause for concern."[13] Pentecost says: "[D]uring this present age, then, while the King is absent, the theocratic kingdom is in abeyance in the sense of its actual establishment on the earth."[14] "Christ's kingdom is presently in abeyance. The promised king came to His own and was rejected. David's throne is vacant. The king is 'exiled' in heaven. . . . Scripture everywhere repudiates and disproves the doctrine that Christ is now reigning as Prince of peace, seeking through the church to extend His kingdom on earth by means of the gospel."[15]

What does Hunt mean by "a Christian elite"? Concerned Christians who run for office and are elected? Dedicated Christians who establish Christian schools? Committed Christians who train up their children for Christian living in all of life?

---

off the potential convert, who may then die and go to hell. Jack Hyles, *Let's Go Soulwinning* (Murfreesboro, TN: Sword of the Lord, 1968).

12. Herschell H. Hobbs, *An Exposition of the Gospel of Matthew* (Grand Rapids: Baker, 1965), p. 422.

13. Dave Hunt, *Whatever Happened to Heaven?* (Eugene, OR: Harvest House, 1988), p. 43.

14. Pentecost, *Things to Come*, p. 471.

15. Charles E. Stevens, "The Church of Christ and the Kingdom of Christ in Contrast," *Prophecy and the Seventies*, Charles Lee Feinberg, ed. (Chicago: Moody Press, 1971), pp. 102-103.

Why does he deny that Christians have "a mandate to set up the kingdom"? Christ established it while on earth (as I noted in Chapter 11). We are *ambassadors* of our king (2 Cor. 5:20).

What does he mean, we labor without "Christ's personal presence"? Does he denigrate the spiritual presence of Christ now? Is not Christ personally present with us: "And, lo, I am with you always, even to the end of the age"?[16]

Regarding the necessity of Christ's physical presence in order for His kingdom to manifest itself on the earth and in history, House and Ice write: "Within the Reconstructionist framework, Messiah is in heaven and only present mystically in his kingdom. His absence from the earth during his kingdom reign robs Messiah of his moment of earthly glory and exaltation. It is a truncated reduction of the true reign of Christ. Since the first phase of Christ's career, his humiliation, was spent physically upon the earth, it follows that there should be a corresponding display of his great glory through his reign on the earth."[17]

Though not intended as such, their statement is really quite demeaning to Christ, for several reasons. In the first place, it diminishes the absolute glory and majesty that is His as He sits enthroned at the right hand of God on high. The New Testament Church looks to its heavenly king as the King of kings enthroned in awe-inspiring majesty, "far above all rule and authority and power."[18] He is the Lord of lords. Shall we say, then, that His rule from heaven is somehow a robbery of the glory due His Name? Is it the case that His present session in heaven is "a truncated reduction" of His reign?

In addition, it speaks rather condescendingly of Christ's rule. It offers to Christ but a "moment of glory" and speaks of His

---

16. Matt. 18:20; Rom. 8:9-11; 2 Cor. 13:5; Gal. 4:19; Col. 1:27; 3:16; Heb. 13:5.

17. H. Wayne House and Thomas D. Ice, *Dominion Theology: Blessing or Curse?* (Portland, OR: Multnomah, 1988), p. 240.

18. Matt. 28:18; Acts 2:30-36; Rom. 8:34; 1 Cor. 15:23, 24; Eph. 1:20; Col. 3:1; Heb. 1:3,13; 10:13 Heb. 12:2; 1 Pet. 3:22.

wondrous mystical presence as if meager: He "is *only* present mystically." But His kingdom is an eternal kingdom, not a momentary one.[19] The indwelling presence of Christ displays itself in the rich blessings that flow forth from His glorious exaltation.[20] Shall we say He "is *only* present mystically"?

Furthermore, this statement forgets that a major aspect of His *humiliation* was the fact that He came to earth.[21] House and Ice overlook the fundamental consequence of His *exaltation:* His return to heaven to take up His manifest glory. In Christ's High Priestly prayer, we read:

> I have glorified You on the earth. I have finished the work which You have given Me to do. And now, O Father, glorify Me together with Yourself, with the glory which I had with You before the world was. . . . As You sent Me into the world, I also have sent them into the world. . . . Father, I desire that they also whom You gave Me may be with Me where I am, that they may behold My glory which You have given Me; for You loved Me before the foundation of the world. (John 17:4, 5, 18, 24)

Why should it be necessary that Christ's kingdom require His physical presence on earth? Does not Satan have a kingdom on earth, although he is only spiritually present (Matt. 12:26; Luke 4:6)? Do not Satan's covenantally faithful servants on earth manifest his power in history? Is Satan's kingdom any less a kingdom just because he is not reigning from a throne on earth?

What kind of necessary glory is it that requires that Christ personally and corporeally rule on earth over a political kingdom that revolts against Him at the end (Rev. 20:7-9)?[22] This

---

19. Isa. 9:6; Luke 1:33; 2 Pet. 1:11; Rev. 11:15; 22:5.

20. John 7:39; Rom. 8:9; 1 Cor. 3:16; 6:19; 2 Cor. 6:16; Gal. 4:6; 1 John 3:24; 4:4.

21. Rom. 8:3; Heb. 2:14; 10:5.

22. Pentecost, *Things to Come*, pp. 547-551.

view insists on a *second humiliation* of Christ. Hunt boldly (and erroneously) states: "In fact, dominion – taking dominion and setting up the kingdom of Christ – is an *impossibility*, even for God. The millennial reign of Christ, far from being the kingdom, is actually the final proof of the incorrigible nature of the human heart, because Christ Himself can't do" it.[23]

"The Scripture Presents a Suffering-Church Motif"

The present theological objection is directly related to the intrinsic, historical pessimism in all non-postmillennial systems. Many argue that it is the Church's ordained lot to suffer through the entirety of history, only receiving its glory beyond the present era. That being the case, there is no room for a long era of righteousness, peace, and prosperity.

William Hendriksen teaches as strongly as conceivable that the gospel age "will finally result in the complete destruction of the church as a mighty and influential organization for the spread of the Gospel. For, finally every tribe and people and tongue and nation will worship antichristian government."[24] This statement is made on the basis of his futurist understanding of Revelation's prophecies of Israel's doom. On the basis of Matthew 10:23, Ridderbos notes: "Jesus is here predicting persecution to the end, although they will always have a refuge to flee to."[25] As an express objection to postmillennialism George Murray writes: "Our Lord's promise to His church in this world is tribulation, rather than ease and comfort."[26]

23. Dave Hunt, "Dominion and the Cross," Tape 2 of *Dominion: The Word and New World Order* (Ontario, Canada: Omega-Letter, 1987). See also Dave Hunt, *Beyond Seduction: A Return to Biblical Christianity* (Eugene, OR: Harvest House, 1987), p. 250.

24. William Hendriksen, *More Than Conquerors* (Grand Rapids: Baker, [1939] 1967), p. 178.

25. Herman Ridderbos, *The Coming of the Kingdom* (Philadelphia: Presbyterian & Reformed, 1962), p. 507.

26. George L. Murray, *Millennial Studies: A Search for Truth* (Grand Rapids: Baker, 1948), p. 86.

Gaffin focuses on this objection in a vigorously argued article. In fact, he calls this his "most substantial reservation" to postmillennialism.[27] His position may be summarily stated: "Over the interadvental period *in its entirety*, from beginning to end, a *fundamental* aspect of the church's existence is (to be) 'suffering with Christ'; *nothing*, the New Testament teaches, *is more basic* to its identity than that."[28] He establishes his case on the basis of three important passages of Scripture: 2 Corinthians 4:7ff.; Philippians 3:10; and Romans 8:17ff. I have dealt with his argument in some detail elsewhere,[29] so here I will give a summary response to Gaffin and this sort of argument.

2 Corinthians 4:7ff

2 Corinthians 4:7-8 reads: "[W]e have this treasure in earthen vessels, that the excellence of the power may be of God and not of us. We are hard pressed on every side, yet not crushed; we are perplexed, but not in despair."

Gaffin comments regarding this passage that "Paul . . . effectively distances himself from the (postmil-like) view that the (eschatological) life of (the risen and ascended) Jesus embodies a power/victory principle that progressively ameliorates and reduces the suffering of the church." He then informs us that "Paul intends to say, as long as believers are in 'the mortal body,' 'the life of Jesus' manifests itself *as* 'the dying of Jesus'; the latter describes the existence mode of the former. Until the resurrection of the body at his return Christ's resurrection-life

27. Richard B. Gaffin, Jr., "Theonomy and Eschatology: Reflections on Postmillennialism," *Theonomy: A Reformed Critique*, William S. Barker and W. Robert Godfrey, eds. (Grand Rapids: Zondervan, 1990), p. 250.

28. *Ibid.*, p. 211 (emphases mine).

29. Kenneth L. Gentry, Jr., "Whose Victory in History?" *Theonomy: An Informed Response*, Gary North, ed. (Tyler, TX: Institute for Christian Economics, 1991).

finds expression in the church's sufferings. . . ; the locus of Christ's ascension-power is the suffering church."[30]

It is quite clear, though, that Gaffin's argument is contra-contextual. As many exegetes note, Paul is here giving an historical testimony of *his own apostolic predicament;* he is *not* setting forth a universally valid truth or a prophetically determined expectation.[31] Consider the context of the passage. A major point in this portion of Paul's letter is the defense of the apostolicity of his ministry against false apostles (2 Cor. 2:14-7:1). Notice the shift between the apostolic *"we"* and the recipient *"you"* (2 Cor. 4:5, 12, 14-15).[32] Interestingly, Gaffin seems aware of this fact, when he admits that "strictly speaking, [Paul's statements] are autobiographical."[33] That is the whole point: these statements were autobiographical. They were not prophecies.

Furthermore, Gaffin's comments are far too sweeping in their assertions: "Over the interadvental period *in its entirety,* from beginning to end, a *fundamental* aspect of the church's existence is (to be) 'suffering with Christ'; *nothing,* the New Testament teaches, *is more basic* to its identity than that." Is suffering (persecution?[34]) throughout the "entirety" of the interadvental period a "fundamental" aspect of the church's existence? Is there absolutely "nothing . . . more basic" in the New Testament? If we are not suffering (persecution?), are we a true Church? Is Gaffin suffering greatly? Gaffin's statements are

---

30. Gaffin, "Theonomy and Eschatology," p. 212.

31. For example, see the commentaries on 2 Corinthians by Philip E. Hughes, F. F. Bruce, A. T. Robertson, John Calvin, Marvin R. Vincent, Albert Barnes, E. H. Plumtree, James L. Price, and F. W. Farrar.

32. F. F. Bruce, *1 and 2 Corinthians* in Ronald E. Clements and Matthew Black, eds., *The New Century Bible Commentary* (Grand Rapids: Eerdmans, 1971), p. 194. Philip E. Hughes, *The Second Epistle to the Corinthians (New International Commentary on the New Testament)* (Grand Rapids: Eerdmans, 1962), p. 135.

33. Gaffin, "Theonomy and Eschatology," p. 211.

34. If persecutional suffering is not in Gaffin's mind here, then all other forms of suffering are irrelevant to the argument contra postmillennialism.

inordinately applied in an attempt to win points for his pessimistic eschatological view. Surely they are overstatements.

Philippians 3:10

In Philippians 3:10, Gaffin's second major reference, Paul writes: "That I may know him, and the power of his resurrection, and the fellowship of his sufferings, being made conformable unto his death." Of this verse Gaffin notes: "Paul is saying, the power of Christ's resurrection is realized in the sufferings of the believer; sharing in Christ's sufferings is the way the church manifests his resurrection-power. Again, as in 2 Corinthians 4:10-11, the locus of eschatological life is Christian suffering" (p. 213). But is Paul's reference to suffering here contrary to postmillennialism? Is Christ's resurrection-power *limited* to the upholding of believers in times of persecutional suffering?

Again, his statements must be understood in terms of his present condition: Paul is writing from prison, where he is being held because of his enemies (Phil. 1:7, 13[35]). As with the case in 2 Corinthians 4, and as Davidson notes regarding Philippians 3, "verses 4-11 are a biographical passage."[36]

Romans 8:17

Romans 8:17 reads: "[I]f so be that we suffer with him, that we may be also glorified together." Of this verse Gaffin comments: "This correlation of future glory and present suffering is a prominent concern in the section that follows. At least two points are worth noting about 'our sufferings' (v. 18): (1) their nature/breadth and (2) their terminus" (i.e., the resurrec-

---

35. Paul was imprisoned many times (2 Cor. 11:23) and suffered much affliction (1 Cor. 15:32; 2 Cor. 1:8-11; 6:5).

36. Francis Davidson, *The New Bible Commentary* (2nd ed.; Grand Rapids: Eerdmans, 1968), p. 1030. Hendriksen suggests that this letter may even be in response to the Philippians' specifically expressed concern about Paul's condition. William Hendriksen, *Exposition of Philippians* (*New Testament Commentary*) (Grand Rapids: Baker, 1962), p. 19.

tion).[37] It is important to note that this passage is something of a conclusion to Romans 6-7. Romans 6 and 7 deal with the *internal* struggle of the Christian against *indwelling sin*, not the *external* buffeting of *persecution*. The postmillennialist does *not* teach that there is coming a day in which Christians will no longer have a sin nature. As John Murray notes on this verse: "Christian suffering ought not to be conceived of too narrowly. In the passages so far considered, and elsewhere in the New Testament (e.g., 2 Co 1:5-10; 1 Pe 4:12-19), suffering includes but is more than persecution and martyrdom."[38]

Even the next reference to suffering by Paul has reference to the decaying condition of the natural world (Rom. 8:19) and is not tied to persecutional suffering by opposition to the Christian faith. Although postmillennialism teaches the advancement of longevity (cf. Isa. 65:17-21), nevertheless death remains throughout the kingdom era (Isa. 65:20; 1 Cor. 15:26). The sufferings of Romans 8 are not evidences against postmillennialism, which promises the reduction to negligible proportions (at least) of suffering for the faith. The great advances of the post-millennial kingdom expansion, even at its glorious height, will still not compare to the glory of the total liberty of the believer in the resurrection as he possesses a glorified, eternal body.[39]

Conclusion

To assess properly the future expectations for the Church, we must consider the specifically positive *prophetic* statements of the New Testament, which I have presented in this book. These actually set before us our divinely ordained victory-oriented expectation for the future, rather than describing our hope amidst present trial when it arises (as it did so universally

---

37. Gaffin, "Theonomy and Eschatology," p. 213.

38. John Murray, *The Epistle to the Romans* (*The New International Commentary on the New Testament*), 2 vols. (Grand Rapids: Eerdmans, 1959), 1:213.

39. See discussion in Murray, *Romans* 1:300-302.

among our first century forefathers). Does not 1 Corinthians 15:20-28 hold before us the prospect of the universal triumph of the gospel of Jesus Christ as He sovereignly reigns from the right hand of God? Do not the statements of cosmic redemption set forth the confident expectation of a redeemed world (John 3:17; 1 John 2:2)? Do we not have the right to hope that the kingdom of God will dominate and permeate the entirety of human life and culture (Matt. 13:31-33)? Are we not commanded to "make disciples of all the nations" under the absolute authority of Christ, who is with us in the project until the end (Matt. 28:18-20)? Does not the prospect of the redemptive New Heavens and New Earth, which began definitively in the first century, speak of an enormous transformation of human culture?[40] These texts do not teach Christianity's historical defeat.

"Postmillennialism Entangles Church and State"

Because the postmillennial advance of the kingdom applies to every area of life, it necessarily impacts on politics. Due to this implication within postmillennialism – especially as promoted by theonomic postmillennialism – some object that this necessitates an illegitimate entanglement of Church and State. A spate of anti-postmillennial books of late have attacked theonomic postmillennialism from this angle: Charles Ryrie's *Basic Theology* (1986), H. Wayne House's *Dominion Theology: Blessing or Curse?* (1988), Dave Hunt's *Whatever Happened to Heaven?* (1988), Hal Lindsey's *The Road to Holocaust* (1989), and Robert Lightner's *The Last Days Handbook* (1991), to name a few. Although more cautious and scholarly analyses do not assert this.[41]

---

40. See: Isa. 65:20ff; 2 Cor. 5:17; Gal. 6:15. See Gary North, *Millennialism and Social Theory* (Tyler, TX: Institute for Christian Economics, 1990), ch. 5. Roderick Campbell, *Israel and the New Covenant* (Tyler, TX: Geneva Divinity School Press, [1954] 1981), ch. 13. J. A. Alexander, *Commentary on the Prophecies of Isaiah*, 2 vols. in one (Grand Rapids: Zondervan, [1875] 1977), 2:452-456.

41. D. Clair Davis writes: "Theonomy can be of great service precisely within the context of the constitution of the American republic" (Will S. Barker and W. Robert

From a practical, American, Constitutional perspective, House expresses this concern when he writes that a "serious reading of Reconstructionism raises monumental doubts about the compatibility of its vision with the guarantees of liberty found in the Constitution, and even with the basic three-part structure of the U. S. Government."[42] In theonomic postmillennialism, he insists, "the state becomes merely an extension of both the invisible *and the visible* church."[43]

This concern is related to a broader and frequently heard objection to theonomic postmillennialism: God's Law was expressly designed and intended for use only in old covenant Israel. Its relevance is only for the special redemptive nation in pre-Christian times, and for no other. Dispensationalists are prone to employ this argument quite vigorously: "The stipulations of Sinai were not for the nations in general but to a people under grace. . . . Since nations around Israel were not called to adopt the Mosaic Covenant, it seems evident that the pagan nations would not be judged by the law of Moses."[44]

Although this might be expected of dispensationalism, with its severe compartmentalization of history, certain Reformed theologians also take a dispensational approach to the matter. Such a dispensational-like argument is clearly visible in the following statement from Reformed theological circles: "Israel *as a nation* was chosen by God 'out of all the peoples on the face

---

Godfrey, *Theonomy: An Informed Critique* [Grand Rapids: Zondervan, 1990], p. 392). Ronald Nash comments that: "For one thing, the people called theonomists don't appear to be dangerous. Efforts to show that they are dangerous do more, I suspect, to dishonor the people raising the charges" (Ronald H. Nash, *Great Divides: Understanding the Controversies That Come Between Christians* [Colorado Springs, CO.: NavPress, 1993], p. 176). See also: Bruce Barron, *Heaven on Earth? The Social & Political Agenda of Dominion Theology* (Grand Rapids: Zondervan, 1992); Mark A. Noll, *The Scandal of the Evangelical Mind* (Grand Rapids: Eerdmans, 1994), pp. 224-225; Bob and Gretchen Passantino, *Witch Hunt* (Nashville: Thomas Nelson, 1990).

42. House and Ice, *Dominion Theology*, p. 77.
43. *Ibid.*, p. 93.
44. *Ibid.*, pp. 128, 129.

of the earth to be his people, his treasured possession' (Dt 7:6). No other nation of the ancient or modern world is like Israel in its place in redemptive history. . . . Before applying a case law from the Old Testament today, therefore, we must consider not only cultural adaptations but also discontinuities that result because of the difference in redemptive status between Israel and any modern society."[45] Here are five counter-responses to this objection.[46]

1. The Church-State objection confuses moral commandments and covenantal form. The moral directives of God's Law are distinguishable from the covenantal system in which they are found. For example, in both the New Covenant and the old covenant (2 Cor. 3), we are commanded to honor father and mother (cf. Exo. 20:12 and Eph. 6:2); we are forbidden to covet (cf. Exo. 20:17; Rom. 13:9); a man must not marry his father's wife (cf. Deut. 22:30; 1 Cor. 5:1); and so forth. This does not mean that the old covenant and the New Covenant are the same. The old covenant form, which included the sacrificial system and other such temporary-typological elements and expected only of Israel, encodes numerous divinely ordained moral requirements, which are the perpetually obligatory commandments of God. Moral requirements may be distinguished from the historical and redemptive trappings in which they are found.

Bahnsen clearly demonstrates that moral commandments (justice-defining) are distinguishable from distinctive ceremonial laws (redemption-expounding), as is evidenced in the Old Testament itself.[47] God contrasts the moral and ceremonial, when He says: "For I desire mercy and not sacrifice, and the knowledge of God more than burnt offerings" (Hos. 6:6).

---

45. Tremper Longman III, "God's Law and Mosaic Punishments Today," *Theonomy: A Reformed Critique*, pp. 47, 48.

46. A more detailed treatment may be found in Greg L. Bahnsen, *No Other Standard: Theonomy and Its Critics* (Tyler, TX: Institute for Christian Economics, 1991).

47. Greg L. Bahnsen, *Theonomy in Christian Ethics* (rev. ed.; Phillipsburg, NJ: Presbyterian & Reformed, 1984), ch. 9.

Elsewhere we witness the same: "Then Samuel said: Has the LORD as great delight in burnt offerings and sacrifices, as in obeying the voice of the LORD? Behold, to obey is better than sacrifice, and to heed than the fat of rams" (1 Sam. 15:22). David writes: "Deliver me from bloodguiltiness, O God, The God of my salvation, And my tongue shall sing aloud of Your righteousness. O Lord, open my lips, And my mouth shall show forth Your praise. For You do not desire sacrifice, or else I would give it; You do not delight in burnt offering. The sacrifices of God are a broken spirit, A broken and a contrite heart; These, O God, You will not despise" (Psa. 51:14-17). See also Proverbs 21:3 and Isaiah 1:10-17.

2. God's Law was in fact designed to be a model for the nations. "Therefore be careful to observe them; for this is your wisdom and your understanding in the sight of the peoples who will hear all these statutes, and say, Surely this great nation is a wise and understanding people. For what great nation is there that has God so near to it, as the LORD our God is to us, for whatever reason we may call upon Him? And what great nation is there that has such statutes and righteous judgments as are in all this law which I set before you this day?" (Deut. 4:6-8).[48] God did not have a double standard of justice (cf. Deut. 25:13-16; Lev. 19:35-37), nor does He have a double standard today.

3. The nations around Israel were often judged for breaching God's moral standards, but never for breaching the Mosaic covenantal form. Israel was warned while preparing to enter the Land: "Do not defile yourselves with any of these things; for by all these the nations are defiled, which I am casting out before you. For the land is defiled; therefore I visit the punishment of its iniquity upon it, and the land vomits out its inhabitants. You shall therefore keep My statutes and My judgments, and shall not commit any of these abominations, either any of your own

---

48. See also: 1 Kgs. 10:1, 8-9; Isa. 24:5; 51:4; Psa. 2:9ff; 47:1-2; 94:10-12; 97:1-2; 119:46, 118-119; Prov. 16:12; Eccl. 12:13.

nation or any stranger who sojourns among you (for all these abominations the men of the land have done, who were before you, and thus the land is defiled)" (Lev. 18:24-27).[49] The same truth may be seen earlier in Abraham's day in the judgment of Sodom and Gomorrah (Gen. 19:15; cf. 2 Pet. 2:9).

4. Church and State were separate in the Old Testament era. There was a distinction between the civil ruler, Moses, and the priestly head, Aaron; between the offices of priest and king; between the temple and palace (1 Sam. 13:11; 2 Chr. 19:5-11; 26:16-21). These distinctions between Church and State should be maintained today. Theonomists have always said this.

5. People from all nations are under obligation to God's Law today. Paul's writings are very clear in this regard: "Who, knowing the righteous judgment of God, that those who practice such things are worthy of death, not only do the same but also approve of those who practice them" (Rom 1:32; this speaks of the complex of sins preceding, not necessarily any one particular sin). A few verses later he writes: "For as many as have sinned without law will also perish without law, and as many as have sinned in the law will be judged by the law (for not the hearers of the law are just in the sight of God, but the doers of the law will be justified; for when Gentiles, who do not have the law, by nature do the things contained in the law, these, although not having the law, are a law to themselves, who show the work of the law written in their hearts, their conscience also bearing witness, and between themselves their thoughts accusing or else excusing them)" (Rom. 2:12-15).

A very clear statement by Paul is found in Romans 3:19: "Now we know that whatever the law says, it says to those who are under the law, that every mouth may be stopped, and all

49. See also: Deut. 7:5-6, 16, 25; 12:1-4; 19:29-32; Amos 1:6 (Exo. 21:16; Deut. 24:7); Nah. 3:4 (Exo. 22:18; Lev. 19:21); Hab. 2:6 (Exo. 22:25-27; Deut. 24:6, 10-13); Hab. 2:12 (cf. Mic. 3:10).

the world may become guilty before God" (cf. 12:19-13:10; 1 Tim. 1:8). The world is guilty; hence, it is under God's law.

All of this is expected in light of the coming of the Messiah, who will teach the nations God's Law: "Now it shall come to pass in the latter days that the mountain of the Lord's house shall be established on the top of the mountains, and shall be exalted above the hills; and all nations shall flow to it. Many people shall come and say, Come, and let us go up to the mountain of the LORD, to the house of the God of Jacob; he will teach us His ways, and we shall walk in His paths. For out of Zion shall go forth the law, and the word of the LORD from Jerusalem" (Isa. 2:2-3). Thus, as noted earlier, God's Law in our era is considered to be "just" (Rom. 7:12; Heb. 2:2) and "good" (Rom. 7:12; 1 Tim. 1:8).

Conclusion

As creatures created in the image of God, we ought to think theocentrically. We ought, therefore, to think theologically. The theological objections to postmillennialism are more serious than the pragmatic objections considered in the preceding chapter. Yet, as I have shown, these objections are not sufficient to overthrow the strong positive case for postmillennialism. In fact, as with so many of the objections to postmillennialism, most of these are based on an improper conception of postmillennialism, rather than on genuine weaknesses in the system. Because eschatology is fundamental to biblical revelation, no eschatological system with major theological problems ought to be held. Postmillennialism is a coherent system that flows naturally from the Scriptural record.

20

BIBLICAL OBJECTIONS

These were more fair-minded than those in Thessalonica, in that they received the word with all readiness, and searched the Scriptures daily to find out whether these things were so. (Acts 17:11)

In the course of the present study I have dealt with a great number of supporting texts and have responded to various alleged negative passages. At this juncture I will give brief exposition to certain other texts that are thought to be contra-indicative to postmillennialism.

Zechariah 14:4

And in that day His feet will stand on the Mount of Olives, which faces Jerusalem on the east. And the Mount of Olives shall be split in two, from east to west, making a very large valley; half of the mountain shall move toward the north and half of it toward the south.

Zechariah has been called "the most messianic, the most truly apocalyptic and eschatological of all the writings of the Old Testament."[1] And surely it is. But Zechariah is greatly misunderstood in dispensationalism. The Zechariah 14 passage, and especially verse 4, is held forth as a solid proof of dispensa-

---

1. George L. Robinson, "Zechariah," *The International Standard Bible Encyclopedia*, James Orr, ed., 5 vols. (Grand Rapids: Eerdmans, [1929] 1956), 4:3136.

tionalism that undermines other views such as postmillennial-ism. I will summarize the view from Dallas Seminary's *Bible Knowledge Commentary* and then give a brief postmillennial inter-pretation of the passage. Parenthetical page references refer to this work.[2]

That the prophecy is thought to contradict postmillennialism is evident in the following comment:

> Zechariah 14 progresses from the initial plundering of Jerusalem near the end of the future Tribulation, through the catastrophic judgment on the Gentile armies at Messiah's Second Advent and the establishment of His millennial reign, to a description of the worship in Jerusalem during the Millennium. The fact that these events have not yet occurred points to a premillennial return of Christ, that is, His return *before* the Millennium. (p. 1569)

The Dispensational Interpretation

Dispensationalists apply verse 1 to a Great Tribulation still in our future, which introduces the earthly millennial reign of Christ, comprising "the day of the Lord." Verse 3 is said to speak of the "military intervention of the Messiah," with verse 4 detailing its accomplishment with the Lord's descending upon the Mount of Olives (p. 1570). Then He will establish His politi-cal kingdom over the earth, accompanied by "changes in illumi-nation, climate, and topography which God will bring on Jeru-salem, Palestine, and no doubt the whole earth during the Millennium," as indicated in a literalistic reading of verses 6-11 (p. 1570).

Zechariah 14:12-15 supposedly is a "parenthetical flashback" describing "the second phase of the invasion of Jerusalem by the confederated Gentile armies" (p. 1571). After this, "the

2. F. Duane Lindsey, "Zechariah," *Bible Knowledge Commentary: Old Testament*, John F. Walvoord and Roy B. Zuck, eds (Wheaton, IL: Victor, 1985), pp. 1569-72. See also: John F. Walvoord, *Prophecy Knowledge Handbook* (Wheaton, IL: Victor, 1990), pp. 332-334.

survivors from all the nations will worship annually in Jerusalem. 'The survivors' are not the Jewish remnant. . . [but are those] from nonmilitary personnel of those nations whose armies were destroyed by Messiah" (p. 1571).

Verses 16-17 are said to indicate that "a newly instituted worldwide religious order embracing both Jews and Gentiles" will be established that "will center in Jerusalem and will incorporate some features identical with or similar to certain aspects of Old Testament worship." Thus, "worshiping annually in Jerusalem will be necessary for the people to enjoy the fertility of crops" (p. 1571).

This whole scheme of things — widely held in dispensationalism — is totally out of accord with the flow of redemptive history, as I have shown before. Such a scheme has been soundly rebutted by evangelicals of every other millennial stripe, including historic premillennialists. As redemptive history progresses to "the last days" instituted by Christ (Isa. 2:2-4; 1 Cor. 10:11; Heb. 9:26) in the "fullness of time" (Mark 1:14-15; Gal. 4:4), the entirety of the Temple order and sacrificial system is forever done away with (Matt. 24:1-34; Hebrews). Accompanying such a removal of a central temple, the worship of God is de-centralized (John 4:21; Matt. 28:18-20). In addition, the peoples of the world are merged into one kingdom without ethnic distinction (Rom. 11:13-24; Eph. 2:12-21; Gal. 6:12-16). This is very much contrary to dispensationalism's hermeneutic reversal of Christ's economy of redemption back to an Old Testament order.

Of course, a major part of the problem with the dispensational viewpoint here is its *a priori* interpretive literalism (see Chapter 8). The postmillennialist would interpret the passage in a much different light. The whole passage – as often with prophecy – is a mingling of literal and figurative prophetic allusions, as we shall see.

The Postmillennial Interpretation

The siege of Jerusalem described in Zechariah 14:1-2 has to do with the A.D. 70 devastation of Jerusalem. Pentecost admits that the disciples who heard the Olivet Discourse would naturally have applied Zechariah 14 to the A.D. 70 destruction of the Temple. But then, he says, such involves a confusion of God's program for the Church with that for Israel.[3] So, he and other dispensationalists interpret the passage literalistically, with all the topographical and redemptive historical absurdities intact. As they do this they totally omit any reference to the destruction of the very city and Temple being rebuilt in Zechariah's day. *This* literal Temple *was* destroyed in A.D. 70, as all agree.

Verses 1 and 2 picture the imperial forces of Rome in conjunction with the various client kings involved in A.D. 67-70. The war was conducted by an empire of "nations" (v. 2) consisting not only of the nation of Italy, but the lands or nations of Syria, Asia Minor, Palestine, Gaul, Egypt, Britain, and others.[4] The consequences are disastrous: much of the population of Israel is led captive. Yet the Lord defends those who are truly His people, insuring their escape from the besieged city (vv. 3-4).

The Lord will fight for His true people "as when he fought in the day of battle" (v. 4). The Lord's feet standing on the Mount of Olives and His fighting for His people need be no more literal than other such references of the Lord's fighting for Israel in the Old Testament. The language is similar to that in Joshua 10:14, 42 and 23:3, where the Lord "fought for Israel." In Joshua these references indicate His providential favor in Israel's victory and deliverance, not His corporeal presence. God's feet are often mentioned when the opposition to His

---

3. J. Dwight Pentecost, *Thy Kingdom Come* (Wheaton, IL: Victor, 1990), p. 248.

4. Joseph Ward Swain, *The Harper History of Civilization*, 2 vols. (New York: Harper & Bros., 1958), 1:198. The Roman empire was composed of imperial provinces, senatorial provinces, and client kingdoms.

people is thwarted and His own are given success against all odds (Psa. 18:9; Isa. 60:13; Nah. 1:3; Hab. 3:5).

The cleaving of the Mount of Olives under Him employs the common imagery of God's conquering and restraining power in Old Testament prophecy. In Micah 1:3-4 we read that "the LORD is coming out of His place; He will come down and tread on the high places of the earth. The mountains will melt under him, and the valleys will split like wax before the fire, like waters poured down a steep place." Even dispensationalists admit this speaks of the Old Testament subjugation of Israel under heathen nations for her sin.[5] The mention of the direction of the cleft "indicates the direction of their flight," i.e., the Christians who flee Jerusalem when God judges it.[6] They ultimately flee to all points of the compass, taking the gospel with them (cf. vv. 8-9 below).

In the latter part of verse 5 the coming judgment upon Jerusalem, which disperses the Christians over the Roman Empire, is ultimately God's coming in angelic judgment ("holy ones" are angels). The destruction of Jerusalem by Rome is providential destruction by "his armies" (Matt. 22:7). It leads to darkness and woe upon Israel (Zech. 14:6-7; cf. Acts 2:20, 22; Matt. 24:29). Yet, as Jerusalem collapses and Christianity is loosed from her Jewish chains, the waters of life begin flowing out into all the world (v. 8). The Lord's kingdom overflows the limited borders of Israel so that the Lord becomes the King of all the earth (v. 9).

The subsequent topographical and liturgical references are figurative images of the ethical and spiritual changes that occur under Christ's spiritual administration as His worship spreads through the earth (vv. 10ff[7]). Even Jerusalem and the Jews

---

5. John A. Martin, "Micah," *Bible Knowledge Commentary: Old Testament*, p. 1477. Walvoord, *Prophecy Knowledge Handbook*, p. 301. Pentecost, *Thy Kingdom Come*, p. 111.

6. G. N. M. Collins, "Zechariah," *The New Bible Commentary*, Francis Davidson, ed. (2nd ed.; Grand Rapids: Eerdmans, 1954), p. 761.

7. See Isa. 40:4; Zech. 4:7; Mark 11:23; Luke 3:5.

shall be nourished by the waters of life eventually (vv. 10-11; cf. Ezek. 47:1ff; John 7:38-39). The enemies of God's people will either be vanquished (vv. 12-13, 14), converted (vv. 16, 20-21) or reduced to insignificance (vv. 14, 17-19).

The Feast of Tabernacles is mentioned, not as a literal rein-stitution of the Old Testament feast, but as the ultimate hope pre-figured in that feast: the time of the fullness of the field and its harvest (cf. John 4:35-38). Those who do not convert will be reduced to servile labors, lacking the blessing of God (vv. 17-19).

Overall, however, the kingdom of God (represented here by a rejuvenated Jerusalem) will be spread throughout the earth. All areas of life will be consecrated to the Lord: even the horses' bells will contain the inscription written on the High Priest's miter (vv. 20-21).

Matthew 7:13-14

Enter by the narrow gate; for wide is the gate and broad is the way that leads to destruction, and there are many who go in by it. Because narrow is the gate and difficult is the way which leads to life, and there are few who find it.

This is a popular passage that seems on the surface to be detrimental to the postmillennial outlook. These words are often cited to show the paucity of the number of saved: "[T]he great mass of humanity are engulfed in the maelstrom of sin, which is sweeping its millions down to graves of destruction (Mat. 7:13), and compared to them, in numbers, the true be-lievers are but a handful. In the Millennium all this will be changed."[8] "The way to salvation is narrow, and only a few find it."[9] "Even the Lord Jesus acknowledged that *few would*

---

8. William E. Blackstone, *Jesus Is Coming* (3rd ed.; Old Tappan, NJ: Revell, 1932), pp. 119-120. Published originally in 1878.

9. Walvoord, *Prophecy Knowledge Handbook*, p. 368.

find the true way, the way *that leads to life* (i.e., to heaven, in contrast with ruin in hell)."[10] "The passage itself contains no clue to the right way except that it is the way of *the few*."[11] There cannot be a billion Christians in the world because "such figures certainly do not square with what Jesus said about many on the broad road and few on the narrow."[12] "There are several passages in the scriptures which refer to the fact that the number of the saved, though a great multitude, is nevertheless, relatively speaking small. Texts such as Matthew 7:14 and 22:14 are referred to in this connection. . . . It is like a narrow way, and there are only a few who enter this way."[13]

There is no doubt that postmillennialists expect a vast multitude of men to be saved, so that we can legitimately anticipate that the "world" will be saved. How do we reply to all this?

It is important to notice, first, that in other places the Bible speaks of the number of the redeemed as a vast and countless multitude. Interestingly, just a few verses later – and apparently soon after stating the words of Matthew 7:13-14 – the Lord speaks seemingly contradictory words in Matthew 8:11: "And I say to you that many [*polus*, the same word in Matt. 7:13] will come from east and west, and sit down with Abraham, Isaac, and Jacob in the kingdom of heaven." Revelation 7:9 speaks boldly of a great number of the redeemed: "After these things I looked, and behold, a great multitude which no one could number, of all nations, tribes, peoples, and tongues, standing before the throne and before the Lamb, clothed with white robes, with palm branches in their hands." And of course there

---

10. Louis A. Barbieri, Jr., "Matthew," *Bible Knowledge Commentary: New Testament*, John F. Walvoord and Roy B. Zuck, eds. (Wheaton, IL: Victor, 1983), p. 34.

11. A. B. Bruce, "The Gospel According to Matthew," *Expositor's Greek Testament*, W. Robertson Nicoll, ed. (Grand Rapids: Eerdmans, [n.d.] 1980), 1:132.

12. John F. MacArthur, Jr., *The Gospel According to Jesus* (Grand Rapids: Zondervan, 1988), p. 191.

13. Herman C. Hanko, "An Exegetical Refutation of Postmillennialism" (unpublished conference paper: South Holland, IL: South Holland Protestant Reformed Church, 1978), pp. 15, 16.

are those prophecies which speak of "all nations" flowing into the kingdom (e.g., Isa. 2:2-4; Mic. 4:1-4).

Obviously, for the evangelical Christian there can be no contradiction in Scripture generally; neither is there any in Christ's teaching particularly. How, then, can we reconcile such seemingly contradictory passages? And more importantly, how does the postmillennialist deal with Matthew 7:13-14 in light of his optimistic expectations?

The resolution to the matter is to realize "our Lord's purpose is rather ethical impression than prophetic disclosure."[14] That is, He is urging His disciples to consider the *present situation* they witness round about them. They are to look around them and see that so many souls are presently perishing, so few men are seeking righteousness and salvation. What will they do about this sad predicament? Do they love Him enough to seek its reversal? Christ's challenge to them is ethical.

In John 4:35 He urges the dim-eyed disciples to see that there was much work to be done: "Do you not say, 'There are still four months and then comes the harvest'? Behold, I say to you, lift up your eyes and look at the fields, for they are already white for harvest!" In Matthew 7 He warns against false prophets that will arise among the people (Matt. 7:15-20). Then He warns that a man must hear *and act* upon His words (Matt. 7:21-27). His disciples must feel the horror of the present vastness of the multitude entering the broad way to destruction.

Certainly the gate is narrow: only He is the Way, the Truth, and the Life (John 14:6). But His statement in Matthew 7:13-14 does not imply that it will *always and forever* be the case that few will be saved in every era of history. In fact, there are numerous indications, as we have seen, that a great multitude of men will be saved, that the *world* as an organic system will experi-

---

14. B. B. Warfield, "Are There Few That Be Saved?" (1915), in Warfield, *Biblical and Theological Studies* (Philadelphia: Presbyterian & Reformed, 1952), p. 338.

ence the redeeming work of Christ, that all of His enemies will be subdued.

The Fall of Adam has taken an enormous toll upon the race of man, to be sure. But the resurrection and ascension of Christ will surely outstrip the effects of the Fall as history unfolds. This is why He delays His coming, so that He may gather the elect in. "The Lord is not slack concerning His promise, as some count slackness, but is longsuffering toward us, not willing that any should perish but that all should come to repentance" (2 Pet. 3:9).[15]

That the Lord is using the statement in Matthew 7:13-14 as an ethical prod rather than a prophetic expectation is evident from His use of it in another context. In Luke 13:23, we read: "Then one said to Him, 'Lord, are there few who are saved?' And He said to them, 'Strive to enter through the narrow gate, for many, I say to you, will seek to enter and will not be able. When once the Master of the house has risen up and shut the door, and you begin to stand outside and knock at the door, saying, "Lord, Lord, open for us," and He will answer and say to you, "I do not know you, where you are from" ' " (Luke 13:24-25). Here He refuses to answer the question regarding the number of the saved. This was one of those questions that was asked in order to evade Christ's call to righteousness. The Lord was not prone to allow such rabbit trails to lead Him away from calling men to commitment. His statement in Matthew 7:13-14 served His purpose. Let us avoid this particular rabbit trail.

---

15. The longsuffering is toward "us" (3:9), who are the "beloved" (3:1, 8, 14, 17), the brethren, the elect (1:10-11). He is not willing that any – i.e, of us – should perish. Indeed, we should "account that the longsuffering of our Lord is salvation" (2 Pet. 3:15). John Owen, *The Works of John Owen*, William H. Goold, ed., 16 vols. (London: Banner of Truth, [1642] 1967), 10:348-349. Election comes to historical fruition "when it pleases God" (Gal. 1:15).

Matthew 13:36-39

Then Jesus sent the multitude away and went into the house. And His disciples came to Him, saying, "Explain to us the parable of the tares of the field." He answered and said to them: "He who sows the good seed is the Son of Man. The field is the world, the good seeds are the sons of the kingdom, but the tares are the sons of the wicked one. The enemy who sowed them is the devil, the harvest is the end of the age, and the reapers are the angels."

A frequent misconception regarding postmillennialism is that it requires an "each and every" *salvific universalism* at the height of the kingdom. That being the case, a passage such as this one is deemed detrimental to postmillennialism. Then there are critics who correctly recognize that theonomic postmillennialists expect eventual *majoritarian Christendom*. Critics employ this parable to show that Christianity will never gain the upper hand in the world, even until the very end at the resurrection.

Amillennialist Hoekema objects to postmillennialism, partly due to this passage:

> In the Parable of the Tares (or Weeds) found in Matthew 13:36-43 Jesus taught that evil people will continue to exist alongside of God's redeemed people until the time of harvest. The clear implication of this parable is that Satan's kingdom, if we may call it that, will continue to exist and grow as long as God's kingdom grows, until Christ comes again. The New Testament gives indications of the continuing strength of that "kingdom of evil" until the end of the world when it speaks about the great tribulation, the final apostasy, and the appearance of a personal antichrist. To suppose, therefore, that before Christ's return evil "will be reduced to negligible proportions" would seem to be a romantic oversimplification of history not warranted by the biblical data.[16]

---

16. Anthony A. Hoekema, *The Bible and the Future* (Grand Rapids: Eerdmans, 1979), p. 180. Cf. Floyd E. Hamilton, *The Basis of the Millennial Faith* (Grand Rapids:

In objecting to postmillennialism, amillennialist Kuiper agrees that there will be a "parallel development of the kingdom of light and that of darkness. . . . That twofold process is being exemplified in current events."[17] Hanko concurs.[18]

Dispensationalists and premillennialists agree. In his treatment of the Parable of the Tares, Walvoord is convinced that "the parable does not support the postmillennial idea that the Gospel will be triumphant and bring in a golden age."[19] Barbieri explains the significance of the parable as indicating "in this period between Jesus' rejection and His future return He the King is absent but His kingdom continues, though in a newly revealed form. . . . This mystery period does not involve a universal triumph of the gospel, as postmillennialists affirm."[20] Premillennialists Moorehead and Erickson agree.[21]

A proper understanding of this parable requires its viewing in its setting, however. It is true that this particular parable, which is found collected among the Kingdom Parables in Matthew 13, does not overtly teach the "universal triumph of the gospel." But it does not need to. The Parables of the Mustard Seed and Leaven (Matt. 13:31-33) teach that concept.[22] That is, the Mustard Seed Parable teaches that the kingdom of Christ will grow until it dominates its setting (the world). The Leaven Parable teaches the method of its victory: through total permeation within, until the whole (world) is leavened.

Eerdmans, 1942), p. 33.

17. R. B. Kuiper, *God-Centered Evangelism: A Presentation of the Scriptural Theology of Evangelism* (Grand Rapids: Baker, 1961), pp. 208-209.

18. Hanko, "An Exegetical Refutation of Postmillennialism," p. 15.

19. Walvoord, *Prophecy Knowledge Handbook*, p. 373.

20. Barbieri, "Matthew," *Bible Knowledge Commentary: New Testament*, pp. 50-51. Cf. J. B. Chapman, "The Second Coming of Jesus: Premillennial," in A. M. Hills, *Fundamental Christian Theology: A Systematic Theology*, 2 vols. (Salem, OH: Schmul, 1980), 2:341.

21. Millard J. Erickson, *Christian Theology*, 3 vols. (Grand Rapids: Baker, 1985), 3:1216. William G. Moorehead, "Millennium," *International Standard Bible Encyclopedia*, 3:2053.

22. See earlier discussion in Chapter 12 above.

The point of the Parable of the Tares is not to reiterate what the Mustard Seed and Leaven Parables teach. Rather, it is designed to illustrate the fact that there will always be a mixture of the unrighteous and the righteous. Neither sin nor sinners will ever *totally* be rooted out of the world in history – not even during the kingdom's highest development in the future, whether in the premillennial or the postmillennial scheme. Consider the boldness of Christ's instruction here *in light of the contemporary setting of the parable*. The gospel was having only a minuscule influence in the world, the Lord Himself was soon to be cruelly crucified. Christ warned His people of the great trials and tribulations through which they must go. Yet He speaks here of what those possessing power should do with sinners in His kingdom! Surely this concern has behind it the concept of a massive influence of His kingdom: concern about what to do with the defenseless leftover people, the wicked.

It is clear upon reading the parable that the entire world is considered God's field, where He desires fully to plant wheat: He "sowed good seed in his field" (v. 24); "the field is the world" (v. 38). The effort – surely a great and purposeful one – is expended in order to create a field of wheat (the righteous, v. 38a) in all of the world (cf. Matt. 28:18-20). An enemy (the devil, v. 39) intervenes and sows tares (the wicked, v. 38b) – surely not equally great and successful, particularly in light of the parables of the Mustard Seed and Leaven. The point of the parable is that tares will be found among the predominant wheat: the tares are the intruders, not the wheat. That to which the Son of Man returns in the parable is a *wheat* field, not a tare field. The tares are to be left alone *for the sake of the wheat*.

Luke 18:8

I tell you that He will avenge them speedily. Nevertheless, when the Son of Man comes, will He really find faith on the earth?

This verse of late has been employed with great confidence by dispensationalists against postmillennialism. House and Ice comment regarding this verse: "This is 'an inferential question to which a negative answer is expected.' So this passage is saying that at the second coming Christ will not find, literally, 'the faith' upon the earth." Of Luke 18:8 Lindsey writes: "In the original Greek, this question assumes a negative answer. The original text has a definite article before *faith*, which in context means *'this kind of faith.'* " Borland agrees: "The faith spoken of is probably the body of truth, or revealed doctrine, since the word is preceded by the definite article in the original. Improvement in the worldwide spiritual climate is not here predicted." Wiersbe follows suit: "The end times will not be days of great faith." It has also been used by amillennialists, such as Kuiper and Hanko.[23]

In response, we may note several avenues of rebuttal. First, we need to note that there is doubt as to whether this question is even dealing with the future existence of Christianity. In the context, the Lord is dealing with the matter of fervent prayer. The definite article that Borland thinks must refer to "the body of truth, or revealed doctrine" seems rather to refer to *the* faith in prayer evidenced in the Importune Widow's persistence: "Then He spoke a parable to them, that men always ought to pray and not lose heart" (Luke 18:1). Christ is asking if *that* sort of persistent prayer will continue after He is gone.[24]

---

23. H. Wayne House and Thomas D. Ice, *Dominion Theology: Blessing or Curse?* (Portland, OR: Multnomah, 1988), p. 229. Hal Lindsey, *The Road to Holocaust* (New York: Bantam, 1989), p. 48. James A. Borland, "The Gospel of Luke," *Liberty Commentary on the New Testament*, Edward E. Hindson and Woodrow Michael Kroll, eds. (Lynchburg, VA: Liberty Press, 1978), p. 160. Warren W. Wiersbe, *Bible Exposition Commentary* (Wheaton, IL: Victor, 1989), 2:249. Kuiper, *God-Centered Evangelism*, p. 209. Hanko, "An Exegetical Refutation of Postmillennialism," p. 16.

24. Warfield suggests that the reference to "the faith" has to do with the *faith-trait* under question in the parable: perseverance. He doubts the reference even touches on whether or not the Christian faith will be alive then, but rather: Will Christians still be persevering in the hope of the Lord's return? As in Matthew 7:13-14, He was urging them to keep persevering. Warfield, "The Importune Widow and

Second, even if it does refer to the Christian faith or the system of Christian truth, why is a negative prospect expected? As with the Matthew 7:13-14 passage, could not Christ be seeking to motivate His people, encouraging them to understand that the answer issue forth in an optimistic prospect. In another context was not Peter's answer to such a query optimistic (John 6:67, 68)?[25] Could it not be that "the question is asked for the purpose not of speculation but of self-examination."[26]

In point of fact, *the question does not "assume" a negative answer at all.* It is not a rhetorical question. The classic Funk-Blass-Debrunner Greek grammar notes that when an interrogative particle is used, as in Luke 18:8, "*ou* is employed to suggest an affirmative answer, *me (meti)* a negative reply. . . ."[27] But neither of these particular particles occurs here, so the implied answer to the question is "ambiguous,"[28] because the Greek word used here *(ara)* implies only "anxiety or impatience."[29]

Third, the terminus is open to debate. Apparently, Christ had in mind the era of His imminent coming in judgment upon Israel, not His distant Second Advent to end history. Christ seems clearly to speak of a *soon* (cf. Rev. 1:1) vindication of His people, who will cry out to Him (cf. Rev. 6:9-10): "I tell you that He will avenge them speedily" (Luke 18:8a). He is urging His disciples to endure in prayer through the trouble-

---

the Alleged Failure of Faith," in *Selected Shorter Writings of Benjamin B. Warfield,* John Meeter, ed., 2 vols. (Phillipsburg, NJ: Presbyterian & Reformed, 1970), 2:698-710.

25. For similar ethical promptings, see Warfield, "Are There Few That Be Saved?"

26. William Hendriksen, *The Gospel of Luke* in *New Testament Commentary* (Grand Rapids: Baker Book House, 1978), p. 818. See also: Francis Davidson, ed., *New Bible Commentary* (2nd ed.; Grand Rapids: Eerdmans, 1954) p. 857.

27. Robert W. Funk, ed., F. Blass and A. Debrunner, *A Greek Grammar of the New Testament and Other Early Christian Literature* (Chicago: University of Chicago Press, 1961), p. 226 (section 440).

28. *Ibid.*

29. William F. Arndt and F. Wilbur Gingrich, *A Greek-English Lexicon of the New Testament and Other Early Christian Literature* (Chicago: University of Chicago Press, 1957), p. 103.

some times coming upon them, just as He does in Matthew 24, which speaks of the first century generation (Matt. 24:34). In fact, the preceding context speaks of Jerusalem's destruction (Luke 17:22-37).

In the final analysis, though, no evangelical millennial view supposes there will be *no* faith on the earth at the Lord's return. Yet, to read the statements regarding Luke 18:8 and its supposed expectation of a negative answer, one would be pressed to assert that Christianity will be totally dead at His return.

Thus, it is clear that this passage is radically misunderstood when urged against postmillennialism. Its *standard* is misinterpreted: The Lord's teaching regarding fervent prayer is changed into a warning regarding the existence of the Christian faith in the future. Its *grammar* is misconstrued: The grammar that is indicative of concern becomes an instrument of doubt. Its *goal* is radically altered: Rather than speaking of soon-coming events, it is made to point to the end of history. Its *final result* is overstated (even if all the preceding points be dismissed): No critic of postmillennialism teaches that "the faith" will have vanished completely from the earth at Christ's Return.

Luke 22:29-30 and Matthew 19:28

And I bestow upon you a kingdom, just as My Father bestowed one upon Me, that you may eat and drink at My table in My kingdom, and sit on thrones judging the twelve tribes of Israel. (Luke 22:29-30)

So Jesus said to them, "Assuredly I say to you, that in the regeneration,[30] when the Son of Man sits on the throne of His glory, you who have followed Me will also sit on twelve thrones, judging the twelve tribes of Israel." (Matt. 19:28)

---

30. Note that Luke's version of this thought substitutes the word "kingdom" for "regeneration."

The approach taken to these verses marks a clear distinction between all premillennial views as opposed to amillennial and postmillennial views. All premillennialists vigorously dispute the non-premillennial positions by interpreting these verses and their parallels in a literalistic fashion. The dispensationalist is especially vigorous in this assertion, although other premillennialists hold that these passages demand a premillennial understanding.[31]

Walvoord employs these and related passages in his argument against amillennialists, and by implication postmillennialists. Of Luke 1:30-33 he writes: "If it is true, as advocates of amillennialism contend, that the Old Testament has been misunderstood and that a literal fulfillment of the Davidic Covenant should not be expected, why would God instruct His angel to use such terminology for Mary?" He continues this line of argumentation: "Later Christ confirmed [the disciples'] expectation in promising them that they would sit on thrones judging the twelve tribes of Israel in the promised period of restoration (Matt. 19:28). This promise was confirmed later in Luke 22:30 when Christ met with His disciples for the Passover the night before His crucifixion. Again, they were assured that they would sit on thrones and judge the twelve tribes of Israel."[32] The expectation held by dispensationalists, then, is clearly a literalistic political governance by the apostles.

The amillennial view also differs with a leading postmillennial interpretation. Amillennialists generally apply them exclusively to the heavenly realm: "So the disciples are not to expect earthly glory and worldly power as a reward, but heavenly joy and a holy vocation in His eternal kingdom."[33] These verses

---

31. For example, see George Eldon Ladd's use of Matthew 19:28 in *A Theology of the New Testament* (Grand Rapids: Eerdmans, 1974), pp. 48, 109, 205, 628, 631.

32. Walvoord, *Prophecy Knowledge Handbook*, p. 65. See also: Barbieri, "Matthew," *Bible Knowledge Commentary: New Testament*, p. 65; Pentecost, *Thy Kingdom Come*, p. 154-155.

33. Norval Geldenhuys, *The Gospel of Luke (NICNT)* (Grand Rapids: Eerdmans,

are said to apply to " 'the restored (or: renewed) universe,' 'the new heaven and earth'. . . ; in other words the reference is clearly to the period beginning with the day of Christ's return for judgment."[34]

Postmillennialists are divided as to whether these passages apply to the eternal state or to the kingdom of Christ in the present. Brown allows either view.[35] The passages may be taken either way without compromising the eschatological system.[36] But they cannot refer to the premillennial conception of a Judaized, earthly, political kingdom. Such a view is based on a simplistic hermeneutic, is contextually erroneous, and involves serious redemptive retrogression.

Focusing on the Luke 22:29-30 passage, I believe that a stronger case may be made for its direct relevance to the earthly aspect of the kingdom in time and on earth, though allowing its eternal implications by extension (just as our present salvation and service have eternal implications). I have shown in detail that the kingdom of Christ was established during His earthly ministry (see Chapters 11 and 12). Here the Lord specifically says: "And I *bestow* upon you a kingdom, just as My Father bestowed one upon Me" (Luke 22:29). The Greek for "bestow" is *diatithemai*, which is the present indicative and which indicates a present bestowal. This fits perfectly with all other

---

[n.d.] 1988), p. 563.

34. William Hendriksen, *The Gospel of Matthew* (*NTC*) (Grand Rapids: Baker, 1973), p. 730.

35. Robert Jamieson, A. R. Fausett, and David Brown, *A Commentary, Critical and Explanatory on the Old and New Testaments*, 2 vols. (Hartford: S. S. Scranton, n.d.), 2:119 (see discussion at Luke 18:30).

36. J. Dwight Pentecost's radical shift of late regarding the Parables of the Mustard Seed and Leaven does not seem to Pentecost to have compromised his eschatological system, even though he is in disagreement with his former views and other leading dispensationalists. Compare Pentecost, *Things to Come* (Grand Rapids: Zondervan, 1958), pp. 147-148 (early printing; nowhere in the more recent printing, which has changed, is there any note that the work has been edited from its 1958 version) with Pentecost, *Thy Kingdom Come*, pp. 222-223. Contrast the later Pentecost with Walvoord, *Prophecy Knowledge Handbook*, pp. 374-375.

references to the presence of the kingdom studied heretofore (e.g., Luke 11:20; 17:20-21; Rom. 14:17; Col. 1:13). He is not speaking of the future eternal and heavenly aspects of the kingdom. Here Christ the King indicates that he is presently *bestowing* formal authority on His apostles; they are His ambassadors (2 Cor. 5:20) who reign with Him (Rom. 5:17, 21).

The kingdom He is here bestowing upon them is not an earthly, political kingdom, for He expressly forbids such carnal kingly trappings: "And He said to them, 'The kings of the Gentiles exercise lordship over them, and those who exercise authority over them are called "benefactors." But not so among you; on the contrary, he who is greatest among you, let him be as the younger, and he who governs as he who serves' " (Luke 22:26). His kingdom is a spiritual kingdom of humble spiritual service rather than regal political glory.

As a consequence of His bestowal of the kingdom, the Lord holds out the promise to them "that you may eat and drink at My table in My kingdom, and sit on thrones judging the twelve tribes of Israel" (Luke 22:30). The reference to the eating and drinking at His table must speak of the Lord's Supper, which He had just instituted a few moments before (Luke 22:13-20). Though He is about to die (Luke 22:21-23), they should not despair, for He will be with them spiritually. This will be particularly evident as they gather for "communion" (1 Cor. 10:16; Rev. 3:20) with Him at "the Lord's Table" (1 Cor. 10:21).

Since the kingdom is a present, spiritual reality, we may not take the sitting on thrones in a literal sense, for the apostles never really sat on thrones. This sitting on thrones has spiritual implications, much like the Pharisees' sitting in "Moses' seat" (Matt. 23:2) – which certainly was not a literal chair. Although here the express reference is to the apostles themselves, elsewhere there is a sense in which all Christians sit on thrones. He "raised us up together, and made us sit together in the heavenly places in Christ Jesus" (Eph. 2:6; cf. Rev. 20:4-6).

Luke 22 links the Lord's Supper with Christ's judicial rule in history. It is a means of exercising spiritual and covenantal judgment among men (cf. 1 Cor. 11:22-34).[37] The Lord's Supper draws a *covenantal distinction* between men, between the saved and the lost. It appears that the express application to His apostles is especially in His mind. The particular concern is that their authority from Him was to be demonstrated in the destruction of Jerusalem. By their preaching the apostles would be "passing sentence on the twelve tribes of Israel, who would reject their ministry as they had done his"[38] (1 Thess. 2:15-16; cf. Matt. 23:32-37; Acts 2:19-20, 37-40). North observes: "Their sitting in judgment over Israel was fulfilled representatively, yet no less definitively, for Old Covenant Israel is no more."[39]

Acts 3:19-21

Repent therefore and be converted, that your sins may be blotted out, so that times of refreshing may come from the presence of the Lord, that He may send Jesus Christ, who was preached to you before, whom heaven must receive until the times of restoration of all things, which God has spoken by the mouth of all His holy prophets since the world began.

This is a favorite passage of dispensationalists and is thought to establish the premillennial expectation against all others. "But Heaven has only received Him until the time of restitution of all things which God hath spoken by the mouth of all holy prophets (Acts 3:21), when He shall come again, to sit in the throne of His Father David. This again proves His coming to be

---

37. See discussion in Gary North, *Millennialism and Social Theory* (Tyler, TX: Institute for Christian Economics, 1990), pp. 215ff.

38. Thomas Scott, *The Holy Bible Containing the Old and New Testaments According to the Authorised Version: with Explanatory Notes, Practical Observations, and Copious Marginal References* (Philadelphia: J. B. Lippincott, 1868), 3:265.

39. North, *Millennialism and Social Theory*, p. 217. See: John Lightfoot, *Commentary on the New Testament from the Talmud and Hebraica*, 4 vols. (Peabody, MA: Hendrikson, [1658] 1989), 2:265-266.

pre-millennial."[40] "The king is 'exiled' in heaven (Acts 3:20-21; 7:55-56). . . . Scripture everywhere repudiates and disproves the doctrine that Christ is now reigning as Prince of peace, seeking through the church to extend His kingdom on earth by means of the gospel."[41] "The declaration is that, if the nation repented and believed, the Messiah would return and establish the promised kingdom."[42] "Acts 3:17-21 shows that Israel's repentance was to have had two purposes: (1) for *individual* Israelites there was forgiveness of sins, and (2) for *Israel as a nation*, her Messiah would return to reign," i.e., in the Millennium.[43]

Amillennialists, of course, hold a fundamentally different conception. Hoekema comments: "Surely the words 'the times of restoration of all things' refer not to an intermediate millennial interval but to the final state."[44]Berkouwer concurs: "There is good reason to believe that this involves an eschatological perspective."[45] Erb and Adams agree.[46]

A postmillennial understanding of this passage is more satisfying than either of these views. In the context Peter is preaching a message most relevant to *the Jews of that day*: He opens with "Ye men of Israel" (Acts 3:12), emphasizing their lineage

---

40. Blackstone, *Jesus Is Coming*, p. 47.

41. Charles E. Stevens, "The Church of Christ and the Kingdom of Christ in Contrast," *Prophecy and the Seventies*, Charles Lee Feinberg, ed. (Chicago: Moody Press, 1971), pp. 102-103.

42. Wiersbe, *Bible Exposition Commentary*, 1:414.

43. Stanley D. Toussaint, "Acts," *Bible Knowledge Commentary: New Testament*, p. 362. Interestingly, Toussaint vigorously argues that this is a re-offer of the kingdom to Israel; Pentecost just as adamantly argues that such a re-offer was impossible until after A.D. 70. Toussaint, "Acts," p. 361. Pentecost, *Things to Come*, pp. 469-476 and Pentecost, *Thy Kingdom Come*, pp. 274-276.

44. Hoekema, *Bible and the Future*, p. 185, cf. p. 282.

45. G. C. Berkouwer, *The Return of Christ* (Grand Rapids: Eerdmans, 1972), p. 403.

46. Paul Erb, *Bible Prophecy: Questions and Answers* (Scottsdale, Penn.: Herald, 1978), p. 133; Jay Adams, *The Time Is At Hand* (Phillipsburg, N.J.: Presbyterian and Reformed, 1974), p. 31.

from "Abraham, Isaac, and Jacob" (3:13a). They are the "sons of the prophets" and the sons of "the covenant" (3:25). These highly favored people were guilty of crucifying the Messiah: "God . . . glorified His Servant Jesus, whom *you* delivered up and denied in the presence of Pilate, when he was determined to let Him go. But *you* denied the Holy One and the Just, and asked for a murderer to be granted *to you*, and [*you*] killed the Prince of life, whom God raised from the dead, of which we are witnesses." "Yet now, *brethren*, I know that *you* did it in ignorance, as did also your rulers" (Acts 3:13b-15, 17).

Keeping this in mind – along with some additional contextual notations to follow – let us now seek to gain the proper understanding of Peter's statement.

After pointing out their guilt in the crucifixion of Christ, Peter notes God's sovereign prophetic ordering of the event (Acts 3:18). Then he exhorts these guilty crucifiers of Christ to "repent therefore and be converted, that your sins may be blotted out" (3:19a). In essence Peter urges: "Let them repent, for their vast evil has not frustrated God."[47] This call to repentance from their sins contextually speaks of their horrible guilt in the crucifixion. With an eye to the coming A.D. 70 judgment, Peter issues a warning from Moses: "And it shall come to pass that every soul who will not hear that Prophet shall be utterly destroyed from among the people" (Acts 3:23). This is reminiscent of his previous allusion to the "blood, fire, and smoke" threatened upon Jerusalem and his urging of his Jewish auditors to "be saved from this perverse generation" (Acts 2:19-21). The issue here is God's way of escape from His negative sanctions.

He then adds to this urgent call: "[S]o that[48] times of refreshing may come from the presence of the Lord" (Acts 3:19b).

47. E. M. Blailock, *The Acts of the Apostles* (Tyndale) (Grand Rapids: Eerdmans, 1959), p. 63.

48. The KJV "when" is most definitely mistaken, as all exegetes are agreed. The Greek *hopos on* must be translated "that" or "so that."

The "times of refreshing" hold forth for Jerusalem the promise of "a respite from the judgment pronounced by Jesus, as it brought the Ninevites a respite from the judgment pronounced by Jonah."[49] These times of refreshing speak of the glorious salvation that God mercifully offers them along with the favor of God that would issue forth from it. This refreshing will be especially glorious, for it stands in contrast to the horrible wrath under which they now live and which will soon crash down upon them.

But perhaps they would lament their having destroyed the only One who could bring them such consolation – a fear much like he had encountered before (Acts 2:37). In order to circumvent such, Peter sets a promise before them. *The promise is that Christ will yet come to them in salvation:* ". . . and that He may send Jesus, the Christ appointed for you" (Acts 3:20 NASB). It is true that He is in heaven physically away from them; in fact, "heaven must receive [Him] until the times of restoration of all things" (3:21). Still, there is the promise that God will send Him to them *in salvation*.[50] Although He is in heaven, He is not beyond their reach, for He comes to dwell in those who have faith in Him (John 14:23). As the gospel is preached, the hearers discern the voice of the living Christ (Eph. 2:17).

This understanding of the "sending" (*apostello*) of Jesus in salvation is no more awkward than is the Second Advent view. Neither the wording for the *sending* of the Son in salvation nor for the sending of the Son in the Second Advent expressly occurs in Scripture. Though in the economy of redemption it is more precise to speak of the Father sending the *Spirit* in the gospel (John 14:26), we must understand that the sending of

---

49. F. F. Bruce, *The Book of the Acts* (*NICNT*) (Grand Rapids: Eerdmans, [n.d.] 1980), p. 91n. See my earlier discussion of the "to make an end of sins" phrase in Daniel 9:24.

50. John Lightfoot, *Commentary on the New Testament from the Talmud and Hebraica*, 4:40-41. Cf. G. C. Berkouwer, *The Return of Christ* (Grand Rapids: Eerdmans, 1972), p. 151.

the Spirit results in the coming (sending) of the Son into the believer (Rom. 8:9). In this context the focus is on what they have done to Christ, who was perfectly subject to God. God fore-announced His incarnation (3:18); Christ was God's "Servant" (3:13, 26), "His Christ" (3:18), whom God sent (3:22). Hence the unusual manner of speaking: Christ is being emphasized as One Who is subject to the Father.

This particular sending of Christ does not await His Second Advent. Why would Peter tell the Jews that if they repent today, God will send the Son thousands of years later? Christ is being presented to them *at that very moment*. In fact, the exaltation of Christ forever provides for the sending of the Son to lost sinners; this is particularly true for those to whom He is speaking: "When God raised up his Servant, he sent him first to you to bless you by turning each of you from his wicked ways" (Acts 3:26 NIV).

Peter continues: Christ must remain in heaven "until the times of restoration of all things" (Acts 3:21a). Peter's use of the word "until" is significant. It relates to *Christ's mediatorial kingdom in history*. Wilmot's point is on target: "The word 'until' which denotes that *during* these times the Lord Jesus will remain in the heavens, having been there 'received' upon His ascension, to the right hand of the majesty on high. This is the context. 'Until,' according to the lexicon, carries the meaning of, 'continuedly, fixing attention upon the whole duration. . . .' [T]he force of 'until' . . . makes the times of restitution simultaneous with Christ's mediatorial session in heaven. He will come again not to introduce the restitution predicted by the prophets, but because He shall then have completed it." Restoration is an aspect of history – *a judicial process through time* – not just the closing of history. Restoration is progressive.

This "restoration of all things" has already begun, having been instituted during the ministry of Christ. In fact, Peter informs his auditors of the events begun in their time: "Yes, and all the prophets, from Samuel and those who follow, as many as have spoken, have also foretold these days" (Acts 3:24). This is also clear from Matthew 17:11, where John Baptist functions as an Elijah introducing the restoration of all things.

The restoration is *a reformation that supplants the old order* (Heb. 9:10). It is a process leading to "the regeneration" of the fallen world as a system (John 1:29; 3:17; 4:42), where Christ's will shall be done in earth (Matt. 6:10) as His kingdom grows and spreads (Matt. 13:31-33; 1 Cor. 15:20-27). It is the fulfillment of all things "which God has spoken by the mouth of all His holy prophets since the world began" (Acts 3:21), as in Isaiah 2:2-4; 9:1-7; 11:1ff. Acts 3:24-25 demonstrates that "these men of Israel who stood listening to Peter were 'sons of the prophets' – not in the OT sense of the words which denoted the professional prophetic guild, but in the sense that they were heirs of the promises made by God through the prophets – promises which had found their fulfillment before their very eyes. So, too, they were 'sons of the covenant' made by God with Abraham, and that in a special sense, for they had lived to see the day when that covenant came true in Christ: 'In thy seed shall all the families of the earth be blessed.' "[51]

This fulfillment progressively grows during "the times" of the "restitution of all things." "The gospel blessings that were to flow from His death and resurrection must spread abroad throughout the world, and then He would return from the right hand of power."[52] Even rebellious Israel will be re-incorporated into the kingdom (Acts 1:6; Rom. 11). Christ will not return bodily until this reformation/restoration/regeneration process has overwhelmed the kingdom of Satan on earth. The battle between these rival kingdoms takes place on earth and in time. It is fought by the representatives of each leader.

---

51. Bruce, *Acts*, p. 93.
52. *Ibid.*, p. 91.

2 Timothy 3:1-4, 13

> But know this, that in the last days perilous times will come: For men will be lovers of themselves, lovers of money, boasters, proud, blasphemers, disobedient to parents, unthankful, unholy, unloving, unforgiving, slanderers, without self-control, brutal, despisers of good, traitors, headstrong, haughty, lovers of pleasure rather than lovers of God. . . . Evil men and impostors will grow worse and worse, deceiving and being deceived.

Employing these or similar verses, premillennialist Kromminga and amillennialists Hoeksema, Berkhof, Hanko, and Morris agree with Hoekema that "the postmillennial expectation of a future golden age before Christ's return does not do justice to the continuing tension in the history of the world between the kingdom of God and the forces of evil."[53] Hendriksen comments on this passage: "These seasons will come and go, and the last will be worse than the first. They will be seasons of ever-increasing wickedness (Matt. 24:12; Luke 18:8), which will culminate in the climax of wickedness."[54]

Dispensationalists agree: "[T]he Bible speaks of things progressing from 'bad to worse,' of men 'deceiving and being deceived' (2 Timothy 3:13), we look out at our world and see how bad things really are."[55] "[W]ith the progress of the present age, in spite of the dissemination of the truth and the availability of Scripture, the world undoubtedly will continue to follow the sinful description which the Apostle Paul gave

---

53. Hoekema, *Bible and the Future*, p. 180. See also: D. H. Kromminga, *The Millennium in the Church: Studies in the History of Christian Chiliasm* (Grand Rapids: Eerdmans, 1945), pp. 72, 265. Louis Berkhof, *Systematic Theology* (Grand Rapids: Eerdmans, 1941), p. 718. Herman Hoeksema, *Reformed Dogmatics* (Grand Rapids: Reformed Free, 1966), p. 817. Herman C. Hanko, "An Exegetical Refutation of Postmillennialism," pp. 16-17. Leon Morris, "Eschatology" *Encyclopedia of Christianity*, P. E. Hughes, ed., 4 vols. (Marshallton, DE: National Foundation for Christian Education, 1972), 4:95. This encyclopedia was never completed.

54. William Hendriksen, *I and II Timothy and Titus* (NTC) (Grand Rapids: Baker, 1957), p. 283.

55. House and Ice, *Dominion Theology*, p. 183

here."[56] "Passages like 1 Timothy 4 and 2 Timothy 3 paint a dark picture of the last days."[57]

Such interpretations are exegetically flawed and anti-contextual. Nothing in these verses is contra-postmillennial. Note that Paul is instructing Timothy on this matter. He is speaking of things that *Timothy* will have to face and endure (v. 10, 14). He is not prophesying regarding the constant, long-term process of history. And though it is true that perilous "times" (*chairoi*) shall come, this does not demand a pessimistic position. The Greek term here indicates "seasons." It is the logical error of quantification to read this reference to (some) "seasons" of perilous times as if it said *all* times in the future will be perilous. The "grievous times" (*kairoi chalepoi*) are "qualitatively complexioned and specifically appointed seasons," rather than like *eschatai hemerai*, which are "purely chronological."[58] Postmillennialists are well aware of the "seasons" of perilous times that beset the church under the Roman Empire and at other times.

The citation of 2 Timothy 3:13 leaves the impression, further, that "things" shall irrevocably become worse in history. But the verse actually says: "[E]vil men and seducers shall wax worse and worse." Paul is speaking of specific evil men becoming ethically worse, not more powerful. He is speaking of their progressive personal degeneration: the progressive anti-sanctification of evil men. Paul says absolutely nothing about a predestined increase in the number and power of such evil men. He is not teaching that evil is rewarded with power in history.

Paul tells Timothy that these evil men "shall proceed no further: for their folly shall be manifest unto all men" (v. 9). God

---

56. Walvoord, *Prophecy Knowledge Handbook*, p. 495.

57. Wiersbe, *Bible Exposition Commentary*, 1:249; see also 2:249. Cf. Charles F. Baker, *A Dispensational Theology* (Grand Rapids: Grace Bible College, 1971), p. 623. Chapman, "The Second Coming of Christ: Premillennial," *Fundamental Christian Theology*, 2:341. Bruce Milne, *What the Bible Teaches About the End of the World* (Wheaton, IL: Tyndale, 1979), pp. 80-81.

58. Geerhardus Vos, *The Pauline Eschatology* (Phillipsburg, NJ: Presbyterian & Reformed, [1930] 1991), p. 7n.

places limits on them. Paul clearly expects victory. How different from the widespread, pessimistic conception of the progressive, limitless power of evil in our day is the Pauline conception of the long-run impotence of evil in history.[59]

Conclusion

For the devout Christian the ultimate issue determining the validity of a particular eschatological system is none other than the Word of the Living God. If there are *biblical* problems with a person's concept of the millennium, he is in serious trouble. Such is not the case with postmillennialists. In this chapter I have examined several of the leading alleged biblical objections to postmillennialism. These, along with others that are touched on in the main text of this book, can be adequately answered from within the framework of postmillennialism. It seems clear to me that the Bible itself sets before the Christian a grand historical hope that is postmillennial in orientation.

I have argued in this book that eschatology is a part of an integrated system of biblical truth. It is not something that sits on the sidelines of theology. Biblical eschatology reveals itself in three ways. *First*, it is consistent theologically (exegetically) with the whole of Scripture. The Bible does not contradict itself. *Second*, it is internally consistent. What it teaches about the Second Advent of Christ fits what it teaches about the kingdom of God in history. *Third*, its view of the kingdom of God in history is consistent with ethical cause and effect as described in the Bible. Does God progressively reward covenant-breakers in history, while bringing covenant-keepers into long term bondage to them? Any eschatological system that teaches that the unrighteous will triumph over the righteous in Church history should also explain how this view of the future fits God's coven-

---

59. See: Kenneth L. Gentry, Jr., *The Greatness of the Great Commission: The Christian Enterprise in a Fallen World* (Tyler, TX: Institute for Christian Economics, 1990), ch. 12: "Pessimism and the Great Commission."

antal promises – God's blessings and cursings in history – in
such passages as Leviticus 26 and Deuteronomy 28.

PART VI

CONCLUSION

CONCLUDING REMARKS

Declaring the end from the beginning, and from ancient times things that are not yet done, saying, "My counsel shall stand, and I will do all My pleasure," calling a bird of prey from the east, the man who executes My counsel, from a far country. Indeed I have spoken it; I will also bring it to pass. I have purposed it; I will also do it. (Isaiah 46:10-11)

Contrary to the perception presented in many popular and even some scholarly approaches to millennial studies, eschatology is a deeply rooted and intricately involved aspect of Christian theology. It should not be approached in a naïve manner or be given superficial treatment. Consequently, no single passage may be expected to present an entire eschatological system – not even the famous Revelation 20 passage.

Eschatology is woven into the whole fabric of Scripture as the story within; it is not painted on it as an embellishment without. Indeed, eschatology serves as the very ligamentation, not the ornamentation of Scripture. A proper comprehension of the eschatological message requires a working knowledge of the whole drift and framework of the revelation of God in Scripture.

The eschatological message of Scripture is one of glorious victory, not only in eternity, but also in time and on earth, before Jesus returns bodily in glory to judge the world. This is the message of both the Old and New Testaments.

A Summary of the Old Testament Evidence

The sovereign plan of God for the world can be adequately understood only when viewed in light of its historical inception: in the Bible's account of the beginning of the universe we discover the very purpose of history. God created man in His own image (Gen. 1:26) as a materio-spiritual being (Gen. 2:7). Man's purpose and destiny are to bring honor and glory to God by exercising godly dominion in the earth (Gen. 1:26-30).

Because God possesses almighty power (Job 40; Isa. 40), and governs by inscrutable wisdom (Isa. 55:8-9; Rom. 11:32-35), the Christian actually should be predisposed to the sort of historical victory envisioned by postmillennialism. The postmillennial system best balances the material and spiritual aspects of Scripture, giving full significance to the temporal and eternal features of God's plan and man's obligation to Him. The Lord created man and history for His glory; therefore, man and history *will* bring glory to Him. "You are worthy, O Lord, to receive glory and honor and power; for You created all things, and by Your will they exist and were created" (Rev. 4:11). "For of Him and through Him and to Him are all things, to whom be glory forever. Amen" (Rom. 11:36).

Postmillennialism teaches that there is coming a time in earth history, continuous with the present and resultant from currently operating, God-ordained spiritual forces, in which the overwhelming majority of men and nations will voluntarily bow in salvation to the Lordship of Jesus Christ. This righteous submission to His gracious scepter will issue forth in widespread righteousness, peace, and prosperity. The eschatological theme in Scripture is a clearly discernible victory theme. It begins with the protoevangelium of Genesis 3:15 (which harmonizes with the creational purpose of God) and weaves its golden cord throughout Scripture all the way to Revelation 22. There is certainly the expectation of struggle in history. But it is a struggle that will triumphantly issue forth in victory rather than stalemate, defeat, or despair. The Seed of the Woman (Christ) will conquer the Seed of the Serpent (Satan) – in time and on earth. This is *the* fundamental truth of biblical eschatology.

The victory theme is traceable through and insured by the sovereign covenant of the LORD God. His is a unified covenantal administration, although it is developed in Scripture through a series of successive and judicially related covenants. Hence, Paul speaks of "the covenants of the promise" (Eph. 2:12). The Adamic (Gen. 1:26-30) and Noahaic (Gen. 9:1-17) covenants set the stage for the dominion of godly man and the victory of the gospel of God's saving grace in history. The Abrahamic Covenant promises the spread of salvation to "all the families of the earth" (Gen. 12:1-3). The gospel is the tool for the spread of the Abrahamic blessings through family generation and evangelistic outreach (see Gal. 3:8, 29). The Davidic Covenant identifies the regal nature of the pre-eminent covenant seed, Jesus Christ, and secures His throne and gracious rule in the plan of God (2 Sam. 7:8-16).

In covenantal harmony, the patriarchal and Mosaic era prophecies foresee a time in earth history, issuing forth from the first Advent of Christ, in which God's glory and righteousness will cover the earth (Gen. 22:17; 49:10; Num. 24:17-19). The prophets of the Old Testament, as prosecuting attorneys of God's covenant lawsuits, continue the hope of victory – despite opposition without and defection within. They command kings and judges of all the earth to bow to Christ, and promise that the ends of the earth will turn to God in salvation (Psa. 2; 22; 72; Isa. 2; 9; Mic. 4; Zech. 14).

Although, early on, the gracious saving work of God is largely confined to the family of Abraham, it is not always to be thus. The victory will be gained apart from Jewish exclusiveness and Old Testament ceremonial distinctives. All people who receive God's grace will be on an equal footing before Him (Jer. 3:16-17; 31:31-34; 48:47; 49:6, 39).

A Summary of the New Testament Evidence

As we enter the New Testament record we are immediately confronted with Christ's birth. The birth of "the Son of David, the Son of Abraham" (Matt. 1:1), gloriously reflects the victory theme of the Old Testament expectation, showing that Christ's first coming began the fruition of the promises (Luke 1:46-55, 68-79). The fullness of time had come in Christ (Gal. 4:4).

The covenanted kingdom of Christ came near in the early ministry of Christ because the "time was fulfilled" for it to come (Mark 1:14-15). Thus, John Baptist is something of a marker separating the fading Old Testament era from the dawning kingdom era (Matt. 11:11-14; Mark 1:14-15).

Christ's power over demons is evidence that the kingdom comes during His earthly ministry (Matt. 12:28). It is not to await some future, bodily coming on Christ's part (Luke 17:20-21). As Christ preaches the gospel, He claims to be king, while on earth (John 12:12-15; 18:36-37). He is formally enthroned as king at Pentecost following His resurrection and ascension (Acts 2:30ff). From then on we hear of his being in a royal position, at the right hand of Almighty God (Rom. 8:34; Eph. 1:20; 1 Pet. 3:22).

Because of this, first-century Christianity proclaim Him as a king (Acts 3:15; 17:7; Rev. 1:5) with regal dignity, authority, and power (Eph. 1:22; Phil. 2:9). Beginning in the first century, people are, at conversion, translated into the kingdom of Christ (Col. 1:12, 13; 4:11; 1 Thess. 2:12). Christ's kingdom rule goes where His people go, for they are the subjects of His kingdom (Rev. 1:6, 9) and are now mystically seated with Him in rulership position (Eph. 1:3; 2:6; 1 Cor. 3:21-22).

The beginning of the victory fruition is with the resurrection of Christ from the dead (Matt. 28:18-20) and His ascension to the right hand of God (Dan. 7:13-14). Accompanying His cosmic victory over sin and death is the empowerment of His people as the Spirit is poured out from on high (Acts 2:16-33).

The kingdom of Christ is essentially a spiritual kingdom (John 18:36-37; Rom. 14:17) that operates from within the heart (Luke 17:20-21). We enter the kingdom of Christ by means of salvation (Col. 1:12, 13; John 3:3). Christ rules His kingdom by His mystical presence from heaven (John 18:36; Eph. 4:8-14) and through the indwelling of the Holy Spirit (John 7:39; Rom. 8:9; 1 Cor. 3:16). The basic power of the kingdom is the "*gospel* of the kingdom" (Matt. 4:23; 9:35; Mark 1:14-15). The basic function of the kingdom is the promotion of God's truth (John 18:37; 2 Cor. 10:4-5).

The kingdom of Christ is not a future, Armageddon-introduced, earthly, political kingdom. The first-century Jews want a political kingdom to overthrow Rome, and when Christ does not offer them this (John 6:15), they reject Him. Even his disciples are confused and disappointed for a time (Luke 24:21-27). Israel as a geo-political entity is once for all been set aside as the specially favored nation of God (Matt. 8:11-12; 21:43), because of their prominent role in crucifying Christ (Acts 2:22-23,36; 3:13-15; 5:30; 7:52; 1 Thess. 2:14-15). The Messianic kingdom includes people of all races on an equal basis (Isa. 19:19-25; Zech. 9:7; Eph. 2:12-17); even great numbers of Jews will eventually enter it (Rom. 11:11-25).

The New Testament-phase Church is "the Israel of God" (Gal. 6:16), "the circumcision" (Phil. 3:3), "the seed of Abraham" (Gal. 3:7, 29), the "Jerusalem above" (Gal. 4:24-29), the "temple of God" (Eph. 2:21), "a royal priesthood" and a "peculiar people" (1 Pet. 2:9-10). Consequently, Jewish promises are applied to the Church (Jer. 31:31-34; Matt. 26:28).

Evangelism is the essential pre-condition to postmillennial, theocratic success. Apart from Christ we can do nothing (John 15:5; Matt. 19:26); in Christ we can do all things (Phil. 4:13, 19; Matt. 17:20). Because He possesses "all authority in heaven and on earth" (Matt. 28:18; Eph. 1:19-22), Christ's Great Commission expects His people to win converts, who are then baptized into His body, and then instructed in "all things" He taught

(Matt. 28:19). Due to the glorious presence of Christ with us, the Great Commission expects the conversion of all nations, as do the prophets (Matt. 28:19; Isa. 2:1-4; Mic. 4:1-4). The kingdom comes gradualistically, growing and ebbing ever stronger over the long run (Dan. 2:35ff; Ezek. 17:22-24; 47:1-9; Matt. 13:31-33; Mark 4:26-29).

The Christian witness involves exposing evil (Eph. 5:11) and calling men to repentance from *all* unrighteousness in *every* realm (Luke 3:8; 24:47), so that "every thought" is taken captive to Christ (2 Cor. 10:5). As citizens of Christ's kingdom, Christians are to live in every area of life with body, soul, mind, and strength (Mark 12:37) to the glory of God (1 Cor. 10:31; Col. 3:17), for they will give an account of every word and deed (Matt. 12:36; 2 Cor. 10:5). God's redemption provided in Christ is designed to bring the world as a system to salvation (John 1:29; 3:17; 1 John 2:2) and to redeem mankind (John 12:31; 1 Tim. 2:6). The falling away of the Jews allow for mass conversions among the Gentiles (Rom. 11:12). Eventually the vast majority of Jews and Gentiles alike will be converted, leading to the "reconciliation of the world" (Rom. 11:15). Thus, Christians cannot omit cultural endeavors as they seek the redemption of all of life to God's glory.

Biblical prophecy expects a time when the majority of the world's population will be converted to Christ by means of the gospel. Christ is presently ruling and reigning from heaven (1 Cor. 15:25a). He will not return in His Second Advent until "the end" of history (1 Cor. 15:24) when He turns His rule over to the Father (1 Cor. 15:28). At Christ's Second Advent, He will have already conquered His enemies (1 Cor. 15:24). His last enemy, death, will be conquered at His Return, when we are resurrected (1 Cor. 15:26).

Christ's gifts to the Church well equip it for its task of winning the world to Christ through its members. The Church has the very presence of Christ (Matt. 28:20; Acts 18:10) and the Holy Spirit (Rom. 8:9; 1 Cor. 3:16). God the Father delights in the salvation of sinners (Ezek. 18:23; Luke 15:10). The gospel is nothing less than "the power of God unto salvation" (Rom. 1:16; 1 Cor. 1:18, 24).

The binding of Satan is effected in principle (i.e., definitively) through the ministry of Christ in history (Matt. 12:28-29), thus casting him down from his dominance (John 12:31; Luke 17:10) on the basis of Christ's redemptive labor (Col. 3:15). Christians may resist the devil, causing him to flee (Jms. 4:7); they may even crush him beneath their feet (Rom. 16:20) because "greater is he that is in you, than he that is in the world" (1 John 4:4).

Conclusion

In accordance with the plan of God and under His almighty hand, Christianity is destined to overwhelm the world so that "the earth shall be full of the knowledge of the LORD as the waters cover the sea" (Isa. 11:9). There is coming a day when the large majority of the human race will bow before the Lord in humble worship, offering up the labor of their hands and the glory of their kingdoms to Him Who is "the King of kings and Lord of lords" (Rev. 17:14; 19:16).

Postmillennialism expects the expansion of Christ's righteousness throughout the earth. According to the clear teaching of Christ (Matt. 5:17-20) and the New Testament (e.g., Rom. 3:31; 7:12; I John 2:3-4), His righteousness is defined by God's law. Hence, consistent, biblically-based postmillennialism is necessarily theonomic.

The glorious message of Scripture – in both Old and New Testaments – is that "every knee shall bow to Me, and every tongue shall confess to God" (Rom. 14:11). Paul confidently asserts that

> Christ has indeed been raised from the dead, the firstfruits of those who have fallen asleep. For since death came through a man, the resurrection of the dead comes also through a man.

For as in Adam all die, so in Christ all will be made alive. But each in his own turn: Christ, the firstfruits; then, when he comes, those who belong to him. Then the end will come, when he hands over the kingdom to God the Father after he has destroyed all dominion, authority and power. For he must reign until he has put all his enemies under his feet. The last enemy to be destroyed is death. For he "has put everything under his feet." Now when it says that "everything" has been put under him, it is clear that this does not include God himself, who put everything under Christ. When he has done this, then the Son himself will be made subject to him who put everything under him, so that God may be all in all. (1 Cor. 15:20-28).

Appendix A

CULTURAL ANTINOMIANISM

But He said, "The things which are impossible with men are possible with God." (Luke 18:27)

According to some advocates of the various pessimistic eschatologies, postmillennialism is not only a spiritually mistaken hope, but is also a culturally dangerous phenomenon. It is a mirage hiding an open pit. In the writings of dispensational populists, such as Hal Lindsey and Dave Hunt, postmillennial eschatology has been most vehemently attacked as a potential social disaster – in Hunt's vision, a social disaster marked by worldwide peace and prosperity.[1] But with the present resurgence of postmillennialism, these are not the only critics sounding such an alarm today.

Calvinistic amillennialists have also entered the fray. Nowhere has the amillennial objection been more vigorously pressed than in the writings of theologians from the Protestant Reformed Church. Despite their strongly Calvinistic heritage and commitments,[2] these writers have tended toward a dispensationalist-like law/grace dichotomy, which generates a form of

---

1. Dave Hunt, *Peace Prosperity and the Coming Holocaust* (Eugene, OR: Harvest House, 1983).

2. "Now it is certainly true that the Reformed faith has always been marked by its deep and continuing regard for God's law. . . ." Bernard Woudenberg, "Hope as an Incentive to Godliness," *Standard Bearer* 66:7 (Jan. 1, 1990) 161.

cultural antinomianism and historical pessimism. Because of this, they greatly fear any society-wide pro-nomian challenge to secular humanistic culture.

An Amillennial Alarm

Protestant Reformed theologian Herman Hanko is quite concerned about postmillennial advocacy:

> I was compelled to *warn* God's people against the *spiritual dangers* involved in postmillennialism. It is my fervent hope and prayer that those who hold to postmillennialism "do not actually *promote the kingdom of Antichrist*;" but Herman Hoeksema was right when somewhere he *warned* God's people of the *spiritual danger* involved. It is not inconceivable that, if the saints are looking for a glorious kingdom on earth, they will be tempted to *identify the kingdom which Antichrist establishes with the kingdom of Christ.* It will be hard enough in that dreadful day to stand for the cause of Christ without putting other *spiritual temptations* in the way.[3] (Emphases mine)

Earlier, Hanko had written of postmillennialism that "it is a *mirage* because the kingdom which the Postmillennialists describe *is, in fact, the kingdom of Antichrist.*[4] I do not doubt that a kingdom of peace, of great plenty, of enormous prosperity and uncounted riches, of beauty and splendor such as the world has never seen, will some day be established. Scripture points us to that. What makes one *cringe*, however, is that this kingdom is described by Scripture as *the kingdom of the beast* (read Revela-

---

3. Herman Hanko, "Response to 'The Other Side' of Postmillennialism," *Standard Bearer* (April 1, 1990) 295.

4. Hanko's concern here is identical with dispensationalist Dave Hunt's concern. See Hunt's *Peace Prosperity and the Coming Holocaust* and *Whatever Happened to Heaven?* (Eugene, OR: Harvest House, 1989). See also: the discussion of the two positions' agreement in Gary North, "Ghetto Eschatologies," *Biblical Economics Today* 14:3 (April/May 1992).

tion 13). This makes postmillennial thinking of *considerable spiritual danger.*"[5]

In the final analysis, argues Hanko, postmillennialism is doomed to failure in this fallen world. Why? The only hope of culture-wide righteousness is in eternity: "The old creation has to be moved aside to make way for the new as the first Adam has to be moved aside to make room for the Second."[6]

Hanko certainly trumpets a chilling alarm regarding the extreme "danger" inherent in postmillennial advocacy: postmillennialism might well promote the cause of *Antichrist* in the looming and fateful eschatological hour! And what is more, the whole idea of Christian cultural renewal is altogether hopeless to begin with. Three fundamental problems beset such a charge at the very outset, however. Let me briefly consider these before actually engaging the ethical backdrop of this pessimistic assessment – cultural antinomianism.

A Postmillennial Response

In the first place, Hanko's argument is guilty of the informal logical fallacy of hasty generalization. He misinterprets the postmillennial hope by placing *a part* of that hope for *the whole*. Then on that truncated basis he charges that there is a real danger involved in such. He only emphasizes a portion of the postmillennial hope while he totally overlooks the driving force and the true nature of the postmillennial kingdom. The kingdom victory that postmillennialists seek is one in which the Lord Jesus Christ will be exalted in all areas of life, the Word of God will be the directive for all of human society, the Triune God of Scripture will be worshiped by all peoples, and right-

---

5. Herman Hanko, "The Illusory Hope of Postmillennialism," *Standard Bearer*, 66:7 (Jan. 1, 1990) 159. Emphases mine.

6. Homer C. Hanko, "An Exegetical Refutation of Postmillennialism" (unpublished manuscript: South Holland, IL: South Holland Protestant Reformed Church, February 28, 1978), p. 23.

eousness and godliness as defined by God's Law will prevail throughout the world. Every one of the elements he mentions as definitive of the kingdom hope – unsurpassed peace, plenty, prosperity, beauty, and splendor – are the *eventual fruits* of the kingdom, not the *whole of the kingdom*. These elements, to be sure, may be temporarily mimicked by the unrighteous. The evangelical postmillennialist does not hold that Hanko's elements are final goals to be sought regardless of biblically-defined righteousness.

The postmillennial hope is in the gospel of God's sovereign redemptive grace through the Lord Jesus Christ. The postmillennialist does not long for just any old worldly peace or for mere materialistic prosperity, devoid of evangelistic success, Christian discipleship, biblical righteousness, and true holiness. Such an empty peace would not serve as a sign of kingdom victory, for *it is a gospel kingdom that we promote*, which entails the widespread influence of the gospel. How a Christian could confuse the promotion of a Bible-based, Christ-exalting culture with a secularistic, man-centered culture is not explained by Hanko. He *presupposes* that visible success is humanistic. Why?

In the second place, Hanko never considers the very real possibility that retreatism itself might be promoting the cause of Antichrist — at this present hour! Surely it is a genuine danger for Christians to retreat from cultural and political leadership and to allow the non-Christian children of the devil to have free reign in society. How could this be any "worse" than for Christians to seek to promote the visible expression of the kingdom of Christ (as if that were intrinsically dangerous)? In light of the very real presence of the sin principle and man's total depravity, sins of omission (retreat from leadership in a fallen world) should be as much a concern as sins of commission (mis-directed cultural concerns by the people of God).

This rejoinder is especially significant because of Hanko's surrender elsewhere. The sin principle, he says, is being worked out in history to its full fruition. "What Scripture constantly teaches is that, with the fall sin entered into the world. From that moment on, as the catholic church is being gathered, the history of the world is characterized by the organic development of sin as 'all those ominous signs (of Christ's coming) become increasingly more apparent.' That organic development of sin finally culminates in the 'man of sin' (II Thessalonians 2:3-12). That is the kingdom of Antichrist."[7]

In the third place, if the retreatist logic of Hanko's concern is taken too readily to heart, it goes too far. Then the Christian should separate himself from church life, as well. Are there not multitudes of liberal churches and denominations today which preach a corrupted gospel? In his report on the Protestant Reformed Church-sponsored conference on postmillennialism, Hoeksema states: "There was also a question raised as to whether even mild, or moderate, postmillennialism does not after all, in fact, with its view of a kingdom of Christ being realized in this present world, end up by laboring for the realization of the kingdom of Anti-Christ and develop into radical and liberal postmillennialism and social gospelism."[8]

"Social gospelism" is promoted through (liberal) churches. Should we avoid all churches – just to be safe? Employing Hanko's logic of concern regarding the possibility of confusing the evil kingdom for the good, should Christians avoid building and attending churches altogether? After all, might they not confuse evil churches for good ones? Could it be that God-fearing Christians who promote church life might end up promoting the ecclesiastical aspect of the kingdom of Antichrist? Does not the Antichrist of the futurist[9] operate through a false

---

7. Hanko, "Response to 'The Other Side' of Postmillennialism," p. 298.

8. H. C. Hoeksema, "An Interesting Conference on Postmillennialism" (unpublished paper: South Holland, IL: South Holland Protestant Reformed Church, 1978), p. 60.

9. The futurist interpretation of New Testament prophecy is contrasted with the preterist interpretation.

church, "Babylon, The Bride of Antichrist"?[10] Hanko certainly would not over-compensate in this direction. And if he can tell the difference between a true church and a false one, why cannot the postmillennialists tell the difference between true Christian cultural victory and false anti-Christian victory?

Also, what are we to make of Hanko's statement that "the old creation has to be moved aside to make way for the new as the first Adam has to be moved aside to make room for the Second"? Is this statement not a bit anachronistic? Is that not, in fact, what has already happened in principle in the coming of Christ *in history*? Christ *is* the second Adam, who displaces the first Adam (Rom. 5:14-15; 1 Cor. 15:45-47). He specifically came "to destroy the works of the devil" (1 John 3:8; Heb. 2:14) and of Adam (Rom. 5:17-21).

Furthermore, is not the "old creation" being moved aside by salvation to make room for "the new creation"? "Therefore, if anyone is in Christ, he is a new creation; old things have passed away; behold, all things have become new" (2 Cor. 5:17). "For in Christ Jesus neither circumcision nor uncircumcision avails anything, but a new creation" (Gal. 6:15). Is not grace more powerful than sin (1 Cor. 6:9-11; 1 John 4:4; 5:4)? Does grace not abound much more than sin (Rom 5:20)? As more and more people become new creations in Christ, might we not justly expect the old creation order to be gradually transformed toward a new creation righteousness (Matt. 13:33; 1 Cor. 15:24-25)?

I have presented in the course of this book the true nature of the postmillennial hope. I am convinced that Scripture sets forth a genuinely optimistic hope for a righteous kingdom rooted in the worship of the Triune God. But I have dealt at length with this issue in the text of the book. Let me turn now

---

10. Herman C. Hoeksema, *Behold! He Cometh: An Exposition of the Book of Revelation* (Grand Rapids: Kregal, 1969), ch. 40: "Babylon, The Bride of Antichrist"; see p. 559.

to another area of confusion in Hanko's thought. Besides the eschatological *non sequitur* characterizing his concern, there is lurking behind it a fundamental cultural antinomianism.

Antinomian Tendencies

By the very nature of the case, evangelical antinomianism tends to be retreatist when it comes to confronting secular culture *and* challenging it with the positive alternative of biblical law. Retreatism is contra-postmillennial by definition. Though the theologians of the Protestant Reformed Church deny that the denomination is retreatist and antinomian, nevertheless, we do find those tendencies in their writings on eschatology.

In a rebuttal of the postmillennial hope for cultural transformation, VanOverloop comments: "Most importantly, the believer's hope is based on God's promise of everlasting life. The believer, with uplifted head, anticipates the return of his resurrected and ascended Lord. He fixes his mind upon the new heaven and earth, which Jesus will bring upon His return."[11] Hanko argues that the antithesis between the world and the church "comes especially to manifestation in the life of men in the world with respect to their view of the future." This is because the world longs "to set up a Kingdom where Satan is king. We walk in hope. They look for heaven here upon earth. We are strangers in the world. They make this world their abiding city. We look for the full realization of the purpose of God in the Kingdom which is to come."[12]

It is true, of course, that to the Christian the prospect of the consummative new heaven and new earth one day in the future is joyful to contemplate. And certainly we must await that day for "the full realization of the purpose of God." Nevertheless,

---

11. Ronald VanOverloop, "The Hope of Every Believer Regarding His Future Earthly Life," *Standard Bearer* 66:7 (Jan. 1, 1990), p. 163.

12. Hanko, *The Christian's Social Calling and the Second Coming of Christ* (South Holland, IL: South Holland Protestant Reformed Church, 1970), pp. 10-11.

(1) the Christian should not so completely "fix his mind" upon the future eternal order that he denies his God-given responsibilities in the present temporal order. (2) Neither should the believer look for contemporary signs of the Second Coming. Such anticipation of an any-moment end of history necessarily distracts from Christian cultural transformation in the long run. These two errors have generated cultural antinomianism in the theology of the Protestant Reformed Church. Like it or not, this outlook engenders retreatism. And this pessimistic tendency to retreatism is undergirded by a cultural antinomianism.

For the cultural antinomian, the Christian's duty is summed up in matters almost wholly spiritual and ecclesiastical. In opposing postmillennialism, Hanko comments: "The kingdom of Christ is manifested in this present age in the preaching of the gospel to the ends of the earth; in the gathering of the church; in the establishment of covenant schools; in the godly and holy walk of the saints as they reveal in all their lives the sovereign rule of the grace of Christ in their hearts; in the throngs of faithful in every age who do not bow the knee to Baal, but bow instead in humble worship of King Jesus."[13]

Certainly the kingdom of Christ is manifested in such godly endeavors – this must be the case! And just as truly do these represent the fundamental starting point of the Christian enterprise – with this the postmillennialist agrees. Nevertheless, two problems plague such a statement as Hanko's.

The Theonomic Response

There is a problem of definition in Hanko's concern: What is the *content* of that which we promote in "the preaching of the gospel"? The "gospel" is "good news" regarding God's saving mercies in Christ. Does this good news have implications for mankind at large and for human culture as such? That is, does the gospel have ramifications for the larger social issues, which

---

13. Hanko, "Response to 'The Other Side' of Postmillennialism," pp. 295-296.

most definitely are concerns to God? Does it not call men and nations to repentance for particular, concrete sins – including social and political sins? But how do we define those sins apart from the Law of God?[14] Is it not fundamentally the case that "sin is transgression of the Law" (1 John 3:4; Rom. 7:7)?

So, what is to be taught in the educational process "in the establishment of covenant schools"? Should not "covenant schools" touch on matters beyond reading, writing, and arithmetic? Should not covenant children be taught *from Scripture* how to operate in society from a Christian perspective in every area of life (2 Tim. 3:17)? Is it not true that we should "do *all* to the glory of God" (1 Cor. 10:31; Col. 3:17) and be "the light of the world" (Matt. 5:14)? Should not Christian education equip our covenant seed for a *particular* calling in life? Should not the Christian student be taught specifically how "the weapons of our warfare" are designed for "pulling down strongholds, casting down arguments and *every high thing* that exalts itself against the knowledge of God, bringing *every thought* into captivity to the obedience of Christ" (2 Cor. 10:4-5)?

What defines a "godly and holy walk for the saints"? How shall we exhibit "the sovereign rule of the grace of Jesus Christ" in our day-by-day life? Is a godly walk a matter of individualistic "taste not, touch not" negativism? Or does it operate in terms of a positive course of action in all areas of life? Is it only through clean living and church attendance? How shall the believing politician walk as a *Christian* politician? The believing businessman walk as a *Christian* businessman? The believing school teacher teach as a *Christian* teacher? Should it not be according to God's directives in their particular areas of life – directives that are found in God's Law? Hanko never says.

Furthermore, there is a problem of truncation in Hanko's theology. God has called us to be cultural creatures (as I have

---

14. See: Kenneth L. Gentry, Jr., *The Greatness of the Great Commission: The Christian Enterprise in a Fallen World* (Tyler, TX: Institute for Christian Economics, 1990).

shown in the Introduction of this work: see Gen. 1:26-30). The entire "earth is the Lord's and the fullness thereof" (Psa. 24:1). This requires us to seek our direction from God. And that source where we receive concrete direction is His sovereign Law-word: the whole Bible, including God's Law. But it is precisely here that the cultural antinomian hesitates.

Hanko's Appeal to a Norm-less Christian Liberty

Hanko rejects the civil precepts contained in God's Law, laws that speak directly to the social and political obligations of man in God's world. Consequently, he leaves Christians without moral guidelines.

> In the third place, all the laws governing Israel's civil and social and political life have also been fulfilled. It is here where we come to the crux of the matter. All these laws have no more validity for the Church of the New Dispensation. They were intended to demonstrate the impossibility of Israel's keeping of the law, and they served their purpose when Israel was brought to Christ. It is true that taken together they still show strong principles of the kingdom of heaven. But: 1) they are not in force any longer as such. Israel's dietary laws have passed away because God told Peter: 'What God hath cleansed, that call not thou common.' (Acts 10:15) Those grievously err when once again they call common what God cleansed. . . . 2) There are many laws which not even the postmillennialists would insist are still in force. Certainly it would be saying too much to enjoin upon men the carrying of a paddle to bury excrement. Nor would even the most ardent observer of the law insist that it is still wrong to sow two kinds of seed in one field. 3) The post-millennialists may not bring us back to the bondage of law upon law and precept upon precept, here a little and there a little. We stand in the liberty wherewith Christ has made us free. (Galatians 5:1) The people of God must refuse to be dragged back into the bondage of the law. Their liberty is a very precious gift of grace and no one may take it from them. 4) The postmillennialists forget that the principles of the kingdom of heaven too

are principles which mean that the antithesis cuts through the whole of the life of the child of God. This is clear from the reference to the Old Testament law in II Corinthians 6:14-18. The principles of the kingdom of heaven apply to all our life. There is no part of it exempt from the demands of the kingdom. In every aspect of life we are called to live lives which are principally and fundamentally different from those of the world. But how each child of God lives his life in his own station and calling and how he applies the abiding principles of the kingdom of heaven to his own place in that kingdom is a matter of Christian liberty. The principles are all in the Scriptures. The application of them is in the sanctified consciousness of the child of God.[15]

On the purpose of God's Law, Hanko adds: "In the Old Dispensation, God gave Israel His law in order to show how Israel had to live in relation to God. But the point was that the law could not disannul the promises of God (Galatians 3:17). God gave Israel all these detailed laws in order that Israel might learn that salvation could never come through the works of the law. The law was, so to speak, a tyrant which followed the Israelite wherever he went."[16] Is he correct? Hardly.

An Analysis of Hanko's Argument

The Purpose of the Civil Law

Hanko assumes what he needs to prove from Scripture. It *may* be that *a* purpose of the governance of Israel through the civil law was to demonstrate that salvation could not come by works. Hanko needed to provide exegetical evidence for such a view of the Law. Instead, Hanko leaves us with his bare word.

Furthermore, even if his view were the case, this surely would not be the *only* purpose of God's Law. The Law was also a positive directive for civil and social living. The Bible express-

---

15. Hanko, "An Exegetical Refutation of Postmillennialism," pp. 20-21.
16. *Ibid.*, p. 20.

ly informs us of this purpose. The Law was expressly given to Israel as a nation so that the nation might be an example of social righteousness to the nations of the world.

> Surely I have taught you statutes and judgments, just as the LORD my God commanded me, that you should act according to them in the land which you go to possess. Therefore be careful to observe them; for this is your wisdom and your understanding in the sight of the peoples who will hear all these statutes, and say, "Surely this great nation is a wise and understanding people." For what great nation is there that has God so near to it, as the LORD our God is to us, for whatever reason we may call upon Him? And what great nation is there that has such statutes and righteous judgments as are in all this law which I set before you this day? (Deut. 4:5-8).

There is no indication here at all that the Law was to show that man cannot be saved by Law-keeping. The text is clear: *the Law governing Israel's social and political realm was a positive moral standard for all nations, given to Israel in order that the nations might emulate it*. As I argued in Chapter 7, the nations outside of geographical Israel were never condemned for failure to keep Israel's ceremonial or symbolic laws, but for their failure to keep the moral *and* civil requirements of the Law.

In fact, the New Testament speaks very highly of God's Law as a standard of personal and civil righteousness. The Law is established (Rom. 3:31), holy, just, good (Rom. 7:12), spiritual (Rom. 7:14), and perfect (Jms. 1:25). The Law defines personal sins (Rom. 5:13; 1 John 2:3-4; 3:4). The Law defines civil crimes (1 Tim. 1:8-10) and exacts God's vengeance on evil doers through the ministration of the civil magistrate (Rom. 12:19-3:4). Thus, the punishments of the Law for infractions are "just" (Heb. 2:2). This means that under the general category of God's Law are the Law's sanctions. Without sanctions, there is no law (Rom. 5:12-14).

On Hanko's basis, would not the fundamental Ten Commandments "demonstrate the impossibility of Israel's keeping of the law"? Christ pointed out the sin in the life of the self-righteous Rich Young Ruler by relating to him the Ten Commandments. By so doing He pointed out the man's love of money, his covetousness (Matt. 19:16-23). The self-righteous Pharisee, Saul of Tarsus, learned of the futility of meritorious work by the Tenth Commandment (Rom. 7:7-13). Why, then, are the Ten Commandments not done away with on Hanko's position, i.e., that particular laws were given to show the futility of perfection? Yet Hanko allows their continuance.[17]

Objections to the Civil Law

Hanko attempts to illustrate that there "are many laws which not even the postmillennialists would insist are still in force." Here at least he offers some exegetical insights. But it is very interesting that he provides only two examples, neither of which is helpful to his cause. One is accounted for by the theonomic system; the other law, upon closer consideration, surely is still in effect. Hanko's essay is left without biblical support.

Hanko mentions the sowing of two kinds of seed in one field. Gary North has clearly indicated the symbolic nature and fulfillment of these laws within the theonomic hermeneutic and ethical system.[18] They were symbolic laws that governed the protection of the seed line in the land until the Redemptive Jubilee, the first coming of Christ. Hanko's second example has to do with soldiers burying their excrement. What is the fulfillment of this law? This is a sanitation law (with no civil sanction) that is still morally binding for reasons of health. Hanko will

---

17. *Ibid.*, pp. 19-20.

18. Gary North, "The Hermeneutics of Leviticus 19:19: Passing Dr. Poythress' Test," in *Theonomy: An Informed Response*, Gary North, ed. (Tyler, TX: Institute for Christian Economics, 1991), ch. 10.

have to provide more compelling examples before this portion of his argument can bear any weight.

Hanko is concerned with the theonomic postmillennialist's position; he claims that it leads to "the bondage of law upon law." But is it necessarily wrong to be in "bondage of law upon law"? Is it wrong, for example, to argue "you shall not kill"? And "you shall not steal"? And "you shall not commit adultery"? And "you shall not covet"? Is this an illegitimate "bondage" engendered by adding "law upon law"? Surely not!

Is it true that the civil laws are included "in the liberty wherewith Christ has made us free (Galatians 5:1)"? Here another attempt at exegesis fails Hanko. Contextual exegesis shows that the freedom Paul speaks of here – the freedom that we have in Christ under the New Covenant – is a freedom from the fulfilled *ceremonial/symbolic* laws, not the moral or civil laws. We are still in "bondage" (i.e., under obligation) to civil authority in the New Covenant era (Rom. 13:1-4; 1 Pet. 2:13-14). Paul's point in Galatians has to do with requiring the keeping of *ceremonial* laws in order to *gain salvation*. Paul is condemning the use of the Law (particularly the ceremonial law) by the Judaizers as a means of redemptive merit before God (such as in Acts 15).

This Judaizing approach to Law-keeping is clearly under Paul's scrutiny in Galatians. Paul's concern is with a corrupted "gospel" of salvation by works – a gospel that is under a curse (Gal. 1:6-9). He is arguing "a man is not justified by the works of the law but by faith in Jesus Christ, even we have believed in Christ Jesus, that we might be justified by faith in Christ and not by the works of the law; for by the works of the law no flesh shall be justified" (Gal. 2:16). He warns the Galatians: "I do not set aside the grace of God; for if righteousness comes through the law, then Christ died in vain" (Gal. 2:21). He insists that "no one is justified by the law in the sight of God" (Gal. 3:11).

The problem among those in Galatia was that "they have become estranged from Christ, who attempt to be justified by law"; they "have fallen from grace" (Gal 5:4). And it is the ceremonial elements of the Law that are being pressed by these Judaizers – particularly circumcision (Gal. 2:3-4; 5:2, 3, 11; 6:12-13), but also ceremonial festivals (Gal. 4:10). There is no mention of the civil laws, or of the moral law; neither is included in Paul's denunciation of law keeping (of course, the keeping of these cannot merit salvation, either).

The Sanctified Conscience

The final statement by Hanko in his dismissing of the civil laws is clearly antinomian: "But how each child of God lives his life in his own station and calling and how he applies the abiding principles of the kingdom of heaven to his own place in that kingdom is a matter of Christian liberty. The principles are all in the Scriptures. The application of them is in the sanctified consciousness of the child of God."[19] This differs little from House and Ice's "wisdom" approach to the Law of God.[20] House and Ice are dispensationalists, hence antinomian in tendency.[21]

Does God allow His children to choose to apply laws according to their own determination? Or does He expect us to follow His revealed laws in obedience? May we pick and choose among God's commandments according to our "sanctified consciousness"? "Woe to you, scribes and Pharisees, hypocrites! For you pay tithe of mint and anise and cumin, and have neglected the weightier matters of the law: justice and mercy and faith. These you *ought* to have done, without leaving the others undone" (Matt. 23:23). "Thus you have made the commandment of God of no effect by your tradition" (Matt. 15:6b).

---

19. Hanko, "An Exegetical Refutation of Postmillennialism," p. 21.

20. H. Wayne House and Thomas D. Ice, *Dominion Theology: Blessing or Curse?* (Portland, OR: Multnomah, 1988), pp. 86-137.

21. John H. Gerstner, *Wrongly Dividing the Word of Truth: A Critique of Dispensationalism* (Brentwood, TN: Wolgemuth and Hyatt, 1991), chaps. 11-12.

Does not the Holy Spirit within us move us to keep God's Law? "What the law could not do in that it was weak through the flesh, God did by sending His own Son in the likeness of sinful flesh, on account of sin: He condemned sin in the flesh, that *the righteous requirement of the law might be fulfilled in us* who do not walk according to the flesh but according to the Spirit" (Rom. 8:3-4)? Does not the "carnal mind" resist obedience to the Law of God, while the spiritual mind is led by the Spirit to keep the Law? "The carnal mind is enmity against God; for it is not subject to the law of God, nor indeed can be. So then, those who are in the flesh cannot please God. But you are not in the flesh but in the Spirit, if indeed the Spirit of God dwells in you. Now if anyone does not have the Spirit of Christ, he is not His" (Rom. 8:7-9). Hanko ignores all this.

Did Christ pick and choose among the commandments of God? May we pick and choose according to "sanctified consciousness"? "Now by this we know that we know Him, if we keep His commandments. He who says, 'I know Him,' and does not keep His commandments, is a liar, and the truth is not in him" (1 John 2:3-4). Hanko ignores all this.

The Promises of God

When Hanko points out that "the law could not disannul the promises of God (Galatians 3:17)," what is his point? The *truth* of the matter is that *the Law cannot disannul the promises of God*. The theonomic postmillennialist does not deny this fundamental reality. The *history* of the matter is that the Law came after the promise (Gal. 3:17-18). Would Hanko say that the Jews were not obligated to God's Law, since it cannot disannul the promises of God? Would a Jew living under Moses have been righteous to have declared that he was living under promise and therefore was not obligated to obey the Law? Obviously the Law of God is not inimical to the promise of God, when used rightly. God's Law is not a standard of salvific merit; it is a standard for sanctified living. Thus, this same Paul could say:

"[W]e know that the law is good if one uses it lawfully" (1 Tim. 1:8).

Hanko speaks of the Law of God as a "tyrant which followed the Israelite wherever he went."[22] But is this the conception of the Law held by the saint redeemed by the grace of God, who longs to honor and glorify His Savior? The Law, which Hanko calls a "tyrant," is deemed by the righteous man as a delight (Psa. 1:1-2), an object of loving adoration (Psa. 119:97), a source of moral strength (Psa. 119:97), the foundation of civil wisdom and understanding (Deut. 4:6, 8), a blessing to be sought by the redeemed (Isa. 2:2-3), a standard for holiness, justice, and goodness (Rom. 7:12). Truly the Law becomes a "tyrant" to those who wrongly use it as a means of justification and merit (1 Tim. 1:8; Gal. 2:16; Jms. 2:10). The abuse of ceremonial merit is indeed a "burden" (Acts 15:10, cf. 15:1). But we must not confuse *abuse* with *use*.

Conclusion

Hanko's pessimistic eschatology, when coupled with his cultural antinomianism, leaves him shouting in vain against the darkness. Light overcomes darkness; shouting only confuses.

> What is that calling [of the Christian]? Not to change the world. That is impossible. But we do have a solemn calling. Negatively it is to condemn the world for her sin and for her rebellion against God and against Christ. We must do this constantly. . . . And on the other hand, positively, we must witness to the truth. We must witness to the fact that the Kingdom of Christ is heavenly, that the Kingdom of Christ will come when our Lord comes back again. We must stand in the midst of a world which madly rushes down the road to destruction and shout at the top of our voices, "Jesus Christ is King. . . !" We must do that specifically in connection with the problems of life; specifically in connection with each individual social problem that

---

22. Hanko, "An Exegetical Refutation of Postmillennialism," p. 20.

comes up. Insist upon that. These problems are solved in the Cross; in the Church; in the context of the Church and in the Kingdom of Jesus Christ which shall presently come. In the world there is no solution. We must say that with courage. And it will take courage. . . .[23]

This truth must be maintained in the preaching from the pulpit on Sunday. That will make the preaching "relevant." If you ask me the question, "can this be done in some kind of concerted action?", I see no principle objection to that. . . . As long as the purpose is not to change the world. . . ."[24]

We must recognize that things in the world are not going to get better. We know that from Scripture, too. We are not on the edge of a national and international revival. The world is not going to turn to Christ, nor is this country. We mustn't expect that. . . . Things will get worse and worse; that we know.[25]

I have shown throughout the course of the present work that that which Hanko deems "impossible" is not only theoretically "possible" (on the basis of the "gospel which is the power of God unto salvation," Rom. 1:16), but is, in fact, ordained in God's Word (which "will not return unto Me void," Isa. 55:11).

Hanko's pessimistic message of historical anti-hope is being proclaimed today by the majority of modern evangelical Christians. It is being shouted loudly. With the triumph of dispensationalism (an eschatology that shares amillennialism's pessimism regarding the church's earthly future) in twentieth-century evangelicalism, we have also seen the accelerating decline of Christian influence on society. The age of the dominance of eschatological pessimism has become the age of the dominance of humanism – the bloodiest century known to man.[26]

---

23. Hanko, *The Christian's Social Calling*, pp. 13-14.
24. *Ibid.*, p. 14.
25. *Ibid.*, p. 15.
26. Gil Elliot, *The Twentieth Century Book of the Dead* (New York: Scribner's, 1972).

Norman Shepherd has rightly complained:

> One of the most insidious weapons which Satan has been able to wield against the advancement of the Kingdom of God is the inculcation of the belief that though the Kingdom must be proclaimed throughout the world, the church really cannot expect that such proclamation will meet with any significant degree of success. One prominent writer in the field of inter-national missions has given expression to the commonly held expectation in this way: "The New Testament clearly predicts that in spite of great victories of the Gospel amongst all nations the resistance of Satan will continue. Towards the end it will even increase so much that Satan, incarnated in the human person of Antichrist, will assume once more an almost total control over disobedient mankind (II Thess. 2:3-12; Rev. 13)."
>
> These words really constitute a confession of faith. More accurately they are a confession of anti-faith – anti-faith in anti-Christ. If we were to find them in the anti-confession of a modern Satanist cult, they would not surprise us. At least we cannot conceive of a Satanist solemnly confessing that toward the end of human history, the Son of God, incarnate in the person of Jesus Christ, will assume an almost total control over obedient mankind.
>
> Why are we as Christians so much more confident with respect to the victory of anti-Christ than we are with respect to the triumph of Jesus Christ? Is the worldwide dominion of Satan toward the end of history so much more obviously and unambiguously a revealed truth of Scripture than is the worldwide dominion of Jesus Christ?[27]

Shepherd makes an important point. The Church of the Lord Jesus Christ needs to be armed with the Word of God in order to fully engage her hope-filled calling. She needs theonomic postmillennialism rather than antinomian pessimism.

---

27. Norman Shepherd, "Justice to Victory," *Journal of Christian Reconstruction* 3:2 (Winter 1976-77) 6.

I opened this book with the words of the great Christian psalter hymn: "Christ Shall Have Dominion." This hymn is based on Psalm 72. Perhaps it would be fitting at this point to cite Psalm 72, as a reminder of the hope for the progress of the gospel of Jesus Christ in all of human culture.

Psalm 72

"A Psalm of Solomon"

Give the king Your judgments, O God,
    And Your righteousness to the king's Son.
He will judge Your people with righteousness,
    And Your poor with justice.
The mountains will bring peace to the people,
    And the little hills, by righteousness.
He will bring justice to the poor of the people;
    He will save the children of the needy,
    And will break in pieces the oppressor.
They shall fear You
    As long as the sun and moon endure,
    Throughout all generations.
He shall come down like rain upon the mown grass,
    Like showers that water the earth.
In His days the righteous shall flourish,
    And abundance of peace,
    Until the moon is no more.

He shall have dominion also from sea to sea,
    And from the River to the ends of the earth.
Those who dwell in the wilderness will bow before Him,
    And His enemies will lick the dust.
The kings of Tarshish and of the isles
    Will bring presents;
The kings of Sheba and Seba
    Will offer gifts.

Yes, all kings shall fall down before Him;
  All nations shall serve Him.

For He will deliver the needy when he cries,
  The poor also, and him who has no helper.
He will spare the poor and needy,
  And will save the souls of the needy.
He will redeem their life from oppression and violence;
  And precious shall be their blood in His sight.

And He shall live;
  And the gold of Sheba will be given to Him;
Prayer also will be made for Him continually,
  And daily He shall be praised.

There will be an abundance of grain in the earth,
  On the top of the mountains;
Its fruit shall wave like Lebanon;
  And those of the city shall flourish like grass of the earth.

His name shall endure forever;
  His name shall continue as long as the sun.
And men shall be blessed in Him;
  All nations shall call Him blessed.

Blessed be the LORD God, the God of Israel,
  Who only does wondrous things!
And blessed be His glorious name forever!
  And let the whole earth be filled with His glory.
  Amen and Amen.

The prayers of David the son of Jesse are ended.

Appendix B

POSTMILLENNIALISM AND SUFFERING

Blessed are those who are persecuted for righteousness' sake, for theirs is the kingdom of heaven. (Matthew 5:10)

In Chapter 19, I responded briefly to Richard Gaffin's particularly vigorous employment of the suffering motif in Scripture as a theological objection to postmillennialism. The suffering theme is often deemed as a contra-indicative to postmillennialism, which is classified (dismissed) as "triumphalist" by adherents to pessimistic eschatologies. Some have felt that postmillennialism has absolutely no place for suffering in its historical scheme of things. Postmillennialists have responded to such objections before.[1] But due to this continuing perception, I would like to offer this Appendix as a brief study on the role of suffering in redemptive history.

The Debate Context

In contemporary Christianity, two widely disparate views of Christian suffering are popularly held. Both of these, I believe,

---

1. See for example: John Jefferson Davis, *Christ's Victorious Kingdom* (Grand Rapids: Baker, 1986), pp. 127-128. Roderick Campbell, *Israel and the New Covenant* (Tyler, TX: Geneva Divinity School Press, [1954] 1981), pp. 277ff. Gary North, *Millennialism and Social Theory* (Tyler, TX: Institute for Christian Economics, 1990), ch. 9. North, *Westminster's Confession: The Abandonment of Van Til's Legacy* (Tyler, TX: Institute for Christian Economics, 1991), pp. 176-180.

are extremes from the biblical point of view. As such each is also in contradiction to postmillennialism.

Health-and-Wealth

On the one hand, there is the remarkably popular "health-and-wealth" gospel that is held among many in the charismatic renewal movement. This view absolutely eliminates suffering as a factor for *faithful* believers. This doctrine is based on a misunderstanding of such passages as Mark 11:24 and 3 John 2. "The faith movement teaches that divine health and prosperity are the rights of every Christian who will appropriate enough faith to receive them."[2] In these circles, the faithful believer may expect continual prosperity and good health – the total elimination of all forms of suffering, from physical affliction to societal persecution. Indeed, suffering is deemed evidence of a *lack of faith* among health-and-wealth proponents.

Affliction and Poverty

On the other hand and at the other extreme, the mainline view expects the age long affliction of God's people in history. The Church Militant, it is argued, is established to be a suffering community. It is against the backdrop of this view that I develop a brief postmillennial study of the theme of suffering.

Postmillennialism's glorious historical optimism expects evil gradually to be reduced to minority proportions in the historical long haul. Because of this postmillennialism is deemed out of accord with the biblical record, which clearly speaks of persecution and suffering for the faith. In demonstration of the extremely widespread expectation of age long suffering, let me cite a few quotations randomly selected from various evangelical

---

2. James R. Goff, Jr., "The Faith That Claims," *Christianity Today* (February 19, 1990), 21.

authors. These samples will indicate how pervasive is the notion that the Church is to expect *constant suffering throughout history*.

According to amillennialist Herman Ridderbos' view of the Church's experience in history, "Jesus is here predicting persecution to the end, although they will always have a refuge to flee to."[3] As an express objection to postmillennialism, George Murray writes: "Our Lord's promise to His church in this world is tribulation, rather than ease and comfort."[4] As noted in Chapter 19, Gaffin put the matter very strongly: "Over the interadvental period *in its entirety*, from beginning to end, a *fundamental* aspect of the church's existence is (to be) 'suffering with Christ'; *nothing*, the New Testament teaches, *is more basic* to its identity than that."[5] Amillennialist Anthony Hoekema concurs: "God's people will continue to suffer injustice until the end of this age." Also, "[T]ribulation [is] a sign of the times which is to be expected by his people throughout the period between his first and second coming." "Because of the continued opposition of the world to the kingdom of God, Christians must expect to suffer tribulation and persecution of one kind or another during this entire age."[6]

Other Christian writers, both premillennial and amillennial, follow suit. Amillennialist R. B. Kuiper: "The Bible teaches that every true disciple of Christ is bound to suffer persecution at the hands of the world."[7] Amillennialist Herbert Schlossberg: "The Bible can be interpreted as a string of God's triumphs

---

3. Herman Ridderbos, *The Coming of the Kingdom* (Philadelphia: Presbyterian & Reformed, 1962), p. 507.

4. George L. Murray, *Millennial Studies: A Search for Truth* (Grand Rapids: Baker, 1948), p. 86.

5. Richard B. Gaffin, "Theonomy and Eschatology: Reflections on Postmillennialism," *Theonomy: A Reformed Critique*, William S. Barker and W. Robert Godfrey, eds. (Grand Rapids: Zondervan, 1990), p. 211 (emphases mine).

6. Anthony A. Hoekema, *The Bible and the Future* (Grand Rapids: Eerdmans, 1979), pp. 72, 149, 150-151.

7. R. B. Kuiper, *God-Centered Evangelism* (Grand Rapids: Baker, 1961), p. 90.

disguised as disasters."[8] Dispensationalist C. Sumner Wemp: Paul "assures that persecutions await all who will live godly."[9] Historic (non-dispensational) premillennialist Edith Schaeffer: "Job's cry here shows an understanding that there is no balanced solution until the resurrection."[10] Historic premillennialist George Eldon Ladd: "[I]t is clear that Jesus taught that all his disciples could expect in the world was tribulation and persecution. . . . The only difference between the normal role of the Christian in the world and the time of the Great Tribulation is the intensity of the persecution."[11] Amillennialist G. C. Berkouwer: "There are ominous dangers and hazards connected with the service one gives in the Kingdom of God. Persecution and imprisonment, bodily harm and even death are never far removed from man in this life."[12]

I could multiply examples. The theme of relentless suffering for the Church throughout history is pervasive in contemporary Christian literature. The point is clear: the pessimistic eschatologies interpret the suffering theme in Scripture as *prophetically ordained for all times.*

The postmillennialist does not deny the expectation of personal sufffering in history. Suffering is an important feature of God's governance of His people. But we must consider two important questions relative to suffering:

What role does suffering play in the divine scheme of things?

---

8. Herbert Schlossberg, *Idols for Destruction: Christian Faith and Its Confrontation with American Society* (Washington, D.C.: Regnery, [1983] 1990), p. 304.

9. C. Sumner Wemp, "II Timothy," *Liberty Commentary on the New Testament*, Edward E. Hindson and Woodrow Michael Kroll, eds. (Lynchburg, VA: Liberty Press, 1978), p. 626.

10. Edith Schaeffer, *Affliction* (Old Tappan, NJ: Revell, 1978), p. 55.

11. George Eldon Ladd, *The Last Things* (Grand Rapids: Eerdmans, 19), p. 62. See also pages 58-64.

12. G. C. Berkouwer, *The Return of Christ* (Grand Rapids: Eerdmans, 1972), p. 55. See also pages 115-122.

Is suffering ordained to continue *throughout the entirety of history until the end?*

The postmillennial position is that suffering is ethically necessary in many times, but not predestined for all times..

The Role of Suffering in History

It is abundantly clear from Scripture that the people of God can expect suffering in their temporal experience. Given the sinful condition of the fallen world, the righteous are a stumbling block and an offense to the unrighteous. Believers are in the world but not of it (John 15:19). Christ warns His disciples: "Remember the words I spoke to you: 'No servant is greater than his master.' If they persecuted me, they will persecute you also" (John 15:20a) and "in this world you shall have trouble" (John 16:33). Paul and Barnabas carry forth this caution by "strengthening the disciples and encouraging them to remain true to the faith" and instructing that "we must go through many hardships to enter the kingdom of God" (Acts 14:22). Paul later reminds Timothy of the trial that lay before him: "In fact, everyone who wants to live a godly life in Christ Jesus will be persecuted" (2 Tim. 3:12). Peter urges his reader not to "be surprised at the painful trial you are suffering, as though something strange were happening to you" (1 Pet. 4:12).

The Case of Job

The book of Job is the classic demonstration of the purpose of the suffering among God's people in history. It specifically addresses the question: "Why do the righteous suffer?" In Job, we discover at the very outset that suffering does occur to "the perfect and upright" (Job 1:1), contrary to health-and-wealth advocates.[13] Job's suffering was very real and quite grievous:

---

13. This may be seen also in the persecution and illness endured by faithful

he lost his wealth, health, and children (Job 1:13-19; 2:7-8). We also discover early on that his trials, though administered by Satan, were under the sovereign control of God (Job 1:12; cf. Psa. 103:19; Luke 22:31-32). Suffering is not random; rather, it is wisely governed to a good end by a loving, holy, and sovereign Lord.[14]

In Job's experience we see the overarching moral and spiritual purpose of suffering: the testing and, therefore, the strengthening of faithful obedience to God.

> Then the LORD said to Satan, "Have you considered my servant Job? There is no one on earth like him; he is blameless and upright, a man who fears God and shuns evil." "Does Job fear God for nothing?" Satan replied. "Have you not put a hedge around him and his household and everything he has? You have blessed the work of his hands, so that his flocks and herds are spread throughout the land. But stretch out your hand and strike everything he has, and he will surely curse you to your face." The LORD said to Satan, "Very well, then, everything he has is in your hands, but on the man himself do not lay a finger." Then Satan went out from the presence of the LORD (Job 1:8-12; cf. 2:2-6).

Other Saints

The same is true of the saints of God elsewhere in history. During his suffering, Joseph learns patience in discovering God's good intentions for the long run. To his treacherous brothers who sell him into slavery, he says: "You intended to harm me, but God intended it for good to accomplish what is now being done, the saving of many lives" (Gen. 50:20).

Christians in the New Testament. Persecution: Paul (1 Cor. 4:9-11) and Stephen (Acts 7:59). Illness: Paul (Gal. 4:13), Dorcas (Acts 9:36-37), Epaphroditus (Phil. 2:25-27), Timothy (1 Tim. 5:23), and Trophimus (2 Tim. 4:20).

14. North, *Westminster's Confession*, ch. 6: "The Question of God's Predictable Historical Sanctions."

The psalmist views patient endurance of affliction as instructive of the will of God. He writes: "It was good for me to be afflicted so that I might learn your decrees" (Psa. 119:71). In fact, this helps return him to the straight and narrow: "Before I was afflicted I went astray, but now I obey your word" (Psa. 119:67). This, of course, is the universal expectation in all godly suffering, for we are to "know then in your heart that as a man disciplines his son, so the LORD your God disciplines you" (Deut. 8:5). The Christian should welcome times of suffering even though "no discipline seems pleasant at the time, but painful. Later on, however, it produces a harvest of righteousness and peace for those who have been trained by it" (Heb. 12:11).

Manasseh learns through grievous trials: "So the LORD brought against them the army commanders of the king of Assyria, who took Manasseh prisoner, put a hook in his nose, bound him with bronze shackles and took him to Babylon. In his distress he sought the favor of the LORD his God and humbled himself greatly before the God of his fathers. And when he prayed to him, the LORD was moved by his entreaty and listened to his plea; so he brought him back to Jerusalem and to his kingdom. Then Manasseh knew that the LORD is God" (2 Chr. 33:11-13).

Scripture even says of Christ that "He learned obedience from what he suffered" (Heb. 5:8). And Christ is our ultimate example: "To this you were called, because Christ suffered for you, leaving you an example, that you should follow in his steps" (1 Pet. 2:21).[15] Extended periods of suffering are designed by God to test and, therefore, to strengthen His people.

Though Job descended into his grievous trials from a plane of great wealth and comfort, he engaged the struggle with faith before God. During the course of his extended struggles, however, there arise times of despair (e.g., 3:13-22; 9:22; 17:15)

---

15. Cf. John 13:15; 1 Cor. 11:1; 1 Tim. 1:16; 1 John 2:6.

alternating with periods of confidence (13:16; 19:25-26). His faith is sorely tested.

The Message of Suffering

Ultimately, Job learns the message God has for him. At the end of his trials he replies as a man of faith, who learns much. "Then Job replied to the LORD: 'I know that you can do all things; no plan of yours can be thwarted. You asked, "Who is this that obscures my counsel without knowledge?" Surely I spoke of things I did not understand, things too wonderful for me to know' " (Job 42:1-3). In humility, he bowed before the Lord. Because of this, Job becomes an example of suffering and patience: "As you know, we consider blessed those who have persevered. You have heard of Job's perseverance and have seen what the Lord finally brought about. The Lord is full of compassion and mercy" (Jms. 5:11).

Suffering is an instrument of God for the humbling and purification of His people for the long run. This is why the predominate theme involved in suffering is patient persever-ance.

"We also rejoice in our sufferings, because we know that suffering produces perseverance" (Rom. 5:3).

"Be joyful in hope, patient in affliction, faithful in prayer" (Rom. 12:12).

"If we are distressed, it is for your comfort and salvation; if we are comforted, it is for your comfort, which produces in you patient endurance of the same sufferings we suffer" (2 Cor. 1:6).

"You, however, know all about my teaching, my way of life, my purpose, faith, patience, love, endurance, persecutions, sufferings – what kinds of things happened to me in Antioch, Iconium and Lystra, the persecutions I endured. Yet the Lord rescued me from all of them" (2 Tim. 3:10-11).

"Therefore, among God's churches we boast about your perseverance and faith in all the persecutions and trials you are enduring" (2 Thess. 1:4).

"You know that the testing of your faith develops perseverance" (Jms.1:3).

"Brothers, as an example of patience in the face of suffering,
take the prophets who spoke in the name of the Lord" (Jms.
5:10).

"I, John, your brother and companion in the suffering and
kingdom and patient endurance that are ours in Jesus" (Rev.
1:9).

"If anyone is to go into captivity, into captivity he will go. If
anyone is to be killed with the sword, with the sword he will be
killed. This calls for patient endurance and faithfulness on the
part of the saints" (Rev. 13:10).

Christianity is an historical faith designed for the long run.
The faithful are to be diligently laboring now amidst trials and
tribulations with an eye to the future. It is the tendency of
sinful man to seek short-cuts to attaining his goals, but the
Christian is to labor against difficult circumstances expecting
the gradualistic development of God's kingdom good in history.
We as Christians are to learn this through our trials and tribulations, through our affliction and suffering.

The Progressive Reduction of Suffering in History

Because suffering is designed to teach humble patience
before God it becomes a *strategic means* for the training of God's
people. It is not an *historical end* for them. Suffering is a characteristic of the Church in evil times; it is not the definition of the
Church for all times. It is an instrument to a greater goal: the
ultimate blessing of godly man. Suffering is not a goal; it is a
means.

Job Revisited

In Job's case we have a wonderful illustration of this. He
genuinely suffers. And though he wavers somewhat, he learns
obedience through his trials. Because of this we read of his final

temporal estate (not his heavenly estate): "After Job had prayed for his friends, the LORD made him prosperous again and gave him twice as much as he had before. All his brothers and sisters and everyone who had known him before came and ate with him in his house. They comforted and consoled him over all the trouble the LORD had brought upon him, and each one gave him a piece of silver and a gold ring. The LORD blessed the latter part of Job's life more than the first. He had fourteen thousand sheep, six thousand camels, a thousand yoke of oxen and a thousand donkeys. And he also had seven sons and three daughters" (Job 42:10-13).

Job's patient learning to wait upon God paid off in time and on earth. This is the hope set before the Christian: "As you know, we consider blessed those who have persevered. You have heard of Job's perseverance and *have seen what the Lord finally brought about.* The Lord is full of compassion and mercy" (Jms. 5:11). As the Church of the Lord Jesus Christ, we are directed to see "what the Lord finally brought about" for Job. This is to promote long-term labor and expectation in the body of believers. The whips and thorns of the evil one teach us patience; patience brings us victory.

The New Testament Message

In Matthew 5:5 the Lord promises: "Blessed are the meek, for they will inherit the earth." Meek endurance for the long-run goes against the sinful grain of man. Consequently, enduring suffering breaks the weak, but steels the faithful for greater glory. Thus, in the long run and after much suffering, the meek will inherit the earth, as the Bible teaches and postmillennialism expects. Suffering is a short-term means for long-term dominion.

Christ comforts His disciples for the long run: "In this world you will have trouble. But take heart! I have overcome the world" (John 16:3). The Suffering Christ comes forth from the grave as the Victorious Christ. As it is in the school of life, glory follows suffering. Of Christ, our perfect example, we read: "Did not the Christ have to suffer these things and then enter his glory?" (Luke 24:26). "He predicted the sufferings of Christ and the glories that would follow" (1 Pet. 1:11b). Christ no longer suffers *on earth* after the resurrection. His exaltation glory begins with His bodily resurrection, *in time and on earth*. This is the divine pattern for His Church, as well.

Paul speaks of his own *patient endurance* of persecutional suffering in a context that expects *earthly victory*. He presents it as an example for Timothy to follow: "You, however, know all about my teaching, my way of life, my purpose, faith, patience, love, endurance, persecutions, sufferings – what kinds of things happened to me in Antioch, Iconium and Lystra, the persecutions I endured. Yet the Lord rescued me from all of them. In fact, everyone who wants to live a godly life in Christ Jesus will be persecuted" (2 Tim. 3:10-12). Preceding this statement, Timothy was assured by Paul of the failure of the evil men and impostors of history, who often are the instruments of suffering: "But they will not get very far because, as in the case of those men, their folly will be clear to everyone" (2 Tim. 3:9).

Second Timothy 3:12 is more of an ethical statement than a prophetic one: "In fact, everyone who wants to live a godly life in Christ Jesus will be persecuted." That is, given the historical setting, the godly may expect their godliness to stir up persecution. This, however, need not always and everywhere be the case. Paul is not establishing a *universal principle*. The premillennialist and dispensationalist surely do not believe that in the millennium this will be true. Neither does the amillennialist believe such will be the case for those who live godly lives in the New Heavens and the New Earth. Paul is instructing Timothy what he is to expect, while living among an ungodly majority. He is also instructed that the ungodly will be exposed eventually (2 Tim. 3:9).

Back to the Old Testament

The ultimate outcome of the long period of suffering which the Church endures is destined to be historically glorious. This is the purpose of God-inflicted suffering. He promises to bless covenantal faithfulness (Deut. 28:1-14), but to curse covenantal disobedience (Deut. 28:15ff). This blessing is cultural, involving all aspects of social life: population growth (vv. 4, 11), economic productivity (vv. 11-12), political stability (vv. 7, 13), agricultural abundance (vv. 4-5, 8, 11), increased health (contra vv. 27-29), favorable weather (v. 12), and so forth.

Of Israel's trial in the wilderness we learn: "He gave you manna to eat in the desert, something your fathers had never known, to humble and to test you *so that in the end it might go well with you*" (Deut. 8:16).

David is confident in the eventual blessing of the Lord, despite tribulation. This is the message of Psalm 37:

> Do not fret because of evil men or be envious of those who do wrong; for like the grass they will soon wither, like green plants they will soon die away. Trust in the LORD and do good; dwell in the land and enjoy safe pasture. Delight yourself in the LORD and he will give you the desires of your heart. Commit your way to the LORD; trust in him and he will do this: He will make your righteousness shine like the dawn, the justice of your cause like the noonday sun. Be still before the LORD and wait patiently for him; do not fret when men succeed in their ways, when they carry out their wicked schemes. Refrain from anger and turn from wrath; do not fret – it leads only to evil. For evil men will be cut off, but those who hope in the LORD will inherit the land. A little while, and the wicked will be no more; though you look for them, they will not be found. But the meek will inherit the land and enjoy great peace. The wicked plot against the righteous and gnash their teeth at them; but the Lord laughs at the wicked, for he knows their day is coming. The wicked draw the sword and bend the bow to bring down the poor and needy, to slay those whose ways are upright. But their swords will pierce

their own hearts, and their bows will be broken. Better the little that the righteous have than the wealth of many wicked; for the power of the wicked will be broken, but the LORD upholds the righteous. The days of the blameless are known to the LORD, and their inheritance will endure forever. In times of disaster they will not wither; in days of famine they will enjoy plenty. But the wicked will perish: The LORD'S enemies will be like the beauty of the fields, they will vanish – vanish like smoke. The wicked borrow and do not repay, but the righteous give generously; those the LORD blesses will inherit the land, but those he curses will be cut off. If the LORD delights in a man's way, he makes his steps firm; though he stumble, he will not fall, for the LORD upholds him with his hand. I was young and now I am old, yet I have never seen the righteous forsaken or their children begging bread. They are always generous and lend freely; their children will be blessed. Turn from evil and do good; then you will dwell in the land forever. For the LORD loves the just and will not forsake his faithful ones. They will be protected forever, but the offspring of the wicked will be cut off; the righteous will inherit the land and dwell in it forever. The mouth of the righteous man utters wisdom, and his tongue speaks what is just. The law of his God is in his heart; his feet do not slip. The wicked lie in wait for the righteous, seeking their very lives; but the LORD will not leave them in their power or let them be condemned when brought to trial. Wait for the LORD and keep his way. He will exalt you to inherit the land; when the wicked are cut off, you will see it. I have seen a wicked and ruthless man flourishing like a green tree in its native soil, but he soon passed away and was no more; though I looked for him, he could not be found. Consider the blameless, observe the upright; there is a future for the man of peace. But all sinners will be destroyed; the future of the wicked will be cut off. The salvation of the righteous comes from the LORD; he is their stronghold in time of trouble. The LORD helps them and delivers them; he delivers them from the wicked and saves them, because they take refuge in him.

Conclusion

This same David is confident that the world's rage against Christ in an attempt to displace Him would be totally unsuccessful. The determination to destroy the work of the Lord would result in its ultimate establishment and victory:

> Why do the nations conspire and the peoples plot in vain? The kings of the earth take their stand and the rulers gather together against the LORD and against his Anointed One. "Let us break their chains," they say, "and throw off their fetters." The One enthroned in heaven laughs; the Lord scoffs at them. Then he rebukes them in his anger and terrifies them in his wrath, saying, "I have installed my King on Zion, my holy hill." I will proclaim the decree of the LORD: He said to me, "You are my Son; today I have become your Father. Ask of me, and I will make the nations your inheritance, the ends of the earth your possession. You will rule them with an iron scepter; you will dash them to pieces like pottery." Therefore, you kings, be wise; be warned, you rulers of the earth. Serve the LORD with fear and rejoice with trembling. Kiss the Son, lest he be angry and you be destroyed in your way, for his wrath can flare up in a moment. Blessed are all who take refuge in him (Psa. 2).

Therefore, it is the unshakable confidence of the Suffering Church that she one day will be the Victorious Church. Her persecuted members will rule in the midst of the enemy: "To him who overcomes and does my will to the end, I will give authority over the nations – 'He will rule them with an iron scepter; he will dash them to pieces like pottery' – just as I have received authority from my Father. I will also give him the morning star" (Rev. 2:26-28). Amillennialists do not agree.

In amillennialism's eschatology of predestined historical suffering, Christians are told to expect Christianity's influence to diminish steadily in history. They are expected to suffer ever-greater persecution at the hands of rebellious covenant-breakers. Christians are expected to prove their faith by experiencing ever-greater sickness and poverty, in contrast to the message of the fundamentalists' health-and-wealth gospel. The amillennialist elevates the instrumental function of suffering to the level of a predestined eschatological goal. Amillennialists preach ever-greater suffering unto cultural defeat; postmillennialists preach ever-reduced suffering unto cultural victory.

Appendix C

A CRITIQUE OF HYPER-PRETERISM

An extreme form of preterism has made its presence felt in evangelical circles since the early 1980s. Generally the view is labeled "consistent preterism." But orthodox preterists label it "hyper-preterism." The hyper-preterist believes that *all* prophecy is fulfilled in the A.D. 70 destruction of the Temple, including the Second Advent, the resurrection of the dead, the great judgment, and so forth.

There are numerous exegetical and theological problems I have with the hyper-preterist viewpoint. I deem my historic, orthodox preterism to be *exegetical preterism* (because I find specific passages calling for specific preterist events); I deem the preterism of Max King and Ed Stevens to be *theological preterism* or *comprehensive preterism* (they apply exegetical conclusions drawn from several eschatological passages to *all* eschatological passages, because of their theological paradigm). Let me list some of my present objections

Creedal Failure

First, hyper-preterism is heterodox. It is outside of the creedal orthodoxy of Christianity. No creed allows any Second Advent in A.D. 70. No creed allows any other type of resurrection than a bodily one. Historic creeds speak of the universal, personal judgment of all men, not of a representative judgment in A.D. 70. It would be most remarkable if the entire church that came through A.D. 70 missed the proper understanding of the eschaton and did not realize its members had been resurrected! And that the next generations had not inkling of the great transformation that took place! Has the *entire* Christian church missed the *basic contours* of Christian eschatology for its first 1900 years?

Second, hyper-preterism has serious implications for the perspicuity of Scripture. This viewpoint not only has implications for the later creeds, but for the instructional abilities of the apostles: no one in church history knew the *major issues* of which they spoke — until very recently! Are the Scriptures *that* impenetrable on an issue of *that* significance? Clement of Rome lived through A.D. 70 and had no idea he was resurrected! He continued to look for a physical resurrection (*Clement* 50:3). Jude's (supposed) grandsons still sought a physical resurrection (cf. Eusebius, *EH* 3:24:4). Whoever these men were, they come right out of the first generation and in the land of Israel — with absolutely no inkling of an A.D. 70 resurrection or a past Second Advent. See also the *Didache* 10:5; 16:1ff (first century); Ignatius, *Trallians* 9:2; *Smyrnaens* 2:1; 6:1; *Letter to Polycarp* 3:2 (early second century); Polycarp 2:1; 6:2; 7:1. See also Papias, Irenaeus, Justin Martyr.

Berkouwer rightly notes that the reason the resurrection found early creedal acceptance was because of the clear emphasis of the New Testament. The hyper-preterist view has serious and embarrassing implications for the perspicuity of Scripture — and despite the fact we are now (supposedly) in our resurrected states and have the outpoured Holy Spirit and His gift of teachers who were to protect us from every wind of doctrine (Eph. 4).

Third, the hyper-preterist system leaves the New Covenant Christian (in our post A.D. 70 era) without a canon. If all prophecy was fulfilled prior to A.D. 70 and if the entire New Testament spoke to issues in the pre-A.D. 70 time frame, we do not have any directly relevant passages for us. The entire New Testament must be transposed before we can use it.

Hermeneutic Failure

Fourth, hyper-preterism suffers from serious errors in its hermeneutical methodology. When a contextually defined passage applies to the A.D. 70 event, the hyper-preterist will take *all* passages with *similar* language and apply them to A.D. 70, as well. But similarity does not imply identity; Christ cleansed the Temple twice and in virtually identical ways; but the two events are not the same. Furthermore, we must distinguish *sense* and *referent*; there are several types of "resurrection" in Scripture: the dry bones of Eze. 37; spiritual redemption in John 5:24; physical redemption at the grave in John 5:28; Israel's renewal in Christ in Rom. 11:15; and of the Beast in Rev. 13:3. I hold that passages specifically delimiting the timeframe by temporal indicators (such as "this generation," "shortly," "at hand," "near," and similar wording) are to be applied to A.D. 70, but similar sounding passages may or may *not* be so applied.

Resurrection Errors

Fifth, there is a serious problem with the removal of the physical resurrection from systematic theology. Christ's resurrection is expressly declared to be the paradigm of our own (1 Cor. 15:20ff). Yet we know that His was a physical, tangible resurrection (Luke 24:39), whereas ours is (supposedly) spiritual. What happens to the biblically defined analogy between Christ's resurrection and ours in the hyper-preterist system?

Sixth, there are numerous other theological and exegetical problems with a spiritual-only resurrection. For one thing, the hyper-preterist view tends to diminish the significance of the somatic implications of sin: Adam's sin had *physical* effects, as well as judicial and spiritual effects; where are these taken care of in the hyper-preterist system? Death's implications are not just judicial and spiritual, but also physical (Gen. 3:14, 19; Rom. 6:23). If Christians *now* are fulfilling the resurrection expectation of Scripture, then the gnostics of the early Christian centuries were correct! The physical world seems to be superfluous, in the hyper-preterist viewpoint. The anthropology of hyper-preterism is defective in this, not allowing the theological significance of the body/soul nature of man (Gen. 2:7). This can also have implications for the person of Christ and the reality of His humanity.

Seventh, regarding the teaching of Christ and the Apostles, we must wonder why Paul was mocked by the Greeks in Acts 17 for believing in the resurrection, if it were not a physical reality. We must wonder why Paul aligned himself with the Pharisees on the issue of the resurrection (Acts 23:6-9; 24:15, 21). We must wonder why we Christians still marry and are given in marriage, since Christ said in the resurrection we will *not* marry (Luke 20:35). We must wonder why the apostles never corrected the widespread notion of a physical resurrection, which was so current in Judaism (cf Josephus, Talmud, etc.). We must wonder why we "resurrected" Christians must yet die; why should we not leave this world like Enoch and Elijah? Furthermore, where and what is the resurrection of the lost (John 5; Rev. 20)? Paul considered Hymeneaus and Philetus as having made ship-wreck men's faith by saying the resurrection is past (2 Tim. 2:17-18). A wrong view of the resurrection is a serious matter to Paul.

Eighth, practically I wonder on the hyper-preterist view what the difference our resurrection makes in this life? We get ill and are weak on the same scale as those prior to the A.D. 70 resurrection. Did this glorious resurrection of the "spiritual body" have no impact on our present condition? A hyper-preterist analysis might leave us to expect that Paul looked to A.D. 70 as an agent of relief from the groanings and the temptations of the flesh (Rom. 7:25), yet we still have such — despite the supposed resurrection.

Christology Implications

Ninth, Acts 1 clearly defines Christ's Second Advent in terms of His ascension, which was physical and visible. For example, in Acts 1:8-11 Luke is careful to say the disciples were "beholding" Him as He ascended; He was received "from the eyes of them" (v. 9b); they were "gazing" as He was "going" (v. 10); they were "looking" (v. 11); they "beheld" (v. 11). Clearly His ascension was a visible and glorious phenomenon involving His tangible resurrected body. And there was an actual visible cloud associated with it (v. 10). The angelic messengers resolutely declare "this same Jesus" (i.e., the Jesus they knew for over three years, who is now in a tangible resurrected body) will "so come *in like manner* as you saw Him go into heaven" (v. 11). The Greek *on tropon* literally means "what manner." The Greek phrase "never indicates mere certainty or vague resemblance; but wherever it occurs in the New Testament, denotes identity of mode or manner" (J.A. Alexander, *Acts*, ad loc.). Consequently, we have express biblical warrant to expect a visible, bodily, glorious return of Christ paralleling in kind the ascension. The hyper-preterist position goes contrary to this clear teaching of Scripture.

Tenth, if A.D. 70 ends the Messianic reign of Christ (cf. hyper-preterist view of 1 Cor. 15:24, 28), then the glorious Messianic era prophesied throughout the Old Testament is reduced to a forty year inter-regnum. Whereas by all accounts it is a lengthy, glorious era. A problem with premillennialism is that it reduces Christ's reign to 1000 literal years; hyper-preterism reduces it further to forty years! The prophetical expressions of the kingdom tend to speak of an enormous period of time, even employing terms that are frequently used of eternity. Does Christ's kingdom parallel David's so that it only lasts for the same time frame?

History and Church Errors

Eleventh, hyper-preterists eternalize time, by allowing history to continue forever. This not only goes against express statements of Scripture, but also has God dealing with a universe in which sin will dwell forever and ever and ever. There is no final conclusion to the matter of man's rebellion; there is no final reckoning with sin. Christ tells us that the judgment will be against rebels in their *bodies,* not spiritual bodies (Matt. 10:28). The hyper-preterist system does not reach back far enough (to the Fall and the curse on the physical world) to be able to understand the significance of redemption as it moves to a final, conclusive consummation, ridding the cursed world of sin. The full failure of the First Adam must be overcome by the full success of the Second Adam.

Twelfth, hyper-preterism has serious negative implications for ecclesiastical labor. Is the Great Commission delimited to the pre-A.D. 70 era, due to the interpretation of "the end" by hyper-preterists (Matt. 28:20)? Is the Lord's Supper superfluous today, having been fulfilled in Christ's (alleged) Second Advent in A.D. 70 (1 Cor. 11:26)?

BIBLIOGRAPHY

General Works on Eschatology

Bock, Darrell L., ed. *Three Views of the End of History*. Grand Rapids, MI: Zondervan, 1997. Advocates of progressive dispensationalism (Craig Blaising), amillennialism (Richard Gaffin), and reconstructionist postmillennialism (Kenneth Gentry) present and defend their positions.

Clouse, Robert G., ed., *The Meaning of the Millennium: Four Views*. Downers Grove, IL: InterVarsity Press, 1977. Advocates of the four major views of the millennium present each case.

Erickson, Millard J. *Contemporary Options in Eschatology: A Study of the Millennium*. Grand Rapids, MI: Baker, 1977. Examines modern views of eschatology: the millennium and the great tribulation.

Grenz, Stanley J., *The Millennial Maze: Sorting Out Evangelical Options*. Downers Grove, IL: InterVarsity, 1992. A balanced, objective assessment of the four major millennial views.

Hill, Charles E. *Regnum Caelorum: Patterns of Future Hope in Early Christianity*. Oxford: Clarendon, 1992. A study of patristic eschatology showing errors of dispensational analysis.

Pate, C. Marvin, ed., *Four Views of the Book of Revelation*. Grand Rapids, MI: Zondervan, 1997. A debate book presenting the futurist, historicist, idealist, and preterist (Kenneth Gentry) approaches to Revelation.

Works Defending Postmillennialism or Preterism

Adams, Jay. *The Time Is At Hand*. Phillipsburg, NJ: Presbyterian and Reformed, 1966. An amillennial, preterist interpretation of the book of Revelation.

Alexander, J. A. *The Prophecies of Isaiah*, *A Commentary on Matthew* (complete through chapter 16), *A Commentary on Mark*, and *A Commentary on Acts*. Various Publishers. Works by the nineteenth-century Princeton Seminary Old Testament scholar.

Boettner, Loraine. *The Millennium*. Revised edition. Phillipsburg, NJ: Presbyterian and Reformed, (1958) 1984. A classic study of millennial views, and a defense of postmillennialism.

Brown, John. *The Discourses and Sayings of Our Lord* and commentaries on *Romans*, *Hebrews*, and *1 Peter*. Various Publishers. Brown was a nineteenth-century Scottish Calvinist.

Campbell, Roderick. *Israel and the New Covenant*. Phillipsburg, NJ: Presbyterian & Reformed, (1954) 1981. A neglected study of principles for the interpretation of prophecy. Campbell examines major themes of New Testament biblical theology. The book is easy to read; its chapters are short; the biblical references are numerous.

Chilton, David. *The Days of Vengeance: An Exposition of the Book of Revelation*. Ft. Worth, TX: Dominion Press. A massive postmillennial commentary on the book of Revelation.

Chilton, David. *The Great Tribulation*. Ft. Worth, TX: Dominion Press, 1987. A popular exegetical introduction to the postmillennial interpretation of this important but long-fulfilled prophecy.

Chilton, David. *Paradise Restored: A Biblical Theology of Dominion*. Ft. Worth, TX: Dominion Press, 1985. A study of prophetic symbolism, the coming of the Kingdom, and the book of Revelation. Deeply exegetical.

Clark, David S. *The Message from Patmos: A Postmillennial Commentary on the Book of Revelation*. Grand Rapids, MI: Baker, 1989. A brief preterist and postmillennial commentary.

Davis, John Jefferson. *Christ's Victorious Kingdom: Postmillennialism Reconsidered*. Grand Rapids, MI: Baker, 1986. A biblical and historical defense of postmillennialism by a professor at Gordon-Conwell Seminary.

DeMar, Gary and Peter Leithart. *The Reduction of Christianity: A Biblical Response to Dave Hunt*. Ft. Worth, TX: Dominion Press, 1988. A detailed critique of the pietist and openly retreatist pop-dispensational theology of best-selling author and accountant Dave Hunt. Also, an historical and biblical defense of postmillennialism.

Edwards, Jonathan. *The Works of Jonathan Edwards*. 2 volumes. Edinburgh: The Banner of Truth Trust, (1834 ed.) 1974. Volume 1 includes Edwards' "History of Redemption." Edwards is generally regarded as America's most influential theologian. He was a defender of postmillennialism.

Gentry, Kenneth L., Jr. *The Beast of Revelation*. Tyler, TX: Institute for Christian Economics, 1989. A preterist study of the identity of the beast in Revelation.

Gentry, Kenneth L., Jr. *Before Jerusalem Fell: Dating the Book of Revelation.* (2d ed.: Bethesda, MD: International Scholars Publications, 1996). A Th.D. dissertation of the dating of Revelation: prior to A.D. 70. Corrected edition.

Gentry, Kenneth L., Jr. *The Greatness of the Great Commission: The Christian Enterprise in a Fallen World* (2d. ed.; Tyler, TX: Institute for Christian Economics, 1995). In-depth study in and application of Christ's Great Commission in Matthew 28:18-20.

Gentry, Kenneth L., Jr. *Perilous Times: A Study in Eschatological Evil* (forthcoming). In-depth exegesis of five key preterist passages: Daniel 9, Matthew 24, 2 Thessalonians 2, Revelation 13, and Revelation 17.

Henry, Matthew. *Matthew Henry's Commentary.* 6 volumes. New York: Fleming H. Revell, (1714). A popular commentary on the whole Bible by a still-popular seventeenth-century theologian.

Hodge, A. A. *Outlines of Theology.* Enlarged edition. London: The Banner of Truth Trust, (1879) 1972. A nineteenth-century introduction to systematic theology: question-and-answer form.

Hodge, Charles. *Systematic Theology.* 3 volumes. Grand Rapids, MI: Eerdmans, (1871-73) 1986. A standard Reformed text by Princeton Seminary's most renowned nineteenth-century theologian. Volume 3 includes a discussion of eschatology.

Kik, J. Marcellus. *An Eschatology of Victory.* N.J.: Presbyterian and Reformed, 1975. Preterist exegetical studies of Matthew 24 and Revelation 20.

McLeod, Alexander. *Governor of the Nations of the Earth.* Elmwood Park, NJ: Reformed Presbyterian, 1993 [rep. 1803]. A presentation of the postmillennial hope from a nineteenth century minister.

Murray, Iain. *The Puritan Hope: Revival and the Interpretation of Prophecy.* (Edinburgh: Banner of Truth, 1971). Historical study of postmillennialism in England and Scotland, beginning in the eighteenth century.

North, Gary, ed. *The Journal of Christian Reconstruction*, Symposium on the Millennium (Winter 1976-77). Historical and theological essays on postmillennialism.

North, Gary. *Millennialism and Social Theory.* Tyler, TX: Institute for Christian Economics, 1990. A study of the failure of premillennialism and amillennialism to deal with social theory as an explicitly biblical enterprise.

Owen, John. *Works*, ed. William H. Goold. 16 volumes. Edinburgh: The Banner of Truth Trust, 1965. The seventeenth-century Puritan preacher and theologian; volume 8 includes several sermons on the Kingdom of God, and volume 9 contains a preterist sermon on 2 Peter 3.

Rushdoony, Rousas John. *God's Plan for Victory: The Meaning of Postmillennialism.* Fairfax, VA: Thoburn Press, 1977. A short theological study of the implications of postmillennialism for economics, law, and reconstruction.

Rushdoony, Rousas John. *Thy Kingdom Come: Studies in Daniel and Revelation.* Phillipsburg, NJ: Presbyterian and Reformed, 1970. Exegetical studies, full of insightful comments on history and society.

HE SHALL HAVE DOMINION

Shedd, W. G. T. *Dogmatic Theology*. 3 volumes. Nashville, TN: Thomas Nelson, (1888) 1980. A nineteenth-century Reformed text in systematic theology.

Strong, A. H. *Systematic Theology*. Baptist postmillennialist of late nineteenth and early twentieth centuries.

Sutton, Ray R. "Covenantal Postmillennialism," *Covenant Renewal* (February 1989). Discusses the difference between traditional Presbyterian postmillennialism and covenantal post-millennialism. Published by the ICE, P. O. Box 8000, Tyler, TX 75711.

Terry, Milton S. *Biblical Apocalyptics: A Study of the Most Notable Revelations of God and of Christ*. Grand Rapids, MI: Baker, (1898) 1988. Nineteenth-century exegetical studies of prophetic passages in Old and New Testaments; includes a complete commentary on Revelation.

Warfield, Benjamin B., *Biblical and Theological Studies* (Phillipsburg, NJ: Presbyterian and Reformed, 1952). Several helpful articles defending postmillennialism, despite dispensationalism's assuming Warfield was an amillennialist.

Eschatology and the Jews

De Jong, J. A. *As the Waters Cover the Sea: Millennial Expectations in the Rise of Anglo-American Missions 1640-1810*. Kampen: J. H. Kok, 1970. A general history of millennial views; throughout the text it mentions the importance of prophecies concerning the Jews.

DeMar, Gary and Peter Leithart. *The Legacy of Hatred Continues: A Response to Hal Lindsey's **The Road to Holocaust***. Tyler, TX: Institute for Christian Economics, 1989. A brief but thorough refutation to Hal Lindsey's claim that all nondispensational eschatologies are anti-Semitic. Lindsey has never replied in public to this book, published one month after his *The Road to Holocaust*. He did not revise any of its numerous factual errors in the subsequent paperback edition. Prior to the publication of *The Road to Holocaust*, he refused repeatedly to meet individually in private with either Gary North or Gary DeMar, although both men formally requested such a meeting.

Fairbairn, Patrick. *The Prophetic Prospects of the Jews, or, Fairbairn vs. Fairbairn*. Grand Rapids, MI: Eerdmans, 1930. Nineteenth-century scholar Fairbairn changed his mind about the conversion of the Jews. This volume reproduces his early arguments for the historic postmillennial position, and his later arguments against it.

Holwerda, David E. *Jesus and Israel: One Covenant or Two?* Grand Rapids, MI: Eerdmans, 1995. One of the finest treatments available on the question of the Jews and eschatology. Shows Jesus as the fulfillment of the Jewish purpose.

LaRondelle, Hans K. *The Israel of God in Prophecy: Principles of Prophetic Interpretation*. Berrien Springs, MI: Andrews University Press, 1983. An extremely helpful study of the place of the Jews in prophecy and a critique of the dispensational viewpoint. From an unusual source: LaRondelle is a Seventh Day Adventist (so be careful!)

Lightfoot, John. *Commentary on the New Testament from the Talmud and Hebraica*, 4 vols. Peabody, MA: Hendrickson, 1989 [rep. 1642]. Prominent Westminster divine and Hebraist scholar. Helpful for particular preterist texts (Matthew - 1 Corinthians).

Murray, John. *The Epistle to the Romans: New International Commentary on the New Testament*, 2 vols. Grand Rapids, MI:

Eerdmans, 1965. Chapter on the Jews from Romans 11 is worth the price of the book. Clearly shows Murray's postmillennialism.

Schlissel, Steve and David Brown. *Hal Lindsey and the Restoration of the Jews*. Edmonton, Alberta, Canada: Still Waters Revival Books, 1990. A Jewish-born Reconstructionist pastor responds to Hal Lindsey's claim that Christian Reconstruction is anti-Semitic. Schlissel's work is combined with David Brown's work that demonstrates that *postmillennialism* is the "system of prophetic interpretation that historically furnished the Biblical basis for the most glorious future imaginable for the Jews!"

Sutton, Ray R. "A Postmillennial Jew (The Covenantal Structure of Romans 11)," *Covenant Renewal* (June 1989). Sutton has a conversation with a postmillennial Messianic Jew.

Sutton, Ray R. "Does Israel Have a Future?" *Covenant Renewal* (December 1988). This examines several different views of Israel's future, and argues for the covenantal view.

Toon, Peter, ed. *Puritans, the Millennium and the Future of Israel: Puritan Eschatology 1600-1660*. Cambridge: James Clarke, 1970. A detailed historical study of millennial views with special attention to the place of Israel in prophecy.

Works Critical of Dispensationalism

Allis, Oswald T. *Prophecy and the Church*. Phillipsburg, NJ: Presbyterian and Reformed, 1945. A classic comprehensive critique of the theology of dispensationalism by a postmillennialist Old Testament scholar. It has never been refuted and is rarely mentioned by dispensational scholars.

Bacchiocchi, Samuele. *Hal Lindsey's Prophetic Jigsaw Puzzle: Five Predictions That Failed!* Berrien Springs, MI: Biblical Perspectives, 1987. It examines Lindsey's failed prophecies, arguing for an imminent (any-moment) Second Coming.

Bahnsen, Greg L. and Kenneth L. Gentry. *House Divided: The Break-Up of Dispensational Theology.* Tyler, TX: Institute for Christian Economics, 1989. A detailed response to the book by H. Wayne House (then of Dallas Seminary) and Thomas Ice, *Dominion Theology: Blessing or Curse?* It includes a comprehensive discussion of eschatological issues written by Gentry.

Bass, Clarence B. *Backgrounds to Dispensationalism: Its Historical Genesis and Ecclesiastical Implications.* Grand Rapids, MI: Baker, 1960. A massively researched history of dispensationalism, with focus on J. N. Darby.

Boersma, T. *Is the Bible a Jigsaw Puzzle: An Evaluation of Hal Lindsey's Writings.* Ontario, Canada: Paideia Press, 1978. An examination of Lindsey's interpretive method, and an exegesis of important prophetic passages.

Bray, John L. *Israel in Bible Prophecy.* Lakeland, FL: John L. Bray Ministry, 1983. An amillennial historical and biblical discussion of the Jews in the New Covenant.

Brown, David. *Christ's Second Coming: Will It Be Premillennial?* Edmonton Alberta, Canada: Still Water Revival Books, (1876) 1990. A detailed exegetical study of the Second Coming and the Millennium by a former premillennialist who became postmillennial.

Cox, William E. *An Examination of Dispensationalism.* Philadelphia, PA: Presbyterian and Reformed, 1963. A critical look at major tenets of dispensationalism by former dispensationalist who became amillennial.

Cox, William E. *Why I Left Scofieldism*. Phillipsburg, NJ: Presbyterian and Reformed, n.d. A critical examination of major flaws of dispensationalism.

Crenshaw, Curtis I. and Grover E. Gunn, III. *Dispensationalism Today, Yesterday, and Tomorrow*. Memphis, TN: Footstool Publications, (1985) 1989. Two Dallas Seminary graduates take a critical and comprehensive look at dispensationalism.

DeMar, Gary. *The Debate Over Christian Reconstruction*. Ft. Worth, TX: 1988. A response to Dave Hunt and Thomas Ice after their 1988 debate with Gary North and Gary DeMar. Includes a brief commentary on Matthew 24. The book was co-published by American Vision, Atlanta, GA. Audiotapes and a videotape of this debate are available from ICE, P. O. Box 8000, Tyler, TX 75711.

Feinberg, John A. *Continuity and Discontinuity: Perspectives on the Relationship Between the Old and New Testaments*. Westchester, IL: Crossway, 1988. Theologians of various persuasions discuss relationship of Old and New Covenants; evidence of important modifications in dispensationalism.

Fuller, Robert. *Naming the Antichrist: The History of an American Obsession*. New York: Oxford, 1995. Scholarly research into the embarrassing naivete of American dispensationalism.

Gerstner, John H. *A Primer on Dispensationalism*. Phillipsburg, NJ: Presbyterian and Reformed, 1982. A brief critique of dispensationalism's "division" of the Bible.

Gerstner, John H. *Wrongly Dividing the Word of Truth: A Critique of Dispensationalism*. Brentwood, TN: Wolgemuth & Hyatt, 1991. A blistering attack on dispensationalism as a theological system, not just as an eschatological system.

Mathison, Keith A. *Dispensationalism: Rightly Dividing the People of God?* Phillipsburg, NJ: Presbyterian and Reformed, 1995. A critique of some of the leading errors of dispensationalism by a Reformed Theological Seminary graduate.

MacPherson, Dave. *The Incredible Cover-Up*. Medford, OR: Omega Publications, 1975. A revisionist study of the origins of the pre-trib rapture doctrine. He traces it to private revelations in 1830 by a 20-year-old mystic and follower of Edward Irving, Margaret Macdonald.

MacPherson, Dave. *The Rapture Plot*. Simpsonville, SC: Millennium III, 1995. A continuation of MacPherson's exposé of dispensationalism's origins.

Mauro, Philip. *The Seventy Weeks and the Great Tribulation*. Swengel, PA: Reiner Publishers, n.d. A former dispensationalist re-examines prophecies in Daniel and the Olivet Discourse.

Miladin, George C. *Is This Really the End?: A Reformed Analysis of **The Late Great Planet Earth***. Cherry Hill, NJ: Mack Publishing, 1972. A brief postmillennial response to Hal Lindsey's prophetic works; concludes with a defense of postmillennial optimism.

Nash, Ronald H. *Great Divides: Understanding the Controversies That Come Between Christians*. Colorado Springs, CO: NavPress, 1993. Though not technically a critique of dispensationalism, this work chastises the dispensational assaults upon Christian Reconstructionists. Nash is not a Reconstructionist.

North, Gary. *Rapture Fever: Why Dispensationalism Is Paralyzed*. Tyler, TX: Institute for Christian Economics, 1993.

Pate, C. Marvin and Calvin B. Haines, Jr., *Doomsday Delusions: What's Wrong with Predictions About the End of the World*. Downer's Grove, IL: Inter-varsity, 1995. Insightful lamentation over date-setting by progressive dispensational scholars. Holds an unusual preterist-futurist approach to New Testament eschatology (even citing favorable Gentry's *The Beast of Revelation*).

Provan, Charles D. *The Church Is Israel Now: The Transfer of Conditional Privilege*. Vallecito, CA: Ross House Books, 1987. A collection of Scripture texts with brief comments.

Vanderwaal, C. *Hal Lindsey and Biblical Prophecy*. Ontario, Canada: Paideia Press, 1978. A lively critique of dispensationalism and Hal Lindsey by a preterist amillennialist.

Weber, Timothy P. *Living in the Shadow of the Second Coming: American Premillennialism 1875-1982*. Grand Rapids, MI: Zondervan/Academie, 1983. This touches on American dispensationalism in a larger historical and social context.

Wilson, Dwight. *Armageddon Now!: The Premillenarian Response to Russia and Israel Since 1917*. Tyler, TX: Institute for Christian Economics, (1977) 1991. A premillennialist historian studies the history of failed dispensational prophecy. He warns against "newspaper exegesis."

Woodrow, Ralph. *Great Prophecies of the Bible*. Riverside, CA: Ralph Woodrow Evangelistic Association, 1971. An exegetical study of Matthew 24, the Seventy Weeks of Daniel, and the doctrine of the Anti-Christ.

Woodrow, Ralph. *His Truth Is Marching On: Advanced Studies on Prophecy in the Light of History*. Riverside, CA: Ralph Woodrow Evangelistic Association, 1977. An exegetical study of important prophetic passages in Old and New Testaments.

Theonomic Studies in Biblical Law

Bahnsen, Greg L. *By This Standard: The Authority of God's Law Today*. Tyler, TX: Institute for Christian Economics, 1985. An introduction to the issues of biblical law in society.

Bahnsen, Greg L. *Theonomy and Its Critics*. Tyler, TX: Institute for Christian Economics, 1991. A detailed response to the major criticisms of theonomy, focusing on *Theonomy: A Reformed Critique*, a collection of essays written by the faculty of Westminster Theological Seminary (Zondervan/Academie, 1990).

Bahnsen, Greg L. *Theonomy in Christian Ethics*. Nutley, NJ: Presbyterian and Reformed, (1977) 1984. A detailed apologetic of the idea of continuity in biblical law.

DeMar, Gary. *God and Government*, 3 vols. Brentwood, TN: Wolgemuth & Hyatt, 1990. An introduction to the fundamentals of biblical government, emphasizing self-government.

Einwechter, William O. *Ethics & God's Law: An Introduction*. Mill Hill, PA: Preston/Speed, 1995. A helpful, brief introduction to theonomy by a reformed Baptist pastor.

Gentry, Kenneth L., Jr. *God's Law in the Modern World: The Continuing Relevance of Old Testament Law*. Phillipsburg, NJ: Presbyterian and Reformed, 1993. A compact summary of the theonomic position. Excellent resource for lay Bible studies.

Gillespie, George, *Wholesome Severity Reconciled with Christian Liberty*, in Christopher Coldwell, ed. *Anthology of Presbyterian & Reformed Literature*, vol. 4 (Dallas: Naphtali, 1991). Work by prominent Scottish member of Westminster Assembly. Presents so strong a defense of a theonomic understanding of Matthew 5:17 you will think it was written by Greg Bahnsen.

Jordan, James. *The Law of the Covenant: An Exposition of Exodus 21-23*. Tyler, TX: Institute for Christian Economics, 1984. A clear introduction to the issues of the case laws of the Old Testament.

North, Gary. *The Dominion Covenant: Genesis*. Tyler, TX: Institute for Christian Economics, (1982) 1987. A study of the economic laws of the Book of Genesis.

North, Gary. *Leviticus: An Economic Commentary*. Tyler, TX: Institute for Christian Economics, 1995. A study of the economic laws of Leviticus.

North, Gary. *Moses and Pharaoh: Dominion Religion vs. Power Religion*. Tyler, TX: Institute for Christian Economics, 1985. A study of the economic issues governing the Exodus.

North, Gary. *Political Polytheism: The Myth of Pluralism*. Tyler, TX: Institute for Christian Economics, 1989. A 700-page critique of the myth of neutrality: in ethics, social criticism, U.S. history, and the U.S. Constitution.

North, Gary. *The Sinai Strategy: Economics and the Ten Commandments*. Tyler, TX: Institute for Christian Economics, 1986. A study of the five-point covenantal structure (1-5, 6-10) of the Ten Commandments. Includes a detailed study of why the Old Covenant's capital sanction no longer applies to sabbath-breaking.

North, Gary. *Tools of Dominion: The Case Laws of Exodus*. Tyler, TX: Institute for Christian Economics, 1990. A 1,300-page examination of the economics of Exodus 21-23.

North, Gary. *Westminster's Confession: The Abandonment of Van Til's Legacy*. Tyler, TX: Institute for Christian Economics, 1991.

Refutes, chapter by chapter, the criticisms offered in Westminster Seminary's *Theonomy: A Reformed Critique*. North shows that the seminary has returned to natural law theology in order to defend political pluralism. North says that this is by far his best polemical book. Rushdoony has publicly said so, too. It reprints H. L. Mencken's 1937 obituary of J. Gresham Machen.

North, Gary, ed. *Theonomy: An Informed Response*. Tyler, TX: Institute for Christian Economics, 1991. A 400-page symposium refuting Westminster Seminary's *Theonomy: A Reformed Critique*. Essays by DeMar (3), Gentry (3), Sutton, North, and Rev. John Maphet.

Rushdoony, Rousas John. *The Institutes of Biblical Law*. Nutley, NJ: Presbyterian and Reformed, 1973. The foundational work of the Christian Reconstruction movement. It subsumes all of biblical law under the Ten Commandments. It includes three appendixes by Gary North.

Strickland, Wayne, G., ed. *The Law, the Gospel, and the Modern Christian: Five Views*. Grand Rapids, MI: Zondervan, 1993. A popular "debate" book on five approaches to the Law of God. The theonomic position is presented and defended by Greg L. Bahnsen.

Sutton, Ray R. *That You May Prosper: Dominion By Covenant*. Tyler, TX: Institute for Christian Economics, 1987. A detailed study of the five points of the biblical covenant model, applying them to church, state, and family. Second edition, 1992. Sutton became the president of Philadelphia Theological Seminary (formerly: Reformed Episcopal Seminary) in 1992.

SELECT SCRIPTURE INDEX

1:46-55	220	1:29	273-274
1:68-71	221	2:19-21	260, 371
1:72	328	3:10, 12	162
2:32	370	3:17	265, 273-274
3:8	271	3:30	222
4:17-21	326	4:24	368
12:16-21	451	4:35	488
13:23	489	5:19, 30	226
13:24-25	489	5:22	300
13:33	209	5:24-29	430
13:36-39	490-492	5:27	300
16:16	224	5:28-29	297, 301
17:10	266	5:39	336
17:20-21	154, 224, 233-234	6:14-15	162
		6:15	233, 515
18:8	492-495	6:39	337
18:28-30	123	6:44	253
21:20	358, 371	7:38	260
21:20-22	418	12:12-15	225
22:26	498	12:31	266, 427
22:29-30	495, 497	12:32	276, 277
22:30	496	12:32-32	252-253
24:17-21	162	12:48	303
24:25-26	162	14	339
24:21	233	14:3	280-281
24:25-27	233	14:6	282
24:26	550	14:16, 18	281
24:32	161	15:5	268, 467
24:45	161	15:5-6	263
24:44-47	176	15:20	544
24:46-49	264	16:3	549
24:47	269	16:7-15	265
24:47-49	269	16:33	544
		17:4, 5	469
John		17:18, 24	469
1:1	370	17:11, 13	282
1:14	370	17:17	31, 100
1:21	382	17:20-21	247

SUBJECT INDEX

beautiful, 425, 426

Christians and, 264, 418, 422

city of, 204, 207-208, 322-323, 415, 481, 502

Babylon as, 392-393, 424

Christians flee, 422, 485

Egypt as, 396

fall of (see also: Temple — destruction), 283, 311-314, 330, 359-361, 400ff, 427ff

fame of, 392-393

heavenly, 154, 155, 171, 367, 375, 376, 395, 415, 515

holy city, 324, 358, 421

New (see: Jerusalem — heavenly)

physical changes in, 150

siege of, 420, 484

wife of Jehovah, 394

Jesse, 213

Jesus (see: Christ)

Jews (-ish) (see also: Israel; Jewish War with Rome)

Christ's focus on, 329

conversion of, xix, xxvii, 55, 92, 93, 214, 237, 515

exalted, 200, 236, 363

fulfillment of prophecy and, 86, 502

future destruction, 360, 398

gentiles and, 131, 176, 211, 232, 236, 375, 513

God's plan and, 275, 500, 515

holocaust (World War II), 440

kingdom view, 234, 235, 515

race, 353

rejection of Christ, 162, 234ff, 354, 360ff, 396ff, 412, 504, 516

remnant, 482

writings, 313

Jewish War with Rome, 327n, 402, 405, 412, 421-422, 424

jigsaw puzzle (see: eschatology — jigsaw puzzle)

Job, 544-549

John the Apostle, 430, 432

John Baptist, 161, 221, 222, 251, 380-384, 504, 514

Jonah, 198, 502

Joseph, 545

Jubilee, 321-322, 326, 328, 362, 400

Judah, 173, 201, 208, 417

Judaism, 117n, 155, 164, 275n, 427, 558

Judaizing (see: Zionism)

Judea, 237, 419

judgment(s) (see also: consummation — final judgment)

eschatology and , 252, 282, 283, 497

judgment coming of Christ, 362, 411-413, 451

Julius Caesar (Gaius Julius Caesar) (102 B.C.-44 B.C.), 416n, 423

justice, 139, 299

inordinate influence of, 52,
511
Jewish nature, 235
positions, 54-65
orthodoxy and, 76
postmillennialism and,
348n, 429-431
rare in Scripture, 52
rise of views (see: eschatology — rise of millenni-
al views)
term, 51
miracle worker, 405
Mishnah, 415n
missions, 438, 440, 537
Moab, 214
mockers, 312
modernism (see: liberalism/
modernism)
Montanism (-ists), 81
Moody, Dwight Lyman (1837-
1899), 466n
moon, 160, 419
morality (see: good and evil;
ethics)
Mormons (see: cults)
Moses, 109, 137, 142, 466, 479,
498, 501
mountain(-s)
shake, 159, 264, 485
Scripture and, 208, 259,
366, 480
Mount of Olives, 357, 481, 484,
485
mustard seed parable (see:
parables — mustard seed)
mystery, 105, 176, 468

**National Association of Evan-
gelicals**, 304n
nations, 227, 269, 512, 516
natural law, xi, 103, 104, 131
Near East, 361
Nebuchadnezzar, 141
neo-orthodoxy, 439, 455, 456,
463
Nero Caesar (Nero Claudius
Caesar Drusus Germanicus)
(A.D. 37-68)
emperor, 389ff, 402ff, 411,
418, 422, 426
persecution by (see: persecution — Neronic)
suicide, 423
neutrality: judicial (see: law —
judicial neutrality)
New Age, 454
new birth, 251, 375
New Covenant (see: covenant
— New)
new creation (see also: new
heavens and earth)
Christ as head of, 375
Scripture and, 173, 310-
315, 373-378, 432, 497,
524ff
new heavens and earth, xxv,
18, 221, 308, 447, 475 (see
also: new creation)
New Scofield Reference Bible, 158,
251n, 303n, 366, 453
newspaper exegesis, xliv, 443,
446-447
Nicene Creed (see: Creeds —
Nicene)
Nicodemus, 161

AUTHOR INDEX

ABOUT THE AUTHOR

Kenneth L. Gentry, Jr., is an ordained minister in the Presbyterian Church in America since 1977. He is pastor of the Reedy River Presbyterian Church outside of Greenville, South Carolina. He and his wife, Melissa, have three children, Amanda, Paul, and Stephen.

He is a graduate of Tennessee Temple University (B.A., cum laude), Reformed Theological Seminary (M. Div.), Whitefield Theological Seminary (Th. M.; Th. D., summa cum laude). He also attended Grace Theological Seminary for two years, while a dispensationalist.

He is a member of the Evangelical Theological Society and is a Contributing Editor to *The Counsel of Chalcedon* magazine, and is on the Church Council Committee of the Coalition on Revival. He has published articles in numerous periodicals including *Christianity Today, Christianity & Society, The Banner of Truth, The Presbyterian Journal, The Fundamentalist Journal, The Freeman, The Journal of Christian Reconstruction, Antithesis.*

He also serves as Adjunct Faculty member of the Southern California Center for Christian Studies (P.O. Box 328, Placentia, CA 92871), the late Dr. Greg Bahnsen's ministry. He has written several books on eschatology, including *The Beast of Revelation, House Divided: The Break-up of Dispensational Theology, Before Jerusalem Fell: Dating the Book of Revelation,* and *The Greatness of the Great Commission: The Christian Enterprise in a Fallen World.*

He frequently conducts seminars and lectures on eschatological themes, including a condensed survey of the Book of Revelation. He has a writing instruction ministry called "Righteous Writing," which provides tape and correspondence instruction in proper techniques of reading, researching, writing, publishing, and marketing books. Write: Kenneth L. Gentry, Jr., Righteous Writing, P.O. Box 328, Conestee, SC 29636. Or contact him through CompuServe: INTERNET:102544.2500@compuserve.com.

He also publishes a monthly newsletter through the Institute for Christian Economics. This newsletter, *Dispensationalism in Transition*, provides a critique and analysis of dispensationalism. It is available only via e-mail:

Send to: list-request@metanet.net

Write in text box: subscribe transition-list

The Beast of Revelation
by Rev. Kenneth L. Gentry

One of the greatest mysteries of all time is the identity of the dread Beast of the Book of Revelation. The Bible describes him as the ultimate villain in human history. He is the archetype of evil. He is the very incarnation of wickedness and perversion. It is not at all surprising then that many of the brightest minds throughout history have sought to identify and expose him.

Unfortunately, a great majority of those diligent detectives missed one of the most important clues—if not the most important clue—to solving the mystery. That clue according to Kenneth L. Gentry, Jr., is when and to whom the Apostle John actually wrote the Book of Revelation in the first place.

Following that clue, he is able to blow away the dusts of time that have masked the evil culprit's identity for so very long. Like any good detective, Dr. Gentry lets the evidence speak for itself. And he lets you weigh all the facts to decide for yourself. But be forewarned: He has constructed an iron-clad case. This book is thus likely to revolutionize your interpretation of the mystery of the Beast—and the rest of the Book of Revelation as well.

209 pp., indexed, paperback: $9.95; hardback: $25.00
Institute for Christian Economics, P.O. Box 8000, Tyler, Texas 75711

Order all 3 books advertised here (a $38.85 value) for 40% off and pay no shipping! Send a check to I.C.E., P.O. Box 8000, Tyler, TX 75711 for $23.31.

House Divided
The Breakup of Dispensational Theology
by Greg L. Bahnsen and Kenneth L. Gentry

The year 2001 will bring a new millennium: the seventh after the creation and the third after the birth of Jesus Christ. This is the greatest opportunity for evangelism in world history. The world will change drastically. Will it be for the better or the worse? Dispensationalists automatically answer: "Worse!" But their system is in deep trouble.

Many people believed that the Rapture would take place in September, 1988. It didn't happen. Fooled again. And a lot of Christians vowed: Never again! (How about you?)

Meanwhile, the movement known as Christian Reconstruction was spreading in dispensational circles. Spokesmen for the dispensational camp in 1988 concluded that dispensationalism's forty-year tactic of the academic black-out could no longer work. They would have to respond publicly to the Reconstructionists' detailed published criticisms of the dispensationalist system. They would have to refute the Reconstructionists' claim that God's Old Testament civil laws are still valid for society and that there is a bright future ahead for Christianity before Jesus returns.

What house Divided demonstrates is that dispensational theology has now been shattered by its own defenders. They are no longer willing to defend the original system, and their drastic modifications have left it a broken shell. They are also deeply divided among themselves on; the crucial questions of biblical interpretation and social activism. In short, today's defenders of dispensationalism "destroyed the system in order to save it." No one has attempted to put this shattered theological system back together. No one will even outline its main points.

411 pp., indexed, hardback, $19.95
Institute for Christian Economics, P.O. Box 8000, Tyler, TX 75711

The Greatness of the Great Commission
The Christian Enterprise in a Fallen World
by Rev. Kenneth L. Gentry

"Save Souls, Not Cultures!" This has been the motto of twentieth-century evangelism. Having encountered heavy resistance to the prophets' message of comprehensive revival and restoration in history, modern evangelical Christianity has abandoned the prophets. Unlike Jonah, who grew weary of life in the belly of a whale, modern evangelicalism has not only grown accustomed to the Church's cultural irrelevance today, it has actually proclaimed this pathetic condition as God's plan for the "Church Age." But is it? Not according to Jesus' instructions to His Church: the discipling (putting under God's discipline) of all nations (Matt. 28:19-20).

Paul makes it clear that the progressive expansion of Jesus' kingdom in history will continue until all things are under His dominion, on earth, before He returns physically to judge the world (I Corinthians 15:25-26). This was David's message, too (Psalm 110:1-2).

This book presents a biblical case for God's salvation and restoration in history. Sin is comprehensive; God's healing grace is no less comprehensive. Wherever sin reigns today, there God speaks to sinful man and offers a way of escape (I Cor. 10-13). To argue that the Great Commission does not include every aspect of today's cultures — all of Satan's kingdom — is to argue that there is no way of escape in many areas of life.

The war between God's kingdom (civilization) on earth and Satan's kingdom (civilization) on earth is total, encompassing every aspect of life. The Great Commission calls the Church (in this "Church Age") to make a full-scale attack on modern humanist civilization, but always in terms of a positive message and practical program: a better way of life in every area of life. This is the greatness of the Great Commission. It must not be narrowed to exclude culture from God's special grace.

184 pp., indexed, paperback, $9.95; hardback, $25.00
Institute for Christian Economics, P.O. Box 8000, Tyler, Texas 75711

Order all 3 books advertised here (a $38.85 value) for 40% off and pay no shipping! Send a check to I.C.E., P.O. Box 8000, Tyler, TX 75711 for $23.31.